The Origin of Concepts

Oxford Series in Cognitive Development

Series Editors
Paul Bloom and Susan A. Gelman

The Origin of Concepts

SUSAN CAREY

OXFORD
UNIVERSITY PRESS

2009

OXFORD
UNIVERSITY PRESS

Oxford University Press, Inc., publishes works that further
Oxford University's objective of excellence
in research, scholarship, and education.

Oxford   New York
Auckland   Cape Town   Dar es Salaam   Hong   Kong   Karachi
Kuala Lumpur   Madrid   Melbourne   Mexico City   Nairobi
New Delhi   Shanghai   Taipei   Toronto

With offices in
Argentina   Austria   Brazil   Chile   Czech Republic   France   Greece
Guatemala   Hungary   Italy   Japan   Poland   Portugal   Singapore
South Korea   Switzerland   Thailand   Turkey   Ukraine   Vietnam

Published by Oxford University Press, Inc.
198 Madison Avenue, New York, New York 10016
www.oup.com

Oxford is a registered trademark of Oxford University Press

Library of Congress Cataloging-in-Publication Data
Carey, Susan.
The origin of concepts / Susan Carey.
    p. cm.—(Oxford series in cognitive development; 3)
Includes bibliographical references and index.
ISBN 978-0-19-536763-8
1. Concepts. I. Title.
BF443.C37 2009
153.2'3—dc22
2008029129

9 8 7 6 5
Printed in the United States of America
on acid-free paper

For Ned and Eliza

Acknowledgments

In 1997, I was honored to give the Jean Nicod lectures in Paris, which if I had had the sense to publish them then would have been a slim volume. Somehow when I set out to cash the promissory notes in those lectures, the project grew into a totally different work—this one, which has little overlap with that hypothetical volume. I am truly indebted to my hosts from the Institute Jean Nicod for setting this book into motion, and for probing and insightful critical responses to my work that informed its development over the last decade.

This book reflects a career of trying to understand the human conceptual apparatus—what it is like, what it is good for, and how it arises, especially over ontogenetic and historical time. My work has been profoundly shaped by that of several colleagues, friends, and students.

My vision of core cognition reflects the ideas of and sometimes heated arguments with: Elizabeth Spelke, Marc Hauser, Rochel Gelman, Alan Leslie, Randy Gallistel, Renée Baillargeon, Gergely Csibra, and Gyorgi Gergely. Two critical events led me to the study of core cognition. First was Elizabeth Spelke's visit to MIT on her first sabbatical in 1982. Her brilliant work on infants' object representations was in full flower at that time, and together with that of Renée Baillargeon, is the starting point for the material in Chapters 2 and 3 on core object cognition. The second event that set my thinking about the initial state of the human mind along the path I have taken for the past 20 years was a working group at the Center for the Advanced Study of the Behavioral Science at Stanford organized by Rochel Gelman. Rochel, Frank Keil, Ann Brown, Randy Gallistel, and I wrote a paper together that year, drawing out the implications of ethological studies of animal learning for how to conceptualize human domain specific learning mechanisms. Only in retrospect do I see how much this experience shaped my further thought.

My work on conceptual change dates back to my 1972 PhD thesis, entitled "Are Children Little Scientists with False Theories of the World?", carried out under the supervision of my mentors Jerome

Bruner and Roger Brown. Tom Kuhn guided Marianne Wiser and me through our historical study of the Florentine Academy sketched in Chapter 10, and my understanding of the nature of the bootstrapping episodes that underlie conceptual changes in intuitive and scientific theory reflects the work of Nancy Nersessian and of Dedre Gentner.

For many years, I was in the same department at MIT (the Psychology Department, then the Department of Brain and Cognitive Sciences) with Jerry Fodor. His work on the language of thought, and on concepts, framed the issues for me. He will not believe a word of what I say about concepts in these pages. For even longer, I have been married to another philosopher, Ned Block, who like Jerry, takes psychology seriously. His work on two factor theories of concepts has always seemed right on to me.

The research from my laboratory reported here has all been carried out in collaboration with students, who are identified as the work is described. Several deserve special mention for their role in the development of the theoretical ideas developed in this book. The implications of the work on core object cognition for Quine's picture of the initial state was developed with Fei Xu (see chapters 2 and 3). My work on infant number representations was largely in collaboration with Lisa Feigenson (chapter 4), and my work on the acquisition of counting has been largely in collaboration with Mathieu LeCorre and Barbara Sarnecka. Work with Susan Johnson, and subsequent work by her, profoundly influenced my view of core cognition of agency. The work on infants' causal representation reported in Chapter 6 grew out of collaborations with Rebecca Saxe and Paul Meuntener. Finally, much of my work on conceptual change has been in collaboration with Carol Smith and Marianne Wiser, and their work on the role of conceptual modeling activities in conceptual changes is one of the main sources of my characterization of Quinian bootstrapping.

Finally, many people have generously commented on earlier drafts of chapters—students in seminars, graduate students and post-docs, and colleagues. Marianne Wiser and Nancy Nersessian provided valuable feedback on the chapters on conceptual change, and Ned Block, Greg Murphy, and Tania Lombrozo commented on the chapter in which I draw out the implications of the picture of conceptual development I sketch here for a theory of concepts. I thank them all; I hope that everybody who commented will see the fruits of their suggestions in the final version. But especially, I would like to acknowledge the careful reading and extensive comments on the whole book by the editors of this series at OUP—Paul Bloom and Susan Gelman. Their contribution to this book was heroic—they engaged the local arguments throughout, and provided valuable suggestions about how to reorganize and rewrite so as to make the whole project clearer.

Contents

The Origin of Concepts

I

Some Preliminaries

Human beings, alone among animals, come to possess rich conceptual understanding of the world—understanding formulated in terms of such concepts as *evolution, electron, cancer, infinity,* or *galaxy.* This book offers an account of that human capacity for conceptual representation. Different types of processes, operating over three different time courses (individual learning, historical/cultural construction, and evolution), underlie the formation of our conceptual repertoire. Some concepts, such as *object* and *number,* arise in some form over evolutionary time. Other concepts, such as *kayak, fraction,* and *gene,* spring from human cultures, and the construction process must be understood in terms of both human individuals' learning mechanisms and sociocultural processes. Humans create complex artifacts, as well as religious, political, and scientific institutions, that themselves become part of the process by which further representational resources are created.

Cognitive science seeks a precise, explanatory account of the origin of concepts in general, and of some especially important concepts in particular. For example, when it comes to the concept *integer,* what are the relevant innate representational resources bequeathed to us by evolution? In creating such a concept, must we go beyond innately given representations? In what ways, and by what processes, do individuals and groups of individuals construct new representational resources? How is knowledge culturally constructed and maintained? These questions must be answered case by case—there is no reason, at the outset, to expect the answers for concepts of causality or human agency to be the same as the answers for mathematical or biological concepts, or for the concepts that articulate our knowledge of chess or baseball.

This book develops several case studies in some detail: the concepts *object* (chapters 2 and 3), *intentional agent* (chapter 5), *cause* (chapter 6), *integer* (chapters 4 and 7), *rational number* (chapters 9 and 11), and *matter, weight,* and *density* (chapters 10 and 11). In the course of exploring these cases, many others are touched upon. What really matters to me is not the cases (although I do admit finding each one intrinsically fascinating), but the lessons to be drawn from them. My goal here is to demonstrate that the disciplines of cognitive science now have the empirical and theoretical tools to turn age-old philosophical dilemmas into relatively straightforward scientific problems. I shall illustrate the progress science has made in resolving debates about the existence, nature, content, and format of innate knowledge. I consider the thesis that conceptual resources are continuous throughout the life span. I debate the nature of concepts and intuitive theories, and also how to distinguish between conceptual change and belief revision and I show how these controversies bear on the relations between language and thought.

This introductory chapter introduces the problem I seek to solve, states the major theses that are developed in the chapters to come, and provides an overview of the book. As this is a book on the origin of concepts, I begin by sketching what I mean by the term "concept." Concepts are mental representations. Indeed, they make up only part of our stock of mental representations, so discussions of them must distinguish among types of mental representations, saying which ones are concepts. The book's first major thesis is that there are two types of conceptual representations: those embedded in systems of core cognition and those embedded in explicit knowledge systems, such as intuitive theories. The book's second major thesis is that new representational resources emerge in development—representational systems with more expressive power than those they are built from, as well as representational systems that are incommensurable with those they are built from. That is, conceptual development involves theoretically important discontinuities. The book's third major thesis is that the bootstrapping processes that have been described in the literature on the history and philosophy of science underlie the construction of new representational resources in childhood as well.

Concepts and Mental Representations

Concepts are units of thought, the constituents of beliefs and theories, and those concepts that interest me here are roughly the grain of single lexical items. Indeed, the representations of word meanings are paradigm examples of concepts. I take concepts to be mental representations— indeed, just a subset of the entire stock of a person's mental representations. Thus, I use phrases such as "the infant's concept *number*" to mean whatever infant representations (if any) have numerical content, having argued independently that the representation in question (e.g., of number) should be considered a concept, as opposed to a percept or a sensory representation. I assume that representations are states of the nervous system that have content, that refer to concrete or abstract entities (or even fictional entities), properties, and events. I do not attempt a full philosophical analysis of the concept of mental representation itself; I will not try to say how it is that some states of the nervous system have symbolic content. Such a theory would explain how the extension of a given representation is determined, as well as providing a computational account of how that representation fills its particular inferential role, how it functions in thought.[1]

Of course, any theory of the origin of concepts requires some idea of what concepts are and how their content is determined, just as any theory of conceptual content must comport with our best account of how concepts are acquired. Here, I sketch the assumptions that have guided my inquiry from the outset: I assume that there are many components to the processes that determine conceptual content, and that these fall into two broad classes: (1) causal mechanisms that connect a mental representation to the entities in the world in its extension, and (2) computational processes internal to the mind that determine how the representation functions in thought. In broad strokes, then, I assume a dual theory of conceptual content (Block, 1986, 1987).

In order to study the origin of concepts, one must characterize their developmental and evolutionary trajectories, and to do that one must discover what kinds of mental representations and which specific concepts nonhuman animals and human infants and children have. In the pages to come, I work backwards from behavioral evidence for a given representation's extension and inferential role to characterize that representation's nature and content, and whenever possible, to specify something of its format. Chapter 14 draws out some implications for a theory of concepts provided by my picture of their origins.

There are many different types of mental representations, and one challenge faced by cognitive science is to find the principled distinctions among them. Indeed, several historically important views of conceptual development posit shifts in the types of mental representations available to children of different ages, and such claims presuppose distinct kinds of representations. I shall argue that different types of representations may well have theoretically relevant differences in origins, in developmental trajectories, in types of conceptual roles, and in extension-determining mechanisms. Chapter 2 considers one picture of infants' mental lives in which the infant's mind is articulated in terms of representations very unlike those of linguistically and theoretically competent adults. William James famously believed that the infant's world was "one great blooming, buzzing confusion" (James, 1890/1981, p. 496). Quine (1977) suggested that infants begin with a perceptual similarity space that is transformed through learning, especially through learning language, into a system of representations articulated in terms of natural-kind concepts. Similarly, Piaget (1954) proposed that infants begin life with a repertoire of sensori-motor representations, achieving truly symbolic representations only at the end of second year of life.

The views of James, Quine, and Piaget are related in their assumption that a major distinction can be made between sensory representations, on one end of a continuum, and conceptual representations, on the other end. All three theorists posited that sensory/perceptual representations are developmentally primitive, and that uniquely human mental capacities underlie the developmental processes through which sensory/perceptual representations are transformed into conceptual ones. Sensory representations can, of course, be distinguished from perceptual ones, as I shall show in chapter 2, but these writers did not draw a clear distinction between them. For present purposes, the important contrast is between sensory/perceptual representations, on the one hand, and conceptual ones, on the other. All three authors believed that nonhuman animals, just like human babies, do not entertain conceptual representations. Chapter 2 examines the thesis that infants begin with a representational repertoire that is limited to sensory/perceptual representations and that conceptual representations are constructed only later in development, relating this view to the empiricists' theory of the origin and nature of human concepts.

Examining this thesis requires distinguishing the two types of representations (sensory/perceptual vs. conceptual), which is notoriously tricky to do. Modern cognitive science justifies the Empiricists' confidence that representations of the perceptual aspects of the phenomenal world (what things in the world look like, feel like, sound like, smell like, and taste like) result from many levels of processing of the information in physical stimulation impinging on sense organs. That is, as the empiricists knew, there are causal connections between patterns of light, sound, and physical forces and the perception of shape, pitch, depth, and the effort expended in causing something to move. An intuitive first pass at capturing the distinction between perceptual and conceptual representations begins with the observation that representations of such features of immediate experience differ in many respects from clear examples of conceptual representations. The latter represent what things in the world are, categorizing entities into abstract, theory-laden kinds, and positing entities for which we have no sensory evidence.

This first pass at drawing the distinction between sensory/perceptual and conceptual representations presupposes that one can do so on the basis of their content. It assumes one can see, on the face of things, that representations of shapes such as square are sensory or perceptual and that representations of living things or numbers are conceptual. But that can't be quite right, for we certainly have concepts of sensed features of the world. Conflicting with the assumption that shape representations are paradigmatically perceptual, we have words for shapes, develop explicit geometric theories of shapes, and have theories of how shape representations are computed from patterns of retinal input. Conversely, as we shall see, we have perceptual processes that create from sensory input representations of abstractions such as number, agent, and cause.

No doubt there are many dimensions along which clear examples of sensory/perceptual representations differ from clear examples of conceptual ones. Chapter 2 discusses several in the course of exploring the empiricists' proposal (shared by many modern-day cognitive scientists) that the mind begins with a representational vocabulary that is limited to sensory/perceptual primitives. Sensory/perceptual representations are likely to differ from conceptual ones with respect to both important aspects of mental representation—the mechanisms through which their extensions are fixed and the nature of the inferential processes they contribute to. They will also (sometimes) differ in format; I assume many perceptual representations are iconic or analog, whereas at least some conceptual representations are stated over discrete, arbitrary symbols (i.e., are language-like).

One reason for the empiricists' belief that we start out with sensory/perceptual representations and build up concepts from them is that they could imagine how these can be appropriately connected to the world. And they wanted their theory of development to mirror their theory of the determination of content. Although they did not have Darwin to appeal to, they assumed that sense organs guarantee the appropriate causal connections between properties of real-world entities and our perceptual ideas of these entities. I accept this view: the mechanisms of shape perception, for example, are largely innately specified and guarantee that our representations of round things pick out round things. Concepts, for the most part, require different mechanisms to guarantee that a given representation is causally connected to the entities it refers to. Evolution did not provide us with an input analyzer that identifies electrons, justice, or 3,462,179. While there certainly is also a causal story to be told about how the content of the concept *electron* is determined, it will have a very different flavor from the explanation for how the content of *round* is determined. I shall argue, in the course of this book, that inferential role plays a part in the causal processes through which conceptual representations pick out their referents. Additionally, I accept that the principles of content determination for concepts importantly involve social interactions among people and metaphysically necessary features of the entities they refer to. According to philosophers such as Saul Kripke and Hilary Putnam, the extensions of natural kind concepts are fixed not just by the mind but also by some social process of ostensive definition and by the essential nature (a metaphysical matter, not an epistemological one) of the entities so dubbed (Kripke, 1972/1980; Putnam, 1975; see also Burge, 1979). The discovery of the extension of the concept *gold* or of *wolf* is a matter for science, not for philosophy, linguistics, or psychology. As for the psychology of natural-kind concepts, they fall under the assumption of what Susan Gelman calls "psychological essentialism" (Gelman, 2003; Medin & Ortony, 1989). According to the doctrine of psychological essentialism, it is a fact about our mind that we assume (usually correctly, as it turns out, but it needn't be) that individuals of a given natural kind have hidden essences that determine their very existence, their kind, and their surface properties. We assume this even in the face of no guesses as to a kind's essential properties.

In sum, there are many causal processes that are involved in connecting representations in a mind to their referents, and these are likely to differ systematically for sensory/perceptual representations, on the one hand, and conceptual representations, on the other. Whether or not inferential role plays a part in content determination, there is no doubt that perceptual representations and conceptual representations differ in many aspects of their inferential role. Sensory/perceptual representations have different and more impoverished inferential roles from concepts. They represent the here and now, and almost nothing else follows from the fact that something is red, whereas rich inferences are licensed by identifying something as an agent or identifying the substance a given entity is made of. Conceptual representations, but not sensory/perceptual ones, are embedded in conceptual structures such as intuitive theories that support this rich inferential role. Conceptual representations articulate causal and explanatory structures and are integrated with other conceptual representations.

Focusing on conceptual role, the philosopher Jerry Fodor (1983) argued that a systematic distinction between kinds of representations can be drawn in terms of how they are processed in the mind. He distinguished between modular input analyzers and central processes. For the most part, sensory/perceptual processes are modular and conceptual processes are central. Modular processes are data driven, automatic, fast, and encapsulated. (A process is encapsulated if it operates on proprietary input and ignores available information that is relevant to the computation at hand.) Perceptual illusions make the notion clear. Consider the familiar Muller-Lyer illusion (Figure 1.1). You know (because I tell you or because you measured them) that the two horizontal lines are the same length, but you still see the lower one as longer than the upper one. Your perceptual representation is encapsulated from (uninfluenced by) your conceptual representation of the actual relative lengths. Central processes,

innateness is onto the problem of understanding what learning is. Nonetheless, I believe that this contrast is both coherent and that it matters in the debate about which representations are innate. This book is an extended exploration of learning mechanisms, but for present purposes, we can characterize learning processes as those that build representations of the world on the basis of computations on input that is itself representational. Clear examples are mechanisms that chose among alternative hypotheses on the basis of rational processes that weigh evidence (as in Bayesian learning processes), operant conditioning, connectionist supervised and unsupervised learning algorithms, habituation, and so on.

Notice that claiming that representations of red or round are innate does not require that the child have some mental representation of red or round in the absence of experience with red or round things. The capacity for forming color or shape representations could be innate (i.e., not constructed through learning), even though no representations of colors or shapes are ever activated until entities are seen. Notice also that "innate" does not mean "present at birth." Many representational capacities arise from maturational processes. An example is stereoscopic representations of depth, which emerge in humans quite suddenly around 6 months of age. Even though stereoscopic depth perception is not present at birth, I would want to say it is innate, for the child does not have to learn to compute depth from the discrepancies between the two images on the two retinas. Another reason some innate (unlearned) representations may not be evident at birth is that the child has not yet encountered the input to the processes that construct them or may not be yet able to represent their inputs. Chapters 2 through 5 provide examples of this sort. For a sophisticated discussion of the concept of innateness as it applies to mental representations, see Spelke and Newport (1998).

I take it that any theory of conceptual development must specify the stock of innate representations, as well as the mechanisms (both maturational and learning mechanisms) that underlie change. Framing the problem this way leaves all the room in the world for cantankerous disagreement. Are the initial representational primitives limited to sense data, as the British empiricists such as Locke would have had it? Or to sensori-motor schemes, as Piaget would have had it? Or to a perceptual similarity space, as Quine would have had it? Or is it theories all the way down, as Allison Gopnik and Andrew Meltzoff would have it?[3] Insofar as learning underlies conceptual development, are the learning mechanisms domain-general or specifically tailored to particular conceptual content? If domain-specific, what are the domains and what are the mechanisms of learning within each? If domain-general, are they powerful pattern abstractors, such as those well modeled in connectionist systems, determinate computational algorithms formulated over symbolic machinery, or bootstrapping mechanisms that draw on nondeterminate processes such as analogical mapping, inference to best explanation, and inductive guesses?

The proposals for the initial stock of representational primitives and for the types of learning mechanisms that underlie cognitive development are logically independent, although there are inductive relations between them. Typically, researchers who believe that the initial state of the baby consists of sensory representations alone also believe that domain-general learning mechanisms of various sorts subserve conceptual development. This position (innate sensory representations/domain-general learning mechanisms) is discussed in chapter 2. A second view (innate conceptual representations/domain-general learning mechanisms), held most forcefully by Gopnik and Meltzoff (1997), is that the initial stock of representational resources includes conceptual representations embedded in intuitive theories and that development is driven by domain-general causal learning mechanisms of the sort that underlie theory development in science. I endorse a version of this position, but not with respect to the characterization of the initial state. Chapter 3 contrasts this position with a third position (innate conceptual representations/domain-specific learning mechanisms), which holds that the initial stock of representational resources includes conceptual representations embedded in core domains and that development is driven, at least in part, by domain-specific learning mechanisms.

It is important to note that the existence of innate conceptual representations and domain-specific learning mechanisms does not preclude the existence of sensory and perceptual representations and domain-general learning mechanisms, or even that there are learning mechanisms capable of taking perceptual representations as input and outputting conceptual ones. Building rich and accurate representations of the physical, social, and biological worlds is so important—to humans especially, but to all animals really—that many distinct representational and learning mechanisms are likely to have been selected for. As Gallistel (2000) commented, speaking of the proposal that there only one learning mechanism, "From a biological perspective, this assumption is equivalent to assuming that there is a general purpose sensory organ that solves the problem of sensing."

A variety of considerations lead individual scientists to favor one or another picture of the initial state and of the processes that yield adult conceptual capacities. Some reduce to matters of scientific strategy, such as the dictum that it is scientifically preferable to assume the least possible in the way of innate representations, in order to explore how much of the adult state could be accounted for under any particular minimal assumptions (e.g., sensory primitives, associationist learning mechanisms). But scientific strategy must not be promoted to principles of theory choice with truth-relevant status, as when it is claimed that such a picture is more parsimonious than alternative pictures and thus should be considered right until proven wrong.

Other scientific strategies lead to a different picture. For example, some scientists bet that human learning processes will be continuous with those of other animals—an assumption that generates an expectation of highly domain-specific and structured learning mechanisms. There are myriad examples of specialized learning mechanisms in other animals—ranging from passerine song learning, to vervet learning to identify predators, to spatial learning in rats, to migratory birds learning the azimuth of the night sky (Gallistel, Brown, Carey, Gelman, & Keil, 1991, review these particular cases). In each of these cases, innately specified representations and domain-specific learning processes are essential parts of the mechanisms that achieve the adult state.

Two Examples of Animal Core Cognition

I now turn to two examples from the ethological literature that show that it is not problematic to attribute innate representations and domain-specific learning mechanisms to nonhuman animals. These examples illustrate what is meant by core cognition, and they raise the question: What core systems has evolution endowed humans with?

Indigo Buntings Learn to Identify North from the Night Sky

Consider the mechanism through which indigo buntings (a species of migratory songbird) learn to identify north from the night sky. In today's night sky, Polaris is the North Star, the star in the region of the sky that reliably indicates north. Because the stars change position over time, Polaris will not always indicate true north, nor will true north in the future be predictable from the constellations of today, for the constellations them-selves migrate and change over evolutionary time. Indeed, 100,000 years ago there was no Big Dipper, no Orion. Thus, evolution probably could not have built a map of the sky in the brain of the indigo buntings on which Polaris is identified as north, yet indigo buntings have such a map. Presented with a stationary simulacrum of the night sky in a planetarium in autumn, they take off as if to fly south as specified by the North Star, no matter how the planetarium's night sky has been oriented with respect to true north in the actual world. Indigo buntings must have learned some-thing equivalent to where the North Star is; how could they have done so?

Steven Emlen (1975) uncovered the mechanism by which nestling indigo buntings achieve this feat. Because the earth rotates on an axis that goes through true north, the North Star, positioned as it is at present above the North Pole, marks the center of rotation for the night sky. Emlen showed that nestling indigo buntings observe the rotating sky and register the center of the rotation as a privileged direction. He showed this by raising indigo buntings in a planetarium in which he could make arbitrary skies rotate around arbitrary centers, and then observed which direction the birds took off in the autumn, when their hormones told them it was time to fly south. There is a critical period for this learning device; if the buntings do not learn the North Star while they are nestlings, they never do.

This is a paradigm species-specific, domain-specific learning device. Clearly, not every animal will spontaneously note the center of rotation of the night sky, nor will every animal infer true north from the obser-vations if they happen to make them; thus, this device is species-specific. With respect to domain specificity, this device is of no use in learning what food is safe to eat, what the indigo bunting song is, or anything else other than where north is. This device exemplifies other properties of core domains, as well. Innate perceptual mechanisms allow the bird to identify the sky and to represent its rotation. And this device is a learning mechanism; innately specified computations concerning the representation of celestial rotation ensure that the buntings end up representing something important that they must, by logical necessity, learn: how to tell north from the night sky.

That some state of the indigo bunting's nervous system represents the night sky is shown not only by the fact that it is activated by the night sky but also how it plays a role in the computations that determine the azimuth and direction of flight during migration. This is an example of what I mean by taking behavioral evidence regarding the extension and inferential role of some representation as evidence regarding its content. Finally, these representations also exemplify the senses in which core cognition is conceptual, but not fully so. The inferential role of the representations of a view of the night sky go beyond the specification of what it looks like (points of light distributed against a black background); nothing in the description of what the sky looks like has the content north. Still, the inferential role of bunting representations of the azimuth is limited (as far as we know) to guiding navigation. In spite of a lack of studies on the matter, it's a safe bet that buntings do not create theories of the earth and the heavens in terms they can use to explain why the center of rotation of the night sky provides information about compass direction on the earth. Thus, it would be a mistake to suppose that the bunting's representations of the night sky are anything like ours.

Conspecific Recognition

Ever since the pioneering work of Konrad Lorenz (1937), we have known that many birds have an innate learning mechanism that enables them to identify conspecifics, and that these representations are input to a learning process that enables them to identify one important conspecific: their mother. The learning device Lorenz discovered and called "imprinting" causes chicks to attend to and seek proximity to the first large thing that moves in certain ways. Countless beginning psychology and ethology students have seen the footage of Lorenz walking through the countryside with a line of goslings imprinted on him, following behind. In this case, the perceptual analyzer that initially identifies mother (or conspecific) does so on the basis of movement of a certain sort.

Goslings and chicks will imprint on a large red shiny ball if that is the only object they see moving during a critical period after birth—or so we thought until the work of Mark Johnson and his colleagues (M. Johnson, Bolhuis, & Horn, 1985). These researchers showed that mother/conspecific identification is such an important problem that evolution has provided at least two redundant learning devices to support it. A newborn chick presented with a moving ball or person and also a stationary stuffed hen will huddle near the stuffed hen.

Thus, Johnson and his colleagues demonstrated that chicks must have an innate perceptual analyzer that specifies what a conspecific looks like. Indeed, these researchers specified the nature of these innate representations. The innate representation of conspecific appearance is very sketchy—there must be an overall bird shape, with a head with eyes and a beak on a neck on a body; if these elements are not in the right configuration, the chick does not recognize the object as a conspecific. However, a chick will huddle close to a stuffed duck or eagle or owl. Johnson and his colleagues have much to say about this fascinating story, bearing on the relations between the two different learning mechanisms, their critical periods, and their neural substrates. My point here is simply that there is an innate representation of hen that specifies roughly what hens look like and contains the inferential role "stay close to that." This representation is part of a domain-specific learning device; the representation is sketchy so it can be filled in with the details of the chick's own mother. In this way it is similar to the innate representations human babies have of conspecifics (two eyes above a mouth within an oval, in a certain configuration—representations that play a role in human babies' identifying others like them and learning to recognize individual caregivers; Morton, Johnson, & Maurer, 1990).

This book argues for many controversial conclusions, but the claim that some representations are innate is not meant to be one of them. The controversy comes when we begin to consider the content and nature of innate representational systems. There certainly are innate sensory representations. Also, innate input analyzers, constrained to accept only some classes of stimuli (bird-shaped entities, face-shaped entities, the night sky), create representations that clearly go beyond sensory content and underlie learning about entities in the world that are crucial to individual survival.

Thesis 2: Discontinuities in the Course of Conceptual Development

This book's second major thesis is that human beings, alone among animals, have the capacity to create representational systems that transcend sensory representations and core cognition. That is, human beings create new representational resources that are qualitatively different from the representations they are built from. Many cognitive scientists, such as Jerry Fodor (1975, 1980) and John Macnamara (1986), deny the very possibility of true cognitive development in this sense, endorsing instead a strong version of the continuity thesis. The continuity thesis is that all the representational structures and inferential capacities that underlie adult belief systems either are present throughout development or arise through processes such as maturation.

Fodor's (1980) argument for the continuity thesis was a one-liner: one cannot learn what one cannot represent. In the famous debate between Piaget, on the one hand, and Fodor and Chomsky, on the other (Piatelli-Palmarini, 1980), Fodor argued that all known learning mechanisms (e.g., parameter setting, correlation detection, prototype formation) are variants of hypothesis testing, and one cannot confirm a hypothesis unless one can already represent it. That is, learning involves choosing between already formulated hypotheses, setting a previously specified parameter, noting a correlation between already represented states of affairs, and abstracting what is common among a set of represented exemplars. These mechanisms, by their very nature, cannot yield a capacity to represent anything that was previously unrepresentable.

Fodor (1975) is famous for an application of this general argument, leading to the conclusion that all lexical concepts are innate. This conclusion requires extra assumptions about lexical concepts—namely that they are atomic, or can't be decomposed into primitives. I eventually address this version of Fodor's continuity thesis in chapter 13, but for now my concern is the more general argument. I do not contest the truism that all learning involves building new representations from antecedently available ones, nor that that all learning in the end can be analyzed as forms of hypothesis fixation. My concern is where the hypotheses come from. As I demonstrate in chapters 8 and 11, learning processes exist that can create representations more powerful than their input. These then allow hypotheses to be formulated over concepts that cannot be expressed in the vocabulary and syntax available at the outset of the learning episode.

Fodor's argument has a crucial weakness. It is falsified by a single counterexample that shows that novel representational capacities, with more expressive power than their input, must have been formed through some learning process. Piaget (1980) invoked an excellent set of counterexamples in his own reply to Fodor. Drawing from the history of mathematics, Piaget pointed out that concepts of rational, real, and complex numbers, and the mathematical notations required to express them, cannot plausibly be attributed to infants, children, or even adults lacking sufficient education in mathematics, and they do not plausibly develop through maturation. Rather, such concepts arise as one learns mathematics. Fodor might reply that infants must innately have the representational resources to express these concepts, but there is an ambiguity in that reply. Of course, they innately have the capacity to construct those representational resources—that is not in dispute. What's actual is possible, and many mathematically literate people represent rational numbers. The question is whether infants could express concepts such as *one-third* or *pi*. I take these questions up in chapters 8 and 9.

Chapter 8 shows that the issue arises even in the case of the positive integers. The integer list is a cultural construction with more representational power than any of the core representational systems on which it is built, thereby providing a genuine counterexample to the argument that conceptual discontinuities are in principle impossible. Chapter 9 sketches the later (in history and in ontogenesis) construction of the concept *rational number,* which equally well transcends the representations available at the outset of the construction process (namely, representations of integers created by children during their preschool years). In these cases, discontinuity is cashed out in terms of vast increases in expressive power.

The study of cognitive development provides many further counterexamples to the continuity thesis. In the course of acquiring intuitive theories of the world, children create new concepts that are incommensurable with those from which they are built. In such cases, discontinuity is cashed out in terms of the creation of new concepts not translatable into the concepts available at the outset of the episode of conceptual change. Chapters 10 and 11 discuss case studies of conceptual change in the history of science and also in childhood.

If such existence proofs show that Fodor's argument is wrong, however, they do not show what is wrong with it. In particular, they do not show us how the infant, child, mathematician, or scientist can use his or her current representational resources to learn new ones. That is the real challenge to cognitive science raised by Fodor's argument, and it is still unmet.

Those who deny the continuity thesis actually face two distinct challenges, one descriptive and one explanatory. First, descriptively, we must provide a satisfactory characterization of what it means for a representational system to be qualitatively different from, to transcend, those that preceded it. We must also provide evidence for two successive points in cognitive development, the later of which contains a representational capacity that transcends what was previously available. Second, with respect to explanation, we must then specify a learning mechanism that accounts for how new representational capacity could come into being.

Thesis 3: Quinian Bootstrapping

This book's third important thesis is that the explanatory challenge is met, in part, by bootstrapping processes such as those described in the literature on history and philosophy of science. I call the kind of bootstrapping process we need to understand conceptual discontinuity "Quinian bootstrapping" because Quine (1960, 1969) developed particularly colorful metaphors in trying to explicate the idea (e.g., building a chimney, pressing against the sides to support oneself as one scrambles up it, building a ladder, and then kicking the ladder out from under, and Neurath's boat, in which one builds a structure to support oneself while already at sea). To "bootstrap" means, literally, to pull oneself up by one's own bootstraps—something that is clearly impossible. The metaphor captures what is hard about the process of creating new representational resources that are not entirely grounded in antecedent representations. Chapters 8 and 11 offer an account of the bootstrapping metaphors of historians and philosophers of science in terms of the resources from current cognitive science.

The Quinian bootstrapping that underlies discontinuous conceptual development must be distinguished from a different kind of learning, also called bootstrapping, that is debated in the contemporary literature on language acquisition. In the language-acquisition literature, bootstrapping processes are invoked to explain how children solve a mapping problem. Suppose children know, thanks to innately supported universal grammar, that there will be nouns, noun phrases, transitive verbs, verb phrases, adjectives, prepositions, quantifiers, and so on, in natural language. Suppose, moreover, that they create innately supported representations for individuals and kinds of individuals for actions, stuffs, intentional causation, and so on. Children still face the formidable problem of identifying how their own particular language expresses these and other universal features of language and thought. Semantic bootstrapping—the use of semantic information to infer syntactic categories—gives the child a beginning wedge into the problem of discovering a particular language's syntactic devices. For example, the language learning mechanism might include the heuristic that representations of kinds of physical objects ought to be mapped onto count nouns. Then, if the child can figure out that a word is being used to refer to a kind of object, the child may assign it to the lexical category count noun and use this assignment to figure out how count nouns are marked in their language (see, for example, Pinker, 1984). Syntactic bootstrapping exploits innately given initial mappings of this sort to solve the converse problem—that of discovering that particular words express particular concepts. For example, if the concept *give* includes a giver, a receiver, and a gift, then the child may exploit syntactic evidence that a given verb has three arguments to guess that it might express this concept (see, for example, Gleitman, Cassidy, Napa, Papafragou, & Trueswell, 2005). Both syntactic and semantic bootstrapping require antecedent conceptual and linguistic representations, and they support solving a very difficult mapping problem. However, these bootstrapping processes do not deny continuity—no totally new representational resources are being created.

Some earlier students of language acquisition also appealed to Quinian bootstrapping as a process underlying language acquisition. Isaac Schlessinger (1982), for example, hypothesized that initially linguistic elements receive only semantic interpretations, such that creating syntactic categories required constructing representations previously unrepresentable.

Rather than just solving a mapping between previously available types of representations, the process envisioned by Schlessinger creates a new type of representations. That is, he suggested that syntactic categories are created by a bootstrapping process of the sort envisioned in the history of science literature (see also Braine, 1963). It is beyond the scope of this book to consider whether Quinian bootstrapping is needed in the course of syntactic development—at issue in that debate is how rich the innate language acquisition device is. But I will show that Quinian bootstrapping definitely has a role to play in explaining the origin of concepts.

1.7. Intuitive Theories—Explicit Conceptual Representations

As I mentioned at the beginning of this chapter, I distinguish two types of conceptual representations: those that articulate core cognition and those that articulate later developing linguistically encoded knowledge structures like intuitive theories. Intuitive theories differ from core cognition in each of its distinctive features: they are not innate, the entities in their domain are not identified by innate input analyzers, their format is most probably not iconic, and they are not continuous throughout development. Quinian bootstrapping mechanisms underlie the human capacity to create theoretical knowledge that transcends core cognition.

Although there are many knowledge structures worthy of study (scripts, schemas, prototypes, the integer list representation of number, the alphabet), many students of cognitive development assume that one kind of knowledge structure—intuitive theories—plays a particularly important role in cognitive architecture. I endorse this assumption, and here I focus on a class of intuitive theories—those that Henry Wellman and Susan Gelman call "framework theories" (Wellman & Gelman, 1992; see also Carey, 1985; Gopnik & Meltzoff, 1997; Keil, 1989). These are the theories that ground the deepest ontological commitments and the most general explanatory principles in terms of which we understand our world. One task (but by no means the only task) in the study of cognitive development is to account for the acquisition of framework theories.

It is worth stepping back and considering what is being presupposed by the choice of the term intuitive theory rather than the more neutral cognitive structure. Intuitive theories, like scientific theories, play several unique roles in mental life. These include: (1) determining a concept's most important features (the properties seen as essential to membership in a concept's extension); (2) representing explicitly held causal and explanatory knowledge; and (3) supporting explanation-based inference. Furthermore, the mechanisms underlying theory development, including Quinian bootstrapping, differ from those that underlie the acquisition of different types of conceptual structures. It is an empirical question whether children have intuitive theories, and whether knowledge acquisition in childhood involves the process of theory change. Those who talk of "intuitive theories" and "framework theories" are explicitly committing themselves to an affirmative answer to those empirical questions. This commitment does not deny that there are important differences between children as theorizers and adult scientists (hence the qualifier, intuitive). Children are not metaconceptually aware theory builders (D. Kuhn et al., 1988). In spite of these differences, the research enterprise in which this work is placed presupposes that there are important substantive similarities between scientific theories and intuitive theories. Of course, the merit of this presupposition depends on the fruitfulness of the research it generates. Chapters 10 and 11 present case studies framed within this research tradition.

As mentioned above, intuitive theories differ from core cognition in many ways. One of the goals of this book is to account for the origin and development of theory-embedded conceptual knowledge, given a beginning state of perceptual representations and core cognition. Many researchers have blurred the distinction between core cognition and intuitive theories. For example, Alan Leslie is one of the most articulate advocates of the core cognition position, and he—like me—characterizes core cognition as modular, encapsulated, supported by innate perceptual analyzers, and unchanging during development. Confusingly, in discussing the infants' beginning state, he characterizes core cognition in much the way I have, yet he dubs his modules Theory of Mind Module and Theory of Bodies Module (Leslie, 1994). That is, he characterizes core cognition, but he calls systems of core cognition "theories." This is not merely a squabble about terminology, for if I am right that core cognition exists and differs from explicit conceptual knowledge in the ways specified above, then failing to adopt contrasting terminology conflates fundamentally different kinds of mental representations.

Gopnik and Meltzoff (1997) go further than merely calling infant conceptual knowledge "theories"; they deny the distinction between core cognition and theories. They explicitly characterize infants' early developing knowledge of bodies and agents as theoretical knowledge, claiming that the mechanisms that underlie acquisition of knowledge in these domains are the same as those that support theory development by adult scientists. This leads to the seemingly absurd (and false, I shall argue) conclusion that the processes by which infants achieve object permanence are the same as those through which Darwin formulated the theory of natural selection.

The confusion between core cognition and intuitive theories is intelligible, for two of the paradigm cases of each have overlapping content. Core cognition of objects overlaps with knowledge of intuitive physics, and core cognition of intentional agents overlaps with an intuitive theory of mind. This overlap in content arises because the output of the core cognition systems is part of the input to theory building. The case studies in this book constitute an extended argument for the position that theory building can, and does, transcend core cognition.

Overview of the Book

The chapters to come distinguish the representations that constitute core cognition from two other types of representations: sensory/perceptual representations and conceptual representations embedded in explicit intuitive theories. Chapter 2 examines the hypothesis that the developmental primitives are sensori-motor or perceptual. Chapters 3, 4, and 5 characterize core cognition and provide evidence for several domains of human core cognition that exemplify its distinctive features. Chapter 6 considers the question of whether all innate representations with conceptual content are embedded within core cognition systems, or alternatively, whether there are also innate central representations. Chapter 7 touches on some relations between core cognition and language. Chapters 8 through 11 take on both parts of Fodor's challenge to cognitive science. They provide descriptions of discontinuous conceptual development in which concepts come into existence that were not expressible given earlier conceptual resources, and they characterize the bootstrapping mechanisms that underlie the change. Finally, the two concluding chapters summarize my account of the origins of concepts (chapter 12) and draw out the implications from these case studies for a theory of human concepts (chapter 13).

NOTES

1. An excellent overview of competing accounts of concepts in the philosophical and psychological literatures is provided in the collection of classic papers assembled by Margolis and Laurence (1999). See also their own superb and comprehensive tutorial essay in the same volume.

2. See Carey & Spelke, 1994; R. Gelman, 1991; Leslie, 1994, and Spelke, Breilinger, Macomber, & Jacobsen, 1992, for related characterizations of core cognition.

3. Different pictures of the initial representational repertoire have articulated theories of conceptual development in the Western philosophical/scientific traditions at least back to the time of Greek thinkers. Here I am referring to works by Gopnik & Meltzoff, 1997; Locke, 1690/1975; Piaget, 1954; Quine, 1960, 1977.

2

The Initial Representational Repertoire: The Empiricist Picture

In this chapter I begin to build the argument for core cognition by marshaling evidence against the empiricist hypothesis that the initial state is limited to sensory representations. Many modern thinkers, as disparate as Piaget, Quine, eliminitivist connectionists, and systems dynamic theorists explicitly or implicitly share this empiricist assumption (e.g., Elman et al., 1996; Piaget, 1954; Quine, 1960, 1977; Thelen et al., 2001). This hypothesis has a certain plausibility. All evidence we have of the particular world we live in comes through our senses. Doesn't this mean that all of our knowledge must be able to be formulated in terms of sensory primitives?

Here I counter this seductive argument, while summoning evidence that some early developing representations are conceptual. The chapter has some secondary goals as well. I discuss the methods I draw upon throughout the first half of this book. Also, different methods yield apparently conflicting data, and I give some sense of how conflicts might be resolved. Finally, I lay out the arguments that convince me that some conceptual representations are innate.

The Empiricist Picture

According to British empiricists such as John Locke, all human concepts are grounded in a set of primitive representations—in Locke's terms, "ideas." The primitive ideas are the output of sense organs—they are sensory representations. They are primitive in two different senses. First, these ideas are definitional primitives. All concepts are either primitive or complex, and all complex concepts are defined in terms of primitive ones that themselves are understood without any definition (Locke, 1690/ 1975; see Margolis & Laurence, 1999, for a superb tutorial on the empiricist theory of concepts). Second, these ideas are developmental primitives. The acquisition of concepts is explained by a specification of the set of innate primitives and by the associative mechanisms through which complex concepts are built from them.

The 18th-century British empiricists' picture of conceptual development finds articulate and ardent defenders to this day. This staying power has two explanations. First, the empiricists staked out an ambitious set of phenomena that a theory of concepts must be responsible for. They sought to explain how concepts refer, how people categorize, how concepts function in thought, how human knowledge is warranted, and how human knowledge is acquired. They offered a comprehensive theory that provided an integrated account of all of these phenomena and more. Few contemporary theories of concepts have anything like the scope of the empiricists'. Second, the theory contains important grains of truth.

That the primitive ideas are sensory was important to the empiricist program. The empiricist explanation of reference depended on the view that sensory representations refer to certain aspects of the world by virtue of the operation of the sense organs. That is, they took as unproblematic the view that our concepts red and round are based on the cases in which red and round things cause us to have sensory representations of red and round. As long as the referential potential of primitive concepts is guaranteed by how sensation works, and as long as all concepts may be defined out of primitive concepts, then the referential potential of all concepts is explained. That is, the extensions of complex concepts are determined by their definitional structure and the extensions of the primitives from which they are built.

This is not the place for a full exposition and critique of the empiricist view of concepts. Every part of the view has come under fire (see chapter 13). Most obviously, the project of defining all concepts in terms of sensory primitives is unworkable. Most representations underlying human natural language are not perceptual representations. Human beings represent nonobservable entities (beliefs, protons), nonobservable properties of observable entities (functions, essences), abstract entities (numbers, logical operators), and fictional entities (Gods, ghosts, Hamlet). Concepts for such entities are not themselves the output of sense organs. Of course, the empiricists held that these concepts are nonetheless definable in terms of perceptual primitives. No adequate definition has ever been provided for most concepts (Fodor, Garrett, Walker, & Parkes, 1980; Laurence & Margolis, 1999), and certainly no definitions for many concepts in terms of perceptual primitives can even be attempted. Try doing so for the concepts *justice* or *sin*, let alone the concept *God*.

This line of argument defeats the position that all human representations are either perceptual or defined in terms of perceptual representations. However, it does not defeat the argument that the innate primitives are perceptual, as long as one provides a learning mechanism that could account for the creation during development of nonperceptual representations, given a beginning stage containing only perceptual representations. I believe that the bootstrapping processes that are characterized in chapters 8 through 11 underlie discontinuities in conceptual development, and thus I do not accept a general learnability argument for the impossibility that the initial state may consist only of perceptual, sensori-motor representations. Rather, if we wish to characterize the innate representational primitives, we have no alternative but to do the hard empirical work of finding out what representations young infants have.

The empiricists certainly got two important points right. There are innate sensory representations and their content is ensured by how our sense organs work. The empiricists did not know that they could thank natural selection for making this is so, but Darwin gave us a way of understanding how the right causal connections between properties of the world and states of the nervous system can be established and maintained. It is because sense organs were selected to work as they do that humans can see color and movement, can taste salt and sweet, can hear tones and feel heat. The operation of evolutionarily constructed input analyzers guarantees that the relevant representations refer to aspects of the environment that are important to survival.

A Historical Aside: The Rationalist/Empiricist Debate About Perception

Sensory representations may be roughly characterized as those representations that are the output of the sense organs. They are what psychologists call proximal representations—those representations that maintain the point of view of the pattern of stimulation on sense organs. For example, a retinal projection is a proximal representation, as is a representation of a pin prick on the back of my hand. As has been well known for centuries, the information in the proximal stimulus greatly underspecifies the distal world that was the source of the stimulation in the first place. Distal representations capture aspects of the external world—they exhibit constancies. Perceived size compensates for the fact that proximal representations of the sizes of objects are determined by distance; the retinal projection of a quarter is much larger at arms' length than 5 feet away, yet our perceptual representation of the actual size of the quarter is accurate over these distances. Similarly, perceived shape is three-dimensional, in spite of the fact that retinal projections are two-dimensional.

Because the empiricists were committed to the view that developmental primitives were sensory, they faced a formidable challenge in accounting for our capacity to perceive the true shapes of objects, the true depth relations among them, and so on. One arena of the historical debates between empiricists such as Berkeley and Hume and rationalists such as Descartes was their solutions to this challenge (e.g., Berkeley, 1732/1919; Descartes, 1637/1971[1]). Consider the representation of depth as an example. Empiricists such as Berkeley and Hume attempted to show how representations of depth could be learned by associative mechanisms operating over sensory primitives. They considered sensory primitives such as proximal representations of size and shape, interposition cues, convergence of the eyes (felt effort in the muscles being greater as a function of how converged the eyes are), and accommodation of the lens (also conceptualized as felt effort). They then assumed that these cues are associated, through learning, with cues to depth from other sensory modalities—for example, proprioceptive cues to the difference between reaching and contacting a nearby versus a more distant object, or between walking to a nearby object and walking to a more distant object. According to the empiricists, the veridical representation of depth is built up from and constituted by this associative structure.

Nativists such as Descartes presented a very different picture. Descartes did not deny that the information from which depth representations were computed must be the output of sense organs. Nativists do not believe in magic. Rather, he believed that there are innate inferential mechanisms (today we would say computational mechanisms) that instantiate constraints derived from geometry that take this input and transform it into veridical representations of depth. His example was the geometrical inference from convergence to depth, an argument ridiculed by Berkeley (1732/1919) thus:

> But those lines and angles, by means whereof mathematicians pretend to explain the perception of distance, are themselves not at all perceived, nor they, in truth, ever thought of by those unskillful in optics. I appeal to any one's experience, whether, upon sight of an object, he compute its distance by the bigness of the angle made by the meeting of the two optic axes? Or whether he ever think of the greater or lesser divergence of the rays, which arrive from any point to his pupil? Nay, whether it be not perfectly impossible him to perceive by sense the various angles wherewith the rays, according to their greater or lesser divergence, do fall on his eye. Every one is himself the best judge of what he perceives, and what not. In vain shall all the mathematicians in the world tell me, that I perceive certain lines and angles which introduce into my mind the various ideas of distance; so long as I myself am conscious of no such thing. (pp. 15–16)

Of course, we now know that Descartes was entirely right—exactly those computations are instantiated in the mind and they do contribute to the perception of depth. Modern models of perception do not require that the representations that enter into modular perceptual computations be consciously accessible. Another example in the tradition of Descartes would be the computation of depth from information derived from the degree of mismatch between the images of an object derived from each eye (stereopsis). Berkeley could similarly ridicule this idea by saying that he is not aware that the two eyes yield different proximal images of an attended object, and that even if he were aware of this fact, he wouldn't know how to calculate depth from it.

As far as I can tell, there is hardly any classical debate from the history of philosophy of mind that has been more conclusively settled. Every textbook on perception details the computations carried out over sensory representations that yield veridical representations of depth, and all agree that such computations are subconscious, operate on proprietary information, and are encapsulated (i.e., are modular, in Fodor's sense, at least to some degree). Showing Berkeley wrong, the evidence that at least some of these computations are innate is overwhelming. Eleanor Gibson's famous work on the visual cliff provided some of the first evidence in support of innate mechanisms for depth perception: newborn animals who have had no opportunity to form associative structures over different sensory cues to depth avoid the deep end of a visual cliff (Gibson & Walk, 1960). With respect to human infants, Alan Slater's demonstrations of size constancy in newborns require that the infant represent depth (Slater, Mattock, & Brown, 1990).

I draw two morals from this story. First, the question of whether development begins with a stock of merely sensory primitives, or whether evolution endowed us with computational devices that yield veridical representations of the distal world, is settled in favor of the existence of Descartes-like innate perceptual input analyzers. Second, there is no in-principle argument against the hypothesis that evolution endowed animals with input analyzers that yield representations that are further along the continuum between sensory representations and conceptual ones than are depth representations. Representations further along this continuum will be couched in the vocabulary of abstractions rather than that of appearances and spatio-temporal relations. They will be central, interacting with the output of other input analyzers, will be accessible, and will have relatively rich inferential roles.

The Initial State: Perceptual/Sensori-motor Primitives

Important 20th-century psychologists and philosophers, as different as Jean Piaget (1954) and W. v. O. Quine (1960), also held that the initial repertoire of mental representations is limited to a set of sensory or perceptual developmental primitives. Piaget's position was that infants begin life solely with representations that subserve innate sensori-motor reflexes. All mental life, according to Piaget, is constructed from this initial representational repertoire. For Piaget, the important properties of sensory representations that distinguished them from conceptual ones included their being the output of sense organs (and restricted to single-sense modalities) and their content being limited to currently experienced sensations.

Quine was no empiricist. He denied that theoretical terms or the terms in natural languages could be defined in terms of perceptual primitives (or even that the notion of analytic definition made sense; he denied the analytic/synthetic distinction). Nonetheless, he held that the infant's initial representational resources were limited to an innate perceptual vocabulary, which he called a "prelinguistic quality space" and which he conceptualized as an innate perceptual similarity space. In a series of influential writings Quine developed three interrelated theses about conceptual development (Quine, 1960, 1969, 1977):

1. Infants' representations are radically different from those of their elders, and are formulated with respect to a perceptual similarity space.
2. The concepts that articulate commonsense ontological commitments are a cultural construction.
3. In the course of mastering natural language, each child acquires adult ontological commitments through a bootstrapping process.

This book is an extended meditation on these three theses. In these early chapters I argue, contrary to Quine, that many infant representations are conceptual and that many of our commonsense ontological commitments are innate. However, I agree with Quine that some, indeed most, of our commonsense ontological commitments are a cultural construction, and in chapters 8 through 12 I will spell out how the bootstrapping processes he envisioned work.

Whether there are innate conceptual representations is an empirical question. Because both Piaget and Quine focused their discussions on representations of objects (as did the British empiricists), I begin with a case study of infant object representations. Both Piaget and Quine agreed that young infants cannot achieve representations of objects that exist independently of the infants' own sensory experience of them.

Why Object Is Not a Perceptual Representation

Perhaps the most studied topic regarding infant representational capacities is the concept object, in the sense of representations of substantial, three-dimensional, material bodies that exist independently of the observer. Are

Piaget and Quine correct that: (1) object representations are non-perceptual; (2) object representations are not available to young infants; and (3) object representations are built from sensory or perceptual primitives in the course of development?

Object representations, like depth representations, are clearly non-sensory, for they represent distal entities. Sensory representations capture object appearances such as color, retinally specified size and shape, and so on, but they do not represent objects as objects. Between them, Piaget and Quine offered several distinct reasons to consider object representations to be nonperceptual as well as nonsensory. First, Piaget argued that if perceptual representations are the output of modality-specific sensory analyzers, then object representations are not perceptual because they are multimodal. For adults, the representation of a visually perceived object specifies what it will feel like, where it will be if one reaches for it, and so forth. Piaget, along with the British empiricists, and along with Quine, believed that infants had to learn the cross-modal correspondences among the sensory representations of object appearances. This was no problem for their theories; indeed, the British empiricists believed that learning those cross-modal correspondences constituted building the complex concept object.[2] Of course, learning contingencies among sensory representations in different sense modalities does not require nonsensory vocabulary. But the learning of such contingencies, Piaget thought, was the first step in transcending the initial sensori-motor primitives. Second—and here Piaget and Quine are also in agreement—if perceptual representations are limited to what currently experienced entities look like, feel like, taste like, and move like, objects cannot be represented as individuals that persist through time, independently of the observer. Quine agreed with Piaget that there would be no representations of permanent objects. As Quine pointed out, a perceptual vocabulary does not include fundamental quantificational devices. The child could not represent a given object as the same one as one seen earlier, for sensory representations do not provide criteria for numerical identity.

According to Quine, the infant endowed only with an innate perceptual quality space can sense similarity among experiences that are represented in this space (flesh-colored, milk-smelling experience at time 1; flesh-colored, milk-smelling experience at time 2), and the stable configurations of these qualities (color, shape, smell, sound) could certainly be learned. This would enable the child to recognize instances of mama-experience. In Quine's words, "his first learning [of the word 'mama'] is a matter of learning how much of what goes on around him counts as the mother" (1960, p. 92). But being able to recognize instances of mama-experience is not the same as representing one enduring mother —the same one today as yesterday.

Quine emphasized how much an ontology exhausted by a perceptual quality space differs from one articulated in terms of enduring individuals. For example, in one passage, he speculated that the baby reconceptualizes his mother once he has mastered the scheme of enduring and recurring physical objects. He also insisted that our adult commonsense ontology is a cultural construction, just as the concepts that articulate scientific theories are cultural constructions. Just as explicit theories embody their ontological commitments in language and formalisms, so too our commonsense ontology is captured in language. Indeed, the process Quine envisioned though which babies transcend the innate perceptual quality space and master the ontology of enduring and recurring physical objects crucially involves language acquisition. Quine proposed that the child bootstraps the new ontology by gradually learning the quantificational devices of natural languages—quantifiers, determiners, the is of numerical identity, and so forth. Chapters 8 through 12 present a sympathetic characterization of Quinian bootstrapping processes, arguing for their role in the construction of new representational resources. My disagreement with Quine is straightforwardly empirical; in my view of conceptual development, he might be right. Rather, his picture of the infant just turns out to be false.

What Piaget wrote about under the rubric of "object permanence" comes to the same thing as what Quine wrote about as "divided reference" and quantificational capacities. When babies reach for a hidden object, and we attribute to them an appreciation of object permanence, we assume that they represent the object they seek as the same object, the same one, that they saw disappear. Otherwise, it isn't object permanence, but rather is some learned contingency, such as an appropriate instantiation of "reach where I saw some visual property disappear and some visual property or tactual property will be there." The latter generalization is formulated in the language of sensori-motor, perceptual, and spatio-temporal primitives; whereas "reach for the object that went behind the screen; it will still be there" is not, for "the object" and "it" pick out a single individual's persisting through occlusion. The criteria for individuation and numerical identity for ordinary objects go beyond perceptual primitives. In the adult state, representations of objects are constrained by the principle of spatio-temporal continuity (objects do not go into and out of existence). Although perceptual primitives can specify a currently perceived, bounded entity and its current path of motion, they do not specify that the entity continues to exist when we lose perceptual contact with it. This construal is provided by the mind; and the question raised by both Piaget and Quine was how representations of permanent individuated objects, quantified as discrete individuals tracked through time, come to be formed.

Before we consider how infants form representations of object permanence, how they create criteria for individuation and numerical identity of objects, we must consider when they do so, for Piaget's and Quine's theories of how depend crucially on when—so, too, for cross-modal representations of objects. Piaget claimed that cross-modal correspondences among perceptual properties of objects were learned by 7 months (by the end of what he called the "stage of secondary circular reactions"), but that infants' representations of objects as permanent, existing apart from their own sensori-motor schemas, emerged only between 18 and 24 months (heralding the end of the stage of sensori-motor intelligence). Quine claimed that the capacity to represent "objects as such" emerged only when the child mastered the quantification devices of natural language (i.e., between ages 2:0 and 3:0). Therefore, evidence that 2- to 6-month-olds have these representational capacities challenges Quine's and Piaget's proposals. Nonetheless, the question of innateness is still open, for infants might form these representational capacities from perceptual primitives during the first two months of life. At the end of this chapter, I shall return to the question of innateness.

Piaget's and Quine's Evidence

Quine, a philosopher, did not consider actual empirical evidence for his claim that the initial state consists solely of perceptual representations. Rather, he discussed possible observations, considering whether they could possibly show that prelinguistic infants' representational capacities are the same as yours or mine. He argued that any piece of behavior we observe is consistent with radically different ontological commitments on the part of the behaving subject. The child who points to a bottle and says "bottle," or who picks up a bottle and drinks from it, may have the capacity to represent to individual bottles and to represent generalizations such as "that bottle has milk in it," or may simply have learned associations between perceptual features of bottle, on the one hand, and a spoken word or an action, on the other. Of course, it is this line of argument writ large that ends in Quine's views of radical indeterminacy, for the same considerations bear on adult linguistic capacities as well. In Quine's view, ontological commitments are fixed only up to the indefinite number of schemes that are consistent with the grammatical commitments of a given language. I believe Quine is wrong, and we can bring evidence to bear on the child's quantificational capacities and ontological commitments.

Piaget's genius was at bringing empirical data to bear on classic philosophical questions, and his experiments on object permanence are justly among the most celebrated in developmental psychology. He reported observations that are consistent with the claim that young infants lack representations of permanent, multimodally specified, objects. With respect to intermodal correspondences, he observed infants being startled when they made a fast movement of their own hand across their visual field, and he assumed this meant that they did not know what their own hand looked like and that they could not relate a representation of a visually located visual experience with a proprioceptive representation of the location of limb. He also made observations of infants' examining their own hands or feet and he assumed that these provided the experience the infants needed to make intermodal representations of their own bodies. These could then scaffold, associating the visual, tactual, and spatial correspondences among the sensory representations of external objects.

With respect to object permanence, Piaget made a two-part empirical argument that infants did not represent objects as spatio-temporally continuous. First, he showed that below 8 months of age or so, an infant reaching for a desired object will abort the reach if the object is hidden under a cloth or cup, or if it is hidden behind a screen, in spite of the fact that the infant has the motor capacity to remove the barrier. Piaget thought that this behavior showed that the infants did not represent the object as continuing to exist when out of sight. Second, he argued (like Quine) that the 8-month-olds' success does not necessarily mean that they do represent objects as existing spatio-temporally continuously. Indeed, he discovered a second important phenomenon, the A-not-B error, which he took as knockdown evidence that they do not do so. After retrieving an object in hidden location A, if it is next hidden in location B, the infant will search again in location A. Piaget's interpretation was that infants had simply learned a rule, "look where something has disappeared and something interesting will happen," rather than that they were tracing the identity of the object through changes in location. It was not until 18 months or so, when infants could solve the hidden displacement pro-blems, that Piaget (1954) was willing to credit them with a representation of object permanence. In the hidden displacement problems, an object is hidden by hand in location A, and the infant sees the closed hand move from A to B. The infant looks first in A and succeeds on this problem when, not finding the object at A, the child goes immediately to B. Piaget argued that this behavior requires representing the absent object and reasoning about its unseen movements.

These Piagetian observations are extremely reliable. They have been replicated replicated countless times, and were even incorporated into an infant "IQ test," because reaching these milestones markedly later than Piaget found sometimes reflects mental retardation (Bayley, 1969). Nonetheless, recent methodological advances have provided a wealth of data that reveal that Piaget underestimated the representational capacities of young infants.

Intermodal Representations

The empiricists believed that learning the intermodal correspondences between sensed properties of objects is the process through which representations of objects are built. The relevant correspondences include how visual appearance of texture is correlated with how that texture feels when touched, how visual appearance of shape is correlated with how that shape feels when touched, and so on, as well as correspondences between visually specified locations and the effects of reaching to proprioceptively specified locations. For the empiricists, there was nothing more to object representations than representation of such correspondences. Piaget disagreed with the empiricists on the issue of whether representations of objects can be cashed out in sensory and spatio-temporal vocabulary, but he agreed with them that intermodal representations such as those listed above had to be learned and that this learning is an essential part of the process through which nonperceptual representations of objects are built.

The empiricist position misses the mark in two ways. First, even once all those intermodal representations are formed, infants still would not have representations that go beyond sensory vocabulary—no representations of individuated, spatio-temporally continuous objects that exist independently of themselves. Second, there is now massive evidence that intermodal representations are innate and certainly not learned through the associative mechanisms Piaget and the empiricists imagined. Neonates orient visually to a location specified by a sound; neonates represent the correspondence between visually and tactually specified shapes; and neonates represent the correspondence between visually specified and proprioceptively specified facial gestures. Two experimental results can stand as examples from this large and convincing literature.

In the first example, Andrew Meltzoff and his colleagues allowed neonates to suck on a strangely shaped pacifier—either a smooth cube or a sphere with bumps all over it. These babies were only a few days old and had never had anything in their mouths other than nipples and their own hands. The babies were not allowed to see the pacifier. At the same time (or later in some experiments), the infants were shown two pictures —one of a cube and the other of a sphere with bumps. The babies preferentially attended to the picture that matched the pacifier on which they sucked. Thus, the infants innately recognized the correspondence between the visually and tactually specified shapes/textures (Meltzoff & Borton, 1979). A second example also comes from Meltzoff's laboratory. He and Keith Moore showed that neonates would imitate the facial gestures of an experimenter (mouth opening, tongue protrusion). Chapter 5 considers the significance of this result for the characterization of core cognition of human agents, but for now it is enough to show innate representations of the correspondence between what another's face looks like and the actions and feel of their own face (Meltzoff & Moore, 1977;

see Myowa-Yamakoshi, Tomonaga, Tanaka, & Matsuzawa, 2004, for a replication with an infant chimpanzee).

These data, along with those reviewed above ("A Historical Aside"), show that representations of people and objects, including their locations in space, are specified intermodally in neonates. Infants do not have to learn which sensations in one modality predict those in another—either in the service of learning the associations that the empiricists took to constitute depth representations nor the associations that they took to constitute object representations.

Criteria for Individuation and Numerical Identity of Objects; Object Permanence

My targets in this chapter are Piaget and Quine. My aim is to convince you that infants have an innate capacity to represent objects as existing independently from themselves and an innate capacity to quantify objects just as do adults. I will proceed in two steps: first, by reviewing the evidence that by 2 to 5 months of age infants have these capacities and then by turning to the question of innateness.

By 2 months of age, infants represent objects as spatio-temporally continuous. Not only do they represent objects as continuing to exist behind barriers, they also take evidence of spatio-temporal discontinuity as evidence for numerical distinctness. The methods that show this were not available to Piaget. The literature I review in these early chapters draws on patterns of looking to diagnose infants' representations of the world, especially experiments using the violation-of-expectancy looking-time methodology. In this paradigm, infants watch as events unfold before them. On some occasions, a magic trick is performed, creating an impossible or highly improbable event. The robust result is that infants look longer at improbable or impossible events than at ordinary ones, presumably because violations of expectancy are attention grabbing. Babies cannot react to a violation of the expected unless there is some mismatch between their representation of a current outcome and their representation of the antecedent events, and thus the researcher can use patterns of elevated versus nonelevated looking times as a source of data concerning the infant's representations of the ongoing events. In chapters

3 through 5 I consider further the nature of the infant's representations of these events. Here, I merely argue that infants' representations of these events are articulated in terms of a concept object, and they begin to characterize that concept in terms of evidence concerning the extension of the representation and its conceptual roles.

Renée Baillargeon, Elizabeth Spelke, and colleagues (1985) carried out the first violation-of-expectancy study that was brought to bear on infants' representations of objects as continuing to exist when out of sight. Four-month-old infants were habituated to a screen rotating 180°, as shown in Figure 2.1a. After habituation, an object was placed in the path of the screen on its downward trajectory, and one of two events ensued. In possible outcomes, the screen was rotated until it touched the object and then rotated back to its initial position (Figure 2.1b). In impossible outcomes, the screen was rotated through the space occupied by the object by the full 180° (Figure 2.1c). Infants looked longer at the

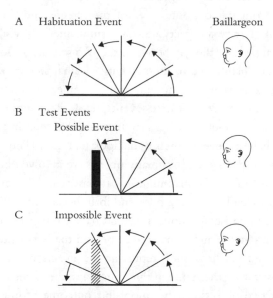

Figure 2.1. Diagram of Baillargeon, Wasserman, & Spelke (1985) rotating screen paradigm. a: habituation events. b: possible outcomes. c: impossible outcomes. Reprinted from Baillargeon, R., Spelke, E. S., & Wasserman, S. (1985). Object permanence in 5-month-old infants. *Cognition, 20*, 191–208, with permission from Elsevier.

impossible outcome than at the possible one. Later studies revealed this pattern of results in infants as young as 2 months of age. These data were the first to suggest that very young infants represent an object placed behind a barrier to exist even when out of sight, as well as that infants' representations of object motion are constrained by the principle that one object cannot pass through the space occupied by another.

I more fully illustrate the logic of violation-of-expectancy studies with another design from Spelke's laboratory (Spelke, Kestenbaum, & Simon, 1995). This study was also aimed at exploring whether young infants represent objects as continuing to exist when out of sight. It is particularly relevant here for it raises the issue of how babies individuate objects and trace numerical identity over time, thus bearing specifically on Quine's claims concerning the quantificational capacities of pre-linguistic human infants.

Figure 2.2a schematically depicts an event shown to infants in this typical violation-of-expectancy looking-time experiment. Two screens are placed on an empty stage, and two objects are brought out, in alternation, from the opposite sides of the screens and then returned behind them. The two objects are never simultaneously visible, and no object ever appears in the gap between the two screens. In some studies, infants are fully habituated to these events; in other studies, they merely are familiarized to them by showing some number of iterations. In full habituation, infants watch these events until their interest in them declines by some preset ratio (e.g., to the point that their final looking at the event is half the level of their initial looking times). The question we want to pose to infants is: How many objects are involved in this event? For adults, the answer is unambiguous: at least two. This event cannot consist of a single object going back and forth because its path would be spatio-temporally discontinuous; it would have to dematerialize behind the right-hand screen and rematerialize behind the left-hand screen.

We ask infants how they represent the events by removing the screens and showing them one of two outcomes: the expected (to adults) outcome of two objects, or the impossible outcome of just one object (thanks to a simple magic trick; one of the objects is surreptitiously removed through a trapdoor in the rear of the stage). Then the stage is cleared, the familiarization event repeated, and the other test outcome

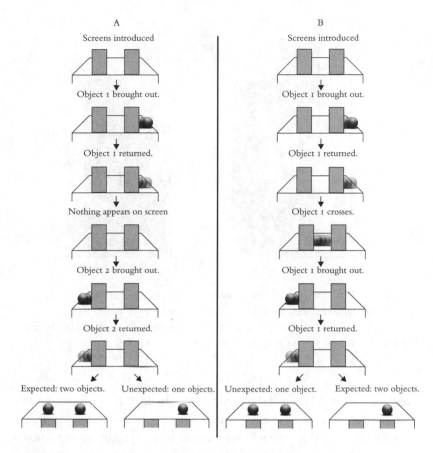

Figure 2.2. Diagram of the Spelke, Kestenbaum, & Simons (1995) split-screen spatio-temporal continuity paradigm. A: discontinuous motion condition. B: con-tiuous motion condition. Redrawn from Spelke, E. S., Kestenbaum, R., & Simons, D. J. (1995). Spatiotemporal continuity, smoothness of motion and object identity in infancy, with permission from the *British Journal of Developmental Psychology*, *13*(2), 113–142. © The British Psychological Society.

revealed. Usually in these experiments there are three pairs of possible/ impossible trials, alternating, with order counterbalanced across infants.

In these studies, infants look reliably longer at the impossible outcome of one object than at the expected outcome of two (see Figure 2.3a for typical data; Xu & Carey, 1996). These are the only actual data (the numbers) from an infant violation-of-expectancy looking-time study I will present in this book. (For most experiments, I present the pattern of data

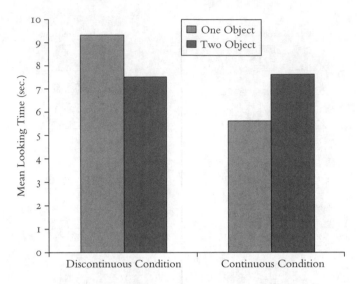

Figure 2.3. Ten-month-old infants' looking times during the test trials in the split-screen spatio-temporal continuity study (Xu and Carey, 1996). Reprinted from Xu, F., & Carey, S. (1996). Infants' metaphysics: the case of numerical identity. *Cognitive Psychology, 30,* 111–153, with permission from Elsevier.

only qualitatively.) I present the numbers here to illustrate for those of you who have never read a technical paper using this method what exactly is meant when I say that infants looked longer at one type of outcome than at another (truth in advertising). Notice that the difference in looking times to the expected outcome (two objects) and the impossible outcome (one object) is small—less than 2 seconds, averaging across the 16 babies who were tested. Still, this is a very reliable result. Of 16 babies, 13 showed this pattern, and those who looked longer at the expected outcome showed a smaller difference in looking times between the two outcomes than did those who looked longer at the impossible outcome. Statistical analyses allow us to distinguish this pattern of data from random responding. Furthermore, this very pattern of data has been replicated many times. All of the looking-time studies I use for my arguments in this book have these characteristics: reliable and replicable differences in looking times between the expected and unexpected outcomes.

Of course, one must consider alternative explanations for any given pattern of results. In this case, perhaps infants are not representing the path of the object(s) emerging from behind the screen at all. Perhaps the most salient aspect of these arrays during the familiarization part of the experiment is that there are two screens. The preference for one object in the outcome arrays might be a novelty preference: an array of one object is more novel, relative to the two-screen familiarization arrays, than is an array of two objects. This alternative hypothesis requires that infants distinguish arrays of one object from arrays of two objects, but it does not require that they represent the objects as continuing to exist behind the screen, nor that they use evidence regarding spatio-temporal continuity as a basis for computations concerning numerical identity.

A control for this alternative is to show the object appearing in the gap during familiarization (Figure 2.2b). The simplest interpretation of this event is that it involves a single object going back and forth behind the screens, and indeed, that is the interpretation 10-month-old infants apparently prefer. When the screen is removed and the outcomes revealed, infants now look longer at the two-object outcomes than at the one-object outcomes (Figure 2.3b). The differentiation of patterns of looking in the discontinuous event and the continuous event shows that infants indeed analyzed the paths of the object(s) emerging from behind the screens and established representations of two objects in the two-object events on the basis of spatio-temporal discontinuity.

The original experiment using this design was carried out by Elizabeth Spelke and her colleagues with 4-month-old infants. Andréa Aguiar and Renée Baillargeon (1999, 2002), using essentially the same method, have shown that 2-month-old infants also expect objects to move on spatio-temporally continuous paths, even through occlusion.

Karen Wynn's (1992b) famous "addition/subtraction" experiments support the same conclusions: that infants use evidence of spatio-temporal discontinuity as a basis for individuating objects, and that they represent hidden objects as existing behind screens. Wynn used the violation-of-expectancy looking-time paradigm to explore whether infants could update a representation of a hidden object or objects when additional objects were added or subtracted from the set. Her first study tested 5-month-olds on $1 + 1 = 2$ or 1, $2 - 1 = 2$ or 1, and $1 + 1 = 2$ or 3 events. Take $1 + 1 = 2$ or 1 as an example. The familiarization events were as in the top panel of Figure 2.4a. Infants watched as a single object was placed on an empty stage, and a screen was rotated up that hid the object. Then the infants watched as a hand brought in a second object and as the hand was withdrawn empty. The screen was then lowered, revealing either the expected outcome of two objects, or the unexpected outcome of one object. Looking times to outcomes of one and two objects in this condition were contrasted with those from the $2 - 1 = 2$ or 1 condition (Figure 2.4b, in which case, the two-object outcome is unexpected and the one-object outcome is expected). Infants' patterns of looking were different in the two conditions; in the subtraction condition they looked reliably longer at the two-object outcome, whereas in the addition condition they did not. Wynn also found that infants succeeded in the $1 + 1 = 2$ or 3 condition, looking longer at the unexpected outcome of three objects. Infants' attention is drawn whenever any number of objects other than precisely two is revealed after a $1 + 1$ event.[3]

The implications of these results for our understanding of infants' representation of number will be explored in chapter 4; here, I wish to emphasize their implications for the Quinian/Piagetian position. To succeed on Wynn's tasks, infants must represent the object as continuing to exist behind the screen. Furthermore, because the objects are physically identical, the child must use spatio-temporal evidence as a basis for individuation; the infant has no other information relevant to whether the second object is numerically distinct from the first. In the $1 + 1$ event, the infant must represent the object behind the screen, use the fact that the object being introduced in the hand is spatio-temporally distinct from that one, and thereby take it to be a numerically distinct object, and update the representation of the hidden array by including a representation of a second hidden object.

Not only do these experiments reveal that infants expect objects to be spatio-temporally continuous, they also show that infants' object representations are governed by criteria for individuation and numerical identity. Contrary to Quine, infants command the logic of divided reference before they have learned the quantificational apparatus of their natural language; they distinguish one object seen on different occasions from two numerically distinct objects.

Aside: Why Do Infants Fail on Search Tasks?

Remember, Piaget's evidence that infants do not represent objects as continuing to exist in the absence of current sensory evidence of them

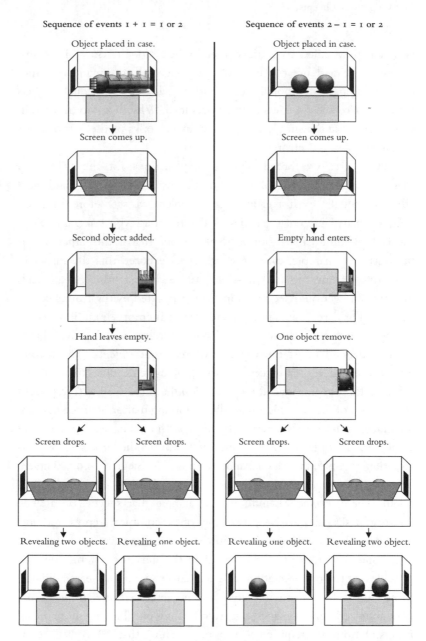

Sequence of events 1 + 1 = 1 or 2

Object placed in case.

Screen comes up.

Second object added.

Hand leaves empty.

Screen drops.   Screen drops.

Revealing two objects.   Revealing one object.

Sequence of events 2 − 1 = 1 or 2

Object placed in case.

Screen comes up.

Empty hand enters.

One object remove.

Screen drops.   Screen drops.

Revealing one object.   Revealing two object.

Figure 2.4. Diagram of Wynn (1992) addition/subtraction paradigm. 1 + 1 condition and 2 − 1 conditions. Redrawn from Wynn, K. (1992b). Addition and subtraction by human infants. *Nature*, *358*, 749–750, with permission from Macmillan Publishers Ltd.

was that they failed to retrieve them when hidden. But I have just reviewed the evidence that by 2 months of age, at least, infants represent objects as spatio-temporally continuous, tracking individual objects through space and time, even when occluded. Why then, do they fail in search tasks like the simple object-permanence tasks or the versions that reveal the A–not-B error?

There are two broad types of explanations for the failure on Piagetian tasks in the face of success on the looking-time tasks, and these are not mutually exclusive. First, any problem we set before an infant requires many different capacities. A failure on a given task may reflect the lack of some capacity other than the one that is the target of our interests. For example, many researchers have noted that the Piagetian tasks differ from the looking-time studies in requiring means-ends planning and various executive functions supported by the frontal cortex (maintaining a representation in short-term memory, inhibiting competing responses). These processes have a developmental course that is partly independent of the capacity to represent objects. The second explanation for earlier success on the looking-time tasks than on the reaching tasks begins with the observation that the capacity to represent some aspect of the world is not an all-or-nothing matter. Representations are graded in robustness or strength, are constructed in real time, and are subject to multiple interacting influences during the processes of construction (Munakata, McClelland, Johnson, & Siegler, 1997; Thelen, Schoner, Scheier, & Smith, 2001; Uller, Carey, Huntley-Fenner, & Klatt, 1999). These interacting influences guarantee that success on a wide range of tasks all putatively drawing on a common representational capacity will be task-dependent. Furthermore, there are many different visual and motor maps of the world in the nervous system, and it is possible that the representations that play a role in guiding search differ in some respects from those that guide eye movement. For example, Yuko Munakata and her colleagues suggested that it is possible that more robust representations are required to support reaching than to evaluate consistency of visual models of the world.

Although it is easy to see how explanations like these might account for failures on some tasks in spite of the infants' having the representational capacity seemingly needed for those tasks, it is not easy to find evidence for any particular version. It is not impossible, though. For the sake of illustration, let's see how some of these ideas play out in understanding the developmental course of the A–not–B error, which wanes between ages 8 and 12 months or so.

Possible Explanation 1: Frontal Cortex Maturation

Adele Diamond and Patricia Goldman-Rakic offered an explanation of the first type—of the failure of young infants in the A–not–B task, in spite of the capacity to individuate and track objects through occlusion—in terms of a lack of a necessary prerequisite for task performance (Diamond, 1991; Diamond and Goldman-Rakic, 1989). Diamond and Goldman-Rakic began with the observation that the A–not–B task closely resembles a task used to diagnose frontal lobe function in monkeys—delayed response (DR). In DR, an item (usually food) is hidden in one of two wells, a delay is imposed in which the animal is not allowed to orient toward the correct well, and the animal is then allowed to search for the item. As in the A–not–B task, a crucial determinate of success in DR is whether the food in the immediately previous trials was hidden in the same well as in the current trial or the opposite one.

There is massive evidence for frontal lobe involvement in DR. Lesions in prefrontal cortex (specifically dorsolateral prefrontal cortex) of adult monkeys disrupt performance in DR tasks. Monkeys with such lesions can still succeed at the task when there is no delay, but performance falls apart at delays as short as 2 seconds. Lesions in other memory or visual systems (such as the hippocampus or parieto-temporal areas) do not affect DR. Also, there is excellent evidence for a maturational contribution to the development of DR during infancy. In *Rhesus* monkeys, 1.5-month-old infants perform on DR as do adults with lesions in the dorsolateral prefrontal regions. Between this age and 4 months of age, the delay that can be tolerated increased from 2 seconds to 10 seconds or more; 4-month-old infant *Rhesus* monkeys perform as well as do adults with intact prefrontal cortex. That maturational changes in prefrontal cortex play some role in this improvement is shown by the fact that lesions in this area at 1.5 month preclude the developmental improvement in DR, and the same lesions at 4 months have the same effect on performance on DR as do such lesions in adulthood—to wit, they disrupt so that performance falls to the level of 1.5-month-old infants.

Diamond and Goldman-Rakic suggested that the maturational change in prefrontal dorsolateral cortex taking place in infant *Rhesus* monkeys between ages 1.5 and 4 months occurs in infant humans between ages 7.5 and 11 months, and it at least partially underlies the developmental changes seen in Piaget's Stage IV of the object concept. Diamond gave the same version of the A-not-B task to human infants at this age, to infant *Rhesus* monkeys, and to adult *Rhesus* monkeys who had been lesioned in the prefrontal dorsolateral cortex. She found that the developmental changes in human infants matched, in parametric detail, those of the monkeys, except that the development was a bit slower in humans (over 2.5 months in monkeys, over 4.5 months in humans). In both species, the delay at solving the A-not-B task increased from 2 seconds at the youngest age to 10 seconds or more at the oldest age. In both species, errors were predominantly on trials in which the correct choice differed from the correct choice on the previous trial (i.e., switch trials). In both species, details of the infants' behavior on the switch trials suggest they represented where the objects was; sometimes they did not even look in the well they had uncovered before reaching for the correct well, and sometimes they stared at the correct well even as they reached for the incorrect one. These behaviors occurred at comparable rates in the two species. Finally, the adult *Rhesus* monkeys with lesions in the prefrontal dorsolateral areas, as expected, failed the A-not-B task at delays over 2 seconds (like the 1.5-month-old *Rhesus* and the 7.5-month-old humans), and made errors predominantly in the crucial switch trials in which the bait was placed in a different well from that of an immediate preceding successful trial.

Diamond concluded that immaturity of dorsolateral prefrontal cortex contributes to the 7.5-month-old's failure on the A-not-B task. Seeking convergent evidence for this conclusion, she reasoned that if maturation of the structure underlies the parametric improvement on this task between ages 7 and 12 months of age, then other tasks that diagnose prefrontal dorsolateral function in primates should show a parallel course of development. She confirmed this prediction in a series of studies of babies reaching for objects in transparent Plexiglas boxes. Problems of differential difficulty are posed for the infant as a function of where the opening of the box is placed. Young infants (7.5-month-old humans, 1.5-month-old *Rhesus*) cannot solve this problem unless the direct line of sight between the infant and object is through an opening. If the opening is to the side, for example, infants of both species of these ages keep reaching directly for the object, hitting the Plexiglas wall, and trying again and again until giving up in frustration. Diamond charted a series of stages infants between 7.5 and 12 months go through before complete success at this task; and she showed that infant *Rhesus* monkeys go through parallel stages between ages 1.5 months and 4 months, and that adult *Rhesus* monkeys with lesions in prefrontal dorsolateral cortex fail at this task, performing like 1.5-month-old infants of their species.

There is no obvious conceptual similarity between the A-not-B task and the Plexiglas box task. In the former, the object is hidden, and memory is a critical component (performance is a function of delay). In the latter, the object is visible through the box, so memory plays no role whatsoever. What unifies these two tasks is their reliance on an intact, functioning dorsolateral prefrontal cortex. Functionally, it is likely that the aspect of executive function being tapped in both tasks involves inhibiting a prepotent response (reaching along the direct line of sight in the Plexiglas box task, repeating the previously successful reach in the A-not-B task). Also, the prefrontal cortex is crucially involved in working memory, a critical component of the A-not-B task. Diamond argues that these are aspects of executive function supported by the prefrontal cortex, and these are not required in the violation-of-expectancy looking-time studies. Diamond's work gives us evidence that the A-not-B error does not reflect a limit in the infant's representation of objects as spatio-temporally continuous, continuing to exist when occluded but, rather, reflects immature executive function that limits the means/end problem solving of infants under 1 year of age.

Possible Explanation 2: The Dynamic Systems Account

In a series of influential writings, Esther Thelen, Linda Smith, and their colleagues have discovered several new phenomena and have systematized the empirical literature concerning the A-not-B error (e.g., Smith, Thelen, Titzer, & McLin, 1999; Thelen et al., 2001). They argue that the error could arise from complex interactions among the multifaceted processes that enter into motor planning, processes that unfold over time. Thelen, Smith, and their colleagues stress that whether the infant makes the error or not is dependent on many factors, such as how many repetitions of hiding at A before the switch to B, the delay, the salience of the object, the distinctiveness of the two locations, whether the infant is in the same position during the A trials and the first B trials, and so on. Their model makes such novel predictions (which have been confirmed) as that the probability of the error will decrease if the child changes posture between successive trials!

In Thelen's model of motor planning, three distinct representations are built up over time, each having its own dynamics (rate of buildup, capacity for stability and self-maintenance, time course of decay), and they interact in a common motor workspace to create a plan to reach to A or B (or neither). The three distinct representations are (1) a representation of the task environment (that establishes the locations of A and B, and maintains them as distinct or as equally or differentially salient); (2) a representation of the cued location of a given trial; and (3) a representation of the previous movements, in which this representation is influenced by the entire history of movements, highly weighting the most recent ones. These representations are integrated in the process of planning a movement; a movement to A or to B ensues when a threshold of activity in the motor workspace is reached. The various context effects discovered and reviewed by Thelen and Smith are modeled in terms of parameters that influence the dynamics of the formation and mainte-nance of each of the three types of representations in motor space, and the developmental change between 8 months (A–not–B errors likely at delays greater than a few seconds) and 12 months (A–not–B errors unlikely, within a wide range of task parameters, at delays as long as 10 seconds) is modeled in terms of a change in a parameter called cooperativity. Cooperativity reflects the differentiation within motor space and the capacity for creating and maintaining a stable representation of the cued location.

Although Thelen and Smith's account differs from Diamond's in many respects, both place the A–not–B error in the context of the inter-action of two different memories: memory for the cued location (or for the object's location) and memory of the past action. Memory of the past action has a much longer time course of decay, the limits of which, as Thelen et al. point out, have not been systematically studied. If the pro-cesses that form and maintain the short-term memory of the cued location are fragile, an A–not–B error is thereby likely to occur. In sum, Thelen and Smith, on the one hand, and Diamond, on the other, agree that the A–not–B error arises from the interaction of object or location representations with other representations involved in the planning of a reach.

Thelen, Smith, and their colleagues draw what seem to be stronger conclusions than those outlined in the first explanation. They sometimes deny the usefulness of the construct object representation or even representation at all. I find this puzzling. Their own model explicitly depends on three different types of representations: the task context, the cued location, and past acts. That these representations are formulated over motoric space, that they evolve over time, and that they interact in complex ways does not make them nonrepresentations.

Although these models of dynamic systems crucially depend on representations, the representations in this case are certainly sensori-motor ones. At other places, Thelen and her colleagues argue that it does not make sense to ask when infants "have" representations of objects. They claim that this is a badly mistaken question because representations are always manifested in behavior and thus their expression is always subject to the dynamic interaction of many different processes. This is undoubtedly true, and I will often rely on this fact in the pages to come (e.g., in explaining infants' failures on A–not–B tasks in spite of their capacity for object representations!). But this observation does not discharge the responsibility to account for the origin of the capacity to represent objects. Either this capacity is innate or it is built by some learning process, and such a learning process would necessarily occur at some particular point in time.

It is true that representations of objects play no role in Thelen and Smith models at all. The representations are representations of locations, with strengths determined by stimulus salience and dynamic factors. The only possible role for perceptual representations of the objects is that their salience might affect the degree of activation of the location in which they were hidden. In support of the claim that representations of objects are playing no role in this task, Smith and her colleagues discovered that infants will reach into the containers even when there are no objects in them, and that merely waving one of the visible lids, or touching it, would induce a reach into a particular one. That is, a wave or a touch would serve as a specific cue to a location on a particular trial (Smith et al., 1999).

It is not surprising that a model of the last stages of planning a reach is formulated in a motor workspace that includes representations of locations, but it is also unlikely that a full model of the dynamics of the planning, memory, and motivational processes that interact in determining a reach can dispense with representations of the goal of the reach —a particular object. Could it be true that representations of specific unseen objects do not ever guide reaches at the ages of children of the age of the A–not–B error? I think not.

My colleagues and I have recently developed a search task that can be used to explore object representations in 10- to 12-month-old infants. Several studies using this method demonstrate that representations of objects guide the reaches of 10- to 12-month-old infants (Feigenson & Carey, 2003; Van de Walle, Carey, & Prevor, 2000). In this task, infants are introduced to a box into which they can reach but cannot see. We measure infants' search behavior as a function of what they have seen placed into the box. For example, on some occasions infants see two objects placed into the box and on other occasions they see only one object placed inside, after which the box is handed to the baby. There is always only one object in the box (the other having been surreptitiously removed on the two-object trials). The infant reaches in and retrieves the object, and the measurement period of interest is that which follows. Does the infant demonstrate, by his persistence of search, that he represents a second object inside it? Success on this task is longer searching on two-object trials because there should be a second object in the box than on one-object trials because the only object the child saw emerging from the box has been retrieved. Both 10- and 12-month-olds succeed in this version of the task. Apparently, infants of this age can represent the difference between one and two objects being in the box, and their reaches into the box are guided by representations of the objects hidden within it. Thus, a full model of the planning process must contain representations of the hidden objects themselves, not only the locations to which the child will reach.

Although I have criticized Thelen and Smith's arguments against mental representations in general, and their claims that it does not make sense to ask whether infants' "have" representations of objects, their models provide insight into why infants with the capacity to represent hidden objects make at the A–not–B error. Both Thelen and Smith's work and Diamond's provide detailed accounts of the complex processes involved in tasks that are used to characterize infants' representational abilities (in this case, in Piagetian search tasks). Variables that influence these processes can produce apparent failures on a given task even if the representational capacity in question is in place. Of course, positive evidence for that capacity is still required; in the present case, the positive evidence that young infants have the capacity to form representations with the content object derives from the looking-time studies reviewed above.

Are Object Representations Innate?

I have argued that very young infants represent objects as spatio-temporally persisting. The computations through which young infants establish representations of objects embody criteria of individuation and numerical identity. Contrary to Quine, a child does not need the ladder constructed from the explicit quantificational devices of natural language in order to create representations of objects that divide reference, that distinguish between the same one and a different one. Contrary to Piaget, a child does not need the full period of sensori-motor development (until 18 to 24 months) to create representations of enduring objects that exist even when the child has no direct perceptual access to them. Quine's and Piaget's specific accounts of the origin of the capacity to form object representations cannot be right.

Still, the youngest age of participants in the violation-of-expectancy looking-time studies reviewed so far in this chapter is 2 months. Is it possible that younger babies' representations are formulated over sensory or perceptual primitives? Could the capacity to represent and quantify over objects displayed in these looking-time experiments be built between birth and 2 months of age? In the last pages of this chapter, I present arguments that convince me that perceptual input analyzers that yield representations of objects are most likely innate.

This question is particularly trenchant because there is one piece of evidence from a looking-time paradigm that suggests that the capacity to compute object representations is not innate. The phenomenon in question is the capacity for amodal completion of single objects, two ends

of which protrude from behind an occluder (see Figure 2.5a). This
phenomenon differs from those discussed so far in this chapter, for it does
not concern when infants represent whole objects that disappear behind
barriers as continuing to exist there. Nonetheless, at issue are the processes that result in object individuation. Under what circumstances,
if any, does the infant establish a representation of a single, spatio-
temporally continuous (i.e., connected throughout) object extending
behind the barrier, rather than two numerically distinct objects? Philip
Kellman and Elizabeth Spelke used the violation-of-expectancy looking-
time method to answer this question (Kellman & Spelke, 1983). They
found that if the visible ends of the occluder move together, 4-month-
old infants establish a representation of a single object, as shown by the
fact that upon removal of the barrier, they look longer if a broken rod
(Figure 2.5b) is revealed than if a continuous rod (Figure 2.5c) is revealed.
Building on this work, Scott Johnson and Richard Aslin have shown

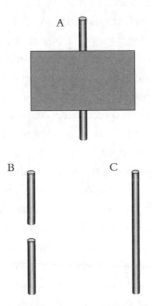

Figure 2.5. Diagram of stimuli for the Kellman & Spelke (1983) broken rod
experiments. a: habituation stimulus (rod moves back and forth behind the screen). b:
two rod outcome. c: single-rod outcome. Redrawn from Kellman, P. J., & Spelke, E.
S. (1983). Perception of partly occluded objects in infancy. *Cognitive Psychology, 15*(4),
483–524, with permission from Elsevier.

that 2- to 4-month-old infants are sensitive to almost all of the same information that adults are in computing representations of a single rod in this situation, but that 2-month-olds need more redundant information than do 4-month-olds (Aslin & Johnson, 1996; Johnson & Aslin, 1995).

Newborns, however, are different. Alan Slater and his colleagues found that newborn infants display the opposite pattern of looking times (Slater, Morison, Somers, Mattock, & Brown, 1990). Habituated to the array in Figure 2.5a, they look longer at the completed rod (Figure 2.5c) than at the broken rod (Figure 2.5b), as if the former were a novel stimulus for them. Slater's findings have been taken to show that between birth and 2 months of age, infants learn that common motion of two visible portions of objects protruding from behind a barrier is likely to be part of one and the same object.

There are, however, alternative explanations for the neonate's failure in the face of 2-month-olds' success, other than that the processes that create object representations are constructed through learning in the first two months of life). Just as Diamond argued in the case of developmental changes in the A–not–B error, it is possible that maturation of capacities other than those that create object representations per se underlie the change between newborns and 2-month-olds. Alternatively, it is possible that neonates need more redundant information still, compared to 2-month-olds, just as 2-month-olds do compared to 4-month-olds, for amodal completion, and that the pattern of looking reveals a familiarity preference rather than a novelty preference. Upon meeting the habituation criterion, the neonates may still be in the process of building the representation of a single object.

How might we decide between an explanation of the developmental change that involves learning that a single object is likely to be found behind the barrier and one that involves developmental changes in processes that are inputs to an innate computational device? Three empirical considerations lead me to favor the nativist view that the capacity for amodal completion is the product of evolution and it does not have to be constructed through learning processes.

First, it is not hard to imagine ancillary capacities that might await development before infants can succeed at completing the rod behind the barrier. They must notice the correlated motion of the two ends of the rod: this is the input to the computation that creates a representation of the single rod. Young infants have a notorious difficulty deploying their attention. Two sources of data suggest that one problem faced by very tiny babies is just this failure to notice the correlated motion: Two-month-olds are less likely to complete the rod behind the barrier if the barrier is wider, and increasing width plausibly makes it more difficult to notice the common motion (Condry, Smith, & Spelke, 2001). Confirming the necessity of doing so, eye-tracking studies show that 3-month-olds complete the rod only if they scan between the two ends of the rod during familiarization (Amso, Davidson, & Johnson, 2005). The Amso et al. study showed that young infants' attention is captured by the motion of one portion of the rod along the edge that specifies the occluder.

Second, even stronger than evidence consistent with some possible way of explaining away a failure is positive evidence that neonates have the capacity. A recent study of neonates presented the stimuli strobo-scopically, showing the end points of the movement only and thus removing interference from the encoding of relative motion along the edges. The neonates generalized habituation to the complete rod, just as do 2-month-old and older infants (Valenza, Gava, Leo, & Simeon, 2004). Thus, amodal completion appears to be innate in humans.

Finally (and this is indirect evidence), the capacity for amodal completion is innate in chickens (Regolin & Vollortigara, 1995). Neonate chicks imprinted on a red triangle, partially hidden behind a barrier, huddle next to a completed triangle, rather than on a broken one, the first time the barrier is removed (Figure 2.6). These newborn chicks had no opportunity to learn what stimulus conditions predict a complete figure as opposed to a broken one under these circumstances. Indeed, even the spatio-temporal continuity implicated in object permanence is the output of innate perceptual analyzers in chicks. Newborn chicks, imprinted on a ball, which have never in their lives seen any object go behind a barrier (and thus could not have learned about spatio-temporal continuity), search behind a screen for the ball the first time it disappears there. They even avoid the A-not-B error! Of course, that object permanence is innate in baby chickens does not mean it is innate in human babies. Nonetheless, these studies provide an existence proof that it is possible for the capacity to represent objects as spatio-temporally continuous, even under conditions of occlusion, to be manifest without learning.

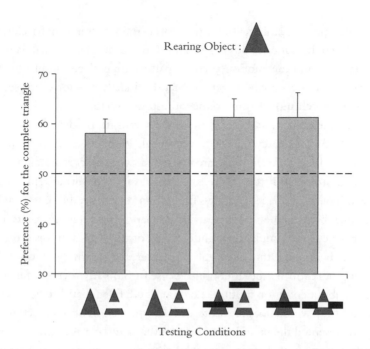

Figure 2.6. Preference for the complete (or amodally complete) stimulus of each comparison pair. Group means +/- standard error depicted. From Regolin & Vallortigara, 1995. Regolin, L., & Vallortigara, G. (1995). Perception of partially occluded objects by young chicks. *Perception & Psychophysics, 57*(7), 971–976. Reprinted with permission from Psychonomic Society, Inc.

Even if we did not have these empirical results in hand, other considerations would bear on deciding between the learning account of the change in performance between 0 and 2 months of age and the alternatives. Those who favor a learning account of the change between birth and 2 months of age need to sketch one. Quine's linguistic boot-strapping process was his answer to this question, and that hypothesis is already ruled out by the existence of object representations and the capacity for divided reference in clearly prelinguistic infants. What learning process could create representations of complete objects that persist behind barriers taking only perceptual primitives as input? Similarly, how could infants learn that whole objects that disappear completely behind barriers continue to exist there? It is easy to see how infants could learn statistical regularities stated over perceptual and spatio-temporal primitives—noting that certain patterns of occlusion predict certain patterns of reappearance, for example, or that certain patterns of common motion predict spatio-temporal continuity of the elements that are moving together. Statistical analyses—for example, of the sort so well modeled in connectionist architectures—could accomplish such learning; and indeed, there are successful models that do just that (e.g., Munakata et al., 1997; Mareschal, Plunkett, & Harris, 1999). However, these generalizations are not stated over object representations. Furthermore, even if they were, they would not constitute representations of object permanence unless the system represents the object as the same one that went behind the barrier. As Gary Marcus (2001) points out, either the current simulations cannot do so or they build in this capacity from the beginning, thus accomplishing interesting learning, but not the learning of spatio-temporal continuity itself . Similarly, even if generalizations about common motion and connected, filled spatial regions were learned, they would not constitute amodal completion of an object unless they represented the completed object as the same one as unites the parts that had been visible before. If it is true that object representations cannot be expressed in a sensori-motor or perceptual vocabulary, there is a serious learnability issue of how they could be learned from statistical generalizations over that vocabulary.

The debates over whether connectionist models could take perceptual input and construct representations of objects that embody criteria of individuation and numerical identity engage the learnability issue in just the right way. Any learning model that could accomplish this feat would defeat in principle a learnability argument that object representations cannot be built from perceptual primitives. It is still an open question whether one can imagine, in principle, a learning mechanism that could accomplish the task. Of course, even if we could imagine one, we wouldn't know that we were right. It would still be a logical and empirical possibility that object representations are innate in human infants, just as representations of the night sky are innate in nestling indigo buntings. A proposal for a plausible learning mechanism would be an important first step toward an empirical investigation of whether object representations could be built from perceptual primitives, for such a proposal would certainly make testable empirical predictions. But even a successful proposal for a plausible learning mechanism would not settle the issue; we'd still have to see whether learning in fact proceeds in the hypothesized manner.

In the following pages, I appeal to learnability considerations, as well as evidence that capacities are innate in other species, in my arguments that a given representational capacity might be innate in humans. I also appeal to one additional type of empirical argument. One source of evidence concerning the content of the representations that underlie infants' performance in any given task is their inferential role. What inferences are embodied in the constraints under which infants apply these representations in ambiguous situations? Elizabeth Spelke has specified principles other than spatio-temporal continuity that constrain young infants' representations of three-dimensional objects, and has pointed out that the principles, in concert, determine still other constraints on object interactions. For example, Spelke notes that infants represent objects as bounded and what she calls coherent (filled in at every point), as well as continuously persisting. These two principles (continuous spatio-temporal persistence and coherence) entail that one solid object cannot pass through another. For object A to pass through object B, object B would have to be noncoherent (like water), or object A would have to dematerialize upon hitting object B and rematerialize on the other side.

This set of interrelated constraints on infants' representations will take center stage in chapters 3 through 6. Here, I wish to illustrate how these facts might bear on the nativist/empiricist debate with respect to the origin of any target representational capacity. The idea is simple: if observed developmental changes are accomplished by statistical generalizations over sensory representations, one would expect it to be piecemeal, depending on the statistical information available in the input. And certainly, much learning in infancy is exactly of this sort. If, however, some developmental changes result from the maturation of capacities that prevented antecedently existing representations from being activated, one would expect that as soon as these capacities mature, the full integrated representational system would be manifest. Observation of the latter pattern supports the nativist position. Here, I sketch how this argument might play out in the case in question: whether object representations are innate or constructed from sensory primitives. I ask whether infants provide evidence for sensitivity to solidity at the same age as they first provide robust evidence of

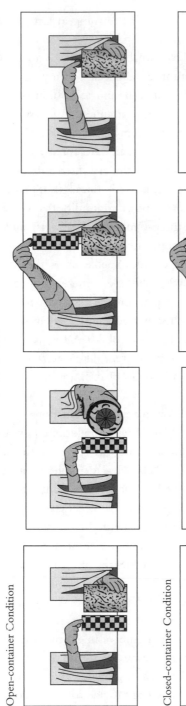

Test Events

Open-container Condition

Closed-container Condition

Figure 2.7. Diagram of test trials in the Hespos and Baillargeon (2001) solidity experiment. Top panel, cylinder inserted into container open at the top. Bottom panel, cylinder apparently inserted through solid closed top. Reprinted from Hespos, S., & Baillargeon, R. (2001). Reasoning about containment events in very young infants. *Cognition, 78,* 207–245, with permission from Elsevier.

amodal completion (Figure 2.5) and spatio-temporal continuity (Figures 2.1–2.4)—namely, at 2 months of age.

Three separate series of studies indicate that 2-month-old infants look longer at events in which one object has apparently passed through the space occupied by another than they do at otherwise identical events in which object motions do not violate the constraint of solidity (Baillargeon, 1987; Hespos & Baillargeon, 2001; Spelke, Breilinger, Macomber, & Jacobsen, 1992). To take just one example, Sue Hespos and Renée Baillargeon showed one group of 2-month-old infants a hollow cylinder and another group an identical cylinder closed on top (Figure 2.7). The cylinder was then placed upright, such that the infant could not see the top. A rod was then picked up and slowly inserted into the cylinder, a possible event in the hollow cylinder case, violating solidity in the closed cylinder case (for the rod would have to pass through the solid top). The infants looked longer at the latter, impossible event. Recall that 2 months is the earliest age at which infants are adultlike in the Kellman and Spelke amodal completion paradigm and in the split-screen object individuation paradigm. It seems that as soon as young infants are able to form object representations under the conditions of these studies, their representations are constrained to reflect boundedness and spatio-temporal continuity in complex ways. It is unlikely that piecemeal learning of local statistical regularities could accomplish the coherently interrelated representations observed by 2-month-old infants.

Conclusions

I have argued here that the Piagetian/Quinian view of the young infant's representational capacities being exhausted by a perceptual similarity space, or a set of sensori-motor primitives, is most probably wrong. The argument had three steps. First, I argued that representations of object cannot be stated in the vocabulary of perception. Second, I reviewed some of the evidence that that young infants represent objects themselves as spatio-temporally continuous, quantifying over these representations as do adults. Third, I considered whether infants' performance in the experiments might better be explained in terms of generalizations stated over a perceptual vocabulary. This is still a hotly debated issue, but evidence concerning the inferential role of infants' representations, together with learnability considerations, lead me to favor the richer interpretation of the currently available data.

Grant, for the moment, that infants' representations of the world reflect an ontology of individuated, spatio-temporally continuous, middle-sized, middle-distanced objects that interact with each other according to the laws of contact causality. Grant, contrary to Quine, that the capacity to quantify over objects is not a cultural construction and does not result from a bootstrapping process that involves learning the quantificational devices of natural language. Grant, contrary to Piaget, that the capacity to represent objects as existing independently of the child, as spatio-temporally continuous even through occlusion, does not await the end of the sensori-motor period of development. Granting all this still tells us little about what kinds of representations, what kinds of knowledge, we are talking about. What is the format of representation? What knowledge is explicit and what is embodied in the computations carried out over explicit representations? What happens to infants' representational capacities in the course of development—how are they built upon and how are they transformed? The core cognition hypothesis stakes out a position on these issues. Chapters 3 through 5 spell out the core cognition hypothesis, continuing with the example of object representations (chapter 3), and then turning to number (chapter 4) and agent (chapter 5) representations. These chapters further differentiate core cognition from perceptual representations and also begin to distinguish core cognition from intuitive theoretical knowledge.

NOTES

1. This aside draws heavily from the excellent discussion of the history of this debate in Spelke & Newport, 1998.

2. No empiricist actually gave a definitional decomposition of the concept object in terms of perceptual primitives—as Piaget and Quine saw clearly, this would be impossible. Rather, what they had in mind was that our concept of object was nothing but a set of associations between the different sensory impressions of the objects of our experience.

3. As is the case with all of the experiments I draw on in my argument, Wynn's results have been replicated in many laboratories: With 4-month-olds, Simon, Hespos, & Rochat (1995) and Koechlin, Dehaene, & Mehler (1998); with

7-month-olds, Feigenson, Carey, & Spelke (2002); with 8-month-olds, Uller, Carey, Huntley-Fenner, & Klatt (1999). Koechlin et al.'s study is particularly interesting. The objects behind the screen were on a rotating plate, such that the infants could not predict the spatial layout of the outcome arrays. This shows that infants were not merely creating a model of the spatial array, and were reacting when there was a new position occupied or when a previously occupied position was empty.

analysis devices that identify the entities that fall under core domains continue to operate throughout life. Core cognition is elaborated during development because core cognition systems are learning devices, but it is never rendered irrelevant. It is never overturned or lost, in contrast to later developing intuitive theories, which are sometimes replaced by subsequent, incommensurable ones. Fourth, systems of core cognition are domain-specific learning devices (remember the indigo buntings learning to identify the azimuth, cited in chapter 1). Fifth, some core cognition (including that of objects) is shared by other animals. At least some early developing cognitive systems in humans have a long evolutionary history. And sixth, the format of representation of core cognition is iconic rather than involving sentence-like symbol structures.

Understanding the mind requires characterizing its architecture—its parts and their relations to each other. It is an empirical claim that there are systems of representation that exemplify the six properties listed above. Later-developing explicit knowledge differs from core cognition in every single one of these six properties, so if the core cognition hypothesis is correct, the theories all the way down hypothesis cannot be. Similarly, because core knowledge is organized into distinct systems of representation for distinct domains of experience, it presents a different picture of cognitive architecture from one that is exhausted by a developmentally primitive vocabulary of perceptual features and domain-general learning mechanisms, such as those captured in many connectionist architectures.

It is an understatement to say that not all researchers concerned with the infant mind agree with my characterization of the initial state. The hypothesis that young infants' representational capacities include several systems of core cognition—as core cognition is characterized in these pages—is highly controversial. As mentioned in chapter 1, some of the controversy derives from differences in scientific taste. Psychologists are drawn to the empiricist characterization of the initial state, either as a general theory (as in the case of Piaget or Quine), or in particular cases, as when Les Cohen seeks to explain the development of causal representations as learning contingencies among sensory primitives (Cohen & Chaput, 2002), or as Yuko Munakata and her colleagues seek to explain the development of object permanence in terms of learning contingencies among sensory primitives (Munakata, McClelland, Johnson, & Siegler, 1997). Some of the controversy is empirical. Many people prefer leaner interpretations of the data I will offer in favor of core cognition, seeking to explain them in terms of generalizations that infants have formulated over sensory or perceptual primitives (e.g., Bogartz, Shinsky, & Speaker, 1997; Haith, 1998; Haith & Benson, 1998). One goal I have in chapters 2 through 7 is to make the case for a richer picture of the initial state.

The core cognition hypothesis provides part of the solution to our quest for the origin of human concepts, for it consists of systems of innate conceptual primitives. But it also provides a challenge, for later-developing conceptual knowledge differs so radically from it. Chapters 7 through 12 take on this challenge, explaining how human beings, and only human beings, have the capacity to transcend core cognition.

Object representations exhibit all of the hypothesized properties of core cognition; in demonstrating this I both illustrate the characteristics of core cognition and give a sense of the evidence for it. Chapter 2 presented arguments that object representations satisfy the first two properties of core cognition: they are conceptual and they are created by innate input analyzers. I will return to both of these features of core cognition in this chapter as well; here, I concentrate on the other four. I begin with a property of core cognition not emphasized at all in chapter 2: the representations that articulate core cognition of objects continue to operate throughout life. This feature is central to the core cognition thesis, for it is one of the respects in which core cognition differs from explicit theoretical knowledge. Theories change, sometimes radically, such that even the deepest ontological commitments are revised. Indeed, theories may and do overturn, at an explicit level, tenets of core cognition, even while core cognition representations are also still computed. For example, the belief that objects are made up of particulate matter is not part of core cognition and even violates the solidity constraints discussed at the end of chapter 2. Matter can and does pass through objects such as people and tables, and anybody who has an understanding of modern physics knows this. So what is the evidence, then, that core object cognition is constant, in the face of changes in our explicit theories of objects?

Continuity

That infants and adults both apparently have representations with com-mon content (e.g., *object*) is not sufficient to establish continuity. Both occlusion. In what follows I first sketch the evidence for these signatures of the processes that articulate mid-level object representations, and then I sketch the evidence that infant object representations reveal the same processing signatures.

The Signatures of Adult Mid-Level Object Cognition

The two literatures—that on mid-level object-based attention (mid-level because the representations fall between low-level sensory processing and high-level placement into kind categories) and that on object representations in infancy—involve parallel problems, including uncovering the bases of object individuation and numerical identity. Establishing continuity is complicated by the existence in adults of at least two distinct representational systems that underlie object individuation. One is fully conceptual, and is the kind-based system that we draw upon when we decide that a person ceases to exist when she dies, in spite of the continued existence of her body, or that a cup seen on a counter on Monday cannot be numerically identical with a cat seen there on Tuesday. The second is the mid-level visual system that assigns spatio-temporal indexes to attended objects and creates object-files. It is this second system that is identified with object representations in young infants, and it is this second system that is characterized by the signature property of almost exclusive reliance on spatio-temporal features (relative to property/kind features) in object individuation and computations of numerical identity.

Figure 3.2 illustrates the operation of the two systems in establishing numerical identity. Imagine that you lose perceptual contact with the scene in Panel A, and return 5 minutes later to view the scene depicted in Panel B. How would you describe what has happened? I assume you would say that the rabbit has moved from above and to the left of the circle to below and to the right of it, while the bird has moved from the bottom left to the top right. That is, you would report the movements of the individuals as in Panel C. In this account, numerical identity is being carried by kind membership; it is the rabbit and the bird each of whom you assume has moved through time. The conceptual, kind-based system of individuation is responsible for establishing the object tokens in this case. Now, imagine that the center is now a fixation point, and Panels A and B

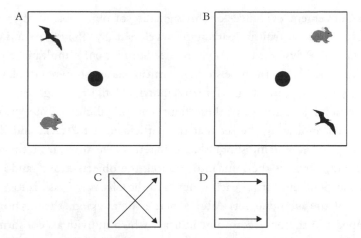

Figure 3.2. Two competing bases of solving the problem of numerical identity. The problem is which individual in Panel A is the same individual as which individual in Panel B. If numerical identity is traced relative to kind or property, one sees a rabbit and a bird moving diagonally (Panel C). If numerical identity is determined by minimizing the total amount of motion, one sees two cases of a rabbit turning into a bird or vice-versa (Panel D).

are projected one after the other onto a screen while you maintain fixation on the common point. If the timing of the stimuli supports apparent motion, which individuals do you see in motion? Rather than seeing a bird and a rabbit each moving diagonally, you see two individuals each changing back and forth between a black bird-shaped object and a grey rabbit-shaped object as they move side to side, as in Panel D.

The visual system that computes numerical identity of the objects that undergo apparent motion in cases such as this works to minimize the total movement even if the result is a change in kind. This system takes into account property or kind information only when spatio-temporal considerations are equated (see Nakayama, He, & Shimojo, 1995, for a review). The mid-level object tracking system is responsible for establishing the object tokens in the case of apparent motion, and it settles on a different solution than does the kind-based system. That is, one of its signatures is that it privileges spatio-temporal information over kind or property information in computations of object individuation and numerical identity.

Convergent evidence for this signature of object-based attention derives from a fruitful paradigm developed by Pylyshyn and his colleagues (Pylyshyn, 2001; Pylyshyn & Storm, 1998): multiple object tracking, or MOT. In these studies, participants are shown a display, as in Figure 3.3, consisting of many individual figures (e.g., eight in this example). A subset of these figures are highlighted (four, in this example), indicating the set that the participant is to track, and then those again become indistinguishable, in terms of features, from the rest. The entire array is then put into motion; the objects move randomly and independently from each other, and the observers' task is to keep track of the attended set. After a period of tracking, the motion is stopped and the observers must indicate which individuals constituted the attended set. Consistent with the claim that object tracking is based on spatio-temporal continuity, and that feature changes do not cause the opening of new object-files, object tracking in the MOT studies is not disrupted by the indexed objects' changing color, size, shape, or kind during their motion.

Additionally, a recent study by Brian Scholl and his colleagues (Scholl, Pylyshyn, & Franconeri, 1999) underscores the primacy of spatio-temporal information in the establishing and tracking of object-files. In the MOT paradigm, if the motion of all the objects is stopped, at which time one of the tracked objects disappears, the participants can indicate that object's last seen location and direction of motion. But if objects are changing properties during tracking, participants are not

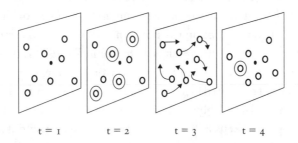

t = 1   t = 2   t = 3   t = 4

Figure 3.3. Schematic depiction of the design of Pylyshyn's Multiple Object Tracking experiments. Figure from Pylyshyn, Z. W. (2001). Visual indexes, pre-conceptual objects, and situated vision. *Cognition, 80*(1–2), 127–158, with permission from Elsevier.

aware of the last seen color or shape of a tracked object. Not only is spatio-temporal continuity the basis of tracking, but also participants have conscious access to the spatio-temporal address of a currently attended object, though not always to other features of the indexed object.

MOT studies also provide empirical support for the two other signatures of mid-level object representations mentioned above. First, the original studies found that the number of objects that may be tracked in parallel is sharply limited. Performance is excellent when sets of one, two, three, and sometimes four objects are tracked, but it falls apart thereafter. This is part of the empirical basis for the claim that there is a limit to the number of indexes that may be assigned at any one time, although later studies suggest that the sharp limit of four objects represented in parallel may be better thought as a limit on working memory rather than a limit on attentional indexes (Alvarez & Franco-neri, in press). Second, tracking in the MOT paradigm illustrates the third psychophysical signature as well: it is not disrupted by barriers that occlude the tracked entities, so long as they disappear at the barrier, as would real objects' going out of sight by regular deletion along the leading contour and reemerging from the other side by regular accretion along the opposite contour. If they pop out of existence, popping back into existence when their trajectory would have taken them to the other side, or if they shrink to nothing concentrically to a point as they approach the barrier, expanding from a point on the other side, tracking is totally disrupted. The system of mid-level object-based attention distinguishes an object's going behind an occluder from the point of its going out of existence and being replaced by another object's coming into existence (Scholl & Pylyshyn, 1999).

Another fruitful paradigm—change detection—provides data that support the signature set-size limit on mid-level object representations. Participants are shown a small array of objects, as in Figure 3.4, for a fraction of a second. After a delay of a second or more, a second array is displayed, identical to the first one or differing in only one feature on just one of the objects. The task is to detect the changes that occur. Participants can detect the changes in arrays of one to three or four, after which performance falls apart. This is true independently of the number of features that might vary. The limit is three to four objects, even if the objects differ in only one feature (e.g., shape, as in Figure 3.4) and if only

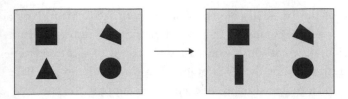

Figure 3.4. Schematic depiction of the Luck and Vogel change detection paradigm. Redrawn from Vogel, E. K., Woodman, G. F., & Luck, S. J. (2001). Storage of features, conjunctions, and objects in visual working memory. *Journal of Experimental Psychology: Human Perception and Performance, 27*(1), 92–114, with permission from American Psychological Association.

that feature changes between arrays (i.e., the shape of one of the entities). The limit is exactly the same (three or four), even if the objects differ in color, size, shape, orientation, or presence/absence of an internal hole, and any of these features can vary on changed arrays (Vogel, Woodman, & Luck, 2001). That is, there is no cost to monitoring changes in color, size, shape, orientation, or so on, over monitoring changes in any one of these features alone. Apparently, working memory has a limit on the number of object-files that can be simultaneously tokened, but many features may be bound to each object-file.

In sum, the computations that maintain indexes to attended objects rely heavily on spatio-temporal information: objects are tracked on the basis of spatio-temporal continuity. Once an object-file is opened, features may be bound to it and updated as they change through time. The Scholl study just described shows that features are not automatically bound in open object-files, perhaps because of the high attentional demands of tracking three or four independently moving objects at once. Up to four object-files may be held in working memory, after which performance falls apart.

The Signatures of Infant Object Representations

Experiments show that the young infant's object representations reveal these same psychophysical signatures. I first sketch the evidence that spatio-temporal features of the input are privileged in the computations of numerical identity early in infancy, and then turn to two other psy-chophysical signatures that support the continuity of core object cognition through the life span.

Signature 1: Primacy of Spatio-Temporal Information in Infant Object Individuation

Daniel Richardson and Natasha Kirkham (2004) modeled an infant study on the object-file experiment of Kahnemann et al. described above. They exposed 7-month-old infants to a computer display consisting of two identical boxes arranged vertically (see Figure 3.5). While the infant watched, a duck was revealed in one box and quacked, the box then returning to its featureless state. Then a bell was revealed in the other box and it rang, and then this box returned to its featureless state. After these events repeated several times, the identical boxes went slowly into motion until they were arranged horizontally, equally distant from the midpoint of the display. At this point, either a quack or a ring was played and the dependent measure was where the infants looked: the box in which the matching object/sound had been revealed during habituation. Analogously to the Kahneman et al. priming studies, these infants had established representations of individual objects, bound features (the identity of the stresses of the sounds that emerged from them), maintaining the binding as they traced the identify of the objects through time on the basis of spatio-temporally continuous paths.

This experiment suggests that infants have object-file representations available to them. However, the thesis under consideration here is that the object representations that were the focus of chapter 2 are object-files. To establish this we must show that the computations that establish object representations early in infancy display the same signatures as those that compute object-files. I begin with the primacy of spatio-temporal information.

The two screen studies and the infant 1 + 1 studies described in chapter 2 (Figures 2.1 and 2.3) show that infants as young as 2 months of age draw on spatio-temporal information in object individuation and tracking. Because the objects in those studies were perceptually indistinguishable from each other, spatio-temporal discontinuity must have driven representations of two distinct objects in these studies. However,

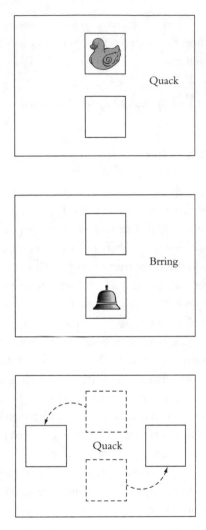

Figure 3.5. Schematic depiction of the infant version of the Kahneman et al. object-file experiment (Richardson & Kirkham, 2004). Richardson, D. C., & Kirkham, N. (2004). Multi-modal events and moving locations: Eye movements of adults and 6-month-olds reveal dynamic spatial indexing. Journal of Experimental Psychology: General, 133(1), 46–62. Reprinted with permission from American Psychological Association.

these studies do not show that spatio-temporal information is privileged, for they did not explore whether infants could also use perceptual property differences (e.g., red vs. blue, cup-shaped vs. duck shaped) or kind distinctions (e.g., cup vs. duck) as a basis for object individuation.

Recent studies, mainly by Fei Xu, establish that under many conditions in which spatio-temporal information is sufficient for object individuation, young infants fail to use property or kind differences among objects for this purpose (Xu & Carey, 1996; Xu, Carey, & Welch, 1999). Imagine the following scenario: One screen is put on a puppet stage. A red cylinder emerges from behind the screen and returns behind it, and then a blue ball emerges from behind the same screen and then returns (see Figure 3.6). How many objects are behind the screen? For adults, the answer is clear: at least two—a cylinder and a ball. But since there is only a single screen occluding the objects, and because we never see both objects at once, there is no clear spatio-temporal evidence that there are two objects. We must rely on our knowledge of perceptual properties or object kinds to succeed at this task.

In our studies, 10- and 12-month-old infants were shown the above event. The objects contrasted in kind and properties (in the above example, a cylinder vs. a ball; a red cylindrical plastic object vs. a blue round rubber object). Some objects were toy models (e.g., truck, duck, elephant) whereas others were from highly familiar everyday kinds (e.g., cup, bottle, book, ball). On the test trials, the screen was removed to reveal either the expected outcome of the two objects or the unexpected outcome of only one of them. If infants have the same expectations as adults—that these kind or property differences signal two distinct objects —they should look longer at the unexpected outcome of one object. The results, however, were surprising: 10-month-old infants did not expect that there should be two objects behind the screen, whereas 12-month-old infants did.

Control conditions established that the method was sensitive to infant representations of distinct individuals. Ten-month-old infants succeeded at the task if they were given spatio-temporal evidence that there were two numerically distinct objects (e.g., if they were shown the two objects simultaneously for 2 or 3 seconds at the beginning of the experiment). Furthermore, Xu and I (1996) showed that infants are sensitive to perceptual or kind differences under the circumstances of this

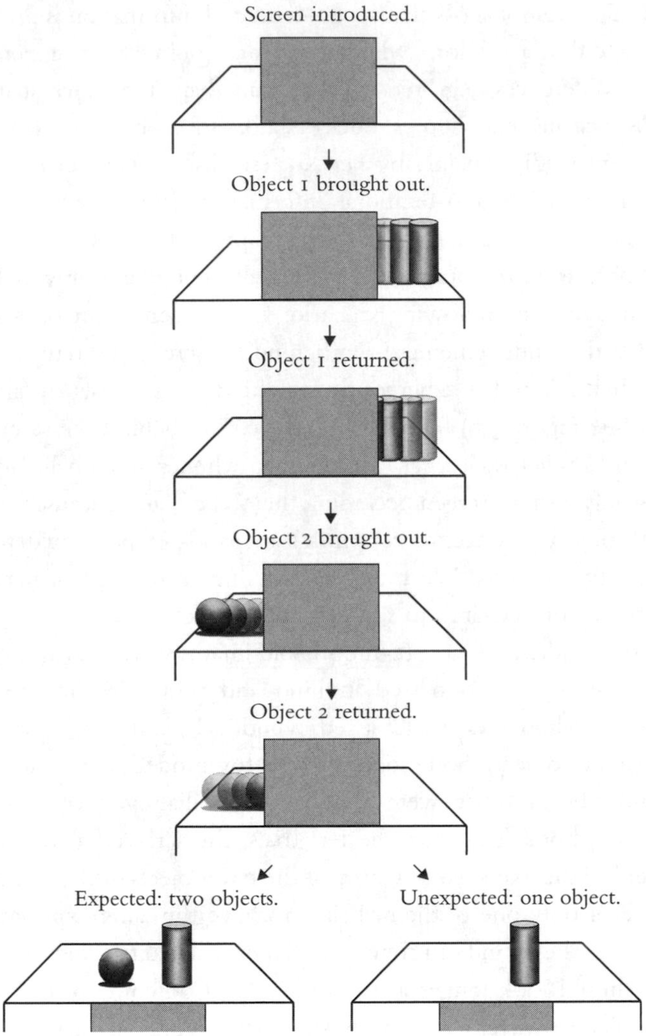

Screen introduced.

Object 1 brought out.

Object 1 returned.

Object 2 brought out.

Object 2 returned.

Expected: two objects.   Unexpected: one object.

Figure 3.6. Schematic depiction of design that explores when infants use property or kind information as a basis for computations of numerical identity (Xu & Carey, 1996). Redrawn from Xu, F., & Carey, S. (1996). Infants' metaphysics: the case of numerical identity. *Cognitive Psychology, 30,* 111–153, with permission from Elsevier.

experimental paradigm: it takes infants longer to habituate to a duck and a car alternately appearing from each side of the screen than to a single car (or duck) repeatedly appearing from behind the screen. Ten-month-old infants are sensitive to the property or kind differences, but they do not use these differences as a basis of object individuation, at least under these circumstances.

In this task, 10-month-old infants failed to draw on kind-based individuation over a wide range of kinds, such as duck, truck, animal, vehicle, cup, bottle, and book. They also failed to draw on perceptual contrasts, such as the contrast between being yellow, duck-shaped, and rubber versus being red, car-shaped, and metal. Gretchen Van de Walle, Mary Prevor, and I (2000) used the manual-search paradigm described in chapter 2 to provide convergent evidence for the claim that infants below 12 months of age are more sensitive to spatio-temporal information than kind or property information in computations that underlie object individuation. In this paradigm, the dependent measure is how long infants search for objects inside a box into which they cannot not see. In the studies that explored the basis of object individuation, three types of trials were contrasted: (1) one-object trials, in which the same object (e.g., a toy telephone) was removed from the box twice and replaced twice; (2) two-object trials in which objects of different kinds (e.g., a telephone and a ball) were removed one at a time and replaced in the box, such that the two were never seen together; and (3) two-object trials in which two different objects were removed one at a time, but shown together before being returned into the box. In the second type of trial, infants must rely on property or kind contrasts as a basis for object individuation; the third type provided spatio-temporal information as well.

After one of these introductions to the contents of the box, the box was pushed into the child's reach, and patterns of search revealed how many objects the child had represented in it. In these experiments, we surreptitiously removed one of the objects on two-object trials, so there was in fact only one object in the box. We could then measure persistence of search for a second object. The question was whether infants search for a second object after having retrieved one on two-object trials (types 2 and 3) but not on one-object trials. Both 10- and 12-month-olds differentiated the one- and two-object trials when given *spatio-temporal* evidence for two objects. Twelve-month-olds also succeeded when given *property/kind* information alone. In contrast, the 10-month-olds failed in this condition; their pattern of reaching on the two-object trials was the same as on the one-object trials. Ten-month-olds failed to use kind differences, such as telephone, duck or car, book, or property differences, such as black, yellow, telephone-shaped, duck-shaped, rubber, or plastic, to establish representations of two numerically distinct objects in the box.

Other laboratories have replicated these findings (e.g., Bonatti, Frot, Zangl, & Mehler, 2002; Wilcox & Baillargeon, 1998). In our original writings on this topic, Xu and I (1996) made a blanket claim that infants under 11 or 12 months of age never use property information or kind information in the service of object individuation. This claim is too strong (e.g., Tremoulet, Leslie, & Hall, 2000; Wilcox & Baillargeon, 1998). Just as is the case in mid-level vision, property information is sometimes drawn upon in object individuation. The resolution of just when and how property information is used for object individuation and in object tracking, whether by adults or by infants, is beyond the scope of this chapter (see Xu & Carey, 2000). For the point I am making here, all that is necessary is that spatio-temporal information is primary, and that infants fail to draw on property or kind information under conditions under which they succeed when provided unambiguous spatio-temporal information. This pattern of findings has been widely replicated.

In sum, results from these manual-search studies are completely consistent with those from the looking-time studies. Two important conclusions follow from these data. First, they are consistent with the claim that kind-based object individuation is architecturally distinct from mid-level object indexing and tracking (see Figure 3.2 and surrounding discussion). They support the possibility that a second system of object individuation, a kind-based system, emerges at around 12 months of age. Of course, the data presented so far do not show that kind distinctions rather than property distinctions underlie the older infants' success; chapter 7 takes up this issue and discusses the mechanisms that might underlie the construction of a new representational system—kind-based object representations—that goes beyond the core cognition system of mid-level object files and object indexing. Second, they support the identification of the young infants' object representations with those of the mid-level object tracking system, for they show that under these circumstances at least 10-month-old infants fail to draw on property/kind information in the processes that establish whether an attended object is numerically identical or different from another, under conditions in which they do draw on spatio-temporal information for this purpose. Just as in adult mid-level object representations, spatio-temporal evidence is privileged by infants in object individuation.

Signature 2: Set-Size Limitations on Working Memory

Results from several paradigms converge to show that by the end of the first year of life, infant working memory limits are in the same range as those of adults (Rose, Feldman, & Jankowski, 2001; Ross-Sheehy, Oakes, & Luck, 2003). In one series of studies, Shannon Ross-Sheehy, Lisa Oakes, and Steven Luck adapted the change-detection paradigm for infants in order to explore the development of infants' working memory. Infants watched two simultaneously presented displays, each consisting of arrays of one, two, three, four, or six entities. Each display was presented for a half a second, followed by a short delay, after which a new array appeared. In one of the displays, there was no change between arrays, whereas in the other, one of elements (chosen at random) changed color. Ross-Sheehy and her colleagues reasoned that if infants could hold the representation of the first array in working memory, they would detect the change, and they would be more interested in the changing display than in the constant array. They found that 4- and 6-month-olds could hold single elements in working memory, for they preferred the arrays in which color changed to the constant arrays when set size was one entity. However, at these young ages infants failed to discriminate the changing arrays when set sizes were two or higher. By 10 months of age, infants differentiated the changing arrays from the constant arrays for sets of two, three, and four, but not for six entities. Thus, it appears that working memory capacity matures over the first year of life, reaching the adult level of three to four object-files by 10 months of age.

Like the Richardson & Kirkham (2004) results, these experiments again show that infants have an object-file system that resembles that of adults. But what we want to know is whether the mid-level object representation system of adults underlies the object representations studied in the tradition of Piagetian studies. That the manual-search paradigms used to explore infants' representations of objects show comparable limits on working memory suggests that the answer is yes. Take, for example, the paradigm in which infants search for objects in a box into which they can reach but cannot see. Above, we were concerned with the criteria for individuation that infants use to establish representations of the distinct individuals in the box. But this task can also used to characterize the limits on infants' working memory, for the infant must hold in mind a model of the objects placed in the box to guide subsequent searches.

In the relevant experiments, only spatio-temporal evidence for individuation is provided—the objects are identical to each other. Infants watch as a number of objects, all seen at the same time, are placed in the box, one at a time. The box is then given to them to retrieve the objects. On crucial trials, some of the objects have been surreptitiously removed before the box is given the child. Success consists of less search on one-in/ one-out trials, or two in/two trials (expected empty) than on two in/one out, or three in/one out, or three in/two out trials (more expected). Several studies have found success on one versus two comparisons (longer search on more expected trials than on expected empty trials), at both 12 and 14 months of age (Feigenson & Carey, 2003, 2005; Van de Walle et al., 2000).

Lisa Feigenson explored the upper limit of infants' representations under these circumstances. She found that infants succeed just when the total number of items placed in the box is three or fewer, but performance falls apart at four entities. For instance, infants of these ages search for more objects if they have seen three go in and have retrieved just two or one, but they fail if they have seen four go in and have retrieved two, and they even fail if they see four go in and have retrieved only one. Dwell on this last result. Infants search no longer upon having seen four go in and having retrieved only one than if they have seen just one go in and have retrieved only one. It's not that the child represents *nothing* in the box when he or she saw four go in; the infant does reach in and retrieve one. Infants represent something in the box, but they cannot form a representation of a set of four items under these circumstances.

Studies of spontaneous choice between two sets of objects provide data entirely convergent with those from the manual-search paradigm (Feigenson & Carey, 2005; Feigenson, Carey, & Hauser, 2002). Ten- and 12-month-old infants were shown a certain number of graham crackers placed in one bucket, one at a time, and a different number placed in another bucket, also one at a time. The infants could not see the crackers in the buckets. After watching the crackers being placed, the infants were allowed to crawl to one or the other bucket. At issue was whether they would go to the bucket with the larger number of crackers. This is what they did, when the choice is one versus two, one versus three, or two versus three. Performance was at chance at three versus four, two versus four, three versus six, and even one versus four. Performance fell apart if one of the sets exceeded three items. Just as in the above experiment, it isn't that the infants represented nothing when there were four or more objects—performance was random, not systematically, in favor of the smaller number in one versus four, two versus four, and three versus six comparisons. Furthermore, when the choice was four versus zero, the infants reliably crawled to the bucket with four. When there were four or more graham crackers in a bucket, infants represented "graham cracker in that bucket" but failed to establish a representation consisting of one object-file for each object.

Consider three versus two and four versus one comparisons. In both cases the total number of graham crackers was five, and this number, by hypothesis, exceeds the upper limit of three that infants can hold in working memory under these circumstances. Yet children succeeded in the former case and failed in the latter one. Apparently, infants can create two short-term memory models of attended objects, up to the limits on parallel individuation, and compare them in memory. We do not currently know how many models may be represented at once. The important lesson for us now is this: the limits on working memory in adult visual cognition studies is in the same range as the limits on the numbers of objects infants can simultaneously represent in working memory. This fact supports the identification of the representations underlying object-based attention and working memory in adults with the object representations of infancy.

Signature 3: Occlusion versus Existence Cessation

Another parallel between the two systems is that adults' representations of indexed objects in the multiple object–tracking experiments, as with infants' representations of objects in the experiments described in chapters 2 and 3, survive occlusion. Brian Scholl and Zenon Pylyshyn (1999) showed that object tracking in the MOT paradigm was not disrupted by the objects going behind real or virtual occluders, so long as the way the object disappeared specified occlusion and not going out of existence. Almost all of the infant studies cited above involve occlusion—objects are hidden behind screens, in boxes, or in buckets.

Eric Cheries and his colleagues (Cheries, Feigenson, Scholl, & Carey, 2005) have recently demonstrated that infants' object tracking is disrupted by exactly the same stimulus manipulations as is adult object tracking. Cheries habituated infants to small sets of disks (say, three) moving slowly, independently of each other. Also present in the display were two vertical bars that served as occluders. When the disks encountered a bar they either (1) disappeared as if passing behind it though ordinary deletion along their forward contours, reemerging on the same trajectory from the other side of the barrier by ordinary expansion along their back contour; or (2) shrank symmetrically to nothing at the same rate of disappearance upon encountering a barrier, reemerging on the same trajectory by expanding symmetrically from a central point. After habituation, the barriers were removed, and the infants were shown, in alternating test trials, either the same number of moving disks (three, in this example) or a new number (two, in this example). Importantly, the test trials were identical in all conditions, depicting continuously moving arrays of disks. Infants who were habituated to the type of deletion at boundaries that specifies occlusion dishabituated to the novel number, whereas those who were habituated to the type of deletion that specified shrinking to nothing did not. We interpret this result as reflecting the child's ability to track the individuals in the normal deletion condition, such that there were exactly three throughout the whole habituation period. When objects shrank out of existence and new objects expanded into existence, there was no fixed number present during habituation and so the child did not dishabituate to a novel number.

The infant's object tracking system and the object tracking system tapped in adult MOT studies use the same characteristics of events to distinguish two types of disappearance of currently attended objects: (1) disappearance that specifies continued existence of the objects behind the barriers and (2) disappearance that specifies existence cessation. This is the third signature, along with privileging spatio-temporal features in object individuation and a limit of three or four object-files in working memory, that favors identifying object representations in infancy with the adult object-file system of representation.

Conclusions from the Identification of the Two Literatures

Researchers in both traditions—those studying infant object representations and those studying mid-level object-based visual cognition—have been studying the same natural kind. This discovery has important implications for the characterization of core cognition. First, the computations that establish object-indexes and object-files, that individuate and trace objects through time and store these representations in visual working memory, operate throughout the life span, exemplifying one of the hypothesized properties of core cognition. Second, adult object-file representations are the output of domain-specific, encapsulated, perceptual input analyzers, thus exemplifying another hypothesized characteristic of core cognition. Adults may know that ducks do not change into rabbits, but typically the mid-level system that computes numerical identity in apparent motion studies does not use that knowledge To a first approximation, the processes that compute figure-ground, assign surfaces to distinct objects, and assign indices to attended objects work the same no matter whether an object picked out is a member of a familiar kind or not (see Carey and Xu, 2001; Peterson, 1994). So, too, for young infants' object representations.

The Evolutionary History of Object-File Representations

I now turn to another property of core cognition systems: deep evolutionary history. Often, but not always, core cognition is shared with other animals. This fact is important, for evidence that a knowledge system is shared among a wide range of species with a common ancestor, but with very different ecological niches and different learning histories, supports the hypothesis that the system is innate and was shaped by evolutionary selection pressures.

Chapter 2 described the work of Regolin and her colleagues on newborn chicks' representations of spatio-temporal continuity of objects—representations that support the search for occluded objects. This work provided an existence proof that representations of objects as spatio-temporally continuous may be innate. Do such results suggest that the mid-level object-file and object-indexing systems shared by human adults and young human infants have a long evolutionary history, perhaps arising early in vertebrate evolution? No, they don't. That chicks can form representations of objects that respect their spatio-temporal continuity does not warrant the conclusion that a system of representation with all of the properties of mid-level object-based attention underlies their performance. To explore this issue, we would need to characterize the conceptual role of chicks' object representations (e.g., do chicks represent object motion as subject to the solidity constraint?), and we would need to study how chicks individuate objects and whether they can create working-memory representations of multiple objects at once. No relevant studies have been carried out, so it is an open empirical question.

However, we do know that the evolutionary history of human core cognition of objects extends at least into our primate past. Marc Hauser and his colleagues have used all of the methods reviewed in chapter 2 and this chapter (violation-of-expectancy looking-time methodology, manual search for hidden objects, choice between two sets of hidden objects) with nonhuman primates (e.g., Hauser & Carey, 1998, 2003; Hauser, Carey, & Hauser, 2000; Hauser, MacNeilage, & Ware, 1996). The results converge with the data from young infants in great detail. Hauser's work has great methodological import. He was the first to show that the violation-of-expectancy looking-time methods yield interpretable data with nonhuman primates, both free-ranging *Rhesus* macaques and laboratory-housed new world monkeys, cottontop tamarins.

Results from the violation-of-expectancy looking-time methods show that both species of monkeys can use spatio-temporal evidence for object individuation and represent objects as continuing to exist when occluded. Hauser's first violation-of-expectancy study (Hauser, MacNeilage, & Ware, 1996) was a replication of Wynn's $1 + 1 = 2$ or 1 addition/subtraction study with free-ranging *Rhesus* macaques on Cayo Santiago, an island off the coast of Puerto Rico that is home to about 900 *Rhesus*. Subsequent studies from Hauser's group also replicated Wynn's study with laboratory-housed cottontop tamarins (Uller, Hauser, & Carey, 2001).

Hauser and I extended this findings to the same range of conditions under which success is obtained with 4- to 10-month-old human infants: 1 + 1 = 2 or 3 (showing that it is exactly two objects the monkeys expect; 1 + 1 = 2 or big one (showing that monkeys are not solely encoding total expected eggplant volume). Furthermore, performance breaks down at four objects; monkeys succeed at 2 + 1 = 2 or 3, but fail at 2 + 2 = 4 or 3, consistent with there being an upper limit of three or four on the number of objects a monkey can track at once (Hauser & Carey, 2003). We also established another processing signature in common to the computations both infants and *Rhesus* macaques deploy when creating object-file working-memory models of small sets. In both populations, success is dependent on the number of updates in short-term memory that are required to build a representation of the set behind the screen. Monkeys and babies succeed in a 2 + 1 = 2 or 3 condition, but they fail at a 1 + 1 + 1 = 2 or 3 condition. Following Uller, Carey, Huntley-Fenner, & Klatt (1999), we interpret these findings as reflecting constraints on computations that can be carried out on models being held in working memory.

Another paradigm that yields convergent results across the two subject populations is the cracker-choice study described above. Actually, this paradigm was originally carried out on Cayo Santiago, with apple slices rather than graham crackers as the food item placed in the buckets. Monkeys watched as two experimenters placed one set of apple slices in one bucket, one at a time (e.g., 1 + 1 + 1), after which the other experimenter placed the another set in the other bucket (e.g., 1 + 1 or 1 + 1 + 1 + 1). Monkeys succeeded when the choices were one versus two, two versus three, and three versus four. Just like the babies, monkeys' performance fell apart when one of the sets exceeded a certain limit —in this case, four rather than the three of the infants. Particularly important are failures at two versus five, four versus eight, and three versus eight; these choices involve highly discriminable numbers, with ratios much greater than those between small sets at which monkeys succeed (two versus three and three versus four; see Barner, Wood, Hauser, & Carey, in press; Hauser et al., 2000). Again, the pattern of performance is extremely similar to that of the babies and reveals the set-size signature of object-file representations

Thus, insofar as the issue has been studied, the processes that create object representations in nonhuman primates reveal the same signatures as do those of human infants. All the work to date suggests that the core cognition of objects exhibited by young infants has a long evolutionary history. Cottontop tamarins, who last shared a common ancestor with human beings well over 100 million years ago, exhibit it, as do our more closely related cousins, *Rhesus* macaques.

Core Cognition and Learning: Specialized Learning Mechanisms?

Another hypothesized feature of core cognition systems is that they are learning devices. There is no doubt that infants learn many generalizations about objects during their early months. Thus, the processes that yield object representations yield representations of endities about which the infant learns. What we do not yet know is to what extent the processes that support learning about objects are within module and domain-specific or domain-general central processes. Because the representations that are the output of the perceptual input analyzers are central, no doubt domain-general central learning mechanisms (e.g., association, causal learning) operate over them. But if human core cognition is like animal core cognition (remember the indigo buntings), we would also expect that some knowledge about the entities in each domain is acquired by within-module domain-specific learning mechanisms. This issue has not been systematically studied.

Consider just one case of learning about objects. Renée Baillargeon (1998) showed that infants do not innately know that unsupported objects fall. In one series of studies, infants watched during habituation trials while a small block was slowly pushed across a large supporting block, beginning on one end of the support and ending at the other, still fully supported (see Figure 3.7, familiasization). Then infants were presented a series of test trials, probing their expectations concerning when the block should fall (Figure 3.7A–F). On some trials the small block was pushed off the large one until it was completely unconnected, and thus totally unsupported by it, apparently suspended in mid-air (Figure 3.7A). On other trials, it remained in contact with the block, but in various configurations that to adults either would seem possible (Figure 3.7D and F) or would not seem possible (Figure 3.7B, C, and E).

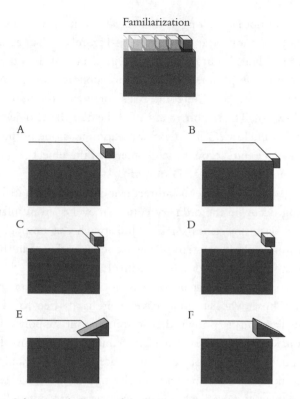

Figure 3.7. Schematic depiction of the Baillargeon support experiments. (Baillargeon, 2001; Baillargeon & Hanko-Summers, 1990). Redrawn from Baillargeon, R., & Hanko-Summers (1990). Is the top adequately supported by the bottom object? Young infants' understanding of support relations. *Cognitive Development, 5,* 29–53, with permission from Elsevier. Emmanuel Dupoux (Ed.), Language, Brain, and Cognitive Development: Essay in Honor of Jacques Mehler, pp. figure: Infants' physical knowledge of acquired expectations and core principles, © 2002 Massachusetts Institute of Technology, by permission of the MIT Press.

Infants' expectations unfold in a regular sequence over a long period of development. At 3 months of age, infants show no differential interest in these events. Even the unsupported object (Figure 3.7A), hanging in mid-air, is not particularly attention grabbing. Just a few weeks later, though, this impossible event draws markedly longer looking than does the possible event they were familiarized to. The child has begun to learn something about support. Infants first make a categorical distinction between contact/noncontact, and do not pay differential attention to objects that do not fall so long as there is any contact with the support. That is, they look longer at outcome A in Figure 3.7 than at any other outcome, including B, but do not differentiate any of the others. They gradually refine the parameters relevant to support. Next, the contact must be from below (now outcome B also draws attention, but none of the rest, C–F, do). Then, more than half of the base of the object must be supported from below (C also draws attention, but none of the rest do). Finally, they take into account the geometry of the object (Figure3.7E is attention grabbing but not 3.7D or 3.7F).

Baillargeon (1998) presents indirect evidence that the initial stages of this learning occur, in the ordinary course of events, from infants' own attempts to place objects on surfaces. Infants who sit unsupported will progress through the early steps of this sequence earlier than those who do not yet sit alone—consistent with the hypothesis that infants learn about support by placing objects on surfaces and observing the outcomes. Those who sit alone have their hands free to manipulate objects. Baillargeon has shown that learning about support can also be driven from observational evidence. In training experiments she shows infants contrasting cases of objects being placed on surfaces and falling or remaining supported, and she finds acceleration in the above sequence.

The objects involved in the support studies are unfamiliar to the babies; that is, they have not had experience with those very objects. This suggests that their previous experiences with objects in general are driving the developmental progressions Baillargeon observes in these studies. Experiments such as Baillargeon's certainly show that infants learn about objects, but they leave open whether the processes that support this learning are at least partly domain-specific. It is easy to see how the learning from observation in the support studies could be well modeled by domain-general associative mechanisms that extract statistical regularities from representations of events. The sense in which domain-specific learning mechanisms *may* be involved is limited, but important. There may be domain-specific constraints on the features and relations that enter into the statistical analysis.

An analogy from the literature on animal learning clarifies the sense of domain-specific learning at issue here. There is absolutely no doubt that animals learn associations between stimuli. Rats can easily learn that the occurrence of a particular sound predicts the occurrence of a shock from their water feeder, and they can also learn that a distinctive taste in the water predicts nausea two hours later. However, the reverse pairing (that a sound predicts nausea, that a taste predicts shock) is much harder to learn. This shows that there are domain-specific constraints on the associative pairings that can be learned. The appeal to domain specificity in this example is much weaker than in the case of the domain-specific learning mechanism that enables indigo buntings to extract north from the rotation of the night sky, for this latter mechanism involves a computation that is unique to the learning problem it evolved to solve. In the case of the rat, the associative mechanisms are very general, applying to a huge variety of cases of learning that involve computing statistical covariation in the environment. The domain specificity comes in constraints on the salience weighting of particular features in particular contexts. Although weaker, nonetheless, this is a bona fide type of domain-specific constraint on learning (see Gallistel, Brown, Carey, Gelman, & Keil, 1991, for an extended discussion of species-specific and domain-specific constraints on associative learning).

How would we find out whether the processes that extract the statistical generalizations concerning support are domain-specific in the sense of being constrained to weight some features more heavily than others? It is possible to imagine a relevant program of research. For example, one could take a variety of contrasts among objects that are salient to infants—for example, shape contrasts—and provide statistical evidence that these covary with whether objects remain supported or fall in the observational learning paradigm of Baillargeon and her colleagues. That is, one could try to teach the generalization—a cylinder covered with blue glitter, supported from below on three-fourths of its surface, does not fall; but a red striped block, supported from below on only one-fourth of its surface, does fall. What generalization does the child learn—the geometric one concerning the amount of surface supported, or that that cylinders don't fall and blocks do, or that blue glittery things don't fall but red striped things do? If the child is biased to analyze the geometric relations between the object's base and the support, this would be evidence for domain specificity in this learning mechanism. If human core cognition resembles animal domain-specific learning devices, we would expect that at least some such constraints on statistical learning will be observed. To my knowledge, no studies have yet explored this issue.

Modularity: Are Object Representations Encapsulated or Informationally Promiscuous?

As discussed in chapter 1, in *The Modularity of Mind,* Fodor (1983) argued that rather than trying to distinguish perceptual from conceptual *content,* the conceptual/perceptual contrast is more perspicuously drawn on the basis of processing characteristics. He suggested that perceptual processes are modular, and he characterized modular processes as fast, automatic, primarily data driven by sharply limited input, inaccessible, and encapsulated. By "encapsulated" he meant that other knowledge does not affect processes internal to the module. He contrasted modular perceptual processes with central cognitive processes, which are slow, effortful, optional, accessible, and informationally promiscuous. By "informationally promiscuous" he meant freely used in inference. For informationally promiscuous representations there are no restrictions on what data bear on which inferences; it is a matter of theory building to discover the inferential relations among real-world phenomena. Fodor suggested that the architecturally important distinction is between modular and central processes. According to Fodor, it doesn't much matter whether one uses the terms "perceptual" and "conceptual" for the two respective types.

Unambiguously perceptual processes (such as computing depth) are indeed modular and unambiguously conceptual ones (such as creating the theory of natural selection) are indeed nonmodular and central. Notice that if one draws the distinction between perceptual and conceptual this way, many representations that do not have sensory content, such as syntactic representations, turn out to be perceptual. What about *object* representations? I argued in chapter 2 that object representations themselves have conceptual content in the sense of not being able to be stated in terms of perceptual primitives, and in the sense of having a rich conceptual role. Nonetheless, like syntactic representations, the input analyzers that create object representations are most likely modular, and thus perceptual on Fodor's definition. One reason to think so is that the processes that underlie object individuation are encapsulated from property and kind information that the infant undoubtedly represents. The core cognition thesis concurs that core cognition representations are perceptual in this sense. Indeed, it is important to the thesis, for the existence of evolutionarily created innate perceptual input analyzers at least partially solves the problem of how the representations in core cognition have the content they do. This aspect of core cognition representations explains how they are causally connected to the entities in the world they represent.

However, the *output* of the innate perceptual input analyzer—as with all perceptual modules—is part of a central system that is cognitive by Fodor's characterization. Object-files themselves seem accessible and participate in slow, optional, inferentially promiscuous processes. They are inferentially related to the outputs of other systems of core cognition.

Take, first, the question of accessibility. Of course, it is virtually impossible to know whether a representation in a prelinguistic creature's mind is widely accessible. But *adult* object-files are certainly accessible. We have phenomenal access to them and we can carry out a wide variety of optional computations, under executive control, over them. Accepting the identification of object-files with infant object representations implies that object-files are accessible for infants as well. Furthermore, we have at least indirect evidence that object-files are accessible to infants. Object-files support voluntary action—infants reach for objects, even hidden ones. The box-search and bucket-choice studies reviewed above show that infant object representations, like object-files, are individual symbols that can be placed in short-term memory, and such short-term memory representations are accessible for adults.

What clinches the matter for me is evidence that that infant object representations interact inferentially with representations that are the output of distinct input modules. Because this is such an important point, I will belabor it. Individuating distinct domains of core cognition is far from a trivial matter. It is not clear, for example, whether computations of Michotte contact causality are part of core cognition of objects or a separate system whose outputs are interrelated with it (a point taken up in chapter 6). But on just about every analysis, spatial representations are a distinct input system from object-file representations, as are number representations, quantity representations, and representations of intentional agency. Yet object representations are integrated with representations from all of these domains. Thus, while the computations that yield representations of object-files are modular and encapsulated, the object-files themselves are inputs to a variety of central computations. With respect to inferential role, then, the object representations that are part of core cognition are seen to be rich conceptual representations. Let me remind you of the bases of these assertions.

First, young infants represent the spatial relations among objects. I have reviewed massive evidence that shows they represent objects behind barriers, inside boxes, and inside buckets. To give just one more demonstration of this, Kristine Onishi and Renée Baillargeon (2005) habituated infants to two identical blocks being moved into the center of the stage from the sides, one (e.g., the one from the left side) always placed on top of the other. Looking times were measured to the static array. After habituation, the blocks were again moved to the center of the stage, but the previously bottom block was placed on top. The resulting array was identical in appearance to the one that the infant was habituated to, but if they distinguished the two object tokens and represented which one was on top, their attention might be drawn to the change, and, indeed, it was.

Second, with respect to number representations, we have already seen that infants can compute 1–1 correspondence over object-files to establish numerical equivalence (see also chapter 4). Chapter 4 will also show, with respect to quantity representations, that infants can sum over continuous variables bound in object-files to choose between sets on the basis of total volume.

Third, with respect to agency, chapter 5 will show that infants as young as 5 months old represent objects as goals of others' intentional actions, and chapter 6 will show that 7- to 12-month-old infants infer a previously unseen agent to explain the motion of a known inanimate object.

Notice that, on the view of core cognition developed here, some of the representations that articulate core cognition are *not* conceptual—those that are within module and encapsulated. I have made an extended argument that *object* itself is a conceptual representation, but knowledge of spatio-temporal continuity and cohesion probably are not. The computations that create representations of objects make use of evidence for spatio-temporal continuity and boundedness, and embody a commitment to these pro-perties of objects in further computations, but there is no reason to believe that the child explicitly knows principles such as "objects continue to exist behind barriers," "objects do not fall apart and reassemble," or "one object cannot pass through the space occupied by another."

The Content of Object-Files

Recognizing that object representations (both young infants' and adults' object-files) are the output of modular input analyzers, at least partially encapsulated from representations of object kinds, and hence *mid-level,* may raise questions about the argument of chapter 2 that object representations are conceptual. There, I argued that young infants' representations of objects, which we now see to be object-files, are conceptual because their content cannot be stated in spatio-temporal vocabulary or in the vocabulary of sense data, and also because of their rich inferential role. As just mentioned, chapters 3 through 7 provide much more evidence concerning the rich inferential role of young infants' object representations—they are integrated with infants' representations of number, causality, and intentional agency and they are expressed in the child's earliest explicit language.

But what exactly is the content of object-files? What concepts do they represent? It is difficult enough to characterize the content of a given mental symbol if the creature we are studying can express that symbol explicitly in language. But what of nonlinguistic creatures like chicks and monkeys and preverbal humans? I see no other route to specifying a representational system's content than by studying what entities in the world cause the tokening of the mental symbol in question—that is, by studying the extension of the symbol. And, also, we must study that symbol's inferential role. These two aspects of the functioning of symbols determine content, and thus whatever evidence we can glean about a symbol's extension and inferential role allows us to characterize its content. In what follows I illustrate, first, how one might appeal to evidence concerning extension and, then I illustrate how one might draw on evidence concerning inferential role to answer the question of what the content is of object-files.

The Extension of Object-Files

I have been assuming that object-files symbolize physical objects, by which I mean bounded, coherent, 3-D, separable, spatio-temporally continuous wholes. This claim, that object-files represent real 3-D objects, hardly may seem surprising, but in fact there are reasons to doubt it. In virtually all of the adult studies done on mid-level vision, as well as in many of the infant studies, the stimuli are actually 2-D entities on computer screens (e.g., Cheries, Feigenson, Scholl, & Carey, 2008; Johnson & Aslin, 1995; Kahneman et al., 1992; Pylyshyn & Storm, 1998; Richardson & Kirkham, 2004; Scholl & Pylyshyn, 1999). Does the fact that 2-D bounded entities activate object-files mean that their content is more perceptual—perhaps *closed shape*? Should object-files be called "closed shape-files" or "perceptual individual-files"? No, they should not. For computer displays to work, we must present many of the cues for depth in 2-D arrays, and surfaces arrayed in 3-D are routinely perceived in such displays. That the system can be fooled into accepting 2-D entities as objects does not mean that it is not representing the stimuli as real objects, just as the fact that the system can be fooled into seeing depth in 2-D displays that provide perspective and interposition cues does not mean it is not representing the stimuli as arrayed in 3-D space.

But what reasons do we have for believing that the system is being fooled by these computer displays, and is representing them as real 3-D objects in spite of the fact that they are not? If 2-D closed shapes are not in the extension of object-files, but object-files are activated by these computer displays, then the mid-level object tracking system is *misrepresenting* these stimuli. Jerry Fodor (1990) has provided a way of thinking about misrepresentation. Misrepresentation is a problem for any naturalistic theory of representation, but Fodor is mainly interested in one kind of naturalistic theory, one that holds that content is determined by a causal link between the entities in the world and a symbol token in the mind. Fodor's asymmetric dependence theory of referential content proposes a solution to this problem. He illustrates the solution with the example of a horse seen in the distance on a misty day being misidentified as a cow. The real-life horse caused the tokening of the cow symbol; and if content is determined by such causal links, doesn't this mean that the content of the cow symbol is *horse* as well as *cow*? No, says Fodor. When one fleshes out the causal story, one sees that the *reason* that the horse can cause the cow symbol to be activated depends on the causal links between cows and that symbol, but that the reason cows cause the cow symbol to be activated does not depend in any way on whether horses do so. This asymmetry allows us to see that the symbol really represents cows, not horses.

Even if Fodor's analysis has problems, it works well enough for the purposes of this book (for discussion of the problems, see Adams & Aizawa, 1994; Godfrey-Smith, 1989). I accept the causal theory of content determination for representations in core cognition, so Fodor's analysis applies to the case at hand. That 2-D individuals cause object-files to be activated is dependent on the causal relations that ensure that object-files refer to 3-D objects; and in the case of core cognition (unlike concepts such as *cow*), we have at least a sketch of what the relevant causal processes are. Through natural-selection input analyzers have evolved that create representations of objects from the information in the physical stimulation of sense organs. It is clear how Fodor's asymmetric dependency theory allows that 2-D entities might be misrepresented as objects, and there is evidence it is on the right track. One reason to believe that infants misrepresent 2-D pictures as real objects is that, under at least some circumstances, they attempt to pick them up. Systematic studies have shown that attempts to handle and pick up pictured objects are readily elicited in children under 1 year old and disappear completely only around 18 months of age (Deloache, Perroutsakos, Uttal, Rosengren, & Gottlieb, 1998). This observation does not require that babies completely fail to distinguish 3-D and 2-D objects—and they don't (they always reach more for a 3-D than a 2-D version), for there is conflicting evidence coming from the pictures. The situation is the same as when we adults see depth in a picture: we represent the depth while at the same time representing the picture's 2-D quality.

Another line of evidence that 2-D entities are actually being represented as objects is that the properties that constrain object representation clearly reflect the properties of real objects. For example, I have reviewed evidence that the processes that establish and maintain object-file representations are sensitive to the spatio-temporal information that specifies either occlusion or existence cessation. Occlusion and existence cessation are properties of real physical objects, not disks of light displayed on computer screens. The implosion/disappearance studies provide data concerning the extension of object representations by probing what does *not* cause their tokening: entities that shrink to nothing or suddenly disappear fail to elicit object indexing and tracking.

Two series of studies with 8-month-old infants confirm that mere perceptual boundedness is *not* sufficient to cause object-files to be set up.

Object-files are not closed-shape files. These studies confirm that the individuals being tracked in the infant studies are physical objects, and not just any perceptual objects specified by figure/ground processes, such as disks on computer screens or piles of sand or blocks.

A hallmark of physical objects is that they maintain their boundaries through time. Other entities that are bounded in space while stationary, such as a pile of sand or a pile of separate little blocks, do not maintain boundaries if grasped from above, and in this sense are not objects. Several studies have compared infant representations of such non-cohesive entities with their representations of cohesive entities fashioned to look identical to the non-cohesive ones while are rest. It is only upon viewing such entities in motion (do they fall apart or do they maintain their boundaries?) that unequivocal evidence for their ontological status is obtained. Consistent with the claim that object-files represent objects, two series of studies establish that infants track real objects that are perceptually identical to piles of sand or piles of little blocks, under conditions where they will not track the perceptually identical non-objects (Huntley-Fenner, Carey, & Solimando, 2002; Chiang & Wynn, 2000).

Take the studies by Gavin Huntley-Fenner and his colleagues (2002) as an example. We carried out a series of $1 + 1 = 2$ or 1 experiments involving sand poured behind screens or sand-pile look-alike objects lowered behind screens. Stimulus type was a between-participant variable, and infants were familiarized with the stimuli before the study by handling the sand or the sandlike object. In all of the studies, 8-month-old infants succeeded in the conditions involving objects that looked like piles of sand, but they failed in the sand conditions. The failure in one of these studies was especially striking, for it shows that infants fail to compute "sand permanence" under conditions in which they easily compute "object permanence." In this study, diagrammed in Figure 3.8, the infant watched as a pile of sand was poured onto the stage floor and then covered by a screen. A second, spatially separate, screen was introduced and a second pile of sand poured behind it. The screens were then removed, revealing either two piles of sand (one behind each screen) or only one (the original pile initially seen on the stage floor). Eight-month-olds did not differentiate the two outcomes, although they succeeded if the stimuli were sand-pile shaped objects lowered as a whole onto the stage floor.

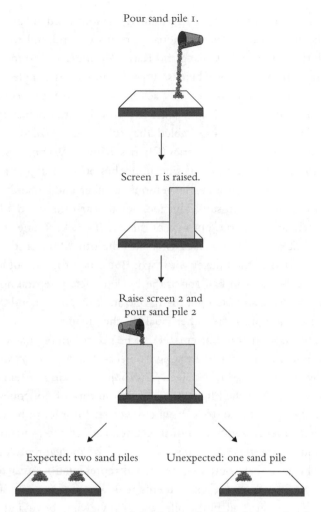

Pour sand pile 1.

Screen 1 is raised.

Raise screen 2 and
pour sand pile 2

Expected: two sand piles   Unexpected: one sand pile

Figure 3.8. Schematic depiction of the design of sand tracking or "sand permanence" studies (Huntley-Fenner, Carey & Solimando, 2002). Redrawn from Huntley-Fenner, G., Carey, S., & Solimando, A. (2002). Objects are individuals but stuff doesn't count: Perceived rigidity and cohesiveness influence infants' representations of small groups of discrete entities. *Cognition*, *85*(3), 203–221, with permission from Elsevier.

To succeed at this task, the infant need only represent "sand behind this screen, sand behind that screen." Why did they fail at "sand permanence"? As mentioned in chapter 2, object permanence requires an individual object whose identity is being tracked; it is the *same* object we represent behind the screen. Apparently, 8-month-old infants cannot establish representations of individual portions of sand and trace them through time. Wen-Chi Chiang and Karen Wynn (2000) found exactly the same results with piles of blocks. If the pile moved as a single coherent object, 8-month-old infants could track it and represent it as continuing to exist behind a barrier. If they were shown this entity being separated into five blocks and then reassembled, they subsequently failed to track it.

A recent study by Erik Cheries (Cheries, Mitroff, Wynn, & Scholl, in press) brings home how devastating noncohesion is to object tracking. Cheries began by replicating Feigenson's cracker-choice study with a two–versus–one comparison. The individuals each consisted of half a graham cracker. If cheries put two of these half-crackers, one at a time, into one bucket and one half-cracker into the other bucket, the infants reliably crawled to the bucket with two. But if he brought out a whole cracker and broke it in half above the bucket, clearly separating it into two half-crackers, and then put them, one at a time, into it and then put one half-cracker into the other bucket, the infants were at chance. Apparently, as soon as an object is seen to be noncoherent, infants cannot track it and they cannot easily assign object-files to parts of an object originally parsed as a single object. The object tracking system fails to track perceptual specified figures that have a history of noncohesion.

Let us stop and take stock of where we are. In order to be sure that infants have mental symbols with the content *object,* we must study the real-world entities that cause the tokening of the mental representations that might have that content—the mental representations that underlie infant performance in the experiments reviewed in chapter 2 and this chapter. The sand- and block-pile studies reviewed above add data in support of the claim that the content of what we are calling *object representations* are indeed real-world objects.

I now turn to another line of relevant data bearing on the content of object-files, deriving from studies of the inferential role of infant object representations.

The Inferential Role of Object-Files and Infant Object Representations

There has been no work on the inferential role of adults' object-file representations, but if we accept the identification of adult object-files with infant object representations, then the infant work bears on both adult and infant conceptual roles. Chapter 2 developed the argument that young infants' object representations articulate physical knowledge. I showed there that infants as young as 2 months old represent physical relations between objects such as *inside* and *behind*, and their representations are constrained by knowledge of solidity—a property of real objects but not of 2-D visual objects. Besides expecting objects to be solid, and thus not to pass through other ones, slightly older infants (6-month-olds) also expect objects to be subject to the laws of contact causality (see chapter 6), represent objects as the goals of human action (see chapter 5), and represent self-moving agents as the cause of motion of inanimate objects (see chapter 6).

Thus, the conceptual role of the infant's object representations is to support inferences about the relations among real objects in the world: objects are represented as solid entities in spatial and causal relations with each other. This fact gives us another reason to conclude that object-file representations have conceptual content, beyond the fact that they cannot be reduced to sensory or spatio-temporal primitives—namely, that they are inferentially interrelated with other representations that themselves cannot be reduced to sensory primitives, other representations that are the outputs of different core systems and of domain-general learning processes. Thus, they play a central conceptual role, one of the hallmarks of nonmodular, conceptual processes.

Interim Conclusions: The Six Properties of Core Cognition

Chapter 2 (conceptual content, innateness) and this chapter (conceptual content, continuity, learning mechanism, long evolutionary history) have sketched the current state of evidence that object representations exemplify the features of systems of core cognition. The only feature not yet discussed is iconic format. I take up the issue of the format of representation of symbols in core cognition in chapter 4. Here, I consider two different challenges to the core cognition hypothesis. The first is theoretical: one might question just how *cognitive* systems of representation with these six properties are. The second is empirical: one might question the evidence, especially from the violation-of-expectancy methods that are drawn upon so heavily in this literature, that is offered for core cognition.

Challenges to the Core Cognition Hypothesis: What Kind of Cognition Is Core Cognition?

Some writers (including me, in my earliest writings on core cognition) claimed knowledge of objects to be conceptual in a much stronger sense than I have argued here (e.g., Baillargeon, 1993; Spelke, 1988). These writers spoke of infants' "beliefs" that objects persist when occluded, infants' "knowledge" that two objects cannot occupy the same place at the same time, infants' "reasoning" and "inferences" about the interactions of occluded objects, and their "surprise" or "puzzlement" at impossible events. There is nothing inherently wrong with such language as long as the writer is clear what kinds of representations constitute the beliefs and knowledge in question, what kinds of computations constitute the reasoning and inference, and what kinds of states constitute the puzzlement and surprise.

However, most researchers now prefer not to use such highly cognitive language in describing the representations and computations of young infants because the term "belief" can be taken to imply a language-like format, that the beliefs are in some sense explicit, and that the computations carried out over them are logical inferences defined over propositions. Most researchers who endorse the core cognition hypothesis do not now see it that way (Carey & Spelke, 1994, 1996; Gelman, 1990; Leslie, 1994; Scholl & Leslie, 1999). Rather, much of the knowledge in core cognition is embodied in constraints on the processes that create the representations of ongoing events. I assume that core cognition representations are iconic (see chapter 4 for an extended discussion of representational format) and that the representations that articulate core cognition are created by modular systems whose computations are constrained by the principles revealed by experiments such as those reviewed in these pages.

For example, the computations that create representations of objects' disappearing behind occluders embody a commitment to spatio-temporal continuity. This is analogous to the computations that create representations of depth from binocular disparity, embodying a commitment to different images in the two eyes arising from a single source. It would be decidedly odd to say that the 5-month-old infant "believes" that the images to the two eyes each derive from a single source in the world and thus provide information about depth, even though that infant undoubtedly uses that information to create representations of objects in depth (e.g., Held, Birch, & Gwiazda, 1980). The infant represents depth and objects, but binocular disparity and the spatio-temporal continuity constraint are most probably embodied only in the computations that yield representations of depth and of objects.

That the representations that articulate core cognition are similar to perceptual representations in all these ways is important to the story I am telling in this book. Some concepts—those in core cognition—have the content they do for the same reasons that some perceptual representations have the content they have. Both types of representations are causally connected to the entities in the real world, thanks to perceptual input analyzers crafted through natural selection. But it is equally important to the story I am telling here that at least some of the representations that articulate core cognition, such as the object-files themselves, have conceptual content. It is for this latter reason that I use the term "cognition" in the name I call these core representational systems.

Empirical Challenges to the Core Cognition Hypothesis

In addition to the theoretical challenges to the core cognition hypothesis, there have been empirical challenges. Many researchers in the field reject the evidence from looking-time studies that are the main source of evidence concerning young infants' mental representations. Because the general points that the skeptics raise are excellent ones, it is worth laying them out and thinking about them. The criticisms boil down to two observations that are undoubtedly right: (1) infants' looking patterns are determined by many factors in addition to responses to violations of expectancy, and it is difficult to rule out alternative interpretations of the patterns of looking obtained in any given experiment; (2) the very late emergence of some explicit representations (representations that can guide action, for example) of knowledge putatively contained within core cognition raises questions about the very existence of core cognition. Let me take up these two objections, in turn, focusing on knowledge of solidity as a case study.

Alternative Explanations of the Looking-Time Patterns in the Solidity Experiments

The first objection to inferences from looking-time studies draws on the observation that infants' attention is drawn not only by violated expectancies but also by simple perceptual novelty or familiarity—and, even more basically, by intrinsic perceptual preferences. Thus, any looking-time study must control for these latter bases of looking adequately before patterns of attention may be taken as reflecting sensitivity to a violated expectancy. The critics claim that the controls are not adequate and that the observed patterns of looking reflect simple perceptual preferences or familiarity/novelty preferences.

We can see how this debate plays out by considering Spelke's solidity experiments (Spelke, Breilinger, Macomber, & Jacobsen, 1992). In those experiments, 4-month-old infants were habituated to an object's being lowered behind a screen, after which the screen was removed, revealing the object on the stage floor (see Figure 3.9). In the test trials, a solid shelf was introduced into the apparatus, the screen was replaced, and the object was lowered, as before, behind the screen. The screen was then removed, revealing either a possible outcome of the object resting on the shelf (A), or an impossible outcome of the object resting on the stage floor as before, apparently having passed through the solid barrier (B). Infants looked longer at the impossible outcomes, suggesting that the models infants build of the events unfolding before them are constrained by the principles that one object cannot pass through the space occupied by another.

Critics of these studies have suggested that the outcome in which the object appears enclosed (between the shelf and the apparatus floor) may be more visually interesting to infants than the outcome in which the object is outside, perhaps because of greater contour density. Of course this is possible, but all experimenters using these techniques are aware of such possible confounds and take care to eliminate them. Often, baseline conditions involve showing infants just the outcomes of a series of test trials, thereby establishing whether there are intrinsic preferences. There is

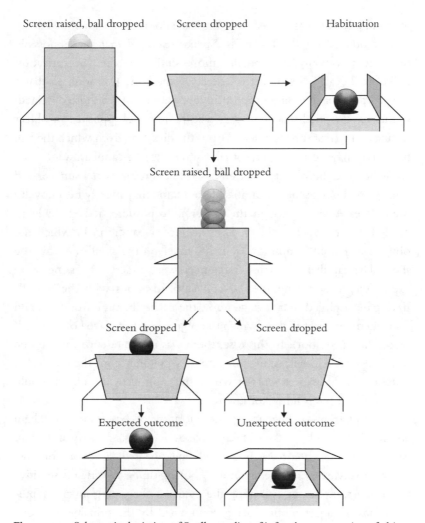

Screen raised, ball dropped   Screen dropped   Habituation

Screen raised, ball dropped

Screen dropped   Screen dropped

Expected outcome   Unexpected outcome

Figure 3.9. Schematic depiction of Spelke studies of infants' representation of object solidity, or the principle that one object cannot pass through the space occupied by another object. Redrawn from Spelke, E. S., Bilinger, K., Macomber, J., & Jacobsen, K. (1992). Origins of knowledge. *Psychological Review, 99*, 605–632, with permission of the American psychological Association.

no baseline preference for the outcome in which the object appears enclosed.

A slightly different line of criticism relies on novelty preferences rather than intrinsic preferences. Remember, infants were first habituated to the object's being lowered onto the stage floor, after which the barrier was introduced for the test trials. Spelke reasoned that the impossible outcome is actually perceptually more similar to the familiarization outcome (because the object is in exactly the same position), so that a novelty preference would support the opposite results to those obtained. Critics have replied that it may as well be just the opposite: an object resting on the first surface reached from the direction from which the ball has come may be more perceptually similar to the familiarization outcome because the object is not enclosed but is resting on a surface, and thus the preference for the impossible outcome may merely be a novelty preference. Again, although this is certainly possible, it is possible to control for and Spelke did so. She included a condition in which the object was placed in position by hand either on the shelf or below the shelf. The familiarization/test sequences were exactly the same as in the solidity experiments (i.e., several familiarizations with the object's having been placed on the stage floor, the barrier being introduced, and then alternating test trials in which the object is either placed on the shelf or on the stage floor). In this case, there was no preference for the one outcome over another, ruling out a novelty preference for the impossible outcome in the experiments in which the motion of the object would have violated the solidity constraint.

Although researchers using the violation-of-expectancy paradigm attempt to rule out perceptual preference or perceptual novelty artifacts, it is always possible that somebody will find one that accounts for one, or even many, results in the literature. Looking times are certainly sensitive to such factors. But in evaluating the evidence for young infants' representations of object motion being constrained by the principle that one object cannot pass through the space occupied by another, we must consider the huge amount of convergent evidence from many different paradigms. Consider the Baillargeon rotating-screen studies (see Figure 2.1, chapter 2), the Baillargeon box-on-track experiments (Baillargeon, 1986), the Baillargeon sand-in-cylinder experiments (Baillargeon, 1995), the Hespos and Baillargeon rod/cylinder experiments (see Figure 2.6, chapter 2), and the Spelke experiments described above. Convergent evidence from many different studies, each with different controls for perceptual preferences or perceptual novelty, ultimately convinces me of the case.

I will not belabor discussion of the controls in each study I cite. Nonetheless, I would like to reassure the skeptical reader by going through one design in detail—the Sue Hespos and Renée Baillargeon solidity study mentioned in chapter 2; see Figure 2.6 for a diagram of the test events in this study. Recall that 2-month-olds looked longer at an impossible event in which a rod apparently was lowered through a remembered lid on a container than when it was lowered into an empty container. Hespos and Baillargeon successfully controlled for novelty and familiarity effects. In these studies, the events began with the rod's being picked up and raised over the cylinder. This familiarized the infants with the hand, the rod, the motion of the rod, and so forth, but it provided no information about the upcoming test events. After familiarization, in a between-participants design, the cylinder was turned, revealing either a closed top (half of the participants) or an open cylinder (half of the participants; see Figure 2.6). The rod was then inserted into the cylinder (impossible outcome for those participants shown the closed top and possible outcome for the other group; these are the test trials depicted in Figure 2.6). Those infants for whom the event violated the solidity constraint looked over twice as long as did those for whom it did not.

Consider this design. Both the open-cylinder and the closed-cylinder groups saw exactly the same events during familiarization and during test; the only difference was what was revealed when the cylinder was turned. Since there was only one outcome during the test trials of the experimental condition (the rod was lowered into the container), a simple perceptual preference for one outcome over another could not have accounted for the results. The familiarization events in both the experimental and control baseline conditions were identical (the rod was lifted and held above the container), so greater perceptual novelty of one of the outcome events relative to the habituation events could not account for the results. A final possibility is that the closed top was more interesting than the open tube, and so infants looked longer during the test events in the closed-top condition just because of that. Hespos and Baillargeon controlled for this as well, running two more groups in a series of test trials that were identical to the familiarization trials (the rod remained perched above the cylinder). Between the familiarization and test trials, half of the participants were exposed to the open container and half to the closed. But during the test trials, the rod remained raised

Baseline Events

Open-container Condition

Closed-container Condition

Figure 3.10. Schematic depiction of baseline condition in Hespos & Baillargeon (2001) solidity study. Reprinted from Hespos, S., & Baillargeon, R. (2001). Reasoning about containment events in very young infants. *Cognition*, 78, 207–245, with permission from Elsevier.

above the cylinder (see Figure 3.10). There was no difference between the groups; having seen a closed tube did not by itself cause greater interest in the events. As far as I can see, this leaves no explanation for the pattern of looking other than the violation of the solidity constraint.

It is beyond the scope of this book to include all the controls for perceptual preferences and perceptual novelty/familiarization effects that have been included in the experiments I report. I advise the interested or skeptical reader to look at the research papers I cite. This is not to say that the controls have always been adequate; there are no guarantees in science. No doubt, the interpretations of some particular studies will be modified in the future, as alternative interpretations of the observed patterns of looking times are corroborated. Nonetheless, the conclusions I draw from the experiments cited in these pages are supported by a great deal of convergent evidence from many different paradigms.

Looking Time versus Reaching

As we saw in chapter 2, infants' failure to reach for hidden objects has led many researchers to doubt that young infants actually do represent objects as existing behind barriers. Chapter 2 laid out my response to these doubts. Performance limitations, owing to immature executive function or to parameters of the motor system that guides the reach, partly account for failures to search in such tasks. Development within these systems can be independent of the capacity to form representations of hidden objects.

However, sometimes success in looking-time procedures predates success in reaching procedures by a matter of years! These dramatic age lags have cast doubt on the conclusions from the infant studies. How can infants "know" something that 2-year-olds cannot demonstrate knowledge of? At the very least, such dramatic lags will require different explanations from the accounts of performance limitations appealed to above.

The solidity studies provide a particularly striking example of a much earlier manifestation of understanding in looking-time procedures than in procedures that rely on search. Two-month-olds succeed in the looking-time studies, whereas it is not until over *2 to 3 years* of age that children succeed in manual-search versions of the same tasks (Hood, Carey, &

Prasada, 2000; Berthier, DeBlois, Poierier, Novak, & Clifton, 2000). Bruce Hood, Sandeep Prasada, and I carried out four object-search studies closely modeled on the Spelke shelf studies, and in all four cases, 24-month-old toddlers (2-year-olds) failed.

Let's consider one of these studies as an example. Toddlers were familiarized with an object's being dropped onto a stage floor. Then a barrier was introduced above the stage and a screen with two doors, one at barrier level and one at floor level, was introduced in front of the apparatus (see Figure 3.11). The object was dropped behind the screen, and the infant was allowed to search for the object. Two-year-olds searched at the floor level, where they had seen the object before, and not at the barrier level, where the object must be if its motion was arrested by the barrier.

The studies of Rachel Keen (formerly Clifton) and her colleagues are all the more striking (Berthier et al., 2000; Butler, Berthier & Clifton, 2002; Mask, Novak, Berthier, & Keen, 2006; Shutts, Keen, & Spelke, 2006). Their task is more difficult, involving four doors and four possible locations of the barrier (see Figure 3.12). But unlike in our studies, they gave the child considerable training. The child watched the ball roll down the incline with the doors open and the barrier placed at each of the four locations, seeing it stop in front of the barrier each time. Also, they were given multiple trials, with feedback. In our studies, 30-month-olds succeed, whereas in Keen's, robust success is not obtained until 36 months of age. This is almost three years after success at the looking-time studies by 2-month-olds!

A first response to these studies is to doubt the infant work. How can 2-month-olds know that one object cannot pass through another when 2-year-olds search for an object as if it had fallen right through a solid shelf? Some of the explanations offered in chapter 2 for the A-not-B error in search tasks probably play a role in this case as well. The toddler's search shows the influence on search of previously viewed locations of the object. Thus, part of the answer lies in developing executive function, which must adjudicate between competing representations of locations. Perhaps there is further development of the system of planning that computes over representations in motor work space. But I do not think this is the whole story, because of the extreme magnitude of the gap. The difference between 2 months and 3 years suggests a principled difference

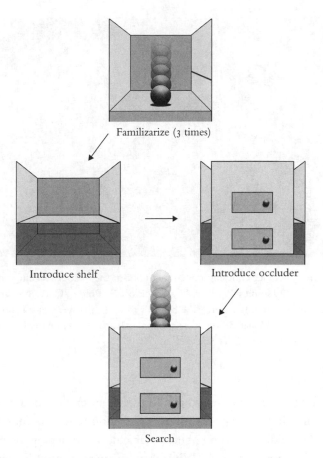

Familizarize (3 times)

Introduce shelf   Introduce occluder

Search

Figure 3.11. Schematic depiction of toddler reaching version of Spelke infant solidity experiment (Hood, Carey, & Prasada, 2000). Redrawn from Hood, B., Carey, S., & Prasada, S. (2000). Predicting the outcomes of physical events: Two-year-olds fail to reveal knowledge of solidity and support. *Child Development, 71*(6), 1540–1554, with permission from Blackwell Publishers.

in the kinds of knowledge being tapped in these two different paradigms. Indeed, I believe there are two kinds of knowledge involved here: within-module encapsulated representations and explicit representations that are output of the perceptual device that creates representations of object-files. Only the latter can be drawn upon in the service of prediction.

Keen and her colleagues have shown that the toddlers who fail at her four-door task are not encoding the position of the shelf relative to the

Figure 3.12. Toddler choosing the correct door in the 4-door reaching version of the Spelke solidity studies. Berthier, N. E., DeBlois, S., Poirier, C. R., Novak, M. A., & Clifton, R. K. (2000). Where's the ball? Two- and three-year-olds reason about unseen events. *Developmental Psychology, 36*(3), 394–401. Reprinted with permission from American Psychological Association.

doors, and thus are not using that information in predicting the location of the ball. Thus, the 2-year-olds' representations of object motion may respect the solidity constraint, but 2-year-olds fail to deploy the relevant information to plan a reach. Why, then, do they succeed in the infant studies? In the infant studies, infants are shown an object falling behind a screen, and then the screen is removed, revealing the location of the object relative to the shelf. At this point, the infant need only draw upon a memory representation of the motion of the ball (falling from above) to recognize that the path of motion would have passed through the shelf. This violates a constraint on object motion, drawing attention. On this view, the child is not predicting where the ball is, relative to the shelf, when both are hidden in the infant studies; the violation is detected only upon seeing the final disposition of the event, where the shelf and the location of the ball are both visible and available to reconstruct the path the ball must have taken through the shelf.

What changes between 24 and 36 months, such that the child now succeeds? We do not know the answer to that question. There are several possibilities, not mutually exclusive. First, the child may come to explicitly represent the spatial relations among all of the objects behind the screen, aided perhaps by explicit spatial language. Second, the principle that objects do not pass through the space occupied by other objects may become explicitly formulated by the child, allowing a prospective prediction. Third, developments within executive function help the child overcome perserverative responses. Although it would be interesting to work this out, the important suggestion I am making here is that the toddler failures do not undermine the interpretation of the infant successes, for the toddler experiments do not draw on the same within-module computations that the retrospective infant experiments do. I suggest there are two kinds of knowledge at stake here: that embodied within module in the form of constraints on model building and that represented in terms of symbols that are input to central reasoning processes.

Conclusions

My goals in this chapter were twofold. My first goal was to show that infants' knowledge of objects displays several of the hypothesized properties of core cognition. Representations of objects are created by modular, encapsulated, perceptual input analyzers that have a long evolutionary history, extending deep into human beings' primate heritage. These representations continue to articulate our representations of the world throughout life. (The format of representation will be discussed in chapter 4.) Only one signature property of core cognition has not yet been fully explored—the existence of domain-specific learning mechanisms.

My second goal in this chapter, as well as my goal in chapter 2, was to explore what kind of cognition core cognition is. Object–files are conceptual representations, in that they cannot be defined in perceptual primitives and as shown by their accessibility and rich conceptual role (of which much more will be said in chapters 4–6). However, they are also perceptual representations, being the output of innate, modular, input analyzers and having iconic format. Both features of these representations are important to the role core cognition plays in conceptual development. As the empiricists understood, we have the beginnings of a causal theory of reference for perceptual representations. The requisite causal connection between entities in the world and symbols in the head is guaranteed by natural selection. Thus, we have the beginnings of a theory of how the symbols in core cognition come to have the content they do. But core cognition also provides the starting point for conceptual development, and to play this role, it is crucial that it is conceptual in the ways that it is.

The next three chapters characterize two additional systems of core cognition—one for representing intentional agency and one for representing number—and consider the nature of causal representations that centrally integrate the output of distinct core cognition systems. I then turn to the question of how core cognition is transcended in the course of cognitive development, to how children create fully conceptual representational systems with *none* of the properties of core cognition.

NOTE

1. Baillargeon, 2001; Carey & Spelke, 1996; Gallistel, 1990; Gelman, 1990; Leslie, 1994; Spelke, 2000. Spelke calls the systems of knowledge "core knowledge" rather than "core cognition." Because knowledge is, roughly, justified true belief, the term "knowledge" implies more than I want—that the representations are veridical and warranted.

4

Core Cognition: Number

Representations of number play a huge role in human mental life, as they are central to mathematics and science, as well as to modern commerce. Less obviously, representations of number articulate human language. In languages like English, those with a count/mass distinction, every sentence we speak requires us to make quantificational commitments. Are we speaking about individuals or nonindividuated entities, one or more than one?

Accounting for the origins of human numerical abilities seems to pose a formidable challenge. Number is a quintessential abstract entity. Piaget believed that numerical representations are built from logical capacities (the capacity for linear order and the capacity to represent and operate over sets), logical capacities that were not themselves constructed until the early school years. Accordingly, he believed that children could not represent number until then and, indeed, offered his famous work on number conservation as evidence for his view (Piaget, 1952).

Chapters 2 and 3 presented data that undermine Piaget's position. The object-file system of representations embodies criteria of individuation and numerical identity for objects, and infants create working-memory models that distinguish sets with two numerically distinct objects from those with three objects or one object. As we will see in this chapter, infants also create working-memory models of sets of different types of individuals—individual events, individual tone bursts—and these working-memory models have many structural similarities to those that represent small sets of objects. As I discuss at length below, these "individual file" representations are numerical in ways that conflict with Piaget's position. Furthermore, there is another core cognitive system that more directly represents number and hence is flatly incompatible with Piaget's view—the system of representation Dehaene (1997) calls the "number sense." The number sense is a paradigm example of core cognition. Thus, this chapter lays out the evidence for two distinct systems of core cognition with numerical content, contrasting the two.

Core System 1: Analog Magnitude Representations of Number

Human adults, human infants, and nonhuman animals deploy a system of analog magnitude representations of number. Number is represented by a physical magnitude that is roughly proportional to the number of individuals in the set being enumerated. The following is an external analog magnitude representational system in which lengths represent number:

number   symbol

1:         —

2:         ——

3:         ———

4:         ————

7:         ———————

8:         ————————

and so on.

    A psychophysical signature of analog magnitude representations is that the discriminability of any two magnitudes is a function of their ratio; that is, discriminability is in accordance with Weber's law. Examining the external analogs above, it is easy to see that the lengths that represent numbers 1 and 2 should be more discriminable than are those that represent 7 and 8 (what is called the magnitude effect). Similarly, it should be easier to discriminate the length that represents 1 from that representing 3 than to discriminate the length that represents 2 from the one that represents 3 (what is called the distance effect). And indeed, studies of numerical discrimination robustly reveal both magnitude and distance effects, which follow from Weber's law (Dehaene, 1997; Gallistel, 1990).

Evidence for Analog Magnitude Representations of Number in Animals

I will provide evidence for two separate claims: (1) that animals represent number, and (2) that one system of number representation is analog. To establish the first, I must show that animals have representations with cardinal values in their extensions, and that these representations have number-relevant inferential roles. That is, I must show that animals discriminate sets on the basis of cardinal value (rather than other features of the arrays correlated with number, such as their total surface area or volume) and that at least some number-relevant computations are supported by the representations that underlie such discriminations. To establish the second, I need to show that the representations in question reveal the psychophysical signatures of analog magnitude representations. In particular, I will be at pains to show that they conform to Weber's law.

In this section I provide more data than usual because, for those who are practiced at reading graphs, the data tell a story better than words can. Figure 4.1 shows data from an experiment in which rats were trained to press a bar a given number of times before a feeder was armed. What is plotted is the number of bar presses before the rat checked the feeder. Panel A shows that the mean of each distribution of number of presses is just a little higher than the correct number for that condition (4, 8, 16,

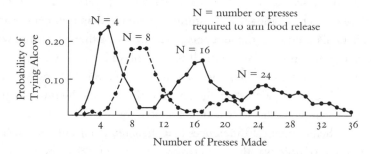

Figure 4.1. Data from Platt & Johnson (1971). Each curve shows the probability distribution of number of presses before the rat checked whether the feeder was armed. N = the correct number of presses needed to arm the feeder. Reprinted from Platt, J. R., & Johnson, D. M. (1971). Localization of position within a homogeneous behavior chain: Effects of error contingencies. *Learning and Motivation, 2,* 386–414, with permission from Elsevier.

or 24), as if rats were tracking the number of presses and were conservative. What is also shown is that the standard deviation around those means becomes greater as the means do. These data exhibit what is called "scalar variability": the ratio of the standard deviation to the mean is a constant (Platt & Johnson, 1971).[1] Scalar variability is a reflection of Weber's law that the discriminability of two magnitudes is a strict function of their ratio.

These data establish that some analog magnitude representation is underlying the rats' decision of when the feeder is likely to have been armed. However, they do not unequivocally show that it is an analog magnitude representation of number of presses, because in this study the number of bar presses was confounded with other correlated quantities, such as the total amount of effort expended or the total time taken for a sequence of presses. Others have deconfounded these variables, showing that number is indeed represented. Here I sketch two relevant studies, and I refer the interested or skeptical reader to the excellent reviews in Dehaene's *The Number Sense* (1997) or Gallistel's *The Organization of Learning* (1990).

In another landmark study of animal number representations, Russell Church and Warren Meck (1984) taught rats a discrimination between two sequences of tones. Rats were trained to press one bar if presented with a sequence of two tones, each 1 second long, and another if presented with a sequence of eight tones, each 1 second long. Rats readily learned this discrimination, but again, this does not tell us on what basis they were discriminating, for the stimuli differed both in number of tones and in total duration of the sequences. The rats were then presented with a series of discriminations in which the stimuli differed only in number, holding total duration constant, or only in duration, holding number constant (see Figure 4.2). They generalized the learned discrimination in both cases, showing that they had represented the original stimuli in terms of both their numerical differences and their temporal differences. The other result of note was that the crossover point in both series was at the geometric mean. That is, rats experienced four tones and two tones as the same distance from each other as they experienced eight tones and four tones, and they experienced 4 seconds and 2 seconds as the same distance from each other as 8 seconds and 4 seconds. Discriminability is a function of ratio, as dictated by Weber's law.

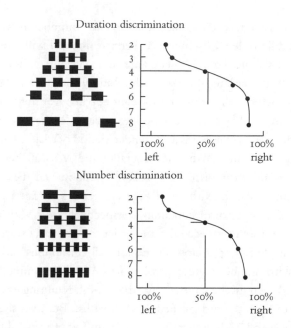

Figure 4.2. Data from test trials in Church & Meck (1984). Top graph: number of tones held constant, total duration of tones varied between 2 and 8 seconds. Bottom graph: total duration of tones held constant, number of tones varied between 2 and 8. Church, R. M., & Meck, W. H. (1984). The numerical attribute of stimuli. In H. L. Roitblatt, T. G. Bever, & H. S. Terrace (Eds.), *Animal Cognition* (pp. 445–464). Hillsdale, NJ: Erlbaum. Reprinted with the permission from Taylor and Francis Ltd. (http://www.tandf.co.uk/journals).

As a final example, Elizabeth Brannon and Herb Terrace (1998) demonstrated that *Rhesus* macaques are sensitive to number and represent sets differing in cardinal value as numerically ordered. These researchers began with Terrace's previous demonstrations that *Rhesus* macaques can learn to order arbitrary sets of simultaneously presented stimuli. Presented with an array of four objects randomly distributed on a touch screen on each trial—for example, a red circle, a brown table, a black cat, and a blue flower—the monkeys can learn to touch the stimuli in a specified order. Thus, Terrace's earlier work suggests that the capacity to represent serial order is itself part of our evolutionary endowment and does not await the end of Piaget's stage of "preoperational" thought for its emergence (Swartz, Chen, & Terrace, 1991; Terrace, Son, & Brannon, 2003).

Brannon and Terrace established that *Rhesus*'s number representations are intrinsically ordered (Brannon & Terrace, 1998). I will illustrate with data from two monkeys, Rosencrantz and Macduff. They were first taught to do the ordered-list task with arbitrary lists such as, "first circle, then table, then cat, then flower." Of course, whenever they were shown four new stimuli, they could have no idea what order they were supposed to touch them in, so there was an extended period of trial and error before they learned the order. After Rosencrantz and Macduff became good at that trial-and-error discovery process, Brannon and Terrace started giving them lists such as those in Figure 4.3. As you can see, each list consisted of four pictures containing, respectively, sets with one, two, three, and four items. In each list, the order the monkeys were supposed to press was 1, 2, 3, 4. Across all the lists, all continuous variables confounded with number were controlled for. At the beginning, the monkeys treated each list the same as any arbitrary list, requiring extensive trial and error to learn the order called for on that list. But over the course of learning 35 such lists, Rosencrantz and Macduff got faster and faster. This could be because they were becoming ever more efficient at the trial-and-error strategies for learning whatever arbitrary list the experimenter had in mind, or it could be because they had learned a numerical rule.

To decide between these two possibilities, Brannon and Terrace gave Rosencrantz and Macduff 150 trials in which they saw new lists only once, thus preventing any trial-and-error learning. They did as well as on these lists as on those at the end of the 35 training-sets series, where they saw each list 60 times. They had learned a numerical rule. But which one? "Press one object, then two objects, then three objects, then four objects?" Or "press in order of increasing numerical magnitude?" To find out, Brannon and Terrace then presented the monkeys with novel trials including sets of five, six, seven, eight, and nine items. Now the task was simply to order two stimuli: for example, 2 versus 4, 3 versus 6, or 5 versus 9. Some included numbers within the trained lists, and some were entirely novel pairs. Each pair was shown only once. Again, both monkeys transferred the rule to the novel lists including numbers outside of the training set. Apparently, they had learned the rule, "touch in order of increasing numerical magnitude."

Analog magnitude representations of number underlie performance on this task. Clear evidence for distance effects was observed: accuracy

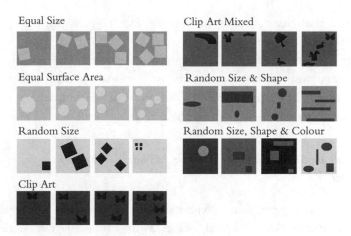

Equal Size

Clip Art Mixed

Equal Surface Area

Random Size & Shape

Random Size

Random Size, Shape & Colour

Clip Art

Figure 4.3. Examples of stimulus lists from Brannon & Terrace (1998). From Brannon, E. M., & Terrace, H. S. (1998). Ordering of the numerosities 1 to 9 by monkeys. *Science, 282,* 746–749. Reprinted with permission from AAAS.

was a function of the numerical distance between the stimuli (e.g., the monkeys' ability to order 6 and 9 was more accurate than their ability to order 7 and 8). Recent data from Brannon's laboratory confirm these generalizations. Monkeys were trained to touch two arrays in numerical order; all training pairs were taken from sets of one to nine elements, and over all pairs other variables were controlled as in the Brannon and Terrace studies. After training, sets of 10, 15, 20, and 30 were added. Again, monkeys continued to succeed at the task upon first encountering these larger sets, and their performance accorded with Weber's law (Cantlon & Brannon, 2006).

These experiments are illustrative of many in the literature: animals studied include rats, crows, pigeons, a parrot, monkeys, apes, and dolphins (at least, these are the studies on analog magnitude number representations I am aware of). These data support the existence of an evolutionarily ancient representational system in which number is encoded by an analog magnitude proportional to the number of objects in the set. These representations support computations of numerical equivalence and numerical order. There is also evidence that animals can add analog magnitudes. For example, *Rhesus* macaques shown four objects placed behind a screen, followed by another four objects, look longer if the screen is removed to reveal four objects than if to reveal eight (Flombaum, Junge, & Hauser, 2005).

In sum, that these analog magnitude representations are number representations is shown by the fact that they track number rather than other properties of the attended sets, and by the fact that numerically relevant computations are defined over them.

Evidence for Human Infants' Analog Magnitude Representations of Number

In the past five years, four different laboratories have provided unequivocal evidence that preverbal infants form analog magnitude representations of number (Brannon, 2002; Brannon, Abbot, & Lutz, 2004; Lipon & Spelke, 2003, 2004; McCrink & Wynn, 2004a; Wood & Spelke, 2005a; Xu & Spelke, 2000; Xu, Spelke, & Goddard, 2005). The first paper in this flurry of studies is by Fei Xu and Elizabeth Spelke, who solved the problem of how to control for other possible bases of judgment (cumulative surface area, element size, density) in a large number habituation paradigm. Xu and Spelke habituated 6-month-old infants to displays containing 8 dots or to displays containing 16 dots (see Figure 4.4). Possible confounds between number and other variables were controlled either by equating the two series of stimuli on those variables or by making the test displays equidistant from the habituation displays on them. Habituated to 8-dot displays, 7-month-old infants recovered interest when shown the novel 16-dot displays, while generalizing habituation to the novel 8-dot displays. Those habituated to 16-dot displays showed the reverse pattern. Subsequent studies duplicated this design (and the positive result) with 16-dot versus 32-dot comparisons and with 4-dot versus 8-dot comparisons. Thus, the infants showed a sensitivity to cardinal values of sets outside the range of object-tracking mechanisms, when potential confounds were strictly controlled for.

That analog magnitude representations support these discriminations is shown by the fact that success is a function of the ratio of the set sizes. In all of the above studies, in which infants succeeded with a 2:1 ratio, they failed in comparisons that involved a 3:2 ratio (i.e., they failed to discriminate 8-dot from 12-dot arrays, 16-dot from 24-dot arrays, and 4-dot from 6-dot arrays). Also, these researchers have found that sensitivity

Habituation

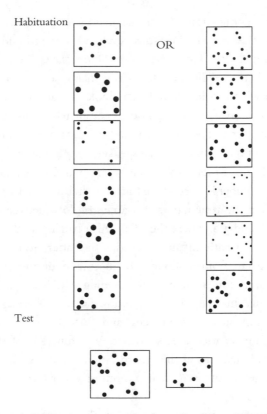

OR

Test

Figure 4.4. Sample habituation sequences and test stimuli from Xu & Spelke (2000). Reprinted from Xu, F., & Spelke, E. S. (2000). Large number discrimination in 6-month old infants. *Cognition, 74*, B1–B11, with permission from Elsevier.

improves by 9 months of age. Infants of this age succeed at 3:2 comparisons across a wide variety of absolute set sizes, but fail at 4:3 comparisons.

These baby experiments involve dot arrays. As reviewed above, animals create analog magnitude representations of number of sounds, number of bar presses, and number of key pecks. Infants also represent the cardinal values of sets of individuals that are not visually specified. Jennifer Lipton and Elizabeth Spelke (2003, 2004) showed that 6-month-old infants discriminate 8 from 16 tones, and also 4 from 8 tones, when continuous variables are controlled in a manner analogous to the Xu and Spelke studies, and they fail to discriminate 8-tone from 12-tone sequences or 4-tone from 6-tone sequences. The alert reader might wonder how one does a looking-time study when the stimuli are a stream of tones. Basically, the sequences of tones are played from one of two speakers, each to a different side of the infant, and if the infants are interested in what is being played, they look to that speaker, continuing to attend to it even after the sequence is completed. Thus, looking times can reflect interest in this paradigm, and if infants notice a difference in the number of tones coming from a speaker, their attention is drawn to it.

Not only do 6-month-old infants create analog magnitude representations of number in a sequence of tones, their sensitivity to numerical differences is in the same ratio as for arrays of dots (between 2:1, where they succeed, and 3:2, where they fail). Also paralleling the results with dot arrays, by 9 months infants succeed at this latter ratio, distinguishing 8-tone sequences from 12-tone sequences and distinguishing 4-tone sequences from 6-tone sequences. Succeeding at 3:2 ratios, irrespective of set size, infants this age fail at 5:4 ratios, failing to distinguish 5-tone sequences from 4-tone sequences and also 10-tone from 8-tone sequences. Thus at each age, sensitivity is a function of the ratios of the number of elements in the sets to be compared, with older infants showing greater sensitivity (3:2 at 9 months; 2:1 at 6 months; Lipton & Spelke, 2003, 2004).

Furthermore, infants also represent the number of jumps in a sequence of jumps with the same sensitivity. Justin Wood and Elizabeth Spelke (2005a) showed that 6-month-olds distinguish 4-jump sequences from 8-jump sequences, but not from 6-jump sequences, whereas 9-month-olds succeed at 4-jump versus 6-jump comparisons.

In all of the above studies we can be confident that it is number the infants are responding to, because every other variable is equated either across the habituation stimuli or across the test stimuli. In these studies, the child's attention is drawn when there is a different number of dots, jumps, or tones in a test set from the number in each of the habituation sets, and discrimination follows Weber's law. Thus, the child is using the analog magnitude system to compute numerical equivalence. Of course, if the analog magnitude representations underlying performance in these habituation studies are truly numerical representations, number-relevant computations other than establishing numerical equivalence should be defined over them, and indeed this is so.

Elizabeth Brannon showed that 11-month-old infants represent numerical order among sets sets. Infants were habituated to sequences of three arrays, always increasing in number by a ratio of 2: 1 (e.g., 2, 4, 8; 4, 8, 16; 1, 2, 4). Continuous variables were controlled as in the Xu and Spelke studies. After habituation, infants were shown a novel increasing sequence (3, 6, 12) or a decreasing sequence (12, 6, 3). They generalized habituation to the former and dishabituated to the latter. Another group of infants were habituated to decreasing sequences; they generalized habituation to the test sequence that decreased in numerical value and dishabituated to the one that increased (Brannon, 2002).

Finally, Koleen McCrink and Karen Wynn (2004a) showed that 9-month-olds can manipulate sets of objects in the analog magnitude range to support addition and subtraction. Shown five objects move behind a screen, followed by another five, infants look longer if the screen is removed, revealing a set of five than if a set of ten is revealed. Conversely, if the first set was ten objects, and five objects were seen to leave, infants looked longer if, upon the screen's removal, ten were revealed. These objects were each constantly expanding and contracting so that it was possible to control for summed continuous variables as a basis of response. McCrink and Wynn also showed that infants are sensitive to the ratio between two sets of dots; habituated to arrays of dots of two colors, such that there were always two times as many red dots as blue dots, infants dishabituated to arrays when the ratios were reversed (McCrink & Wynn, 2004b).

In sum, analog magnitude representations of number are available at least by 7 months of age. Preverbal infants represent the approximate cardinal value of sets, and compute numerical equivalence, numerical order, addition, subtraction, and ratios over these representations. Given the ancient evolutionary history of analog magnitude number representations, it is very likely they are the output of innate perceptual analyzers.

Continuity Through the Life Span

Under a wide variety of conditions, adult humans create analog magnitude representation of number of individuals. For example, analog magnitude representations of number are deployed when participants must estimate the number of individuals in large sets under conditions when they cannot or do not count. For illustration, I draw on recent experiments by Hilary Barth, Nancy Kanwisher, and Elizabeth Spelke (2003). Barth and her colleagues displayed arrays of large numbers of dots (20–200), with total area covered, density of dots, and size of dots varying from array to array. Arrays were displayed sequentially (e.g., 35 followed by 60; 120 followed by 95). The participants' task was to indicate whether the second array was numerically larger or smaller than the first array. Participants could do this task. The reaction times and accuracies were predicted by the ratios of the numbers; 20 was discriminated from 30, as was 40 from 60, as was 80 from 120. These numbers way exceed the set-size limits on parallel individuation, and performance respects Weber's law; thus, we can be fairly confident that analog magnitude representations underlie performance.

Barth found parallel results when the stimuli were sequences of tones or flashes of light, when these sequences were also constructed to control other dimensions of the stimuli (e.g., total length of the sequence, density of the individuals, total amount of energy, length of individual tones/flashes). Thus, like infants and nonhuman animals, human adults create analog magnitude representations of numbers of quite different kinds of individuals.

Two further results bolster the conclusion that these are number representations. First, there was near perfect intermodal transfer. When the task was changed such that the first stimulus was a sequence of tones or light flashes and the second stimulus was an array of dots, participants could discriminate the numbers, indicating which one was greater, with the same accuracy, reaction times, and Weber fraction as when both stimuli were arrays of dots. Furthermore, in addition to supporting computations of more/less, analog magnitude representations support least four other number-relevant operations: addition, subtraction, multiplication, and division. Consider one example from Barth's studies as a demonstration of this. Participants were shown two dot arrays colored in blue (e.g., 40, 65) followed by a dot array colored in red (e.g., 75). The participants' task was to indicate whether the red array contained more or fewer dots than the sum of the blue arrays. Participants' performance on this task was at almost the same level as the previous ones, with success dictated by the ratio between the total number of blue dots (the sum of two arrays) and the number of red dots.

One might object that cognition of symbolic arithmetic might be playing a role in the tasks that involve computation—perhaps participants establish approximate cardinal values of the sets via analog magnitude representations; map them onto verbal numerals; and then add, subtract, multiply or divide using symbolic arithmetic rules. Although adult participants deny doing this, we can ensure that analog magnitude representations themselves are supporting the calculations by using participants who do not yet know the symbolic arithmetic facts—preschool children. Barth and her colleagues have carried out a series of such studies, showing that 4- to 6-year-olds succeed at addition, subtraction, multiplication by 2, and division by 2 (Baron, Barth, & Carey, 2005; Barth et al., 2006).

Barth's studies illustrate the operation of analog magnitude representations of number in tasks that do not involve explicit linguistic number representations. John Whalen, Randy Gallistel, and Rochel Gelman (1999) have recently confirmed that human adults have mapped linguistic numerals onto analog magnitude number representations. Whalen and colleagues asked participants to tap their fingers a given number of times (between 7 and 40) without counting. Participants said that they were not counting, and various details of the data suggest that they actually were not. For example, the rate of tapping was much faster than the rate of nonverbal counting, and inter-tap intervals were unrelated to the length of the corresponding words. Figure 4.5a shows the data from one participant; note the linear relation between the number requested and the number of taps, and note also that the data display scalar variability (standard deviation linearly related to set size). All participants' data showed these patterns; for everyone, the ratio between the mean number of taps and the standard deviation was constant. In a second version of the task, the stimulus was a sequence of tones presented too fast to count. Counting was also precluded by a concurrent articulation of "the, the, the . . ." during the stream of tones. The participants' task was to say the number of tones that had been presented. One participant's data, typical of all, is displayed in Figure 4.5b. Again, the number produced was a linear function of the number of individuals displayed and the variability was scalar.

These studies show that adult humans deploy analog magnitude representations of number, and that they have constructed a mapping between analog magnitude representations and the verbal integer list.

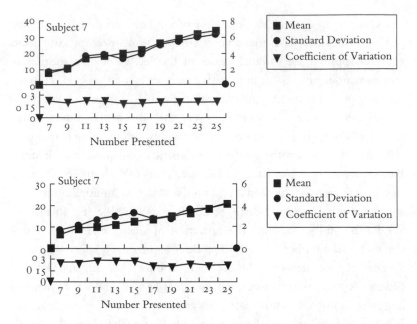

Figure 4.5. An individual participant's data from Whalen, Gallistel, & Gelman (1999). Top curve: target is verbal numeral, response is number of taps. Bottom curve: target is number of tones, response is verbal numeral. Whalen, J., Gallistel, C. R., & Gelman, R. (1999). Nonverbal counting in humans: the psychophysics of number representation. *Psychological Science, 10*, 130–137, with permission from Blackwell Publishers.

Indeed, even when questions are posed in terms of the verbal integer lists, adults often automatically activate the analog magnitude representations and use them to compute the answer. For example, the reaction time to say which of two numbers is larger shows the magnitude and distance effects typical of Weber's law. It is faster to decide that 6 is less than 8 than to decide that 26 is less than 28 (Dehaene, 1997; Moyer & Landauer, 1967). Dehaene and his colleagues provided a particularly striking demonstration of this phenomenon. The task they gave to adults was simple—indicate whether each of these numbers was more or less than 5: 1, 4, 6, 9. Even after thousands of trials, participants were much faster at saying that 1 was less than 5 than saying that 4 was less than 5, and they were much faster saying that 9 was more than 5 than saying that 6 was more than 5. This result is surprising. In counting, we have recited "4, 5,

6" countless times; the order in this list is about as well entrenched as any we could imagine. Yet when asked to judge which number is larger, adults apparently activate the underlying mental magnitudes, finding it easier to discriminate magnitudes relatively far apart on the underlying number line.

Space precludes reviewing all of the convergent lines of evidence for analog magnitude representations of number in human adults. The interested reader should consult Stan Dehaene's *The Number Sense* (1997) and Brian Butterworth's *What Counts* (1999) for additional evidence from studies of discalculia following brain damage and from studies of developmental discalculia, and from imaging studies using PET and fMRI technology. That analog magnitude representations constitute one system of number representations deployed by human adults has been established beyond any reasonable doubt.

Characterizing the Input Analyzers that Create Analog Magnitude Representations of Number

Why are analog magnitude representations of number really number representations? It is not the format of the representation—that they are analog magnitudes—that makes them so. Animals, including humans, create analog magnitude representations of many different quantities (distances, temporal durations, lengths, weight, area, volume, mass, and so on). Rather, what establishes that these are representations of numbers is that the animal or infant can track the number of individuals in an attended set, rather than other variables correlated with number, as reviewed above. Other relevant data reviewed above is derived from studies of the numerical computations that are defined over these representations: computations that establish numerical equivalence, numerical order, numerical differences, numerical sums, and numerical ratios.

As in any putative system of core cognition, one important challenge is to characterize the input analyzers that create its symbols. Doing so provides further evidence concerning the content of those symbols. In this case, if we understand how analog magnitude representations are computed from perceptual input, we can see that it is number they are representing. In fact, there are many different proposals for how the input analyzers might work, and in each proposal their output is an estimate of the cardinal value of the attended set (Church & Broadbent, 1990; Church & Meck, 1984; Dehaene & Changeux, 1993; Verguts & Fias, 2004).

The earliest proposal was the accumulator model of Russell Church and Warren Meck (1984). Their idea was simple: suppose the nervous system has the equivalent of a pulse generator that generates activity at a constant rate and a gate that can open to allow energy through to an accumulator that registers how much as been let through. When the animal is in a counting mode, the gate is opened for a fixed amount of time (say 200 ms) for each individual to be counted. The total energy accumulated is then a linear function of the number of the individuals in the set, and thus can serve as an analog representation of number. Meck and Church's model seems best suited for sequentially presented entities, such as bar presses, tones, light flashes, or jumps of a puppet. Gallistel (1990) proposed that this mechanism functions as well in the sequential enumeration of simultaneously presented individuals.

The gate is opened for a fixed amount of time for each individual to be enumerated, irrespective of other properties of that individual, such as its kind, size, brightness, length, loudness. This is what ensures that the resulting analog magnitude is a linear function of number rather than some other variable. Randy Gallistel and Rochel Gelman (1992) pointed out that the accumulator model is formally identical to the explicit counting procedures defined over culturally constructed lists of integer words, "one, two, three, four, five ...". The accumulator model instantiates the counting principles that ensure that such lists also encode number. In the accumulator representations, the successive states of the accumulator play the same role as successive number words in the list—as mental symbols that represent numerosity. States of the accumulator are stably ordered, gate opening is in 1–1 correspondence with individuals in the set, the final state of the accumulator represents the number of items in the set, there are no constraints on individuals that can be enumerated, and individuals can be enumerated in any order.

Thus, the accumulator model of the input analyzers that yield analog magnitudes shows them to be number representations—it instantiates a counting mechanism. Unfortunately, considerable evidence militates against the accumulator model. Analog magnitude representations of number are not constructed by a sequential, iterative process—or at least not always. The accumulator model has been most directly tested with infants. Justin Wood and Elizabeth Spelke (2005b) tested how fast infants could encode dot arrays in the habituation paradigm discussed above. For example, 5-month-old infants were presented 4-dot or 8-dot arrays for 1 second each, 1.5 seconds each, or 2 seconds each, and then tested with new 4-dot or 8-dot arrays. The controls of Xu and Spelke ensured that success would be based on number. At this age, infants succeeded only at the 2-second encoding time, but it did not matter whether the habituation arrays contained 4, 8, or 16 dots. Thus, although it of course takes time for the child to encode dot arrays in terms of analog magnitude representations of the number of dots, it takes no longer to encode 16 dots than 4 dots. This is not consistent with an iterative, serial encoding process because time for encoding should increase monotonically with N for any iterative counting process.

Studies with adults provide additional evidence against the accumulator model. Subjects are able to discriminate visually presented numerosities under conditions of stimulus size and eccentricity in which they are not able to attend to individual elements in sequence (Intriligator & Cavanagh, 2001). Their numerosity discrimination, therefore, could not depend on a process that involves a response to each entity in turn, and thus cannot rely on a counting mechanism. Problems such as these led Russell Church and Hilary Broadbent (1990) to propose that analog magnitude representations of number are constructed quite differently from Meck and Church's accumulator mechanism, most significantly in that the Church-Broadbent model does not include an iterative process. Focusing on the problem of representing the numerosity of a set of sequential events (e.g., the number of tones in a sequence), they suggested that animals perform a computation that depends on two timing mechanisms. First, animals time the temporal interval between the onsets of successive tones, maintaining in memory a single value that approximates a running average of these intervals. Second, animals time the overall duration of the tone sequence. The number of tones is then estimated by dividing the sequence duration by the average intertone interval. Although Church and Broadbent did not consider the case of simultaneously visible individuals, a similar noniterative mechanism could serve to compute numerosity in that case as well, by directly representing the average density of individuals in a set, representing the total spatial extent occupied by the set of individuals, and dividing the latter by the former. Relatedly, Dehaene and Changeux (1993) described a parallel encoding mechanism that could create an analog symbol for the number of simultaneously presented visual individuals in a different manner, also through no iterative process.

The encoding processes in the Church and Broadbent model (as well as in the Dehaene and Changeux model) differ from the original Meck and Church accumulator model in a number of important ways. Because the processes that construct these representations are not iterative, the analog magnitudes are not formed in sequence and therefore are less likely to be experienced as a list. Moreover, the process that establishes the analog magnitude representations does not require that each individual in the set to be enumerated be attended to in sequence, counted, and then ticked off (so that each individual is counted only once). That these mechanisms do not implement any counting procedure becomes important to my argument in chapter 8, where I take up the question of how children learn the meaning of verbal numerals such as "three" and "seven." Nonetheless, the proposed input analyzers ensure that the quantity encoded by the mental magnitude is number; the magnitude computed is a linear function of the cardinal value of the attended set.

Iconic Format

The system of analog magnitude representations of number exemplifies most of the features of core cognition I have discussed in chapters 2 and 3. Number representations are conceptual; their content goes beyond spatio-temporal and sensory vocabulary. The domain-specific perceptual analyzers that encode number, as well as the arithmetic computations defined over the resulting representations, are evolutionarily ancient, most likely innate, and operate throughout the life span. In addition, this case study illustrates issues I have not explicitly discussed before, including specification of the exact nature of the perceptual input analyzers that create analog magnitude representations of number, a question that should be addressed as we study any system of core cognition. The iterative accumulator model was contrasted with parallel models, with evidence favoring the latter.

Also, this case study exemplifies one of the six features of core cognition not yet touched upon—that the format of representation is iconic. Iconic representations are distinguished from language-like symbolic representations along many dimensions, but one is in being analog. In analog iconic symbols, such as a realistic picture of a dog representing a dog, parts of the symbol represent parts of the represented entity: the ears on the picture represent the ears of the dog, respecting spatial relations that hold in reality. The word "dog," in contrast, contains no information about ears or any other part of a dog. Analog magnitude number representations are analog in this very sense: the symbol for 3 (———) contains the symbol for 2 (———), respecting the actual numerical relations between 2 and 3. Just as a full account of any system of core knowledge will specify the nature of the input analyzers in detail, so too will it specify the format of representation—what the symbols are like.

The evidence points to a system of representation in which number is encoded in the brain by some neural quantity that is a linear or logarithmic function of number. If this is right, we can say more about what is represented explicitly and what implicitly by this system. The symbols themselves are explicit. They are the output of the input analyzers and are available to central processors for a wide variety of computations. They can be bound to sets of quite different types of individuals. And various arithmetical computations are defined over them—numerical comparisons, addition, subtraction, and ratio computations.

But much of the numerical content of this system of representation is implicit. There is no explicit representation of the axioms of arithmetic, no representation that 1–1 correspondence guarantees numerical equivalence. These principles are implicit in the operation of the input analyzers and in the computations defined over analog magnitudes, but they need not be available for the child to base any decisions on. This case illustrates that once one has a well-confirmed model of some representational system, one can examine that model to establish exactly what is represented and how. Analog magnitudes are explicit symbols of approximate cardinal values of sets. Other numerical content is embodied in operations that compute over these symbols; that latter knowledge is not symbolized and thus is not input to further computations.

Representations of Sets

Piaget believed that it was not until the end of "preoperational thought" (around 5 years of age) that children were capable of set-based quantification. I turn to the set-based quantification that underpins the semantics of natural language quantifiers in chapter 7, but Piaget's insistence that the representations of sets and representations of number are intertwined is well founded. In the literature on mathematical cognition, analog magnitude number representations are sometimes called "numerosity" representations, for they are representations of the cardinal values of sets of individuals, rather than fully abstract number representations. There is no evidence that animals or babies entertain thoughts about 7 (even approximately 7) in the absence of a set of entities they are attending to. Still, cardinal values of sets are numbers, which is why I speak of analog magnitude number representations rather than numerosity representations.

The analog magnitude number representations discussed in these pages require representations of sets. At any given moment, an indefinite number of possible sets to enumerate are in the visual field; attentional mechanisms must pick out a particular set to enumerate. Analog magnitude representations are predicated of particular sets of individuals, and thus demand that the animal or infant represent which set is being assigned which approximate cardinal value. Thus, in addition to the analog magnitude symbols themselves (e.g., ———, the analog magnitude symbol for 3), the baby must at least implicitly represent {box} or {red object} or {object on table}, where { } designates a set and the symbol therein represents the kind of entity contained in the set. An analog magnitude representation of three boxes must at least implicitly include the information symbolized {box} and ———.

Little is known about how infants or animals select sets as input to analog magnitude computations, but Justin Halberda and his colleagues have recently begun to study this issue with adults. In one study (Halberda, Sires, & Feigenson, 2006), they presented adults with clouds of dots that were a single color, two colors, three colors, four colors, five colors, or six colors, all interleaved, for a couple of seconds. After the dots had been masked, subjects were given a color and asked to report approximately how many dots of that color there had been. Participants

could do this for up to three colors, showing that they could select sets of
dots on the basis of color and enumerate up to three sets in parallel.
Performance when there had been four, five, or six colors showed that
participants randomly selected three sets to encode. Thus, the number of
sets that can be simultaneously indexed is subject to the limits on working
memory for individuals (i.e., about three, see chapter 3). In conclusion,
core cognition includes mechanisms for selecting sets of individuals and
quantifying over them with analog magnitude number representations. I
now turn to a second core system with numerical content, in which
number itself is only implicitly represented.

A Second Core System with Numerical Content: Parallel Individuation of Small Sets

Science moves rapidly, and the infant studies reviewed above came relatively late in the history of studies designed to show that infants are
sensitive to number. The first studies, some 20 years earlier than Xu's and
Spelke's studies on analog magnitude representations, concerned small
sets—discriminations of 2 from 3 or 1 from 2. Indeed, in chapters 2 and 3,
I reviewed some of these studies in the service of demonstrating that
infants must represent, at least implicitly, criteria for individuation and
numerical identity. There, I was concerned with the Quinian/Piagetian
thesis that young infants cannot represent the concept *object* with the
quantificational force of a count noun. In some cases the studies were
originally intended to address the Quinian/Piagetian issues (for example,
Spelke's split-screen studies concerning spatio-temporal criteria for object
individuation), but they nonetheless required that infants distinguish one
individual from two. In other cases, the studies were intended to show
that the infants were sensitive to number. These include many versus 3
habituation studies and Wynn's $1 + 1 = 2$ or 1 violation-of-expectancy
studies (Antell & Keating, 1983; Starkey & Cooper, 1980, Wynn, 1992b).
In *The Number Sense*, Stan Dehaene reviews these experiments as
demonstrations that infants distinguish small sets on the basis of number
of individuals in them. Dehaene then writes as if these data provide
evidence for analog magnitude representations in preverbal infants.
However, before we draw that conclusion, we need evidence that the

sets are being distinguished on the basis of number rather than other variables confounded with number, and if so, that analog magnitude representations underlie the infant's performance.

Many researchers have suggested that a very different representational system might support infants' number sensitivity in most of these experiments—namely, the object tracking system described in chapter 3 (Feigenson & Carey, 2003; Feigenson, Carey, & Hauser, 2002; Scholl & Leslie, 1999; Simon, 1997; Uller, Carey, Huntley-Fenner, & Klatt, 1999). In this alternative representational system, number is only implicitly encoded; there are no symbols for number at all, not even analog magnitude ones. Instead, the representations include a symbol for each individual in an attended set. Thus, a set containing one apple might be represented as "o" (an iconic object file) or "apple" (a symbol for an individual of the kind apple) and a set containing two apples might be represented as "o o" or "apple apple," and so forth. These representations consist of one symbol (file) for each individual, and when the content of a symbol is a spatio-temporally determined object, it is an object-file. As discussed in chapter 3, several lines of evidence identify these symbols with the object-file representations studied in the adult literature on object-based attention. However, as we shall see below, infants also create working-memory models of small sets of other types of individuals, such as sound bursts or events, and so I shall call the system of representation "parallel individuation" and the explicit symbols within it "individual-files." When those individual-files are object-files, I sometimes refer to them as such.

In what follows I will show that the parallel individuation system, rather than analog magnitude representations, underlies performance on many small number experiments. I will then further characterize the parallel individuation system, considering the format of representation and considering its numerical content. I conclude by contrasting the two distinct systems of core cognition with numerical content: parallel individuation and analog magnitude number representations.

There are many reasons to favor individual file representations over analog magnitude representations as underlying performance in most of the infant small-number studies. In the interest of space, I present just two. First, and most important, success on many spontaneous number representation tasks involving small sets do not show the Weber-fraction signature of analog magnitude representations; rather they show the set-size signature of individual-file representations. That is, individuals in small sets (sets of one, two, or three) can be represented, and sets outside of that limit cannot, even when the sets to be contrasted have the same Weber-fraction as those small sets where the infant succeeds. Second, in these experiments the computations over individual-files most often respect other quantitative variables bound to the individuals-files, such as total volume for objects or total energy for events, rather than number itself. This fact rules out the possibility that a summary representation of number such as an analog magnitude underlies success, and it also provides indirect evidence concerning the format of the representations that underlie infants' performance on these studies. Let me take up these two points in turn.

The Set-Size Signature of Individual-File Representations

As reviewed in chapter 3, the set-size signature of object-file representations is motivated by evidence that even for adults there are sharp limits on the number of object-files that can be simultaneously attended to and held in working memory. If object-file representations underlie infants' performance in some tasks meant to reflect number representations, then infants should succeed only when the sets being encoded consist of small numbers of objects. Success at discriminating 1 versus 2, and 2 versus 3, in the face of failure with 3 versus 4 or 4 versus 5 is not enough to confirm that object-file representations underlie success, for Weber-fraction differences could equally well explain such a pattern of performance. That is, ratios of 3:4 or 4:5 might exceed the sensitivity of the analog magnitude system at that age. Rather, what is needed is success at 1 versus 2 and perhaps 2 versus 3 in the face of failure at 3 versus 6—failure at the higher numbers when the Weber-fraction is the same or even more favorable than that within the range of small numbers at which success has been obtained. This is the set-size signature of individual-file representations.

This set-size signature of object-file representations is precisely what is found in some infant habituation studies—success at discriminating 2 versus 3 objects in the face of failure at discriminating 4 versus 6 objects (Starkey & Cooper, 1980). Similarly, two methods reviewed in chapter 3 provide vivid illustrations of the set-size signature of object-file representations. In one of them, a monkey or an infant watches as each of two opaque containers, previously shown to be empty, is baited with a different number of apple slices (monkeys) or graham crackers (babies). For example, the experimenter might put two apple slices (graham crackers) in one container and three in the other. After placement, the experimenter walks away (monkey) or the parent allows the infant to crawl toward the containers (infant). The dependent measure is which container the monkey or baby chooses. The data from both studies reflect the set-size signature of object-file representations. Monkeys succeed when the comparisons are 1 versus 2; 2 versus 3, and 3 versus 4, but they fail at 2 versus 5, 3 versus 5, 4 versus 5, 4 versus 8, and even 3 versus 8 (Barner, Wood, Hauser, & Carey, in press; Hauser, Carey, & Hauser, 2000). A variety of controls ensured that monkeys were responding to the number of apple slices placed in the containers, rather than the total amount of time the apple was being placed in each container, the differential attention being drawn to each container, or even the total volume of apple placed in each container (even though that surely is what monkeys are attempting to maximize). These data show that *Rhesus* macaques spontaneously represent number in small sets of objects and can compare two sets with respect to which one has more objects. More important to us here, they show the set-size signature of object-file representations; monkeys succeed if both sets are within the set-size limits on parallel individuation (up to four for adult *Rhesus* macaques), and fall apart if one or both of the sets exceeds this limit.

The infant data tell the same story exactly with respect to the set-size signature of object-file representations, except that the upper limit is three instead of four. The lower limit in human babies compared to adult *Rhesus* macaques is not surprising, given maturational considerations. Ten- to 12-month-olds infants succeed at 1 versus 2, 2 versus 3; and 1 versus 3, and fail at 3 versus 4, 2 versus 4, and even 1 versus 4 (Feigenson & Carey, 2005; Feigenson, Carey, & Hauser, 2002). One:four is a more favorable ratio than 2:3, but infants fail at 1 versus 4 comparisons and succeed at 2 versus 3. Not also that five crackers are involved in each choice, so the total length of time of placements is equated over these two comparisons. This is a striking result. Infants could succeed at 1 versus 4 comparisons on many different bases: putting four crackers in a bucket takes much longer, draws more attention to that bucket, and so on, yet infants are at chance. Although infants could solve this problem in many different ways, apparently they are attending to each cracker, creating a model of what's in the container that contains one object-file for each cracker. As soon as one of the sets exceeds the limits on parallel individuation, performance falls apart. This finding provides very strong evidence that parallel individuation underlies success on this task.

Convergent data from a second paradigm involving small sets of objects demonstrate the set-size signature of parallel individuation. Recall the task in which infants search inside a box into which they can reach but not see. When 12- to 14-month-old infants have seen one, two, or three objects placed in a box, they search for exactly one, two, or three, respectively. But when they have seen four objects placed in the box, they are satisfied when they have retrieved only two or even only one. That is, as in the cracker-choice experiments, infants distinguish two from three (see three hidden, retrieve two, expect another in there), but fail to distinguish four from one (see four hidden, retrieve one, do not search further for any more in there; Feigenson & Carey, 2003, 2005). Performance falls apart when the set to be represented exceeds the limit on parallel individuation of objects, not when the ratio of objects exceeds some limit. Again, 4:1 is a more favorable ratio than 3:2, yet infants search for additional objects having seen three placed in the box and having retrieved only two, but fail to search for additional objects having seen four placed in the box and having retrieved only one. This set-size signature of object-file representations rules out the possibility that analog magnitude representations of number underlie the baby's actions on this task.

Numerical Computations Carried out over Parallel Individuation

That infants' performance shows the set-size signature of parallel individuation rather than the constant Weber ratio signature of analog magnitudes shows that analog magnitude representations cannot subserve performance on the small number tasks described above. Rather, these arrays are being represented in short-term memory models that consist of one symbol for each individual in the small set being represented. These symbols represent the individuals in the set, not the number of them (except implicitly, for there is one symbol for each individual). So why I am discussing these parallel individuation models in a chapter on core number cognition?

Two recent studies show that infants carry out computations on these models that are numerical. They compute 1–1 correspondence between representations of small sets held in short-term memory, determining numerical equivalence and numerical order. Lisa Feigenson and I (2003) showed that it is number of objects represented in the box that guides search in the task in which infants reach into a box into which they cannot see to retrieve hidden objects. We carried out a version of this study in which infants saw two small objects—for example, cars, placed into the box, one at a time. We then gave them the box, and they reached in and retrieved a car—either one of the cars they had seen or a car that was twice the surface area and four times the volume but was otherwise identical to the cars they saw hidden. Infants showed by their subsequent search that they expected exactly one more in either case. They were oblivious to the cumulative continuous variables; their reaches were guided by how many objects they represented in the box.

In this study, infants must have created a working-memory model of the set of objects placed in the box. Although they were trying to retrieve those objects they saw placed there, they had no way of knowing for each car they retrieved which of the two original objects it was identical to. They must have created a model of the objects they removed from the box, ceasing to search when this model matched their model of the objects placed in the box. And, given their insensitivity to the size of the objects, the match must have been subserved by a computation of 1–1 correspondence.

Feigenson (2005) also showed that infants are sensitive to number in a simple habituation task, as long as the individuals in the set are distinct from one another. Unlike what happened when the individuals are all identical to each other (see below), when habituated to arrays as in Figure 4.6, infants dishabituated to the array with a novel number. Apparently, homogeneity in properties of individuals facilitates computations of cumulative continuous variables from representations of small sets of individuals, and heterogeneity of properties focuses attention on representations of distinct individuals.

An important feature of this study is that it requires an abstract representation of the sets of objects (sets of one or sets of two). During

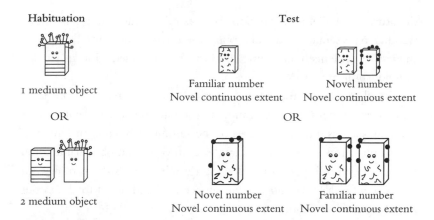

Figure 4.6. Examples of habituation and test arrays from Feigenson (2005): heterogeneous arrays. Reprinted from Feigenson, L. (2005). A double-dissociation in infants' representation of object arrays. *Cognition, 95*, B37–B48, with permission from Elsevier.

habituation, two different sets of heterogeneous objects were presented. Thus a working-memory model of two objects must be abstracted from these habituation arrays, which then must be compared to a model of the outcome array, which in turn contained very different objects from those in each of the habituation arrays, on the basis of 1–1 correspondence. The important conclusion is that 1–1 correspondence computations that establish numerical equivalence and numerical order can be carried out over object-file representations held in parallel in working-memory models, in spite of the fact that in all of the experiments cited in the following section they are not.

Lack of Sensitivity to Number in Properly Controlled Studies of "Number" Representations of Small Sets

I turn now to a second conclusive argument that analog magnitude number representations of number do not underlie success in many infant small number tasks. Very often, it is actually not number at all that is driving performance, even though the studies still reveal the set-size signature of parallel individuation. Besides ruling out analog magnitude number representations as subserving these tasks, these results provide suggestive evidence concerning the format of representation in parallel individuation models.

In all of the habituation studies with small sets in which the individuals are a constant size, number is confounded with continuous variables such as total surface area of the stimuli, total contour length of the stimuli, and so on. For example, in the first number habituation studies the stimuli were black dots of a single size, so the stimuli with novel number also had novel total surface area and novel total contour lengths (Antell & Keating, 1983).[2]

Several recent habituation studies rigorously controlled for continuous dimensions of variation. Some began with replications of the standard findings when number and continuous variables such as total surface area are confounded—infants habituated to arrays of two objects dishabituate when shown arrays of one or of three objects (and vice-versa). They then went on to pit number against cumulative values of continuous variables as a possible basis of response (see Figure 4.7 for a diagram of such a design). In several studies of this sort, when number is pitted against the cumulative value of some continuous variable (e.g., total contour length or total front surface area), after habituation, infants dishabituated to the test stimuli that were familiar in number and novel in some dimension of spatial extent and did not dishabituate to the test stimuli that were novel in number and familiar in spatial extent (Clearfield & Mix, 1999, 2001; Feigenson, Carey, & Spelke, 2002). Thus, representations of number were not driving the novelty response in these studies.

One might object that the response in this habituation study may have been a familiarity preference for common number rather than a novelty response to changed cumulative surface area. After all, the entities in the test series were novel in element size, and this change may have led children to seek a consistent model in terms of number. For this reason, subsequent studies have adopted a design in which continuous variables are strictly controlled, so that they cannot be the basis of response. Thus, any familiarity or novelty preference based on number could emerge. Figure 4.8 provides an example of one such design. The habituation stimuli (all sets of two, for example), vary in the size of elements during habituation. The test stimuli are chosen so that the same number match

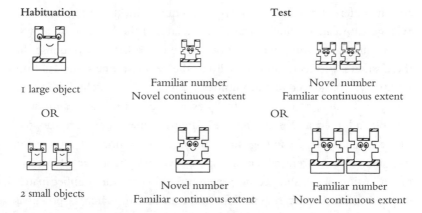

Figure 4.7. Examples of habituation and test arrays from Feigenson, Carey, & Spelke (2002) in which one test array matched the habituation array in number and the other test array matched the habituation array in total front surface area. Reprinted from Feigenson, L., Carey, S., & Spelke, E. (2002). Infants' discrimination of number vs. continuous extent. *Cognitive Psychology, 44,* 33–66, with permission from Elsevier.

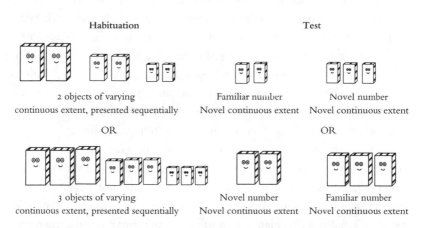

Figure 4.8. Examples of habituation and test arrays from Feigenson, Carey & Spelke (2002) in which each test array differed from the average total continuous extent during habituation by the same ratio, Number is the only possible basis of discrimination. Reprinted from Feigenson, L., Carey, S., & Spelke, E. (2002). Infants' discrimination of number vs. continuous extent. *Cognitive Psychology, 44,* 33–66, with permission from Elsevier.

and the different number match are each equidistant (by ratios) from the average cumulative value of front surface area of the habituation arrays. Thus, cumulative surface area is not available as a basis for response. In these studies, infants respond equally to the two test arrays, showing no sensitivity whatsoever to the number mismatch (or match; Feigenson, Carey, & Spelke, 2002). In another design, the controls for continuous variables adopted in Xu and Spelke's large number studies are adopted (see above), again removing any variable but number as a basis for response. Infants were at chance on sets within the range of parallel individuation. They showed no preference either for the number match (a potential familiarity response) or the number mismatch (a potential novelty response; Xu, 2003). Thus, in all of these studies, infants respond to novelty in cumulative value of continuous variables, and show no response whatsoever to the number of elements in the display, even when continuous variables are removed as a basis for choice.

Consider also Feigenson's cracker-choice experiments. As described above, these experiments reveal the set-size signature of object-file representations. Still open, however, is what quantitative comparison the infants are making. It seems likely that they would try to maximize the total amount of cracker, not the total number of crackers. And indeed, given a choice between one large cracker and two small ones, each one-fourth the size of the large one, the infants chose the bucket with the single large one. And given a choice between one large cracker and two smaller ones, each one-half the size of the large one, the infants were at chance. Thus, in almost all of the experiments on infant representations of small sets, using habituation or ordinal choice, cumulative values of continuous variables are more salient than the number of objects in the set.

These studies have two important upshots. First, infants' performance in these particular studies cannot possibly reflect an analog magnitude representation of number, since infants are not responding to number at all. Second, they bear on further characterization of the system of parallel individuation that subserves performance on these tasks. In the initial formulation of how object-file representations might underlie infant performance on small number tasks, it was assumed that models of different sets of objects were compared on the basis of 1–1 correspondence, thus establishing numerical equivalence and/or numerical more/less (Leslie, Xu, Tremoulet, & Scholl, 1998, Simon,

1997; Uller et al., 1999), and as shown in the previous section, infants can carry out such computations. However, they do not always do so.

The studies reviewed in this section motivate a different model for how object–files might underlie performance. In a revised object–file model (depicted in Figure 4.9), each individual is represented by a symbol (an object–file) for that individual, but values on continuous dimensions for each individual are represented as well, bound to the file that represents it. Models of arrays are then compared on the basis of cumulative values of those continuous dimensions. Notice that although athe infant can sum continuous variables of the individual objects, these must be available in the model itself. Infants cannot be computing surface areas of each individual in some analog magnitude format, and keeping a running sum, because if they were able to do this, there is no reason for the set-size signature of parallel individuation to emerge. Although it is not necessary that the symbols be iconic (as in Figure 4.9), I believe this to be the most parsimonious model of the observed data.

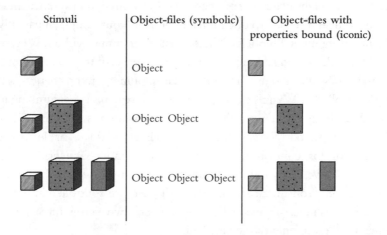

Stimuli	Object-files (symbolic)	Object-files with properties bound (iconic)
	Object	
	Object Object	
	Object Object Object	

Figure 4.9. Two versions of the memory structures that might subserve parallel individuation of small sets of objects. In one, each object is represented by an object–file that abstracts away from specific features (object). In the other, each object is represented by an iconic object–file on which shape, color, texture and spatial extent features have been bound.

Parallel Individuation of Individuals Other than Objects

As shown by the stock of English count nouns, we individuate many types of entities other than objects. We can count naps, jumps, drum beats, hopes, words .... Babies also individuate entities other than objects. Habituation studies show young infants to be sensitive to the distinction between two- and three-syllable words, as well as to the distinction between sequences of two and three jumps (Bijeljac-Babic, Bertoncini, & Mehler, 1991; Wood & Spelke, 2005a; Wynn, 1996). A close look at the studies involving jumps shows how deeply similar are the systems for parallel individuation of small sets of events, small sets of tones, and small sets of objects.

Karen Wynn was the first to show that infants can represent small sequences of events (jumps of a puppet). She habituated 5-month-old infants either to two-jump sequences or three-jump sequences. Each jump was the same height and temporal duration. Total jump sequence length was controlled in one condition and jump density was controlled in another. Infants dishabituated to the sequences with novel numbers of jumps in both conditions. Justin Wood and Elizabeth Spelke (2005a) went on to show the set size signature of parallel individuation in these studies; although infants discriminate two from three jumps under these circumstances, they fail to discriminate two from four jumps. Apparently infants create mental models of the sequences of jumps, with one "event file" for each individual jump, and four jumps exceeds the capacity limit. Wood and Spelke also noted that the total amount of "jump energy" was not controlled in Wynn's studies; there was more cumulative jumping in the three-jump sequences than in the two-jump sequences. They therefore repeated Wynn's studies controlling for this variable in the manner of his controls in his large-number jump-sequence studies reviewed above. They found that, just as when cumulative variables (total volume, total front surface area, total perimeter) are controlled in object habituation studies, infants fail to discriminate two versus three jumps when total jump energy is controlled.

Just as with object-file models, infants compare models on the basis of summed continuous variables in preference to 1–1 correspondence between numbers of events. Finally, if the jumps within a sequence are made different heights and different durations from each other, now infants compute numerical equivalence, just as Feigenson found for parallel individuation models of objects that differed within a set. Infants carry out two types of quantitative computations over event-file representations—summing values of continuous variables and 1–1 correspondence to compare number of jumps. In sum, Wood and Spelke (2005a) have shown a system of parallel individuation of jumps with all of the same signatures as the system of parallel individuation of objects.

Representations of Sets, Redux

The parallel individuation models depicted in Figure 4.9 consist of symbols for individuals that may have properties bound to them and that may be typed for kind. Still, no less than in the case of analog magnitude representations, parallel individuation requires that a set of individuals be selected as input. Further, as the cracker–choice studies show, infants are able to index at least two sets in parallel, keeping track of which consists of {cracker cracker} and which consists of {cracker cracker cracker}. In the cracker–choice studies, the sets are individuated by location. The infant must represent one set in one bucket and another in the other bucket.

Recently, Lisa Feigenson and Justin Halberda (2007) have begun to delimit the bases on which infants select sets for parallel individuation. Remember the box-search task at which 12- to 14-month-old infants fail to represent a set of four objects as more than one. Shown four objects placed in a box into which they can reach but not see, infants of this age are satisfied after having retrieved just one object. Feigenson and Halberda have shown that 14-month-old infants can exceed their limit of three objects in parallel individuation by chunking the objects shown originally on top of the box into two sets. Shown a car, car, shoe, and shoe lined up on top of the box before being placed inside it, infants now search for all four, as they do if shown a car, shoe, car, and shoe. They fail to search for more than one, of course, if shown a car, car, car, and car. The Feigenson and Halberda data show that infants represent the objects in the box as {car car} {shoe shoe}. The capacity to hold two sets in working memory in parallel allows infants to exceed their limits on parallel individuation, just as representing two sets of crackers does in the cracker-choice task. Apparently, sets can be selected on the basis of location (as in the cracker-choice task; see also Feigenson & Halberda, 2004) or on the basis of property/kind information (as in the manual search task). The infants' working-memory representations must index the distinct sets, binding the representation of the contents to each, so the child knows which bucket to choose to maximize the total amount of cracker and so the child knows that when she or he has retrieved a car and a shoe, there are still two more objects in the box.

Finally, the experiments on parallel individuation reviewed above reflect set representations in yet another way. In habituation studies, infants are often never shown the same individuals twice. Thus, they are not indexing particular individuals. By necessity, then, the representations that support generalization or dishabituation capture only that each array consisted of a set consisting of, for example, an object and another object. In cases where the set-size signature of parallel individuation is observed, the representations must at least implicitly contain the information contained herein: {O O}. Infants abstract away from the particular individuals shown—to differing degrees in different contexts. Sometimes these object representations capture the average value on some dimension over which the habituation objects varied, and infants may then compare a model of a currently viewed set with the memory model on the basis of total spatial extent. Sometimes these object representations abstract away from the continuous variables that characterize the individuals, and the memory model is compared to a model of a currently indexed set on the basis of 1–1 correspondence.

In conclusion, infants' capacity to create working models of more than one set of individuals at a time, and their capacity to abstract away from representations of particular individuals, creating memory models that capture that what was in common in successive arrays was that each consisted of sets of one, two, or three individuals, requires that infants attend to, index, and represent sets. Parallel individuation, like analog magnitude number representation, depends on representations of sets and supports quantitative computations over sets.

A Second Core Cognition System with Numerical Content

Although some describe this system of representation as a "small number system," that is a misleading name. The purpose of parallel individuation is to create working-memory models of small sets of individuals, in order to represent spatial, causal, and intentional relations among them. Unlike analog magnitude number representations, the parallel individuation system is not a dedicated number representation system. Far from it. The symbols in the parallel individuation system explicitly represent individuals. Consider again the individual file representations of two boxes depicted in Figure 4.8. There is no symbol that that has the content "two"; rather, the symbols represent the boxes. The whole model {box box} represents two boxes, of course, but only implicitly. Furthermore, as we have seen, the quantitative calculations over parallel individuation models in working memory often privilege continuous variables (such as total event energy, total contour length, total surface area) over numerical equivalence.

For these reasons, many researchers have taken the evidence that parallel individuation underlies infant performance on "number" experiments as undermining the claim that infants represent number. This conclusion is wrong for several reasons. First, and foremost, that infants sometimes fail to represent the number of individuals in small sets does not detract from the evidence that they represent the number of individuals in large sets. There is unequivocal evidence for infant analog magnitude representations of number.

Another reason the conclusion is wrong is that parallel individuation is shot through with numerical content, even though that numerical content is merely implicit in the computations that pick out and index small sets to represent, that govern the opening of new individual-files, that update working-memory models of sets as individuals are added or subtracted, and that compare sets on numerical criteria. The creation of a new individual-file requires principles of individuation and numerical identity; models must keep track of whether this object or jump, seen now, is the same one as that object seen before, or this sound just heard, is the same one as that just heard previously. The decision the system makes dictates whether an additional individual-file is established, and this guarantees that a model of a set of three boxes will contain three box symbols. Computations of numerical identity are (as their name says) numerical computations. Also, the opening of a new individual-file in the presence of other active files provides an implicit representation of the process of adding one to an array of individuals. Finally, working-memory models of two sets of individuals can be simultaneously maintained, and when individual-file models are compared on the basis of 1–1 correspondence, the computations over these symbols establish numerical equivalence and numerical order.

Thus, although the numerical content in parallel individuation systems is entirely implicit, it is sufficient to establish numerical equivalence and numerical order among small sets. And, as we shall see in chapters 7 and 8, this system of representation plays a crucial role in the creation of the explicit verbal numeral list representation of the positive integers.

Conclusions: Relations Between Analog Magnitude Number Representations and Parallel Individuation

That there are at least two distinct systems of core cognition with numerical content raises several questions about the relations between them. In what senses are they distinct? What determines when each is deployed? Do they ever become integrated in a single system for representing number? If so, when and how?

The analog magnitude number system and the system of parallel individuation each take sets of individuals as input and create representations that support quantitative computations. Still, the two differ in many ways. Their qualitatively different processing signatures provide evidence for radically different formats of representation, with mental symbols with very different content. Two distinct processing signatures were highlighted. First, the sensitivity of analog magnitude representations is limited by the ratio of the sets being discriminated, whereas the capacity of parallel individuation is limited (in infants) to three individuals. Second, because object-file and event-file representations consist of symbols for each individual, properties of those individuals (such as the size of a particular object or the height of a particular jump) can be bound to them and quantitative computations can be carried out over continuous variables as well as over discrete ones. These continuous variables are highly salient in the infant parallel individuation system. Analog magnitude representations of number, in contrast, abstract away from properties of the individuals in the set, rendering those properties unavailable for further computation. And indeed, the studies reviewed above showed that infants create representations of the number of individuals in large sets of objects, sounds, or events when continuous variables are controlled, but that they largely fail to do so for small sets of objects, sounds, or events when continuous variables are controlled for. Third, the analog magnitude system creates summary symbols that represent approximate cardinal values of sets, whereas the parallel individuation system does not. Infants' capacity to sum over continuous variables shows that they maintain representations of each individual in their working-memory models of sets of objects or events.

Perhaps the most unexpected finding from these studies is that analog magnitude representations and parallel individuation of small sets seem to be mutually exclusive in infancy. Of course, it is in the nature of parallel individuation models that they cannot represent large sets. But when small sets are involved, infants seem not to deploy analog magnitude representations, leading to striking failures. In all studies that reveal the set-size signature of parallel individuation, such as comparing one to four crackers, two to four crackers or three to six crackers, two to four jumps, two to four sounds, or one to four balls seen placed into a box, infants would succeed, if (1) they represented both sets with analog magnitudes, or (2) they represented the larger set with analog magnitudes and could compare across the two systems of representation. Rather, they seem to fail to deploy analog magnitude representations at all, even though we know they can do so for sets of four or six (as in 4 versus 8 or 6 versus 12 comparisons).

If analog magnitude representations are not defined for small sets in infancy, then there would be a discontinuity between the infant system and the adult system, contrary to one of the hypothesized properties of core cognition. Sarah Cordes and colleagues (Cordes, Gelman, & Gallistel, 2002) found that when estimation tasks are made very difficult, scalar variability is constant from sets of 1 to 30, and Dehaene's (1997) study reviewed above found distance and magnitude effects comparing sets of 1 and 4 (both within the limits of adult parallel individuation) to

5 that were comparable to the comparisons of sets of 6 and 9 to 5 (all outside the limits of adult parallel individuation). These data show that for adults, analog magnitude number representations are computed for small sets. Similarly, in Brannon and Terrace's (1998) number-ordering task, monkeys were trained to order small sets (one through four), all within the limits of adult monkey parallel individuation. Nonetheless, Brannon and Terrace found immediate generalization to large sets in which numerical order was computed over analog magnitudes, and the monkeys had no problems ordering pairs of sets one of which was in the range of parallel individuation and one of which was outside it (e.g., three versus seven). Thus, for human and monkey adults, representations of the number of elements in small sets are seamlessly integrated with analog magnitude representations of larger sets, and in some circumstances scalar variability is observed in estimates of the cardinal values of sets from 1 to 30.

Fortunately for the core cognition hypothesis, at least two studies show that infants can in some circumstances integrate numerical representations across the boundary of small and large sets. For example, in Brannon's (2002) infant ordinal judgment tasks, one of the habituation arrays was 1, 2, 4 and another was 2, 4, 8. Infants' responses to these arrays did not differ from 4, 8, 16. Also, the test array crossed the boundary: 3, 6, 12. More directly, Sara Cordes and Elizabeth Brannon (Cordes, Lutz, & Brannon, 2007) recently showed that infants can discriminate sets of 2 from sets of 8 in the Xu and Spelke habituation paradigm, when all continuous variables are controlled for. This differs from the failures of discrimination of 2 versus 4 cited above.[3] It seems possible that, in these tasks, the analog magnitude system is primed by the presence of large sets, leading the child to apply it to small sets. It is also possible that the perceptual processes that create analog magnitude representations are not well defined for small sets, so larger ratios (e.g., 4:1 instead of 3:2) are needed for discrimination.

I conclude that analog magnitude representations are computable for small sets by infants as well as by adults, but that in many situations infants instead focus on the individuals. In these circumstance, attention to individuals, and the creation of individual-files in working memory, may simply take precedence over analog magnitude representations. It would be nice to have an account of when infants will and when they will not compute analog magnitudes for small sets, but the argument of this chapter does not require such an account. Which system is invoked by a given situation is on the face of it rather unsystematic and context-dependent. An account of exactly how one chooses to activate a given representational capacity might be like the account of the exact forces on a flipped coin—too unsystematic and detailed to be the object of any science. We have no account, nor should we expect one, of how I represent what's on my cluttered desk as I write these words. I can focus on the stacks of papers (approximately 20 of them, my analog magnitude system tells me), or my cup and my cell phone (represented by parallel individuation). What is important to the argument here is that there clearly are two distinct systems, each with its own signatures and each representing number in quite different ways.

In chapters 7 and 8, when I consider how children come to quantify over sets using the conceptual resources that underlie natural language quantifiers and how they learn the meanings of explicit numerals, I return to the question of how and when children integrate the two systems of core cognition. For now, please bear in mind that there is massive evidence for two distinct core cognition systems with numerical content, in one of which (parallel individuation) number is represented only implicitly and in the other, number is represented by a mental magnitude that is proportional to the cardinal value of the set of items under consideration.

NOTES

1. Scalar variability of responses falls out of each of two competing models of analog magnitude representations (magnitudes a linear function of number, standard deviations proportional to the mean, or magnitudes a logarithmic function of number, standard deviations constant). For the purposes of this book, choosing between these two models does not matter.

2. See Antell and Keating, 1983; Starkey and Cooper, 1980. Of course, researchers were aware of this potential confound, and attempted to control for it in two ways. First, Starkey and Cooper contrasted 2 vs. 3 comparisons with 4 vs. 6 comparisons, finding that infants succeeded in the first and failed in the second. Since 4 vs. 6 differs in all continuous variables as does 2 vs. 3, they reasoned, it cannot be that representations of some continuous variables underlie success. This control does show that infants are not directly representing some continuous variable, such as

total surface area, in memory, but it ultimately misses the mark because of the set-size limits on object-file representations. Infants' memory representations of the arrays are subject to the limitation on parallel individuation of object-files, and indeed, that infants succeed in comparisons of 2 vs. 3 in the face of failure at 4 vs. 6 is the set-size signature of object-file representations. It is still possible within the limits of parallel individuation that size may be bound to the object-file representations and representations of the stimuli compared with respect to total area. Second, in some studies (e.g., Starkey & Cooper, 1980; Strauss & Curtis, 1981), the stimuli varied in area from habituation trial to habituation trial. However, since area variation was random, the average total surface area of sets of two objects was less than that of sets of three objects, and in the test trials, on average, the stimulus novel in number will be more different from the average habituation value of total surface area than will be the stimulus of the familiar number. What is needed is a design such as that achieved by Xu and Spelke (2000).

3. I know of one study in which infants succeed in a three versus four habituation design (Wynn, Bloom, & Chiang, 2002). In one condition of this study infants were habituated to three independently moving collections of four objects each. They dishabituated upon being shown four collections of three objects each. As neither the Weber-fraction limit of discrimination nor the set-size signature was systematically probed, it is not clear what system of representation underlies performance here, but clearly infants in this study surpassed the typically found limits of representation of small sets. It would be of interest to probe what made this possible—perhaps it was the fact that the individuals (collections in this case) were moving independently of each other, in the manner of a MOT experiment.

5

Core Cognition: Agency

Chapters 2 and 3 concerned core cognition of the physical world, the world of distinct individual objects and physical constraints on their motion and spatial relations. But the world of human infants is also social. For us primates especially, predicting what others of our kind will do, and influencing them to act in such a way that furthers our own interests, is crucial for our survival. Selection pressures on understanding others so as to be able to manipulate them (what has been called "the Machiavellian mind") may have been a driving force in the shaping of the human brain. On this view, it would not be surprising that evolution bequeathed us humans with core cognition of agents, agents' interactions with each other, and agents' interactions with the physical world, articulated in terms of representations of goals, information, and attentional states.

My review of the literature on infants' representations of agents closely parallels that of objects. First, I characterize the core domain, detailing the concepts of agency that are at issue. I then sketch evidence that infants represent the actions of agents as goal directed, and contrast two different (and not mutually exclusive) proposals for the systems of concepts that are deployed in these representations. I then consider the competing empiricist hypothesis that the relevant innate representations are perceptual, and that the infant learns concepts of agency through some learning mechanism that operates over sensory and spatio-temporal primitives. I then turn to a second aspect of agency—that agents are capable of attending to and providing information about events and things in the world, again sketching the evidence that infants represent agents as such and countering leaner interpretations of the data I present. I then examine whether core cognition of agency exemplifies other key features of core cognition. Do the innate input analyzers that create representations of agency in infancy continue to operate throughout the life span? Also, unlike core cognition of objects, which definitely extends deep into our primate past, if not even further, how evolutionarily ancient is core cognition of agency? I end with some questions unique to this domain.. Is there more than one distinct system of core agency representations, and if so, how are they related? And finally, I have a few words to say about whether and in what ways the preschooler's theory of mind transcends core cognition of agency.

The Central Concepts in the Domain: Agency, Goals, Information, and Attention

Causality in the domain of inert physical objects is contact causality. Inanimate objects go into motion immediately upon and only upon being contacted by another moving object, and change state only upon being contacted by an object or by some source of physical energy. Causality in the domain of agents has a different structure. Agents are capable of self-generated motion and of resisting forces acting upon them. This aspect of our concept of agency interacts with representations of physical causality and is the topic of chapter 6. A second component of causal attributions in the domain of agency concerns our explanations for specific actions. We explain agents' actions in terms of their goals and the states of the world that facilitate or impede attaining these goals. We monitor agents' attentional focus, and expect (at least in the case of people) agents to provide us useful information about the world. Representations of goals and attentional states are aspects of intentional attributions and are the concern of the present chapter.

On some analyses, intentionality is a relation between an agent and the world that is characterized by *aboutness*; an agent's intentional state is about something in the world. On this analysis, having a goal is a paradigmatic intentional state: the agent desires a state of affairs (that she get the toy, eat the apple, and so on), and wanting or desiring is an intentional relation between the agent and the world. Other relations between agents and the world also display the relevant property of aboutness. Agents attend to and perceive objects and events, and attending and perceiving are other paradigmatic intentional relations. Agents also indicate objects in the world (through pointing, spoken language). Referring is another paradigmatic intentional relation.

On other analyses of intentionality, intentional attributions necessarily involve attributions of propositional attitudes to agents. We can see the difference between the richer and leaner interpretations of intentional agency by comparing how we think of light-seeking tropisms of plants and cookie-seeking actions of children. Both are goal directed, but we attribute to the child representations of their goals and beliefs about where cookies are to be found (e.g., "she wants to eat a cookie" and "she believes cookies are in the cupboard"), whereas we attribute neither to the plant. The full-blown schema of intentional causality is clearly in place by age 3 (e.g., Bartsch & Wellman, 1995). The proposals for core cognition of intentional agency stop short of attributing to infants explicit representations of agents' propositional attitudes (what they believe, what they want, what they promise ...). Rather, the proposals for which I will argue credit the infant with representations of agents, their goals, their attentional and perceptual states, and their information providing activities. Sometimes I use the term "intentional agency" to signal that I am attributing more to the infant than representations of self-generated motion and action (those aspects of agency related to physical causality), but I do not mean by this that I am attributing representations of mental representations.

The debates reviewed in this chapter do not concern whether infants are intentional agents. I have no doubt that they are, even in the strongest sense. Infants form mental representations with symbolic content, and their behavior is intentional, goal directed, and mediated by their representations of the world. Rather, what is at issue is whether infants *understand* intentional agency—whether the capacity to form representations of themselves or others as intentional agents is part of core cognition.

Representations of Goal-Directed Action

Imagine the following scenario presented to you on a computer monitor (see Figure 5.1). You are initially shown a stationary scene, depicted in Figure 5.1a. The small ball goes into motion toward the gap in the screen, and the large ball begins to follow it. The small ball goes through the gap, which is too small for the large one to fit, and the large ball goes around,

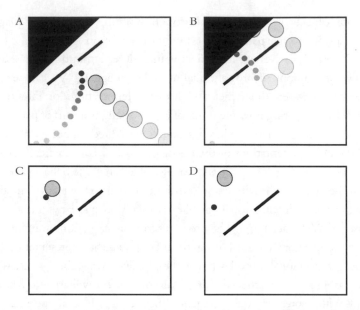

Figure 5.1. Schematic depiction of habituation trials in Csibra et al., 1999. Reprinted from Csibra, G., Gergely, G., Koos, O., & Brockbank, M. (1999). Goal attribution without agency cues: The perception of "pure reason" in infancy. *Cognition, 72,* 237–267, with permission from Elsevier. The small ball goes into motion, passing through the small gap in the barrier, then going out of sight. The large ball appears to follow it toward the gap, then goes around the barrier before passing out of sight.

both balls then disappear out of sight at the edge of the screen (Figure 5.1b). How would you interpret this scene? If you represent it in terms such as "follows," "chases," "tries to catch," "flees," "tries to escape," you are representing the large ball, the small ball, or both, as agents. You are characterizing the goals of agents. It is also possible to represent this scene entirely in terms of descriptions of the motions of each ball—a purely spatio-temporal description of the paths each ball takes. Indeed, Laura Wagner found that when adults describe this scene, their language reflects both types of construals (although the agentive construals are far more common). The question, though, is how infants construe the scene.

Csibra and his colleagues (Csibra, Biro, Koos, & Gergely, 2003) presented evidence that 6- to 12-month-old infants represent the large ball as having the goal of catching the small ball. In one study, they habituated 12-month-old infants to this event. Notice that no completion of the event is depicted during habituation; the infants are not shown what happens on the far side of the barrier. At issue was whether infants would infer the goal of catching. After habituation, test trials revealed what happened behind the screen. Two endings were revealed: "catching" trials versus "passing trials." In catching trials, the small ball stopped and the large ball came to rest, touching it. In passing trials, the small ball stopped and the large ball passed on by, passing off the screen as before. Infants dishabituated to the passing trials, and generalized habituation to the catching trails. Infants apparently had inferred the goal of catching from the chasing event.

Wagner and I (Wagner & Carey, 2005) replicated this study, adding two controls. In our study, infants in the chasing condition were habituated to an event as in Figure 5.1. After habituation, they also were shown two outcomes of this event in alternation. One was identical to the catching outcome of the Csibra study; in the other, the passing outcome, the large ball passed by the small ball, but stopped visibly at the edge of the monitor. Thus, the two outcomes were matched in terms of the number of balls visible at the end of the event. Again, infants generalized habituation to the catching outcome, and dishabituated to the passing outcome.

Wagner and I also wanted to ensure that the outcome with objects separated in space was not intrinsically more interesting than the outcome with the two objects next to each other, but rather that infants found it anomalous given their interpretation of the motion of the large ball as goal-directed. We included a condition in which the motion of the big ball would not be seen as chasing; the small ball went into motion, and the big ball then came in from off screen, bounced off the bottom, and then went off in the same trajectory as in the chasing event. After habituation, infants were shown the two outcomes. Now they did not differentiate the two. These experiments show that 12-month-olds infer an end state in accord with an inferred goal of the large ball's actions. In other studies, Csibra and his colleagues (Csibra, Gergely, Koos, & Brockbank, 1999) have shown comparable findings with 6-month-olds.

Amanda Woodward (1998) and her colleagues have provided convergent evidence that young infants represent actions as goal-directed. In a typical experiment, Woodward habituated 5-month-old infants to a hand moving across a stage and grasping one of two objects that were on opposite sides of the stage. After habituation, the positions of the two objects were reversed, and one of two new events was shown. In one (same goal, different path), the hand took a different path to grasp the same object (a different path, because the original object is now in a different place). In the other, the hand took the same path as before, grasping a different object from before. Apparently, infants had represented the original action in terms of its goal, and their attention was drawn when the hand apparently pursued a new goal.

Several control conditions rule out the possibility that infants are merely representing the final spatial relation between the hand and one of the objects, dishabituating when the hand is touching a new object. In one control, the hand was replaced with a stick with a multifingered sponge at the end as the actor during habituation. In this case infants dishabituated only in the same goal/different path condition. Apparently, they did not reason about the motion of the stick-like entity as goal-directed. Even putting the hand in a gold sparkly glove disrupts the representations of these events as goal-directed for 5-month-olds. Woodward (1998) also showed that actions of human arms and hands are not always analyzed as goal-directed. If the arm just flopped down, hand backwards, through the same path as before, the hand ending in contact with the target, infants reacted as in the stick/sponge condition. They dishabituated only in the different path/same goal condition. In these three conditions (gold glove, stick/sponge, flopping arm), the spatial relation at the end of each habituation trial was the same as in the grasping condition: the object in contact with the target object. But it is only when the action can be interpreted by the child as goal-directed that the child dishabituates when the target of the action (rather than the path of the motion) changes.

Two Proposals for the System of Representations Underlying Infant Attribution of Goals

The Csibra, Gergely and the Woodward experiments all suggest that infants represent some actions as goal-directed by 5 or 6 months of age (see Sommerville, Woodward, & Needham, 2005, for evidence in 3-month-olds). Very young infants are capable of goal attributions. What system of representation supports these attributions?

Proposal 1: The Teleological Stance

Csibra, Gergely, and their colleagues argue that the teleological (i.e., goal-directed) interpretation of such events has a three-part structure (see Figure 5.2): a representation of the goal, a representation of the physical constraints on the action needed to attain the goal, and a representation of the means for achieving the goal, given the constraints. Furthermore, they claim that infants' representations of the actions chosen to achieve a goal are constrained by a "principle of rationality," to wit the most direct, least effortful, action to attain the goal, given the current environmental constraints, should be chosen.

The study described above (Figure 5.1 and surrounding discussion) shows that infants represent the goals of actions. In a variant of this study, Csibra and his colleagues (2003) probed whether 12-month-olds' representations are constrained by the principle of rationality, and whether they analyze the constraints imposed by the environment. They habituated

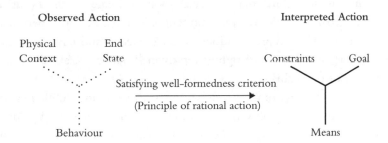

Figure 5.2. The three-part structure of the teleological stance, according to Gergeley & Csibra. Infants analyze behavior relevant to end states and the physical context of the behavior. If the behavior is consistent with being directed toward an endstate, taking into account the constraints of the environment, and following the most efficient path, it is analyzed as goal directed, satisfying the rationality constraint. Gergely, G., & Csibra, G. (2006). Sylvia's recipe: Human culture, imitation, and pedagogy. In S. C. Levinson & N. J. Enfield (Eds.), *Roots of human sociality: Culture, cognition, and human interaction* (pp. 229 to 255). Oxford, UK: Berg Publishers Ltd.

infants to the same beginning events as in Figure 5.1. The test trials were identical to the habituation trials except for one change: the gap in the barrier was enlarged, so that now the large ball could pass through. The two test events consisted of the large object following the small one directly through the gap (a rational action, given the goal of catching) versus the large object following the same trajectory as during habituation. The latter outcome violates the rationality principle. Given that the infant understood the action of the large ball in terms of the constraint imposed by the small gap, and expects the large ball to take the shortest path in pursuit of the small ball, then the event in which the ball continues to go around the barrier is anomalous. Indeed, infants looked longer at the irrational event. It appears, then, that infants' representations of this event include a specification of environmental constraints and a specification of the relative efficiency of means to attain goals. Their attention is drawn if the less rational means are chosen.

Further evidence for this conclusion is provided by a study that shows that infants infer an environmental constraint given evidence for a nondirect path of motion. Csibra and his colleagues (2003) habituated 12-month-old infants to the event depicted in Figure 5.3. After habituation, the screen was removed, revealing a scene in which there either was or was not a barrier in the path toward the goal. The large ball's motion was the same as during habituation. Infants looked longer at the event in which the ball jumped over a nonexistent barrier. Again, this experiment shows that infants' representations of goals, means, and environmental constraints on actions are tightly intertwined and constrained by the principle of rationality.

One final study from Gergely's group shows just how subtle infants' reasoning about rationality is. The study built on earlier work by Andy Meltzoff (1988), showing that 14-month-old infants imitate the means an agent adopts in attaining a goal, even when the means are not obviously rational. Meltzoff demonstrated for the infants that touching a panel with one's head would make it light up. A week later the infants returned to the laboratory, and they imitated the means—they make the panel light up by touching it with their heads, even though that is not the easiest way to make bodily contact with the panel. Gergely and his colleagues suggested that the infants might be reasoning as follows: if touching the panel with hands would work, the actor would have done so, this being the

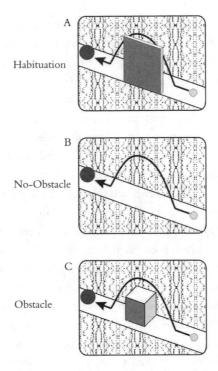

Figure 5.3. Schematic depiction of the experiment from Csibra et al. (2003), showing that infants infer an environmental constraint to make sense of an action that apparently violates the rationality constraint. Infants were habituated to a ball rolling along a path and then apparently jumping while the path is hidden behind a screen (A). During test trials, the screen is removed, revealing an obstacle on the path (C) or no obstacle on the path (B), and the motion of the ball is repeated. Reprinted from Csibra, G., Biro, S., Koos, O., & Gergely, G. (2003). One-year-old infants use teleological representations of actions productively. *Cognitive Science, 27*(1), 111–133, reprinted by permission of Taylor & Francis Ltd, http://www.tandf.co.uk/journals.

more natural, efficient, and thus more rational action; therefore, it must be necessary to use one's head.

Gergely (Gergely, Bekkering, & Kiraly, 2002) showed that infants were engaged in such reasoning by including a condition in which the actor's hands were obviously engaged when he leaned down and touched the panel with its head. The actor pretended to be cold, was given a blanket, and was clutching the blanket around himself when touching the panel with his head. This condition was compared to one exactly like that of Meltzoff's experiment, in which the actor's hands remain on the table, beside the panel, when the actor touched the panel with his head. Infants in the latter condition replicated Meltzoff's findings—they also touched the panel with their heads. But those in the first condition, in which the actor's hands were otherwise engaged, touched the panels with their hands and virtually never used their heads. This study shows that by 14 months of age, the rationality constraint is used not only to predict what an actor will do but it also guides the child's causal analysis if the actor acts in an inexplicably irrational way.

Gergely's and Csibra's proposed schema for the intentional stance has no privileged representation of the agent. The goal is not explicitly predicated of an agent, nor is there any relation between an agent and a desired state explicitly represented. Rather, it is the action itself that is represented as goal-directed. And indeed, Gergely's and Csibra's very first experiments on infants' teleological reasoning suggested that information about the potential agency of the figures played no role in the teleological attribution. In these studies, a ball sailed over a barrier and then nestled against another ball on the other side of that barrier. In one condition, there were ample cues to agency for the geometric figures; they went from rest to motion on their own, they expanded and contracted in apparent response to one another, and they reacted contingently to the barrier. In the other, the circle appeared from off screen already in motion and simply sailed over the barrier, stopping next to the other circle. In both cases, infants' reasoning about the subsequent behavior of the figures was guided by the principle of rationality, and equally so. That is, they apparently saw the action as goal-directed, in spite of no independent evidence in the second case that the actor was an independent agent.

Proposal 2: The Goal-directed Agent

Of course, we do not know from these results that infants did not attribute the goal to agents. Rationality, after all, is actually a property of agents, and goals are something agents have. Proposal 2 differs from Proposal 1 in that intentional states (goals, attention, perception, referring) are predicated of particular agents. Consider again the event in which the ball comes flying from off screen already in motion. There are two cues to goal-directedness in this task. The large ball always ends up nestled next to the small one (equifinality). Furthermore, the screen heights vary over three values during habituation, and the large ball always clears them (variable paths, tracking environmental constraints). But this event is perfectly ambiguous concerning whose goal it is—it could be the ball's, or it could be some other agent's, an agent who is throwing the ball. If infants are indeed assigning goals to agents in these circumstances, then they should be sensitive to cues that disambiguate these two possibilities. In a series of studies that I will describe more fully in Chapter 6, Rebecca Saxe and I have explored this possibility, and found evidence that indeed infants are concerned with assigning agency in such studies.

Saxe (Saxe, Tenenbaum, & Carey, 2005) habituated 10- and 12-month-old infants to real-live versions of the habituation events described above. Infants watched as a figure flew in from offstage over a screen, landing on the other side of the stage. The screens were of variable heights, so the infants had evidence for variable paths, and for equifinality—the figure always landed on the other side of the stage, having cleared the screen. For present purposes, the crucial manipulation was a familiarization period before these habituation events occurred. During this period, babies were acquainted with the nature of the flying entity. For half of the babies, the flying entity was a regular bean bag, and infants had seen it resting on the stage floor motionless for 20 seconds during familiarization. For the other half of the babies, the flying entity was a furry brown puppet with googly eyes and two floppy legs, and the infants had seen it moving around on the stage for 20 seconds during familiarization. Then the experiment unfolded as in the original Gergely experiments. Infants were habituated to the object's flying over three screens of variable heights, always landing in the same place on the other side of the stage. After habituation, a hand appeared, either from the side of the stage from which the bean bag/puppet had appeared or from the other side of the stage. When the flying figure was a dispositionally inert bean bag, infants looked reliably longer at the test events in which the hand appeared from the side different from that from which the bean bag had appeared during habituation, suggesting that they had interpreted a person or hand as the source of the bean bag's goal-directed motion. In contrast, when the flying entity was the puppet, they did not differentiate the two sides, but rather looked longer when a hand appears at either location, suggesting that they interpreted the puppet itself as the source of its own goal-directed motion. Thus, assuming that the equifinality and environmental constraints were sufficient to create goal representations in our version of the experiment, it appears that infants do assign goals to particular agents, although they, like adults, can see an event as goal-directed even when there is ambiguity as to the intentional agent (see Saxe, Tzelnic, & Carey, 2007, for convergent data with 7-month-olds).

Three other lines of studies show that infants are assigning distinct roles to distinct actors in these teleological events. Phillip Rochat and colleagues (Rochat, Striano, & Morgan, 2004) showed showed that infants as young as 3 months of age discriminate displays that consist of one disk "chasing" another from motion of the two disks in which the motion of one is independent of the motion of the other. Of course, this shows only a sensitivity to contingency, not that the infant interprets the events as consisting of one object's chasing another. Adapting an experimental logic first introduced by Alan Leslie (see chapter 6), Rochat habituated 5-, 7- and 9-month-old infants to the chasing events, in which the disks differed in color. For example, the chaser might be red and the quarry blue. After habituation, the colors were reversed. After reversal, the overall contingency and spatio-temporal relations between the figures was the same as before. Nine-month-olds, and 7-month-olds to a lesser extent, dishabituated to the reversal, as if they had assigned different roles to the chaser and to the quarry.

Supporting this conclusion, Anne Schlottman and Luca Surian (1999) habituated 9-month-old infants to a "reaction event." A green rectangle inched toward a stationary red rectangle, with a motion similar to that of a caterpillar. Before the green rectangle reached the red one, and also before the green rectangle stopped moving, the red one inched away. Adults see this display as the red one fleeing the green one, an intentional attribution. However, if the green rectangle stops before reaching the red one, and there is a pause before the red one goes off, the event is not seen as one in which the red rectangle is fleeing the green one. Thus, this "nonreaction" event provides a control for the reaction event—if infants are responding to the spatio-temporal relations alone (first the green one moves, then the red one moves), then a reversal of the event should be equally interesting in both cases. Infants in the reaction event condition dishabituated when the roles were reversed (the green one flees the red one), but those in the nonreaction event condition did not (first the red one moves and then the green one moves). It seems, then, that 9-month-olds represent the reaction events in terms of intentional agency, assigning different intentions to the two actors. These data provide convergent evidence for Rochat's conclusion that the 7- and 9-month-olds in his role-reversal experiment are seeing chases in terms of agency. They also provide convergent evidence that infants assign goals to particular actors—if there were merely representing the teleological structure in the reaction event (there's chasing going on), they would not dishabituate when the roles were reversed, because the teleological structure of the overall event remains the same.

Finally, a recent series of studies by Valerie Kuhlmeier, Karen Wynn, Paul Bloom, and their colleagues (Kuhlmeier, Wynn, & Bloom, under review; Hamlin, Wynn, & Bloom, in press) show how rich infants' representations of agents can be. Infants represent second-order goals—whether one agent's goal is to help or hinder a second agent's attaining its goal—and they make differential attributions about the helper and the hinderer. In these experiments, a geometric figure with eyes (e.g., a red half-circle) is trying to get up a hill, as shown in Figure 5.4. It makes it to the first plateau, and partly up the second hill, before falling back to the plateau. Then, on half of the habituation trials, one of the other geometric figures with eyes (e.g., a yellow triangle) comes down and gently pushes the figure up the rest of the second hill. In these trials, the yellow figure is the helper. On the other half of the habituation trials, the other figure (e.g., a blue square) positions itself between the top of the hill and the figure, and gently pushes it all the way down to the bottom. This blue square is the hinderer.

In a series of studies with this basic design, some involving animations and some involving live action, infants as young as 6 months of age distinguish the helper and the hinderer. Their attention is drawn in test trials if the original figure approaches the hinderer in preference to the helper; and if they are themselves given a choice to pick up or touch either the yellow triangle or the blue square, they choose the helper, not the hinderer. That is, they prefer the helper and they expect the figure whose goal it was to reach the top of the hill to also prefer the helper.

I conclude that by 6 months of age, infants make rich attributions of goals to agents. They represent goal-directed actions in terms of the

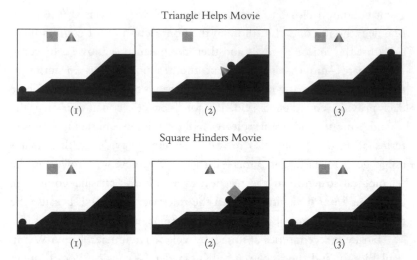

Figure 5.4. Schematic depiction of habituation trials from Kuhlmeier et al. (under review): a: the circle apparently attempts to climb the hill, not succeeding to make it all the way up, b: on ½ of the habituation trials, the triangle comes down behind the circle and apparently helps it up the hill, and c: on ½ of the trials the square positions itself in the way of the circle and apparently pushes it down, causing it to go all the way down to the bottom.

teleological schema depicted in Figure 5.2. In addition, they assign goals and even dispositions to particular actors, and their interpretations of subsequent events are constrained by these dispositional attributions.

Conceptual Representations of Agency or a Leaner Interpretation of the Data?

In some of the above experiments, the actors are geometric figures with no bodily features of agents. In these cases, no evidence concerning the goal-directedness of their actions is provided by the nature of the entities themselves. These objects do not look like known agents; they are not people or animals. Apparently, there is sufficient information in the spatio-temporal properties of these events to support the teleological interpretation. As input to their analysis of the scene, viewers have only the trajectories of the objects, the spatial layout of the environment, and the contingencies between the objects' motions with respect to each other and with respect to the environment. Just as spatio-temporal relations between the movements of perceived surfaces are sufficient to cause the representation of one or two numerically distinct 3-D objects (see chapters 2 and 3), a spatio-temporal analysis of such events as those shown in Figures 5.1, 5.3 and 5.4 supports attributions of goal-directed actions, and of agents and their dispositions. Although spatio-temporal information is sometimes sufficient input to the mechanism that computes teleological descriptions of these events, representations of goals and means, agents, helping, hindering, chasing, fleeing, and computations of rationality go beyond the spatio-temporal description of the scene, and they cannot be reduced to a spatio-temporal vocabulary. The motions could be characterized entirely in spatio-temporal terms—in terms of the trajectories of each figure relative to the others, and to those of each other. Nowhere in these descriptions would we find concepts such as goal.

Thus, infants' representations of agents are conceptual in just the same sense as their object representations are. They cannot be expressed in terms of spatio-temporal primitives, and as documented above, they have a rich infererential role. Of course, the claim that infants' representations are conceptual depends on our being correct in attributing to them concepts of goal, means, agent, chasing, helping, and so forth. It is always possible that infants are merely representing regularities in the motions. Perhaps infants have learned generalizations about motions: if an object repeatedly follows a given path, it will do so in the future, unless there is a change in the environment that permits a straighter path between the starting point and the end point; objects cannot pass through gaps in barriers that are smaller than they are; objects go around or over other objects (owing to the solidity constraint). Could the infant's looking-time patterns in these experiments reflect violations of expectancies formulated directly in terms of the paths of motions themselves? Call this the "lean" interpretation of experimental results such as those reviewed above.

Perhaps the lean interpretation is correct, but I doubt it. How often have infants seen objects jump over barriers much larger than the objects themselves are? How often, really, have infants seen objects begin with the trajectories as shown in Figure 5.1 and end with one object next to the other? One problem with the lean interpretation, on which infants' expectations reflect learned regularities of patterns of motion, is that one has to explain how the child focuses on just these regularities. If the infant's reasoning is guided by the three-part representation of goals, actions, and environmental constraints depicted in Figure 5.2, and by the distinction between agents and dispositionally inert objects, then this problem becomes much more tractable.

Furthermore, evidence concerning interrelations among different aspects of intentional attribution strongly suggests that infants represent events in terms of agency. First, the inferential role sketched in the previous section provides strong evidence for the rich interpretation. Second, several of the studies reviewed above show that the features of the actor do matter. Independent cues to intentional agency are integrated from as early as we have evidence that infants are making intentional attributions at all. Remember Woodward's findings that the motion of a figure across the stage and making contact with a given object is interpreted as a goal-directed action only if the object is a normally reaching and grasping hand. This shows that by 5 months of age, infants have identified "grasping by a human hand" as a special case of agentive action, and that they use this schema to supplement the spatio-temporal and contingency information in these events (which is identical across the grasping hand, flopping hand, stick/sponge, and golden glove conditions).

Not only is information about an agent's kind sometimes taken into account as infants attribute goals to a behaving entity, but agent-specific information is also considered as infants assess rationality. This was shown by infants' taking into account whether there was an explanation (the hands were occupied) for why the person turned on the light with her head rather than with her hands in the Gergely experiment described above.

In sum, several forms of evidence support the view that infants represent goals as goals of particular agents. From as early as when infants create representations of goals from patterns of motion and contingent interaction, they notice if the roles of particular players within the scenario shift, even if the patterns of motion and contingency remain constant. Second, equally early in development, infants draw upon cognition of particular kinds of agents as they build representations of goal-directed action in three different ways: (1) in assigning agency to the moving entity itself or to the source of that entity's motion, (2) in assigning goal directedness to an action at all, and (3) in interpreting what is rational. Some of these phenomena are observed at 5 to 7 months of age—as young as these methods yield systematic results. That the representations are sensitive to multiple sources of information outside of the spatio-temporal features of the events supports the claims that the representations of these events go beyond the vocabulary of the lean interpretations—that is, go beyond the vocabulary of perceptual primitives.

Another type of integration within the domain of intentional agency also supports the richer interpretation. In addition to representations of agents' goals, infants represent agents as indicating, communicating about, and attending to objects. Insofar as representations of these aspects of intentional agency are integrated with those of agents' goal-directed behavior, the rich interpretation of both types of representations is bolstered. But before considering evidence for the integration of the two aspects of representations of intentional agency, I must make the case that infants represent agents as referring to objects in the world.

Attention/Perception/Reference

Imagine the following scenario: you are engaged in intense conversation with a person sitting across the table from you, and she mentions "the book on the table." Her language has content; it refers to something in the world, and you take what she subsequently says to be about the book you decide she is referring to. You are making a referential attribution, as well as an attribution that she is providing information about the book. Suddenly, the person disengages and turns and looks to the side. You follow her gaze. Why? If you are seeking what she is looking at, you are representing her attentional state, as well as representing hat she is looking at and perhaps seeing something. That is, you interpret her look as having content, as being directed at something in the outside world. Similarly, she points and you follow her point. Why? If you are seeking what she is pointing at, again you are assuming that she is referring to something and perhaps about to provide information about it. When we represent others as using language referentially, attending to something, pointing or looking at something, we take these actions as being about something in the world, and in this sense as intentional.

There is decisive evidence that infants in their second year of life (12 to 24 months of age) make this type of intentional attribution. As we shall see, there is good evidence that infants in the first year of life do so as well. Perhaps the clearest manifestation is the toddler's understanding of language as referential. "Cat" refers to cats, and there is much evidence that toddlers know this. Dare Baldwin's (1991) work on 15- to 18-month-olds' interpretation of newly heard words provides one striking demonstration that this is so. Baldwin presented toddlers with a novel object, an object that they knew no name for. She waited until the child was looking at the novel object, and then said "Look at the toopa," using a novel word. The experimenter, however, was looking into a bucket at that moment. Baldwin assessed whether the child mapped the word to the object the child was examining. Toddlers of both ages, 15 and 18 months, looked up at the experimenter's eyes as soon as they heard the novel word, as if they were checking what the experimenter might mean. And the older infants established a mapping between the novel word, "toopa," and the object in the experimenter's bucket, even though they had never seen that object before and never saw it at the same time the word was spoken. These data show that children at both ages assume word usage to be referential; one must establish what a person is indicating in order to know what a newly heard word means, and what that person is looking at when using the term provides relevant information. The relation between words and entities in the world is not merely one of associative pairing; the child does not make an associative mapping between a novel object and a novel word heard when the child is attending to that object. Another person's word usage and looking behavior must be integrated in order to establish what that person is referring to.

Recently, Melissa Preissler and I (Preissler & Carey, 2004) provided convergent evidence for Baldwin's conclusion that by 18 months, at least, the mapping infants establish between words and objects is referential, not associative, and we extended this conclusion to the relations between pictures and objects. Preissler taught 18-month-old toddlers a new word, "whisk," by repeatedly pairing it with a picture of a whisk: "This is a whisk. Can you show me the whisk, point to the whisk ... ?" After the child had learned to pick the picture of the whisk from among pictures of familiar objects, and also from pictures of unfamiliar objects, the child was given a choice between the picture of a whisk and a real whisk, and asked to "show me the whisk." If the child had learned an associative pairing between the word and the picture of the whisk, he would be expected to choose the picture. The child might also pick the real whisk, generalizing the association on the basis of perceptual similarity. However, if he knew that words refer to objects, and also that pictures do, the child would assume that the initial teaching concerned what "whisks" are—namely, the object depicted in the picture. In this case the child would be expected to pick the real whisk, although he might also sometimes pick the picture because we do use language that way—calling a picture of a whisk "a whisk," not "a picture of a whisk."

The toddlers' responses fell into the second pattern. They always (100% of the time) chose the real whisk, even though they had never seen one before and had not heard it paired with the word "whisk." They also sometimes included the picture (40% of the time). Control trials showed that it was not the salience of the real object that drove the responses; given a picture of a whisk and a different novel object, and asked to indicate the "whisk," they invariably chose the pictured whisk. Exactly the same pattern of responses was also observed in 24-month-olds.

These results will not surprise any parent, but their theoretical import bears further discussion. When we show a toddler a picture of a zebra in a book and call it a "zebra," we assume that she knows that the word refers to the real animal. Likewise, when we say, indicating the picture, "We can see a zebra in the zoo," we do not think that the child thinks we will see a picture of a zebra in the zoo. Preissler's data, along with Baldwin's, show that our assumptions are right. By 15 to 18 months of age, at least, toddlers understand the intentionality behind language use: words and pictures are analyzed as symbols. They refer to objects; they are not merely associatively paired with objects.

Gaze-Following, Pointing, and Joint Attention

The phenomona of gaze-following, pointing and showing provide further evidence concerning when infants represent agents as seeking or providing information about the world. By 9 to 12 months of age, children hold up objects for others to look at, checking back and forth between the others' eyes and the object they are apparently attempting to bring to their attention (see Tomasello, Carpenter, Call, Behne, & Moll, 2005, for a recent review of the literature on shared attention). Most researchers agree that such behavior reflects an intentional attribution on the part of the infant: the infant is attempting to get the other to attend to an object and is monitoring success. This behavior presupposes that the infant represents others' as attending to objects. But what of younger infants, those who merely follow the gaze or points of others but who do not yet point to or hold up objects to indicate them?

We know that in normal face-to-face interaction, infants begin to follow the gaze of others at around 6 months of age, and reliably do so by 10 months or so. Point following begins a few months later. Bruce Hood and his colleagues suggested that even younger infants might have the competence to follow another's gaze, but this competence might be masked by very young infants' poor control of their own attentional resources. To turn to look where the communicative partner is looking requires the infant to disengage attention from the partner. However, infants below 6 months or so have great difficulty disengaging from an attended object. To test the hypothesis that difficulty disengaging from an attended object masks competence in following gaze, Hood (B. Hood, Willen, & Driver, 1998) displayed a photograph of a face on a computer monitor in front of an infant. The eyes were centered, as if the face were looking at the infant, and it blinked for 1 second. The eyes then shifted to the left or the right and held their position for 1 second, after which the whole face disappeared (see Figure 5.5). At that point, an object appeared, to either the left or the right side of the monitor. This sudden onset of a new object in peripheral vision, with nothing attended to centrally, would of course draw attention. The question was whether the shift in eye gaze of the face on the monitor had led the infant to begin to shift attention even before the face disappeared. If so, the reaction time to shift gaze to the peripheral object would be faster and more reliable when it appeared on the same side as the eyes gazed toward. This is what was observed, and the youngest infants in the study were only 2 to 4 months old. Consistent with the hypothesis that previous failures to observe gaze-following in infants this young reflect infants' difficulty in disengaging attention, infants failed if the face stayed in place; they often did not even shift their gaze to the new object when it appeared

Perhaps the response was just to a direction of movement—the eyes shifted from center to left, and if the object appeared on the left, infants

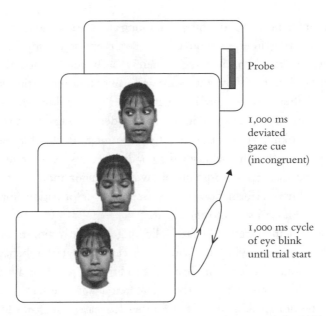

Probe

1,000 ms
deviated
gaze cue
(incongruent)

1,000 ms cycle
of eye blink
until trial start

Figure 5.5. Design of Hood et al. (1998). Reprinted from Hood, B., Willen, J. D., & Driver, J. (1998). Adults' eyes trigger shifts of visual attention in human infants. *Psychological Science, 9*(2), 131–134, with permission from Blackwell Publishers.

shifted their gaze to it more quickly than if the object appeared on the right. To check that any congruent movement would not yield the same pattern of results, Hood et al. ran a condition in which the initial view of the face had a tongue protruding centrally, accompanied by opening and closing of the mouth instead of blinking, and instead of an eye-gaze shift, the tongue moved to the extreme right or left of the mouth before the face disappeared from the monitor. There was no congruency effect in this case. Thus, these experiments establish that by 2.5 months of age, infants shift attention in the direction of another's gaze.

Rich or Lean Interpretation of Infant Gaze-Following?

Although we may all agree that very young infants shift attention in the direction of another's gaze, we certainly will not agree on what this behavior reveals about the mind of the young baby. When the child follows another's gaze or point, does the child make an agentive attribution (namely, that the other is looking at or indicating something)? This is the rich interpretation of gaze or point following behavior. Alternatively, the behavior might merely be a conditioned response (follow the gaze or follow the point and something interesting will be found), or there may simply be an innate reflex to follow the gaze of another—one that does not imply any understanding that the other person is looking at or attending to something. Both of these lean interpretations (that the behavior is a conditioned response or an innate reflex) deny that gaze- or point-following behavior indicates that the infant attributes information-seeking states or information-imparting states or attentional states to the agent.

Hood's demonstration of gaze-following at 2½ to 3 months of age is certainly consistent with the lean interpretation that this behavior is merely an innate reflex. The learned conditioned response alternative seems less likely, given the difficulty children at this age have in disengaging attention, making it difficult for them to learn that if they follow a gaze, something interesting will happen there. Notice that the hypothesized sensori-motor reflex itself has some of the properties of core cognition. It requires representations that identify eyes, such that a shift in direction of the eyes may trigger the child's shift in attention in the same direction. Any innate reflex involves representations, and so the content of those representations is an open scientific question. It seems likely that these would include both eye and face. Indeed, we know that even newborn infants have representations of faces; they preferentially attend to faces over other stimuli of comparable complexity and they imitate facial gestures of others, producing the same gesture themselves (Johnson & Morton, 1991; Meltzoff & Moore, 1994, 1999). Thus, this hypothesized "reflex" requires innate input analyzers and representations with content that go beyond mere perceptual and spatio-temporal vocabulary. But if the reflex hypothesis is correct, these representations do not provide evidence for core cognition of agency. Certainly, with respect to attribution of agency, a lean interpretation of this behavior is plausible. I know of no other converging evidence that would lead us to credit the 2-month-old infant with a representation that the other is looking at or attending to something. In other words, the representations that underlie the infant's shift of attention may well have the content "look there," rather than "look for what the other is looking at."

But although the lean interpretation is plausible, a richer interpretation is also possible, and several lines of evidence lead me to favor it. As we shall see, the ability to interpret gaze referentially has a long evolutionary history, and it has a dedicated neural substrate. Cells in the monkey's superior temporal sulcus respond selectively to direction of perceived gaze, and lesions in the homologous area in human adults disrupt their capacity to tell what others are looking at (Campbell et al., 1990; Perrett et al., 1985, 1990). Of course, that the capacity to detect direction of gaze has a dedicated neural substrate does not tell us what the content of the representations it computes are, but as we will see below, there is good evidence that monkeys and chimpanzees use eye gaze to infer others' attentional states.

Simon Baron-Cohen (1995) argues that the fact that people with autism show a selective deficit at making intentional attributions from eye gaze supports the existence of a specialized system of core cognition in normally developing people. He has shown that people with autism (even adults, in some circumstances) can tell you what direction eyes are pointed, but they cannot tell you what the person is looking at, what the person wants, or what the person is referring to with a label. Normal 3-year-olds effortlessly make all of these intentional attributions from eye gaze.

Whether or not we accept Baron-Cohen's arguments that the existence of selective deficits supports the existence of specialized representational systems (see Karmiloff-Smith, 1998, for a counterargument), can we decide between the richer and the leaner interpretations of infant gaze following on the basis of data from human infants? Two types of considerations are relevant, just as in the case of object representations. First, the more representations of eye gaze are integrated with other reflections of representations of agency, the more likely the rich interpretation becomes. Second, we must consider learnability. Once we grant that infants of a certain age represent agency, if we think that younger infants do not, and if we think that the capacity to do so is learned, we must be able to specify, at least in principle, a learning process that could do the trick.

Early in infancy, the representations that underlie gaze-following are integrated with other representations of agency. Infants much younger than those in Baldwin's word-learning studies monitor others' attentional focus in communicative situations. As mentioned above, by 9 months of age, some infants try to get communicative partners to attend to objects they are attending to, and they actively monitor that their partners are looking at what the infant is indicating. This behavior goes beyond a reflex (or conditioned response) to look in the direction of a shift of gaze, and it suggests that the infant's attempts at communication are guided by an appreciation establishing that joint reference is necessary. By this age, infants appreciate that looking at, or attention, has content.

Similar phenomena are observed in the communicative situation called "social referencing." By 9 months of age, infants look to communicative partners when placed in novel situations, such as a visual cliff (an apparent drop-off in depth, visually, but a clear Plexiglas surface) or a novel object. They monitor the partner's expression. If the partner exhibits fear or disgust, they do hold back; if the partner is happy and encouraging, they explore the novel situation. Using the same logic as in her word-learning studies cited above, Dare Baldwin and Lou Moses (1994) showed that by 9 months of age, in social-referencing situations, infants know that expressions of fear and disgust have content—one is afraid of something or disgusted by something. They showed that infants monitor where the mother is looking when she expresses fear or disgust. If the infant is looking at a novel object when the mother expresses disgust, the infant immediately looks to the mother's eyes. If the mother is looking elsewhere, the infant does not assume that the object he or she was looking at when the mother said "Oh, yuk" in a tone dripping with disgust is disgusting. Emotional terms have content; one is disgusted by something, and where the eyes are pointed is relevant to establishing what that something is.

Recent studies by Yuyan Luo and her colleagues provide evidence that infants integrate representations of an agent's attentional focus with representations of that agent's goals by 6-months of age. These important studies begin with an observation that forces a slight reinterpretation of phenomenon tapped in the Woodward reaching paradigm. Luo and Baillargeon (2005; see also Song, Baillargeon, and Fisher, 2005) showed that infants' look longer when an agent approaches or reaches toward a new goal object in Woodward's paradigm only if both potential goal objects were present during the familiarization/habituation trials. Apparently, infants interpret those familiarization trials as providing evidence concerning an agent's preference between two objects, rather than providing evidence merely that the agent has a goal to reach for a particular object. This is actually quite rational. If you see me reach 9 times for an apple when I have a choice between an apple and a banana, you would be warranted in concluding I prefer the apple and might be surprised if on a 10th trial I reached for the banana. But if you see me reach for an apple 9 times when it is the only food present, you might have no prediction about what I would want when given a choice between an apple and a banana.

Luo asked whether infants understand that an agent can express a preference between two objects only if he or she can perceive both of them. In two studies (12-month-olds: Luo and Baillargeon, 2007; 6-month-olds: Luo and Johnson, in press) Lou found evidence that this is so. In each of these studies infants watched as an agent reached repeatedly and grasped one of two goal objects visible to the child on the stage. However, if one these two objects was not visible to the agent (because the agent had her back to it, or because it was blocked by a barrier that prevented the agent, but not the infant, from seeing it), the child reacted as in the one-object conditions described above. That is, the child did not look longer when the agent now could see both objects and reached for the one that they had not reach for during familiarization.

These experiments show that 6- to 12-month-olds understand what John Flavell called "Level 1 perspective taking." That is, infants appear to understand that an agent can see an object only if there is a direct line of sight between the agent's eyes or face and the object in question. Contrary to the lean interpretation of infants' gaze following, these studies establish that infants understand that attention/perception provides the agent with information about the world, and that the information available to an agent is relevant to that agent's preferences and goals.

Finally, 9- to 18-month-old infants infer more than attentional content and predictions about future goal seeking behavior from people's gaze and emotional expression. If an adult playing with an infant engages in activities that are ambiguous with respect to the intentions, the infant looks to the adult's face. For example, if the infant is playing with an object, the adult might cup her hand over the infant's hands, preventing motion. Is this a game, a tease, or is the adult communicating that there is something dangerous? Or if the infant is reaching for an object, the adult may pull it away just as the infant is about to grasp it. Again, the adult's intentions are ambiguous. These interactions may be contrasted with unambiguous activities, in which the adult merely offers and gives infants interesting objects. In the cases of the ambiguous actions, but not the unambiguous ones, even infants as young as 8 months look to the adult's faces, specifically his or her eyes. Infants are apparently trying to read the adult's intentions (is this a game or something else), not just the adult's attentional focus.

Thus, very shortly after infants have control of their own eye gaze (i.e., can voluntarily control where they look), they seek information from where others are looking to make intentional attributions. They look to another's gaze to establish what that other person was afraid of or disgusted at, what that person can see, whether that other person is attending to what the infants are showing them, and to glean some information about that other person's intentions in ambiguous situations. By this age, representations of where others are looking have a much richer inferential role than merely directing the infant's attention in a reflex manner.

Lean and Rich Interpretations of Gaze-Following—Entities Without Eyes

Both of the lean interpretations of gaze-following (innate reflex, conditioned response) assume that the input to the reflex or learned association is a human face or eyes. But as we saw above, at least in the case of goal attribution, infants and adults reason about the motions of geometric figures, entities without faces or eyes, in terms of the goals of their actions, the environmental constraints, and a principle of rationality. If goal attribution and reasoning about perceptual and attentional states are truly integrated, then infants should reason about the attentional states of entities without eyes or faces as well, and the stimulus characteristics that lead infants to attribute goals should also lead them to attribute attention. What little work there is on the stimulus characteristics that elicit representations of actions as goal-directed suggests that they involve contingency between the actors and the environment. Is the same information used in the attribution of attentional states as well?

Susan Johnson, Virginia Slaughter, and I (1998; following earlier work by Movellan & Watson, not published until 2002) asked whether evidence of communicative contingency between a baby and a robot would be sufficient for the infant to attribute that the robot was capable of attending to objects in the world. In other words, would infants follow a shift in the attention of a faceless or eyeless robot? If so, under what circumstances? The experiment ran as follows: infants were seated on their mothers' laps facing a stuffed robot. The robot was asymmetrical and initially "facing" to the side; it had a light on the top of its highest part. An experimenter faced the robot, said "Hi," upon which the robot "answered" with a single tone. The experimenter then said, "How are you?," upon which the robot "answered" with a three-tone sequence. The experimenter then waved, and the robot flashed the light in response. The robot then turned 90 degrees, so that the same side that had been facing the experimenter now faced the baby.

A 1-minute period ensued such that any vocalization the infant made was answered by the robot, and any hand or foot motion of the baby was answered by a light flash. This was a low-tech robot—hidden experimenters watching the baby controlled the sounds and light flashes. After this minute, the robot "turned" 45 degrees to the left or to the right, "looking at" objects on the wall to the left or the right of the baby. The dependent measure was whether the baby followed the robot's "attention." (Remember, there is no gaze to follow here; the robots lacked faces or eyes.) The answer was yes, and just as much as in a comparison condition in which infants were interacting with a communicative partner who was a human being.

Data from a control condition established that the infants were not simply following the turning of the robot. A second condition was a yoked control to the first; the babies saw the same introductory events. After the robot turned to face the baby, the robot's actions (sounds made and light flashing) were not contingent on the vocalizations or arm/leg motions of that baby, but were rather those that had been contingent on the actions of the previous baby. Thus, infants in the yoked control group saw a behaving robot, indeed, exactly as much behavior as the experimental group they were yoked to. However, when the robot turned 45 degrees, the infants in the yoked control group did not turn to follow its "gaze." The robot must respond contingently to the baby for the infant to represent the turning of the robot to reflect a shift in the robot's attention or the robot's attempt to draw the child's attention to something new.

Two other conditions established that the presence of a face is also sufficient to elicit gaze-following. In these conditions, the robot had a face on the front of the highest protuberance. The light on the top of the head was removed, and now the eyes flashed in response to hand or leg motions. Not surprisingly, the infants in the contingent reaction group turned to follow the gaze of the robot. Indeed, the degree of gaze-following was identical whether the entity was a person, a contingently responding robot with a face, or a contingently responding robot with no face. Importantly, in this condition, the infants in the yoked control group also followed the gaze of the robot—a noncontingently responding entity that made sounds, had flashing eyes, and had a face. Again, the degree of gaze-following was identical to the other three conditions. Apparently, agents capable of attentional states may be identified in two different ways: by analyzing their behavior and from the presence of a face and eyes. These two cues to agency are not additive—the degree of gaze following to a contingently responding robot with a face or to a contingently responding person with a face was no greater than to a contingently responding robot without a face, or a behaving, but noncontingently responding, robot with a face. The failure of the infants to follow the gaze of the faceless robot whose behavior had not been contingent on the baby's behavior tells us that under these conditions at least, contingency is important for the attribution of the referential/attentional aspects of agency. This robot behaved, and even moved on its own; it turned on its own. Even the experimenter's brief modeling of communicating with the robot was not sufficient.

These data support the richer interpretation of gaze-following for two reasons. First, neither lean interpretation (learned association between gaze shift and something interesting in the direction of the gaze, reflexive following of gaze shift) can explain the gaze-following of the faceless or eyeless contingently responding robot. Second, this experiment provides further evidence that by 12 months of age, infants have integrated two different aspects of agency representations; those agents who can respond contingently to the environment are those that attend to it. Inferential integration of different aspects of agency lends support to the rich interpretation of experiments that establish infants' representations of each aspect independently.

Integrated Representatiions of Agents—Goals and Attentional States

As mentioned above, evidence that gaze-following is integrated with representations of an agent's goals provides the basis for a richer interpretation of both the phenomenon of gaze-following and the phenomena that suggest infants make a teleological construal of events. Susan Johnson and her colleagues (Johnson, Shimizu, & Ok, 2007; Shimizu & Johnson, 2004) have extended the gaze-following robot results to a robot even less animal looking than the brown furry one in the above studies— a blue cylindrical plastic object. She finds that if that this object interacts contingently with the child or the child sees it interact contingently with an experimenter, it elicits gaze-following by the child. She also finds that the baby's seeing this object interacting contingently with an experimenter increases the probability of teleological attributions to it when the child sees it subsequently move repeatedly toward a novel goal. Again, representations of attentional states and of goal-directed motion are integrated by infants of this age, supporting the rich interpretation of each.

Melinda Carpenter and her colleagues (Carpenter, Nagell, & Tomasello, 1998) carried out an extensive longitudinal study of 24 infants between the ages of 9 and 15 months to explore the degree to which different aspects of agent representations emerge together. They found that the emergence of joint attentional engagement, gaze- and point-following, imperative and declarative gestures, and imitation of novel actions on objects were positively correlated, whereas these measures were uncorrelated with performance on tasks of object permanence or spatial reasoning. They concluded that representations of actions in terms of goals (necessary for imitation) and of attentional and information providing actions are two instances of the same underlying phenomenon —namely, the representation of intentional agency.

Of course, as many have noted, it is always possible to offer a lean interpretation of all these results. As Povinelli (Povinelli & Eddy, 1996) has argued in the case of chimpanzees, perhaps that child has merely learned very complex rules for predicting others' behaviors—rules like: (1) if an entity responds contingently to another, and the side facing me turns away, that side is likely to be facing something interesting; or (2) if an entity responds contingently to another, and then subsequently moves repeatedly to a particular object, it is more likely to continue to move to that object than if it hasn't been observed responding contingently to another entity; or (3) if there is no object between an entity's face and two objects, and if an entity repeatedly moves toward one of these two objects, the entity is likely to continue to move toward that one. But what would support learning just these rules? Purely inductive statistical learning over perceptual primitives is wildly unconstrained. Core cognition of agency provides the needed constraints. In my view, the more parsimonious interpretation is that contingent response triggers the attribution of agency, including the capacity for attention to external entities (the child himself, the object of the gaze), and it is these representations that are the input to statistical learning mechanisms.

The Input Analyzers?

To reiterate the argument so far, representing events in terms of attentional states, referential states and goal-directedness is part of core cognition of agents. Agent representations are conceptual in the sense of requiring representations not expressible in spatio-temporal vocabulary, as well in the sense of having a rich inferential role, not only drawing together different aspects of agent representations but also integrating agent representations with causal reasoning about inanimate objects (see chapter 6). The most important hurdle for a candidate core domain has been cleared: evidence for a system of representation with conceptual content early in infancy. I now comment on other features of core cognition in this domain.

The claim that agency is a core domain requires that there be innate input analyzers that identify the entities in it. How do infants recognize some entities as agents and some behaviors as goal directed or referential? Elizabeth Spelke and I (Carey & Spelke, 1994) considered two alternatives concerning the nature of the hypothesized input analyzers:

Possibility 1: Innate face recognizers enable the infant to categorize entities as people, and people are innately recognized as agents.

Possibility 2: Agents are identified through analyses of their actions. Contingent reaction to the child or to the environment, self-generated motion, and so on are sufficient for attributions of attentional states and goals.

Notice that on the second possibility, the way infants may come to recognize people as intentional agents is by analyzing their actions.

Spelke and I argued for the second possibility, on the basis of experiments that show that infants see faceless continently reacting bags of cloth and geometric figures on computer screens as agents. But Hood's gaze-following results with 2- to 4-month-olds pose problems for this position. It is possible that infants this young have analyzed the actions of human beings, and have learned that they are agents, what their fronts are from analyses of goal-directed actions, and that eyes are especially informative about attended entities. I think it more likely that the gaze-following mechanism involves a separate innate input analyzer.

I now believe that there is no reason we must choose between possibilities 1 and 2, for both could be true. Agent detection is likely to be a problem of such significance for humans that evolution has built more than one redundant mechanism to contribute to its solution. The situation may be parallel to the imprinting story for chicks. Conspecific/mother identification is so important a problem for the survival of geese and chickens that evolution endowed newborn chicks with two different innate input analyzers dedicated to the problem, one that identifies things that look like birds and one that identifies things that move in a certain way (Johnson, Bolhuis, & Horn, 1985; Lorenz, 1937; see also chapter 1). Similarly, it certainly possible that evolution built specific mechanisms for face and eye detection, including specific computations relevant to representations of agency, and also built mechanisms that identify agentive behavior from patterns of motion and interaction among potential agents and the world. Call the latter the agency-from-action input analyzer.

Infants certainly compute agency from action, as they do so when analyzing the actions of moving geometric figures and nonanimal puppets and robots. But as we saw above, Woodward showed that the identity of the moving entity repeatedly ending in contact with a potential goal (a hand versus a stick with finger-looking sponge appendages) influences whether 5-month-old infants attribute goals to the entity. Subsequent work showed that infants at this young age can attribute goals to such nonhand objects, so long as the spatio-temporal evidence for equipotentiality and multiple paths to the goal is stronger (Gergely & Csibra, 2002). Still, Woodward's demonstration that identifying the moving figure as a hand helps disambiguate an action at 5 months of age holds. It is possible that analysis of contingency is at the root of all goal attribution, including attribution of the goal of reaching, and infants have merely had massive experience with the contingency between grasping human hands and the objects they pick up. That is, the intentionality-from-action input analyzer may underlie learning about hands as potential agents of goals. But is also likely that evolution built in representations of grasping as goal-directed; after all, reaching for objects is probably the first systematic goal-directed activity the child has control over, and thus both reaching and visual recognition of acts of reaching may have innate support.

An Aside: The Like-Me Hypothesis

One of my favorite results from developmental cognitive science is Meltzoff and Moore's (1994, 1999) demonstrations that young infants imitate the facial gestures of people they are interacting with. Open your mouth wide, and your newborn will do the same. Ditto for sticking out your tongue (see Myowa-Yamakoshi, Tomonaga, Tanaka, & Matsuzawa, 2004, for comparable findings with a newborn chimp). These demonstrations converge with other evidence for innate input analyzers that represent human faces. More important here, they show also that infants innately recognize the intermodal correspondence between what some other person's face looks like and their own facial gestures. Building on these and similar observations, Meltzoff has suggested that infants may come to represent other agent's actions as intentional on the basis of an understanding of their own intentional agency, plus the capacity to recognize others as "like me."

The demonstrations that categorization of an actor as a person (or part of a person) increase the likelihood of intentional attributions are consistent with this hypothesis. One of these was mentioned above: Woodward's finding that equifinal motions of hands were treated as goal-directed, whereas equifinal motions of sticks with sponges on the end were not. Indeed, other research by Woodward has shown that infants understand the intentionality in pointing only after they themselves have begun to point. And a recent study by Jessica Somerville, Amanda Woodward, and Amy Needham (2005) provides further evidence that there definitely is something in the Like-Me hypothesis. These authors gave 3-month-old infants experience with a mitten covered in Velcro, such that the infant could pick up fuzzy objects simply by contacting them. Infants quickly learned to use the sticky mitten. After this experience, infants were run in the traditional Woodward paradigm—an adult wearing an identical mitten repeatedly contacted a given object in a given location (one of two objects present in the scene). On test trials, the locations of the objects were switched, and the adult either reached to the old location/new object or the new location/old object. Only infants who had themselves experienced the sticky mitten looked longer when the adult reached for the new object. This result is important for several reasons. First, it pushes the representation of goal-directed behavior down to the youngest age yet—3 months. Second, it shows that in this situation (involving reaching), only if the infant herself has carried out the relevant goal-directed activity does she represent another's action as goal-directed. Note that this is not in general the case—in Gergely and Csibra's experiments described above geometric figures carry out actions that the infant cannot yet do (and in some case will never do).

The Like-Me hypothesis seems likely to be true. Infants' representations of themselves as agents does help them analyze others' actions as goal directed, when these actions are seen as relevantly similar to goal-directed actions in the infants' repertoire. However, it is important to realize that the Like-Me hypothesis is not an account of where the capacity for representations of agency comes from, for two clear reasons. Most important, babies can use their own agency to understand others' only if they represent themselves as agents. Infants not only must be intentional agents (which surely they are), but they must represent themselves so. If they can do that, they already have representations with contents like *goal*, *looking at*, *agent*, and so forth. Second, the Like-Me hypothesis is underspecified. It leaves entirely open what features of similarity to the baby support the identification. The experiments sketched above suggest the person-recognition input analyzers play an important role (the agent must look like a hand or have the features of a face), but we have also seen that infants can use patterns of motion alone as a basis for intentional attributions. Thus, the Like-Me hypothesis, although probably right, does not solve either of the outstanding questions at issue in the present discussion: the origin of agency representations or the nature of the input analyzers that identity agents, their goals, their attentional focus, and their referential intent. It does add another important piece to the story—evidence that the child indeed does represent its own actions as goal directed and can use representations of its own actions in making attributions of agency to others.

Constant Through the Life Span?

One of the earmarks of core cognition is that the innate input analyzers operate throughout the life span. And indeed, adults make intentional attributions on the basis of monitoring both eye-gaze and patterns of contingency among actors. Obviously, adults follow eye-gaze and understand a shift of gaze to reflect a shift of attention. Not so obviously, adults also compute intentionality from patterns of motion alone. Heider and Simmel's (1944) classic studies, in which adults described interacting geometric figures in language rich with intentional attributions, show this. Heider and Simmel created a rich animated clip in which geometric figures moving on a screen are seen to chase each other, escape, hide, try to break down barriers, and so on. Here's a sample description:

> A man has planned to meet a girl and the girl comes along with another man. The first man tells the second to go; the second tells the first, and he shakes his head. Then the two men have a fight, and the girl starts to go into the room to get out of the way and hesitates and finally goes in. She apparently does not want to be with the first man. The first man follows her into the room after having left the second in a rather weakened condition leaning on the wall outside the room. The girl gets worried and races from one corner to the other in the far part of the room. Man number one, after being rather silent for a while, makes several approaches at her; but she gets to the corner across from the door, just as man number two is trying

to open it. He evidently got banged around and is still weak from his efforts to open the door. The girl gets out of the room in a sudden dash just as man number two gets the door open. The two chase around the outside of the room together, followed by man number one. But they finally elude him and get away. The first man goes back and tries to open his door, but he is so blinded by rage and frustration that he cannot open it. So he butts it open and in a really mad dash around the room he breaks in first one wall and then another. (pp. 246–247)

And the exception that proves the rule—one adult in Heider and Simmel's original sample of 34 described the movies thus:

A large solid triangle is shown entering a rectangle. It enters and comes out of this rectangle, and each time the corner and one-half of the sides of the rectangle form an opening. Then another, smaller triangle and a circle appear on the scene. The circle enters the rectangle while the larger triangle is within. The two move about in circular motion and then the circle goes out of the opening and joins the smaller triangle, which has been moving around outside the rectangle. Then the smaller triangle and the circle move about together and when the larger triangle comes out of the rectangle and approaches them, they move rapidly in a circle around the rectangle and disappear. The larger triangle, now alone, moves about the opening of the rectangle and finally goes through the opening to the inside. He [sic] moves rapidly within, and finding no opening, breaks through the sides and disappears. (p. 246)

Many subsequent studies have confirmed the finding that adults attribute intentionality to displays of moving geometric figures, and researchers have begun to explore the psychophysical bases of these judgments (e.g., Gelman, Durgin, & Kaufman, 1995). Although the actual movies presented to infants in the studies described above have not been systematically studied, I have seen these movies and there is no doubt that this adult automatically sees the actions displayed there in terms of intentional agency. Wagner and I had naïve adults describe the movies depicted in Figure 5.1. Their descriptions used intentional language and/or personified the balls in 75% of their descriptions of events in which infants inferred a goal (Figure 5.1), as opposed to only 13% of the movies in which the infants did not infer a goal.

Susan Johnson (2003) pursued the question of continuity much more systematically. She showed adults videotapes of an experimenter interacting with the robot (with or without eyes, responding contingently or not), after which the robot turned. The adult was simply why the robot turned. The language used to describe the robot was shot through with intentionality in exactly the same three conditions that babies followed the robot's gaze; in the condition in which the babies did not follow the gaze (faceless, noncontingent behavior), adults used almost no intentional language. For example, in explaining the turning of the faceless contingent robot: "Maybe it was looking for someone and tried to figure out where it was," and description of the faceless, noncontingently beeping and flashing, robot: "The thing turned due to a program. It was programmed according to the sounds. After so many, the thing rotated."

Thus, it appears that the input module that derives representations of agency from action continues to operate throughout the life span. The representational systems that accomplish these feats display common psychophysical and processing signatures in infancy and in adulthood. Core cognition of agency is continuous over development in the same sense as is core cognition of objects (chapter 3) and number (chapter 4). Recently, Henry Wellman and his colleagues have tested a strong prediction of the continuity thesis (Wellman, Phillips, Dunply-Lelii, & LaLonde, 2004; Wellman, Lopez-Duran, LaBounty, & Hamilton, 2007). Systems of core cognition are learning mechanisms. Later developing representations of agents are built from those in core cognition. If this is true, then individual differences in the robustness or elaboration of agent representations in infancy might be reflected in individual differences in the course of later developments in theory of mind. In two different studies, Wellman and his colleagues found just that.

Phillips, Wellman and Spelke (2002) had studied the integration of infants' representations of agents' focus of attention with their representations of agents goals. They found that at 14 months of age, infants looked longer when an agent looked at and expressed positive emotion toward one of two objects, and then reached for and picked up the other of the two (as opposed to picking up the object that was the focus of the attention and positive emotion). The Phillips study used a lengthy familiarization procedure, in which infants saw an agent repeatedly express positive emotion toward and pick up one of the objects; in a Woodward type design, the test trials involved a switch of the two objects, such that the surprising outcome involved picking up the object that had been picked up during familiarization. The authors noted that infants differed in their degree of habituation during the familiarization period. Some barely decreased looking at all whereas others quickly became bored. Wellman and his colleagues brought the children who had been in the infant studies back to the lab several years later. In two different studies (Wellman et al., 2004, in press), individual differences among infants in the decrement of attention to these events during habituation predicted performance on a preschool theory of mind battery at age 4.

But wait—we know that speed of encoding during infancy predicts later IQ (Bornstein & Sigman, 1986; Fagan & McGrath, 1981), and IQ is highly correlated with measures of individual differences in executive function. We wouldn't be surprised to learn that children with higher IQs achieve the preschool theory of mind milestones earlier than do children with lower IQs. But Wellman showed that the prediction of individual differences in the preschool theory of mind tasks was undiminished if he controlled variance in IQ or executive function.

In sum, core cognition of agency is continuous throughout development in two related senses. The input analyzers that compute agency from patterns of interaction among entities continue operate throughout life, and the representations of agents that are the output of these analyzers are one source of later developing conceptions of agents.

Why So Late? Are Representations of Agency the Output of Innate Input Analyzers?

Although some of the phenomena described in this chapter are observed in infants under 6 months of age (Hood's gaze-following phenomena and Woodward's goal-directed reaching phenomena), most are not robust until 6 to 9 months of age or later. Should such late emergence raise doubts concerning core cognition in this domain? Does it undermine the hypothesis that the representations in this domain are the output of innate input analyzers? As we have seen in the case of core object cognition, the core cognition hypothesis is consistent with late emergence of behaviors that reflect it. First, in some cases performance factors unrelated to the representations articulating core cognition interfere with the behaviors that might reveal it. Examples we have considered include frontal lobe immaturity masking competence in tasks reflecting representations of spatio-temporally continuous objects (chapter 2) and immaturity in control of attentional resources masking competence in gaze-following. Second, in other cases, the neural substrate of the innate input analyzers or domain-specific learning mechanisms may itself mature relatively late. Late emergence may have a maturational explanation rather than a learning explanation. I do not know whether such maturational factors play a role in this case, but there are reasons to think they may. Available evidence supports frontal lobe involvement in the representations of other minds, and the frontal lobes are late maturing (Diamond & Goldman-Rakic, 1989). Finally, the core cognition hypothesis is not incompatible with learning. Quite the contrary, core cognition systems are domain-specific learning devices (remember the indigo buntings). Even assuming core cognition of agency, learning dependent upon innate conceptual representations would certainly be implicated in the current case. Infants must learn what agents look like in order to form categories of kinds of intentional agents. Infants must analyze patterns of contingency in order to learn about particular goals or particular environmental constraints. And it is possible that cognition in this domain is supported by partially distinct systems of core cognition (e.g., the eye-gaze computation device, the agency-from-action input analyzer) and that learning is required to integrate them.

Indeed, there is only one learning account that is inconsistent with core cognition of intentionality, and that is the empiricist position that the innate representations in this domain are perceptual or sensori-motor. On the empiricist view, the capacities to represent agents, goals, and attentional states emerge as the result of some learning mechanism that takes perceptual or sensori-motor representations as input and yields representations with such content as output. Many psychologists hold a version of the view. For example, consider Jean Mandler's (1992, 2004) account of the origin of the concept *animal* (see also Rakison & Poulin-Dubois, 2001, for a closely related proposal). Mandler maintains that the concept *animal* has a conceptual core (self-moving agent), and that the capacity to represent this conceptual core is learned. The problem, then, is how it is learned. Mandler posits, and I obviously agree, that infants are sensitive to properties of motion—paths, self generation, contingency. These can be cashed out in spatio-temporal terms. But the question is how representations of agency might be learned, even given sensitivity to such parameters of motion. The question, which should now be familiar, is how learning generalizations stated in sensori-motor vocabulary could ever lead to a representation with the content *goal* or *agent* or *attention*.

Here is how Mandler thinks about this problem. She is concerned with the transition between perceptual representations and conceptual ones, and she thinks of the distinction as one of processing. Conceptual representations support memory and action, and they serve as the core of kind representations. She suggests that the infant produces conceptual categories from perceptual input through a process of active, attentive, perceptual analysis. Visual information is redescribed into a simpler and explicitly realized form, most likely in the format of an image schema, but perhaps in a more abstract format. The content of these explicit representations includes the paths objects take, plus various relations among objects such as containment, support, contact, and contingent relations. So far, these contents are still statable in a sensori-motor vocabulary. These redescribed representations are conceptual in the sense of being explicit and accessible—an image schema constitutes a symbol in memory that supports recall, computations in working memory, and so on.

I find these suggestions plausible. But the question that concerns me is the origin of representations that are conceptual in a different sense—in the sense of having content that goes beyond spatio-temporal vocabulary. There is no known way that perceptual analysis alone could do the trick of transforming representations of spatiotemporal properties into representations of intentional agency. Abstracted image schemas of paths, contingent interactions, and so on still represent paths, contingent interactions, and so on. I agree with Mandler that the format of representations of intentional agency is likely to be iconic, just as for other core cognition systems (see chapter 4). But the question is where image schemas with the representational content of the domain of agency come from. How does an image schema come to represent attentional states, goals, and agents rather than self-generated motions, movement from

A to B, simultaneity? If one cannot define agency in spatio-temporal vocabulary (even though spatio-temporal representations provide suffi-cient input to perceptual analyzers that output representations of agents, their goals, and their attentional states), then the problem of how these concepts arise has not been solved.

In addition to these bare learnability considerations, this chapter has developed many other arguments against the empiricist learning account. In some cases the age of the infants, along with considerations of lim-itations on the inputs they could possibly have experienced, casts doubt on some plausible learning accounts. To repeat, that 2-month-olds shift attention in response to shifts in another's gaze is very unlikely to be the result of a learned generalization: look in the direction those black circles inside white circles shift direction toward, because something interesting will be found there. Children so young cannot easily disengage attention from an attended face, so they are unlikely to have the experience that would be the input to learning this generalization. Similarly, but more weakly, doubts were raised about the possibility that infants learn about chasing and approaching events involving jumping over huge barriers or squeezing between gaps in barriers by observation, simply because they probably never see such events. In addition, I summarized the evidence that different aspects of agency representations are closely integrated throughout development. This integration is important for two reasons. It provides evidence for the conceptual role of these representations and makes it unlikely that the behaviors we see should be characterized in merely spatio-temporal vocabulary. Also, that the representations of different aspects of agency emerge together in development is not what would be expected on a view of piecemeal learning of contingencies among environmental events described in a spatio-temporal vocabulary.

These arguments are not conclusive, of course. The empiricist/ rationalist debate has engaged thinkers for over 2,000 years. It will be no easier to settle in a particular case than it has been to settle in general. Still, these considerations lead me to favor the core cognition hypothesis over the empiricist alternative in the case of agent representations, just as in the case of object representations.

Long Evolutionary History?

As reviewed in chapter 3, the evolutionary history of the core cognition of objects extends far into our primate past. Similarly, the hypothesis that there is core cognition of intentional agency presupposes that representations of goals, agents, and attentional/referential states arose during evolution as the result of selection pressures. Two possibilities are consistent with the core cognition hypothesis. Mind-reading abilities may be a specific human adaptation, one of the central capacities that distinguishes us from our nonhuman primate ancestors. Alternatively, like object representations, the capacity for agent representation may be part of our primate heritage.

Many people have argued for the first possibility—that nonhuman primates, even chimpanzees, do not represent agents and their actions in terms of goals, referential actions, attentional or perceptual states. Primates do not establish shared attention; they do not point, indicate, or monitor whether their partner shares attention on a third object. Also, primates do not teach and, to a first approximation, they do not imitate. Seeing a human or another primate acquire something attractive via some kind of tool use does make it more likely that a chimpanzee will explore that tool, but it will be as likely to discover a nonmodeled means to an end as the modeled one. Thus, it seems as if the chimpanzee fails to analyze the modeler's actions telelogically or causally. These observations are certainly consistent with the hypothesis that nonhuman primates lack the core cognition of agency exhibited by young infants (e.g., Povinelli, 2000; Tomasello & Call, 1997).

On the other hand, nonhuman primates have neural mechanisms that specialize in the detection of eye gaze, and chimpanzees follow a gaze shift. In the wild, *Rhesus* macaques and other primates have been observed hiding objects from the gaze of dominant individuals. Of course, such observations are consistent with both lean and rich interpretations. Following a shift in eye gaze may be a reflex, and primates may simply learn to take into account eye gaze in the prediction of future actions of conspecifics.

Indeed, Daniel Povinelli and Timothy Eddy (1996) provided striking data in support of the lean interpretation of chimpanzee eye gaze. They first confirmed that their chimpanzee subjects followed eye gaze and they also set up a situation in which chimpanzees knew to beg from a human in order to be given a goodie on a plate in front of the person. Povenelli then put two humans, each in front of a plate with good stuff on it, varying whether each human could know what was on the plate. For instance (see Figure 5.6), one was turned toward the plate, one away; one had her eyes covered and one her mouth; one had a bucket over her head and one did not. The dependent measure was which one the chimpanzees begged from. The chimps were dreadful at this task, succeeding (and this only after months of experience) only in the condition of Figure 5.7a, where one person was turned entirely backwards. From these studies, Povenelli and Eddy concluded that chimpanzees do not understand the relations between seeing and knowing.

However, recent work questions this conclusion. Brian Hare and his colleagues (Hare, Call, Agnetta, & Tomasello, 2000) noted that chimpanzees, like other primates, do not beg food from each other. Primates simply do not use shared attention in the service of cooperation. Hare reasoned that nonhuman primates might display an understanding of the relation between seeing and knowing in experimental situations that exploited their competitive, as opposed to their cooperative, motivational structure. This finding would be consistent with observations of primates in the wild hiding food or an erection from a more dominant animal. In the first study to explore this hypothesis, Hare set up situations such as those diagrammed in Figure 5.7. A subordinate chimpanzee watched as a piece of food was hidden. The important experimental manipulation was whether the dominant chimp, visible to the subordinate one, also saw where it was hidden. When released into the area of the food, the subordinate chimpanzees went for the food that the dominant ones had not seen hidden, as if they realized that this was food that the latter would not know about and thus would not compete for.

Laurie Santos and her collaborators have extended these results to Rhesus macaques. They carried out their research on the island of Cayo Santiago, off the coast of Puerto Rico, that was described in chapter 4. The macaques there forage for tasty food to supplement their adequate but rather boring diet of monkey chow. The monkeys are particularly interested in the fruits that the humans bring for lunch when they are carrying out observational studies on the island. Monkeys will sometimes try to steal a piece, although they are usually afraid to approach a human.

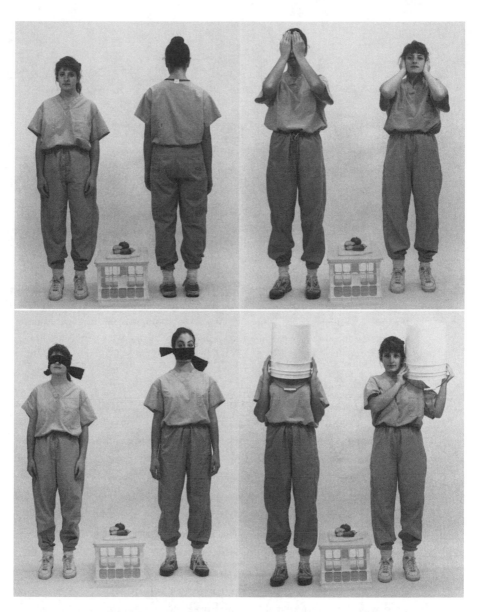

Figure 5.6. Examples of pairs of people chimps must chose between to beg for food.
From Povinelli & Eddy (1996). Povinelli, D. J., & Eddy, T. J. (1996). What young chimpanzees
know about seeing. *Monographs of the Society for Research in Child Development, 247*, with permission
from Blackwell Publishers.

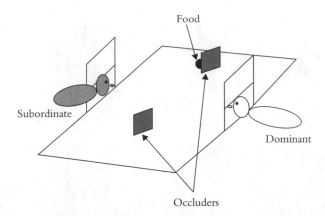

Figure 5.7. Schematic depiction of the design of one of the trials in Hare, Call & Tomesello (2000). The subordinate chimp watches the food being placed; the dominant chimp does not see the placement. The dependent measure is whether the subordinate chimp tries to get the food, relative to trials where the dominant chimp can see the food. Both chimps are free to move around. Reprinted from Hare, B., Call, J., Agnetta, B., & Tomasello, M. (2000). Chimpanzees know what conspecifics do and do not see. *Animal Behaviour, 59,* 771–786, with permission from Elsevier.

Johnathan Flombaum and Laurie Santos (2005) carried out a series of studies in which two humans approached a single monkey, stopping some meters away, equally spaced to the left and the right of the monkey. They put two platforms on the ground, each having one grape on it. What was varied was the experimenters' visual access to the grape (see Figure 5.8). In one study one experimenter had his back turned to the monkey, whereas the other looked at the grape. In another, one experimenter's eyes pointed to the side, whereas the other looked at the grape. And in still another, one experimenter covered his eyes with a square of paper while the other covered his mouth. In each of these cases, the monkey retrieved the grape from the platform of the experimenter who was not looking at it (Flombaum & Santos, 2005).

Both groups of researchers (Hare et al., Flombaum & Santos) have confirmed these results in different related paradigms. For example, if a grape seen by the monkey rolls from one location to another, the monkey uses whether the experimenter/competitor could have seen this motion (because it is screened or not) to decide whether to try to retrieve

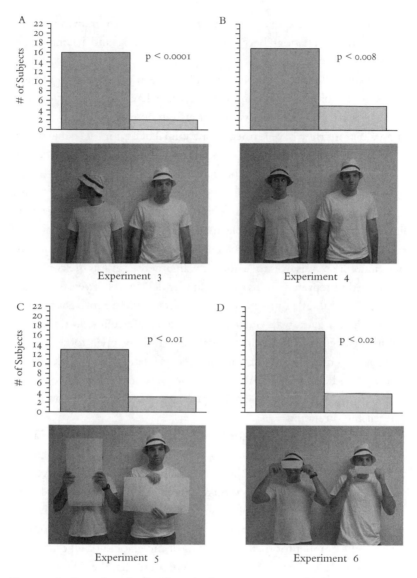

Figure 5.8. Examples of pairs of people rhesus macaques could choose among if attempting to steal food from one of the them (from Flombaum & Santos, 2005). Reprinted from Flombaum, J. I., & Santos, L. R. (2005). Rhesus monkeys attribute perceptions to others. *Current Biology, 15,* 447–452, with permission from Elsevier.

it. Altogether, these studies make a strong case that nonhuman primates understand the relations between seeing something and having information about it.

Of course, just as in the infant studies, a lean interpretation of these results is possible. Povinelli and his colleagues have argued that the primates' behavior in competitive situations can be understood in terms of generalizations they have learned about animal behavior—generalizations such as "where somebody is looking predicts where he will go" or "where somebody is looking predicts what he will reach for"—rather than generalization about seeing and information. As in the case of the related controversy between rich and lean interpretations of the infant literature, it is nearly impossible to provide conclusive arguments that might decide between the two classes of interpretation. In the animal case we cannot help ourselves to learnability arguments, for it is the content of primate adult representations that are under debate. As of yet, there have been fewer studies of just how interconnected these representations of primate looking are with other representations of agency, so this line of argumentation for the rich interpretation is also not open to us. Indeed, there has been little study of primates' representations of actions as goal-directed, and we know that primates are deficient, relative to young babies, in many aspects of agent representations (joint attention, social referencing, imitation).

Santos and her collaborators make what I consider a decisive argument for the rich interpretation (Santos, Flombaum, & Phillips, 2006). First, as I argued for infants, they point out that the lean interpretation leaves it a mystery how the monkey picks the correct statistical generalizations about behavior. For instance, every time eyes are pointed at an object, so are mouths and noses, yet in the above studies, the monkeys avoided the competitor that was looking at the grape, not whose mouth was pointing at the grape. Second, they point out that the Rhesus studies involve spontaneous behavior. These animals have not been trained. In Povinelli and Eddy's cooperative behavior studies, months of training led chimpanzees to form the generalization that people whose whole body is facing them are more likely to cooperate if begged from than are people whose whole body is facing away. Povenelli's studies show that the kind of learning procedure called for in the lean interpretation surely exist. But in Santos's studies, the monkeys selectively focus on eyes in a first and only trial. Given the competitive ecological niche the monkeys exist in, core cognition of eye gaze predicting the information another animal will have would be expected to be drawn upon spontaneously in competitive situations.

In the light of these results, Tomasello (Tomasello et al., 2005) has modified his earlier hypothesis that nonhuman primates lack representations of agency, attentional states, or goals. He now argues that these representational capacities extend far into our evolutationary past. Still, one must not forget that the human capacities for imitation, shared attention, and referential behavior are dramatically greater than are those of non-human primates. Several researchers are at work trying to characterize how human core cognition of agency may be richer than that of nonhuman primates, Tomasello's current working hypothesis is that a particular representational/motivational capacity distinguishes humans from other primates: a capacity for shared intentionality and cooperation. In a closely related proposal, Gergely and Csibra (2006) suggest that a representational/motivational capacity for pedagogy distinguishes humans from other primates. However these working hypotheses play out, non-human primates have richer representations of agency than were acknowledged even a decade ago.

In sum, I take the upshot of the primate literature to be that non-human primates represent conspecifics and human beings as agents with goals, perceptions and attentional states. Like object representations, core cognition of agency has a long evolutionary past. However, unlike object representations, in which the full core cognition system is observable in primates, it is likely that hominid evolution contributed to the enrichment of core cognition of intentional agency. It is true that primates do not generally establish joint attention, do not show and point out things to each other, do not teach, do not generally engage in cooperative problem solving, and do not analyze others' action in service of imitation.

Transcending Core Cognition: A Representational Theory of Mind?

This chapter has developed the argument that infants and nonhuman primates represent agents; specifically, they represent the agents' attentional states, referential actions, and goals. I have been careful not to claim that infants and nonhuman primates have the capacity to express the mental states of agents in terms of propositional attitudes. We must distinguish between intentional states represented as direct connections between agents, on the one hand, and objects and states of affairs in the world, on the other hand—as when an agent is represented as wanting or seeing an apple that is in the world, contrasted with intentional states represented as propositional attitudes such as "believes that there is an apple behind that screen," in which the agent is represented as having a representation of the apple in relation to the screen. One crucial difference between these two types of representation is that only the latter allows another's behavior to be predicted or explained in terms of his or her false beliefs. Many eminent scholars have offered analyses of a conceptual system 1/conceptual system 2 (CS1/CS2) transition between an early developing conception of agents that cannot express representational mental states and a later one that can. For representative examples, Perner's distinction between a want/belief psychology and a want/prelief psychology (Perner, 1991), or Bartsch and Wellman's (1995) distinction between a desire psychology and a belief/desire psychology. These researchers have hypothesized two fundamentally different forms of intentional attribution to make sense of the striking failures of 3- and young 4-year-old children on a wide range of explicit theory-of-mind tasks. The most well-known of the explicit theory-of-mind tasks are the false-belief tasks introduced into the literature by Heinz Wimmer and Joseph Perner (1983). In one classic paradigm, the child is shown a vignette in which an actor (e.g., Mary) watches as something (e.g., a cookie) is hidden. Mary then leaves. While Mary is absent, the cookie is moved to a new hiding place, after which Mary returns. The child is then asked "Where does Mary think the cookie is?" or "Where will Mary look for the cookie." Since 1983, now hundreds of studies have used this basic paradigm, or variations on it, and found that young 3-year-olds say that Mary will think the cookie is in its true location and that Mary will look there for it. The transition to adult performance (Mary will look for the cookie where she saw it hidden before she left, because that is where she thinks it is) occurs around the 4th birthday (see Wellman, Cross, & Watson, 2001, for a meta-analysis of the factors that influence behavior on many replications and variations of this basic false belief paradigm).

It is easy to see how adult performance requires a representational theory of mind—this task requires that the child reason explicitly about another's beliefs, to recognize that those beliefs may be false, and to predict another's behavior on the basis of that person's beliefs rather than merely on his or her goals and the actions needed to realize those goals. None of the infant studies reviewed so far require that the child distinguish between true beliefs and false beliefs. However, as should now be familiar, the failures of 3-year-olds on the standard false-belief tasks are consistent with two broad classes of interpretation. On the one hand, Flavell, Wellman, Perner, De Villiers, and others may be right. A representational theory of mind (CS2) may be qualitatively different from the cognition of agency available to infants and non-human primates (CS1), and CS2 may require conceptual change for its construction. Alternatively, developmental changes (perhaps maturationally driven) in some ancillary processes required to succeed on the false-belief tasks themselves—processes unrelated to the capacity for representing beliefs—may underlie the developmental changes observed on the false-belief tasks. For example, many authors have explored the role that maturationally driven changes in executive function play in helping the child adjudicate between two competing responses based on where the object really is and where the agent last saw it (e.g., Carlson, Moses, & Hix, 1998; Frye, Zelazo, & Palfai, 1995; Leslie, German, & Polizzi, 2005).

Many hundreds of papers and many books have explored the developmental changes in preschoolers' theory of mind, and it is beyond the scope of this book to do justice to this subtle and voluminous literature. I have not come to any conclusion for myself with respect to whether the developmental changes observed in normally developing children during the fourth year of life constitute a case of discontinuous development. Must the child build a representational system with more expressive power than its input? Is conceptual change required? I see good arguments in favor of the developmental continuity position and good arguments in favor of the conceptual change position. In what follows I sketch some of the arguments for both positions. Chapters 8 through 11 take up cases where I believe the arguments for conceptual discontinuity are conclusive.

Considerations in Favor of the Conceptual Change Position

One source of evidence for the conceptual change position derives from an analysis of spontaneous speech of toddlers that is available in the Child Language Data Exchange System (CHILDES) data base, which consists of publicly available transcripts of conversations between adults and children. Karen Bartsch and Henry Wellman (1995) analyzed the transcripts of several children whose language was taped regularly from before they were 2 until age 4 or later. They identified mentalistic use of terms expressing desires, goals, preferences (such as "wants" or "likes", on the one hand, and terms expressing epistemic mental states (such as "knows" or "thinks"), on the other. From the earliest ages (less than age 2), children used desire and goal language mentalistically, in sentences such as "He likes chocolate ice cream; I like vanilla," "He wants to go to the zoo." In contrast, no uses of mentalistic language expressing epistemic states emerged until age 3 or so (as in "I thought my socks were in the drawer, but they were under the bed)." These differences emerge whether the child is talking about true or false beliefs, about realized or frustrated desires. Bartsch and Wellman showed that children command the linguistic structures needed to use epistemic language, and that they talk about mental states a lot, and that their input contains as much talk about epistemic mental states as desires, preferences and so on. Bartsch and Wellman concluded that 2-year-olds' failure to talk about beliefs and cognition reflects the lack of the relevant concepts, rather than (or in addition to) problems in ancillary representational or computational abilities needed for success on the false-belief tasks themselves.

Also, success on the false-belief task is correlated with success on a wide range of other tasks that reflect a representational theory of mind, even tasks that place very different information processing demands on the child. These include tasks that reflect explicit awareness that seeing leads to knowing, tasks in which children must articulate how they know something (by seeing it, feeling it, or inferring it), tasks which require distinguishing appearance from reality, tasks that require explicit reasoning about others perspectives, tasks that require access to warrants for beliefs, and many others (e.g., Flavell, Green, & Flavell, 1986; Flavell, Everett, Croft, & Flavell, 1981; O'Neill & Gopnik, 1991). One example will have to suffice to give you a feel for this wonderful literature. In an experiment on children's understanding of the sources of cognition, Danielle O'Neill and Allison Gopnik (1991) introduced children to a pink fur rabbit and a blue plastic horse. They then put one of the objects into a large tube and the child's task was to figure out which one was in the tube. On some trials a semitransparent opening allowed the color (but not the texture) to be seen. On other trials the child put their hands in the tube and felt the object. On still other trials, a puppet whispered "psst— it's the rabbit." On all of these trials both 3- and 4-year-olds correctly identified which object was in the tube. The crucial question was this: "How did you know? Did you tell by seeing it was the rabbit? By feeling it was the rabbit? Because somebody told you it was the rabbit?" Three-year-olds were at chance and 4-year-olds succeeded, and success is correlated with success on the false-belief task. This finding exemplifies many that show correlations among quite different reflections of an explicit representational theory of mind—in this case, between understanding the sources of cognition and understanding of the possibility of and some of the conditions leading to false beliefs.

Jill de Villiers and her colleagues (2005) provided another argument for the conceptual change position. They proposed (and provided evidence for) a bootstrapping process that may underlie the construction of an explicit representational capacity for representing beliefs. They point out that one particular type of linguistic structure is particularly important in expressing epistemic propositional attitudes, and that it is relatively late to develop. These are linguistic expressions with embedded propositions such that the overall sentence can be true even if the embedded sentence is false. This semantic feature, opacity, holds for complement structures such as "John said that Kerry won the election," or "Frank thinks that Kerry won the election." Both sentences could be true; John could be a liar and Frank could be remarkably clueless. De Villiers found that children do not begin using complement structures of this sort until their 4th year of life, and the appearance of these linguistic forms in free and elicited speech is correlated with success on the false-belief tasks. This correlation holds even for nonverbal false belief tasks, and tasks in which the question posed to the child is where the actor will look—that is, even ones that do not use this construction in the task itself. Deaf children learning sign language relatively late in life do not succeed on false-belief tasks until they command complement structures, and training studies on communication verb complement structures help children pass a wide range of theory-of-mind tasks that emerge at age 4. These data are consistent with a bootstrapping story in which learning the semantics of complement structures, especially opacity, plays a necessary role in creating a representational theory of mind. I am quite sympathetic to this possibility; chapters 8 to 11 discuss the role that bootstrapping processes of the sort de Villiers is suggesting play in conceptual change.

Arguments Against Developmental Discontinuity

In spite of these considerations in favor of the conceptual change position in this case, there are reasons to doubt it, at least in the form of a change from a CS1 that is incapable of representing epistemic states to a CS2 that is. Children do not reliably pass the false-belief tasks, the appearance/reality tasks, the sources-of-cognition tasks, and so on, until late in their fourth year or early in their fifth year. But a variety of task manipulations dramatically lower the age of success. For instance, merely asking "where will the agent look first for the cookie?" increases success rates, as if the child interpreted the standard questions "where will she look?" and "where does she think it is" as questions about her eventual behavior or beliefs, once she's found it (Garnham & Ruffman, 2001). Bartsch and Wellman's CHILDES analysis found the onset of epistemic mentalistic language to be around 3:0, not 4:0. And finally, if one analyzes children's looking, rather than their answers to questions, one finds that as young as 2:9, when asked where the agent will look for the cookie, toddlers reliably look first at the location where the agent last saw it, even though they eventually respond to the explicit question incorrectly (Clements & Perner, 1994). These data, along with convincing analyses of the performance difficulties posed by the explicit false-belief tasks (Leslie et al., 2005) and correlations between executive function measures and success on false-belief tasks (Carlson et al., 1998; Frye et al., 1995), are consistent with the claim that coming to succeed on the false-belief task around age 4 does not reflect conceptual change.

Recent infant studies from three different laboratories provide dramatic data that undermine the conceptual change position (Onishi & Baillargeon, 2005; Surian, Caldi, & Sperber, in press). These data suggest that preverbal toddlers represent epistemic states of actors. Specifically, infants use what information an agent has about the location of a desired object in predicting where that person will look for it.

All of these studies begin with the Woodward paradigm that elicits representations of actions as goal-directed. Kristine Onishi and Renée Baillargeon (2005) showed 15-month-old infants events in which an actor placed a plastic watermelon slice into one of two boxes, and then, on two familiarization trials, reached into the box as if to reach for the slice therein. (Figure 5.9a). After this brief familiarization, infants were shown a "belief induction trial." The slice moved, in full view of the infant, from its original box into the other box. The crucial manipulation was whether the actor could see this motion or not. In the latter case, the back of the stage was completely closed off, blocking the view of the actor (Figure 5.9b). After this belief induction trial, the actor (now visible again) reached into one of the boxes. There was only one test trial per infant, so comparisons of looking times are between subjects. In the case where the actor saw the movement into the new box, infants looked longer when the actor reached into the old box than into the new box. This is simply a replication of Woodward; the infant expects the actor to continue reaching for the same object and tracks the change of location of that object. The only difference from Woodward's paradigm is that the actor is reaching for a hidden goal object. But, when the actor did not see the watermelon move (Figure 5.10b), infants looked longer when the actor reached into the new box (where the child knew the slice to be) than in the old box (where the actor last saw the slice).

Further conditions ruled out lean interpretations of these data based on low-level strategies; infants did not expect the actor to reach where the object was actually hidden, where the hand had previously searched, or where the actor had last attended. Onishi and Baillargeon (2005) conclude, "Whether the actor believed the toy to be hidden in the green or the yellow box, and whether this belief was in fact true or false, the infants expected the actor to search on the basis of her belief about the toy's location. These results suggest that 15-month-olds already possess (at least in a rudimentary and implicit form) a representational theory of mind. They realize that others act on the basis of their belief, and that these beliefs are representations that may or may not mirror reality."

In sum, Onishi and Baillargeon appeal to infants' representing the agent's representation of the location of the apple or the slice—the agent's beliefs or the agent's information about where the object is. Clearly, this rich interpretation is consistent with these data, but can we also understand them in terms of conceptual machinery we have already granted prelinguistic infants—representations of agents' goals and attentional states? Conceivably, we can. Perhaps the computations concerning what an actor

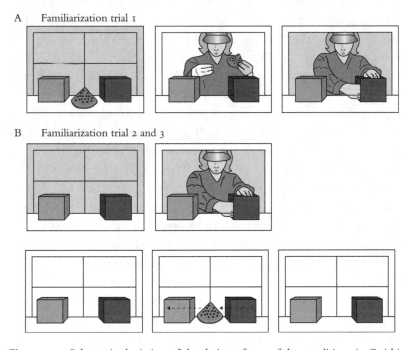

Figure 5.9. Schematic depiction of the design of one of the conditions in Onishi and Baillargeon (2005). A and B—familiarization files. Person puts object in blue box and then reaches for it. C. One version of belief induction trial—when the person cannot see, the object moves from blue box to yellow box. From Onishi, K. H., & Baillargeon, R. (2005). Do 15-month-old infants understand false beliefs? *Science, 308* (5719), 255–258. Reprinted with permission from AAAS.

will do take into account where the actor was attending during previous events. On this leaner interpretation these data provide even stronger evidence that any we have seen so far that the two threads of infants' agent representations (attribution of goals and attributions of attention and seeing) are integrated, but they do not show that infants' expectations are guided by representations of beliefs.

As these data are brand new, at present we have no way of deciding between a desire/attention psychology and a desire/belief psychology interpretation of them. Personally, I favor the richer interpretation. The simplest interpretation of why the baby monitors perceptual access when the locations are switched is that the baby realizes that the agent gains information from what he or she sees. Otherwise, the rules the baby is following are unmotivated.

That children are reasoning about the information available to the agent is strongly suggested by another in the line of studies from Onishi and Baillargeon. In this study, the slice is put into the green box, and then, when the actor is not looking, the locations of the whole green and yellow boxes are switched. In this case, apparently infants reason that the actor can figure out where the object is, because they look longer if the actor reaches into the yellow box, even though the yellow box is in the location into which the actor has reached before. In the companion condition, the two boxes are the same color (both green). As before, the infant sees the slice put into the left-most box, and is familiarized with the actor reaching into it. Again, when the actor is not looking, the locations of the whole boxes are switched. Now the infant looks longer if the actor reaches into the right-most box, apparently because they reason that the actor has no information (perceptual or inferential) about where the slice really is. At this point, any lean interpretation of the sort sketched above breaks down.

I conclude, tentatively, that prelinguistic infants represent the information a person gains from attending to objects and events in the world. Prelinguistic infants have the capacity to represent an agent's epistemic mental states as well as its goals and attentional states. If this is so, then the wide-ranging developmental changes in children's theory of mind that take place between ages 2 and 4 do not reflect conceptual change between as CS1 in which epistemic states cannot be represented to a CS2 in which they can. Of course, this conclusion leaves a great mystery to be solved—namely, understanding 2- and 3-year-olds' failures on the battery of theory-of-mind tasks that reflect a representational theory of mind. Why, if infants understand that seeing leads to cognition, do 3-year-olds fail the sources-of-knowledge tasks? Why does command of complement structures in language predict success on tasks that reflect the child's theory of mind?

There are several, not mutually exclusive, ways of resolving this paradox. It is possible that representations of others' informational access in core cognition are implicit, embodied in the computations that operate over representations of goals and attentional states. On this view, language learning is required to create representations that contain explicit mental symbols for concepts like *thinks, believe, information, cognition.* We will see an example of this type of mental construction when we consider the origin of mathematical concepts (chapters 8 and 11) and when we consider the origin of explicit scientific cognition (chapters 10 and 11). More weakly, even if core cognition itself is articulated in terms of mental symbols for such concepts, perhaps the creation of an explicit, verbal, system of representation makes mental state attributions more salient and robust, more stable and more likely to be recruited in the complex ebb and flow of ongoing events. This would be an example of what is sometimes called "weak Whorfianism" in the literature on the effects of language and thought, and we shall see examples of this type of learning in the pages to come as well (see chapter 7).

Conclusions: Core Cognition of Intentionality

This chapter makes a case for a third system of core cognition, in addition to object representations (chapter 3) and number representations (chapter 4). I do not mean to imply that these three exhaust core cognition; it is an open empirical question whether there are other core domains. Rather, my goal has been to demonstrate the existence of core cognition and to illustrate its properties. The identification of a candidate core domain generates issues for further research. When in development (during phylogeny or ontogeny) does the eye-gaze-detection device output intentional attributions—that an agent is looking at something, indicating something, attending to something, gathering information about something? How many subsystems of core cognition are dedicated to the problem of agent representation, and how are they related? Are their outputs integrated from the beginning? How far back in our evolutionary history did our ancestors create agent representations with the same content and computational roles as those of human infants? Finally, what underlies the transition to an explicit representation of beliefs that we do not see robust evidence for until the fourth year of life?

These questions are very much open and many talented researchers are at work answering them. Before turning to the question of how core cognition is transcended in the course of conceptual development (chapters 7 through 11), chapter 6 considers the possibility that there may be innate representations with conceptual content that are not embedded within systems of core cognition.

6

Representations of *Cause*

Contrary to the theories of the British empiricists, as well as those of Piaget and Quine, the representational primitives from which the human mind is constructed are not *solely* perceptual or sensori-motor. Concepts such as *object* and *agent* are the output of innate input analyzers, embedded in distinct systems of core cognition. Thus, core cognition is the source of *some* innate representations with conceptual content. This line of argument raises an important question: Might core cognition be the source of *all* innate concepts? Are all innate representations with conceptual content embedded within one or another distinct system of core cognition? If so, transcending core cognition will require integrating representations from different core cognition domains.

As we shall see in the chapters that follow (chapters 8 through 11), new representational resources are indeed built in just this way—by integrating what were previously distinct systems of knowledge. Some thinkers have speculated that the capacity for such integration requires language (and indeed, the bootstrapping processes described below require external symbols), and thus that the capacity for such integration may be uniquely human (e.g., Mithen, 1996; Spelke, 2003). Counter to this speculation, it is also possible that some innate conceptual resources are central, and thus integrative, rather than encapsulated within core cognition.

Representations of *cause* present an ideal case study for exploring these possibilities. However the vexed question of the metaphysics of causation plays out (are there really causes in the world, or merely conditional probabilities and spatio-temporal relations among events?), there is no doubt that human beings represent the world in terms of a rich causal texture. Our language is shot through with causality ("he made it happen, he broke it"), and children master these constructions very early in language acquisition (Bowerman, 1974; Hood, Bloom, & Brainerd, 1979). There is a huge literature on adults' causal perception (Michotte, 1946/1963), and on the psychological process that lead participants in studies to infer causation from patterns of statistical relations among events (Cheng & Novick, 1990; Dickinson & Shanks, 1995; Gopnik et al., 2004; Pearl, 2000).

For adults, causal representations certainly integrate distinct domains of knowledge. We represent causal relations across core domains (e.g., an agent's hitting an inanimate object causes the latter to move) as well as between events not embedded in any domain of core cognition (e.g., smoking causes cancer, building a dam creates a lake, watering one's crops causes growth.). To be sure, causal representations are also part of each domain of core cognition: representations of contact causality are part of our core cognition of objects (an object at rest goes into motion upon being contacted by a moving object) and representations of tele-ological causality articulate core cognition of agents (see chapter 5).

The question here is how the human capacity for causal repre-sentations arises. The broad outlines of how this question might be answered should now be clear. There may be no innate representation of *cause*, and some processes (as yet not discussed) through which human beings transcend innate knowledge yield the capacity to represent the world in causal terms. The empiricist hypothesis that causal representa-tions are built from sensory primitives is an example of this constructivist family of theories, and it has its present-day adherents (e.g., Cohen, Amsel, Redford, & Cassasola, 1998; Cohen & Chaput, 2002). Another possibility from this family of theories is that causal notions are con-structed from noncausal resources from core cognition, as I have argued that a vitalist biology is constructed from resources from core cognition that lack a concept *alive* (Carey, 1985; 1999).

Alternatively, the capacity for causal representation may be innate. This position, too, has its modern adherents; indeed, we may distinguish several nativist proposals. Causal representations may initially be embedded within a single system of core cognition—*either* core cognition of objects and their interactions *or* core cognition of agents and their capacity to effect changes in their worlds. Finally, a third possibility not yet considered in these pages presents itself: the capacity for causal representations may be an innate, but central, part of an innate representational resource that is neither modular nor domain-specific. For example, there may be innate learning mechanisms that take computations of conditional probability as input and that output causal representations (e.g., Gopnik et al., 2004).

Each of these nativist positions privileges a different aspect of our mature concept of causality as its developmental source. Albert Michotte posited core representations of mechanical causality (as when a moving billiard ball hits another, causing it to go into motion) as the ontogenetically primary ones. This view highlights the transmission of causal power, a primitive mechanistic notion, as the source and essence of our concept of *cause*.

Others, such as Michotte's contemporary Maine de Biran, suggested that core cognition of human agency includes a concept of internally generated causal power—that which supports the capacity for self-generated motion. Representations of intentional action entail a capacity to effect changes in the world, and this is a causal notion. According to de Biran:

> A being who has never made an effort would not in fact have
> any idea of power, nor, as a result, any idea of efficient cause. He
> would see one movement succeed another, e.g. one billiard ball
> bump into another and push it along; but he would be unable to
> conceive, or apply to this sequence of movements, the idea of efficient
> cause or acting force, which we regard as necessary if the series is to
> begin and continue. (quoted in Michotte 1946/1963, p. 11)

De Biran's view highlights agency—a causal agent effecting changes in the world through the action of internally generated force—as the source and essence of our concept of *cause*.

Still others posit an innate capacity to compute causal representations from patterns of statistical dependence. Those who credit animals with causal representations of the contingencies in operant and classical conditioning paradigms fall in this camp, as do those who see causal representations as a constrained network of conditional probabilities, called a "Bayes-net representation," and see causal learning as the process of constructing such representations from representations of the conditional probabilities among events. This view highlights the idea of difference making and counterfactual representations (if the cause did not happen, the effect would not happen) as the source and essence of our concept of cause (Gopnik et al., 2004, Pearl, 2000; Sloman, 2005; Spirtes, Glymour, & Scheines, 2000; Tenenbaum & Griffiths, 2001; J. Woodward, 2003).

My discussion of these options unfolds as follows. First, I lay out Michotte's proposal that human causal representations are part of core cognition of objects and of object motion. I then turn to the evidence that young infants represent Michottian contact causality, considering leaner interpretations for the phenomena that have been taken as evidence for infants' causal perception in Michottian events. The data strongly suggest that by 6 months of age infants have rich causal representations of Michottian launching, entraining, and expulsion events. Nevertheless, these same data undermine Michotte's hypothesis concerning the domain-specific and modular source of these causal representations. The data reveal a role for representations of human agency in infants' interpretations of physical causality. I conclude with a discussion of the current status of rationalist versus constructivist theories of the source of causal representations, and with some speculations concerning the existence and nature of innate central conceptual representations.

Michotte's Picture

In his landmark book *The Perception of Causality*, Albert Michotte offered a theory of the psychological origin of human causal representations. Michotte discovered the phenomenon of *causal perception*. He showed that under specifiable circumstances, "certain physical events give an immediate causal impression, and that one can 'see' an object *act* on another object, *produce* in it certain changes, and *modify* it in one way or another" (Michotte, 1946/1963, p. 15, emphasis in original). One example is the launching event: object A approaches and contacts object B, and then immediately afterwards object B goes into motion, or changes motion path and/or speed. Using the reports of trained observers, Michotte detailed the conditions necessary to produce an impression of causality. He found that launching is perceived when and only when the two motions have parameters consistent with a single motion or causal impetus transferred from one object to a second, perceptually distinct object. Based on his experimental results, Michotte proposed the existence of a special mechanism in the mind that transforms privileged inputs—visual sequences of events with certain spatio-temporal parameters—into a domain-specific output, a "genuine causal impression" of motion events.

All of the data Michotte collected relied on verbal reports by adult observers. Nonetheless, he took a strong position on the origin of causal representations, claiming that the input analyzer that yields causal perceptions is innate and is the source of all subsequently developing causal representations. Michotte did not have the theoretical vocabulary to talk of core cognition and modularity. Still, this is what he was proposing. A module is a cognitive mechanism that is obligatory and encapsulated; the translation from privileged input to domain-specific output within a module is not (or is minimally) influenced by other beliefs or knowledge in the mind of the observer. Michotte hypothesized that the privileged input to causal perception was spatio-temporal parameters of the inter-actions among moving entities. He hypothesized that causal perception was highly domain specific in its output as well—limited to caused motion alone. He acknowledged that adults represent causal relations involving state changes, but he believed that these causal representations were extensions of the initial module, which takes spatio-temporal data as input and outputs representations of caused motion. Michotte, of course, did not know of the Spelke and Baillargeon work on core cognition of objects, but his proposal places the origin of causal representations within this domain. Indeed, Spelke formulated the three constraints on object motion that guide infants' model building in this domain as the "three Cs—cohesion, continuity, and contact (causality)."

Michotte's evidence for modularity included the observation that even when the observers knew that an actual causal interaction was impossible, because the entities involved were moving lights or marks on paper, the impression of causality was not reduced. Furthermore, the psychophysical parameters that determine whether causality is per-ceived are not faithful to the properties of real causal interactions in our friction-full Newtonian world, making it unlikely that these para-meters are determined by explicit knowledge of (or even experience with) the physical world. The claim that the input analyzer that computes launching causality is innate, and operates continuously through devel-opment, is a paradigm example of hypothesized core cognition.

Since Michotte, Anne Schlottmann and her colleagues (Schlottmann & Shanks, 1992) have provided convergent evidence for the robust encapsulation of perceptual causality representations. In one experiment, Schlottmann directly pitted the spatio-temporal signature of launching against patterns of covariation. Subjects watched an interaction in which object A approached object B, and sometime later object B went into motion. What actually predicted the onset of object B's motion was a change in the color of object B. The results revealed two independent systems for detecting causal interactions: while subjects were able to explicitly judge that the color change was necessary and sufficient for object B's motion, they also reported perceiving launching (i.e., that object A transferred its motion to object B, making object B go) when and only when the spatio-temporal conditions for a launching event were met. These causal perceptions were independent of the color change. Even with many blocks of experience with the actual contingencies, the factors that affected perceived causality remained the spatio-temporal parameters Michotte described.

As mentioned above, Michotte held that the inputs to the caused motion input detector are specified purely in spatio-temporal terms; the device is blind to the ontological status of the objects involved. Schottmann, and her colleagues (Schlottmann, Allen, Linderoth, & Hesketh, 2002) tested this prediction in an experiment with participants from 3 years of age through adulthood. Observers indicated whether they saw each event as launching, chasing, or as two independent motions. The objects involved in each event moved either nonrigidly (a little like a caterpillar), specifying animate motion, or rigidly, consistent with inanimacy (Michotte, 1946/1963; Kanizsa & Vicario, 1968). This study yielded stable explicit judgments from the youngest children of any to date. Consistent with Michotte's views about the developmental history of perception of launching, Schottmann found that even the youngest children saw these events as causal, just as did adults. Also consistent with Michotte's views on modularity, the children were utterly impervious to the ontological status of the moving entities in these events. Whether children saw an event as involving mechanical causality (launching), chasing, or neither was entirely determined by its spatio-temporal parameters. This was largely true of adults as well, although the judgments of adults were slightly modulated by whether the entities moved as caterpillars or as blocks.

Schlottmann's experiments support the encapsulation of the mechanism for perceived causality: beliefs about the actual contingencies or mechanisms governing a particular causal interaction, or about the properties and causal dispositions of the entities, do not easily infiltrate the computation of a causal impression. Schlottmann's studies also provide evidence for the continuity of causal perception through childhood into adulthood. All of this evidence, though, comes from studies of young children and adults, not infants. Michotte's developmental claims concerning the ultimate origins of the capacity for causal representations must be addressed with studies of creatures who are closer to the original state—young infants.

Causal Perception: Do Infants Represent the Causality in Michotte Launching Events?

The question of just when infants first interpret Michotte-type launching events in causal terms must be approached in two steps. First, we will want to know whether infants are sensitive to the spatio-temporal parameters of launching. Then, we will want evidence that infants' representations of launching have at least some causal content. To summarize the current state of the art, there is no doubt that young infants are sensitive to the spatio-temporal parameters that distinguish contact causality from noncausal interactions. Although it is much more difficult to show that they attribute causality in these events, this chapter presents an extended argument that they do.

The simplest experiments exploring infants' representations of launching events are habituation studies. They begin by letting infants watch an event in which object B goes into motion immediately upon being contacted by object A. After habituation, infants are shown either more launching events or events in which there was a temporal delay or a spatial gap. Events with spatial or temporal gaps retain the simple sequence of one event followed by another, but they do not yield a perceptual experience of causality in adults. As young as 4 months, infants successfully make this discrimination, expressed by regaining interest (increasing looking time) to the spatial or temporal gap events (Leslie, 1982; Cohen et al., 1998). Similarly, if habituated to an event with a spatial or temporal gap, infants recover interest to a launching event. These results show that infants are sensitive to the spatio-temporal parameters that determine the adult perception of launching, but they do not demonstrate that infants perceive this distinction in terms of causality.

The challenge, of course, is to show that the infants' representations have some content that goes beyond generalizations stated in perceptual or spatio-temporal vocabulary. Many have risen to this challenge, most notably Alan Leslie and Les Cohen and their collaborators. The first approach was to demonstrate that infants' representations give different status to the agent and the patient in launching events, in the face of failure to do so when two events follow regularly, one after another, but are not causally related. Alan Leslie (Leslie & Keeble, 1987) habituated two groups of infants to events in which one object A approached and made contact with a stationary object B from the left and stopped, after which object B went into motion to the right and then stopped. The only difference was that in one group object B went into motion immediately upon being contacted, specifying launching for adults, and in the other group there was a pause before object B went into motion, such that adults do not perceive a causal relations between the two motions. In spatio-temporal terms, each motion could be described in terms of direction and speed of motion of each object and spatio-temporal relations between the two motions (motion of object B follows motion of object A, either simultaneously upon contact or upon a temporal gap). If this is the vocabulary in which the infants were representing the events, then reversing the motion (having object A be stationary at the beginning, having object B emerge from the right, move toward, and contact object A, after which object A moves to the left and stops) should be equally novel in the two cases. But if the original launching event is represented as A *causes* B to move, and the original nonlaunching event is seen merely as A moves and then B moves, then it is possible that reversing the launching event, in which the roles of the agent and patient are reversed, will be more noticeable to the baby than reversing the nonlaunching event. This is what happened: 6-month-old infants dishabituated to the reversal of the launching event whereas they did not dishabituate to the reversal of the nonlaunching event. This experiment suggests that young infants represent launching events in terms of concepts that go beyond spatio-temporal descriptors.

Leslie Cohen and Lisa Oakes (Oakes & Cohen, 1990) attacked the problem of establishing whether young infants represent launching events causally in a second way, asking if infants categorize different spatio-temporal patterns together on the basis of whether they specify a causal interaction or not. In one series of studies, they habituated babies to launching events or to events that are seen by adults as noncausal for one of two reasons: either there was a period of time after contact by object A before object B started to move (a temporal gap), or object A stopped short of object B before object B went into motion (a spatial gap). The habituated event was then contrasted with each other event. By 6 months of age, infants generalize habituation from one noncausal event to another while dishabituating from either noncausal event to the causal one. Thus, at the same age infants are sensitive to the role reversal in Michottian launching events, but not in events with gaps, they categorically distinguish causal from noncausal interactions.

These experiments suggest that infants perceive causality in these events, just as do adults, but of course they do not conclusively show this. Convergent evidence for this conclusion derives from experiments on infants' causal *inferences* in which they do not see the causal interaction. As I describe these data, please keep two points in mind. First, these data greatly increase our confidence in attributing representations with the content *cause* to young infants. Second, at the same time they undermine Michotte's contention that the sole source of our causal representations is a data-driven modular input analyzer that yields representations of cause from spatio-temporal evidence alone, for they show that causal inferences are influenced by representations outside of Michotte's hypothesized module (spatio-temporal input alone, solely caused motion as output) as young as we have evidence for causal representations at all.

Causal Inferences: Beyond Data-Driven Causal Perception

Michotte explicitly distinguished between the causal impression that is the output of a perceptual analyzer, on the one hand, and inferential extensions and applications that the observer makes using that causal impression, on the other. Only the perceptual component is delivered by the operation of the perceptual module. If infants' earliest causal representations are determined exclusively by the operation of the perceptual module, Michotte would therefore predict that, at some ages, infants perceive causality in simple interactions like launching events, but they cannot make inferences about unseen causal interactions.

William Ball (1973) carried out the very first experiment using the violation-of-expectancy looking-time method, using it to address infants' understanding of contact causality. In his study, he required infants to make an inference about unseen causal interactions. Ball habituated infants to events, similar to those shown in Figure 6.1. An event began with a screen visible on a stage floor with object B (in this case a block) partially visible at its right edge. A second object, A (another block), moved onto the stage from the left and went behind the screen. After timing consistent with a launching event, the block went into motion and stopped, visible, to the right of the screen. Infants' looking at the outcome of this event was monitored, and the trial was terminated when they looked away from the outcome array for 2 seconds or more. The whole stage was then covered by curtains, after which the curtains were opened, showing the beginning array, and the event was repeated as before. Infants were shown this event over and over until they habituated to it—that is, until their looking at the outcome arrays was half of its initial levels.

How had the infants interpreted this event? Did they think that the first block had caused the motion of the second via contact? To address this question, Ball then showed infants two new events, in alternation: an expected event (as defined by adult expectations) and an unexpected event. The events were exactly like the habituation event, except that there was no screen. In the expected event, in which contact causality explains the motion of the second block, the first emerged from the right edge of the stage, moved toward and hit the block, after which the block immediately went into motion and then stopped as before (Figure 6.1, expected outcome). The unexpected event was identical, except that the first block stopped short of the second, and after a short period of time, the block went into motion and then stopped as before (Figure 6.1, unexpected outcome).

The participants in Ball's experiments (ages 2 to 26 months) looked longer at the unexpected event than at the expected event (Ball, 1973; for replications see Kosugi, Ishida, & Fujita, 2003; Muentner & Carey, 2007; Spelke, Phillips, & Woodward, 1995). Ball concluded that the event in which there was no contact between the balls was unexpected for infants,

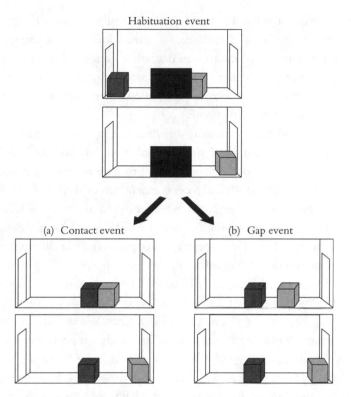

Figure 6.1. Schematic depiction of the design of Ball (1993); Muentner & Carey (under review) replication. During habituation, a block comes from off stage, passes behind a barrier after which a partially hidden block goes into motion and stops at the stage edge. During test trials, the barrier is removed and on ½ of the trials, the train hits the block, upon which the immediately goes into the motion and on the other ½ of the trials, the train stops short of the block, upon which the block immediately goes into motion.

just as it is for adults, and thus that infants represent Michotte contact causality. Ball's experiment was never published, but subsequent studies have replicated his result in infants as young as 6 months of age. This pattern of looking at the test trials is not observed when the habituation trials are omitted from the experiment: observing the occluded interaction during habituation is necessary to produce asymmetric looking behavior on the test trials. That is, even though contact between the two objects was not visible during the habituation trials, infants treat the contact test event as familiar based on the partially occluded habituation event. For this to be so, infants must form an inference or expectation about the unseen causal interaction occurring during habituation. Thus, as young as there is evidence that infants perceive causality in Michotte's launching events, they recruit these representations even when not part of a data-driven perceptual process.

Although infants are making an inference in this experiment, the inference does not transcend the vocabulary of Michottian launching events (i.e., the inferences concerned the relative motions and contact between two objects). In a recent extension of Ball's study, Paul Meuntner and I (2007) explored whether 8-month-olds' inference of contact in these events is *restricted* to this vocabulary. That is, consistent with Michotte's claims for the restriction of perceived causality to motion events, would infants fail to infer causality in such events if the effect was a state change rather than caused motion? Before we tested infants, we wanted to make sure that adults would infer a contact causality in the state change events we planned to show infants. We showed adults the events infants would be habituated to, in which a train went behind a barrier that that partially hid a block, after which the block underwent some change (motion or a state change). We asked the adults to describe the events and then we had them predict what was happening behind the screen. Adults used causal language and predicted that the train would contact the block before both state changes and the motion of the block. Not astonishingly, adults' inferences concerning causal interactions transcend motion events, even if Michotte is right that there is no direct causal perception in cases of state change. More interestingly, adults expect contact between the train and the box as part of the causal event for state changes as well as for block motion.

We then asked how infants encode these events. The habituation events are diagrammed in Figure 6.2 (top panel, color change and music; bottom panel, box collapse). The full design was modeled on Ball's study (Figure 6.1). As in Ball's studies, at the outset of each habituation trial infants saw an object (in this case a block) partially hidden behind a screen. They were habituated to a moving object (in this case a train) entering behind the screen, after which an outcome occurred. The full experiment had three groups of infants, with three different outcomes. One outcome was motion of the block, as in Ball's experiments (Figure 6.1). The other outcomes were state changes—the block either changed color and made a sound *or* fell apart into six separate pieces (Figure 6.2). We expected to, and did, replicate Ball's finding in the motion outcome. That is, in test trials infants looked longer at gap events in which the train approached the block and stopped short of it before the block went into motion than they did at events in which the train made contact with the block before it went into motion. The question we were interested in was whether infants would also expect contact in the state change events. In neither of the state change events did infants differentiate the two types of test trials. Their attention was not drawn to events in which the state change occurred in spite of no contact between the train and the block.

This pattern of results has two possible interpretations. First, infants may not have made a causal construal of the initial state change event. Alternatively, they may have construed the habituation event causally, but may have no expectation that contact is needed for events in which the motion of one object causes a state change in the other. Subsequent experiments, described below, confirm the first interpretation. The results presented so far are consistent with Michotte's proposal that initially causality is represented only in the case of motion events, even while confirming that these causal representations already support inferences by infants 6 to 8 months of age.

However, further experiments undermine Michotte's hypothesis concerning the domain specificity of the information relevant to attributions of causality early in infancy (spatio-temporal information only). Contrary to claims of encapsulation, infants' causal inferences are robustly influenced by information other than spatio-temporal parameters of the interaction, some of which are most definitely derived from core cognition of agents. Additionally, infants can interpret these state changes as caused by contact with a possible agent at roughly the same age as they show the first evidence of interpreting Michottian motion events causally.

Infants' Causal Inference: Beyond Spatio-Temporal Information

Both Michotte and the researchers who have followed him provide substantial evidence that the causal impression produced by a launching

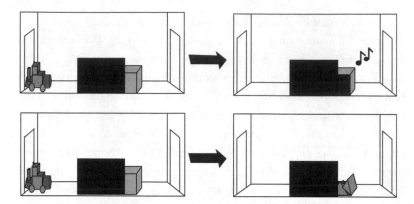

Figure 6.2. Schematic depiction of the habituation events in the Muentner & Carey (under review) state-change version of Ball's causal inference study. Top panel: train goes behind screen, after which the box's front panel lights up and the box plays a tune. Bottom panel: train goes behind screen, after which the box breaks into 6 pieces.

event depends on the spatio-temporal properties of the two entities' motions, but not on any intrinsic properties of the entities themselves. Michotte concluded that "the causal impression which appears in the Launching Effect is independent in principle ... of the phenomenal aspect of the objects—their size, shape, color and constitution" (1946/ 1963, p. 85). A causal impression could even be evoked by the right sequence of motions involving a wooden ball (object A) and a circle of light (object B). If the original idea of cause is the output of this modular perceptual mechanism, then at the earliest ages when infants perceive causal impressions of launching, their causal inferences should be similarly blind to the nature of the entities in the interaction. It simply is not so.

A large body of recent work shows that, in addition to perceiving causal impressions, very young infants track the ontological status and stable causal dispositions of the participants in causal interactions, and they use this information to inform their interpretation of the causal interaction itself. Within a single causal interaction, two entities play distinct roles: I call these roles the "situational agent" and "situational patient," respectively. For example, in an archetypal causal sequence, a hand moves a billiard cue, which hits the white ball, which rolls across the table to hit the red ball. The white ball plays the patient role in one specific causal interaction (with respective to the agentive billiard cue), and then the agent role in the subsequent interaction (with respect to the red ball as patient). Research on infants' inferences about the participants in a given causal interaction can be divided into two streams: (1) studies investigating infants' causal inferences as a function of their representations of the entities in the patient role, and (2) studies investigating the role of representations of the entities in the agent role. Consider first how representations of the stable causal dispositions of entities in the *patient* role influence infants' causal inferences.

Effects of the Entity in the Situational Patient Role

Infants' inferences about partially occluded launching events, as in Ball's experiment described above, depend critically on the ontological status of the entity the infant sees in the patient role. The results described above —longer looking at noncontact than contact test trials—applies only when the entity in the patient role is an inert inanimate object. Elizabeth Spelke and her colleagues (Spelke et al., 1995) showed infants events modeled on Ball's experiment, except that the objects A and B were human beings. Six-month-old infants in the new people version did not differentiate contact and noncontact test trials; a person going into motion without having been contacted by another person did not draw more attention than a person going into motion after having been contacted by another moving person (see also Kosugi & Fujita, 2002).

The object in the patient role has a particularly important and clear effect when infants make inferences about noncontact events. When an event fulfills the spatio-temporal criteria for launching, a perceptual input analyzer produces a "causal impression"—independent of the identities of the interacting objects. But what if the event does not fit the criteria for launching, because of a spatial gap? Laura Kotovsky and Renée Baillargeon (2000) argued convincingly that 7.5-month-olds' response to noncontact events depends on their prior categorization of the object in the patient role. As mentioned above, many previous studies have reported that, prior to habituation, infants do not look longer at launching events with or without a spatial gap. This might seem surprising. If launching without a spatial gap is infants' paradigm instance of a causal interaction, then one might expect the gap event to be surprising even without habituation. On the contrary, Kotovsky and Baillargeon argued that infants in each of these previous studies directly observe object B moving without contact, and therefore categorize object B as dispositionally capable of self-generated motion. In these experimental contexts—using unfamiliar objects presented either live or on a video screen—there is no reason a priori to categorize the novel objects as self-moving or inert, so neither categorization is inherently surprising, and infants look equally at both gap and no-gap events.

Kotovsky and Baillargeon provided evidence for this interpretation in a new experiment in which 6-month-old infants are given robust and consistent evidence that the entities in the interaction were inert, both outside of the experimental room and during the experimental procedure. Instead of habituation, infants are simply familiarized to the apparatus: a ramp (the path for object A), object B lying stationary near the bottom of the ramp, and between them a barrier that either completely blocks access from the ramp to object B or has a gap. The bottom half of the barrier and the near end of object B are then occluded by a screen, and infants see object A placed at the top of the ramp and released, and then roll down the ramp and disappear behind the screen. Object B then moves across the stage, in a manner consistent with launching by object A.

The critical features of this experiment are that (1) infants have evidence to classify object B as dispositionally inert, but (2) there are no habituation trials. Nevertheless, infants show increased looking (i.e., their attention is drawn) when object B moved in the full-barrier case where contact was not possible, relative to the part-barrier condition where contact would have occurred. That is, if the entity in the patient role is categorized in advance as inanimate and inert, then infants look longer at an apparent noncontact event even on the very first trial.

Kotovsky and Baillargeon showed that the reverse is also true: if object B (categorized as inert) does not go into motion after object A disappears behind the occluder, infants look longer when contact was possible than when it was impossible, as if they are surprised that the inert object in the patient role can resist the causal impetus of the first motion. Recent studies from Baillargeon's laboratory show that 5-month-old infants are surprised if an inert object resists contact causality (i.e., does not move when hit) but are not surprised by this event if the patient was previously categorized as self-moving (Luo, Kaufman, & Baillargeon, in press).

These results highlight the dissociation between the output of the perceptual module—which detects the spatio-temporal profile of launching independent of the ontological status and stable causal dispositions of the interacting entities—and the overall behavior of the infant, which includes inferences based on that status.

Effects of the Entity in the Situational Agent Role

Other experiments investigate the interactions between infants' causal inferences and the identity of the object in the situational agent role. The experiments present infants with events that are ambiguous with respect to the spatio-temporal parameters of Michottian perceptual causality and explore the causal inferences infants make.

Recall the Muentner studies described above (Figure 6.2). Eight-month-old infants apparently did not infer that a train caused the state change of a box (either a color change or a collapse). Muentner repeated these studies, replacing the train with a hand. Consider the collapsing box version. Infants were first familiarized to a solid box. In habituation trials, the curtain was lowered to reveal the box half hidden behind a screen. A hand then entered from the side of the stage opposite to the box and went behind the screen, after which the box collapsed into pieces. This event was repeated until infants habituated. On test trials, the screen was removed and the hand approached the box, either making contact with it before it collapsed or stopping just short of it before it collapsed. Unlike in the train case, where infants did not look longer at gap test trails than contact test trials, now infants recovered interest in the gap events. The same pattern of results was observed in the color/sound state change events.

This pattern of results is consistent with two interpretations: First, unlike the train events described above, when object A is a hand—a paradigmatic dispositional agent—infants see the state change events as causal and expect contact for the effect to occur. Or, second, infants saw the hand as engaged in an intentional action (reaching for the box) and recovered interest when the hand did not attain its apparent goal (see chapter 5). Muentner ruled out the second interpretation with the following experiment. Infants were habituated as before and were shown identical test trials, except on these test trials the box did not break into pieces. If infants merely expected the hand to reach its goal, they should have shown the same pattern of looking in this experiment as in the original one—longer looking to the gap events. However, if their sensitivity to contact derived from a causal analysis, their looking-time pattern should reverse: attention should be drawn when the hand contacts the box and it does not fall apart, whereas the gap event (no contact/ no effect) is not surprising at all. The looking-time pattern did reverse. Infants looked longer when the hand made contact with the box and it did not collapse than they did when the hand failed to contact the box and there was no state change.

This pattern of results shows that infants are sensitive to the stable dispositional properties of agents (in this case, the hand as a likely cause of effects) in their causal inferences, and that they expect contact for state changes as well as motion events. When the situational agent in a possible causal interaction has the stable dispositional properties of an agent (in this case, if it is a hand), the event is interpreted causally—otherwise (in this case, if it is a train) not. These results increase our confidence in attributing causal representations to infants, but undermine Michotte's claims that causal representations derive solely from the schema of causal perception of launching events. Causal inferences are not restricted to motion events, as they encompass reasoning about state changes, and they are penetrable by representations of the entities in the events

Sabina Pauen and Brigitte Trauble (2007) provided convergent data for the latter conclusion. The Michottian causal interaction at issue is entraining, not launching. In a paradigmatic entraining event a stationary object is contacted by a moving one, and then they move together, maintaining contact. In Pauen and Trauble's experiment, the event was ambiguous. The screen was lowered, revealing two distinct objects already moving together. The participants were 7-month-old infants who watched this ambiguous motion event, in which a ball attached to a furry animal-like tail bounced and rolled erratically around a small stage. Since both the ball and the tail always moved together, situational causal roles could not be assigned based on spatio-temporal cues. Then, the ball and the tail were separated, and lay stationary in separate parts of the stage. Although the infants' exposure to the two objects (ball and tail) moving was equivalent, the looking behavior to the stationary objects was asymmetrical. Infants looked preferentially at the tail, as if they expected the tail, but not the ball, to continue to move following separation. Pauen and Trauble's data suggest that when two entities moved together, 7-month-old infants parsed the spatio-temporally ambiguous motion event into a causal interaction based on cues to dispositional agency. The infants assigned the furry tail (a more plausible agent in the enduring, dispositional sense) to the situational agent role, just as adults do with the same stimuli.

These recent results confirm Alan Leslie's (1984) conclusions from his earlier study of causal agency in an entraining event. In that experiment, 7-month-old infants watched a film of a hand either (1) move in from off-screen and stop near a stationary doll (reach) or (2) start near the doll, and then move off the screen together with the doll (pick-up). In addition, each film involved either contact (in which the hand grasped the doll) or no contact. Leslie observed that the infants who are habituated to a pick-up event recover interest on the test trials if the contact relation changed (in either direction, from contact to no contact or vice-versa). But infants do not react to a contact change in a reach event. When a dispositionally inert object (a stick) is the candidate situational agent, infants do not recover interest to a contact change for either pick-up or reach events. Taken together, these results suggest that 7-month-olds see an event in which a hand and an inanimate object move together as a causal interaction, and they attend to contact between the hand and the object; an event which two inanimate objects move together equivalently is not perceived as an interaction for which contact/no contact is relevant (i.e., is not perceived as causal).

Remember that, according to the logic of the Oakes and Cohen and the Leslie experiments, 6 months is the age at which we have good evidence that infants *perceive* causality in Michottian launching events. Pauen's and Leslie's experiments suggest that infants also perceive causality in more complex Michottian entraining events. But contrary to Michotte's view, the infant's perceptual analysis is constrained by representations of the dispositional agency of the participants in the events. This is so by 7 months of age—just about the same age we have evidence infants are imputing causality at all, even in straightforward causal perception studies.

Joint Effects of the Entities in the Situational Agentive and Patient Roles

In a series of studies, Rebecca Saxe and I (Saxe, Tzelnic, & Carey, 2007; Saxe, Tenenbuam, & Carey, 2005) have shown that the young infant's causal inferences are impressively sophisticated, simultaneously integrating representations of the stable causal dispositions of entities in the situational agentive *and* patient roles. As in Ball's studies, in Saxe's studies the infant never sees the interaction between the potential situational agents and patients, and in some of the studies, the infant must *infer* the presence/nature of a situational agent from the fact that the moving entity is a dispositionally inert object. In these latter studies, during habituation not only do infants not see the causal interaction, they don't see the potential situational agent at all.

I introduce Saxe's studies with the simplest one—one in which the child need not infer the identity or nature of the situational agent. Nine-month-old infants were first familiarized to two beanbags lying motionless on the stage floor, thus providing evidence that these are inert entities. Then, during habituation, on each trial a bean bag came flying out from behind one of two small screens on the side of the stage (Figure 6.3), landing in the middle of the stage and remaining inert until the infant looked away. The order of emergence from each of the two sides was unpredictable; on half of the trials a beanbag emerged from behind the left screen and on half of the trials from behind the right screen. After habituation, on each test trial the screens were lowered, revealing a hand behind one of them and a toy train engine behind the other. On test trials the screens were then raised again, and a beanbag came flying out from behind one of the screens. Infants recovered interest, relative to the last habituation trial, only if the beanbag emerged from behind the screen where the train was; they maintained their habituated looking when it emerged from behind the screen where there was a hand (Saxe et al., 2007).

Apparently, infants reason about the source of motion of the beanbag, and consider hands to be better candidates for situational agents than toy trains. This result does not tell us what it is about a hand that makes it a good situational agent. Is it that infants have represented hands, per se, as throwers of small objects like beanbags? Or are hands represented as entities capable of self-generated motion, and any self-moving

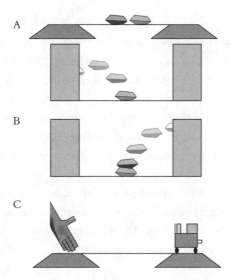

Figure 6.3. Schematic design from Saxe et al., 2007. Top panel, familiarization display. Next two panels: habituation events—a single bean bag emerges in flight from behind either the left screen or the right screen, unpredictable. During test trials, a hand is revealed behind one of the screen and a train behind the other, the screen are replaced and the bean bag emerges in flight from behind the screen with the hand (expected event) or the train (unexpected event). Saxe, R., Tzelnic, T., & Carey, S. (2007). Knowing who-dunnit: Infants identify the causal agent in an unseen causal interaction. *Developmental Psychology, 43*(1), 149–158. Redrawn with permission from American Psychological Association.

entity is a candidate situational agent? Or is it that hands have the mechanical properties of potential throwers and the train does not? These possibilities are not mutually exclusive, of course; infants' causal reasoning could possible integrate information about dispositional agency in general, about particular agents infants have had experience with, and about mechanical and functional affordances of objects. That is, their inferences could be central and nonmodular in the extreme.

We have just begun the studies that will allow us to tease apart these possibilities. In one study, infants were familiarized to a small brown furry puppet, with eyes and spindly legs, but no arms (Figure 6.4). Very thin black strings, invisible against the black backdrop, supported the puppet as it gently hopped around the stage, apparently moving by itself. Infants were then habituated, as before, to beanbags flying out from behind the each of the two screens. Now, when the screens were lowered, the puppet (now stationary) was revealed behind one and the toy train behind the other. The issue here is whether infants would accept the puppet as a candidate agent of a beanbag's motion, just as they had the hand. The answer is yes. Infants again generalized habituation to those test trials on which a beanbag flew out from the screen where the puppet had been revealed, whereas they recovered interest when the beanbag flew out from behind the screen where the train had been revealed.

Apparently what it is about hands that makes them good candidate situational agents extends to entities the infants have never seen throw anything before—entities that do not have throwing limbs (the puppet). Of course, we do not yet know what it was about the puppet that made it a good dispositional agent—its morphological properties (eyes, legs, fur) or the fact that it had been shown to move by itself. Ongoing studies address this issue. Nonetheless, the completed studies converge with those cited above, demonstrating that infants' representations of

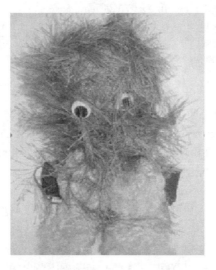

Figure 6.4. Self-moving agent from Saxe et al., 2005, 2007. Reprinted from Saxe, R., Tenenbaum, J., and Carey, S. (2005). Secret agents: 10 and 12-month-olds infer an unseen cause of the motion of an inanimate object. *Psychological Science, 16*(12), 995–1001, with permission from Blackwell Publishers. Saxe, R., Tzelnic, T., & Carey, S. (2007).

particular motion events integrate information about the stable dispositional properties of candidate situational agents. Further studies that
build on these results demonstrate just how complex the infants' reasoning is.

Saxe (Saxe at al., 2005; 2007) was the first to show that infants *infer* a
situational agent, even if they have seen neither the causal interaction nor
the candidate agents themselves prior to the test trials. One experiment is
similar to the beanbag-throwing study diagrammed in Figure 6.3. That
study showed babies potential agents and asked whether they formed
expectations about which beanbag would come flying out from behind
the screen. The study under consideration here never showed babies the
candidate agents, and asked instead whether their representations of the
event led them to posit the existence of a hand.

Consider the following situation: Infants are again familiarized with
an inert beanbag. The curtains open on a stage with two boxes, one on
each side of the stage. The beanbag comes flying out of one box,
landing on a white platform between the two boxes. The curtain closes,
opens again to reveal the two boxes, and again the beanbag comes
flying out of the same box, landing on the white platform. There is only
one beanbag in this study, and it always emerges from the same box.
Infants are habituated to this event. The question is, do they reason
about the (invisible) source of the beanbag's motion? In a series of
experiments, we have shown that 7- and 10-month-old infants do
indeed do so. On test trials, the box again flies out of the same box as
during habituation, and then the fronts of the boxes are lowered,
revealing a hand in one of them and a brightly colored block in the
other. Looking times are measured to these outcomes. At issue is
whether infants look longer at the outcome in which the block is
revealed in the box from which the beanbag had emerged and the hand
is revealed in the other box, relative to the reverse pattern. They do. If
infants have had previous evidence that the beanbag is an inert object,
they infer a hidden causal agent (e.g., a human hand) as the source of the
motion (inside the box) and are surprised if an inert object is revealed in
the source position instead (Saxe et al., 2007).

Note that information about the ontological categories of the entities
is actually playing two different, and critical, roles in these inferences.
First, the infants categorize the moving entity (the beanbag) as inert, and

therefore seek an external causal explanation of the beanbag's motion. Second, infants categorize the potential causal agents, and judge that a human hand is more likely causal agent than is an inert toy train or a block.

The assumption that if the moving object is categorized as self-moving, then infants do not seek an external cause was tested in a final experiment—an experiment that also confirmed that if infants categorize a moving entity as dispositionally inert, they infer a hidden cause of its motion (Saxe, Tenenbaum, & Carey, 2005). The set up is diagrammed in Figure 6.5. In some conditions, as in the above studies, 10- and 12-month-old infants were familiarized to an inert beanbag. Then, during habituation, the curtain was lowered, revealing a barrier in middle of the stage. The bean bag came flying in from one side of the stage (say, the left), sailed over the barrier, landing on the other side (Figure 6.5a). On different trials, the barriers were of different heights and colors; the beanbag always cleared them and landed on the other side of the stage. You may have noticed that this is a real-live version of the Gergeley & Csibra (2006) event described in chapter 5, minus a goal object reached by the flying one. Gergeley and Csibra were interested in whether infants would see the motion of the flying object as goal-directed. Here, our interest is whether they see it as caused by a situational agent, and what entities they might accept as situational agents. To explore this, after habituation, a hand emerged either from the side of the curtain from which the beanbag had been emerging (the left; Figure 6.5b), or from the opposite side of the stage (the right; Figure 6.5c). In three different replications of this design, infants looked longer when the hand emerged from the side of the stage from which the beanbag had *not* come.

The natural interpretation of this finding is that infants inferred a situational agent as the cause of the beanbag's motion, and that a hand is a good candidate for this agent. Two further studies bolstered this interpretation, while ruling out obvious alternative interpretations of the results. One alternative is that infants merely represent these events as motion from the left to the right, and so motion from right to left was novel. To rule this interpretation out, the experiment was rerun, but the entity that emerged from the left or from the right during test trials was our solid wooden toy train, not a hand (Figure 6.6d). Infants did not differentiate these test trials. Thus, their looking patterns in the hand

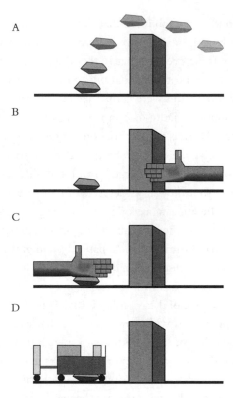

Figure 6.5. Schematic design from Saxe et al., 2005. After familiarization with an inert beanbag on stage floor, the habituation trials involved a beanbag flying in from offstage, clearing a wall, and landing on the other side of the wall (top panel). The side of emergence is constant during the habituation trials (e.g., always from the left in the condition diagrammed here). In test, the beanbag sails over the wall as before, followed by a hand emerging either from the same side from which the beanbag emerged (panel b) or the opposite side (panel c). In another condition of this experiment, the hand is replaced by a train during test trials, the train emerging either from the same side from which the beanbag emerged, or the different side (panel d). Reprinted from Saxe, R., Tenenbaum, J., and Carey, S. (2005). Secret agents: 10 and 12-month-olds infer an unseen cause of the motion of an inanimate object. *Psychological Science, 16*(12), 995–1001, with permission from Blackwell Publishers.

studies are not determined by a low-level expectation that all motion will be from a single side of the stage. Also, these results confirm all the others reviewed in this chapter that hands are good candidate situational agents and dispositionally inert objects such as small wooden trains are not.

The final condition established that the representation of the figure, the *beanbag*, as dispositionally inert is playing a crucial role in infants' representations of these events—that is, that dispositional representations allow infants to represent it as a situational patient or a situational agent. In this last condition, infants were familiarized to the brown googly-eyed, spindly-legged puppet (Figure 6.4) moving around on the stage, rather than to a beanbag. During the habituation events, it was the *puppet* that came flying from off-stage over the barrier. The test trials were as before —after habituation, a hand emerged from the side from which the puppet had come or from the other side. In this case, infants looked reliably longer at the appearance of a hand during test trials than in the beanbag conditions, and they did not differentiate the trials as a function of which side the hand came from. Apparently, when the moving figure is itself categorized as a dispositional agent, infants do not infer a situational agent as the cause of its motion.

The overall message of these studies is that 6- to 7-month-old infants already form expectations with causal content that cannot be explained by the output of Michotte's module for perceptual causality. Their inferences rely on the categorization of the entities in the situational agent and patient roles in terms of enduring causal dispositional status. These results are not incompatible with the existence of a perceptual module in early infancy. Richly integrated causal inferences may exist alongside an encapsulated module. But clearly, not all of an infant's earliest causal representations are modular. Thus, these results weigh clearly against Michotte's contention that the perceptual module is the single original source of all true causal concepts, while at the same time bolster our confidence in attributing representations of cause to young infants.

Are We Justified in Attributing Representations with the Content *Cause* to Infants?

Below, I consider how the data summarized to this point bear on the innateness of the concept *cause,* as well as on Michotte's particular hypothesis concerning the nature of innate causal representations. But before turning to these considerations, let us first step back and consider whether the rich interpretation of these experiments in terms of causal representations by 6 months of age is justified. The experiments reported above have been taken to show that by 6 months of age, infants have a concept *cause*. The dialectic around this claim should now be familiar, for we have seen it before concerning representations of the concepts *object* and *agent*. Not astonishingly, developmental psychologists with empiricist leanings prefer a leaner interpretation of the results reviewed here. Might they be right? Might infants' behavior be understood entirely in terms of representations of contingencies among events in the world specified entirely over a sensory or perceptual vocabulary?

None of these experiments provides absolute, knock–down evidence that preverbal infants interpret Michotte launching events causally. Just as infants may have learned the contingent relations among the spatio-temporal features of launching, so too they may have learned restrictions on those contingencies stated over perceptual features of the entities involved (and hence be sensitive to parameters correlated with disposi-tional agency), and they may have learned generalizations concerning the relative sizes of objects and relative extents of motions. The Leslie and Keeble study (1987) is more difficult to reinterpret in this way, but one may imagine an empiricist response. An empiricist might argue that infants bring previous learning of the spatio-temporal contingencies in launching events to the representation of the events that satisfy the schema of Michottian launching, but have no relevant experience with events in which there is a temporal delay between object A's contacting object B and object B's subsequent motion. Exactly why this would lead to an interest in the reversal of the events only in the former case is not clear, however. Also, Leslie and Keeble did not find differential rates of habituation to the two classes of events.

Although the empiricist has responses to the rich interpretations that credit infants with causal representations in the above studies, I doubt them, for two reasons. First, attributing representations of the schema *the motion of object A causes object B to move* to the infant is the most parsi-monious account of how the young infant learns the generalizations revealed in the above studies. If causal notions organize infants' repre-sentations of launching events, we can make sense of their distinguishing agents and patients, of their learning generalizations of what can be agents and patients, and of their learning properties of motion contingent on which is which. As always, those who believe that the child is merely gathering reliable statistics about the events unfolding around him owes an account of how the child constrains which properties to notice, which correlations to store.

Second, and related, attributing the concept *cause* to infants by 6 months of age makes sense of a very striking finding that emerges from the above review. As early in development (i.e., 6 months) as there is evidence that infants *perceive* Michotte launching, expulsion, and entraining events in causal terms (i.e., distinguish the situational agent and patient roles, see launching events as categorically distinct from both spatial gap and temporal gap events), they make complex causal infer-ences integrating representations of dispositional agency into their causal interpretation of specific events. A few seconds' experience with our brown googly-eyed puppet moving on its own is all that is required for the child to interpret it as the source of its own motion and as the possible source of the motion of a beanbag. The child has seen no interactions between this entity and others, and so can have learned no contingencies between its motion and that of others. The relevant generalizations (and thus learned contingencies) are stated over an abstract vocabulary, and the learning looks anything but piecemeal. This is what would be expected if representations of cause are organizing the child's representation of these events and hence of their learning about the entities that participate in them.

Are Representations of *Cause* Innate?

Suppose we accept that by 6 months of age infants represent causality. The fact that there is no evidence for representations of causality before this age cannot be taken as evidence, in itself, that there is no innate concept *cause*. Those who believe that the concept can be built from noncausal sensori-motor primitives need to specify what those primitives might be and what learning process operative in the first 6 months of life might yield representations of *cause* from them. No such account is on offer.

Cohen and Chaput (2002) present a connectionist model that purports to solve this problem. Their interesting model learns the spatio-temporal factors that predict when motion of one entity is followed by motion of another. However, this prediction is still formulated over spatio-temporal vocabulary—there is no representation with the content *cause*.

Evaluating Michotte's Hypothesis: The Origin of Causal Representations

The studies reviewed above provide very strong evidence that by 6 to 7 months of age, infants perceive and interpret launching events, entraining events, and expulsion events causally. Learnability considerations favor the conclusion that some mechanism for computing causality from perceptual input is innate. Nonetheless, the evidence is quite strong against Michotte's hypothesis concerning the nature of that mechanism. That is, the data reviewed in this chapter militate against Michottian perceptual analyzers as *the* source of the human capacity for causal representations. If this were so, there should be a point in development at which we could find evidence for causal perception in fully visible launching or entraining events (as in the Leslie and Keeble studies,1987, or the Oakes and Cohen studies, 1990), and no evidence for causal inference, especially inferences integrating mechanical causality with other types of causal representations. No such point in development has been discovered yet; rather, just the opposite is true. As soon as there is any evidence for causal representations, infants integrate their representations of the spatio-temporal parameters of events with information about the ontological status and stable causal dispositions of the interacting entities. Infants' causal representations of motion events are exquisitely sensitive to whether a candidate situational agent is a hand, a puppet with eyes and legs, a toy train, or a block. The fact that *state* changes of a box are interpreted as caused by a hand making contact with it, but not a moving train doing so, provides additional evidence that some of the ultimate sources of causal representations are outside of Michotte's perceptual module, either in addition to it or in conjunction with it.

Furthermore, the existing literature does not provide any evidence for Michotte's claim that the perceptual module itself is innate. By the time experimentalists can find robust evidence of causal perception, infants have already had 6 months of experience observing causal interactions, presumably including launching, entraining, and expulsion.

More important, we have shown that other causal information (about the phenomenal and ontological aspects of objects) is integrated with representations of mechanical causality as young as we can find evidence that mechanical causality is itself represented. It is therefore possible that infants learn to recognize launching, entraining, and expulsion as causal, informed by data interpreted through the lens of this "other" causal information—for example, from the infants' own experience of effort (along the lines of the de Biran hypothesis), and/or from the analysis of conditional probabilities (along the lines of Bayes-nets causal learning proposals). To belabor my point here, the Michottian schemata might be learned, even if the capacity to represent causality per se is innate and plays a role in learning them.

Which other sources of causal representations that might contribute to construction of Michottian launching causality? That hands are privileged as candidate situational agents provides some support for Maine de Biran's hypothesis that the ontogentic and conceptual core of causal representations is the schema of an agent exerting effort and affecting the world. Just as infants are influenced by knowledge of their own intentional actions in representing others' actions as intentional (see chapter 4), so too might they be influenced by knowledge of their own causal interventions on the world in providing causal analyses of events not involving themselves. And they may thus project their own sense of internally generated effort onto their representations of the capacity of situational agents to effect motion and state changes. If this hypothesis has merit, we might expect to find that, just as infants interpret state changes causally if the situational agent is a hand more easily than if the situational agent is a toy train, so too 4- and 5-month-old infants may succeed in Ball's paradigm exploring launching causality more easily if the situational agent is a hand than if it is a ball or a toy train.

Still, I do not think that the infant's own sense of causal interventions on the world can be the sole source of causal representations, for reasons analogous to those that convince me that the infant's sense of its own intentionality cannot be the sole source of the capacity for intentional attributions. The infant may well represent his or her own effort, and his or her own goals with respect to changing the environment, but representing effort, goals, and means is not the same as representing causality. I could try all I like to lift my car with my bare hands, experiencing great effort. To know whether my efforts have actually had an effect on the world, I need some other way of representing causality— either Michotte's (my action resulted in a perception of launching or entraining) or an analysis of the probabilities of outcomes conditional upon my actions, as in a Bayes-net representation.

Carolyn Rovee-Collier (e.g., Rovee & Rovee, 1969) has demonstrated that 2-month-olds can learn to kick their legs in order to make a mobile move and that 6-months can learn to press a lever to make a train move (Hartshorn & Rovee-Collier, 1997). In the mobile experiments, the infants' legs in fact are connected to the mobile by a ribbon, but it is unlikely that the child is aware of that, for after the child has learned the behavior, the child kicks in the presence of the mobile even if the ribbon is not tied to her leg. This is, of course, standard operant conditioning, and Rovee-Collier was not primarily interested in causal representations; rather, she used this behavior to explore infants' memory for the mobile or the train. However, many have argued that operant conditioning implicates causal representations (e.g., Dickinson & Shanks, 1995; Gallistel, 1990). These authors analyze operant condition as a learning mechanism that computes causality from patterns of conditional probabilities, a special case of the learning that establishes Bayes-nets causal representations. It would be very important to see whether infants younger than 6 months of age can make causal attributions from observing the patterns of conditional probabilities among events not involving themselves. If so, this capacity could underlie both the development of causal perception (coming to see launching, entraining, and expulsion events as causal) and correctly interpreting which of one's own actions are causally effective.

This third mechanism (computing causality from patterns of conditional probabilities) is a paradigm domain general central process. If it is indeed the root of human causal representations, then this case study provides an example of conceptual representations with innate support that are not limited to a domain of core cognition. It is also possible that all three mechanisms for identifying causal interactions in the world exist and are initially independent of each other, but have begun to be integrated already by 6 or 7 months of age. However, there is another possibility not anticipated in Michotte's debates with Maine de Biran over the ultimate source of human causal representations. As the rationalists insisted, representations with the content *cause* may be innate, but they may be part of a central conceptual system that integrates information from *all three* sources of evidence (contingency, direct perception of mechanical causality, sense of one's own causal effort and efficacy in the world) from the outset. Given the rich interconnections between infants' representations of the sources of motion of inert objects and their representations of dispositional causal agents documented in the present studies, this alternative picture is very much alive.

Conclusions

This chapter completes my comments on the initial representational systems that ground conceptual development. Core cognition is one source of representations with innate conceptual content, and chapters 2 to 5 provided evidence for several distinct core domains and characterized the nature of core cognition. But core cognition need not be the only source of representations with innate conceptual content. Core cognition representations are input to central conceptual processes, and there is no reason there may not be central representational systems with innate conceptual content that is distinct from that of core cognition systems. The example considered here is the capacity to represent *cause,* and there may well be others.

I turn now to the second half of my account of the origin of concepts. The chapters to come describe discontinuities in conceptual development and sketch an uniquely human learning mechanism that underlies the human capacity to create new representational resources— that is, to create concepts not available in or definable in terms of antecedent representations.

7

Language and Core Cognition

Noam Chomsky made nativism respectable in the face of the dominant empiricist behaviorism of the first half of the last century. His concern was language acquisition, not conceptual development. Many modern cognitive scientists agree with Chomsky that domain-specific learning devices support the mastery of natural language, although there is much disagreement on the details of what aspects of language are innate and what kinds of domain-specific acquisition devices exist (e.g., Chomsky, 1965; Pinker, 1984, 1989; Spelke & Newport, 1998; Wexler & Culicover, 1983; Gleitman, Cassidy, Nappa, Papafragou, & Trueswell, 2005). I will assume, with these authors, that human evolution bequeathed us with innate knowledge of language, which we can imagine takes the form of a language acquisition device (LAD). The LAD guides the learning of natural language syntax, morphology, and phonology.

Although an account of the acquisition of syntax, morphology, and phonology is beyond the scope of this book, the lexicon stands right in the middle of any theory of conceptual development. Words express concepts, and most of the concepts I have been concerned with are of the grain of single lexical items. How is it that language comes to be integrated with nonlinguistic representations, such that it is a vehicle for expressing thought? Must prelinguistic thought be transformed in any ways for this to happen?

These questions are at the heart of the scientific study of the relations between language and thought. For most cognitive scientists, this topic brings to mind the Whorfian hypothesis that languages differ from each other in the representational resources they make available or make salient. Recent years have seen a resurgence of interest in Whorfian claims (see Bowerman & Levinson, 2001; Gentner & Goldin-Meadow,

2003, for recent reviews), and I shall not attempt to review this burgeoning literature. Rather, I focus on an issue that is logically prior to the question of whether language learning leads speakers of different languages to think differently about the world. The issue that concerns me here is whether language learning (any language) leads infants to think differently about the world from how they thought about it before language learning. Is language learning itself a source of concepts? Does language learning require building representational resources that transcend core cognition, and if so, in what ways and how is this possible? These questions are logically prior to Whorfian hypotheses for a simple reason. If language learning cannot transform thought, as continuity theorists would hold (see Fodor, 1975; Pinker, 1994; Macnamara, 1982; 1986), then it would be impossible for distinct languages to express qualitatively different representational systems.

My discussion of these issues unfolds as follows: I distinguish the strong linguistic continuity hypothesis that emerges from the language-acquisition literature with two broad ways language learning might affect thought, which I call "weak linguistic influence" and "Quinian linguistic determinism" respectively. At issue is the continuity thesis mentioned in chapter 1: the thesis that the resources needed to express all concepts humans can represent are available throughout development, even at the beginning. As in all discussions in this book, specific case studies illustrate what is at stake and how the arguments go. I make no effort to review how these issues play out in every case in which they have been examined. The cases discussed here include the representations that underlie natural language quantifiers, especially the singular/plural distinction ("is" versus "are," "a" versus "some," "-s"), and basic-level sortal concepts, like *dog* or *table*. I review evidence for an influence of language learning on nonlinguistic representations in each of these cases, and I conclude with arguments that these particular cases reflect weak linguistic influences, at most, and not Quinian linguistic determinism.

Strong Continuity: Lexical Learning as a Mapping Problem

Many linguists have articulated a view of lexical development that presupposes strong continuity, at least underlying the aspects of meanings of lexical items that contribute to their syntactic role (Gleitman et al., 2005; Grimshaw, 1987; Pinker, 1984, 1989). They suggest:

1. Infants' representations of the world are articulated in terms of conceptual distinctions that directly map onto syntactic distinctions.
2. LAD includes representations of the semantic and syntactic categories that underlie all natural languages.
3. LAD includes innate mappings between semantic categories and linguistic ones.

These principles do not require that all concepts are innate—infants' representations need not include concepts like *mortgage, quark, carburetor,* or *persecute*. But the concepts that underlie the meanings of the closed-class vocabulary (bound morphemes, quantifiers, determiners, and so on) and that underlie contrasts between lexical categories (count versus mass versus proper nouns, nouns versus adjectives, and so on)—the concepts that embody the basic ontological commitments made by language—are innate, as are expectations about how these will be realized in language.

This picture of language acquisition gives rise to theories of lexical learning called in the language-acquisition literature "semantic bootstrapping" and "syntactic bootstrapping." This is confusing nomenclature, for semantic and syntactic bootstrapping differ greatly from the bootstrapping mechanisms envisioned in the history and philosophy of science literature. Semantic and syntactic bootstrapping theories seek to explain how children might solve a killingly difficult mapping problem. Even if children were endowed with rich innate conceptual knowledge, and rich knowledge of the possible linguistic categories, they still have to learn their particular language—which syntactic, semantic, and morphological devices it has and how exactly they are expressed.

To get a feel for how semantic bootstrapping mechanisms works, suppose the child knew innately that labels for kinds of objects were count nouns (an innate mapping rule between a conceptual category, object kind, and a linguistic one, count noun.) Then as children figure out that "dog," and "table," and "man" refer to kinds of objects, they would infer that they were count nouns, and this would help them learn how the syntactic reflections of count nouns represented in LAD are expressed in their language (number marking, determiners, adjectives, branching structures, verb agreement, and so on). Once that is learned, hearing "a great idea," would be sufficient to categorize "idea" as a count noun, which would then constrain the meanings children assigned to this word (i.e., that it is an individuated entity). This latter inference is an example of syntactic bootstrapping. Once some of the syntax of the language has been mastered, the innate (or learned) mapping rules enable the child to use syntactic context as a source of evidence for word meaning. Gleitman and her colleagues (2005) have shown how syntactic bootstrapping plays an important role especially in the learning of verbs. For example, hearing a verb in a structure with three arguments rules out its having a meaning like *sleep*, which must be realized as an intransitive verb.

The evidence that children make use of both syntactic and semantic bootstrapping is overwhelming. The field divides upon whether the mapping rules are innate or learned, but nobody can deny that knowledge of semantics/syntax correlations would constrain further learning of both syntactic and lexical information. For present purposes, it is important to recognize that what linguistics call semantic and semantic "bootstrapping" is actually embedded in a theory strongly committed to continuity. The learning processes support mappings between antecedently available conceptual and linguistic categories.

Language as the Source of Concepts: Quinian Linguisitic Determinism

Continuity theorists such as Jerry Fodor (1975), John Macnamara (1982), and Steven Pinker (1984, 1994) deny that language learning shapes our concepts in any interesting ways, let alone that language learning is part of a process that creates new concepts that embody new ontological commitments. These writers would certainly allow weaker effects of language on thought during cognitive development. The language spoken might select among different possible conceptual distinctions to mark explicitly (and even obligatorily), and learning language might make some antecedently represented concepts more salient to and more automatically deployed by the child.[1] Such effects are not inconsistent with conceptual and linguistic continuity throughout the life span. Call these effects "weak linguistic influence," to contrast them to Quinian linguistic determinism.

The continuity thesis stands in stark contrast to Quine's doctrine of strong linguistic determinism (see chapter 2). Quine (1960, 1969, 1977) claimed that there are episodes of conceptual development in which:

1. Infants' representations are radically different from those of their elders.
2. Adult representational resources are a cultural construction, expressed in natural languages.
3. Adult representational resources are acquired by each child through bootstrapping processes in the course of mastering natural language.

As you will recall from chapter 2, Quine, along with the British empiricists, Piaget, and many modern-day psychologists, held that infants' representations of the world are formulated in terms of perceptual primitives. Quine, like Piaget, pointed out that such representations differ qualitatively from those that natural languages express, especially in term of their quantitative capabilities. Quine's view of the depth of the difference between a representational system formulated over an innate perceptual quality space and one formulated over concepts with the quantificational structure of natural languages was emphasized when he insisted that commonsense ontology is a cultural construction, just as the concepts that articulate scientific theories are cultural constructions: "Theory may be deliberate, as in a chapter on chemistry, or it may be second nature, as in the immemorial doctrine of ordinary enduring middle-sized objects" (1960, p. 11). And "analyze theory-building how we will, we must all start in the middle. Our conceptual firsts are middle-sized, middle-distanced objects, and our introduction to them and to everything comes midway in the cultural evolution of the race" (1960, pp. 4–5).

Chapter 2 explored Quine's claims, concluding that they fail on premise number 1. Infants' representations are not formulated over a perceptual or sensori-motor quality space (only), and thus are not radically different from those of their elders in the ways Quine envisioned. I bring up Quine's view again because of his view of linguistic determinism. Quine hypothesized that the processes through which infants create new representational resources crucially implicate language learning. Quine saw the child's mastery of the linguistic devices of noun quantification—the machinery by which natural languages manage divided reference—as the process through which the child's ontology comes to match his or her elders'. That is, the child works out meanings of quantifiers, determiners, the "is" of numerical identity, the count/mass distinction, the common noun/proper noun distinction, and so forth—by learning how these linguistic devices are interrelated and used, and in so doing, acquires the commonsense ontology these devices express. Quine appealed to bootstrapping metaphors in describing this process:

> The contextual learning of these various particles goes on simultaneously, we may suppose, so that they are gradually adjusted to one another and a coherent pattern of usage is evolved matching that of one's elders. This is a major step in acquiring the conceptual scheme we all know so well. For it is on achieving this step, and only then, that there can be any general talk of objects as such. (1969, pp. 9–10)
>
> The child scrambles up an intellectual chimney, supporting himself against each side by pressure against the others. Conceptualization on any considerable scale is inseparable from language, and our ordinary language of physical things is about as basic as language gets. (1960, p. 93)

I will have much more to say about bootstrapping processes in chapters 8 through 11. Quine did not even try to characterize these learning processes with enough detail that would begin to satisfy a modern cognitive scientist. But the basic ideas of Quine's bootstrapping metaphors are clear enough. The linguistic devices are learned initially, in part, only with respect to each other ("they are gradually adjusted to one another" 1969, p. 9). They are not, and cannot be, fully interpreted in terms of the innate perceptual similarity space, for the latter does not have the expressive power to represent the *is* or *same* of numerical identity, the *dog* or *bottle* that is a kind of individual that divides reference. It is the pattern of interrelations among the newly learned linguistic devices that constitutes the sides of the chimney that supports the learner as he or she simultaneously climbs. When these linguistic devices are fully learned and stable, the child has achieved a representation of the commonsense ontology they express, which reorders and reinterprets the features of the innate perceptual similarity space.

Chapters 2 through 4 argued against the empiricist (and Quinian) picture of the initial state, and I will not belabor those arguments. The child's initial systems of representation do have the expressive power to represent the *is* or *same* of numerical identity (they distinguish numerically distinct individual objects from each other). Rather, I bring up Quine again because of his proposal for how children acquire the ontological commitments they putatively lack innately. He held that the route to mastery of those concepts is language learning itself. If this were right, then language learning would shape the concepts the child represents, making possible thoughts not representable before. This is Quine's picture, which I call "Quinian linguistic determinism."

While much of the adult conceptual repertoire may be continuous with the representational resources of infants—that is, continuous with core cognition, innate central representations, and the representations in the language acquisition device—Quinian linguistic determinism may characterize the ontogenetic origin of some concepts. Indeed, chapters 8 through 11 argue that this is so. Possible cases in which language learning plays a role in the construction of or wide deployment of representational resources must be examined one by one. Even within the case of the representations that articulate the quantificational resources of natural languages (Quine's own example), there is room for linguistic determinism, and these are the cases I will examine further in the rest of this chapter. I illustrate how one explores the possibility of linguistic determinism, and how in these cases doing so leads to the discovery of innate representational resources I had not earlier anticipated and to evidence for weak linguistic determinism. Chapters 8 through 11 provide examples of Quinian linguistic determinism.

The concepts that articulate the quantificational semantics of noun phrases in natural languages go beyond the resources core cognition described in chapters 2 through 4 in many ways, and here I discuss two of them. First, natural languages include explicit symbols for quantifiers that are not represented in the parallel individuation and analog magnitude quantificational systems. Second, natural languages deploy concepts for individuals other than spatio-temporally defined objects; they include sortals like "dog, table," and "cup." Initial evidence suggests that language learning may play a role in shaping infants' conceptual development in each of these cases. Might these be examples of Quinian linguistic determininism?

Possible Linguistic Determinism: Case 1—Quantifiers

The quantificational devices of natural language noun phrases go beyond those implicit in the computations carried out over object-files and analog magnitude representations. Natural language quantifiers are explicit symbols (in English, the determiners, the numerals, plural morphemes, "some, many, each, few...," and so on). In parallel individuation representations the only symbols are those for particular individuals and, at least implicitly, for the set being represented. The quantificational force of parallel individuation is carried by computations defined over those representations of sets of individuals. In analog magnitude representations the only symbols are symbols for particular quantities (e.g., the approximate cardinal value of a set), and the only computations defined over these representations are arithmetical. There are no concepts in either of these systems of core cognition with the content *some, all,* or *a*.

As we will see below, the first explicit lexical contrasts with quantificational force that children learn in English are singular/plural markers, such as the contrast between "is a X" and "are some Xs." Even the singular/plural distinction is not naturally expressed in terms of the two core systems discussed in chapter 4.

Consider a representation of sets of 1, 2, and 3 objects that works as parallel individuation does:

This representation contains explicit symbols for each object, and

1 object:	OBJ		
2 objects:	OBJ	OBJ	
3 objects:	OBJ	OBJ	OBJ

implicitly represents the sets by having selected sets of 1, 2, or 3 particular objects to represent. There are no explicit symbols for *each, every, some, more, a, plural*... on this figure. Nor does this system of representation mark the distinction between a single individual, on the one hand, and multiple individuals, on the other, collapsing across distinctions among pluralites. And, of course, this system of representation cannot even implicitly represent pluralities greater than 3. This system does not have the representational force of set-based quantification.

Now consider a representations of cardinal values of sets that works as do analog magnitudes:
and so on.

1 object:	_
2 object:	__
3 object:	___
4 object:	____
5 object:	_____
6 object:	_____
7 object:	_____
8 object:	_____

This system of representation contains explicit symbols for cardinal values of the sets that are implicitly represented through having been selected by some attentional mechanism. There are no explicit symbols for *each, every, some, more, a, plural,* and so on, on this figure, either. And this system also fails to collapse across distinctions among pluralities, treating 8 as equivalent to 2, distinct from 1. Rather, this system distinguishes any two cardinalities whose ratio exceeds its limit of discrimination. Thus, this system also fails to have to the representational force of set-based quantification. Furthermore, in chapter 4 we saw that these two systems of representation are not well integrated with each other in infancy. Pluralities, in contrast, encompass sets of 2 and 3 as well as sets of 4 or 10, or 100 or more.

Moreover, chapters 3 and 4 reviewed evidence that suggests that at least sometimes 12- and 14-month-olds do not draw upon the singular/ plural distinction when it would serve them well to do so. Remember the cracker-choice and the box-reach studies, and the set-size signature of parallel individuation representations. Infants failed in these tasks with contrasts of 1 versus 4. These are extremely surprising results. Shown one cracker placed into one box and four crackers into another box, infants were at chance in choosing which box to crawl to. All they need to have done to succeed was to represent 4 as more than 1—as plural compared to singular, as *some* rather than *one*,—but they did not. Similarly, shown four objects placed into a box, and then allowed to retrieve one, infants did not reach back in to retrieve any more. Again, if they had merely represented 4 as more than 1, as *plural*, they would have succeeded, but they did not (Feigenson & Carey, 2005).

We found these results so remarkable that we have tested older children on the box-reach task. Eighteen-month-olds succeed at 3 versus 1 comparisons, as do 12- and 14-month-olds, but still fail at 4 versus 1 comparisons. And 20-month-olds also fail at 4 versus 1 comparisons. Shown four objects together on the top of a box, which are then put into the box through a slit infants can reach but not see through, 20-month-old English learning infants, as well as younger ones, reach in and retrieve one. After getting one, they are satisfied. These data are consistent with the possibility that not only are there no explicit symbols for *plural* in the two core cognition systems with numerical content discussed in chapter 4, neither are there computations that treat all sets greater than 1 as equivalent and different from *one*.

What is needed, beyond the core cognition systems of analog magnitudes and parallel individuation, to represent the singular/plural distinction? Linguists such as Genaro Chierchia (1988) and G. Link (1987) show how the quantifiers of all languages, as well as the count/mass distinction, the distinction between nouns in classifier languages and nouns in languages with the count/mass distinction, and much else, can be defined over the semi-lattice depicted in Figure 7.1, which creates all of the possible sets from a domain of atoms or individuals. This structure makes explicit the contrast between individuals (the bottom line) and all of the sets composed out of them. One needs explicit symbols with the content set and individual, plus distributive and collective computations over those symbols, to capture the meanings of natural language quantifiers, including even the singular/plural distinction. I call this system of representation "set-based quantification."

Note that aspects of set-based quantification are implicit in parallel individuation systems; some attentional process selects a set of individuals to represent in parallel, and various computations with quantitative import are licensed over these data structures. But the system of parallel individuation has no symbols for quantifiers, not even *one* versus *some*, and it has an upper limit of sets of 3. The representations in parallel individuation are input into set-based quantification, as are the representations of sets

$$\{a, b, c, d\} \ldots\ldots$$
$$\{a,b, c\} \quad \{a, b, d\} \ldots\ldots$$
$$\{a,b\} \qquad \{b , c\} \quad \{a, c\} \quad \{c,d\} \ldots\ldots$$
$$a \qquad b \qquad c \qquad d \qquad \ldots\ldots$$

Figure 7.1. The semi-lattice of sets comparised of a domain of individuals. Bottom line: the individual atoms in the domain. Next: all the sets of 2 atoms that can be constructed. Next: all the sets of 3 atoms that can be constructed. Top line; set containing all of the atoms in the domain.

that are the input to analog magnitudes. The system of set-based quantification defines quantifiers in terms of the structure in Figure 7.1.

Acquiring Explicit Linguistic Symbols for Quantifiers—Singular and Plural Markers

Since the seminal work of Roger Brown (1973), the father of empirical studies of language acquisition, we have known that the first linguistic quantifiers English-learning children produce are the singular determiner "a," plural marking of various types (on verbs, on nouns, on pronouns), "more" and "some." By the time children have acquired (and properly analyzed) the linguistic symbols for the singular/plural distinction ("a" vs. "some," "is" vs. "are," "noun-Ø" vs "noun-s," and so on), they must represent the conceptual distinction between individuals and sets of multiple individuals. Brown found that between 24 and 30 months of age, children begin producing the plural marker on nouns in 90% of obligatory contexts. Carolyn Mervis and K. Johnson (1991) presented one case study of a child who began marking nominal plurals at 20 months. Thus, children begin marking plurals in production before their second birthday. These studies leave open when children come to comprehend plural marking.

In my laboratory we have recently completed two series of studies, with two different methodologies, on the earliest comprehension of the singular/plural distinction. In both methods, we began by using linguistic contrasts that marked the distinction redundantly: "There are some blickets" versus "There is a blicket." Both methods provided convergent

results: 20-month-old infants, as a group, do not yet command the linguistic distinction and 24-month-old infants do.

One study, by Justin Wood and collaborators (Wood, Kouider, &
Carey, in press), adapted the box-reaching method we have used for
many other purposes. Wood reached under a table and said "I am putting
some balls into the box." He then brought out the box and said, "There
are some balls in the box," and pushing the box within the child's reach,
"Can you get the balls?" Alternatively, he said "I am putting a ball into
the box. There is a ball in the box. Can you get the ball?" Whichever he
said, the box contained only one object. The measure of interest was how
persistently the child searched in the box after retrieving that first object.
We reasoned that if the child reached longer in the plural context, he
must know that plural morphology is used to refer to more than one
individual. Twenty-month-olds did not reach differentially in the two
linguistic contexts whereas 24-month-olds did.

The other study, by Sid Kouider and collaborators (Kouider,
Halberda, Wood, & Carey, 2006), used looking times as a dependent
measure. Two video screens each displayed unfamiliar objects (e.g., a
vacuum tube on one and eight honey dippers on the other). The child
was told either "Look, there is a blicket," or "Look, there are some
blickets." If the child comprehends plural morphology, he should look at
the set of eight in the latter case—whatever blickets are, the only screen
that could contain some of them is the one with eight objects. Whereas
there is no absolute right answer in the singular case (the screen with eight
blickets contains a blicket, after all), the pragmatics of the situation might
lead the child to choose the set of 1 as a better example of "a blicket."
Twenty-four-month-old infants looked at the appropriate screen in each
of the linguistic contexts (i.e., the eight-object screen with plural markers;
the one-object screen with singular markers), 20-month-olds in neither.
Because looking times were being tracked frame by frame, Kouider and
his colleagues could determine which linguistic markers of plurality
guided attention to the relevant display. Infants' looking to the two arrays
began to diverge immediately after they heard "is" vs. "are," and continued to diverge through the quantifiers. Performance was driven by the
contrast between "is a" and "are some." In both looking time study and
the box search study, 24-month-old toddlers failed if cued by plural noun
morphology alone ("blicket" or "ball" vs. "blickets" or "balls").

Notice that in the looking-time study, the plural sets contained eight objects, whereas in the box-search study, the plural sets contained two objects. Thus, the toddler's "are some noun-s" encompasses sets of object both in the range of parallel individuation and analog magnitudes. These findings, which reflect comprehension rather than production, converge with the data on production. We can be confident that English-learning children begin to appreciate the force of the contrast between "is a noun-Ø" versus "are some noun-s" between the ages of 20 and 24 months.

Data that Suggest that Language Learning Plays a Role in Creating the Concepts of Individual and Set of Multiple Individuals

English-learning infants master some of the linguistic markers of the singular/plural distinction between 20 and 24 months. Furthermore, infants demonstrate in the nonlinguistic box-search task that they spontaneously represent a set of four balls as *plural, some,* or *more than one* at 22 months of age, but not at 20 months. This coincidence of the apparent age of acquisition of the linguistic and nonlinguistic reflections of the distinction between individuals and sets of multiple individuals raises the question of the relations between these two developmental achievements.

David Barner and his colleagues (Barner, Thalwitz, Wood, & Carey, 2007) have recently tackled this question in the case of English-learning infants. Barner studied 20-, 22-, and 24-month-old toddlers from monolingual English-speaking households. He asked parents to indicate whether their infants were yet producing plural morphemes on nouns (*never, sometimes, often*) and he also ran each infant in the nonverbal box-search task. In this task, infants watched as either four balls or a single ball were placed on top of the box and their attention was drawn to them. The balls/ball were placed in the box and the child was allowed to reach in and retrieve one (the other three, in the four-ball condition, having been surreptitiously removed). That single ball is then taken from the child and the critical measurement period ensues. Success consists of more persistent search in the four-ball condition, when there should be more balls in the box, than in the one-ball condition, when the child has already removed the only ball seen placed in the box. As mentioned already, 20-month-olds fail, whereas 22- and 24-month-olds succeed.

Barner also found that the parents of the 20-month-olds overwhelmingly said that their infants were never producing plurals, whereas the parents of the 22- and 24-month-olds said their infants sometimes or often did so. Furthermore, among the 22- and 24-month olds, who were overall succeeding on both measures, the two measures were correlated. Success on the nonverbal box-reach task was carried by those infants whose parents said they were producing plural markers on nouns.

These studies establish a connection between the two developmental achievements, but of course they tell us nothing about the nature of that connection. They do not even speak to the direction of causal influence. It could be that some maturational or learning process makes the conceptual distinction between individuals and sets become available between 20 and 22 months of age, and it is this conceptual development that makes it possible for children to acquire the contrast between "is a noun" and "are some noun-s." Alternatively, it could be that language learning somehow makes that conceptual distinction available (Quinian linguistic determinism) or more salient (weak linguistic influence).

Influence of Language Learning on Nonlinguistic Thought

Peggy Li and David Barner and colleagues (Li, Ogura, Barners, Yange & Carey, in press) carried out two parallel studies to explore causal relations between mastery of plural marking in English, on the one hand, and the deployment of a nonlinguistic distinction between one and more than one in the box-search task, on the other hand. They reasoned that if mastery of explicit plural marking played a role in formulating this distinction, or making it more salient and thus more likely to be spontaneously deployed in nonlinguistic contexts, then children learning a language with no plural marking would succeed on the box-search task later than do English learners. Classifier languages, like Japanese and Chinese, are such languages. They do not have singular determiners (no word that means "a") and do not mark plurality on nouns or verbs. Barner tested Japanese-learning children in the box-reach task and found success at the same age as English learners succeed. Li tested Mandarin-learning children and also found success at the same age at which English learners succeed. Thus there is no evidence that learning explicit linguistic representations for set-based quantification underlies the changes observed in English learners between 20 and 22 months on 4 versus 1 comparisons in the box-reach task.

These data suggest that set-based quantification is part of the machinery children bring to the task of language learning, either as part of the language-acquisition device or as part of general representational capacities. Other considerations also militate against the proposal that Quinian bootstrapping is necessary to construct the representational capacity for set-based quantification. Quinian bootstrapping takes time, and the external linguistic symbols must first be uninterpreted or at least partially misanalyzed, as they are gradually adjusted to one another. This case does not appear to fit this bill. As soon as the child begins producing plural markers, between 20 and 24 months of age, these markers are correctly analyzed, as shown by the fact that children both produce them in appropriate contexts and comprehend them. Also, John Macnamara and his colleagues (Katz, Baker, & Macnamara, 1974) showed that infants before their 2nd birthday understand the semantic force of the distinction between "a blicket" and "Blicket," taking the former to refer to an individual of a kind, blicket, and the latter to refer to an individual named "Blicket." As soon as the singular determiner "a" is learned, it seems to be interpreted correctly; there is no evidence for a protracted process of adjusting the meanings of placeholder symbols to each other, creating representations with semantic force previously unavailable.

There is a second source of evidence that could settle the issue. If LAD contains set-based quantification, along with innate mapping rules between the syntactic expression of quantifiers and conceptual representations of quantifier meanings, we should be able to find some evidence for those conceptual representations in prelinguistic infants. And if set-based quantification is part of our general representational abilities, we might even be able to find evidence for it in nonlinguistic primates. David Barner and Justin Wood have recently found such evidence (Barner, Wood, Houser, & Carey, in press; Barner, Thalwitz, Wood, & Carey, 2008). They have shown that under some circumstances 15-month-old infants and *Rhesus* macaques spontaneously represent the distinction between individuals and sets of multiple individuals. The cases in which infants and monkeys fail to represent sets that exceed the limits on parallel individuation as "some" or "plural" or "more than 1" are cases that elicit parallel individuation, cases in which each individual moves independently of others and is salient as an individual. Monkeys and prelinguistic infants display a previously undocumented pattern of success and failure if the sets of multiple objects move as a rigid whole. Consider the monkey experiments. Using two different methods (the food-choice task, and simple habituation), these authors have found success at discriminating 1 from other set sizes (1 vs. 2, 1 vs. 3, 1 vs. 4, and 1 vs. 5) in the face of failure at 2 versus 3, 2 versus 4, and 2 versus 5. This pattern of success and failure cannot be accounted for by analog magnitude representations because the ratio of 2 to 5, at which monkeys fail, is more favorable than the ratio of 1 to 2, at which they succeed. Nor can it be accounted for by the system of parallel individuation, as monkeys are failing at 2 versus 3 and 2 versus 4 comparisons (within the range of parallel individuation) and succeeding at 1 versus 5 comparisons (and 5 is outside of the range of monkey parallel individuation). Apparently, under these circumstances, monkeys are representing these arrays as *individual* or *one* versus *plural* or *some*, and failing to represent any further information about quantity in the plural sets. Barner et al. (2008) elicited the same pattern of response in the box-search task with 15-month-olds, so long as the sets moved as united wholes.

These data provide strong evidence that acquiring the singular/plural distinction does not require Quinian bootstrapping, as nonlinguistic creatures such as 15-month-old infants and *Rhesus* macaques spontaneously deploy it in some special circumstances. It is available to support learning the meaning of the contrast between "is a noun-Ø" and "are some noun-*s*."

Science is particularly fun when it produces mysterious findings. Why on earth would monkeys ever treat pluralities as equivalent, not distinguishing between a set of 2 and a set of 5? We know that they can distinguish these set sizes with the machinery of analog magnitude representations. Why would they need a representation with content *some* or *plural*? And what is changing between ages 20 and 22 months such that the contrast between one and more than one becomes spontaneously deployed in a nonlinguistic task that previously elicited only parallel individuation? I have no conclusive answers to these questions—they await further thinking and research—but here is my speculation. The machinery of set-based quantification supports the distinction between kinds and individuals; hence the double function of the singular determiner: it introduces a single member of kind into the discourse. Kinds typically have more than one individual in them, and monkeys may sometimes find it useful to encode the fact that there are multiple individuals of a kind, while not at that moment caring how many individuals there are. Relatedly, between 18 and 20 months, children learning all languages are mastering words for basic-level kinds, words like "dog" and "cup" and "shoe." Indeed, morphological development in the earliest stages of language learning is closely linked to vocabulary growth. Perhaps what is changing between 20 and 22 months is an increase in the vocabulary for kinds of objects, and this indirectly makes set-based quantification more salient. It also supports the learning of explicit linguistic quantifiers. This hypothesis is testable. If it is right, then success at the nonlinguistic 1 versus 4 condition in the box-search task should be correlated with noun vocabulary size in learners of languages with a count-mass distinction and in learners of classifier languages alike.

Whatever the answers to these mysteries, we have found another representational ability available to prelinguistic creatures: the capacity for set-based quantification and the distinction between *one* and *some*. These representational capacities are not made possible by language learning. If there is any influence of language learning on thought in this case, it is of the weak variety. It is possible that deploying set-based quantification in language (merely by using count nouns) makes it more salient, and thus more likely to be deployed in nonlinguistic contexts. Further research is needed to establish even this.

Possible Linguistic Determinism: Case 2—Kind Sortals

The literatures on metaphysics and philosophy of language dub concepts that provide criteria for individuation and numerical identity "sortals." I shall use the term "sortal" to refer both to sortal concepts, such as *dog*, and the words that express sortal concepts, such as "dog." Sortals come in many varieties. I shall use the term "kind sortal" to refer to what are sometimes called in this literature "substance sortals"—sortals such that if an individual ceases to fall under that sortal, that individual ceases to exist.[2] Thus, *dog* is a kind-sortal because, when an individual ceases to be a dog (i.e., it dies), it ceases to exist. When my dog Domino died, there was one fewer entity in the world. *Puppy* and *pet*, while sortals, are not kind-sortals because when an entity ceases to be a puppy or a pet, it does not go out of existence. *Puppy* is a stage-sortal; *pet* a phase-sortal.

The term "kind sortal" has two parts—"kind" and "sortal." These do different, but related, work in the full analysis of kind-sortals. A concept is a sortal by providing criteria for individuation and numerical identity. A concept is a kind-concept by being inductively deep; kind concepts fall under the assumptions of psychological essentialism. We assume, in the case of essentialized kinds, that hidden causal processes explain the existence of members of that kind, determine their identity throughout their existence, their surface properties, and their causal powers (S. Gelman, 2003). Not all kind-concepts are sortals. For example, some substance terms such as "gold" refer to essentialized kinds, but do not provide criteria for individuation or numerical identity.

If *dog* is a kind-sortal, then *is a dog* is not a property like other properties that do not provide criteria for individuation and numerical identity or are inductively shallow, such as *red* or *big* or *water*. We cannot count the red in the room, the bigness, or the water, but we can count the dogs in the room. Language marks this distinction in many ways. In languages with the count/mass distinction, such as English, sortals are lexicalized as count nouns; count nouns pick out the individuals that properties are predicated of.

As reviewed in chapter 2, Piaget (and Quine) conjectured that infants represent no sortals. Contrary to these authors, the concept *object* characterized in chapters 2 and 3 is a sortal with spatio-temporal criteria for individuation and numerical identity. Notice that the criteria for individual and numerical identity are not explicitly represented—they are not spelled out in the form of a definition, for example. Rather, they are implemented in the computations that govern the opening and closing of object-files, the computations that determine whether a given object is the same one or a different one from one seen previously. Because of these computations, *object* is a sortal.

However, in the adult conceptual system, *object* is not the only sortal in terms of which we individuate physical objects. Many intuitions reveal that specific sortals provide different criteria for individuation and numerical identity than do object-files. Take *dog*, for example. The criteria for individuation and numerical identity for dogs are not spatio-temporal.

Most simply, a dog ceases to exist when it dies, even though the dog's body is spatio-temporally continuous with the resulting corpse. Some sortals individuate portions of existence even less than a life—for example, *passenger, puppy*; a given person may be counted many times when American Airlines is reporting the number of passengers it flew across the country in 1999, and when my beloved Labrador retriever Domino was 13, she was the same dog I got at a farm those many years ago, but not the same puppy, in spite of exquisite spatio-temporal continuity.

The core cognition systems we have described so far leave open the following possibility concerning the infants' representational capacities. It is possible that the only sortal in terms of which material entities are individuated by young infants is *object*. Unlike adults, young infants may not represent kind-sortals for specific objects (dog, person), and may not distinguish kind-sortals from properties (for infants both redness and dogness may be properties that can be bound to spatio-temporally specified objects). This proposal has empirical support. In addition, there is evidence for a role of language in constructing kind-sortals. Below, I review the evidence for these claims, concluding by considering whether the role language learning plays on conceptual development is a case of weak linguistic influence or Quinian linguistic determinism.

The Relatively Late Emergence of Object Kind-Sortals

Chapter 3 described Fei Xu's (Xu & Carey, 1996) and Gretchen van de Walle's (Van de Walle, Carey, & Prevor, 2000) studies in which infants under 12 months of age failed to draw on kind contrasts among objects in the service of object individuation.; Shown a yellow rubber duck drawn from behind and returned behind a screen or inside a box, followed by a red metallic truck, 10-month-old infants failed to infer that there were two numerically distinct objects behind the screen or inside the box. I appealed to these data in my arguments that young infants' object representations are built by the object tracking mechanisms of mid-level vision, for spatio-temporal information dominates property or kind information in computations of numerical identity in that system as well.

In these studies, we presented the children with contrasts such as duck/car, book/bottle, cup/ball, and telephone/dog as possible bases for individuation. In these experiments, then, infants failed to reveal knowledge of object kind-sortals. The distinction between an elephant and a truck, between a ball and a book, and so on, does not suffice for the child to establish and maintain in memory representations of two numerically distinct objects in these events. Results from a third paradigm extended this pattern of results to an individuation problem in which short-term memory was not required. Consider the display in Figure 7.2. The duck-shaped part is yellow and rubber; the car-shaped part is red and metalic. How many objects are there? If your intuition is like that of other adults in our studies, you will have parsed this display into two distinct objects, a duck and a car, and you would predict that if the duck's head is grasped and lifted, only the duck will rise.

Infants were habituated to this stationary display with a hand perched above it. Another display was a cup on a shoe. After habituation, the hand reached down, grasped the top of the top object, and lifted. On one half of the trials (move apart outcomes), just the top object came up. On the other half of the trials (move together outcomes), the duck-car or the cup-shoe rose as a single object, lifted by the top of the duck or the top of the cup. Twelve-month-olds looked reliably longer at the anomalous move-together outcomes than at the expected move-apart outcomes, but 10-month-olds failed to allocate attention differentially to the two outcomes. Like the 10-month-olds in the experiments described above, infants of this age failed to use the kind distinctions between the duck and the car or between the cup and the shoe to conclude that two distinct objects were involved in the display (Xu, Carey, & Welch, 1999). And again, the method was sensitive to the knowledge sought, for 12-month-olds succeeded. Further, if provided spatio-temporal evidence that the duck was a distinct object from the car or the cup from the shoe, 10-month-olds succeeded. That is, if at the outset of each habituation trial, the top object was moved slightly laterally, relative to the bottom, the 10-month-olds looked longer in the anomalous move-together test outcomes.

When adults are asked to describe such events, their descriptions support the assumption that they encode the duck/car array as a duck on a car—that is, in terms of the spatial relations between two individuals specified by kind-sortals. Similarly, adults encode the screen and box events as a car comes out, then an elephant comes out—that is, in terms of the successive emergence of two individuals specified by kind-sortals.

Habituation

Apart
(Expected)

Together
(Unexpected)

Figure 7.2. Diagram of one pair of stimuli from Xu, Carey, & Welch, 1999. Infants were habituated to a stationary duck on top of a car. During test, the hand lifted the duck, which either separated from the car (apart trials) or remained connected to the car, such that the duck and car was lifted as a single object (together trials). Reprinted from Xu, F., Carey, S., & Welch, J. (1999). Infants' ability to use object kind information for object individuation. *Cognition, 70,* 137–166, with permission from Elsevier.

Ten-month-olds, in these experiments, fail to do so, as shown by their robust failure to posit two objects in any of these three paradigms. These data suggest that an important aspect of the empiricists' (and Quine's and Piaget's) description of infants' minds may be correct. Infants 10 months and under may not have yet constructed kind-sortals anything like the adult concepts *duck, car, animal, vehicle, book,* or *bottle.* At the very least, they do not deploy these concepts in the service of object individuation under the conditions of these tasks, failing to recruit them for the central logical work of sortals in these tasks.

Twelve-month-old infants succeed at these experiments. It is possible that the capacity to recruit specific sortals for object individuation develops between 10 and 12 months of age. However, another representational possibility is consistent with the 10- to 12-month-old shift. It may be the case that the only sortal concept even these older infants represent is object, and by 12 months of age children have learned generalizations about whether objects with certain properties are likely to transform into objects with other properties, or whether objects with certain properties move independently from objects with other properties. The question is whether the 12-month-old infants' representational system makes a principled distinction between sortals such as *duck* and properties that can be bound to sortals such as *yellow, soft, flexible,* or *small.*

Twelve-Month-Olds' Success—Object Properties or Object Kind-Sortals?

In all of our experiments, the two objects also differed in terms of perceptual properties—color, texture, shape, size—as well as in kind. If an unfamiliar irregularly shaped black plastic object emerges from behind a screen and returns, followed by an unfamiliar, spherical, green fuzzy object, adults would represent this event in terms of two different objects even if they had not encoded them as a telephone and a tennis ball—indeed, even if they had never seen telephones and tennis balls before. Although the representations of properties such as color and texture and size are not sortal concepts, experience with objects could lead to the generalization that properties such as these do not change over this time course, and thus, objects contrasting on such properties must be numerically distinct objects. The 10-month-olds' failure shows not only that they fail to individuate on the basis of kind distinctions but also on the basis of property distinctions where adults would.

These considerations raise an important question: Is the success of the 12-month-olds based on property differences rather than kind differences? If this were so, then we would still have an interesting developmental shift on our hands (from not being able to draw on property distinctions as a basis for individuation under a wide range of circumstances to being able to do so), but this developmental shift would not reflect the emergence of kind-sortals or their deployment in the service of object individuation. This is a real possibility. Studies from many laboratories demonstrate that under some circumstances 12-month-olds or even younger children (Needham & Baillargeon, 1998, 1999; Tremulet & Leslie, 2002; Wilcox & Baillargeon, 1998; Xu & Baker, 2005) draw on property contrasts in object individuation. However, these demonstrations do not take away from the failure to do so in the studies under consideration here, or answer the question of whether success in these studies at 12 months is due to property contrasts or kind contrasts.

To begin to address this question, Xu and I have recently carried out a series of studies on the basis of the 12-month-old's success (Xu, Carey, & Quint, 2004). We used our original paradigm, in which infants saw two objects emerge from opposite sides of a screen, one at a time, each then returning behind it. In this new series, the objects differed only in their properties. We looked at individuation based on size contrast alone (e.g., a big cup versus an otherwise identical small cup), based on color contrasts alone (e.g., a green ball versus an otherwise identical red ball), based on contrasts in pattern and color and size (e.g., a small green solid colored bottle versus a large yellow polka-dotted bottle), and based on a within basic level kind-shape contrast (e.g., a tea-cup versus an identically sized and colored two-handled, nippled, sippy cup). In each case, the 12-month-olds failed to draw on the property contrasts to establish representations of two numerically distinct objects behind the screen; that is, they did not look longer at the anomalous outcome of one object. Importantly, other data revealed that the babies encoded the property differences—they took longer to habituate to successive appearances of objects with different properties than to successive appearances of identical objects. They simply failed to recruit these property differences to draw conclusions concerning the number objects involved in the event. However, in cases of a between basic-level kind shape contrast alone (e.g., a tea-cup versus an identically sized, patterned, and colored ball), the 12-month-olds succeeded.

It appears, then, that 12-month-olds make a principled distinction between representations of kind-sortals and representations of properties, such that the former provide criteria for individuation in these experiments and the latter do not. By 12 months of age, specific object kind-sortals such as *duck, bottle, book*, and *cup* play the same direct role in object individuation as the concept *object* does much earlier in development. By 12 months of age, the predicate *is a duck* plays a different computational role in individuation than does the predicate *is red*. In sum, these data are consistent with the suggestion that a crucial component of noun-phrase semantics, the distinction between sortals and properties, is not part of core cognition and becomes part of the child's representational repertoire between 10 and 12 months of age.

Creating Kind-Sortals—A Role for Language?

There is striking evidence that language might play some role in the developments we see at the end of the first year of life. The emerging capacity to individuate objects on the basis of kind distinctions is closely tied to linguistic competence. In Xu's and my original experiments (illustrated in Figure 3.6), in one of the series of studies, we used a set of objects the names of which are comprehended by some 10-month-olds (ball, cup, bottle, book). According to the parents, about three-fourths of the 10-month-olds participating in our studies did not comprehend these words, and these infants failed to individuate the objects on the basis of the kind contrasts alone. But those whose parents said that they understood the words for the objects succeeded, even though the objects were not named during the individuation task. Thus, those 10-months-olds who already know the basic-level count nouns that refer to the objects emerging from behind the screen succeed at this task. Most 10-month-olds do not yet know these words, so 10-month-olds as a group fail (Xu & Carey, 1996).

In a new set of studies, Xu (2002) has shown that labeling the objects during the trials themselves facilitates individuation in this paradigm. She tested 9-month-old infants in the original Xu & Carey (1996) paradigm. Infants were provided verbal labels for the objects. For example, when a toy duck emerged from behind the screen, the experimenter said, in infant-directed speech, "Look, [baby's name], a duck." When the duck returned behind the screen and a ball emerged from the other side, the experimenter said, "Look, [baby's name], a ball." On the test trials, infants were shown an expected outcome of two objects, a duck and a ball, or an unexpected outcome of just one object, a duck or a ball. Infants looked longer at the unexpected outcome of a single object. That is, when the objects are labeled, success is observed three months earlier than when they are not. In a control condition, the infants heard "a toy" for both the duck and the ball, and their looking-time pattern on the test trials was not different from their baseline preference. Thus, the facilitation observed is not due merely to the fact that labeling facilitates attention to objects; infants were making use of the evidence from contrastive labels in this study of Xu's. In several additional conditions, two contrastive tones, or two contrastive environmental sounds, or two contrastive emotional expressions ("ahh," "yuk") were used instead of two contrastive labels. Infants robustly failed to look longer at the one-object outcome. The negative finding with all of these nonlexical contrasts suggests that perhaps language in the form of labeling plays a specific role in signaling object kind-sortals for the infants.

In sum, the development of kind-sortals presents some parallels to that of explicit quantifiers. There is an apparent developmental shift (in this case between 10 and 12 months of age, rather than between 20 and 22 months of age) in which sortals more specific than *object* are first deployed in at least some object individuation tasks. Furthermore, there is evidence that language learning plays a role in this developmental shift. Might this be a case of Quinian bootstrapping? I think not, just as I think not in the case of explicit linguistic quantifiers. We already have one reason in hand to doubt that the construction of kind-sortals between 10 and 12 months requires Quinian bootstrapping. Xu's data suggest that applying words to entities influences individuation by 9 months of age, and at this age infants certainly have not built an external placeholder linguistic structure to scaffold a bootstrapping process. Furthermore, there is evidence from other paradigms that 9- or 10-month-olds (and even 7-month-olds) distinguish kinds from properties.

Evidence Young Infants Represent Kinds: Categorization and Inductive Inference

Success at drawing on the distinction between ducks and cars, shoes and balls, bottles and books in individuating entities might possibly be accounted for without appeal to kind-sortals. Perhaps generalizations stated over a perceptual quality space underlie success. Perhaps children have learned that shape differences are particularly reliable in predicting when objects move independently of each other, relative to other property differences, and that shape differences tend to be preserved when objects move on spatio-temporally continuous paths. Perhaps, but considerations concerning the input infants receive relative to such generalizations militate against this empiricist hypothesis. Statistical generalizations concerning objects as they move through visible spatio-temporally continuous paths come out the wrong way—size, color, texture, and the like almost never change under these conditions, whereas shape often does. Many objects are flexible and malleable (rubber ducks, cloth toys) or have articulated parts (animals and people and hands, many artifacts). These change shape while maintaining spatio-temporal continuity as a whole. Indeed, in the same experiments in which 8-month-old infants failed to trace the numerical identity of piles of sand or piles of separately movable blocks (see chapter 3), infants succeeded in tracking unique flexible objects, even those that assumed three radically different shapes during their trajectories. Furthermore, studies of infant categorization and inductive inference (to which I now turn) support the conclusion that, by the end of the first year of life, infants' representations of object kinds are distinguished from representations of properties of objects—even shape.

Object kind-sortals do much more work in our conceptual system than providing criteria for individuation and numerical identity. Like all concepts, kind-sortals also provide criteria for categorization. That is, we classify objects together on the basis of all being animals, or ducks, or tables, just as we may classify objects together on the basis of all being red, or striped, or bigger than a breadbox. Although all concepts determine categories, categorization on the basis of kind differs from categorization on the basis of nonkind properties in many ways (S. Gelman, 2003; Markman, 1989). As mentioned above, kind categorization is inductively deeper. Far more follows from knowing that an entity is a duck than from knowing that an entity is red. Similarly, it is kind-sortals that enter into psychological essentialism.

A series of studies by Jean Mandler and her collaborators (Mandler, 2004; Mandler & McDonough, 1993, 1996; McDoough & Mandler,

1998) suggest that infants represent kind concepts, at least by 9 months, perhaps by 7 months. Mandler's studies draw on two methodologies we have not yet considered: habituation of manual exploration as a measure of categorization and generalization of imitation as a measure of inductive inference.

In manual habituation, infants are presented toys or small objects, one at a time, and allowed to play with each one as long as they like. The dependent measure is the amount of time spent in active exploration (inspecting the object, trying out what activities it can participate in). Merely banging the object, mouthing the object, or holding it while attending elsewhere do not count. There are two types of evidence for categorization: (1) decreasing times of exploration as additional objects from the same category are presented (relative to control groups presented with the same number of objects not from a single category and (2) recovery of active exploratory interest when an object from a novel category is presented (relative to control groups presented with a new object from the original category). Mandler and her colleagues have found evidence that infants as young as 7- to 9-months-old categorize on the basis of a variety of global kind categories: animals, vehicles, furniture, and tools. A global kind is more general than a basic-level kind such as *dog* or *horse*; Mandler calls these kinds "global," rather than "superordinate," because *superordinate* implies hierarchy, and Mandler has evidence that infants represent the more abstract kinds before they represent the lower-level ones, at which point there is no hierarchy.

In these studies, Mandler asked whether the categorization is more likely to be based on shared kind or shared perceptual properties (shape, color, texture ...). She argues for shared kind. First, the stimuli are equated for color, texture, and so on. And whereas basic-level kinds like *dogs* and *tables* and *hammers* share shapes, global kinds like *animals* and *furniture* and *tools* do not. Infants categorize together a turtle, a fish, a bird, and a mammal, and they categorize together a boat, a motorcycle, an airplane, a truck, and a car. These items do not obviously share common shapes.

Obviously, there must be some perceptual bases for the child's identifying an entity as a member of a global kind (e.g., animal or vehicle). It is unknown what these bases are. What is in question here is whether the child's categorization behavior is being driven by some perceptual contrast that is independent of global kind. At least some attempts to discover perceptible properties that could underlie the categorization behavior have failed. Van de Walle (Van de Walle & Hoerger, 1996) took the animal/vehicle contrast as a case study. She pointed out that animals differ from vehicles along two perceptual dimensions: (1) vehicles (both real vehicles and the toys used in these experiments) are more rectilinear; animals are more curvilinear; and (2) the part boundaries of vehicles are more salient. For example, color contrasts co-occur with part contrasts in vehicles (wheels, being black and rubber, are different parts from the body, being red and metalic), whereas color contrasts on animals do not (the black patches of a pinto do not respect the boundary between leg and body or head and body).

Van de Walle began by demonstrating that 9-month-old infants are sensitive to these perceptual properties. She made small toys out of clay that were not the shape of any particular animal or vehicle, making some of them rectilinear with clear part boundaries and some curvilinear with color changes not at part boundaries. If habituated to stimuli that were curviliniar and had unclear part boundaries, infants of this age recovered interest to a rectilinear object with clear part boundaries, and vice-versa. Thus, we have a candidate perceptual basis for the discrimination Mandler finds by 9 months of age. However, Van de Walle showed that these perceptual distinctions did not account for the preferences in an animal/vehicle comparison. Allowed to explore a series of animals, infants did not recover exploratory interest to a rectilinear object with clear part boundaries that was not an animal.

There is a general lesson to be drawn from Van de Walle's work. The claim that low-level perceptual properties might underlie the discriminations in Mandler's manual exploration experiments requires positing what perceptible properties could do the trick, and then showing that they actually do underlie the infants' performance. The only serious attempt to do so, so far—Van de Walle's—failed to support the perceptual hypothesis.

Van de Walle (1999) approached the question of a perceptual basis for exploration in the manual habituation paradigm in yet another way—by pitting an obviously perceptual contrast (color) against a kind contrast (animal/vehicle). She habituated infants to a series of vehicles all the same color (e.g., a red car, a red boat, a red motorcycle, a red truck) and then presented them with either an animal of the same color (e.g., a red horse—familiar color, novel kind) or a novel vehicle of a different color (e.g., a blue airplane—novel color, familiar kind). Nine-month-old infants recovered interest to the exemplar of the novel kind and not to the exemplar of the novel color. Thus, infants seem to be categorizing on the basis of global kind in these studies, in spite of the fact that objects that are members of a global kind such as *animal* do not share any obvious perceptual similarity and in spite of the availability of a salient perceptual property as a possible basis of categorization.

The second paradigm Mandler and her colleagues (Mandler & McDonough, 1998) used to study infant categorization explores the basis of inductive generalization. Data from this paradigm corroborate that young infants represent global categories that are not based on shared shape. The experimenter modeled kind-dependent actions on a single exemplar of a category. For example, she modeled putting a dog to sleep, saying "night, night," or putting a key to the side of a car and saying "vrooom, vroom"). She then assessesd the likelihood that the infants would imitate this action given a bed and another object, or a key and another object. The transfer objects either shared global kind with the original exemplar or not, and if they did, they were either perceptually similar or not. For example, after being shown a dog being put to bed, the child might have been handed a cat and a bed (same kind, perceptually similar), a fish and a bed (same kind, not perceptually similar) or a car and a bed (different kind, not perceptually similar). As young as 9 months of age, infants imitated the actions with objects of the same global category, and were completely uninfluenced by perceptual similarity (e. g., they were as likely to put a snake or a turtle or bird to bed as a cat, but they would not put a chair or a truck or a hammer to bed). Thus, it appears that by 9 months of age infants categorize objects on the basis of global kind, and kind representations are differentiated from representations of similarity based on perceptual properties.

These experiments support the conclusion that kind distinctions play a different role in 9-month-old infants' categorization than do property distinctions, just as kind distinctions play a different role in individuation than do property distinctions. But notice that the ages here are several months younger—children apparently categorize entities on the basis of global kind before they draw on these distinctions in individuation. Thus, it seems likely be 9-month-old, may represent some kind-sortals.

Some Kind Distinctions Support Individuation by 9 to 10 Months of Age

Data from two different laboratories show that 10-month-olds use some kind distinctions as a basis for object individuation in the Xu and Carey paradigm. So, not only do 9- and 10-month-olds represent some kind concepts, but also some function as sortals. Luca Bonatti and his colleagues (Bonatti, Frot, Zangl, & Mehler, 2002) showed that the distinction between human heads (well, dolls' heads) and inanimate objects served as the basis of individuation for 10-month-olds, and at this age children do not know the words *face, head,* or *person* nor were the objects labeled in Bonati's studies. Similarly, Luca Surian (Surian, Caldi, & Piretta, 2004) showed that the distinction between an entity that moved on its own and one that did not served as a basis of individuation at this age, again in the absence of any linguisitic support. Thus, some kind-sortals are represented at this age, and are most likely constructed without linguistic support.

Consider these experiments in turn. Luca Bonati and his colleagues (2002) asked whether there were really no kind differences that could support object individuation before 10 months. Perhaps the kinds tested by Xu and her colleagues (bottle, shoe, cup, book, toy duck, toy car, toy telephone, ball ...) are not yet represented as kind-sortals, but what about the distinction between human beings and other objects? Standing in for human beings were very realistic dolla' heads on top of featureless bodies—porcelain, rubber, and plastic heads of dolls. Bonatti showed babies the head mounted on a stick with cloth draped below it, like a robe, emerging from one side of a screen and returning, followed by a toy inanimate object, also mounted on as stick with cloth draped below it, emerging from the other side of the screen and returning. He found that both 10- and 12-month-olds succeeded at this task. Ten-month-olds failed if the contrast was between two toy inanimate objects (replicating Xu's and my studies), but they succeeded if the contrast was between a human head and an inanimate object or between a human head and a dog's head

Of course, the stimuli in these studies are representations of people, dogs, and inanimate objects—they are toys. Still, how are we to understand the earlier success in Bonati's study than in all of Xu's and my studies, which have explored dozens of sortal contrasts? Has the child learned that objects with the properties of human faces tend to maintain spatio-temporally continuous paths and not turn into other objects? Human faces are notoriously difficult to track spatio-temporally —they don't stay where you left them! A more likely account is that human beings are represented as kinds (indeed, the central kinds in core cognition of intentional agency, see chapter 5), and kind distinctions support individuation. Some kinds may be innate, part of core cognition, or acquired without the help of linguistic input.

Luca Surian (Surian et al., 2004) recently provided support for this interpretation. He also replicated the Xu and Carey study, showing failure at individuation when a toy animal was moved out by hand from one side of the screen, followed by a toy vehicle moved out by hand from the other side of the screen. As in Xu's and my studies, the objects were then left for the child to encode fully, before being moved back behind the screen. Ten-month-old infants failed to create a representation of two objects behind the screen, just as Xu and I had found. He then repeated the study, except now the toy animal moved out from behind the screen on its own steam, making a sound with each step, stayed stationary while the infant looked at it, and then moved back behind the screen, followed by the toy vehicle's being rolled out by hand, making a constant sound while rolling, remaining stationary while the infant looked at it, and then being rolled back. Under these circumstances, where the type of motion provided evidence for different global kinds (animal and vehicle), infants created representations of two distinct individuals and looked longer at outcomes when one object was revealed behind the screen.

These data provide very strong evidence against the hypothesis that Quianian bootstrapping is required for the construction of kind-sortals. Prelinguistic infants represent kinds and clearly have the logical capacity to bring kind membership to bear on object individuation.

Language and Kind Categorization

Remember, labeling two entities with distinct words leads young infants to create representations of two distinct individuals. Conversely, labeling distinct entities with a common label increases the likelihood that infants as young as 9 months of age will find the categorical similarity between them, both at the basic level and at superordinate levels (Balaban & Waxman, 1997; Waxman & Markow, 1995). For example, infants told, "Look, a vehicle," each time they are handed a vehicle, show a faster decline in exploration time of successive vehicles than those in a no-label condition ("Look at this"), and also are more likely to rekindle their attention to an exemplar of a novel category (e.g., an animal or a tool).

Thus, by the time infants are 9 months of age, labels have consequences for kind categorization and for kind-based individuation. Furthermore, Sandra Waxman, Amy Booth, and their colleagues (Waxman, 1999) have found that by 13 or 14 months of age, English-learning infants have learned to mark the distinction between kind representations and property representations linguistically. Using the manual habituation paradigm described above, Waxman showed 13-month-old infants objects that either shared a global kind (e.g., were all vehicles) or shared a salient property (e.g., were all red). When handing the infants each object to explore, she either described each one with the same count noun, "Look, a blicket" or with the same adjective, "Look, a blickish one." For a third group of infants, the objects were not labeled—they were simply told, "Look at this." Upon hearing a series of objects described by the count noun, infants extracted kind similarity— they habituated faster to the objects that shared kind and dishabituated more robustly to an object from a different kind, compared to infants in the no-label condition. But the count noun did not facilitate categorization on the basis of property similarity (shared color or texture). The adjective, in contrast, facilitated categorization on the basis of shared property as well.

These conclusions have been corroborated in several studies with 14-month-olds that depend on a word-learning paradigm. For example, if shown four purple animals (a horse, an elephant, a giraffe, and a cat) labeled by a noun, 14-month-olds generalize the label to a new animal of a different color. However, if the original four objects are labeled with an adjective, infants do not generalize the label to a new animal. In some cases they map the adjective to the shared property; in other cases adjective use does not lead to a principled distinction between kind and property similarity (Booth & Waxman, 2003; Waxman & Booth, 2001).

Thirteen-month-old infants are many months away from learning the quantificational devices of natural language. Object kind representations are distinguished from object property representations by the end of the first year of life, and each type of representation is drawn upon in different ways in individuation, categorization, and the earliest stages of language acquisition. This distinction is not bootstrapped in the course of mastering natural language quantifiers, even though it is mapped to language very early in development.

The Role of Language in the Construction/Deployment of Kind-Sortals

The above data rule out the hypothesis that the construction of kind-sortals at the end of the first year of life requires Quinian bootstrapping. Even 7- to 9-month-olds represent some kind concepts, and even at 9 to 10 months of age some of these function as sortals. Still, it is not until between 10 and 12 months that infants spontaneously draw on many kind-sortals (e.g., bottle, book, shoe, duck, car, truck) in support of individuation in nonlinguistic tasks, and language learning is implicated in this change. There are several ways (not mutually exclusive) that language might play a role in promoting the deployment of kind-sortals in non-linguistic tasks.

Xu's interpretation of these findings is that from the outset of language learning, infants expect labels to refer to kind-sortals. She supposes that LAD includes innate mapping rules between open-class words referring to objects and object kind-sortals. This is an example of a innate linking rule of the sort that supports semantic and syntactic bootstrapping. That is, eventually this mapping will support, through semantic boot-strapping, infants' learning the syntactic reflexes of count nouns in their language. Such an innate mapping would explain why infants take contrastive labels to indicate distinct individuals (because objects that fall under distinct kind basic-level kind-sortals are necessarily distinct individuals) and would explain why common labels applied to distinct objects would lead infants to search for kind similarities between them. However, even if the logical capacity to represent kind-sortals is innate, and even mapped to labels (or to nouns) as part of LAD, the child must still discover the particular kinds in his or her world. Xu imagines that the putatively innate mapping allows contrastive labels and shared labels to actually play a role in the construction of previously unrepresented kind-sortals. For example, even if the child knows of no causally deep features shared by blickets, that different entities are called "blicket" may lead them to be represented as sharing a kind, much as even in mature representations of kinds the nature of the essential features of those kinds may be unknown (S. Gelman, 2003).

However, Waxman has added an important new chapter in this story: she shows that at 11 months of age, hearing a common novel noun applied to a set of objects facilitates categorization on the basis of common properties (e.g., shared color) as well as shared kind. From this result, Waxman offers a different interpretation of the findings with 9-month-olds from Xu's. Waxman suggests that from the beginning of word learning, children expect common labels (or common open-class lexical items) to refer to entities that share properties. It is experience with count-noun contexts that leads to the narrowing of the hypothesis that count nouns refer to entities that share shape or kind.

Can we decide between Xu's and Waxman's interpretations of these data? Xu can assimilate Waxman's findings that shared labels increase categorization to shared properties as follows: infants expect shared labels to refer to shared kinds, but they have to learn what properties are good cues to kind membership. Waxman's story leaves unexplained how infants create representations of kinds as opposed to properties; Xu assumes this distinction is available from the beginning and is mapped to language, but the child must learn about particular kinds in the world.

Xu has one recent finding that favors her interpretation over Waxman's. She repeated her language and individuation studies with 9-month-olds in the following four conditions: (1) distinct labels/distinct kinds (e.g., "blicket/stad" applied to honey dipper/vacuum tube); (2) distinct labels/identical objects (e.g., "blicket/stad" applied to honey dipper/identical honey dipper); (3) common labels/distinct kinds (e.g., "blicket/blicket" applied to honey dipper/vacuum tube); and (4) common labels/identical objects (e.g., "blicket/blicket" applied to honey dipper/identical honey dipper). Conditions 1 and 3 replicated the earlier studies, although now with novel labels and novel objects: if infants see a vacuum tube and honey dipper, labeled "blicket" and "stad," respectively, as each emerges in alternation from opposite sides of a screen, they establish a representation of two objects behind the screen, in contrast to the condition where the two objects are both labeled "stad." Conditions 2 and 4 asked whether distinctive properties are necessary for individuation under these conditions, as would be the case if contrasting labels heightened interest in contrasting properties, in turn leading to individuation. They were not. Condition 2 patterned with condition 1— in the face of distinctive labels, each applied to identical honey dippers emerging from opposite sides of the screen, infants established representations of two objects behind the screen. And, of course, condition 4 patterned with condition 3—children failed to establish representations of two individuals if they heard only one label, whether or not the features of the objects emerging from behind the screen differed. In a crucial control condition, Xu brought out a single object and gave it two contrastive labels, and then brought out the other (different) object and gave it the same two contrastive labels. Here, the infants did not infer two objects behind the screen—the distinctive labels must be applied to objects for which there is spatio-temporal ambiguity concerning numerical identity. Thus, by 9 months of age, distinctive labels have consequences for individuation by themselves—even in the absence of contrasting properties. If children expect open-class lexical items to refer to kind-sortals, then these results are as expected. It is as if the infant is saying to herself, "I don't see the difference between the entity/entities emerging from opposite sides of the screen, but since they are of different kinds, they must be different objects" (Xu, 2005). Of course, eventually the assumption that membership in different kinds implies distinct individuals is relaxed. As mentioned earlier, there are stage-sortals (*puppy*) and phase-sortals (*pet*) as well as kind-sortals (*dog*)—and even kind-sortals are hierarchically organized (*dog, animal*). Xu's hypothesized linking rule serves in the earliest stages of concept and language acquisition.

One last study from Xu's laboratory (Dewar & Xu, 2007) underlines how specific the mapping is that is guiding children's learning in these cases. The fact that contrast labels lead the child to establish representations of two individuals is consistent with three representational possibilities:

1. Two open-class labels suggests two individuals (no further analysis).
2. Labels are being analyzed as count nouns: two open-class labels suggests two constrasting kinds, which suggests two individuals.
3. Labels are being analyzed as proper nouns: two open-class labels suggests two named individuals.

Xu and her colleagues (Dewar & Zu, 2007) carried out a study confirming the second hypothesis. Children were familiarized to boxes being brought out and opened from the front, revealing either a pair of identical novel objects (e.g., two honey dippers) or a pair of different novel objects (e.g., a vacuum tube and a plumber's T). The boxes always contained one of these pairs of objects, and they were brought out in random order so the child could not predict what would be revealed when the front of the box was opened. The 12-month-old infants were habituated to these events, looking times being measured when each pair of objects was revealed. After habituation, the experimenter looked into a closed box from the top and said either "Look, a blicket," "Look, a stad," or "Look, a blicket; look, a blicket." The box was then opened from the front revealing either the pair of identical objects (the two honey dippers) or the pair of objects from distinct kinds. If hypothesis 1 or 3 were correct, the child should not differentiate these two outcomes, because the language specifies two individuals and there are two individuals in each case. But on hypothesis 2, the child should expect the pair of objects from distinct kinds when hearing "a blicket, a stad" and the pair of identical objects when hearing "a blicket, a blicket." This is what happened. These data provide convincing evidence that young infants expect labels applied to novel objects to be referring to an object kind, and this expectation certainly provides relevant evidence concerning which perceptible differences among objects signal kind distinctions.

Other hypotheses concerning the role of language in kind-based categorization and individuation may also be right. Words for kinds are explicit symbols and must obviously be learned. Words for kinds may be stored directly in working memory, providing an efficient representation. The idea is that these symbols may then directly into representations of events (duck in box). Needham and Baillargeon (2000) call such symbols for kinds "summary representations" and suggest that the availability of summary representations helps infants in Xu's and my difficult individuation tasks. I agree. They propose that what is being learned in the last year of life may or may not be not be kind-sortals themselves, but definitely includes explicit linguistic symbols for kind-sortals. Before the creation of such symbols, representations of events may be articulated in terms of object-files. Object-files are symbols for objects. Representations of properties, such as shape, size, color, texture, and perhaps kind, may be bound to object-files. The infant who has only object-file representations represents the result of an event in which a duck is removed from and returned to a box as *object in object*, perhaps with properties bound in the object-files: *object (yellow, rubber, small, curved, duck) in object (blue, hard, large, rectilinear, box)*. Clearly, such representations are more cumbersome than *duck in box*.

These suggestions for what may be changing between 7 and 12 months or so are not mutually exclusive. The child may create some representations of kind-sortals de novo and the child certainly must learn what members of antecedently represented kinds are called. These linguistic labels are symbols that function in thought, as do count nouns. If the child expects kinds to be labeled by open-class lexical items, language may play a role in all of these developments. These are all paradigm examples of weak effects of language on thought.

The Origin of Kind-Sortals

To summarize the argument to here, Xu's and my studies suggest that Quine and Piaget were largely right in their speculation that young infants do not represent kind-sortals such as *animal, vehicle, dog, car, cup, bottle, book, ball*, even when they can recognize entities from these kinds as familiar and even predict their behavior. My evidence in support of this proposal is that early in infancy there are no quantificational consequences of categorization in terms of these concepts. However, contrary to Quine's and Piaget's speculations, Bonatti's, Mandler's, Surian's, Waxman's, and Xu's studies provide evidence that children have created kind-sortals that cover these entities by 10 to 12 months of age. Thus, the capacity to represent specific object kind-sortals, distinct from properties, does not require Quinian bootstrapping. The child does not learn interrelations among natural language quantifiers, only then reinterpreting the meaning of "dog" in terms of this structure. Nor does it await the end of Piaget's putative sensori-motor stage of development. I agree with Xu that this capacity is most likely innate, and is mapped to language as part of the LAD. Still, we need an account of how new kind-sortals are constructed. That is, language may signal to the child that two entities differ in kind (distinctive labels) or share kind (common labels), but words don't tell the child what the relevant kinds are.

The literature on the emergence of the first kind-sortals reflects the now familiar tension between empiricist and nativist approaches to infants' representations. As in Xu's proposal, the linguistic evidence could lead the child to extract shape as a reliable indicator of shared kind or, as Linda Smith and her colleagues suggest, the relevant generalizations may be stated in a perceptual vocabulary—shared shape begins to be privileged as a basis of similarity. But shared shape is not the same as shared kind, and the evidence reviewed above leads me to favor Xu's and Waxman's conclusions that kinds are distinguished from properties at the very outset of language learning.

So how does the child construct concepts of new kinds? Many things might trigger establishing a new kind representation, including the lexical evidence that Xu and Waxman document infants can use. Other information may be evidence of inductive potential (e.g., a particular shape predicts functional or causal affordances). Consistent with psychological essentialism, kind representations are often placeholders: infants (or adults) can then discover at their leisure, in a process that never ends throughout development, to fill in those placeholders with theories of the causal mechanisms that underlie the inferential potential of any given kind. In the case of animal kinds, infants have the resources of core cognition to begin filling in those placeholders, as the child has evidence that animals are agents (chapter 5). Also, the child has the central causal learning processes discussed in chapter 6 to aid in filling in kind placeholders.

Kinds are reananalyzed throughout life, and new kind-sortals are constructed. Chapters 9 through 11 consider the bootstrapping mechanisms that support the constructions of kind representations that transcend those that draw on core cognition.

Conclusions

The case studies in this chapter—set-based quantification and kind-sortals —turned out to exemplify continuity, as well as the resources needed for semantic and syntactic bootstrapping, rather than Quinian linguistic determinism. The ontology presupposed by at least one natural language —English—is not a construction that has appeared midway during the cultural evolution of human beings. The young infant distinguishes between individuated entities such as objects and nonindividuated entities such as sand, and compares representations of sets of objects with respect to both continuous and discrete quantification. Also, at least by the time the infant is about a year old, he or she has constructed her first object kind-sortals, distinguishing kind-sortals from properties in categorization, individuation, inductive inference, and language. In this case, Quine almost certainly got it completely backwards. Natural languages most likely have the quantification machinery they do because of the quantificational resources of prelinguistic mental representations (both ontogenetically and phylogenetically), as these were drawn upon in creating the language-acquisition device. The ontological commitments discussed here reflect core cognition, supporting learning language rather than resulting from it.

Nonetheless, there is room for genuine effects of language learning on nonlinguistic mental representations. Language learning certainly plays a role in the construction of specific kind-sortals, which are then deployed in infants' encoding of events unfolding around them. Language learning may also play a role in the availability and deployment of set-based quantification. These are weak effects of language on thought, at most— the child is operating within innately given representational resources.

Although these cases did not turn out to involve Quinian linguistic determinism, I am sympathetic to Quine's picture of conceptual development. Chapters 8 through 11 endorse Quine's ideas, presenting cases of developmental discontinuities where Quinian bootstrapping results in the construction of representational capacity more powerful than any antecedently available.

NOTES

1. When different languages mark different distinctions, this mechanism leads to weak Whorfian effects. Many examples of weak Whorfian effects have been attested. Examples include Borditsky's studies of the effects of cross-linguistic variation in gendermarking, gender marking (Boroditsky, 2001; Boroditsky, Schmidt, & Phillips, 2003; Bowerman and Choi's (2003) studies of the effects of cross-linguistic variation in the contrasts underlying different spatial prepositions, and many more.

2. "Substance-sortal" is a misleading term, in my view, because these concepts do not pick out substance kinds like gold or water but rather enduring entities like dogs, trees, and tables.

8

Beyond Core Cognition: Natural Number

When the great constructivist mathematician Leopold Kronecker remarked "The integers were created by God; all else is man-made" (cited in Weyl, 1949, p. 33), he was making a metaphysical claim. Yet, the remark also expresses a natural position concerning the cognitive foundations of arithmetical thought. If we replace "God" with "evolution," the position would be that evolution provided us with an innate input analyzer that outputs representations of the positive integers, the natural numbers. The claim would be that the capacity to represent natural number is part of core cognition. If we continue to interpret Kronecker psychologically, we find he would be saying that all the rest of mathematics, including the rest of the number concepts (rational, negative, 0, real, imaginary, etc.) were culturally constructed by human beings. On this interpretation, Kronecker was espousing the continuity hypothesis with respect to integer representations; they are available throughout human development, both historically and ontogenetically. Indeed, many modern cognitive scientists, most notably Rochel Gelman and Randy Gallistel, have argued for the continuity of integer representations throughout development (Gelman & Gallistel, 1978; Gallistel & Gelman, 1992). This chapter argues that evolution did not give humans the positive integers. Rather, the capacity to represent the positive integers is a cultural construction that transcends core cognition.

I turn, here, to cases of discontinuities in conceptual development. Unlike core cognition, unlike the representations in the language-acquisition device, and unlike innate central representations such as cause, much of the human conceptual repertoire is not continuous through the life span. To convince you of this claim, I must meet two challenges, and these are the challenges I take on in the rest of the book. The first

challenge is *descriptive*: to establish discontinuities in cognitive development by providing analyses of successive conceptual systems, CS1 and
CS2, demonstrating in what sense CS2 is qualitatively more powerful
than CS1. Further, I must provide evidence that children indeed have
these two systems of representations at successive points in development
—that is, I must demonstrate within-child consistency across a wide
variety of tasks reflecting the two different systems of concepts, CS1 and
CS2. Also, if CS2 transcends CS1 in the sense of containing concepts not
representable in CS1, it must be the case that CS2 is difficult for children
to learn. Great difficulty in learning provides indirect evidence that a
given CS2 does indeed require representational resources not available in
CS1. The second challenge is *explanatory*: to characterize the learning
mechanism(s) that get us from CS1 to CS2.

I begin by taking on the descriptive challenge, and after showing that
the acquisition of the capacity to represent natural number meets it, I take
on the explanatory challenge. I elaborate on a particular type of bootstrapping process, Quinian bootstrapping, and I sketch two alternative
Quinian bootstrapping processes that might account for the acquisition of
the capacity to represent natural number.

The Descriptive Challenge

Empirical Arguments for Continuity

In modern cultures, the ontogenetically earliest explicit representational
system (in the sense of being expressed in shared symbols) with the
potential to represent natural number are numeral list systems. Most, but
not all, cultures have ordered lists of words (numerals) for successive
integers (e.g., "one, two, three, four, five, six ..." in English). Numeral
lists are used in conjunction with counting routines to establish the
number of individuals in any given set. In their seminal book on toddlers'
number representations, Rochel Gelman and Randy Gallistel (1978)
argued that if young toddlers understand what they are doing when they
count (i.e., establishing the number of individuals there are in a given set),
then, contra Piaget, they have the capacity to represent number. Gelman
and Gallistel analyzed how numeral list representations work: there
must be a stably ordered list of symbols (the stable order principle). In

counting, the symbols must be applied in order, in 1–1 correspondence to the individuals in the set being enumerated (1–1 correspondence principle). The cardinal value of the set is determined by the ordinal position of the last symbol reached in the count (cardinality principle). These principles indeed characterize counting, and honoring them guarantees that number representations implement the successor function: For any symbol in the numeral list that represents cardinal value n, the next symbol on the list represents cardinal value n + 1. It is the successor function (together with some productive capacity to generate new symbols on the list) that makes the numeral list a representation of natural number.

Gelman and Gallistel made a bold argument for continuity of number representations throughout development. They noted evidence for infant and animal representation of number (see chapter 4; of course, there are now many more relevant studies than were available in 1978). They suggested that infants and animals establish numerical representations through a nonverbal counting procedure. Their hypothesis at that time was that babies and animals represent a list of symbols, or "numerons," such as %,˅, #, $, @, ... Entities to be counted are put in 1–1 correspondence with items on this list, always applying the symbols in the same order. The number of items in the set being counted is represented by the last item on the list reached, and its numerical value is determined by the ordinal position of that item in the list. For example, in the list above, "˅" represents 2 because "˅" is the second item in the list.

Gelman's and Gallisel's argument for continuity drew on evidence that they took to show that toddler's counting is constrained by the counting principles almost from its inception. Toddlers use a stably ordered count list and tag each item in a count only once. Gelman and Gallistel suggested that toddlers' learning of a linguistic count list is guided by their antecedent nonlinguistic count list. Their proposal for the nonlinguistic representation of number is a paradigm example of a continuity hypothesis, for this is exactly how languages with explicit numeral lists represent the positive integers. On their hypothesis, the child learning "one, two, three, four, five ..." need only solve a mapping problem: identify the list in their language that expresses the antecedently available numeron list. Originally learning to count should be on the same order of difficulty as is learning to count in Russian, once one knows how to count in English. If, in contrast, integer representations are discontinuous with core cognition, coming to represent the positive integers should be hard.

Wynn's Difficulty of Learning Argument Against the Gelman/Gallistel Continuity Proposal

Children learn to count during the ages of 2 to 4 years, and contrary to the predictions of Gelman and Gallistel's 1978 numeron-list theory, learning to count is far from easy. Although young toddlers use a stably ordered list and count each object just once, honoring the stable order and 1–1 correspondence principles, they do so for almost a year and a half before they figure out the cardinality principle—that is, before they figure out how counting represents number. This fact in itself does not defeat the continuity hypothesis, for we do not know in advance how difficult is it to learn an arbitrary list of ordered words or to discover that one such list (e.g., "one, two, three...", rather than "a, b, c,..." or "Monday, Tuesday, Wednesday...") is the list in English that represents number. True, but work by Karen Wynn (1990, 1992a) showed that children have difficulty discovering the meanings of specific number words even after they have solved these two problems. The developmental process through which children learn the meanings of the number words, therefore, is at odds with that predicted by the continuity thesis.

Wynn demonstrated that for over a year, young children know the numerical meaning of some words in the count sequence but not others. First, she identified children who could count at least to six when asked how many objects there were in an array of toys. These 2- to 3-year-old children honored 1–1 correspondence in their counts, and they used a consistently ordered list, although sometimes a nonstandard one such as "one, two, four, six, seven..." She went on to show that if such a child were given a pile of objects and asked to give the adult "two" or "three" or any other number the child could use in the game of counting, most 2- and 3-year-old children failed. Instead, young children grabbed a random number of objects (always more than one if the numeral was two or higher) and handed them to the experimenter. Also, shown two cards depicting, for example, two versus three balloons and asked to indicate which card had two balloons on it, young children responded at chance. Thus, in spite of being able to count at least to six, these children did not know the numerical meaning of the words "two," "three," "four," "five," or "six."

There is one more observation of Wynn's that is important to the evaluation of the Gelman/Gallistel continuity hypothesis. She showed that, from very early in the process of learning to court, children know what "one" means. They can pick one object from a pile when asked, and they correctly distinguish a card with one fish from a card with three fish if asked to indicate the card with one fish. Further, they know that the other words in the count sequence contrast with "one." They always grab a random number of objects greater than one when asked to hand over "two, three, four..." objects, and they also successfully point to a card with three fish when it is contrasted with a card with one, even though their choices are random when three is contrasted with two. Such children are called "one"-knowers, for they know the meaning only of the verbal numeral "one." In all of Wynn's studies with 2 ½- to 3 ½-year-olds, she found only one no numeral-knower.

Thus, Wynn's studies provide evidence that toddlers learn the English count list and identify the list as relevant to number very early on (younger than age 2 ½): they know what "one" means, and they know that "two, three, four," and so on" contrast numerically with "one." They are in this state of knowledge for more than a year before they work out the principle that allows them to determine which number each numeral refers to. This state of affairs is impossible on the numeron-list continuity hypothesis, whereby the English count list need only be identified and mapped onto the putative preexisting nonlinguistic numeron list that the infant already uses to represent number. The counting principles, if understood, guarantee that a numeron-list representation of the integers specifies the meaning of all of the symbols on the list.

In sum, in spite of the evidence that prelinguistic infants represent number, core cognition of number cannot have the format of a numeral list system. Even after children have learned the list, know how to count, and know that the list encodes number, they do not immediately infer how the list encodes number. Learning to count in English is not remotely like learning to count in French, once one knows how to count in English. That is, English speakers learning French do not learn the list, going through a stage where they know that it refers to number, but take "deux," "trois," "quatre," and "cinq" to be roughly synonymous with each other, meaning plural or some.

Wynn's argument against the continuity hypothesis is indirect. The difficulty children have learning how the numeral list represents number cannot be explained with the hypothesis that infant representations of number are a nonlinguistic numeral list, and that this representation guides children in learning to count. But direct evidence regarding continuity is also available to us. Chapters 4 and 7 provided positive characterizations of toddlers' quantificational knowledge at the outset of learning to count. We can examine the core cognition systems with numerical content and specify the ways in which integer representations transcend them. The most important task for one attempting to establish conceptual discontinuity is to characterize CS1 and CS2, demonstrating in what sense CS2 contains representations not expressible in CS1.

The reader may be forgiven for being a bit confused at this point, or for suspecting that I am contradicting myself. Haven't I argued that a signal property of core cognition is that it is continuous throughout development? Didn't chapters 2 through 7 demonstrate that the representations that articulate cognition in infancy also play a role in the mental lives of adults? Yes, certainly, and I am not here taking back that infants have core cognition of number: the analog magnitude and the parallel individuation systems described in chapter 4 and the set-based quantification system described in chapter 7. These are continuous throughout development. What is at issue here is whether these systems represent natural number (the positive integers).

In later writings, Gallistel and Gelman (1992) abandoned their hypothesis that infants' number representations are subserved by a nonlinguistic numeron list, instead suggesting that the linguistic numeral list representation of number is continuous with the analog magnitude number representation system. They, along with many others (e.g., Dehaene, 1997; Wynn, 1998), assume that learning what "five" means consists of learning a mapping between the number word and a particular analog magnitude within the system of magnitudes that represent number. This assumption seems warranted by two facts: First, analog magnitude representations constitute a system of core cognition, and thus they are available to infants as they face the problem of language learning. Second, adults (and even preschool children) have constructed a mapping between the numeral list and analog magnitude representations of number (see chapter 4 for evidence that adults have constructed this mapping; for preschoolers, see Huntley-Fenner, 2001; LeCorre & Carey, 2007; Lipton & Spelke, 2005, Temple & Posner, 1998). The continuity hypothesis would be confirmed, then, if analog magnitude representations represent natural number, or if any other system of core cognition did so; and of course it is disconfirmed if they do not. They do not.

Why the Numeral List Transcends Analog Magnitude Representations of Number

Gallistel and Gelman (1992) argued that the Church and Meck accumulator model described in chapter 4 is formally identical to the numeral list representational system of positive integers. The successive states of the accumulator serve as the successive integer values, the mental symbols that represent the cardinal value of the set. Gallistel and Gelman pointed out that the accumulator model satisfies all the principles that support verbal counting: States of the accumulator are stably ordered, gate opening is in 1–1 correspondence with individuals in the set, and the final state of the accumulator represents the number of items in the set. Given that infants represent analog magnitudes, and that the accumulator model of analog magnitude representations implement a counting routine, Gallistel and Gelman argued that this system is continuous with and is likely to be the ontogenetic underpinnings of learning to count and constructing an explicit verbal numeral list representational system of number. This is the position Dehaene (1997, 2001) seemed to endorse as well when he said that the verbal system provides a list of words to express the numerical meanings captured by states of the analog magnitude number representation system.

Unfortunately for this proposal, there is considerable evidence that suggests that the Church and Meck model is false, and that analog magnitude representations of number are not constructed through an iterative process (see chapter 4). If analog magnitude representations were created by an iterative process that implements a counting routine, then the time to enumerate sets should increase monotonically with increasing set size. Instead, over wide ranges in set sizes studied so far, the time to create an analog magnitude representation of sets is constant for both adults and infants (for adults, see Barth, Kanwisher, & Spelke, 2003; for infants, Wood & Spelke, 2005b). Moreover, subjects are able to discriminate visually presented numerosities under conditions of stimulus size in which they are not able to attend to individual elements in sequence (Intriligator & Cavanagh, 2001). Under these circumstances, numerosity discrimination could not possibly depend on a process of counting each entity in turn, even very rapidly.

These considerations have led to models in which analog magnitude representations are computed by input analyzers operating over individuals in parallel (e.g., Church & Broadbent, 1990; Dehaene & Changeux, 1993; Zorzi & Butterworth, 1997). These models differ from the original Meck and Church accumulator model in a number of important ways. Because the processes that construct the analog magnitude representations are not iterative, they are not formed in sequence and therefore are less likely to be experienced as a list. Moreover, the process that establishes the analog magnitude representations does not require that each individual in the set to be enumerated be attended to in sequence, counted, and then ticked off (so that each individual is counted only once). These mechanisms do not implement any counting procedure.

Most important, none of the analog magnitude representational systems, even Church and Meck's accumulator system, has the power to represent natural number. For one thing, there is a highest number any analog magnitude system can represent, owing to the capacity of the accumulator and/or the discriminability of the individuals in a set, whereas base-system numeral lists do not have an upper limit (subject to the coining of new words for new powers of the base). For another, analog magnitude systems provide merely approximate representations of the numbers in their domain, even one, whereas numeral list systems represent each natural number exactly.

All analog magnitude representations differ from any representation of the natural numbers, including numeral list representations, in two crucial respects. Because analog magnitude representations are inexact and subject to Weber fraction considerations, they fail to capture small numerical differences between large sets of objects. The distinction between eight and nine, for example, cannot be captured reliably by the analog magnitude representations of human adults. Also, noniterative processes for constructing analog magnitude representations—those favored by the timing data alluded to above—include nothing that corresponds to the successor function, the operation of adding one to a given integer in order to generate the next integer. Rather, all such systems positively obscure the successor function. Since numerical values are compared by computing a ratio, the difference between one and two is experienced as different from that between two and three, which is again experienced as different from that between three and four. And, of course, the difference between eight and nine is not experienced at all, since eight and nine, like any higher successive numerical values, cannot be discriminated.

In sum, analog magnitude representations are not powerful enough to represent the natural numbers and their key property of discrete infinity. They do not provide exact representations of numbers and they obscure the successor function, which is constitutive of natural number.

Why the Parallel Individuation System Cannot Represent Natural Number

As argued in chapter 4, in addition to analog magnitude representations, there is another core cognition system of representation with numerical content: the parallel individuation system. If this system had the power to represent natural number, then the continuity thesis would stand. This system does not remotely have the capacity to do so. Unlike the analog magnitude number representation system, the parallel individuation system is not dedicated to number representations. Number is only implicitly represented, in that computations of 1–1 correspondence are made over symbols for individuals represented in parallel in models of arrays of objects and events. The system of parallel individuation, like that of analog magnitude number representations, contains machinery for indexing and tracking sets of individuals, but it contains no symbols for cardinal values. The only symbols in such models represent the individuals themselves. Also, the system of parallel individuation has an upper bound at very low set sizes indeed—three for infants. With this system of representation, infants cannot even represent four, let alone seven or 32 or 1,345,698.

Why Natural Language Quantifiers Do Not Represent Positive Integers

Chapter 7 argued for a third innate system of representation with numerical content: the set-based system that underlies natural language quantification. Numerals, when used in sentences, are quantifiers, so this system is clearly implicated in number word meanings. Further, the quantificational semantics of natural languages may distinguish singular (one), dual (two), sometimes trial or paucal (three or several), and most languages have approximate quantifiers like "many" or "some" or "more" that pick out numerical magnitudes. However, barring the numeral list itself, natural language includes no representations of exact cardinal values above three. Natural language quantifiers do not implement the successor function.

Comments on the Use of the Term "Number" in the phrase "Core Number Cognition"

When we say that infants or nonverbal animals represent number, it is very important to be clear on what we are claiming. We must specify the precise nature of the symbol systems that underlie the number sensitive behavior, and ask in what senses they are representations of number—what numbers do they have the capacity to represent and what number-relevant computations do they support? This was the goal of chapters 4 and 7. I have argued that none of the representational systems that underlie infants' or animals' behavior on nonlinguistic number tasks represent number in the sense of natural number or positive integer. Nonetheless, all three systems support number-relevant computations, and the analog magnitude system contains symbols for approximate cardinal values of sets. Because of this each deserves to be called a representation of number. By specifying the format and the computations defined over particular class of representations, one can say precisely what numerical content they have. It then becomes a merely terminological matter whether one wants to use the term "number" only for natural number or for the integers or for the integers plus the rationals plus the reals (in which case there is no core cognition of number) and adopt some other term for the quantificational content of core cognition systems (e.g., parallel individuation, approximate cardinal value, set-based quantification).

Growing up in a culture where counting is salient, like the United States, children construct a representation of the positive integers between ages 3 and 4. At this point they have constructed a representation of the positive integers (or at least a finite, but expandable, subset of them). They deploy their count list in accordance with Gelman and Gallistel's counting principles and this ensures that it implements the successor function.

This case of conceptual development is shaping up well to meet descriptive challenge of providing evidence for a developmental discontinuity. I have characterized CS1 (in fact, three CS1s) and their representational capacities, providing evidence that young children indeed have each CS1. I have characterized a CS2 (the numeral list representation of the positive integers) and its representational capacities, showing how it qualitatively transcends those of its predecessors. Furthermore, as required by the discontinuity hypothesis, it is very difficult to learn.

Within-Child Consistency on Tasks that Reflect CS2

The ways in which CS2 transcends core cognition makes sense of why it takes children a year and a half or two years to figure out how counting represents number. Not only does the discontinuity hypothesis require that constructing CS2 should be difficult, but it also predicts that behavioral measures will reflect a qualitative change in representational capacity as CS2 is constructed. We should see within-child consistency on a whole variety of tasks that reflect CS2. And indeed we do.

Preschool children's performance on tasks that reflect an understanding of how counting represents number has been extensively studied. Dozens of studies have used Wynn's Give-a-Number task, in which children are asked to create sets with a cardinal value named with a numeral ("Give me one," "Give me two," "Give me three," etc.). They all revealed a reliable developmental sequence. First, children are no numeral-knowers—they cannot even reliably give one object when asked for it. Between 24 and 30 months of age, most English-learning children become "one"-knowers. They can reliably give one object but hand over a random number of objects (always greater than one) when any other numeral in their count list is used in the request. They are in this stage for 6 to 9 months. They then become "two"-knowers (can reliably give one or two objects; chose a random larger number for any other numeral), and then "three"-knowers. Although it is much rarer, "four"-knowers have also been observed. Then, around age 3 ½ on average, English middle-class children become cardinal principle knowers—they work out the numerical meaning of the activity of counting and can now reliably produce sets with the cardinal value of any numeral in their count list.

I shall call "one"-, "two"-, "three"- and "four"-knowers, "subset-knowers," because they know the numerical meaning of only a subset of the numerals on their count list. The questions with respect to within-child consistency are twofold: First, is there evidence from a wide variety of measures for a qualitative shift between subset-knowers, on the one hand, and cardinal principle knowers, on the other? Second, how consistent is knower level within subset-knowers? Does a "one"-knower reveal knowledge only of the numeral "one" on every task that probes for such knowledge? Ditto for "two"-, "three"- and "four"-knowers. Many sources of data provide affirmative answers to both questions.

Several measures of within-child consistency suggest a qualitative shift in understanding how counting represents number upon becoming a cardinal principle knower. In Karen Wynn's (1990, 1992a) original studies, subset-knowers almost never counted to produce sets (to give five apples, they merely grabbed a handful), whereas cardinal principle knowers almost always counted out large sets. Also, when simply asked to count a set of objects, children in both groups could do so with few errors, but then after counting, if asked "How many was that?" the cardinal principle knowers almost always merely repeated the last word of their previous count, whereas subset-knowers rarely did so. Rather, subset-knowers recount, or provide a numeral that does not match the last word of their count. This suggests that subset-knowers do not realize that the last word reached in a count represents the cardinal value of the set. Later studies confirmed these findings and extended them. Even cardinal principle knowers sometimes make mistakes when creating sets of a requested number. Children are asked to count and check their answers. When the count reveals an incorrect set-size, cardinal principle knowers virtually always correct appropriately. Subset-knowers, in contrast, leave the set unchanged or correct in the wrong direction (e.g., add more objects when the count revealed that there were already too many) on more than 70% of the trials (Wynn, 1990, 1992a; LeCorre, Brannon, Van de Walle, & Carey, 2006).

Mathieu LeCorre, Elizabeth Brannon, Gretchen Van de Walle, and I (2006) have recently extended the data showing qualitative differences between cardinal principle knowers and subset-knowers. Adapting a procedure introduced into the literature by Rochel Gelman (1993), we studied what numeral children produced when asked simply "What's on this card?" The cards in question depicted sets of objects, ranging number from one to eight. We modeled the use of numerals in the description for the first card in a series. For example, if the first card had eight apples, and if the child said, "some apples," or "apples," we'd say, "that's right, there are *eight* apples." This procedure elicits numeral use. We divided our participants into subset-knowers and cardinal principle knowers according to Give-a-Number, and we found qualitatively different performance on What's-on-this-Card as a function of this division. Subset-knowers rarely produced both a count ("one, two, three, four, five" and a cardinal response ("five apples"), but if they did, the cardinal response often did not match the last word of their count. Cardinal principle knowers, in contrast, very often counted for large sets and always produced a cardinal response that matched the last numeral in their count list. More important, it was possible to divide children into cardinal principle knowers and subset-knowers on the basis of their performance on What's-on-this-Card alone. Cardinal principle knowers produced cardinal responses for all cards, up to sets of eight, whereas subset-knowers could produce them only for sets of one ("one"-knowers), for sets of one and two ("two"-knowers), for sets up to three, or to four ("three"- and "four"-knowers). It is nontrivial that subset-knowers can be identified on this task, for it makes very different processing demands than does Give-a-Number. In Give-a-Number, children must hold a numeral in memory and use counting to produce a set with that cardinality. In What's-on-this-Card, children must merely use counting (or some other method) to determine a cardinal value of a set. Yet, some children could determine a cardinal value for only a subset of the numerals on their count list, and these children rarely used counting to do so. These are the subset-knowers. And the striking result is that subset-knowers on What's-on-this-Card were also subset-knowers on

Give-a-Number, and so too cardinal principle knowers on one measure were cardinal principle knowers on the other (LeCorre et al., 2006).

What children said for sets larger than those for which they could produce a correct numeral was informative. Consider first a "one"-knower. What this child would do, almost always, is say "two apples" for sets of apples ranging in value from two to eight. Similarly, a "two"-knower would typically use just one numeral (e.g., "three"), or just two numerals (e.g., "three" and "four") for all sets larger than two. Children did not produce larger numerals for larger set sizes beyond their knower level. This suggests that not only do subset-knowers not use counting to solve this task but also that they have not mapped higher numerals beyond their knower level onto analog magnitudes. We will return to this result later, when we consider the role mappings to analog magnitudes play in the construction of the integer list representation of natural number, and when we discuss the process through which children create a mapping between their numeral list and analog magnitude representations. For now, though, the important conclusion is that many different tasks provide evidence for a qualitative change in understanding counting upon becoming a cardinal principle knower.

LeCorre extended the evidence for a qualitative change between cardinal principle knowers and subset-knowers to still another task. Making the processing demands on the child as few as he could imagine, he introduced a picky puppet who wanted things just so. The puppet announced he wanted "six" cookies, or "seven" or "eight." Another puppet then counted out a set of puppets, stopping at the number asked for, or one more or one less. The question to the child was simply, "Is that six?" (or whatever the puppet requested). One could solve this task with less than a full appreciation of the cardinality principle (an uninterpreted "last word rule" would do), but surely if the child understood how counting represents number he or she should succeed. Subset-knowers (as assessed on Give-a-Number) failed; cardinal principle knowers succeeded.

The above analyses demonstrate the within-child consistency one would expect if CS2 (commanding the numeral list representation of the positive integers) is qualitatively different from CS1 (being a subset-knower). Children are designated subset-knowers or cardinal principle knowers on the basis of their performance on a single task—Wynn's Give-a-Number task. Subset-knowers fail to demonstrate an understanding of how counting represents number on a wide variety of tasks and cardinal principle knowers demonstrate understanding on all of them.

The within-child consistency is also found within subset-knower level. The term "'one'-knower" means that of all the numerals on her count list, the child knows the numerical meaning only of the numeral "one." Again, children are usually designated "one"-knowers on the basis of performance on Give-a-Number. But if they truly know only the numerical meaning of the word "one," they should fail to demonstrate knowledge of the meanings of higher numerals on any task. And indeed, for three different tasks that diagnose knower-level, "one"-knowers on one task are "one"-knowers according to the others (and ditto for "two"-, "three"-, and "four"-knowers). These are the Give-n task, the Point-to-n task, and the What's-on-this-Card task. To illustrate, consider "one"-knowers' performance on all three tasks. On Give-n, the child can give one object when "one" is requested, but grabs a random number of objects when asked for two, three, four, or any other number on the child's count list. On Point-to-n, when asked to point to the card with one fish, the child points to the card with one when this is contrasted with a set of any other number. Conversely, if asked for a card with two, three, or four fish and provided two cards, one with multiple items and one with one fish, the "one"-knower chooses the card with multiple items, confirming that the child takes all other words in his count list, other than "one", to depict sets that do not contain one individual. The child chooses at random given a choice between two larger sets (e.g., 2 and 3) when probed with either numeral. On What-on-this-Card, the child asserts that a card with a single object has one apple, and uses other numerals randomly for all other set sizes. Very often the child uses "two" to describe sets of two, three, four, five, six, seven, and eight objects. Thus, performance on all three tasks consistently reflects the knower-level assigned on the basis of Give-a-Number alone (for within-child consistency on Give-n and Point-to-n, see Wynn, 1990; for within-child consistency between Given-n and What's-on-this-Card, see LeCorre et al, 2006).

Besides confirming that CS1 and CS2 are stable representational systems, these data constrain an account of the learning process. After having memorized the count list and the count routine, first the child is a no numeral knower, although by 24 months of age, many English-learning children are already "one"-knowers. Being a "one"-knower is a consistent stage children remain in for six to nine months. They then become "two"-knowers, remaining so for several more months. They then become "three"-knowers, and some also become "four"-knowers before figuring out how the numeral list represents natural number. Children stay subset-knowers for 1 to 1 ½ years. When they become cardinal principle knowers, they have created a representation of some positive integers, a numerical representations that transcends core number representations.

Before the Cultural Construction of Integers: Evidence from Adults

If representations of natural number transcend core cognition, then before the cultural construction of representations of the positive integers, adult numerical cognition should be articulated in terms of the representations in the core systems. Even if this hypothesis is correct, it is possible that the episode (or episodes) of cultural evolution that led to the numeral list representation of natural number are lost in historical time, and, given the global economy, there are no cultures today that do not have numeral lists. As the linguist James Hurford (1987) reviewed, many anthropologists in the 19th century described societies whose numerical language was restricted to the quantifiers, including often words that were translated as "one" and "two" (which often become transformed into morphological singular and dual markers) and "many." Of course, those anthropologists did not know about core cognition, and they made no attempt to describe the nonlinguistic number representations of the people they studied.

Recently, the anthropologist Daniel Everett (2005) described an isolated Amazonian culture, the Piraha, with a "one, two, many" system of quantifiers. Their language has explicit quantifiers that express set-based quantification. Although the Piraha sometimes indicate number with fingers, they do not have a finger/toe/body counting system. Rather, they appear to use fingers, and even their words commonly translated as "one" and "two," as approximate numerosities. Michael Frank and colleagues (Frank, Everett, Fedorenko, & Gibson, in press) elicited quantifiers for sets from one to ten objects, either in ascending order (1, 2, 3, . . .) or descending order (10, 9, 8, . . .). They found that the quantifier translated as "one" was used only for sets of one in the ascending-order elicitation, but it was used for sets from one to six in the descending-order series. The quantifier translated as "two" was used for sets from two to ten in the ascending-order elicitation and for sets from ten to four in the descending-order series. Apparently, these quantifiers are better translated with relative quantifiers ("a few," "more than a few," "many"), rather than as "one," "two," "many." There is no evidence that the Piraha have a word in their language that expresses the concept of "one."

The psychologist Peter Gordon (2004) described the Piraha's non-linguistic representations of number (see also convergent results from another Amazonian people, the Munduruku, who have a slightly more elaborate quantifier vocabulary; Pica, Lemer, & Izard, 2004). In a series of tasks in which Piraha adults were to create sets that matched others in number, or reach into a can to remove exactly the number objects they just saw put there, they never used 1–1 correspondence (with fingers or pebbles) to solve these tasks. Nor did they use number words, of course, because there are no number words for cardinal values over 2 in their language. Rather, Gordon found evidence for the two core-knowledge systems described in chapter 4. For numerosities from 4 to 10, the average number produced in a match was a linear function of the cardinal value of the set to be matched, and the standard deviation increased with set size, satisfying scalar variability. That is, the standard deviation around 10 was twice that around 5. This is the signature of analog magnitude representations. For numerosities of 3 or less, performance was much better, sometimes at ceiling. Some other representational system subserved performance at these small numbers—most likely the system of parallel individuation, perhaps also the analog magnitude system. In sum, the Piraha clearly use the three core systems described in chapters 5 and 6 in their quantitative representations of the world, but they provide no evidence of any numerical representations that go beyond them.

Michael Frank and his colleagues (in press) found that Piraha adults can easily be induced to create numerical matches on the basis of 1–1 correspondence. Their experiments differed from Gordon's in that they provided training with feedback for small sets. With this training, Piraha adults could create sets in 1–1 correspondence with a target set, up to sets of ten, without error, so long as both sets were visible and each aligned horizontally, one above the other. When the target set was hidden during the process of set construction, or if one set was aligned vertically and the matching set was to be constructed horizontally, Gordon's results were replicated: analog magnitude representations underlay performance for sets from four to ten. Clearly, words for numerals, embedded in a count routine, provide a memory aid, allowing adults to encode the cardinal values of set and maintain that representation in working memory. This is a paradigm weak influence of language on thought.

Does the success at the 1–1 correspondence task mean that the Piraha have a representation of exact cardinal values in the absence of a numeral list representation of the positive integers, contrary to the conclusions Gordon drew? No, it doesn't. Whereas the inability to use 1–1 correspondence to create sets with the same number of elements would be good evidence that the Piraha lack a concept of the cardinal value of a set, the capacity to do so falls short of the concept. The resources of set-based quantification are sufficient to support this ability. Basically, the Piraaha need only have a concept of all or each. They must create sets where each balloon is paired with a spool of thread and vice-versa, or where all of the balloons have corresponding spools and vice versa. Being able to do so does not mean that they would conceive of the number of items these two sets share as a particular cardinal value, or ever think to use 1–1 correspondence as a way of representing that cardinal value (as in finger counting, or marks on a branch, or knots in a string; see Hurford, 1987). As we will see below, this representational insight is the first step in the cultural bootstrapping of representations of cardinal value, and these data provide no evidence that the Piraha have made this step.

Summary: The Challenge of Describing a Discontinuity in Development Met

To show that conceptual development involves qualitative change, such that a later conceptual system (CS2) has more expressive power than an earlier one (CS1), one must provide a characterization of each, demonstrating the discontinuity. I have shown how the numeral list representation of number transcends the numerical content of the three systems of representation with numerical content that are bequeathed to human beings by natural selection. Furthermore, if constructing CS2 requires conceptual change, it should be hard. Unlike learning the meaning of the plural morpheme, which is a problem of finding a mapping between antecedently available nonverbal representation and a linguistic expression, learning the meaning of "seven" requires constructing a new representational resource. If this is right, then learning should be a protracted process, and the initial meanings children assign to the symbols they are learning the meaning of should be incorrect from the point of CS2. As the system gets constructed, there should be stable intermediate conceptual structures. And finally, if CS2 is a cultural construction, there must have been sometime in history cultures who do not yet command it (although this period may be lost to anthropological or historical record). The numeral list representation of number exemplifies all of these features of conceptual discontinuity.

The Explanatory Challenge

Quinian Bootstrapping

Developmental discontinuities are frequently observed in the course of mathematical development and in the course of theory change. Chapters 9 through 11 provide further examples from the study of conceptual development in children and also from historical case studies. I turn now to the explanatory challenge: what learning processes can create representational resources with more expressive power than, or qualitatively different from, their input?

This explanatory challenge has been extensively discussed by historians and philosophers of science, and many appeal to what are called "bootstrapping" processes as an explanation for how representational resources that transcend their input can be created. For example, as mentioned in previous chapters, Quine offered many different bootstrapping metaphors when discussing how the child, beginning only with perceptual primitives, might create representations of "objects as such" as well as the quantificational capacities to represent individuals and kinds. He explicitly likens these processes to those involved in theory changes. I have argued above (chapters 2, 3, and 7) that Quine's description of the developmental changes in this case were off the mark. Bootstrapping processes are not needed to construct the concept of individual object from perceptual primitives because this concept is part of core cognition and is in this sense innate. Nonetheless, I believe his basic insights about the nature of bootstrapping are right.

As I commented before, the very word "bootstrapping" is a metaphor, meant to capture the deep difficulty of the problem. After all, it is impossible to pull oneself up by one's bootstraps. Neurath's metaphor of building a boat while already in the middle of the ocean also captures the difficulty of the problem—that while not grounded one must build a structure that will float and support you. Not grounded in this case means that the planks one is building the boat with are not interpreted concepts one already represents. In other metaphors, the learner's concepts are partially grounded, as in Quine's ladder metaphor. Here, one builds a ladder grounded in one conceptual system until one has a platform that is self-sustaining, and then one kicks the ladder out from under. And in a final Quinian metaphor, one is scrambling up a chimney supporting oneself by pressing against the sides one is building as one goes along. Quine again captures that the new conceptual system that supports you is being built as you go along. This metaphor stresses, as does Neurath's boat, that the structure one builds consists of relations among the concepts one will eventually attain—it is that structure of interrelations among the to-be-attained concepts (the sides of the evolving chimney, the boat itself, the platform from which the ladder can be kicked away) that serves the crucial bootstrapping role. See Quine (1960, 1969, 1977) for his own elaboration on Quinian bootstrapping.

Although such metaphors are evocative—of both the problem to be solved and the solution—Quine never describes in detail how this learning process operates. These metaphors are hardly satisfying to a cognitive scientist trying to understand bootstrapping mechanisms. In the chapters that come, I flesh out the metaphors with processes that are better understood in computational terms.

Quinian bootstrapping processes require explicit symbols, such as those in written and spoken language or mathematical notational systems. The aspect of the bootstrapping metaphor that consists of building a structure while not grounded is applied as the learner initially learning the relations of a system of symbols to one another, directly, rather than by mapping each symbol onto preexisting concepts (Block, 1986). The symbols so represented thus serve as placeholders, at most only partially interpreted with respect to antecedent concepts. This is one essential component of Quinian bootstrapping. The second essential component is the process through which the placeholders become interpreted. As historian and philosopher of science Nancy Nersessian (1992) argues, these are modeling processes. Often, but not always, processes of analogical mapping are involved. Other modeling processes, such as abduction, thought experimentation, limiting case analyses, and induction, all have roles in Quinian bootstrapping.

Two properties of these mechanisms are important. First, they are not deductive. There are no guarantees in bootstrapping. The structures that are tentatively posited either work, in the sense of continuing to capture the observed data that constrain them, or they do not. Second, they are all problem-solving mechanisms that play a role in thought more generally. They are bootstrapping mechanisms only when harnessed in the service of creating a representational resource with more power than those that are their input.

In the pages that follow, I flesh out how Quinian bootstrapping works in cases where descriptive work reveals discontinuous conceptual development, both in childhood and in the history of science. The childhood cases include bootstrapping the numeral list representation of natural number, bootstrapping an intuitive theory of matter in which weight, volume, and density are differentiated (chapter 11), and bootstrapping a representation of rational number (chapter 11). The historical cases (chapter 11) include Kepler's bootstrapping a physics that was the direct precursor to Newtonian mechanics and Maxwell's bootstrapping the physics and mathematics of electromagnetic fields. As each case unfolds, the abstract characterization of Quinian bootstrapping given above will be clarified.

Bootstrapping the Numeral List Representation of Natural Number

The output of the hypothetical bootstrapping mechanism is the numeral list representation of natural number—an ordered list of numerals such that the first one on the list represents 1 and for any word on the list that represents the cardinal value n, the next word on the list represents n + 1. The successor function is the heart of numeral list representations of integers. The numeral list representation of number is characterized by Gelman and Gallistel's counting principles (the list is stably ordered; individuals in a given count are put in 1–1 correspondence with number words, and the cardinal value of the set is the ordinal position of the word in the count list).

The problem of how the child builds an numeral list representation decomposes into the related subproblems of learning the ordered list itself ("one, two, three, four, five, six . . ."), learning the meaning of each symbol on the list (e.g., "three" means three and "seven" means seven), and learning how the list itself represents number, such that the child can infer the meaning of a newly mastered numeral symbol (e.g., "eleven") from its position in the numeral list. Rather than offering just one bootstrapping proposal, I will offer two. They differ in the planks of the process, in what aspects of core cognition are drawn upon. I offer two proposals to illustrate that it is, in fact, not difficult to imagine how to we might explain conceptual discontinuities, and to illustrate that it is possible to bring empirical data to bear on choosing among specific proposals concerning possible bootstrapping processes.

Each proposal assumes that the child first learns "one, two, three, four, five . . . " as a list of meaningless lexical items. This is the no numeral knower stage documented above. There is no doubt that children have the capacity to learn meaningless ordered lists of words—they learn sequences such as "eeny, meeny, miny, mo," the alphabet, the days of the week, and so on. Indeed, nonhuman primates have this capacity, and so it is likely part of innate computational machinery (e.g., Terrace, Son, & Brannon, 2003). This step in the learning process—learning an arbitrary ordered list ("one, two, three, four, five, six . . .") is a paradigmatic example of one aspect of Quinian bootstrapping: the meanings of the counting words are exhausted, initially, by their interrelations, their relative order in the list. At this point in the process, the verbal numerals are placeholders with respect to the numerical meaning they will come to have.

The two bootstrapping proposals differ in terms of the process envisioned as to how the placeholders come to be interpreted as words for natural numbers. Both proposals must capture what is known, empirically, about the earliest stages in number word learning. Both presuppose that the learning process involves combining antecedently available representations. Proposal 1 assumes that analog magnitude representations of number are the only system of core numerical cognition that is drawn upon in the process. I then present data that decisively undermine Proposal 1. Proposal 2 assumes that the resources of parallel individuation, together with those of set-based quantification, underlie the construction of the numeral list representation of number.

Proposal 1: Numeral List Representations Are Bootstrapped from Analog Magnitude Representations

Dehaene (1997), Wynn (1998), and Gallistel and Gelman (1992, 2000) have all suggested that analog magnitude representations are the numerical foundation for numeral list representations of number. There are several arguments in favor of this proposal. First and foremost, both numeral list representations and analog magnitude representations include symbols for cardinal values of sets, and there is no doubt that eventually a mapping is constructed between verbal numerals and analog magnitude values (see chapters 4 and 9). These facts make plausible the hypothesis that the construction of this mapping is what underlies the learning of the numeral list representational system in the first place. Until recently, however, nobody has ever attempted to explain how a mapping from analog magnitudes to the natural numbers might be constructed by the child, or how constructing this mapping might play a role in the creation of the numeral list representation of the positive integers. Note that these are separate problems. It is logically possible that the mapping is created after children come to understand how counting represents number and thus plays no role whatsoever in the initial creation process.

As required by the empirical data, on Proposal 1 the child learns the arbitrary list ("one, two, three, four, five, six...") and the counting routine (pointing to objects one at a time, while reciting this list) without recognizing the numerical significance of these activities. As in all bootstrapping processes, the initial meanings assigned to the count list are exhausted by their inter-symbol relations—in this case, strict linear order. The bootstrapping proposal must then account for how partial meanings for small numerals are created, for the data show that children assign some numerical meaning to "one," "two" and "three" before they figure out how the numeral list represents number, and then it must account for how they accomplish this latter feat.

As detailed in chapter 4, prelinguistic infants compute analog magnitude representations of the cardinal values of sets, at least in some circumstances, and are sensitive to numerical differences at least in a 2:3 ratio. A problem for Proposal 1 arises immediately in the evidence that analog magnitude representations of small sets are apparently not readily computed, at least by infants. In almost every experiment to date, infants' representations of small sets show the set-size signature of parallel individuation or the signature of singular/plural representations, rather than the Weber-fraction signature of analog magnitude representations (see chapters 4 and 7). To get Proposal 1 off the ground, we must assume that analog magnitude representations of small sets are easily computed. Given that this is so for adults (Cordes, Gelman, & Gallistel, 2002), for the sake of argument, we will grant this is so for 2-year-olds as well. Even with this liberal assumption, we will see that it is by no means easy to bootstrap the numeral list system out of analog magnitude representations alone.

Given the description of the subset-knower period of development, I assume that the first step in the process is that the child learns a mapping between small numerals ("one," "two," and then "three," in that order) and states of the accumulator (——, ———, and ———, respectively). How the child might learn this mapping is far from obvious. If the child already knows that "one" represents a cardinal value of a set, we may imagine that garden-variety lexical learning mechanisms are at play. If the child knows that "one" applies to a cardinal value of a set, then the hypothesis space for what "one" means is highly constrained. Given that the symbol, ——, is also a representation of a cardinal value of a set, the child might simply analyze adult usage and conclude that "one" applies to those sets that are represented by ——. But how does the child come to realize that "one, two," and so on represent distinct cardinal values of sets?

Gallistel and Gelman (1992) suggested that the role of the numerals in counting provides a wedge into the problem. They pointed out that the Meck and Church accumulator model implements a counting routine, and so the fact that the numeral list is also deployed in counting helps children discover its significance. As argued above, there are two problems with this idea. First, as shown in chapter 4, there are reasons to doubt the Meck and Church model. Assuming that analog magnitudes are established in parallel, there is nothing to alert the child to the correspondence between counting and the cardinal values of subsets of the set being counted. Second, before the child has learned the numerical significance of any numerals, how does the child know that the count routine is counting?

It is important to grasp the magnitude of this problem. Remember that originally the counting routine and the numeral list have no numerical meaning. Suppose the child is asked "How many" of a set of five objects. "How many" elicits counting as a meaningless routine. Suppose also that he or she has established an analog magnitude representation of roughly five. As the child counts, nothing guides him or her to attend to a set of one, a set of two, a set of three, a set of four, a set of five during the count. It is only the set of five that has automatically activated an analog magnitude representation (if that's the set the child is indexing). Still, if the child continually practices the counting routine in response to the parent's prompt, "How many?" the child will have access to repeated pairings of "one, two" with sets of two, "one, two, three," with sets of three, etc. To construct the hypothetical mapping, the child has to have figured out at least a "last word" rule—that the last item in the list refers to the numerosity of the set, and this insight is one thing we are trying to explain. Furthermore, there is evidence that children figure out a last-word rule only shortly before they become cardinal principle knowers; "one"-knowers do not understand that the last word in a count has any special significance (Fuson, 1988, LeCorre et al., 2006). Thus, Proposal 1 has a difficult problem of explaining how the child learns a mapping between "one" and ——.

Perhaps children do not learn the meaning of "one" in the context of counting. "One" is much more frequent in speech to the child's input as a quantifier than embedded in the count routine (Sarnecka, Kamenskaya, Yamana, Ogura, & Yudovina, 2007). "Can you give me one?" "Would you like that one?" "I'd like one cupcake." As Paul Bloom and Karen Wynn (1997) argued, from the outset numeral production, children correctly use them in the syntactic positions of quantifiers. The semantics of quantifiers may help children recognize the numerical meaning of "one." As I will argue below, I agree with Bloom and Wynn's conjecture, but it is not clear how this will help us here. As detailed in chapter 7, set-based quantification is at the heart of the semantics of quantifiers, and analog magnitude number representations do not provide the representations drawn upon in set-based quantification (although set representations are necessarily the input to analog magnitude representations of number).

In spite of all these problems, let us assume that the child has made the mapping that initiates the proposed bootstrapping process—the mapping between at least some numeral words in the count list and approximate numerosities represented as analog magnitudes. By the time the child is a "three"-knower, he or she may even have established some associative mapping between higher numerals (e.g., "five") and analog magnitudes. How then does the child learn how the numeral list representation and the counting algorithm work? The child might notice the analogy between two different relations: the temporal relation follows in the ordered count word list and the numerical relation more than in the analog magnitude representations. Notice that this is a true analogy. The order in the count list exhausts its early content, but that order relation is very different from numerically ordered as represented by analog magnitudes (greater analog magnitude). To make this analogy, the child may notice that the magnitude paired with "two" is greater than that paired with "one", and that the word "two" follows the word "one" in the counting routine. Similarly, the child may notice that the magnitude paired with "three" is greater than the magnitude associated with "two," and that "three" follows "two" in the list of number words. And finally, the child might notice that the magnitude paired with "five" is greater than the magnitude associated with "two" and that "five" is later than "two" is the list of number words (if the child has mapped "five" to the analog magnitude symbol for 5, that is). From these observations, the child may come to the induction that each number word is associated with a different numerical magnitude, and that larger magnitudes correspond to words that come later in the count list. There is no deductive necessity that the child notice this analogy; as in all bootstrapping processes, noticing an analogy is a serendipitous matter. If the child entertains the analogy, it becomes a source of hypotheses that can be confirmed in additional contexts in which numerals are used by adults and in additional episodes of counting. Remember, the child counts for one to two years before figuring out how the count list work.

However, this is not yet the full numeral list representation, for it does not represent the arithmetic successor relation between adjacent items on the numeral list as corresponding to the numerical operation of adding 1. Although a child might use her analog magnitude system to discover that numerosity increases monotonically as one proceeds through the count list, nothing in the analog magnitude system would appear to inform the child that each count increases numerosity by exactly 1. On the contrary, because accumulator representations are compared as are representations of continuous variables, and because of Weber-fraction considerations, the difference between __(1) and ——— (2) is not experienced as the same as the difference between ———— (3) and ———— (4). And because representations of adjacent larger numbers are not discriminated, successive discriminable analog magnitude values for larger numbers are not related by + 1 at all.

One possible solution to this problem is as follows. In the course of practicing the counting routine, the child might note that the state of the accumulator for that corresponds the word "two" (——) is achieved when the analog magnitude that corresponds the word "one" is added to the analog magnitude that corresponds to the word "one" (−), and similarly for the relations between the analog magnitudes that correspond to the words for "three" and "two," and for "four" and "three"—in each case the analog magnitude value that corresponds to the numeral next in the list is achaieved by adding the analog magnitude that corresponds to "one" to that that corresponds to the numeral immediately preceding it in the list. This would require that 2-year-olds reliably distinguish analog magnitudes in the ratio of 4:3, which has not yet been shown, but let's grant that to the child for the sake of argument. This regularity, if noticed, may be enough evidence for an induction that there are two states of the accumulator that corresponds to both n and n + 1, for any n, even if they cannot be discriminated. Once this insight has been achieved, the bootstrapping process is complete.

Reasons to Doubt Proposal 1

As currently formulated, Proposal 1 fails to address many of the questions we want to resolve, including the crucial one of how the child creates the initial mappings that get the process started. More important, the proposal faces two critical empirical challenges. First, it offers no explanation for the well-established findings that children begin by learning what "one," means and take "two, three, four, five..." to contrast with "one," well before they learn how "two, three, four, five..."contrast with each other. Nothing in analog magnitudes makes the distinction between ——(1), on the one hand, and ——————— (2), ——————— (3), ————————————— (4), ... , on the other hand, particularly salient, such that all states of the accumulator greater than one should be treated alike.

Even more important, Proposal 1 absolutely requires that before children work out how the numeral list represents number, they have mapped some of the numerals in the count sequence onto approximate analog magnitudes. It also requires that the inductions children make in the process of constructing the counting principles include the generalization that numerals later in the list represent larger numbers, where "larger numbers" means larger analog magnitudes. There is now good evidence (reviewed below) that neither of these requirements is met. Children apparently integrate numerals with analog magnitude representations some six months after they have learned how counting represents number. Thus, Proposal 1 cannot be right.

Two large empirical projects have sought evidence that analog magnitudes are mapped to numerals by subset-knowers—that is, by children who have yet to figure out the counting principles. Any data showing that subset-knowers could estimate the number of elements in a set larger than four without counting would provide unequivocal evidence for mappings between analog magnitudes and large numerals, because parallel individuation cannot support representations of sets greater than four. Kirsten Condry and Elizabeth Spelke (2008) and also Mathieu LeCorre and I (2007) have sought such data. Each group studied 2- and 3-year-olds early in the process of learning to count—those who knew only what "one" meant, or only "one" and "two," or at most "one, two" and "three" (i.e., children who were subset-knowers as diagnosed by Wynn's Give-a-Number task). Condry and Spelke showed children two cards, one with four objects on it and one with eight, and asked "Which one has four?" or "Which one has eight?" Children were at chance. Because even 6-month-olds can discriminate sets in numerical ratios of 1:2, the fact that children could not tell which of these sets had "eight" and which had "four" shows that they had not mapped these numerals to analog magnitude representations of approximately eight, or approximately four, respectively. Providing data convergent with this conclusion, LeCorre showed children cards with from one to ten dots on them for just a few seconds (too fast for counting) and asked children to give an estimate of how many dots were on each card. For all subset-knowers the slope of the average numeral produced as a function of set size in the range of five to ten was 0. That is, subset-knowers used numerals randomly, with no tendency whatsoever to produce higher number words for larger set sizes. Thus, there is no evidence that children map any numerals in the unambiguous range of analog magnitudes onto analog magnitudes before they become cardinal principle knowers. Nor is there any evidence that they have learned a generalization that numerals later in the list pick out larger sets (as determined by analog magnitude representations of number), for if they did, they should produce larger numerals for sets of ten than for sets of five.

The data summarized above are from subset-knowers. Perhaps children make this mapping just as they become cardinal principle knowers, and thus it is difficult to find subset-knowers who have done so. If so, all cardinal principle knowers, at least, should show evidence of understanding that numerals later in the list pick out higher analog magnitudes. To explore this question, LeCorre included 72 young cardinal principle knowers (3- to 5-year-olds) in the estimation task described above. The distribution of slopes relating the average numeral produced as a function of set size between five dots and ten dots was not normal—it reflected two groups of children. One had slopes centered around 0, just as the subset-knowers have, and the other had slopes centered around 1, just as adults do (see Figure 8.1). The latter group—those with slopes of 1, estimate "five" for sets of five, on average, and "ten" for sets of ten, just as do adults. These children have clearly mapped numerals to analog magnitudes (remember, the cards were flashed too fast for them to count), and so LeCorre called these children "mappers." LeCorre separated the cardinal principle knowers who gave the same numerals for sets of six as for sets of eight and ten ("nonmappers") from those whose average numeral produced tracked set size (mappers); Figure 8.2 plots the estimates for each set size for each group. The average age of the 31 cardinal principle knowers who were nonmappers was 4:1, and the average age of the cardinal principle knowers who were mappers was 4:6. Both groups of cardinal principle knowers fully understood how counting represents number; they all counted to produce sets of any size asked for, and if they made mistakes, all knew how to correct immediately. Apparently, children do not map larger numerals in their count list to higher numerals until about six months after they have figured out how counting represents the positive integers.

These data absolutely rule out the possibility that mapping numerals in the range of 5 to 10 to analog magnitudes plays any role in the construction of the numeral list representation of natural number. LeCorre's data establish another previously unknown fact about the construction process. LeCorre found several "four"-knowers among his subset-knowers, and he also found that many "three"-knowers were well on their way toward mapping "four" onto sets of 4 as well. As is obvious from Figure 8.2, all cardinal principle knowers, both mappers and non-mappers, have mapped the numerals "one," "two," "three," and "four" onto core cognition systems. Thus, although "four"-knowers are

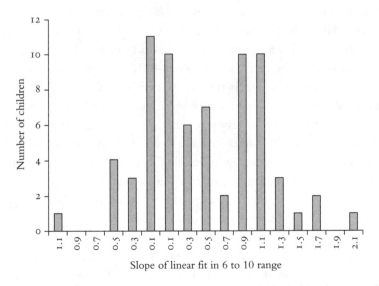

Figure 8.1. Distribution of the slopes from individual childrenof the function of average numerical estimates by set sizes in the 6 to 10 range. Slopes ranged from − 1.1 (e.g., average numerical estimate for sets of 6 = "ten", for 8 = "eight", and for 10 = "six" to over 1. The distribution is bimodal, with one mode around 0 (same estimates for 6, 8 and 10) and the other around 1 (e.g., sets of 6 = "six," sets of 8 = "eight" and sets of 10 = "ten").

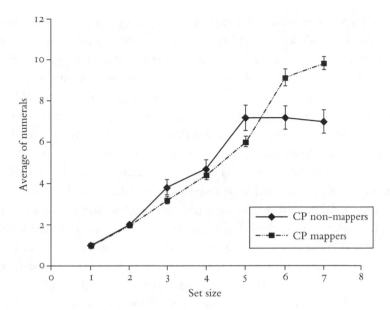

Figure 8.2. Average numeral given as a function of set size for CP-mappers (dotted line) and CP-non mappers (solid line).

relatively rare, it seems that children do not induce the counting principles until they learn the numerical meaning of "one," "two," "three," and "four," for all cardinal principle knowers have done so. Numerical meanings of "one," "two", "three" and "four" and nothing more underlie the construction of the counting principles.

What might these meanings be? Might Proposal 1 be correct, with the emendation that only analog magnitude representations of sets of 1 through 4 are mapped to numerals before the induction? LeCorre's data bear against this proposal as well. Proposal 1's crucial induction on the way to figuring out the successor function is that numerals later in the list pick out larger sets. Even though this might be induced from a mappings between the first four numerals and analog magnitudes, the effect of this generalization, if known, should be seen on the estimation task. That is, children who know this principle should give larger numerals for larger sets throughout their whole count sequence. All cardinal principle knowers in LeCorre's sample could count to 10; many could count to 20 or more. Yet the nonmappers failed to provide larger numerals for larger sets.

Two final empirical considerations militate against Proposal 1. First, Proposal 1 provides no explanation for why no subset-knowers have mapped "five" or "six" or "ten" onto analog magnitudes before inducing the counting principles. Whatever associative process supports mapping "two" to analog magnitudes, or "four" to analog magnitudes, should be available to support mapping "six" or "ten" to analog magnitudes as well. To be sure, higher numerals are less frequent, but the very striking discontinuity at "four" has no ready explanation on Proposal 1.

The last empirical consideration is even more conclusive. The signature of analog magnitude representations is scalar variability; the ratio of the standard deviations for the estimates of each set size is proportional to the mean estimate for that set size. And indeed, LeCorre found scalar variability in the estimates of mappers in the five- to ten-item range. The ratio of standard deviation to mean estimate was about .25 for set sizes of six, eight, and ten, which is very close to the adult level (Cordes et al., 2001; Whalen, Gallistel, & Gelman, 1999). If the numerical meanings of small numerals are also subserved by analog magnitude number representations, then estimates in the small set range should also display scalar variability. Children's estimates of small sets did display variability, but not scalar variability. Standard deviations of the estimates for sets of one to four dots were not proportional to the mean estimates. For example, for cardinal principle knowers who were mappers, the SD/M for estimates of sets with one object was 0, as it was for sets of two objects. For sets of three objects, it was .01, and for sets of four objects, it was .12. It did not reach .20 (the value of scalar variability observed for sets between five and ten) until a set size of five. This pattern of increasing values of SD/M for estimates of sets from one to four held up within each of the three groups (subset-knowers as well as the two groups of cardinal principle knowers) and is not that predicted by the hypothesis that analog magnitude representations provide the numerical meaning for the numerals. Rather, it is that predicted by the hypothesis that representations deploying parallel individuation underlie success (LeCorre & Carey, 2007; Vogel, Woodman, & Luck, 2001).

Although these considerations conclusively rule out Proposal 1, the hypothesis that numeral list representations are ontogenetically grounded in analog magnitude representations may still be correct. A different learning process might exist that would avoid the pitfalls of Proposal 1.

Indeed, Gelman and Lucariello (2002) sketched an alternative in which the initial mapping is between the count list as a whole and analog magnitudes as a whole. I do not consider this proposal here because it, too, requires that the child have access to the generalization that numerals later in the list refer to larger cardinal values as specified by analog magnitudes is available as soon as the child has constructed this initial mapping, a generalization not made until some months after the child has induced the cardinal principle (Condry & Spelke, 2008; LeCorre & Carey, 2007). As will be clear in chapter 9, I am sympathetic to Gelman and Lucariello's proposal for how analog magnitudes are integrated with the numeral list; I just do not believe that this integration is the key to the initial creation of the numeral list representation of natural number.

My goals in considering Proposal 1, and then rejecting it, were threefold. First, I issue a challenge: those who believe that numeral list representations are bootstrapped out of analog magnitude representations must characterize a process through which this could be accomplished. Proposal 1 is my best shot. Second, I offered Proposal 1 as an example of a Quinian bootstrapping process that could do the trick. Like all Quinian bootstrapping, it involves creating a placeholder structure whose meaning is initially exhausted by inter-symbol relations, and it involves modeling processes such as analogy and inductive inference. As Proposal 1 shows, it is not difficult to flesh out bootstrapping proposals that could underlie an important developmental discontinuity. Third, with specific proposals in hand, it is not difficult to evaluate them empirically. If those who believe that analog magnitude number representations underlie the learning of the numeral list can propose a different learning mechanism, it too could be put to empirical test.

What Concepts Underlie the Meanings of "One-" to "Four" for Subset-Knowers?

LeCorre's data suggest that all children have created numerical meanings for the first four verbal numerals before they figure out how the numeral list represents number. His data also suggest that these meanings are unlikely to be analog magnitudes. What might they be? The fact that they are restricted to representations of sets of one, two, three, and four objects raises the obvious possibility that parallel individuation underlies their meanings. Although this is a tempting suggestion, it cannot be that the parallel individuation system that is part of core cognition supports the meanings of the first four numerals by itself. This is because the symbols in this system represent specific individuals. If the representations in this system are modeled as in Figure 4.9 (see chapter 4 for evidence this is so), the working-memory models that make up this system of representation contain no symbols for quantifiers or for numerals.

What could "one" for a "one"-knower mean, or "one" and "two" for a "two"-knower? What is the format of the mental representations that underlie the numerical meanings subset-knowers have created for numerals? What is the process through which a given set is assigned one numeral rather than another? The answer we give to this question must be constrained by what we know about the decidedly unadult nature of the meanings of numerals early in the learning process. That the only meanings assigned are for sets of one through four definitely implicates parallel individuation as playing some role. In addition, the particular partial meanings children create implicate set-based quantification as well.

In chapter 7 we saw that prelinguistic infants and nonhuman primates are endowed not only with parallel individuation and analog magnitude representations but also with a set-based system of quantification that underlies the quantificational resources of natural language. In some circumstances that do not favor parallel individuation, both nonhuman primates and 15-month-old infants make a singular/plural distinction. Furthermore, by 22 months of age, English-learning children have learned some of the syntactic/morphological symbolic expressions for it. The quantifier "a" is of special interest, as its semantic force in many contexts overlaps the meaning of "one." Indeed, in many languages the word for the singular indefinite determiner is the same as the first word in the numeral list.

Semantic treatments of quantifiers require the abstract concepts individual and set. The classic treatment of the singular/plural distinction assumes individuals in some domain and a join operation that combines individuals into sets (see Figure 7.1; Chierchia, 1998; Link, 1987). Natural language quantifiers explicitly distinguish atoms—the individuals on the bottom of this semi-lattice—from the sets that are created by joining atoms. Singular quantification is used when a single individual in the domain is referred to, and plural quantification is used when referring to any set containing more than one individual. Chapter 7 argued that children are endowed with the syntactic category of quantifiers, with the syntactic/semantic distinction between singular and plural, and with the associated semantic notions of "set" and "individual." These notions, together with computational resources of parallel individuation, may provide the initial meanings of the first four numerals.

This suggestion was first made by Paul Bloom and Karen Wynn (1997), who noted that the partial meanings assigned to numeral words by subset-knowers are equivalent to quantifier meanings. For example, children's responses both on Give-a-Number and What's-on-this-Card show that "one" for a "one"-knower is equivalent in meaning to "a," and all other numerals are analyzed as if they meant "some." That is, when asked to give the experimenter one fish, a "one"-knower hands over one fish, but if asked for any other numeral's worth, the child merely grabs a plurality. And when asked to say, without counting, how many bees there are on a card that could contain anywhere from one to eight bees, "one"-knowers say "one" for one bee and "two" for sets from two to eight bees (LeCorre et al., 2006; LeCorre & Carey, 2007; see also Clark & Nikitina, in press, for evidence from diary studies and elicited production that that English-learning children initially analyze "two" as a plural marker).

Bloom and Wynn (1997) pointed out that if children analyzed numerals as quantifiers, and if there were innate or learned expectations about the semantics of quantifiers in place, this would help them break into the meanings of the numerals. They then went on to show that from the very beginning of numeral use, children have indeed analyzed them as quantifiers. They showed that the speech that children hear contains both quantifiers (determiners, "all," "some," etc.) and number words that appear in the quantifier position (e.g., "all brown cows, some brown cows, each brown cow, three brown cows"), and children's own speech respects the adjective-quantifier distinction at two years of age, in number words and in other quantifiers as well. In addition, "a" is one of the first quantifiers children learn, before the child's second birthday (see chapter 7). These observations, along with the nature of the partial meanings subset-knowers assign to numerals, suggest that young children's initial meanings assigned to number words are constrained by the semantics of quantifiers in natural languages.

Barbara Sarnecka and her colleagues (2007) have recently provided striking confirmation of this hypothesis. If quantifier meanings are supporting subset-knowers' initial hypotheses about numeral meanings, those meanings should be affected by the nature of number marking in their own language. As we saw in chapter 7, English-learning children have worked out the meaning of the contrast between "is a blicket" and "are some blickets" by 22 months of age. Children who have learned this aspects of number marking already have available language-relevant hypotheses to support the meaning of "one." Classifier languages, like Mandarin and Japanese, largely lack singular/plural marking, and so children learning such languages will not learn morphemes that mean "singular" and "plural." If explicit quantifier knowledge structures the hypothesis space available for positing the first meanings for verbal numbers, children learning classifier languages may become "one"-knowers much later than children learning a language that marks the singular/plural distinction morphologically (such as English or Russian). This is what Sarnecka found. She showed that Japanese, Russian, and English children learn to recite the count list in the counting routine equally early, and that children in all three language groups get equivalent input with respect to parental use of numerals. Yet, when she administered Wynn's Give-a-Number task to samples of 2:9- to 3:6-year-olds learning Japanese, English, and Russian, she found the Japanese sample to have markedly more no numeral knowers than the other two samples. Japanese children are slower to become "one"-knowers; they remain longer in the stage in which the numeral list is a meaningless list. Being later to break into the system ripples through all the stages—there are also fewer "two-", "three"- and cardinal principle knowers among the Japanese than the other two samples.

Japanese has two verbal numeral lists and children are exposed to both. Perhaps this makes learning the meaning of number words harder. To address this possibility, and to provide further evidence that it may be the lack of morphological number marking that's slowing the children down, Peggy Li and her colleagues (Li, LeCorre, Jia, & Carey, 2008) repeated Sarnecka's study with Mandarin-learning children in China and Taiwan. Mandarin is also a classifier language with virtually no singular/plural marking on nouns or verbs in the child's input, and Mandarin has only one count list. Li et al. found that Mandarin learners become "one"-

knowers six to nine months later than do English-learning children, in spite of evidence from other studies that they learn the numeral list at comparable ages.

These data on the effects of language on numeral learning provide striking evidence for the proposal that linguistic quantifier representations play a role in the earliest learning of the meaning of numerals. If this is so, learning still other linguistic number marking systems (e.g., singular/dual/plural) might interact with the initial partial meanings children assign to spoken numerals. As of yet, nobody has systematically studied this issue, but I know of one relevant study of the acquisition of linguistic number marking in a language quite different from English—Palestinian Arabic. Palestinian Arabic has a dual marker system and also distinguishes plural morphology and collective morphology. In a study of children's learning number marking in Palestinian Arabic, Ravid and Hayek (2003) found that 3-year-olds often used the numeral translated "two" instead of the dual when referring to sets of two objects, whereas older children were unlikely to do this. This finding is consistent with the suggestion that "two" is initially a dual marker.

Furthermore, there is evidence from historical linguistics that the number words have their origins as quantifiers. The linguist James Hurford (1987) summarized the evidence that, historically, the small-number words have a different origin than the larger ones, an origin that implicates them in the business of noun phrase syntax. In all languages with rich morphology, for example, "one" is more widely inflected than is "two," which in turn is more widely inflected than "three." "Four" or "five" and higher are equally, and less, inflected than the first three count words.

What these data suggest is that, historically, the initial meaning of "one" overlapped substantially that of the singular determiner "a," and that the initial meaning of "two" overlapped substantially that for dual markers in languages that have them, and the initial meaning of "three" overlapped substantially that for a trial marker. But what might the representations that underlie the meanings of the singular determiner, dual markers, and trial markers be? What is their format, and what is the process through which sets are assigned numerals? And why is this system of representation limited to representations of sets of one through four objects? LeCorre and I proposed a system of representations that could underlie the meanings of numerals for subset-knowers that draw on the resources both of set-based quantification and parallel individuation, and thus we dubbed it "enriched parallel individuation" (LeCorre & Carey, 2007; see Mix, Huttenlocher, & Levine, 2002, for a similar proposal).

The parallel individuation system that is part of core cognition creates working-memory models of sets. The symbols in these models represent particular individuals—this box, which is different from that one. However, as detailed in chapter 4, even when drawing on parallel individuation alone, infants have the capacity to represent two models and compare them on the basis of 1–1 correspondence. For representations of this format to subserve the meanings of the singular determiner or the numeral "one" for subset-knowers, the child may create a long-term memory model of a set of one individual and map it to the linguistic expression "a" or "one." Similarly, a long-term memory model of a set of two individuals could be created and mapped to the linguistic expression for a dual marker or "two," and so on for "three" and "four." These models could contain abstract symbols for individuals ($\{i\}$, $\{j\,k\}$, $\{m\,n\,o\}$, $\{w\,x\,y\,z\}$) or they could simply be long-term memory models of particular sets of individuals ($\{$Mommy$\}$, $\{$Daddy Johnnie$\}$ ...). What makes these models represent "one" "two" and so forth is their computational role. They are deployed in assigning numerals to sets as follows: The child makes a working-memory model of a particular set he or she wants to quantify $\{$e.g., cookie cookie$\}$. He she then searches the models in long-term memory to find that which can be put in 1–1 correspondence with this working-memory model, retrieving the quantifier that has been mapped to that model.

All of the computational resources required for enriched parallel individuation are known to be available to prelinguistic infants. Prelinguistic infants create working-memory models of at least two separate sets and compare these on the basis of 1–1 correspondence (chapter 4). They also treat sets as objects, quantifying over them as required by natural language quantifiers (chapter 7). Still, it is important to stress that the long-term memory models that support the meanings of singular, dual, and triple markers, as well as the child's first numerals, are not themselves part of core cognition. These must be created in the course of language learning, and for English-learning children this process unfolds for a period of over a year. This why we designate the hypothesized system of representation "enriched parallel individuation."

*Proposal 2: Numeral List Representations Are Bootstrapped from
the Representations of Enriched Parallel Individuation*

In Proposal 2, as in Proposal 1, the two important planks of the boot-strapping process are constructed in parallel, largely independent of each other. As in Proposal 1, the child learns the numeral list and the count routine as a numerically meaningless game. As in Proposal 1, the child also creates numerical meanings for some numerals—in this case "one" through "four." In Proposal 2, these meanings are supplied by enriched parallel individuation.

I envision something like the following for how concepts of enriched parallel individuation are constructed: English-learning children first learn the distinction between singular and plural—"a block" versus "some blocks"—by noting that "a block" applies when the speaker is referring to an array that contains only a single individual, whereas "some blocks" applies when the speaker is referring to an array that contains more than one individual. When learning the singular/plural distinction, children must treat sets of one—the atoms on Figure 7.1—differently from sets of two or three (within the limits of parallel individuation) and from sets of four to eight (beyond it); see chapter 7. This principled distinction underlies the learning of the syntactic marker "a" for the semantic notion *singular*, which applies to atoms—single individual files. The semantic notion *plural* (and the syntactic marker "-s", or "are" versus "is," and quantifiers like "some" when applied to sets of individuals) refers to sets of multiple individuals, not distinguishing whether their number is within the range of parallel individuation or outside it. Thus, learning the plural morpheme might alert the child to the possibility that sets outside the range of parallel individuation should be treated, for some linguistic purposes, in the same manner as sets within the range of parallel individuation.

Second, children learn that the word "one" is a quantifier that picks out individuals by noting that it applies in the same situations as "a," which they have already learned. I propose that the representation that underlies the meaning of "a" and "one" is a model stored in long term memory{atom}, and any working memory model of a single individual the child wants to refer to is called "a" or "one" because the set containing that single individual can be put in 1–1 correspondence with the working memory model. Children also learn that the other number words are quantifiers that pick out sets of individuals, by noting that they apply in the same situations as "some," always in the presence of the plural marker. This step corresponds to the stage discovered by Wynn in which children know the meaning of "one" and know that all the number words above "one" refer to numerosities above one but do not know which numerosities are picked out by each word. It is at this stage of the process that some children misinterpret "two" as a general plural marker (Clark & Nikitina, in press; LeCorre et al., 2006; LeCorre & Carey, 2007). Thus, one of the major embarrassments for Proposals 1— the fact that children treat "two, three, four, five, . . ." as rough synonyms, referring to plurality, in spite of the fact that analog magnitude representations makes no principled distinction between one and more than one—is one of the motivations for Proposal 2.

Third, children learn that the word "two" applies only to a subset of plural representations: those in which the speaker is referring to an array that can be put into 1–1 correspondence with a set that contains two individual files. The word "two" is mapped to a model in long-term memory $\{j\ k\}$, which is deployed as one of the candidate sets to match attended sets to for the purpose of quantifier selection. The same representations underlie the meanings of dual markers in languages that have them. Later, children create a model in long-term memory that analogously supports the meaning of "three," again supported by whatever processes allow children to construct meanings for trial markers in languages that have them. Finally, as LeCorre has shown, they also create a long-term memory model to support the meaning of "four." Note that up through this step, the count list and the counting routine play no role in the process of children's constructing numerical interpretations of the first four numerals.

Independently of the above steps (though perhaps concurrently with them), children learn the count sequence as a meaningless routine. They note the identity of the words "one, two," "three," and "four" which now have numerical meaning, and the first words in the otherwise meaningless counting list. Also, in the course of counting, children discover that when an attended set would be quantified with the dual marker "two," the count goes "one, two," and when an attended set would be quantified with the trial marker "three," the count goes "one, two, three." The child is thus in the position to notice that for these words at least, the last word reached in a count refers to the cardinal value of the whole set.

At this point, the stage is set for the crucial induction. The child must notice an analogy between next in the numeral list and next in the series of models ($\{i\}$, $\{j\,k\}$, $\{m\,n\,o\}$, $\{w\,x\,y\,z\}$) related by adding an individual. Remember, core cognition supports the comparison of two sets simultaneously held in memory on the basis of 1–1 correspondence, so the child has the capacity to represent this latter basis of ordering sets. This analogy licenses the crucial induction: if "x" is followed by "y" in the counting sequence, adding a individual to a set with cardinal value x results in a set with cardinal value y. This generalization does not yet embody the arithmetic successor function, but one additional step is all that is needed. Since the child has already mapped single individuals onto "one," adding a new individual is equivalent to adding one.

Proposal 2 has several advantages over Proposal 1. It makes sense of the actual partial meanings children assign to number-words as they try to fill in the placeholders. The semantics of quantifiers explain these facts. It makes sense of the fact that subset-knowers acquire the cardinal meanings of "one" "two" "three" and "four," and no other numeral, for only sets of these sizes are representable by models of the sets of individuals held in parallel in working memory, thus to be matched via 1–1 correspondence to long-term memory models of sets of one, two, three, and 4 individuals. It makes sense of the patterns of noise in children's choices of numerals to apply to sets of one through four; again, parallel individuation explains this fact.

We sought an answer to two questions. First, how do children assign numerical meanings to verbal numerals, and how do children learn how the list itself represents number? And second, how do they learn the counting principles? The bootstrapping proposals—both of them—answer both of these questions, albeit differently from each other. Proposal 2's answer is that the meanings of "one" through "four" are acquired just as quantifiers in natural languages are—as quantifiers for single individuals, pairs, triples, and quadruples. These words, as well as higher numerals, also get initial interpretations as part of a placeholder structure, the count list itself, in which meaning is exhausted by the fact that the list is ordered. The bootstrapping process explains how children learn how the list itself represents number, which in turn explains how they assign numerical meaning to numerals like "five" and "seven." When children first become cardinal principle knowers—that is, when they are nonmappers who have not yet integrated the count list with analog magnitude number representations—the meaning of "five" is exhausted by the child's mastery of counting. The counting principles ensure that the content of "five" is one more than four, and the meaning of "seven" is one more than six, which is one more than five, which is one more than four.

Summary: Bootstrapping the Numeral List Representation of Natural Number

I have argued here that the numeral list representation of number is a representational resource with power that transcends any single representational system available to prelinguistic infants. When the child, at around age 3½, has mastered how the count sequence represents number, he or she can in principle precisely represent any positive integer. Before that, he or she has only the quantificational resources of natural languages, parallel individuation representations that implicitly represent small numbers, and analog magnitude representations that provide approximate representations of the cardinal values of sets.

Additionally, I have taken on the challenge of specifying a learning mechanism that can underlie developmental discontinuities—Quinian bootstrapping. I provided two possible routes through which explicit numerals for integers might be learned. Both involve, but are not exhausted by, garden-variety learning processes: association, the mechanisms that support language learning, and so on. Both are bootstrapping mechanisms. Like all Quinian bootstrapping processes, they are nondeductive. They both involve noticing analogies and making inductive and abductive leaps. Proposal 1 depends on an analogical mapping between "later on the numeral list" and "larger number as represented by analog magnitudes." Proposal 2 depends on the analogy between next on the numeral list and next state after additional individual has been added to a set. Both proposals require that the child recognize, one way or another, that successive numerals among "one," "two," "three," and "four" refer to sets that are related by +1, and induce that all successive numerals in the count list are so related.

Both proposals exemplify one of Quine's bootstrapping principles: an explicit structure is learned initially without the meaning it will eventually have, and at least some relations among the explicit symbols are learned directly in terms of each other. The list of numeral words and the counting routine are learned as numerically meaningless structures. Whereas order is essential to numerical representations, ordered relations in themselves are much more general and thus not uniquely numerical. In both proposals the ordering of the number words exhausts their initial representational content within the counting routine and plays a role in the mappings and inductions of each proposal.

Both proposals depend on integrating previously distinct representations. This is where the new representational power comes from. The concepts *set, individual, singular, plural, dual,* and *triple* are explicitly available to support the learning of quantifiers, but are only implicit or absent in parallel individuation and analog magnitude representations. In analog magnitude representations, numerical distinctions are explicitly symbolized that are unmarked in natural language quantifiers or parallel individuation (e.g., 35 vs. 40), and although analog magnitude representations may play no role in the child's learning how counting represents number, they are integrated with counting some six months later (LeCorre & Carey, 2007; see chapter 9). And the representations that articulate the parallel individuation system contain computations that embody the successor function, whereas neither of the other systems does. The bootstrapping process (which depends on analogical mapping) creates an explicit representational system with all of these properties, a representational system that maps onto each of its sources and thus serves to integrate them.

An Aside: Can Animals Create a Numeral List Representation of Number?

Language plays two crucial roles in Proposal 2. First, the system of set-based quantification that underlies the meanings of quantifiers provides some of the hypotheses children entertain for the partial meanings of numerals as they try to fill in the placeholder symbols. As shown in chapter 7, *Rhesus* macaques (and presumably other nonhuman primates as well) have the capacity for set-based quantification and represent the singular/plural distinction. Of course, they will have no LAD that constrains general hypotheses about the role of quantifiers in noun phrase semantics. If the latter abilities are necessary, no other animal should be able to build a numeral list representation of natural number. Second, all bootstrapping processes require language or some other explicit symbols to provide a system of placeholder symbols with at least some relations among them directly represented. No other animal creates explicit symbols, and thus, if bootstrapping processes such those detailed here are required to create representations of natural number, there is a second reason to expect no other animal to do so.

Contrary to these predictions, several studies have claimed success at teaching numerals to nonhuman animals, ranging from an African grey parrot to several chimpanzees. These are heroic and extremely interesting experiments that certainly show that nonhuman animals can learn the mapping between numerals (external symbols for cardinal values of sets) and nonlinguistic number representations beyond the range of parallel individuation. The question is what the animals have learned, and how. Evidence that they create these mappings as do children would undermine the claim that Quinian bootstrapping is necessary for the construction of representations of the positive integers. On the contrary, it is likely that the process underlying this achievement is nothing like the process children go through. Years of operant condition was required in each case, and there is no evidence that any animal has induced how the numeral list works (Boysen & Bernston, 1989; Matsuzawa, 1985, Pepperberg, 1987).

For illustration, consider one case: Matsuzawa's (1985) chimpanzee, Ai. Ai can now enumerate up to nine dots without error, showing the same RT functions as do normal adults. Also, Ai knows the ordinal relations among the numerals; she will touch numerals displayed on the screen (e.g., "6, 3, 8, 1") in order of increasing numerical values. Thus, there is no doubt Ai has learned a mapping between numerals (written ones in this case) and some nonlinguistic representations of cardinal values of sets ranging from one to nine.

In her training regimen, Ai was taught the numbers in succession. She first taught to associate "1" with sets with one individual and "2" with sets with two individuals. After this mapping had been mastered, Ai was introduced to the symbol "3" and sets with three individuals. She maintained her high performance on "1" but was at chance at discriminating "2" and "3," indicating that she had first associated "2" with values that included at least two and three. This is reminiscent of the child's "one"-knower stage, where "two" is taken as general plural marker, and is supported by the nonlinguistic set-based quantification system documented by David Barner and colleagues (see chapter 7). After thousands of additional trials, Ai mastered "1, 2, 3" and then "4" was added to the set. She maintained her high performance on "1" and "2," but now fell to chance discriminating the sets that matched "3" and "4.", indicating that she had previously associated "3 with values that included at least three and four. This is reminiscent of the child's "two"-knower stage, and suggests that linguistic dual markers also draw on capacities available to nonhuman primates. After thousands of additional trials, she mastered "1, 2, 3, 4," and when introduced to "5", showed that she had taken the symbol "4" to apply to sets both with four and five members (as would "three"-knowers learning natural language numerals). As her training progressed to higher numerosities, however, Ai never made the induction that each number symbol added to the set was to be associated with a precise numerosity. As each new symbol was introduced, up to "9," she was always at chance between the last item learned "n" and the newly introduced item "n + 1", indicating that she had previously learned that "n" was to be associated with at least n and $n + 1$. No child has ever been seen to continue this pattern of learning beyond "four."

Ai never made the relevant induction, even though she certainly eventually mapped the first nine numerals onto the first nine numbers. Since there is no evidence that Ai ever mastered how the list represents number, it seems likely that she did not really construct a numeral list representation of number. Still, an important question is how she did learn what she did, for her representations of number do go beyond either object-file representations, exceeding as they do the intrinsic limits of parallel individuation, and they also appear to be symbols for precise numerosities up to nine. I can only speculate as to how she and other animals achieve this, but my guess is that Ai probably created an association between numerals and analog magnitude representations. Ai's sensitivity, in the ratio of 8:9, only slightly better than that of unpracticed human adults' analog magnitude number representations (7: 8; Barth et al., 2003). With extensive training, sensitivity to finer numerical distinctions may be accomplished in various ways—for instance, the noise in the analog magnitude representations might be reduced by changing the parameters of the perceptual process that computes numerical magnitudes, as occurs in other cases of training of psychophysical discrimination thresholds. If this is right, Ai's failure to induce the successor relation gives us one more reason to suspect that human children's construction of the numeral list representation does not depend solely on the analog magnitude representations of number.

Why did Ai fail to make the induction children do? Well, she wasn't really given the chance, and neither has any other animal trained to associate numerals with nonverbal number representations. Remember that nonhuman primates, like young children, can learn meaningless lists. But in none of the training studies with nonhuman animals were the animals taught the list itself. Thus, even if they had the capacity for Quinian bootstrapping, they did not have the placeholder structure available to support the induction. Although training animals numeral representations requires several years of work, with several hours of training a day, I fervently hope that somebody will repeat Matsuzawa's study, having trained the chimpanzee on "1, 2, 3, 4, 5, 6, 7, 8, 9" as a meaningless ordered list first. That is, Ai may have failed to make the induction because she did not have planks of the bootstrapping process in place.

If I were to bet, I'd bet against this alternative training regime's making a difference. That is, I very much doubt that nonhuman animals have the capacity for Quinian bootstrapping. I doubt that they have the capacity to use a symbolic structure as a placeholder structure and to engage in the modeling techniques needed to combine previously distinct representational systems. My suspicion is that nonhuman animals lack a crucial tool for combining previously distinct mental representations: They cannot use lexical identity as a clue that previously unrelated representations actually capture the same aspects of reality. Although many animals appear to have very similar capacities to those of humans to track objects, represent analog magnitudes, and even engage in set-based quantification, they cannot use language to enrich or link these and so to create the sides of Quine's chimney, inching up it to arrive at the natural numbers. I do not know whether my suspicions are correct; there are no relevant data. But whether or not they are is a question of great theoretical importance in our quest to understand the origin of the human conceptual repertoire. The capacity for Quinian bootstrapping underlies the construction of new representational resources that allow us to think thoughts we could not previously entertain. We may be the only animal with this capacity.

There is another possible principled reason Ai may never have made the induction children make. This induction requires recursion: 2 is $(1 + 1)$, 3 is $((1 + 1) + 1)$, 4 is $(((1 + 1) + 1) + 1)$, and so on. Marc Hauser, Noam Chomsky, and Tecumsah Fitch (2002) suggested that the capacity for recursion may be one that separates nonhuman animals and human beings. On either hypothesis—nonhuman animals lack the symbolic capacity for Quinian bootstrapping in general or the computational capacity that underlies the induction made in this particular case (and nothing prevents both from being true)—creating a representation of the positive integers would forever elude nonhuman animals.

Conclusions

Kronecker was wrong. Neither God nor evolution gave humans natural number. Natural number is a human construction. I have provided here one worked example of the creation of a new representational resource with more power than the representations upon which it is built. The lessons I wish to draw, however, are very general. Such creations occur repeatedly, both historically and within the individual child. Within mathematical representations, much has been written about the creation of 0, negative numbers, and rational numbers. Each of these developments transcends the power of the numeral list representation that is the focus of the present chapter, and each requires further episodes of Quinian bootstrapping (see chapters 9 and 11 for a discussion of the construction of rational number). Similarly, within the history of science, theory changes that involve conceptual change involve the creation of new representational resources that allow thoughts that were previously unthinkable, and these theory changes also require Quinian bootstrapping (see chapters 10 and 11).

9

Beyond the Numeral List Representation of Integers

Unlike core cognition, which is continuous throughout the life span, much of conceptual development involves qualitative changes and thus discontinuities in the systems of representation that underlie thought. Chapter 8 presented a case study of a developmental discontinuity. None of the original three core systems with numerical content (analog magnitudes, parallel individuation, set-based quantification) can express exact cardinal values such as seven or thirty-two, let alone 6,856,349 or infinity. Thus, the numeral list representation of the positive integers contains representations not expressible in any attested conceptual system from which it is built. As expected by this analysis, learning to use the numeral list to represent number is very difficult; it does not merely involve mapping words to symbols that already exist prelinguistically.

Even when the child has constructed a count list and induced how to deploy it to represent number, the construction of a representation of the positive integers is not complete. Strictly speaking, what the child has constructed by the end of the bootstrapping episode detailed in chapter 8 is capable of expressing only a finite subset of the positive integers, constrained by the length of the child's count list (at most 20 at the time the child first succeeds at using counting to represent number, often only 10 or fewer). The bootstrapping process continues. Part I of this chapter considers how the child who uses counting to represent number (i.e., is a cardinal-principle-knower) integrates the count list with analog magnitude representations, and what this integration buys the child. My goal is to further illustrate the meaning-making capacity of Quinian bootstrapping.

Over the next few years, the child extends the verbal numeral list to "one hundred" and then "one thousand," beginning to command the base system, and coming to the realization that there is no highest numeral. Perhaps we would want to credit a representation of natural number only at this point. The issue here is purely semantic; it depends upon what we choose to count as a representation of natural number. When we study conceptual development we must characterize the child's representational resources at different points, including the computations they support, and then we are in a position to characterize their content.

Equally obviously, mathematical development does not end with the construction of representations of natural number. Both in this history of mathematics and in the conceptual development of the child, increasingly powerful representations are created, and often this process requires further bootstrapping. Many books could and have been written on the historical construction of representations of zero, of rational number, of real number, and of orders of infinity, as well as mathematical structures that are not numbers in any sense. As with natural number, these culturally constructed representations must then be mastered anew by each individual learner.

It is beyond the scope of this book to treat any other episode in the construction of mathematics in the detail I have given to the numeral list representation of natural number. In Part II of this chapter, I present evidence for a second discontinuity in the development of mathematical cognition: the construction of representations of fractions. Chapter 11 then takes up the bootstrapping process that underlies this developmental discontinuity.

Part I: Integrating the Numeral List with Analog Magnitude Number Representations

As chapters 4 and 8 reviewed, adults have integrated the numeral list with analog magnitude representations of number. Even when comparing the numerical values of symbols (e.g., which is more, 5 or 6), adults display the Weber-fraction signature of analog magnitudes. For example, it is harder to say which is larger between 5 and 6 than between 5 and 9 (Dehaene, 1997). Reflect on this fact for a moment. "Five" is the next numeral in the count list after "four", and adults couldn't be more practiced at counting, "one, two, three, four, five ... " Still, when deciding numerical order, they apparently rely on the analog magnitude number sense, for ease of comparison is a function of the ratio between the numbers, not practice at the count list.

Analog magnitudes could not underlie this judgment if they were not mapped to the numerals. And, of course they are. The simplest and most straightforward demonstration of this mapping derives from tasks in which participants are asked to estimate the number of dots on a display, or number of clicks in a stream, when prevented from counting. Randy Gallistel, Rochel Gelman, and their colleagues (Whelen, Gallistel, & Gelman, 1999; Cordes, Gelman, & Gallistel, 2002) showed that adults' estimates are an almost perfect function of number—that is, if there are 20 dots, the mean estimate is 20. But the standard deviation of the estimate is also a linear function of number. That is, the range of responses given to sets of 40 is twice as big as to sets of 20. This is scalar variability and it follows from Weber's law.

Chapter 8 considered and rejected the hypothesis that constructing the mapping between verbal numerals and analog magnitudes simply is the process through which verbal numerals come to have numerical meaning. As detailed in chapter 8, LeCorre showed that children do not construct this mapping until about six months after they have figured out how the count list represents number, so this mapping could not possibly play a role in the child's construction of the numeral list representation of natural number. Still, the mapping is eventually constructed. What does the child gain from it, and how is it achieved?

What Children Gain by Constructing the Mapping

Consider a child who understands how counting represents number, but has not yet made the mapping—a cardinal-principle-knower who is a nonmapper. This child definitely understands the numerical meaning of "seven." He or she knows that seven is one more than six, which is one more than, five, and so on, and can use the numeral list to represent the cardinality of sets. The philosopher of mathematics, Marcus Giaquinto (2007), suggested a way you may get a feel for the state the child is in, assuming you know how binary notation represents number but have not worked with it enough to map it onto analog magnitudes. Take 10101. If you understand how binary notation works, you know that this number is one more than 10100, and you can count up: 1, 10, 11, 100, 101, 110, 111, 1000.... But what number is 10101? You may understand this just exactly as LeCorre's CP nonmappers understand the number 7. That is your understanding may be exhausted by your ability to count in binary. Giaquinto pointed out that your understanding is greatly enriched if somebody tells you that 10101 is the number of circles in Figure 9.1. Mapping 10101 to the innately given and interpreted analog magnitude representation of this set of dots provides a new source of meaning for "10101." Your understanding is also greatly enriched if you learn that 10101 is 21 in decimal notation. Mapping 10101 to 21 brings two new sources of numerical meaning: 21 is mapped onto analog magnitudes already by adults, and so learning that 10101 in binary notation is 21 in decimal notation provides the same additional meaning for 10101 as does learning that it is the number of dots in Figure 9.1. Also, 21 has rich numerical meaning for adults from within the numeral list and the arithmetical system built on it (e.g., 21 is odd, is 3 times 7, and so on), and so 10101 inherits all this meaning when you learn that it expresses the same number as does 21.

Cardinal-principle-knowers who are nonmappers are in an analogous representational state as the person who knows how to count in binary but has no feel for the quantities represented. These children understand how the count list represents number, but have not yet mapped, "five, "six," "seven," "eight," "nine" or "ten" to the analog magnitude representations of sets of these numerosities.

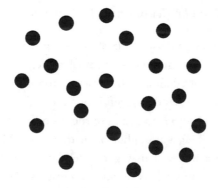

Figure 9.1. 10101 (in binary) dots.

What does constructing this mapping, making the transition between nonmappers and mappers, buy the child? Additional meaning is provided by the content of the symbols in the analog magnitude system, which in turn is partly provided by their innately given conceptual role. For instance, we know that animals and babies use analog magnitude representations to compare sets with respect to which has more (see chapter 4), and that adults rely on analog magnitude representations in comparing numerical magnitudes, even when the input to the comparison is symbolic. That is, number comparison is one of the numerical computations analog magnitude representations support. Perhaps nonmappers will not be able to tell which of two numerals picks out a larger set. CP nonmappers may not be able to compute numerical order from numerals alone. LeCorre (2007; see also Condry & Spelke, 2008) showed just that. Nonmappers (subset-knowers and cardinal-principle-knowing nonmappers alike) are unable determine numerical order among verbal numerals above "four." For example, when asked about closed boxes, one of which was said to have six apples in it and the other ten, "Which box has more apples? This one that has six or this one with ten?" nonmappers responded at random. The children understood the question. Remember, all of these children can count to ten, and all have mapped at least some numerals (e.g., "one" and "two") to core cognition (see chapter 8). All children could answer these questions so long as at least one of the numerals in the comparison had already been assigned a numerical meaning (e.g., a "two"-knower judges that the box with two has less than the box with ten, but responds at chance when asked to compare six with ten).

In contrast, the mappers—children who have mapped numerals to analog magnitudes (i.e., who can provide a verbal estimate of the number of individuals in a set of ten dots using a verbal numeral larger than when providing a verbal estimate the number in a set of six dots; see chapter 8) —answer correctly for all pairs of numerals within their count list. This finding is important for two reasons. First, it provides convergent evidence for LeCorre's conclusion that there are children who understand how counting works who have not yet mapped numerals to analog magnitudes. Not only are the slopes of verbal estimates as a function of set sizes between four and ten zero for nonmappers, but these children cannot carry out a computation known to be subserved by analog magnitudes in adults—say, whether a set with seven apples has more or fewer apples than a set with ten apples. Second, and more important to me here, the finding shows that constructing the mapping between numerals and analog magnitudes provides new numerical meaning for the numerals, even for children who understand how the numeral list represents number. The new meaning created is analogous to that derived from mapping binary strings onto analog magnitudes for adults who understand binary notation only as a counting system.

Creating such mappings between previously distinct systems of representation is part of the process of filling in placeholder structures during bootstrapping episodes (see chapter 8). In this sense, we can conceive of the construction of this mapping as part of the process of bootstrapping a representation of the positive integers, for this mapping provides the meaning to the count list that is inherited from core analog magnitude number representations. Analog magnitude representations support numerical comparison, and also mental arithmetic (at least addition, subtraction, and doubling/halving; see chapter 4). When numerals are mapped onto analog magnitudes, analog magnitudes become a source of representation that supports these numerical processes over numerals.

How the Mapping Is Achieved

Thus, it is clear what constructing the mapping between analog magnitudes and numerals might buy the child. But how does the child construct the mapping? Mathieu LeCorre lays out two possibilities. First, the child may simply associate numerals with analog magnitude representations by observing which sets are represented by which numerals. That is, the child must experience the pairing of "six" with sets of six, and learn the pairing of the analog magnitude symbol for 6 with "six" by association. If this were the only mechanism subserving the mapping, it would have to be made one numeral at a time, number by number. Second, once the child has learned the count list, and how the count list represents number, the child may draw on the order information contained in the count list to infer the analog magnitude that corresponds to any given numeral. That is, the child may infer a rule "later in the list implies greater number," and use this rule along with some mappings achieved associatively to complete the mapping of the entire numeral list to analog magnitudes.

It is fairly obvious that eventually children and adults use the rule-based inferential process. It seems highly unlikely that adults need to experience a pairing of 245 entities with the numeral "245" to be able to estimate, with a numeral, the cardinal value of a set of 245 dots. Experiments with adults show that their numerical estimations require calibration. If simply asked to provide estimates of the numbers of dots in a series of sets, with no information about the range of set sizes involved, adults' estimates are monotonically related to set size, but often way off. However, when given just one calibration value (e.g., being told how many dots are in a sample set of 150 dots), performance improves dramatically when they are subsequently shown sets drawn from the range of 10 to 300 and told how many entities there are. That a single calibration trial has this effect implies that they must have some productive method for generating the mapping (Izard & Dehaene, 2007).

Furthermore, experiments by Jennifer Lipton and Elizabeth Spelke (2005) suggest that by age 5, children make use of the rule-based inferential process. Lipton and Spelke assessed children's counting skills to 100. Children were prompted with triads, such as "65, 66, 67 ..." or "76, 77, 78 ..," and asked to count up from there. Of crucial importance was whether they could manage the decade transition. At age 5, most children have mastered the count list to 40, or even to 60, and about half have done so to 100 or above. A variety of tasks then assessed the children's mapping of numerals onto analog magnitudes. For example, children were shown sets ranging in size from 4 to 120 and asked to estimate how many dots there were in each. Figure 9.2 shows the results from one illustrative experiment. Adults displayed the expected linear relationship between set size and average numeral produced, and so did skilled counters—those who had mastered the count list to over 100. Unskilled counters—who had mastered the count list only to 60—provided a linear relationship between set size and average numeral produced up to 60, but then provided a flat function for sets between 80 and 120.

Skilled and unskilled counters were in the same kindergarten and were the same age. It is extremely unlikely that skilled counters have experienced markedly more pairings of "eighty" with sets of 80 and

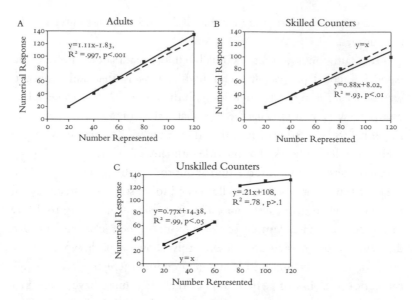

Figure 9.2. Data from Lipton & Spelke (2005). The average numeral produced (y axis) as a function of the number of dots in the stimulus array. a: adult estimates. b: estimates of 5-year-old counters skilled at counting to 100. c: estimates of 5-year-old counters skilled at counting only to 60. Reprinted from Lipton, J. S., & Spelke, E. (2005). Preschool children's mapping of number words to nonsymbolic numerosities. *Child Development, 76*(5), 978–988, with permission from Blackwell Publishers.

"one-hundred with sets of 100 than have unskilled counters, yet the skilled counters made accurate estimates of how many dots there were in sets of 80 and 100 and the unskilled counters did not. It seems likely, then, that children of this age have created the rule-based inferential process that relates place in the count list to analog magnitude representations. Of course, one cannot make use of this inferential process unless one knows the relevant part of the count list, and only the skilled counters did so.

Whether associative pairing of large sets with a given cardinality to specific numerals is necessary to apply the rule that relates position in the count list with analog magnitude number representations could be settled with a training experiment. Unskilled counters could be drilled in reciting the count list, but not given experience actually counting large sets, so that they experience no pairings between large numerals and analog magnitude representations of large sets. If children can infer the mapping from knowledge of the count list itself, then upon becoming skilled counters they should perform as did the skilled counters in the Lipton and Spelke experiments.

That 5-year-olds have constructed the rule-based inferential process by no means implies younger children have. Indeed, LeCorre's data reviewed in chapter 8 very strongly supports the number-by-number associative model for the earliest stages of the process of mapping numerals to analog magnitudes. Recall the nonmappers who understand the cardinal principle. These children can all count to ten (and sometimes higher). They recite the count list effortlessly, and use it to construct sets of any cardinality within those named by numerals they know, and to fix sets that have been miscounted. They spontaneously draw on counting to solve numerical problems. These children are skilled counters (to ten). Yet the construction of a mapping between numerals and analog magnitudes proceeds slowly and in a piecemeal manner. Some children have done so to five, some to six, some to eight, some all the way to ten, and so on.

Thus, the answer to the question of how the mapping between numerals and analog magnitudes is constructed—associatively, and piecemeal, number by number, or by an inferential process that draws on knowledge of order in the count list—is most probably both. Even adults need calibration, showing a role of an associative mapping between numerals and analog magnitude representations of sets. But at the beginning of the process of constructing the mapping, children must build up the mapping numeral by numeral, associatively. Until they have done so, they don't have the basis for forming the rule. Remember, this rule was the proposed centerpiece of the first bootstrapping proposal in chapter 8. Chapter 8 reviewed data that show this rule is learned well after the child has worked out how counting represents number, and thus cannot be the basis of the initial construction of the numeral list representation of natural number. Nonetheless, it is very likely that children do induce the rule that numerals later in the list express larger numbers. This rule enables children to estimate from a numeral's place in the count list what size set it is likely to represent.

In sum, becoming a cardinal-principle-knower is just the beginning of creating an understanding of the positive integers. Once a child has created the numeral list representation of integers, his or her repertoire of represented integers can be extended by merely extending the list, and intuitive addition and subtraction algorithms are generalized from counting. As we have just seen, once the numeral list is integrated with analog magnitude representations, this latter system is also a source of arithmetical generalizations over integers. All of these are important enrichments of numerical representations in the late preschool years, but all build, in a straightforward way, on the representational resources in core cognition and on the culturally constructed and now internalized numeral list representation of the positive integers.

The construction, enrichment, and entrenchment of the numeral list representation of natural number that occur during the preschool years are a great intellectual achievement. Moreover, there are many further episodes of qualitative changes in the course of mathematical development, in which a newly constructed representational system has more expressive power than its input. I will illustrate this point by sketching one example—the construction of representations of fractions. This construction requires conceptual change and a new episode of Quinian bootstrapping (see chapter 11).

Part II: Rational Number

As we have seen, when they are 3 years old, middle-class children growing up in a numerate culture typically construct their first representations of the positive integers—a numeral list deployed in counting. Very soon thereafter, they integrate numerals larger than "four" with analog magnitude number representations. In the immediately following years, children use, and thus entrench, this integrated representational system to invent addition and subtraction algorithms based on the successor function (i.e., by counting up and counting down) to extend their count list to the hundreds, to become conservers of number (i.e., explicitly come to realize that numerical equivalence is guaranteed by 1–1 correspondence; Piaget, 1952), and to realize that there is no highest number (because one can always add 1; Hartnett & Gelman, 1998). The numeral list representation of integers, deployed as licensed by the counting principles, is the symbol system in terms of which preschool children think explicit thoughts about numbers.

As Rochel Gelman (1991) has argued, in this conceptual scheme, there is no place for 1/3 as a number. The extension and conceptual role of the concept *number* are markedly different before and after the construction of representations of the rationals. Clearly, the extension of the concept *number* is vastly expanded when it comes to include rational numbers, and the conceptual framework in which representations of rational number is embedded differs from that exhausted by representations of positive integers in many fundamental respects. Rational numbers are based on division ("x/y" means "x divided by y"), not on the successor function, and division of integers cannot be easily modeled in terms of the numeral list representation of integers. Unlike multiplication of integers, which can be modeled as repeated addition and thus repeated counting on, the division of integers cannot always be modeled as repeated subtraction of whole numbers. To create a representation of rational number, children must develop the following interrelated understandings: that there are numbers between any two successive integers, including between 0 and 1; that the relation between the numerator and denominator in fractions is one of division; and that rational numbers are infinitely divisible and thus there are an infinite number of them between successive integers. When the concept number has come to include the rationals, there is no answer to such questions as "What is the next number after 1/3?" or "What is the next number after three?" When we answer "four" to the latter question, we have interpreted "number" to mean integer.

Several predictions follow from the hypotheses that (1) young children have an entrenched understanding of natural number based on the successor relation and the counting algorithm; and (2) that constructing a representation of the rationals requires the construction of a qualitatively different conceptual scheme from the numeral list representation of natural number. First, constructing a representation of the rationals should be difficult for children to achieve. Second, we should see intrusions from children's representations of integers as they try to make sense of what they are being taught about fractions and decimals. Third, given the analysis of the conceptual discontinuity sketched above, understanding division should be at the heart of constructing a representation of the rationals. And finally, we should see within-child consistency across a wide range of tasks that reflect disparate aspects of the representations of rationals; both CS1 (number restricted to the integers) and CS2 (number includes the rationals) are stably, but differently, interrelated systems of concepts and operations. All of these predictions are born out, as I illustrate below.

Difficulty of Learning; Intrusions from Whole Numbers

Students' difficulty in acquiring the concept of rational number has been well documented. Indeed, above and below the mean (500) on the math Scholastic Aptitude Test (SAT) given at the end of high school reflects an understanding or lack thereof of decimals and fractions. Part of the problem is notational: What does "1/56" mean? Gelman showed that many elementary schoolchildren cannot explain why a given fraction is written with two numerals (R. Gelman, 1991). They do not understand that "1/56" expresses a single number, not two. Not only do children fail at explicitly explaining the mathematical role of the numerator and the denominator in representing fractions, their lack of understanding is also revealed in simple ordering tasks, such as determining whether 1/56 is larger than 1/75. This difficulty has been shown to persist through the high school years in many different countries (c.f., Behr, Wachsmuth, Post, & Lesh, 1984, for the U.S.; Kerslake, 1986, for England; and Nesher & Peled, 1986, for Israel). Children's judgments and justifications for those judgments show their error to be an intrusion from integer representation; they say 1/75 is larger than 1/56 because "seventy-five is a bigger number than fifty-six." Similarly, researchers have found persistent difficulty in ordering two decimals such as 2.09 and 2.9 because "two hundred and nine is bigger than twenty-nine" (Carpenter, Corbitt, Kepner, & Lindquist, 1981; R. Gelman, 1991; Moss & Case, 1999), as well as placing a number like .685 on a number line that goes from 0 to 1 (Rittle-Johnson, Seigler, & Alibali, 2001), and lining up decimals such as 5.1 and .46 so as to add or subtract them

Understanding Division

One cannot understand fractional notation (e.g., "1/75") without understanding division. Children in the grips of CS1 are equipped to understand addition and subtraction on the basis of the successor function and the counting algorithm, and, as mentioned above, multiplication is modeled as repeated addition of whole numbers. Obviously, these models do not apply to fractions. One must understand division to grant the very existence of numbers between 0 and 1, and, of course, to understand that there are infinite rational numbers between any two integers.

Carol Smith, Gregg Solomon and I (2005) explored the degree of within-child consistency in various reflections of children's understanding of fractions and decimals, as well as with their understanding of division. Our sample consisted of middle-class 8- to 12-year-olds, the ages during which many children first construct an understanding of rational number. And indeed, confirming the data in the literature on children's understanding of fraction and decimal notation, half of the participants in our study erroneously judged that 1/75 was a larger number than 1/56. Children's qualitative justifications of this judgment indicated that they saw the two numbers in a fraction as two distinct whole numbers rather than determining a single number determined by division. Conversely, virtually all of those who ordered the numbers correctly articulated a relevant justification. Many envisioned what happened when you cut things into pieces; for example, "It's better to have 1/56 of a pizza than 1/75; the larger the bottom number, the smaller the fraction." Others simply articulated the general rule: "The smaller the denominator, the larger the fraction." Note that in this latter explanation, students explicitly acknowledge a distinction between the numeric value of one part of the fraction and the fraction itself, consistent with their understanding that 1/75 represents one particular number, not two. Similar results were obtained when the children were asked to order decimals such as .65 and .8, and success on one task predicted success on the other.

Following Rochel Gelman, the second way we probed children's understanding of fractional notation was simply by asking them to explain why there are two numbers in a fraction such as 1/7. If children understand a fraction in terms of division, then they should be able to give meaning to the two numerals vis-à-vis an explicit division model. They might directly state that a fraction is merely one number divided by another. Alternatively, they might explain that the denominator indicates the number of parts the whole is divided into, and the numerator indicates the number of parts of that size. We found that about half of the students either had no model of a fraction or had an incorrect model. Those with no model typically said uninformative things, such as "because they are there," "two numbers equal a fraction," "I forget," "don't know—I can't explain," or "top is the numerator, bottom is the denominator." Those with incorrect models all made reference to representations or concrete situations that they had witnessed in teaching, but they provided mistaken interpretations of what the numbers stood for, and thus what concept had informed the teacher's lesson. Fractions are often discussed in terms of cutting pies or other objects, and some students thought the 1 referred to the "whole" and the 7 to the slices (e. g., "1 means one pie; seven equal pieces" or "one whole thing, seven slices"). Others gave incorrect mathematical formulations relating the two numbers in terms of subtraction or multiplication rather than division (e.g., "1 is how many you are taking away; 7 is how many you have," "1 out of 7 is 6," or "1 times 7 equals 1/7").

In contrast, about one-fourth of the sample were able to articulate a clear division model in which they explained that the denominator refers to how many pieces the whole has been divided into and the numerator refers to how many such pieces one has. For example:

- "The top number is how many you used; the bottom number is how many there are altogether in total; how many pieces to make one."
- "The 1 is the numerator; 7 is the denominator. The numerator is how many you have and the denominator is how many it takes to make 1."

The rest of the sample gave ambiguous explanations—ones that could be consistent with either a division or subtraction interpretation. Most typically, these children said 1/7 means "1 out of 7," which could mean either 1 of a whole divided by 7 or 1 taken from a set of 7.

Understanding the Infinite Divisibility of Number; Numbers between 0 and 1

Logically, children must first recognize the existence of numbers between 0 and 1 before they can make the inductive leap that numbers are infinitely divisible. Smith, Solomon, and I (2005) simply asked the participants in our study whether there are any numbers between 0 and 1, and if so, how many they think there are. Almost half initially said there were no numbers between 0 and 1, as is consistent with their interpreting "number" as "whole number." Even when specifically asked about the number 1/2, some denied 1/2 was a number between 0 and 1, although most agreed it was. This latter group ultimately acknowledged the existence of some numbers between 0 and 1, either spontaneously or after being probed, but most of those who had initially denied the existence of any such thing said that they thought there were just a few, naming specific examples such as 1/2, 1/3, and 1/4. Altogether, about half of the children in the same group claimed either that there are no numbers between 0 and 1 or at most just a few.

In contrast, the other half of the sample either said there were an infinite number of numbers between 0 and 1, using the words "infinite" or "continuous" or semantic equivalents such as "numbers go on for-ever," "you can't stop decimals," or there is "an endless amount of numbers,"—or at least they claimed that there were "lots," "hundreds," "millions," or even "trillions" of numbers between 0 and 1, but stopped short of saying there were an infinite number.

To further clarify whether students thought there were an infinite number of numbers between 0 and 1, we devised a number-thought experiment. We asked children what one obtains by dividing 2 in half (answer, 1) and by dividing 1 in half (answer, 1/2). We then asked whether we could divide ½ by 2, and again the resulting number by 2, and whether this process could go on forever. We asked whether the numbers would be getting smaller and whether the process would ever end in 0. There were two coherent patterns of response ("get to zero"; "never get to zero") consistent with different underlying conceptions of number. The get to zero pattern (half the sample) is consistent with an understanding of fractional numbers as occupying finite, separate points on a number line, like integers. Students were coded as having shown this pattern if: (1) they claimed that there are at most only a limited number of numbers between 0 and 1; and (2) they claimed that when one repeatedly divided a positive number in half, one would get to 0, con-sistent with confusing repeated division with repeated subtraction. Some even claimed that one would get to 0 and then pass to negative numbers. To give a feeling for what the data in such a study are like, see some representative excerpts in Figure 9.3. Figure 9.4 gives some excerpts from the "never get to zero" responses.

S3 (Grade 3):

(Any numbers between 0–1?) No.

(How about one half?) Yes, I think so.

(About how many numbers are there between 0–1?) A little, just 0 and half, because it's halfway to one.

(Suppose you divided 2 in half and got 1; and then divided that number in half.... Could you keep dividing forever?) No because if you just took that half a number, that would be zero and you can't divide zero.

(Are the numbers getting bigger or smaller?) Smaller

(Would you ever get to zero?) Yes.

S9 (Grade 3):

(Any numbers between 0–1?) No.

(How about one half?) Yes, because it's not a number.

(About how many numbers are there between 0–1?) 1/2 and there are 4 other pieces. Quarters. There are numbers before 0, negative numbers.

(Suppose you divided 2 in half and got 1; and then divided that number in half.... Could you keep dividing forever?) Yes, it'll soon be just a black line, just numbers.

(Are the numbers getting bigger or smaller?) Smaller.

(Would you ever get to zero?) Yes, because if you have 8 parts, then you minus one and minus one until you get a minus 8, then you'll get 0.

S18 (Grade 4):

(Any numbers between 0–1?) No.

(How about one half?) Yes.

(About how many numbers are there between 0–1?). One: one-half.

(Suppose you divided 2 in half and got 1; and then divided that number in half.... Could you keep dividing forever?) No, I think you might stop. I don't think that there are that much numbers.

(Are the numbers getting bigger or smaller?) Smaller.

(Would you ever get to zero?) Yes because 0 is, most people know it is the last number and if it is then you eventually get to it.

S39 (Grade 6):

(Any numbers between 0–1?) No.

(How about one half?) Yes

(About how many numbers are there between 0–1?) Wait a minute, there's 1 over 2, 1 over 1, 1 over three, 1 over all the way up to 10. (Suppose you divided 2 in half and got 1; and then divided that number in half.... Could you keep dividing forever?) No, after 1 is 0. 0 is nothing esle. If kept dividing, ½, then 1/1 then 1/1 and 0/0 and that's it, because if you just took that half a number, that would be zero and you can't divide zero.

(Are the numbers getting bigger or smaller?) Smaller

(Would you ever get to zero?) Yes, 0 is the last number.

Figure 9.3. Excerpts from protocols that reveal the "get to 0" pattern of response.

S12 (Grade 3):

(Any numbers between 0-1?) Yes.

(Can you give an example?) 0 and a half.

(About how many numbers are there between 0-1?). 0 and a half, 0 and 1/4, 0 and 3/4, 1/8, 2/8, and on and on and on. (How many?) Lots.

(Suppose you divided 2 in half and got 1; and then divided that number in half.... Could you keep dividing forever?) Yes we could just keep on going because if we ran out of numbers we could just make up names for them because numbers go on forever and ever and there's no such thing as counting up to the highest number.

(Are the numbers getting bigger or smaller?) Smaller.

(Would you ever get to zero?) No.

S20 (Grade 4):

(Any numbers between 0-1?) Yes.

(Can you give an example?) 1/2, 1/4, 1/3, .5 fractions of a number.

(About how many numbers are there between 0-1?). It's continuous. I guess, you can keep going and going.

(Suppose you divided 2 in half and got 1; and then divided that number in half.... Could you keep dividing forever?) Yes. Numbers just keep on going.

(Are the numbers getting bigger or smaller?) Smaller.

(Would you ever get to zero?) No because if numbers are getting small, you can't measure them, and anyway, you just keep doing the same thing.

S35 (Grade 5):

(Any numbers between 0-1?) Yes.

(Can you give an example?) 1/2 or .5

(About how many numbers are there between 0-1?). A lot.

(Suppose you divided 2 in half and got 1; and then divided that number in half.... Could you keep dividing forever?) Yes, there always has to be something left when you divide it.

(Are the numbers getting bigger or smaller?) Smaller.

(Would you ever get to zero?) No because there is an infinite number of numbers below 1 and above 0.

S41 (Grade 6):

(Any numbers between 0-1?) Yes.

(Can you give an example?) .5

(About how many numbers are there between 0-1?). 99, no more, infinity.

(Suppose you divided 2 in half and got 1; and then divided that number in half.... Could you keep dividing forever?) Yes there is an infinite amount of numbers.

(Are the numbers getting bigger or smaller?) Smaller.

(Would you ever get to zero?) No, have zero in your problem; it would get before other numbers but never actual number zero.

Figure 9.4. Excerpts from protocols that reveal the "never get to 0" pattern of response.

Most children were classifiable into one of these two patterns; only 10% had transitional patterns. Only slightly more than half (60%) of the 11- and 12-year-olds in our sample showed the adult never-get-to-zero pattern of response, confirming that the construction of even a minimal understanding of rational number is not complete by age 12.

Within-Child Consistency

On each of the measures described above, about half of the sample provided responses consistent with the hypothesized CS1 (number restricted to integers) and about half of the sample reflected a division model of rational number. One purpose of our study was to probe for within-child consistency across the five tasks (asserting that there are numbers between 0 and 1, explaining why there are two numerals in a fraction, ordering fractions, ordering decimals, and get-to-zero thought experiment). Notice that these tasks differ greatly in difficulty. The thought experiment and creating an explanation of the role of the two numerals in a fraction place more analytic demands on the child than do merely asserting that there are numbers between 0 and 1 or ordering fractions and decimals. Further, the latter are specifically taught in the school curriculum whereas the former are not. If each of CS1 and CS2 is a consistent set of concepts that are integrated and mutually constraining, and if they are qualitatively different from each other, then children should respond to all of our probes consistently with one system or the other, with very few children responding in a manner that reveals CS1 on two or three of the five probes and that reveals CS2 on the others. On the other hand, if children acquire insight about fractions, decimals, and the infinite divisibility of number in more graded, piecemeal fashion, merely enriching the concept of number created during the preschool years, then, assuming no ceiling or floor effects, the mixed patterns should be more common than either of the patterns in which all tasks are responded to as if generated either by CS1 or by CS2.

In fact, only 12% of the children gave CS2 responses on two or three tasks and CS1 responses on three or two tasks; the rest were answered consistently as if their responses were generated by CS2 (37%) or by CS1 (51%). What is most striking about the distribution of scores is that those children who showed evidence of some understanding of fractions (i.e., those children who did not answer all probes as dictated by CS1) were three times more likely to provide consistent CS2 answers than to show the mixed pattern of judgments. Moreover, this was as true for the younger as for the older children. Given that more than half of the children were still in the grips of CS1, we can rule out the possibility that this simply reflects a ceiling effect.

In sum, the transition from a numeral list representation of natural number to a representation of number that encompasses the rationals is a qualitative change. I have characterized a CS1 and a later developing CS2, showing how CS2 has more expressive power and is qualitatively different from CS1. I have shown that performance on a wide variety of tasks (and those described here are just the tip of the iceberg, chosen for illustrative purposes) reflects each. As predicted by this analysis, CS2 is very difficult for children to learn, in spite of explicit and intensive school-based instrudtion. Finally, that each reflects a coherent system of representation is shown by the within-child consistency in responses across the different tasks.

Conceptual Discontinuity

One can think about the qualitative change between CS1 and CS2 as I have described it above: the creation of a new representational system with more expressive power than its input. Before the construction of a representation of rationals, children cannot think thoughts about ¾ or .75, 79/80 or .9875, and afterwards they can. In CS2 the computations carried out over explicit numerals been expanded from comparison, addition, subtraction, and multiplication to include division as the inverse of multiplication. Another way to think about the CS1/CS2 shift is as a conceptual change in the concept number.

This latter way of thinking about the CS1/CS2 shift requires an analysis of the very notion of conceptual change, as well as a distinction between conceptual change and belief revision. The remaining chapters of this book explicate conceptual change, defending the notion against its critics, and arguing that it plays a crucial role in distinguishing some episodes of discontinuous development from mere knowledge enrichment. Knowledge enrichment consists of changing beliefs and learning new facts about entities, where these facts and beliefs are stated in terms of concepts already represented. Conceptual change involves creating new conceptual primitives—concepts not able to be stated in terms of the concepts available at the outset of the episode. Conceptual change implies incommensurability of successive conceptual systems, and chapters 10 and 11 take on the challenge of making good on the Kuhn/Feyerabend notion of incommensurability. Here I merely begin this discussion in the context of the CS1/CS2 shift under consideration here.

On the face of it, it might seem that the CS2 encompassing the rationals is merely an enrichment of the CS1 that is natural number. After all, representations of positive integers based on the successor relation continue to play an important role in mathematical thought even after representations of rational number have been constructed. This is so, but coming to see 1/3 as a number on a par with 1 and 3 may nonetheless implicate conceptual change within the concept *number*, involving a reconceptualization of the integers.

Knowledge enrichment consists of changes in beliefs formulated over the same concepts before and after the change, or in the addition of new concepts that do not implicate the revision or abandonment of antecedent ones. Learning that there are new kinds of numbers, in contrast, directly challenges children's initial and entrenched concept of number as counting number. Before the change, 1 and 1/2 are fundamentally different kinds of entities: 1 is a number that occurs in the count list and 1/2 is something else. Some children deny that 1/2 is a number, and, although this might merely be a semantic issue to do with the term "number," even those children in the grip of CS1 who come to agree that 1/2 is a number still often claim that there are only a few numbers between 0 and 1 and that repeated division will get to 0. This implicates differences from CS2 both in the concept *number* and in the concept *division*. Such interrelated and mutually constraining differences typify cases of conceptual change involving incommensurability

After the change, 3 is represented as a number of the same status as 1/3—it is its multiplicative inverse, it can be expressed as "3/1" and, like 1/3, it corresponds to just another point along the number line.

"Conceptual change" means change in individual concepts. One way concepts can change is coalescence of previous concepts that were ontologically distinct and played incompatible conceptual roles in the conceptual systems that are CS1. The coalescence of 3 and 1/3 under a single concept *number* is a classic case. The coalesced concept (that unites numbers like 1/3 and numbers like 3) makes no sense in the original system. Another type of change at the level of individual concepts is differentiation—one concept splits in two. Not just any differentiation implicates conceptual change. The differentiation of the concept *dog* into subordinate concepts *poodle, dalmation, pit bull,* and so on does not, because the concept *dog* had the same extension and conceptual role before and after this differentiation. In cases of differentiation implicating conceptual change, the previously undifferentiated concept makes no sense in the lights of CS2 indeed, it is incoherent from the point of view of CS2. The CS1/CS2 change under consideration here involves differentiating subtraction from division. This is a classic differentiation in which the undifferentiated concept (subtraction/division) is incoherent from the point of view of the attained system. The undifferentiated concept plays no role in mathematics after the differentiation has been achieved. All cases of conceptual change involving incommensurability involve interrelated coalescences and differentiations of this sort, yielding a set of primitives that cannot be expressed in terms of the primitives available at the outset.

Thus, the argument that the core of the concept of positive integer remains essentially unchanged before and after the construction of rational number—because it is based on the successor relation—ignores the fact that in developing a concept of rational number, children have developed an entirely different model of number that has transformed their understanding of positive integers. Numbers are no longer solely the counting numbers, and the positive integers are now a subset of all numbers, occupying points along a seemingly continuous number line.

Implications of the High Degree of Within-Child Consistency in Reasoning about Number

Above, I argued that the extent of the coherence found in children's reasoning about number across widely different tasks designed to reflect CS1 or CS2 supported the claim that the transition from one to another was qualitative—that is, that this is a developmental discontinuity. This type of consistency is entailed by, and thus provides evidence for, the hypothesis that conceptual change is required by this transition. Strong coherence is expected on a conceptual change account, within both CS1 and CS2, because concepts are interrelated differently in the two systems, with understanding of one aspect of each system constraining understanding of others. In contrast, on a knowledge enrichment account, coherence is not an intrinsic part of the change process, as new facts can be added somewhat independently. Further, in the knowledge enrichment view, any coherence that is observed would be seen as resulting from extrinsic factors such as lack of exposure or explicit teaching. In this view, young children may consistently fail on certain tasks when they haven't been exposed to relevant information yet; similarly, older children may consistently succeed when they have been explicitly taught all the items in question. But partial patterns of success and failure should also be abundant, especially because one is typically not exposed to all of the information at once.

Three features of the observed patterns of coherence favor a conceptual change interpretation. First, there was exceptionally strong coherence among the diverse number tasks. Being able to articulate a clear division model of fractions was strongly associated with spontaneously acknowledging the existence of numbers between 0 and 1, being able to order fractions and decimals, and understanding the infinite divisibility of number. Second, coherence was equally striking at both grade groupings. On an exposure account, one might have predicted *less* coherence among the 3rd and 4th grade children than among the 5th and 6th grade children because the younger children have had more experience with fractional than decimal notation. Hence, one might have predicted that many 3rd and 4th grade children would have mixed patterns reflecting only partial mastery of these ideas. Yet this prediction is not borne out. Only one of the 3rd and 4th grade children had a mixed pattern; the rest were either consistently correct (14%) or consistently incorrect (82%). Indeed, the overwhelming failure of the 3rd and 4th grade children on the different fraction problems— despite exposure—is quite striking. A detailed examination of their answers revealed that they had heard of fractions and knew something about them, they just did not understand them correctly as numbers. This pattern of systematic misunderstanding of a new idea—by assimilating it into an earlier entrenched understanding—lends support to the conceptual change rather than to the knowledge enrichment account.

Finally, one of the tasks—the number thought experiment—tapped an understanding that children had not been explicitly taught. The fact that this task patterned as closely with the other tasks that were more related to direct instruction (such as acknowledging the existence of numbers between 0 and 1, understanding the meaning of the two numbers in a fraction, and correctly ordering fractions and decimals) also lends more support to the conceptual change than the knowledge enrichment position. If coherence is an artifact of direct instruction, then children's understanding of the infinite divisibility of number-thought experiment should lag the others; it is not something that has been directly taught. In contrast, if coherence reflects conceptual restructuring, then the internal changes in children's concept of number needed to assimilate the notions of fractions and decimals should be manifest in changed understanding of the number-thought experiment as well.

Making Sense of the Puzzling Things that Children Say

One of the hallmarks of conceptual change can be dubbed the "huh?" phenomenon. Children say things that make no sense if the terms in their language reflected the same concepts as adults use them to express. The transcripts included in Figure 9.3 from the get-to–zero children contain many examples. I urge you to read these carefully. For example, student S39 said, in response to the thought experiment about whether one could keep dividing by 2 forever, "No, after 1 is 0. 0 is nothing else. If kept dividing ½, then 1/1, then 0/1, and 0/0 and that's it." Student S9's response to the question was "Yes, it'll soon be just a black line, just numbers." And in response to the question of whether one would ever get to zero, the student replied "Yes, if you have 8 parts, then you minus one and minus one until you get a minus 8, then you'll get 0." Although these answers seem incoherent from the adult per-spective, they make much more sense when one assumes that children have a concept *division* exhausted by some way of making numbers smaller that is undifferentiated, expressing *subtraction/division* and if one assumes their concept *number* is a natural number.

Of course, it is impossible for us to express the child's undifferentiated concept *subtraction/division* in our conceptual system; such a notion is incoherent. That's the point. Incommensurability is symmetrical. CS2 contains concepts not expressible in CS1 and CS1 contains concepts not expressible in CS2. This raises a paradox that might make the very notion of incommensurability seem unsustainable: How, in the face of putative incommensurability, does a developmental psychologist or a historian understand an earlier conceptual system? This question is taken on in chapter 10, but the short answer is that that incommensurabilities are always local. Enough stays constant to make it possible for the historian or developmental psychologist to engage in bootstrapping in reverse, and learn the concepts that articulate CS1.

Conclusion

Although when 3-year-old children build the numeral list representation of the integers they have created a representational system with more expressive power than those that were its input, there is plenty more learning required in which this representational system becomes consolidated and entrenched. Some of that learning draws upon the very same resources that are implicated in all Quinian bootstrapping episodes. The example I worked through here is children's mapping the numerals to analog magnitudes, in the course of which they induce a rule on the basis of analogical relations between order in the numeral list and order among analog magnitude values.

Part I of this chapter illustrated one of the ways in which bootstrapping creates meaning. By integrating what are initially separate representational systems, each inherits the content and computational capacities of the other.

Part II of this chapter sketched another case of discontinuous conceptual development within the domain of mathematical cognition, in addition to the construction of the numeral list representation of the positive integers discussed in chapter 8. The discontinuity described here is the transition from the preschool child's hard-won numeral list representation of number to the older child's concept of rational number. I characterized CS1 and CS2, showing how CS2 represents concepts that are incoherent from the light of CS1 (division, the number ½, and so on). I provided evidence that each system is coherent and mutually constraining, and that children consistently display one concept of number or the other. I also provided evidence that CS2 is very difficult to learn (indeed, many adults in our society have no understanding of fractions and decimals, in spite of years of schooling aimed at inducing the conceptual change described in these pages). In chapter 11, I briefly discuss the bootstrapping processes that underlie the construction of this new representational resource.

Finally, I suggested that not only is the system of rational number discontinuous with the system of integers in having more expressive power, the two may be incommensurable. Incommensurability is the relation between conceptual systems such that one contains concepts that are not merely absent from the other, but are actually incoherent from the point of view of the other. Chapters 10 and 11 turn to a more complete discussion of incommensurability in the contexts of intuitive theories. They discuss cases drawn from both the history of science and the developmental literatures—cases in which both CS1 and CS2 contain concepts that are unrepresentable and incoherent from the point of view of the other. The historical examples include the transition from the source-recipient theory to the caloric theory of heat, the transition from the phlogiston to the oxygen theory of burning, Kepler's construction of the concept that is an ancestor to Newton's gravity, and Maxwell's creation of electromagnetic theory. The developmental examples include conceptual changes within children's concepts of material entities.

10

Beyond Core Object Cognition

Knowledge represented with explicit, external symbols—the symbols of spoken and written language, the symbols of mathematics and logic, the symbols of graphs and maps—differs from core cognition in many respects: It differs in format (i.e., the explicit symbol systems themselves), it most often is not innate, and it does not remain constant over development. Chapter 7 touched on the processes through which core cognition is mapped to the explicit symbol systems of natural language, and of the effects such mappings have on nonlinguistic thought. Chapter 8 characterized the process through which the first explicit representation of natural number is created, expanding the expressive power of the number representations in core cognition through the mastery of the culturally constructed numeral list. Subsequent developments in mathematics, like the construction of a concept of number that includes the rationals (chapter 9), further expand the expressive power of number representations through the mastery of culturally constructed explicit representations.

I now turn to a type of knowledge structure that is different in many ways from mathematical representations: intuitive theories. Intuitive theories play several unique roles in mental life. These include: (1) representing causal and explanatory knowledge; (2) supporting inferences and predictions; (3) providing the current best guess concerning the essential properties of kinds, which in turn play a privileged role in categorization decisions; and (4) on some views of conceptual content, determining those aspects of conceptual role that separate meaning from belief. Because intuitive theories are such an important part of cognitive architecture, many writers take accounting for theory acquisition is one goal of theories of conceptual development (Carey, 1985b;

Gopnik & Meltzoff, 1997; Keil, 1989; Wellman & Gelman, 1992). Indeed, these writers go further than asserting the importance of accounting for the acquisition of intuitive theories, advocating the theory-theory of conceptual development. The theory-theory has two main tenets. The first is that many important phenomena in the domain of knowledge acquisition must be analyzed in terms of theory development. The second is that intuitive theories share many essential features with explicit scientific theories, and that lessons from the history and philosophy of science apply to theory development in childhood.

Knowledge acquisition sometimes requires radical restructuring of the conceptual and explanatory structures that are the input to the learning process. Clear cases of theory changes involving radical knowledge restructuring have repeatedly occurred over the history of science. As I will show in this chapter and those that follow, conceptual development in childhood sometimes also requires radical theory changes that involve conceptual change. That this is so is one of the central tenets of the theory-theory, which holds that successive intuitive theories of a given domain of phenomena sometimes involve conceptual change, and that the processes underlying conceptual change in childhood are to some important extent the same as those that underlie conceptual change in the history of science.

The theory-theory does not deny that there are important differences between children as theorizers and adult scientists (hence the qualifier, "intuitive"). Children and adult nonscientists are not meta-conceptually aware theory builders; they do not build research programs of systematic experimentation, nor do they attempt to make formal models (Carey, Evans, Honda, Unger, & Jay, 1989; D. Kuhn et al., 1988). In spite of these differences, the research enterprise in which this work is placed presupposes that there are a set of questions that can be asked, literally, of both scientific theories and intuitive theories, and which receive the same answer in both cases. One set of such questions concern discontinuities in theory development, the phenomenon of incommensurability, and the mechanisms underlying conceptual change.

Some adherents of the theory-theory (e.g., Gopnik & Meltzoff, 1997) advocate a "theories all the way down" position, denying the distinction between systems of core cognition, on the one hand, and intuitive theories, on the other. Partly, this is merely a terminological issue; core cognition systems do have many properties in common with intuitive theories, as they embody ontological commitments and causal knowledge, and constrain learning and inference. However, all of the distinctive properties of core cognition are conspicuously not true of intuitive theories. There are no innate perceptual input analyzers that identify the basic ontological kinds for most intuitive theories; intuitive theories are not continuous over development; the format of representation for most intuitive theories is not iconic; and the knowledge embedded in most intuitive theories is accessible and explicit, not implicit and encapsulated. For these reasons, I distinguish intuitive theories from core cognition.

The theory-theory of conceptual development encompasses many topics, but the phenomenon of radical conceptual change is most central to the project of this book: understanding the origin of human concepts. This is because in episodes of conceptual change, new concepts come into being that were not represented, or even representable, at the outset. For this reason, my discussion of the theory-theory of conceptual development focuses on theory change, especially those theory changes implicating incommensurability.

The time has come to subject the very notions of conceptual change and incommensurability to closer scrutiny. I must dispel any worries that the very notion of incommensurability is incoherent, sketching how conceptual change is to be distinguished from knowledge acquisition that does not involve conceptual change (knowledge enrichment), and what kinds of evidence support claims that two successive theories are incommensurable. Conceptual change is (as it says) change at the level of individual concepts. Literally, "incommensurability" means "no common measure." The notion was first applied to the Greeks' discovery that the length of a side of a right triangle and the length of its hypotenuse cannot both be expressed with rational numbers if the same unit of length is used. Since the work of Thomas Kuhn and Paul Feyerabend, the term has been generalized to the relation between conceptual systems in which there is no common set of primitives. That is, it has been applied to conceptual changes within theories as well as within mathematical thought (Feyerabend, 1962; T. Kuhn, 1962).

Conceptual change is implicated in those cases of theory development that involve incommensurability. Although "conceptual change" is a term used loosely in the fields of psychology and education, here I give it its meaning from the history and philosophy of science, where it is contrasted with knowledge enrichment and belief revision. That is, conceptual change is not the same as changing one's mind, acquiring new knowledge, or changing one's beliefs. Rather, it means creating new concepts not expressible in terms of previously available vocabulary. As I use the term, conceptual change requires incommensurability. A given theory at time 1, CS1, and the descendent of that theory at time 2, CS2, are incommensurable insofar as the beliefs of one cannot be formulated over the concepts of the other. Not all theory development involves conceptual change; often theories are merely enriched as new knowledge accumulates about the phenomena in the domain of the theory. Theory enrichment consists of the acquisition of new beliefs formulated over a constant conceptual repertoire.

In cases of two successive incommensurable theories, the differences between the network of concepts articulating CS1 and CS2 can take several forms. Sometimes, new concepts are created that would be unrepresentable in CS1—for example, CS2's *quark* or *spin*, if CS1 is Bohr's theory of the atom. Sometimes, old concepts cease to play any role in CS2—for example, *phlogiston* or *principle*, if CS2 is any chemistry since Lavoisier. Conceptual changes also take place—that is, change within a given concept—such that there is a clear ancestor–descendant relationship between a concept in CS1 and its descendant in CS2. Conceptual changes take several forms. Perhaps the most common is differentiation. In conceptual differentiations involving incommensurability, the undifferentiated parent concept from CS1 no longer plays any role in CS2. Examples include Galileo's differentiation of average from instantaneous velocity (T. Kuhn, 1977) and Black's differentiation of heat from temperature (Wiser & Carey, 1983). Another common type is coalescence. In coalescences involving incommensurability, entities considered ontologically distinct in CS1 are subsumed under a single concept in CS2. Examples include Galileo's abandonment of Aristotle's distinction between natural and artificial motion (T. Kuhn, 1977), and the coalescence of liquids, solids and gases into a single concept of material entities (Jammer, 1961). Conceptual change may also involve the reanalysis of a concept's basic structure (such as the Newtonian reanalysis of weight from a property of objects to a relationship between objects).

And finally, on the common treatment of concepts as having a core/periphery structure, changes in the concept's core constitute examples of conceptual change (Kitcher, 1988).

In what follows I use "conceptual change" to refer to the relation between successive incommensurable theories of overlapping domains of phenomena (for there is a change in the conceptual primitives in terms of which the phenomena are represented and explained), as well as to the relation between particular ancestor–descendant pairs of concepts involved in these theory changes.

I would like to dispel, at the outset, several misunderstandings concerning the claim that the history of science involves conceptual change. It is important to note that the difference between knowledge enrichment and conceptual change is not sharp. Theory changes lie in a multidimensional space that includes clear cases of conceptual change and of knowledge enrichment, as well as a variety of intermediate cases. Also, the analysis of conceptual change endorsed here is not that of the early writings of Kuhn and Feyerabend. These writers were committed to the existence of radical incommensurability, in which theories before and after conceptual change share no conceptual machinery. The incommensurability that occurs in every case of historical and developmental theory building I have personally studied is what in later work Kuhn called "local incommensurability"—incommensurability that implicates only some of the concepts that articulate successive theories (T. Kuhn, 1982). Finally, conceptual change does not occur suddenly. There is not a moment of gestalt shift. It takes time for concepts to change, sometimes centuries in the history of science, always years in the individual scientist or student or child engaged in knowledge restructuring.

What's at Stake

The existence of conceptual change, both in childhood and in the history of science, raises some of the very toughest challenges to an account of the origin of concepts. Characterizing the learning mechanisms that underlie conceptual change is a formidable explanatory challenge. Many classes of learning mechanisms that underlie the major share of knowledge acquisition consist of selection or concatenation over an existing conceptual base. These include hypothesis testing, parameter setting, association, correlation detection, and many others. Additional learning mechanisms, of some other sort, must be implicated in conceptual change, for the conceptual system that is their output cannot be expressed in the conceptual base that is their input. Chapter 11 will address the explanatory challenge, appealing to the Quinian bootstrapping processes introduced in chapter 8 to address conceptual change from one theory to an incommensurable one. Chapter 11 explores both historical and developmental cases of conceptual change.

The distinction between conceptual change and knowledge enrichment, along with the existence of conceptual change in childhood, also raises a fundamental descriptive question for those of us who study cognitive development: Which cases of knowledge acquisition involve incommensurability? Another way of putting the same descriptive question is: Historically, when is one theory incommensurable with a successor? When a student of Galileo's writes that ice mixed with salt and water produces a higher degree of cold than a mixture of the same amount of ice and water without the salt, is he saying something deploying the same concept of cold as we have? Developmentally, when are children's beliefs formulated over concepts incommensurable with ours? The preschool child tells us the sun is alive, or that buttons are alive because they keep your pants up. The preschool child tells us that a grain of rice weighs nothing at all, or that air is nothing and that air and steel can be in the same place at the same time. Is the child making false statements formulated over concepts shared with us? Or is the child saying something true, formulated over different concepts from those expressed by our use of the same terms? If it's the latter, are the child's concepts locally incommensurable with ours?

The theory-theory is committed to these questions receiving comparable answers in the developmental cases as in the historical cases of conceptual change. The child's theory may not correspond to any historically held adult theory, but what is meant by incommensurability, and what counts as evidence for it, had better be the same if the theory-theory is to have any merit. To address these questions, I begin with an analysis of local incommensurability from the historical and philosophical literatures, for this is where the notion first arose. In what follows I first give a sense of what incommensurability is, drawing on historical examples. The historical differentiation of the concepts *heat* and *temperature* from an earlier undifferentiated concept *degree of heat* (part of an extended episode of conceptual change in which CS1 is an Aristotelian theory of thermal phenomena and CS2 is the caloric theory) provides a worked example of a conceptual change and lays the groundwork for what evidence is required to establish episodes of conceptual change in childhood. The rest of the chapter works through a parallel case of conceptual change in childhood: the construction of a theory of matter in which the concept *material* is differentiated from *physically real*, and the concept *weight* from *density*.

Local Incommensurability

A good place to start is with Philip Kitcher's analysis of incommensurability (Kitcher, 1978; 1988). Theories are explicit, formulated in language and other explicit symbol systems. The explicit symbols express concepts. Therefore, incommensurability is a relation that holds between the languages that express theories and between the sets of concepts that articulate theories. Following Kitcher and Kuhn, I will explicate the idea of incommensurability in terms of the languages that express successive theories. To begin, Kitcher endorsed Kuhn's thesis that there are episodes in the history of science at the beginnings and ends of which practitioners of the same field of endeavor speak languages that are not mutually translatable. That is, the beliefs, laws, and explanations that can be stated in the terminology at the beginning, in language 1 (L1), cannot be expressed in the terminology at the end, in language 2 (L2). This is equivalent to the claim that the propositions that can be formulated in terms of CS2 cannot be expressed in terms of the concepts that articulate CS1.

As Kitcher explicated Kuhn's thesis, he focused on the mechanisms through which the referents of terms are fixed. He argued that there are multiple methods for reference fixing. Many kinds of processes support the causal connections between entities in the world and word meaning, and some of these are theory-mediated. A theoretical community expresses definitions, offers descriptions of referents, and draws on theory-relative similarity to particular exemplars in determining the extensions of its theoretical terms. Holders of any given theory presuppose that, for each term, its multiple methods of reference-fixing pick out one and the same set of entities in the world. Incommensurability arises when an L1 set of methods of reference-fixing for a single term is seen by speakers of L2 to pick out two or more distinct entities. In the most extreme cases, the perspective of L2 dictates that some of L1's methods fail to provide any referent for the term at all, whereas others provide different referents from each other. For example, the definition of "phlogiston" as "the principle given off during combustion," fails, in our view, to provide any referent for "phlogiston" at all. However, as Kitcher pointed out, in other uses of "phlogiston," where reference is fixed by the description of the production of some chemical, it is perfectly possible for us to understand what chemicals are being talked about. In various descriptions of how to produce "dephlogisticated air," the referent of the phrase can be identified as either oxygen or oxygen-enriched air.

Kitcher's analysis played an important role in Kuhn's reanalysis of the incommensurability among successive theories, in which Kuhn abandoned the earlier Kuhn/Feyerabend notions of radical incommensurability in favor of what he called "local incommensurability." Kitcher showed how contemporaries who speak incommensurable languages can nonetheless communicate, whereas Kuhn and Feyerabend had insisted that holders of incommensurable theories talked entirely past each other. Kitcher argued that communication is possible between two parties so long as one can figure out what the other is referring to and if the two share some language. Even when L1 and L2 are locally incommensurable, the methods of reference-fixing for many terms that appear in both languages remain entirely constant across them, and even in cases of mismatch of referential potential, there sometimes will be some overlap of referent-fixing mechanisms so that in some contexts the corresponding terms in the two languages will refer to the same entities. This is sufficient to provide enough common ground for some degree of communication, including identifying cases of mismatch of referential potential.

Kuhn accepted much of what Kitcher said, while nonetheless criticizing Kitcher for identifying communication with agreement on the referents of terms. Communication requires more; it requires agreement with what is said about the referents. Agreement on the referents of terms is necessary but not sufficient for communication, and Kuhn argued that the analysis of incommensurability goes beyond the mismatch of referential potential. This is why Kuhn analyzed incommensurability in terms of translation.

Kuhn was concerned with a paradox. If speakers of putatively incommensurable languages can always, with work, come to understand each other, and if we can always, with work, figure out what entities historical texts are referring to, why is it nonetheless true that two theories may sometimes be incommensurable in a theoretically interesting sense? In answering this question, Kuhn moved beyond the referential functions of language. To figure out what a text is referring to is not the same as providing a translation of the text. In a translation, we replace sentences in L1 with sentences in L2 that have the same meaning. Even if expressions in L1 can be replaced with co-referential expressions in L2, we are not guaranteed a translation. For example, replacing every mention of the name "Superman" in a story with "Clark Kent" would preserve reference but would change the meaning of the text. In cases of incommensurability, this process of replacing terms in L1 with co-referential terms in L2 will typically replace an L1 term with one L2 term in some contexts and other L2 terms in other contexts. But it matters to the meaning of the L1 text that a single L1 term was used. For example, it mattered to Priestley that all of the cases of "dephlogisticated" entities were so designated; his language expressed a theory in which all dephlogisticated substances shared an essential property that explained derivative properties. The process of replacing some uses of "dephlogisticated air" with "oxygen," others with "oxygen-enriched air," and still others with other phrases yields what Kuhn called a "disjointed text." One can see no reason that these sentences are juxtaposed. A good translation preserves not only reference; a text makes sense in L1, and a good translation of it into L2 makes sense in L2 as well.

That the history of science is possible is often offered as prima facie refutation of the doctrine of incommensurability. If earlier theories are expressed in languages that are incommensurable with our own, the argument goes, how can the historian understand those theories and describe them to us so that we understand them? Part of the response to this challenge has already been provided. Although parts of L1 and L2 are incommensurable, much stays the same across them, allowing speakers of the two languages to figure out what the other must be saying. What one does in this process is not translation but, rather, interpretation and language learning. The historian of science engages in a bootstrapping process, noting the interrelated uses of terms in L1, seeing how they map to phenomena, and engaging in modeling processes to construct a theory that makes sense of this evidence. Once the historian has learned L1, he or she can teach it to us, and then we can express the earlier theory as well.

Again this seems paradoxical. What is language learning besides expressing the terms of the new language in the terms of the earlier language (in the case of first language learning, into antecedently available nonlinguistic concepts)? Resolving the paradox requires a different picture of language learning. Language learners sometimes learn a whole set of terms together, at least partially interdefined, which at the beginning of an episode of conceptual change are only partly interpreted in terms of antecedent concepts. Recall the characterization of Quinian bootstrapping in chapter 8. Across different theories, these sets of terms can, and often do, cut up the world in incompatible ways. To continue with the phlogiston theory example, one reason that we cannot express claims about phlogiston in our language is that we do not share the phlogiston theory's concepts: *principle* and *element*. The phlogiston theory's *element* encompassed many things not picked out by our *element,* and modern chemistry has no concept at all that corresponds to phlogiston theory's *principle*. But we cannot express the phlogiston theory's propositions that described phenomena involving combustion, acids, gases, and so on without using the concepts of principle, element, and phlogiston, for these concepts are all interdefined. We cannot translate sentences containing "phlogiston" into pure 20th-century language because, when in comes to using words like "principle" and "element" we are forced to choose one of two options, neither of which leads to a real translation:

1. We use "principle" and "element", but provide a translator's gloss before the text. Rather than providing a translation, we are changing L2 for the purposes of rendering the text. The translator's gloss is part of the bootstrapping process whereby the concepts of L1 are taught to the speakers of L2.
2. We replace each of these terms with different terms and phrases in different contexts, preserving reference but producing a disjointed text. Such a text is not a translation because it does not make sense as a whole.

What, then, is the evidence for the existence of episodes in the history of science in which successive theories are not mutually translatable because they are locally incommensurable? As mentioned above, differences at the level of individual concepts implicated in cases of incommensurability come in many different flavors, including differentiations, coalescences, and changes in core. In addition, new primitive concepts are created and important primitives are lost altogether in some episodes of theory changes involving conceptual change. It is important to note that conceptual change always involves whole systems of concepts; one never finds differentiations implicating incommensurability in the absence of coalescences, changes in core, and so on.

Characterizing such changes raises serious problems of both analysis and evidence. Here, I will explore these problems in the case of just one type of conceptual change: conceptual differentiation. Not all episodes in which previously unnoticed distinctions come to be drawn implicate incommensurability. Two-year-olds may not distinguish collies, German shepherds, and poodles, therefore having an undifferentiated concept *dog,* relative to adults, but if that is the only difference between the 2-year-old's and the adult's concept *dog,* the two are not incommensurable. There would be no mismatch of referential potential (i.e., the reference fixing mechanisms for *dog* in both cases would be the same, and the child's and adult's concept *dog* would have the same extensions), and they would have the same meaning-determining conceptual roles. The cases of differentiation involving incommensurability are those in which the undifferentiated parent concept from L1 is incoherent from the point of view of L2, a condition not met by the 2-year-old's concept *dog* under the assumption that the only difference between it and the adult concept is that the child has not created subordinate concepts of breeds.

An Example: On the Differentiation of the Concepts *Heat* and *Temperature*

Consider the claim that before the work of the Scottish physicist Joseph Black in the mid-18th century, *heat* and *temperature* were not differentiated. This would require that thermal theories before Black represent a single concept, in some sense fusing our concepts of heat and temperature. In the language of our current theories, there is no superordinate term that encompasses both of these meanings; indeed, any attempt to wrap heat and temperature together would produce a monster. Heat and temperature are two different types of physical entities; heat is an extensive quantity, whereas temperature is an intensive quantity. The total amount of heat available in two cups of water is the sum of the amounts of heat available in each, whereas if one cup of water at 80° F is added to 1 cup at 100° F, the resultant temperature is 90° F, not 180° F. Furthermore, heat and temperature are interdefined. A calorie is the amount of heat required to raise the temperature of 1 gram of water 1° C. Finally, the two play different and complementary roles in explaining physical phenomena such as heat flow. Every theory since Black's includes a commitment to thermal equilibrium, the principle that temperature differences occasion heat flow. This commitment cannot be expressed without distinct concepts of heat and temperature.

To make sense of the claim that before Black *heat* and *temperature* were undifferentiated, then, we must be able to conceive of how it might be possible for there to be a single undifferentiated concept that is the ancestor to both concepts. Such a concept must have some of the features of each of the descendants, but it cannot simply be a superordinate to them (because, as explained above, there is no single coherent concept superordinate to *heat* and *temperature* in any theory from Black's on). To see how this could be possible requires analyzing the framework theory scientists were working with, the phenomena they sought to explain, and characterizing the concepts that articulated the theory and their explanatory role. The task is parallel to the enterprise of characterizing core cognition systems. As chapters 4, 7, and 8 argued, once we understand the representations of parallel individuation, set-based quantification, and the analog magnitude number system, we can characterize precisely the concepts of number available to the prelinguistic child. Analogously, once we understand the thermal theory any community of scientists was working with, we can answer the question of whether it contained distinct concepts of heat and temperature.

One clue that heat and temperature might not be differentiated in a given theory is that the scientists deploying the theory use only one word, not two, in characterizing and explaining the thermal phenomena in its domain. That is, L1 contains only one term, whereas L2 (any theory since Black) contains two—"heat" and "temperature." Undifferentiated language is a necessary consequence of a lack of conceptual differentiation, but more than one representational state of affairs could underlie any case of undifferentiated language. Lack of differentiation between heat and temperature is surely different, at a representational level, from mere absence of the concept of heat, even though languages expressing either set of thermal concepts might have only one word—for example, "hot." A second representational state that might mimic non-differentiation is the false belief that two quantities are perfectly correlated. For example, before Black's discoveries of specific and latent heat, scientists might have believed that adding a given amount to heat to a given quantity of matter always leads to the same increase in temperature,. Such a belief could lead scientists to use one quantity as a rough-and-ready stand-in for the other, which might produce texts that would falsely suggest that the two were not differentiated.

The only way to distinguish these two alternative representational states of affairs (false belief in perfect correlation and absence of one or the other concept) from conceptual nondifferentiation is to analyze the roles that the concepts played in the theories in which there were embedded. Marianne Wiser and I (1983) analyzed the concept of heat in the thermal theory of the 17th-century Academy of Florence, the first group of scientists to systematically study thermal phenomena, and we indeed found evidence supporting the historians' claim of nondifferentiation (McKie & Heathcoate, 1935). The Academy's publications used undifferentiated language; they used "degree of heat" both in contexts in which we would use "temperature" and in contexts in which we would use "amount of heat." The Academy's heat had both causal strength and qualitative intensity—that is, aspects of both modern heat and modern temperature. The Experimenters (their self-designation) did not separately quantify heat and temperature, and unlike, Black, did not seek to study the relations between the two. Instead, they sought to relate a single thermal variable, degree of heat, to mechanical phenomena. You may think of this thermal variable, as they did, as the strength of the heat and relate it to the magnitude of the physical effects of heating matter (thermal expansion, state changes, and so on). Importantly (and a clue that their system of concepts is different from ours), they also did experiments on another thermal variable, degree of cold, and studied the effects of the strength of the cold on matter (contraction of matter, state changes, and so on). In no theory since Black is cold conceptualized as a real entity on a par with heat).

The Experimenters used the thermometer (an instrument they invented) to measure degrees of heat and cold, but they did so by noting and comparing the rate and/or range of change in the level in the thermometer, rather than focusing on the final level attained by the alcohol in their thermometers. Their thermometers were calibrated with respect to each other rather than to fixed points. To discover fixed points (e.g., the boiling and freezing temperatures of water) requires a concept of temperature differentiated from heat. In sum, the experimenters did not quantify either temperature or amount of heat, and unlike Black, they certainly did not attempt to relate two distinct thermal variables. Finally, their theory necessarily provided a different account of heat exchange from that of the caloric theory or that of modern thermodynamics. The Experimenters did not formulate the principle of thermal equilibrium (which they could not have done without separate concepts of heat and temperature), and indeed their account required no distinct concepts of these variables. Wiser and I dubbed their theory the "source-recipient theory." The source-recipient theory had distinct concepts of heat and cold, conceptualized as distinct substances with opposite mechanical effects. Although the Experimenters saw themselves as opposed to the medieval Aristotelians, the source-recipient theory required the Aristotelian notion of a natural state. It is in the nature of entities with higher degrees of heat or higher degrees of cold than the natural state to transmit heat or cold to the entities they are in contact with. The transmitted heat or cold then caused the mechanical effects the Experimenters discovered, quantified, and attempted to explain. They also speculated about the distinct ultimate sources of heat and cold.

Black's conceptual change included abandoning the concept of cold as a kind of substance/energy with causal powers; the Experimenters' cold suffered the fate of phlogiston—there is no such thing. Conceptual differerentiations involving local incommensurability always accompany other conceptual changes in the same network of interdefined concepts. Because we can characterize the Experimenters' theory in which the undifferentiated concept that conflated heat and temperature played a coherent role, we can be confident in ascribing this undifferentiated concept to these 17th-century scientists. No concept equivalent to the Experimenters' *degree of heat* plays any role in any theory after Black.

The Experimenters' concept, which is incoherent from our point of view, led them into contradictions that they recognized but could not resolve. For example, they noted that a chemical reaction contained in a metal box produced a degree of heat that was insufficient to melt paraffin, whereas putting a sold metal block of the same size on a fire induced a degree of heat in the block that was sufficient to melt paraffin. That is, the block had a greater degree of heat. However, they also noted that if one left the box with the chemical reaction in ice water, it melted more ice than did the heated metal block, also left in the ice water for the same amount of time. Thus, the box had a greater degree of heat. Although they recognized this as a contradiction, they threw up their hands at it. They knew that two different kinds of heat must be involved in these two measures, but they could not resolve the paradox without differentiating temperature from amount of heat. The chemical reaction generates more heat but attains a lower temperature. The melting point of paraffin is a function of temperature, whereas how much ice melts is a function of the amount of heat generated. That holders of CS1 are sensitive to and worried about contradictions that are easily resolved from the point of view of CS2 is one source of evidence for the CS1–CS2 shift and for its involving incommensurability.

Finally, the "huh???!" phenomenon mentioned in the previous chapter provides one very good clue to a conceptual system that is incommensurable with your own. Wiser and I (1983) read the Experimenters' report of their "experiments with the thermometer" over 100 times before we got a hook on understanding their source-recipient theory of thermal phenomenon. Such hooks are often things said or done that make absolutely no sense to you. A principle of charity (the Experimenters were wonderful scientists, being students and collaborators of Galileo) requires that these made sense to them; and understanding how this is possible may require bootstrapping a theory locally incommensurable with your current theory, from whose vantage point the statement or results are senseless. A major suite of the Experimenters' studies involved characterizing the mechanical effects of cold on liquids —water, oil, lemon juice, wines, and so on. I put this their way—they saw the cold as flowing from a source into the liquids and having mechanical effects. Their tables of the course of thermal contraction and then the expansion in the course of freezing as a function of the readings of a thermometer did not make any sense to us, and that is because we were trying to read the tables depicting the mechanical effects as a function of the temperature of the liquids. But the numbers are impossible seen this way. If this is what the Experimenters thought they were doing, they should have put the thermometer in the liquid that was freezing.

Wiser and I then focused on the diagram of their apparatus: the thermometer was not placed in the liquid undergoing the change, but rather in the ice-salt mixture. Huh?! The Experimenters were using the thermometer to measure the strength of the cold (their language again), not the temperature of the liquid (which, as we subsequently realized and as I explained above, they could not have been doing anyway because their thermometers were not calibrated to fixed points).

In Conclusion:

In sum, when we ask whether the language at one point in time (L1) and the conceptual system it expresses (CS1) might sometimes be incommensurable with a later language (L2) and conceptual system that represents overlapping phenomena, we are asking whether there is a set of concepts at the core of CS1 that cannot be expressed in terms of CS2, and vice versa. We are asking whether L1 can be translated into L2 without a translator's gloss. Incommensurablity arises when there are simultaneous additions, deletions, differentiations, coalescences, and changes in type and core between CS1 and CS2, such that the undifferentiated concepts of CS1 no longer play a role in CS2 (indeed, are even incoherent from the lights of C2) and the coalesced concepts of C2 played no role in CS1. In cases of incommensurability, CS1 will lead to unresolvable contradictions easily resolved in CS2, and holders of CS1 will say and do things that make perfect sense from the point of CS1 that are utterly inexplicable to holders of CS2 (the huh? phenomenon).

I now turn to whether there is evidence of exactly the same sort for conceptual change in childhood.

Conceptual Change in Childhood

I have encountered four major reasons that my colleagues doubt that children's conceptual systems may be incommensurable with those of adults:

1. The very notion of incommensurability is incoherent, whether we are talking about theory development in the history of science or in childhood.
2. Adults communicate with children just fine, and psychologists who study cognitive development depict children's conceptions in the adult language.
3. There is no way incommensurability could arise (empiricist version). Children learn their language from the adult culture. How could children establish sets of terms that are interrelated differently from the interrelations adults have established among those sets of terms?
4. There is no way incommensurability could arise (nativist version). Intuitive conceptions are constrained by innate principles that determine the entities we can represent, the entitites about which we can learn. These innate concepts in turn become entrenched in the course of learning.

It is worth dwelling on each of these arguments, although my responses to them are implicit in what has come before. I have countered the first objection (the incoherence of the notion of incommensurability) by offering a positive analysis of what I mean by local incommensurability, and have sketched what counts as evidence that there are episodes of historical development in which it obtains. It is beyond the scope of this chapter to say more about philosophical claims that the very notion of incommensurability is incoherent. Ultimately, one's analysis of concepts constrains one's stance toward the possibility of incommensurability. I will return to this question in chapter 13, arguing that the very possibility of conceptual change depends on whether and how conceptual role contributes to concept individuation and content determination. I prefer to work backwards here, arguing for conceptual change and specifying the mechanisms that underpin it, and then taking up what consequences this work has for how we think about concepts in chapter 13.

The answer to the second objection (adults and children communicate just fine) should, by now, be clear. It is an empirical question just how well adults understand preschool children. In cases of incommensurability, we are failing to do so. More important, incommensurability does not require complete lack of communication. After all, the early oxygen theorists argued with the phlogiston theorists, who were often their colleagues or teachers. Locally incommensurable conceptual systems can and do share many terms that have the same meaning in both languages. This common ground can be used to fix referents for particular uses of nonshared terms (as in a use of "depholgisticated air" to refer to oxygen-enriched air). Similarly, I discussed earlier how it is possible for the historian of science to express in today's language an earlier theory that was expressed in an incommensurable language. We understand the phlogiston theory, to the extent that we do, by interpreting the language in which it was expressed, and this requires creating a conceptual system that is incommensurable with ours (a bootstrapping process in reverse). In creating or learning a translator's gloss, we acquire a whole set of terms together, each of which is only partially interpreted through concepts we already possess. To the extent that the child's language is incommensurable with the adult's, psychologists do not express the child's beliefs in the adult language. Rather, they interpret the child's language, learn it, and teach it to other adults. This is possible because of the considerable overlap between the two, enabling the psychologist, like the historian, to be interpreter and language learner.

The third objection (incommensurability could never arise, empiricist version) is even easier to dispel. The empiricist objection presupposes that language is learned by constructing concepts from a preconceptual theory-neutral vocabulary. Chapter 2 argued against this position. Of course, children learn language from adults, but they bring the rich conceptual resources of core cognition and of constructed intuitive theories to the table. If cultures create representational systems that are incommensurable with core cognition, then children must undergo conceptual change to acquire these systems. In the process of doing so, they may also create explicit intuitive theories that are incommensurable with both core cognition and adult conceptual systems.

Finally, the fourth objection (incommensurability could never arise, nativist version) is merely an argument for continuity. Any demonstration of CS1/CS2 pairs in which the latter differs qualitatively from the former provides a counterexample. Cases of incommensurability in the history of science provide an existence proof that continuity is not logically necessary, and there now are many worked examples of conceptual change in childhood. Stella Vosniadu and William Brewer (1992) showed that preschooler's flat-earth theory is enriched core cognition and they demonstrated that children create novel, but consistent, synthetic models as they attempt to get their mind around the culture's claim that the earth is round like a ball. For another example: by the high school years youngsters have created a rich theory of the motion of macroscopic objects that shares much with the impetus theory of the Middle Ages and is incommensurable with Newtonian mechanics (McCloskey, 1983; McCloskey, Caramazza, & Green, 1980). Similarly, Marianne Wiser (1988) showed that adolescents create a thermal theory that has much in common with the source-recipient model of the Florentine Experimenters, and is incommensurable with the molecular-based thermal theories taught in junior and senior high schools; and Andrew Shtulman (2006) showed that adolescents create a theory of evolution that is incommensurable with the theory of natural selection. The case study in this chapter concerns conceptual change in the children's theories of the material world.

The Case at Hand: Concepts of Matter, Weight, and Density

Jean Piaget discovered many phenomena that captivated generations of developmental psychologists. One, the failure of infants at simple object-permanence tasks, was discussed in chapter 2. Equally well known is his discovery that preschool children are "nonconservers." Ask a 5-year-old to make two balls of clay such that each contains exactly the same amount of clay, and the child will carefully create two balls as close to the same diameter as she can make them. The child will agree that the two balls have the same amount of clay, weigh the same, and take up the same amount of space. If you flatten one into a pancake and ask "Do they still have the same amount of clay (or weigh the same, or take up the same amount of space), or does this one [the ball] have more or does this one [the pancake] have more?" the child will claim that the ball has more clay, takes up more space, and weighs more than the pancake, pointing out its greater vertical extent (or the child chooses the pancake, pointing out its greater horizontal extent; Piaget & Inhelder, 1974). Nonconservation of matter (amount of clay), weight, and volume by 5- and 6-year-olds has been replicated literally hundreds, if not thousands, of times. Relatedly, children of this age, as well as considerably older ones, say that a popped piece of popcorn weighs more than the corn from which it was popped, and that if you add a small bit of clay to a given clay ball, you don't change its weight. In one striking demonstration of nonconservation, 5- and 6-year-old children judged that after a vertically oriented rectangular object is turned on its side, it weighs less than when it was upright.

As any developmental psychologist who grew up in the 1960s or 1970s knows, Piaget argued that nonconservation derived from putative deficiencies in the young child's thought: failures of logic, failures in the capacity to coordinate two dimensions (the greater vertical extent of the ball is compensated for by the greater horizontal extent of the pancake), failures in the capacity to go beyond the perceptually given. Piaget's stage theory of cognitive development located developmental changes at a very abstract domain-general level of description, explaining performance on particular tasks, such as the conservation experiments, in terms putative cognitive stages such as "preoperational thought." But those who have read *The Child's Construction of Quantities* know that Piaget and Inhelder actually gave two theoretical accounts of the phenomena. They showed, first, how the transition from nonconservation to conservation of amount, weight, and volume, plus the differentiation of weight from density, was part of a change in children's underlying theory of matter; and then, second, they argued that the successive theories of matter were constrained by the stage changes in children's logical abilities.

Piaget's and Inhelder's (1974) first interpretation of the transition from being a nonconserver to being a conserver falls within the theory-theory of conceptual development. We may embrace this perspective (as I do) while abandoning Piaget's overall stage theory. Space precludes rehearsing the reasons most developmental psychologists no longer agree with Piaget's stage theory of logical development. Most now reject Piaget's claims that the logical abilities of 4-year-olds are radically different from those of 10-year-olds, which in turn are radically different from those of adolescents (see Carey, 1985a, 1985b; R. Gelman &

Baillargeon, 1983, for reviews of the criticisms of Piaget's stage theory). It is the abandonment of the Piaget's stage theory that made studies of nonconservation go out of style. This is a pity. There may be no domain-general constraints on the intuitive theories a 4-year-old, compared to an adult, can construct. Nonetheless, 4-year-olds do indeed have a radically different theory of matter than do adults, just as Piaget and Inhelder argued. Indeed, the two are incommensurable. Furthermore, the underlying theory change does account for the transition from non-conservation to conservation of amount of matter, weight, and volume, as well as for many other developmental changes in children's explanations for material phenomena.

The Preschool Child's Intuitive Theory of Objects and Substances—CS1

Intuitive theories are the conceptual structures that provide fodder for explanation, and material cause is one of Aristotle's four basic explanatory modes (along with efficient cause, formal cause, and final cause). We explain many fundamental phenomena by in terms of Aristotle's material cause, including appealing to substance kind—why a stick floats but a fork does not; why a log placed into a fire burns but a chunk of solder melts; why Coke tastes sweet but lemon juice tastes sour. Since ancient times philosophers and scientists have offered theories of the basic substances from all things are made, varying from the Greeks' earth, air, water, and fire to the elements of Mendeleev's periodic table. Although young children are not systematizers, and do not seek the primitive materials from which all else is built, nonetheless they surely offer explanations of their world in terms of substance kind. My discussion of CS1 develops two points. First, I review evidence that preschool children represent substance kinds, and that they represent substance kinds as ontologically distinct from object kinds. I conclude the discussion by pointing out that crediting the child with the concept *substance* is not the same as crediting the child with the concept *matter*.

By the time children are 3, they clearly distinguish between objects and the substances from which they are made. By age 3 or 4, and in some studies even by age 2, children project newly heard words ostensively defined over a novel object with an apparently nonaccidental shape on the basis of shared object kind, but one defined over a formless chunk of material over material kind (Prasada, Ferenz, & Haskell, 2002; see also Imai & Gentner, 1997; Kalish & Gelman, 1992; Li, Dunham, & Carey, in press; Soja, Carey, & Spelke, 1991). Soon, this distinction has become entrenched, terms for substances have become full-fledged kind terms, and children's reasoning displays have become distinct ontological commitments with respect to objects and substances. For instance, Susan Gelman and Ellen Markman (1987) showed that preschool children projected substance-relevant properties (e.g., melts when put in an oven vs. burns when put in an oven) on the basis of shared kind labels rather than on the basis of physical features. In these studies, preschoolers were told that one chunk of a substance, called "gold," had one such property (e.g., would melt if placed in an oven), and a very different-looking chunk, called "wood," had a contrasting property (e.g., would burn). They were then shown a third chunk that looked like the wood but was called gold, and they were asked whether it would melt like this gold or burn like this wood (indicating the original samples). Children chose the substance with the same name rather than the same appearance, but only when the property being projected was substance-relevant, such as those in this example (as opposed to a property such as fitting through a hole, where object size and shape were the relevant features of the entities).

Carol Smith, Marianne Wiser, and I (Smith, Carey, & Wiser, 1985) showed that even 3-year-olds know that object kind is not maintained if an entity is broken into pieces, whereas substance kind is. Later, Terry Au (1994; Au, Sidle, & Rollins, 1993) extended these results, characterizing the depth of the preschooler's understanding of the nature of substance. Au explored Piagetian demonstrations of nonconservation more radical than those described above, ones that probed not whether certain measures of substance were conserved over changes of shape but whether substance itself is seen to cease to exist if broken into pieces too small to see. Piaget and Inhelder (1974) found that it was not until age 7 or 8 that children agreed that dissolved sugar added to the weight of a cup of water as much as did undissolved sugar, or that water with sugar in it would taste sweet a few days later. Au reasoned that these Piagetian demonstrations may underestimate children's understanding because the demonstrations require an understanding of what balance scales measure and an understanding of the locution "in two days' time." Au let children taste the sugar and used their own locution for the taste, and used a more intuitive reflection of weight (C. Smith et al.'s (1985) probe concerning being heavy enough to make a cardboard bridge collapse—see below). Au also spelled out the passage of time in terms of "going home, sleeping, getting up, going to school, going home, sleeping."

With these changes to the procedures, Au (1994) found much greater understanding among young children than Piaget and Inhelder had. First, she showed that 3- to 5-year-olds performed above chance when reasoning about substance kinds whose superficial properties across samples were radically different owing to the chunks' being ground into powders or even dissolved in a solvent, apparently vanishing. Children argued that the substance continued to exist over these transformations, and that a portion of the transformed substance main-tained substance kind (e.g., was still sugar) and substance-relevant properties (e.g., would taste sweet, would be healthy or unhealthy to eat, would smell good or "yucky" when burned, and so on). Importantly, they did not conserve object-level properties over these transformations —properties such as total weight or likelihood of being blown away by a puff of air. Furthermore, if shown that a cup of water was not heavy enough to make a cardboard bridge collapse, but that the same water with a tablespoon of sugar was now heavy enough to do so, preschool children were above chance at predicting that a cup of water with a tablespoon of dissolved sugar would also make the bridge collapse.

Au's data complement those of Gelman and Markman, showing that children's representations of substances go beyond representations of perceptual properties. Thus, these data undermine Piaget's claims that preschool children are "perceptually bound." Au argued further that preschool children have made a theoretical construction of substances as homogeneous—wood is wood, through and through. She claimed that representations of substance homogeneity underlie children's ability to conserve substance across transformations as extreme as grinding into a powder or dissolving it. In support of this argument, she showed that judgments of whether there could be portions of a substance too small to see and whether substance-relevant properties were conserved over dissolution held together coherently. For example, in one of her studies, she asked children to make a forced-choice judgment about what happens when sugar is stirred into water: (1) it breaks up into tiny pieces, so small you can't see them, or (2) it disappears. Those who chose the former option were more likely than chance to judge that the dissolved sugar would still taste sweet and cause the bridge to collapse; those who chose the latter were at chance.

Nailing the coherence of these judgments, Au and her colleagues (1993) carried out a series of training studies in which 3- to 5-year-old children were explicitly taught that substance is conserved through grinding into a powder, and through dissolution, because substances can be broken into tinier and tinier pieces until each piece is too small to see. This training improved young children's performance on all of the tasks sketched above in which they had to reason about the sameness of substance-relevant properties over these transformations. This training also improved their reasoning about contamination; those who had received the training were more likely to judge that it is not OK to drink some juice in which a cockroach or a piece of "doggie-doo" had been dropped and removed than were those who had not.

The data reviewed above show that preschool children undoubtedly distinguish objects from the substances from which they are made, and that they take object kinds and substance kinds to be ontologically distinct. Substances survive Pelletier's universal-grinder test (are homogeneous) where objects do not, and substance kind supports different inferences from object kind. Also, it is important to note that in Au's data, the performance of 6- to 8-year olds is markedly better than that of the 3- to 5-year-olds. In Au's own writings, she qualifies her conclusions regarding preschoolers' understanding of the homogeneity of substance (especially its survival of transformations in which it loses macroscropic perceptual properties) by saying " "some preschoolers as young as 3 understand . . . " or "young preschoolers have a fragile understanding. . . . " On many specific questions in Au's experiments, 3-year-olds perform at chance or succeed only when large chunks are broken into smaller ones that are still visibly the same material. Nonetheless, that the training interventions have the effects they do, as well as the robust success of about one-third of the 3- to 5-year-olds, supports Au's claims that young preschoolers have the capacity to understand substance kind as maintained over such radical transformations.

A robust understanding of substance and substance kind is available to children by the end of the preschool years, but does this really challenge Piaget and Inhelder's more general point that children do not construct a representation of matter until many years later? *Matter* is a highly theory-laden concept, one which may merely be a descendent of the child's concept *substance*. To credit the child with a concept of matter we must show that they distinguish material from immaterial physical entities, and explore the inferential work this distinction does for the child. Below I argue for a C21-CS2 transition between the preschooler's intuitive theory of the physical workd articulated in terms of object and substance kinds and the intuitive theory of some adolescents and adults in which material entities have been differentiated from the class of physically real entities. In CS2, but not CS1, the extensive concept *weight* has been differentiated from the intensive concept density, this differentiation supporting the differentiation of the concepts *matter* and *physically real*.

The Conceptual Change

Please pause and dwell on this puzzle: Given that by age 6 or 7, children robustly succeed on Au's tasks, why do they maintain that the weight of a ball does not change if a small piece of clay is added to it? Why do they maintain that the weight of a ball changes if it is flattened, and that a popped piece of popcorn is both bigger and heavier than the kernel from which it was popped? These are "huh?" phenomena that suggest at the very least that the child is using the word "weight" differently from us, and maybe even that the child may have concepts locally incommensurable with ours. A generation of psychologists, including me, became interested in conceptual development upon first encountering the phenomenon of nonconservation. My first experiments (Carey, 1972) involved trying to make sure that children understood what was being asked. I studied conservation of amount of liquid. I provided two small identical glasses and had the child make it so that one had more juice to drink in it the other. I then asked whether they could tell, just by drinking, which one was which. That is, I explained "more to drink" in a quantity-conservation task by having the child drink two portions of juice through a straw (when they couldn't see the amounts), to make sure that they understood what "more to drink" meant—that is, the quantity that took longer to drink took more effort to drink. All 5- and 6-year-olds understood this. Then I switched to differently shaped glasses and established whether children would actually choose the glass with markedly less juice as the one with more to drink—the juice in the tall skinny glass—if given a choice to drink just one. I reminded them that they were to choose choosing the glass with more to drink—the one that would take longer, require more effort to drink (using the locutions they had used when they explained how they could tell which was more when they had drunk through the straws). Nonconservers chose the glass that actually had less juice—the quantity in the tall thin glass rather than in the low wide glass—even though they had seen three times as much juice poured into the wide glass than into the tall thin glass. Then I let them drink both quantities, such that the glass they judged had less juice to drink actually took three times as long and three times as many sucks to finish. Indeed, the quantity difference was exactly the same as they had discriminated perfectly when they had told "just by drinking" which glass had more juice. One-third failed to notice the contradiction, and one-third noted it but could not resolve it (Carey, 1972). I had attempted to make entirely clear what question I was asking (what "more to drink" means) and to provide counterevidence to their generalization that, of two glasses, the one with greater vertical extent had more to drink. I put them into a state of contradiction that they noticed but could not resolve. At this point I realized that understanding the child's conceptual system was going to be difficult, and indeed, I worked on this case of conceptual change, among others, for the next 15 years.

So why is the CS1 described by Au, in which objects are differentiated from substances, and in which substances are conceptualized as homogenous, not sufficient to support conservation of amount of substance, or conservation of weight, or of volume? The short answer is that these conservations require explicit measures of the amount of matter, which requires that the child not only conceptualize substance kind but also take on the question of which physical entities (liquids, powders, solids, gases, heat, light, electricity) are material and which are the extensive measures of the amount of matter. Considering weight as a measure of amount of matter requires more than conceptualizing substance as homogeneous. The child must be able to think of the total amount of a portion of matter, the total weight of that portion of matter, and the total volume of that portion of matter as the sum of the amounts, weights, and volumes of arbitrarily small subportions. The child must not only conceive of substance as homogeneous; he or she must also be able at least to entertain the possibility that it is continuous (infinitely divisible).

Au couches her results in terms of preschoolers' understanding of the continuity of matter, but her experiments fall way short of demonstrating this. As I said above, matter is a theory-laden concept; the above experiments do not show that preschool children and early elementary-age children distinguish between material and immaterial physical entities. Also, a continuous theory of matter is opposed to a particulate theory, a theory which posits a minimal unit, such that further division does not maintain material kind. Our particulate theory also posits space between particles of even the most solid of materials. Clearly none of the above demonstrations show that (or ever test whether) preschool children have a theoretical commitment to either a particulate or a continuous theory of matter.

To establish that the phenomenon of nonconservation reflects a CS1 that is incommensurable with the CS2 that is the commonsense adult theory, we must describe CS1 and CS2, detailing the conceptual changes. The rest of this chapter takes on this challenge. I shall ask whether (and when) children create a representation of matter when they represent matter as continuous, and what they take to be the central features of material (as opposed to immaterial) physical entities. In particular, I shall ask when weight and occupying space come to be seen as central features of material entities that distinguish them from immaterial ones; and when each is conceptualized as an extensive variable that provides a measure of amount of matter; and when these variables are differentiated from density, an intensive variable along which substance kinds characteristically differ from each other. And I shall ask how these concepts are interrelated in development. Only then will we be in a position to address the CS1–CS2 shift with respect to whether it reflects conceptual change in childhood.

A Plausible False Start

As I mentioned above, Piaget and Inhelder (1974) argued that the developmental transition from nonconservation to conservation reflected a theory change, and they attempted to characterize the conceptual changes involved. Consider the nonconservation of weight. Many writers faced with the Piagetian nonconservation phenomena, including Piaget and Inhelder themselves, interpreted them as reflecting a lack of differentiation between two kinds of bigness—big in size and big in weight. This hypothesis is certainly consistent with children's judgments that the weight of a ball of clay or a rectangular block changes when its vertical extent changes, and that a piece of popped corn weighs more than the original kernel. Carol Smith, Marianne Wiser, and I (C. Smith et al., 1985) set out to test this hypothesis by seeing whether children would make judgments on the basis of size that adults would make based on weight, and vice versa. We found that children as young as 3 years old had perfectly differentiated concepts of size and weight. For instance, when deciding whether a given object would fit into a box, even 3-year-olds ignored weight, and when deciding whether an object would make a sponge bridge collapse, they ignored size. Furthermore, judgments were no less accurate when size and weight were not correlated than when they were—judgments concerning very light large objects or very heavy small objects were as accurate as those for very heavy large objects and very light small objects. If the two concepts were even partly undifferentiated, relative values on one dimension should intrude on judgments based on the relative judgments on the other dimension. Furthermore, young children's nonconservation judgments do not reflect the false belief that size differences are good predictors of weight differences. When asked to judge relative weights, they always pick up or weigh the objects; they never think it is sufficient just to look at them.

Piaget and Inhelder (1974) claimed a second conceptual change in this domain—a change from a conceptual system that lacked the concept of density altogether to one that included that concept. They claimed that children do not achieve the concept of density until they reach the stage of formal operations in adolescence, for before then they lack the mathematical tools to represent ratios and proportions—tools needed to represent intensive quantities explicitly. As we will see below, there is truth to these hypotheses, but Piaget and Inhelder aren't quite right. Children in the grips of CS1 have an undifferentiated concept of weight/density, rather than lack representations of density at all.

I review these false starts to illustrate a point: documenting cases of conceptual change requires testing hypotheses concerning what changes at the level of individual concepts might underlie the visible changes in behavior we observe. And, as I shall also illustrate, just as in the historical cases, to be confident in our analysis we must characterize the theories in which the concepts are embedded.

An Undifferentiated Weight/Density Concept

So, if an undifferentiated size/weight concept does not underlie Piagetian nonconservation of weight, what does? To answer that question, we need a fuller characterization of the child's concept of weight, including a characterization of the conceptual system within which it functions. As shown above, young children represent weights of objects, have mapped this property to the words "weight" and "heavy," and know some causal consequences of weight. There is, however, a crucial nondifferentiation involving weight. While weight is perfectly well differentiated from size, it is undifferentiated from density. After demonstrating that this is so, I shall try to show you how that could be so. I shall argue that in CS1, weight is not seen as an intrinsic property of all matter. Differentiating weight from density is part of a conceptual change in which material entities are distinguished from nonmaterial ones; matter comes to be seen as continuous; and weight, as an extensive quantity, comes to be taken to be (along with occupying space) a core defining property of material entities. I shall show how these conceptual changes are mutually supportive, and I shall provide evidence from within-child analyses that they reflect a coherent theory change.

Density is a ratio, weight to volume, and like all intensive quantities, it is not additive. The density of a given chunk of matter is not the sum of the densities of the materials that make it up, but rather is an average of them. It is only when children have differentiated weight from density that they can solve Piaget's popcorn problem, appealing to the change in density (rather than in weight) resulting from the popping. The conceptual change implicated here is deeply parallel to the change within thermal concepts between the time of the Florentine Experimenters and Black (see above). From the point of view of any conceptual system in which weight and density are differentiated, an undifferentiated weight/density concept is incoherent, just as an undifferentiated heat/temperature concept is incoherent from the point of view of any representational system that has constructed extensive measures of heat and intensive measures of temperature. Weight is an extensive quantity and density is an intensive quantity, and furthermore, they are interdefined. Density equals weight divided by volume. The parallels in these two cases demonstrate the fruits of considering intuitive theories from the vantage point of analyses of explicit historical theories.

We require evidence in three steps to support the claim that the concepts of weight and density are not differentiated by young children. First, to rule out the possibility that young children simply lack the concept of density, we must show that heaviness relativized to size plays some role in their judgments. Second, we must show that judgments based on weight intrude on those where density is the relevant factor, and vice versa; and that there are no contexts in which each concept is appropriately drawn upon. And third, we must sketch the conceptual system that supports these judgments in which the undifferentiated concept plays a systematic and fruitful inferential role.

Consistent with Piaget and Inhelder's (1974) claims, albeit for younger children, Smith, Wiser, and I (C. Smith et al., 1985) found that many young children (3- to 5-year-olds) appear to lack the concept of density. We asked children to compare objects on the basis of the heaviness of the kind of stuff they are made of, or to sort painted objects on the basis of material (a task that requires accessing the density of the unknown material—e.g., to recognize that a small heavy object must be made of a different material from a big light one). Just as Piaget and Inhelder would have predicted, all of their judgments were based on total weight alone. But just slightly older children's judgments suggested a conflation of the concepts of weight and density. To explore this possibility systematically, we created a series of tasks, both verbal and nonverbal, that required children to distinguish absolute heaviness from heaviness for size. In these tasks, heaviness for size was often presented as a property of substance kind, which, as we have seen above, even preschool children have differentiated from object kind. Heaviness was presented as a property of objects. For example, we showed children pairs of objects made of different metals and asked "Which is heavier?" or "Which is made of the heavier kind of metal?" Nonverbal tasks involved predicting which objects would make a sponge bridge collapse (weight being the relevant factor) and sorting the objects into steel and aluminum families (density being the relevant factor). In the steel-and-aluminum-family task, children were first shown several pairs of identical-size cylinders, and it was pointed out that steel is a much heavier kind of stuff than is aluminum. This was true within each pair, even though the absolute weight of the smallest steel cylinder was less than the absolute weight of the largest aluminum one. Then children were given new pairs of objects and asked to sort them into the steel and aluminum families. Children under 8 (and many older children as well) showed intrusion of absolute weight on judgments we would base on density, judging a large aluminum object as made of a heavier kind of stuff than a small steel one, and sorting a large aluminum object into the steel family. Conversely, they made density intrusions into the weight task, sometimes judging that a small steel object would make the bridge collapse, while correctly judging that a larger, heavier, wood object would not. These mutual intrusions are what one would expect if the concepts of weight and density are not differentiated.

Carol Smith and her colleagues (Smith, 2007; Smith et al., 1997; Smith, Snir, & Grosslight, 1992; Smith & Unger, 1997; Snir, Smith, & Grosslight, 1993) have corroborated these results with other simple tasks, extending the ages tested from 8 up to 12. They provided children with scales and with sets of objects that varied in volume, weight, and material kind and asked them to order the objects by size, by absolute weight, and by density (explained in terms of heaviness of the kind of stuff). The ordering required no calculations of density. For instance, if one object is larger than another, but they weigh the same or the smaller is heavier, we can infer without calculation that the smaller is denser. Prior to instruction, few children as old as 12 were able to correctly order the same set of items differently on the basis of absolute weight and density. Mistakes reveal intrusions of weight into the density orderings and vice versa. These results are underscored when children are asked to depict in a visual model the size, weights, and densities of a set of such objects. Only children who show in other tasks that they have at least partially differentiated weight and density produce models that depict, in some way or other, all three physical magnitudes.

Another task, based on one originally introduced by Piaget and Inhelder, provided convergent evidence for the lack of differentiation of weight and density. Smith, Wiser, and I showed children large balls of clay and of play dough. The balls were identical in size, and children all agreed that the ball of clay weighed much more. We then divided each in half, formed one half of the material of each into smaller, equal-size balls, and asked if the clay ball would still weigh more than the other. Children were asked to imagine repeating this process, and asked whether the clay ball would always weigh more than the other one. Only half of the 8- to 9-year-olds agreed that no matter how small the balls, the clay ball would always weigh more. Rather, the younger children and half of the older ones argued that when the balls got small enough, they would weigh the same as each other—nothing at all. For these latter children, the intensive quantity of weight/size and the extensive quantity of total weight of each ball were not distinguished.

Besides reflecting the weight/density lack of differentiation, this thought experiment also suggests young children fail to conceptualize matter as continuous and as necessarily weighing something, such that the total weight of a portion of matter is the sum of the weights of its arbitrarily small constituents. Weight in CS1 is the felt weight of the total object, not a measure of arbitrarily small portions of matter. Constructing such a concept of matter supports the differentiation of the extensive concept of weight from the intensive concept of density.

Just as the Experimenters' undifferentiated heat/temperature con-cept led them to contradictions they could not resolve, children's weight/density concept leads them into outright contradiction. We presented children in this conceptual state with two bricks, one of steel and one of aluminum. Though the steel was smaller, the two weighed the same and children were shown that they balanced exactly on a scale. They were then challenged: "How come these weigh the same, since one is so much bigger?" They often answered, "Because that one [the steel] is made of a heavier kind of stuff," or "Because steel is heavier." They were then shown two bricks of steel and aluminum, now both the same size as each other, intermediate in size between the original two bricks, and asked to predict whether they would balance or whether one would be heavier than the other. Now they answered that they would weigh the same, "Because the steel and aluminum weighed the same before" (see Figure 10.1). Children give this pattern of responses because they do not fully realize that the claim that a given steel object weighs the same as a given aluminum object is not equivalent to the claim that steel and aluminum weigh the same, even though they also understand that if

E: How can they weigh the same?

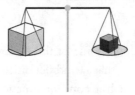

S: Steel is heavier kind of stuff

E: Will these weigh the same or will one weigh more?

S: They will weigh the same, because they weighed the same before.

Figure 10.1. (From Carey, 1991). Eliciting a contradiction the child with an undifferentiated concept *weight/density* cannot resolve. Carey, S. (1991). Knowledge acquisition or conceptual change? In S. Carey & R. Gelman (Eds.), *The epigenesis of mind: Essays on biology and cognition* (pp.133–169). Hillsdale, NJ: Erlbaum. Reprinted with the permission.

a small steel objects weighs the same as a large aluminum one, this is possible because steel is heavier than aluminum. It is not that children are unmoved by the contradiction in these assertions. They, as well as adults, strive for consistency, and they are upset by this contradictory state of affairs. Just as the scientists in the Florentine Academy were unable to resolve the contradictions owing to their undifferentiated heat/temperature concept, so too children cannot resolve the contradictions resulting from their undifferentiated weight/density concept.

How an Undifferentiated Weight/Density Concept Functions in Thought

The previous section outlined some of the evidence that 6- to 12-year-old children have a concept that is undifferentiated between weight and density. But how could such a concept function in a CS1, given the contradictions it leads the child into? The short answer is that the contexts in which children deploy their weight/density concept do not, in general, elicit these contradictions. This is the same answer as for the Experimenters' concept *degree of heat* (undifferentiated between heat and temperature) or for Aristotle's concept *speed* (undifferentiated between average and instantaneous velocity).

A sketch of the purposes for which children do use their concept provides a slightly longer answer. The child's concept is heaviness (degree of weight). Children appeal to the heaviness of objects to explain some effects of those objects on themselves or on other objects, including but not limited to how heavy the objects feel when they lift them. A heavier object is more likely to break something it is dropped on, resist movement more when pushed, and so on. "Heavy," like other dimensional adjectives such as "big," is a relative term. Something is heavy relative to some standard, and the child can switch fluidly among different standards. An object can be heavy for objects of that type (e.g., a heavy book), heavy for the objects on the table, heavy for me but not my mother, or heavy for objects of that size. For the child with an undifferentiated weight/density concept, relativizing heaviness to a standard determined by size is no different from other ways of relativizing heaviness in order to assign the adjective "heavy" or "light." Children differentiate weight and density as they realize that heaviness/size is an independent physical magnitude, one that is an intrinsic property of kinds of stuff and is related systematically to distinct phenomena in the world.

Achieving the full answer to how children can have an undifferentiated weight/density concept that functions effectively within their conceptual system requires characterizing that conceptual system (CS1). Noting that weight is undifferentiated from density in CS1 does not exhaust the differences between the child's concept of weight and the adult's; indeed, it could not. Because an undifferentiated weight/density concept is incoherent from the point of view of a CS2 in which the two are differentiated, it must be embedded in a very different conceptual system to function coherently in the child's thought. We should expect, therefore, that the child's concept of heaviness differs from the adult's in many ways, beyond its being undifferentiated between weight and density. And indeed it does.

The Material/Immaterial Distinction

The concepts *weight* and *density* are embedded in an intuitive theory of matter. Weight is proportional to the quantity of matter; density is the ratio of the quantity of matter to volume. The concepts *weight, volume, density, matter,* and *quantity of matter (mass)* have a long intellectual history (Jammer, 1961; Toulmin & Goodfield, 1962). Since Newton, the central concept is mass. As historian of science Max Jammer tells the story, the late 19th century saw the flowering of the substantial concept of matter, which identified matter with any entity with mass. The concept of inertial mass had been formulated by Kepler and systematized by Newton, who also fused it with the medieval concept of quantity of matter. A typical statement from the beginning of the 20th century was, "If I should have to define matter, I would say: Matter is all that has mass, or all that requires force in order to be set in motion" (Charles de Freycinet, 1896, quoted in Jammer, 1961, p. 86). According to this view, mass is the essential property of matter and provides a measure of the quantity of matter. Clearly, prior to the formulation of the concept *mass*, having mass could not be taken as the essence of material entities. Prior to Newton, weight was not differentiated from mass (the weight of a por-tion of matter is a function of its mass and the strength of the gravitational field). And indeed, Jammer claims that prior to the formulation of the concept of mass, weight was not seen as a candidate measure of the quantity of matter, nor was having weight (even on earth) seen as nec-essary and sufficient for an entity's being material. The Greeks and the medieval scholastics had concepts of matter and weight that were dif-ferent from those of post-Newtonian physicists. According to Jammer, Aristotle had no concept of the quantity of matter, and he saw weight as an accidental, and partly intensive, property of some material entities, akin to odor. Even if the Greeks had had a concept of the quantity of matter, weight could not have served as its measure because some material entities, such as air, were thought to possess intrinsic levity. For the Greeks, weight was not even a single extensive quantity. There were no fixed units of weight. In practical uses, even within the same nation, different substances were weighed in terms of different standards. Further, the weight of material particles was thought to depend on the bulk of the object in which they were embedded. That is, Aristotle thought that a given clump of clay would itself weigh more when part of a large quantity of clay than when alone. Neither did the alchemists consider weight to reflect the quantity of matter; they fully expected to be able to turn a few pounds of lead into hundreds of pounds of gold. Density was also taken to be an irreducible intensive quality, like color, odor, and other accidents of matter. Density was not defined as mass/volume (or weight/volume) until Euler did so. What was actually quantified by the ancients was specific gravity (the ratio of the weight of a given volume of a substance to the weight of the same volume of water), not density. For example, Archimedes never used a term for density in his writings.

If weight was not taken to be an essential property of material entities, what was? Jammer details many proposals. Euclid proposed spatial extent—length, breadth, and depth. This was one dominant possibility throughout ancient Greek and medieval times. Galileo listed shape, size, location, number, and motion as the essential properties of material entities—spatial, arithmetical, and dynamic properties. The spatial notions included impenetrability; that is, material entities were seen to uniquely occupy space. In another thread of thought, material entities were those that could physically interact with other material entities. Again, weight was seen as irrelevant; according to this view, heat, while weightless, is certainly material. Finally, another line of thought posited that being inert, or passive, was the essence of matter. This view was the precursor to considering mass as the criterial property of matter; material entities are those that require forces for their movement or forms for their expression.

The substantial concept of matter (the identification of matter with mass) occupied a brief moment in the history of science. Since Einstein, the distinction between entities with mass and those without is not taken to be absolute because mass and energy are intra-convertible. It is not clear that the distinction between material and immaterial entities plays an important role in today's physics, given the existence of particles with no rest mass, such as photons, which are nevertheless subject to gravity; and as Jammer has pointed out, the concept of mass itself is far from unproblematic in modern physics.

Given the complex history of the concepts *matter, weight, mass,* and *density,* what CS2 should we be probing for in the child? Ours would be a good bet; that is, that of the nonscientific adult. What is the adult's intuitive concept of matter, and how is it related to the commonsense concepts of weight and density? Although this is an empirical question, I shall make some assumptions. I assume that commonsense physics distinguishes between clearly material entities such as solid objects, liquids, powders, and gaseous forms of known material kinds (e.g., steam), on the one hand, and clearly immaterial entities, such as abstractions (e.g., numbers, virtues) and mental entities (e.g., ideas), on the other. Adults also conceptualize quantity of matter. Probably, the essential properties of matter are thought to include spatial extent, impenetrability, weight, and the potential for causal interaction with other material entities. Most probably, the majority of adults do not realize that these four properties are not perfectly coextensive. Weight is seen as an extensive property of material entities, proportional to quantity of matter, whereas density is an intensive property, a ratio of amount of matter to volume. This view is closely related to the substantial conception of matter achieved at the end of the 19th century, but it differs from that in not being based on the Newtonian concept of mass and being unclear about the status of many entities (e.g., air, heat, and so on.)

There are two reasons commonsense physics might be identified so closely with one moment in the history of science. First, in general, commonsense science has as its domain everyday phenomena; it is not the grand metaphysical enterprise of the ancient Greek and medieval philosophers. For example, in two relevant aspects of intuitive physics, commonsense science has been shown to accord with the concepts employed in the first systematic exploration of the relevant domains of phenomena. Commonsense theories of motion share much with medieval impetus theories (e.g., McCloskey, 1983), and commonsense thermal theories share much with the source-recipient theory of the Florentine Academy (e.g., Wiser, 1988). The commonsense theory of matter I attribute to adults in our culture is similarly close to the ordinary phenomena lay people use their framework theory to explain.

A second, specific, reason to credit adults with the material/ immaterial distinction, in which weight is conceptualized as an extensive measure of amount of matter, is that both the impetus theory of motion and the source-recipient theory of thermal phenomena require just this concept of quantity of matter. The impetus theory posits a resistance to impetus that is proportional to quantity of matter, and the source-recipient theory of heat posits a resistance to heat that is proportional to quantity of matter. That scientifically untutored adults hold these theories is one reason to credit them with a pre-Newtonian concept of quantity of matter. Also, the developments of theoretical physics find their way into commonsense physics, albeit at a time lag and in a watered-down and distorted version. The mechanisms underlying this transmission include the assimilation of science instruction (however badly), making sense of the technological achievements made possible by formal science and learning to use the measuring devices of science, such as scales and thermometers.

When and How Children Draw the Material/Immaterial Distinction

The problem we face is ubiquitous in studies of conceptual development Many properties children represent will distinguish some material entities from some immaterial ones. Before we credit the child with a material/ immaterial distinction, we must assess more fully whether there is any concept with enough overlap of extension and conceptual role with the adult concept *matter* to credit children with that theory-laden concept.

As we saw in chapters 2 and 3, infants represent coherent, separately moveable objects in terms of properties that we take as reflecting materiality. Most salient in this regard is solidity, which is represented in the form of the constraint on motion that one object cannot pass through the space occupied by another. Infants also represent generalizations concerning motion that we would attribute to amount of matter—larger objects move less far than smaller objects when contacted by a given object moving at a given speed. However, these generalizations are not enough to credit infants with a distinction between material and immaterial entities, for these generalizations are more likely formulated over the concepts of object and object size, not matter and amount of matter.

Material entities encompass other forms of matter besides solid objects. What we would need to see to credit infants or young children with a material/immaterial distinction is that they treat different forms of matter alike with respect to some material-relevant properties. Also, we would need to see evidence that the relevant distinction is material/immaterial and not merely physically real/unreal. We can see what's at issue by considering two claims from the literature. First, David Estes and colleagues (Estes, Wellman, & Woolley, 1989) claimed that preschool children know that mental entities are immaterial. Second, Piaget (1960) claimed (and Rheta DeVries, 1986, endorsed the claim) that until age 8 or so, children consider shadows to be material. These works credit the young child with one true belief (ideas are immaterial) and one false belief (shadows are material) formulated over the concept of material.

What Estes and his colleagues' (1989) important studies actually showed was that children understand that objects (e.g., cookies) differ from mental entities like thoughts or mental images (e.g., of cookies) with respect to properties we know to derive from the material/immaterial distinction. These include objective perceptual access (can be seen by both the child and somebody else) and causal interaction with other material entities (cannot be moved or changed just by thinking about it). Objective perceptual access and causal interaction with other material entities, like uniquely occupying space, are properties that in our conceptual system are central to the material/immaterial distinction. Although Estes did not study other forms of matter, it is very likely that children would treat noncohesive forms of matter such as liquids and powders as they do cookies in this regard. On the other hand, children would also most likely treat nonmaterial entities such as shadows, heat, and light as they do cookies, suggesting that the distinction tapped in these studies might better be glossed as physically real/mental representation rather than material/immaterial.

The Piagetian claim is based on children's statements like the following: "A shadow comes off you, so it is made of you," "It's always there, but the darkness hides it," and "The light causes the shadow to reflect; otherwise it is always on your body." Huh? DeVries studied 223 children, ages 2 to 9. None of the younger children and only 5% of the 8- and 9-year-olds understood that shadows do not continue to exist at night, in the dark, or when another object blocks the source causing the shadow. Virtually all children spoke of one shadow being covered by another, or of the darkness of two shadows being mixed together, making it impossible to see the shadow, even though it was still there. Again, these results show that children attribute to shadows some properties of what we take to be material entities (i.e., independent existence and permanence)—properties we assume they would assign to liquids and powders as well as objects. But again, the relevant distinction may be physically real/unreal rather than material/immaterial; after all, shadows are physical entities rather than mental or abstract ones.

How would we decide whether children represent the concept *matter*? First, we must explore more systematically the extension of the child's concept, tying them to conceptual distinctions we know children represent that might form the core of a material/immaterial distinction. We must also explore what children take to be a measure of quantity of matter.

To establish whether children represent the material/immaterial distinction Carol Smith and I (Carey, 1991; Smith, 2007; Smith et al., 1997) explored whether material-dependent properties of objects are attributed to nonsolid substances. Given that even infants expect that nonsolid substances (sand and salt) should not pass through the space occupied by solid objects, we expected that preschool children would also generalize the solidity constraint to liquids. We showed 4- to 12-year-old children a box, and asked them to imagine a cube of wood and a cube of steel, each cut so that it just fits into the box and fills it completely. The question posed to the children was whether the wood and the metal could both fit into the box at the same time. All were certain that the answer was no. We then asked them to imagine the box filled with water, and asked whether the water and the steel cube could fit into the box at the same time; again, all but one 4-year-old was sure that the answer was no; this 4-year-old believed the water could be compressed (Carey, 1991). Thus, by age 4 children certainly consider liquids and solids on a par with respect to their uniquely occupying space, consistent with the claim that they unite material entities under a single category. However, other data from our lab, and from many others' labs, belie that conclusion.

As a second attack on the problem of characterizing the existence and extension of a concept of material entities, Smith and I have each elicited 4- to 12-year-old children's judgments concerning what entities in the world "are made of some kind of stuff," thus attempting to ground the distinction with the concept of substance characterized by Au in the studies described above. In one illustrative study (Carey, 1991) I introduced children to the issue by telling them that some things in the world, such as stones and tables and animals, are made of some kind of stuff, are material, and are made of molecules whereas other things that we can think of, like sadness and ideas, are not made of anything, are not material, and are not made of molecules. Thus, I elicited the distinction I was after with clear examples of material and immaterial entities and with a locution they would surely understand (made of some kind of stuff) and locutions they might have learned (are material, are made of molecules). I then asked the children to sort the training examples (stones, tables, sadness, ideas) and new entities (car, tree, sand, sugar, cow, worm, Styrofoam, Coca-Cola, water, dissolved sugar, steam, smoke, air, electricity, heat, light, shadow, echo, wish, and dream) into a pile of material entities and a pile of immaterial entities (the entities were presented verbally, their names written on cards and read to the child). I credited children with the material/immaterial distinction if they sorted objects, liquids, and powders as material and wish and dream as immaterial, and provided a relevant justification for their sort. The pattern of judgments, as well as the justifications, provided evidence for what children took the essential properties of material entities to be.

At all ages, children sorted the car, tree, and Styrofoam as material and the wish and dream as immaterial, showing that the examples and locutions at least tapped an object/nonobject distinction. However, for 60% of the 4-year-olds and 25% of the 6-year-olds, this task elicited no evidence of a material-immaterial distinction. Some children systematically applied a distinction between inanimate objects, on the one hand (judged as being made as some kind of stuff), and everything else, on the other hand. These children denied that gases, liquids, powers, animals, electricity, heat, light, echo, and shadows are material entities (half of the 4-year-olds). A few answered randomly. The data suggest that a concept of material kind encompassing all solids, liquids, and powders is not represented by all preschoolers. Of course, this task may have failed to elicit a distinction that was nevertheless represented by these young children. They may have taken "made of some kind of stuff" to mean "manufactured," for instance. But these data at least show that the relevant concept is not readily accessible or not mapped to the locution "made of some kind of stuff."

Still, almost half of the 4-year-olds, three-fourths of the 6-year-olds, and all of the 10- and 12-year-olds sorted all liquids, solids, and powders as material and denied that the wish and dream were, demonstrating a material/immaterial distinction or a physically real/unreal distinction. Nonetheless, their sorts revealed a very different distinction than that tapped by this task in the case of scientifically naïve adults. Clearly, weighing something, or having mass, was not taken as a criterial property of material entities. Only one of the 40 children provided an adult sort, judging all entities with mass as material and all massless entities as nonmaterial. Some of the oldest children took mass to be criterial, but thought gases to be massless. But all of the remaining children sorted on the basis of physical reality and/or having physical consequences. These children judged an entity material, made of some kind of stuff, made of molecules if it could be seen, touched, or had physical effects on other objects. This led to heat, echos, shadows, light, and electricity to be classified as material. Children with such sorts (the majority of 6- and 10-year-olds) appealed to perceptual accessibility of the entities they judged material—you can see and feel them. (It is important to note that, for the most part, children did not apply a single criterion systematically.) For example, a child might judge heat to be material because one can feel it, and light because one can see it, but deny that shadows and echoes are material, in spite of the fact that these entities can also be perceived. The child has clear examples of material entities—objects, liquids, powders—and a set of properties that distinguish these from clearly immaterial entities; and the child has not yet systematized these properties into a consistent set of criteria. The differentiation of physically real from material had begun; these children do not judge all physically real entities on their lists as made of some kind of stuff, as material, as made of molecules, whereas they do judge all liquids and solids so. In sum, the majority of preschool children and some 6-year-olds had not begun to construct a concept of material entities, and virtually all of the 6- to 10-year-olds who had begun to do so had not fully differentiated material from physically real.

Smith and her colleagues (Smith, 2007; Smith et al., 1997) include a matter-sorting task in the pretests of most of their curricular interventions with junior high school students, and they corroborate these findings. Prior to systematic instruction, only about 10 % of the highest science-track junior high school students include air and exclude heat as material when asked to sort according to the material/immaterial distinction. Like the younger children described above, even up to ages 12 and 13, children justify judgments of materiality by appeals to perceptual access and causal interaction with other material entities. By this age children certainly draw a distinction between prototypical material entities, on the one hand, and mental entities and abstractions, on the other, but material and physically real are not fully differentiated.

That children do not take having mass or weight as central to being material plays two roles in my argument here. First, it is part of the evidence for the undifferentiated concept *material/physically real*. Second, it is likely that coming to see that weighing something as central to materiality is part of the process of constructing a measure of matter, and constructing a measure of matter is part of what drives the differentiation of material from merely physically real. This type of mutual dependence is typical of bootstrapping episodes, in which concepts are acquired in a suite together.

A Digression: An Undifferentiated Air/Nothing Concept

Until age 12, more than three-fourths of the children tested in our sorting tasks deny that air is made of some kind of stuff, deny that air is material, deny that air is made of molecules. In the same set of questions about whether steel and wood, or steel and water, could be in a box at the same time, we also probed children's intuitions concerning whether air and the box-filling steel cube could be in the box at the same time. Virtually all of the 4- and 6-year-olds, and about half of the 10- and 12-year-olds, said, "Yes, they could," explaining that "air doesn't take up any space; air is all over the place," "Air is just there—the metal goes in, air is still there," "Air isn't anything," and so on. One said simply, "Air isn't matter."

One could take these data as suggesting that children have another false belief about matter, in addition to the false belief that shadows are material—namely, that air is not material. Although this belief is easy enough to state, a moment's reflection reveals it to be bizarre. If air is not material, what is it? Perhaps children consider air to be an immaterial physical entity, like an echo. But several said outright. "Air is nothing," or "Air isn't anything." However, air" is not simply synonymous with "nothing" or "empty space," for children this age know that there is no air on the moon or in outer space, that one needs air to breathe (and hence spacesuits and scuba gear), that wind is made of air, and so on. Indeed, in a different interview in which we probed whether children of this age considered dreams and ideas to be made of some kind of stuff, an interview in which "air" was never mentioned, several different children spontaneously offered "air" as the stuff of which dreams and ideas are made. This set of beliefs is formulated over another undifferentiated concept, *air/nothing* or *air/vacuum*—part of the interrelated concepts of CS1 that are locally incommensurable with the adult CS2.

Interim Conclusions: Distinguishing Material from Immaterial Entities

Preschool children distinguish solids, liquids, and powders, on the one hand, from entities such as wishes and dreams, on the other, in terms of properties related to the distinction between material and immaterial entities. These include uniquely occupying space, not being changeable by thought alone, being perceptible, and having the capacity to interact causally with other entities. By age 6, most children, and all children from age 8 on up, have related this distinction to the concept *stuff* or *substance,* but they do not yet see weight or uniquely occupying space as necessary features of material substances. Virtually all children who deemed solids, liquids, and powders material also judged some weightless entities that do not take up space (electricity, heat, light, echoes, or shadows) material. These data reflect an undifferentiated concept *material/physically real.*

Even though children do not consider weight and occupying space a necessary property of material/real entities, nonetheless perhaps they consider these to be properties of prototypical material/real entities (solids, liquids, and powders). If so, volume or weight might be considered a measure of the amount of matter, at least for these entities, and coming to measure matter might be part of the process through which children differentiate material from physically real. Carol Smith and her colleagues (Smith, 2007; Smith et al., 1985; 1992; 1997) now have copious data showing that young children do not expect even this relation between materiality/reality and weight or materiality/reality and occupying space. The phenomenon Smith discovered turns out to be one of the keystones to understanding the conceptual change between CS1 and CS2. It is a genuine "huh?" phenomenon, even though it doesn't necessarily strike one as such at first glance.

When given the choice "weighs a lot, a tiny amount, or nothing at all," young children judge that a single grain of rice, a single lentil, a single grain of sugar, or a small piece of Styrofoam weighs nothing at all. This phenomenon is related to the Piagetian observation that young children claim that adding a small piece of clay to a ball does not change its weight. Virtually all children judge Styrofoam to be material in the sorting task, and virtually all of these children judge that if a piece of Styrofoam is small enough, it will weigh nothing at all—0 grams. By now we have engaged hundreds of adults and children, aged 4 through 12, in a thought experiment in which they imagine a piece of Styrofoam being cut in half, cut in half again, until the remaining piece is too small to see. The question is whether we will ever arrive at a piece that weighs nothing. Below age 10, most children claim that point to be reached when the piece is still visible, and even half of the 12-year-olds claim that a piece too small to see will weigh nothing at all.

This may seem a fairly innocuous error, reflecting a concept of weight closely tied to felt weight. After all, such a small piece will feel like nothing at all and have no measurable weight on any scale the child knows anything about. But these data show that children, like the ancient Greeks, do not take weight as a truly extensive property of substances. They do not conceive of the total weight of an object as the sum of weight of arbitrarily small portions of the substance of which it is constituted. This is one very important way in which the child's concept *degree of heaviness* differs from the adult's concept *weight*. The child's *degree of heaviness* is neither systematically extensive nor systematically intensive, as is required if the child's concept is undifferentiated between *weight* and *density*.

Matter's Homogeneity and Continuity

As sketched above, Au showed that by age 3 (some children) to 6 (virtually all children) understand that there can be pieces of substance too small to see and that some properties of material kinds (e.g., sweetness, capacity for contamination) and some properties of the total amount of material (e.g., weight) are conserved even in the face of dissolution in a solvent. Children who affirmed that substances can be broken up into pieces too small to see, or who were taught so, were more likely to make these judgments. She concluded that preschool children represented matter as homogeneous (same at all points) and continuous (infinitely divisible), and that each portion, however arbitrarily small, maintains material properties.

The weight-thought experiment sketched above should engender some doubts about those conclusions. Au showed that children understand that the properties of the aggregate (sweetness, total weight, contamination, etc.) are maintained when the total aggregate is ground into powder or dissolved, but she did not show that children thought each portion maintains these properties. Four other results, dating back to Piaget and Inhelder (1974), confirm that it is not until age 12 or so that children simultaneously construct a concept of matter and take matter to be continuous (Carey, 1991; Smith et al., 1985; 2005). Of course, matter is not continuous, in the sense of being infinitely divisible, because matter is particulate. However, a particulate theory of matter follows, developmentally, a continuous theory, and as Smith has argued persuasively, requires the prior construction of a continuous theory.

The four results:

(1) As described above, children do not maintain the relative weights of two equal-size portions of material (e.g., clay and play dough) through repeated division, and they do not maintain that a portion of material, obtained by dividing a portion that does weigh something in half, will weigh something. Although this phenomenon reflects a conception of weight as an accidental feature of some physical objects, it may also reflect problems with representing matter as continuous—that is, as repeatedly divisible maintaining its essential properties. To explore the latter possibility, we have carried out a series of related thought experiments.

(2) Most directly, we asked children whether a given portion of play dough was a lot or little bit of material, and asked them to imagine cutting it in half and half again, each time repeating the same question. After several repetitions, we asked whether we would ever reach a point through repeated division that there was no material. Children under 8 claimed that there is point reached where there is no matter at all.

(3) In a related thought experiment, children were asked whether a piece of Styrofoam takes up a lot of space, a little space, or no space at all. They then were asked to imagine the Styrofoam cut in half, half again, half again, and so on, each time. By age 6, all children understood the locution "take up space," judging that the large piece took up quite a bit. But until age 12, half of the children judged that continued halving would yield a piece of Styrofoam so small that it took up no space at all.

(4) Many elementary aged children lack the geometric construction of space that defines points that may or may not be occupied by material bodies. This fact could explain why children failed the above thought experiment, and so we devised one last thought experiment to probe children's understanding of the continuity of matter. We showed children a steel cylinder, told them it was made of iron and was solid, and asked if they could see all the iron. Virtually all children, age 6 and older, said no, because there was iron inside and we can only see the surface. We then asked them to imagine repeated halving, asking of each resultant half whether one could see all the metal now. The question was whether, if our eyes or a microscope were powerful enough, for any given piece of iron we'd ever get to a piece small enough that we could see all the iron in at. Again, until age 12, half of the children said that we would eventually reach a piece where we could see all the iron.

The two thought experiments about continuity of matter occupying space and each piece always having an "inside" are quite different from each other. Yet there was strong within-child consistency on these two measures. Those 6- to 10-year-olds who judged that repeated halving would yield a piece of Styrofoam that occupied no space were the same children who judged repeated halving would yield a piece of iron where we could see all the iron, and those who denied one, denied the other. Almost all 12-year-olds succeeded on both tasks. We concluded that it was not until age 12 that American middle-class children have consolidated a continuous theory of matter.

Measures of Matter

Smith (2007) points out that if weight in CS1 is felt weight, represented in some analog magnitude format and not differentiated from density, then children with CS1 should not understand the measurement of weight. Although they may know how to place objects (or themselves) on a scale and read out the numbers, they should not understand that the total weight of an object is an additive function of the weights of nonoverlapping portions of matter that constitute the object. To explore what children understood about weight and volume measurement, she showed children a $3 \times 3 \times 3$ cm cube in balance with 9 1 gram weights on a scale. Thus, the volume of the object was 27 cc and the weight was 9 grams. The child was simply asked what the weight of the object was and what its volume was. Children who have not yet differentiated weight from density (assessed by the measures described above, such as being unable to order four cylinders both by weight and by heaviness of the metal from which they are made) failed this task.

Conclusions

To establish that children undergo conceptual change in the course of conceptual development, one must first characterize successive conceptual systems, providing evidence that one precedes the other developmentally. One must demonstrate that the two systems are incommensurable, characterizing the concepts in each that can not be expressed in terms available in the other. One must confirm that each provides a coherent, mutually constraining system of representations through which the child makes sense of the world. Finally, one must show that CS2 is indeed difficult for children to achieve, as required by incommensurability. I have discharged all of these obligations. Let me review.

As Carol Smith points out, the explanatory agenda of CS1 and CS2 differ. In CS1, the child is concerned with delimiting physical reality, distinguishing real entities from abstractions and from the world of the mind, and understanding the causal interactions that obtain among physically real entities. Physically real entities include inanimate objects, animals, liquids, powders, shadows, echos, heat, and gases such as steam, and there is indeed much to learn about the causal potential of each kind of entity. In CS2, the material world has been differentiated out of the world of the merely physical real, although this differentiation does not in itself implicate incommensurability. After all, even in CS2, material entities are a subset of physically real entities. But the explanatory agenda of CS2 is completely new, including explaining why entities that weigh different amounts might be the same size, explaining which objects sink and which float, explaining thermal expansion, explaining what is in common among ice, water, and steam, and so on.

Incommensurability requires change at the level of individual concepts, such that a whole set of interrelated concepts are mutually adjusted together.

- Differentiations that implicate incommensurability include: (1) undifferentiated concept *weight/density*, which is neither systematically intensive or systematically extensive, being resolved into an extensive, additive concept *weight* and an intensive concept *density* (i.e., weight per unit volume); and (2) undifferentiated concept *air/nothing* being resolved into the concepts *air*, a gaseous form of matter, and *vacuum*, space unoccupied by matter.
- Coalescences include solids, liquids, and gases being analyzed as different forms of a unitary ontological kind—matter.
- Changes in the cores of concepts include: (1) matter/substance—from perceptual access and capacity for causal interactions to having weight and occupying space; (2) weight—from property of some real entities to necessary property of all matter, providing extensive measure of amount of matter.

Thus, the change from CS1 to CS2 implicates the construction of a new ontological kind, matter. The concept *matter* plays no role in CS1. Weight and volume come to be seen as extensive variables that provide measures of amount of matter, and weight comes to be differentiated from density. The undifferentiated concept *weight/density* functions coherently in CS1, but plays no role whatsoever in CS2 (indeed, is incoherent from the point of view of CS2).

Carol Smith, in explaining the incommensurability, asks us to imagine telling children "Matter is all that which has weight and occupies space." This sentence, which holders of CS2 deem to be true, cannot be expressed in CS1, for CS2 has no concept of matter, nor of weight (distinguished from density), nor of occupying space (in the sense of filling a location specified in some Euclidean coordinates). Holders of

CS1, making sense of this sentence best as they can, would deem it false, for they know of clear examples of physically real objects made out of some kind of stuff that they believe weighs nothing. Conversely, the concepts they would be entertaining are not expressible in CS2. When the child says "This grain of rice weighs nothing at all," she is expressing a true statement in terms of CS1. Although we can translate this sentence into CS2 by replacing "weighs" with "has a felt weight," this translation does not fully capture the child's concept, for her felt weight does not have CS2's weight as a constituent. The two systems are not mutually translatable.

The claim that CS1 and CS2 are each coherent intuitive theories, locally incommensurable with each other, has the consequence that there should be within-child consistency in performance across the various tasks that diagnose them. And indeed there is. Children's judgments and justifications on the open-ended matter/nonmatter sorting task predict whether they have differentiated weight from density, whether they conceive of matter, weight, and volume as continuous, and whether they understand the measurement of weight and volume. Of course, within-child consistency on this wide battery of tasks could be explained by the facts that CS2 responses are more adult, and that smarter or better educated children are more likely to have learned (independently for each piece) the adult responses on these tasks. While within-child consistency is required by the conceptual change position, the abovementioned demonstrations do not, by themselves, provide overly strong evidence for it.

However, in the context of teaching interventions, stronger evidence for the relevant within-child consistency is forthcoming. Basically, one can see whether progress is made piecemeal or in an integrated manner. In a teaching intervention testing bootstrapping models of conceptual change to be described in chapter 11, Smith (2007) found that the half of the 8th graders who began the intervention with a felt-weight pattern of judgments on the Styrofoam thought experiment progressed to an additive-extensive concept of weight after the intervention, whereas for the other half of the 8th graders, their concept of weight was unmoved. There was no difference among these two groups at pretests of weight/density differentiation, matter/immaterial distinction, and measurement of weight and volume. Smith then asked whether progress from on the CS1 pattern of judgment to the CS2 pattern of judgment on the Styofoam thought experiment predicted performance on all of the other tasks in the pretest/posttest battery. It did. The concepts developed as an interrelated whole.

Finally, the CS1/CS2 shift certainly meets the difficulty-of-learning test for conceptual change. Instruction concerning the phases of matter, the measurement of matter, and weight/density differentiation usually is part of the middle school (7th to 9th grade) curriculum. As in other studies of the effectiveness of science instruction, systematic probing of pre- and post-instruction conceptual change often finds little or no progress. Even at the end of high school, many students do not command CS2, and one study of adults studying to be elementary school science teachers showed that a six-week curriculum was needed to induce CS2 in them!

In sum, the transition from physical theory 1 (CS1) to physical theory 2 (CS2) is a case of conceptual change in childhood. Let us turn, in chapter 11, to the explanatory challenge: How is the creation of new conceptual systems, incommensurable with those that precede them, accomplished?

11

The Process of Conceptual Change

Chapter 9 argued that a numerical system that encompasses fractions and decimals is incommensurate with the preschool child's hard-won numeral list representation of the positive integers. Similarly, chapter 10 argued that a physical theory in which weight is conceptualized as a continuous quantity that provides a measure of the amount of matter, and in which weight and density are differentiated, is incommensurate with the preschooler's physical theory, in which material is not differentiated from physically real, and in which the concept of heaviness conflates those of weight and density. In each case, I characterized the structures of two successive conceptual systems, CS1 and CS2. I characterized the incommensurabilities; I provided evidence that children hold each as coherent, stable, symbolic structures; and I showed how hard it is for youngsters to master the respective CS2s. To distinguish the two CS1–CS2 transitions, I will call the successive numerical systems Numerical System 1 (NS1; numeral list representation of integers) and Numerical System 2 (NS2; rational number), and I shall call the two Physical Theories 1 and 2 (PT1 and PT2). In both cases, many high school students in the United States have not made the CS1–CS2 transition, in spite of extensive instruction.

Although, as expected, it is difficult to construct CS2 in each of these two cases, it obviously is not impossible. Some students do so with little instruction, and most can succeed with proper teaching. The challenge to understanding the transition from CS1 to CS2 derives from the incommensurability of the two successive conceptual systems. In cases of incommensurability, the child cannot express the propositions of CS2 in the conceptual vocabulary of CS1. Simply telling children, "Fractions are numbers resulting from dividing one number by another" clearly does not help because children limited by NT1 do not distinguish division from subtraction and reject 2/3 as a number. Similarly, telling children "All matter takes up space and has weight" does not help because those who have only PT1 represent the world in terms of concepts that do not include *matter* or *weight*, concepts that are incommensurable with those the holder of PT2 is expressing with that sentence.

So how is a CS2 that is locally incommensurable with a currently held CS1 that covers the same domain of phenomena constructed? In this chapter I argue that Quinian bootstrapping underlies conceptual change, illustrating with examples drawn from conceptual change in the history of science as well as from conceptual change in childhood. But before I turn to my positive proposal, I begin by mentioning three accounts of the processes involved in theory construction that have wide currency: (1) historically, CS2 is socially constructed, and each child's individual construction is also a social process; (2) the transition between CS1 and CS2 is achieved via noting contradictions and inconsistencies within CS1 itself or as it applies to the world; (3) domain–general cognitive development yields resources the child can draw upon for the purpose of theory construction. None of these accounts is wrong; that is, CS2s that transcend core cognition or antecedent conceptual systems are usually (I would guess always) socially constructed; consistency seeking is a major impetus for conceptual change; and certainly cognitive development witnesses the expansion of information processing and conceptual skills that play a role in conceptual change. But each of these proposals fails to fully engage the problem. In what follows I show how each falls short of the account we want, and I then turn to my positive proposal.

CS2 Is Socially Constructed

There is no doubt that both NS2 and PT2 were originally socially constructed and that children acquire them via social processes. They learn them from adults, through making sense of adult language, through making sense of the artifacts whose development played a role in the construction of each (e.g., mathematical notations, balance scales), and as the result of explicit teaching. While this is certainly true, it does not solve the basic problem of how each child comes to master a set of concepts that are incommensurable with those they currently command.

How do children learn facts and causal accounts that they do not have the concepts to express? This is the basic problem of science education. Consider the problem of how the child constructs the PT2 concept of material entity, superordinate to solids, liquids, and gases. The child can certainly learn, if explicitly told or merely by noting the language adults use, that solids, liquids, and gases are forms of matter. However, they have no choice but to represent this newly learned fact in terms of the PT1 concept of material, which is undifferentiated between physically real and material. The core of the PT1 concept of matter is visibility and tangibility—properties air, a gas, palpably does not have. Being told that air is material may reinforce the physically real/causally efficacious features of the undifferentiated concept, also reinforcing the categorization of heat, electricity, and light as material. But the sentence "Solids, liquids, and gases are forms of matter" implies that nothing else is —that is, not heat, electricity, or light. Thus, the child is led to contradictions he cannot resolve until he has constructed PT2. Initial learning of new facts, by necessity, must be formulated in terms of the available conceptual repertoire, or they must be represented as placeholder structures, not yet interpreted in terms of available concepts.

Contradiction/Inconsistency Detection Is the Engine that Underlies Conceptual Change

Without a doubt, striving for internal consistency is an important part of the process of conceptual change. Children notice failed predictions and internal contradictions among their beliefs. Carol Smith (2007) put children with PT1 in the following quandary. They observed that 50 lentils placed on one side of a miniature seesaw weigh enough to topple it, and they explained this by the weight of the 50 lentils. They then observed that with a narrow enough fulcrum, 1 lentil will topple the card —two related observations being inconstant with their belief that a single lentil weighs 0 grams. They recognized this contradiction but could not resolve it. To do so requires an extensive concept of weight. Similarly, as shown in chapter 10, children with PT1 are concerned that they predict that a given piece of steel will weigh the same as an identical-size piece of aluminum because two pieces of steel and aluminum (differing in size) weighed the same before; and yet, when the pieces are placed on the balance scale, this prediction is falsified. They are concerned, but they do not have the conceptual resources to resolve such contradictions—to do so requires distinguishing weight from density. Chapter 10 pointed out that the scientists in the Florentine academy similarly recognized a contradiction their undifferentiated concept *degree of heat* led them into. Its resolution awaited 150 years of scientific development culminating in Black's differentiation of the concepts *heat* and *temperature*. The Experimenters were metaconceptually sophisticated scientists, students and colleagues of Gallileo. Clearly, adult conceptual capacities do not by themselves guarantee conceptual change.

Noting inconsistencies in one's beliefs serves a motivational role, even for preschool children, and also pinpoints where the cracks in PT1 are (i.e., in the above example, within the concept of weight). But noticing inconsistencies does not provide an answer to the question of where PT2 will come from. How is PT2 constructed, such that it enables the child to differentiate the concepts *weight* and *density* and construct an additive, extensive, concept of weight that is a measure of amount of matter? Appeals to inconsistency detection do not begin to provide an answer to this question.

Domain-General Cognitive Development

Piaget's stage theory purported to describe changes in logical and metaconceptual capacities that occurred during childhood (e.g., only upon reaching the formal operational stage of development in adolescence are children able to reason in accord with propositional logic; see Flavell, 1963, for a tutorial on Piaget's theory). Piaget believed that the domain-general capacities that became available in adolescence made theory building possible. Although Piaget's own formulations of what changes with development have fallen from favor (Carey, 1985a, 1985b; R. Gelman & Baillargeon, 1983), there is no doubt that 10-year-olds have many cognitive resources that 4-year-olds do not—resources that play a role in their capacity for theory development. Increases in information-processing capacity allow the child to consider more aspects of some phenomenon at once, so as to notice contradictions and failed predictions (e.g., Case, 1991; Kail, 1986). Increased meta-conceptual understanding of the nature of knowledge allows the child to monitor his or her comprehension of phenomena (e.g..; Flavell, Speer, Green, & Aughts, 1981), which also may contribute to knowledge restructuring. And older children construct successively more sophisticated epistemologies, specifically of theoretical knowledge, which also would be likely to play a role in the process of theory construction (e.g., Carey, Evans, Honda, Unger, & Jay, 1989; Carey & Smith, 1993; D. Kuhn et al., 1988).

Although it is true that domain-general cognitive development yields new resources for theory development, it is also obvious that cataloguing these resources does not provide a complete explanation for the acquisition of NS2 or PT2. The concepts in NS2 and PT2 are domain-specific; they are constitutive of a particular theory or mathematical system, embodying its ontological commitments and articulating the explanations it provides for the phenomena in its, and only its, domain. Development brings increased information-processing capacities, plus greater meta-conceptual understanding of the nature of knowledge, as well as greater meta-conceptual grasp of theories, of mathematics, of learning, of evidence, and of the importance of belief consistency. Nonetheless, these capacities cannot by themselves explain how the child manages to create a concept of weight differentiated from density, material differentiated from physically real, division differentiated from subtraction, or the concept of a fraction.

What Else Is Needed?

To reiterate what we are looking for: We seek the processes by which new domain-specific concepts, new representational systems, come into being. The process may well be a domain-general one, but it must have the form of taking specific input and outputting new representational resources. Quinian bootstrapping is one such learning process. I make no claims here that it is the only one. For example, the learning algorithms that create Bayes-net representations of causal structure can, in certain circumstances, posit previously unknown variables; and connectionist associative learning algorithms create new systems of representations in hidden layers. Rather, I focus on Quianian bootstrapping because it is a learning mechanism for which there is ample evidence in both the historical and the developmental literatures and because it is capable of explaining developmental discontinuities involving incommensurability.

We necessarily begin with a full account of the concepts available at the beginning of this process, since the conceptual system that the child begins with in any episode of conceptual change is the most important source of the new one. In accounting for the 3-year-olds' construction of the integers, we began with a characterization of number-relevant core cognition (the parallel individuation system, analog magnitude representations, natural language quantification), as well as domain-general skills such as the capacity to represent serial order. The most important sources of NS2 and PT2 are NS1 (characterized in chapter 8) and PT1 (characterized in chapter 10). Nonetheless, we must not lose sight of the problems posed by the local incommensurability of the core concepts of each of these initial conceptual systems with the later ones. In neither case are the new concepts of CS2 definable in terms of those available to CS1, nor are those of CS1 definable in terms of those available in CS2. This is the reason that neither presenting the tenets of CS2 as unproblematic nor creating conflict between evidence and the child's current concepts can be the sole engine of conceptual change. What the child witnesses or hears is assimilated to CS1.

Insights into the mechanisms underlying conceptual change in childhood may be gleaned from accounts of the mechanisms underlying conceptual change in the history of science. This literature suggests that Quinian bootstrapping, as characterized in chapter 8, plays a central role in all episodes of conceptual change. To remind you of the characteristics of Quinian bootstrapping: (1) relations among symbols are learned directly, in terms of each other; (2) symbols are initially at most only partly interpreted in terms of antecedently available concepts; (3) symbols serve as placeholders; (4) modeling processes—analogy, inductive inferences, thought experiment, limiting case analyses, abduction—are used to provide conceptual underpinnings for the placeholders; (5) these modeling processes combine and integrate separate representations from distinct domain-specific conceptual systems; and (6) these processes create explicit representations of knowledge previously embodied in constraints on the computations defined over symbols in one or more of the systems being integrated.

The philosopher Ned Block (1986) vividly illustrated the role of placeholders in conceptual change:

> When I took my first physics course, I was confronted with quite a bit of new terminology all at once: "energy, momentum, acceleration, mass" and the like. As should be no surprise to anyone who noted the failure of positivists to define theoretical terms in observation language, I never learned any definitions of these new terms in terms I already knew. Rather, what I learned was how to use the new terminology—I learned certain relations among the new terms themselves (e.g., the relation between force and mass, neither of which can be defined in old terms), some relations between the new terms and old terms, and most importantly, how to generate the right numbers in answers to questions posed in the new terminology. (p. 648)

In this passage, Block appeals to the process of creating a placeholder structure in which symbols are learned together, in terms of each other. Some of the meaning of these new symbols is provided merely by their conceptual role with respect to each other. Other meaning is provided by their relations to antecedently known terms and concepts. Block is describing the process I call Quinian bootstrapping, but he says little about how these initially largely empty terms become meaningful—that is, about the modeling processes and their consequences that are items 4 through 6 in the above list of characteristics of bootstrapping. Rather, he seems to say that merely learning to use the new terminology is sufficient for assigning meaning to it. This is not so, or at least there is more to say about what is required for learning to use the new terminology. What more there is to say is the topic of the rest of this chapter.

Cognitive-Historical Analysis

In the last quarter of the last century, a small number of cognitive scientists joined forces with historians and philosophers of science in the service of what Nancy Nersessian (1992) dubbed "cognitive-historical" analysis. The source materials of the history of science (publications, notebooks, lab records) are analyzed from the point of view of characterizing the conceptual changes the scientists were undergoing, using and informing cognitive analyses of concepts and of the mechanisms underlying knowledge acquisition. Internalist history and philosophy of science from the mid-20th century, as pioneered by Paul Feyerabend, June Goodfield, N. K. Hanson, Mary Hesse, Thomas Kuhn, Steven Toulmin, and others (e.g., Feyerabend, 1962; T. Kuhn, 1962; Toulmin & Goodfield, 1962) set the stage for these analyses, for these historians and philosophers characterized how successive conceptual systems differed, and they spoke about the role that apprenticeship, analogies, and modeling techniques played in these conceptual transitions. However, the psychological theories available at the time (basically behaviorism and Gestalt psychology—before the cognitive revolution of mid-century) were not up to the task of adding much insight from cognitive science (which did not yet exist) to their project. For example, the best Thomas Kuhn (1962) could do, drawing on psychology to give insight into conceptual change, was to appeal to gestalt shifts as in the Necker cube or duck-rabbit illusion. Nersessian's (1992) cognitive-historical analysis, in contrast, has the explicit models of mental representation from artificial intelligence and cognitive psychology to draw upon.

I have already referred to some of the fruits of cognitive-historical analysis. Work in this tradition places historical analyses and cognitive analyses side by side, using one to illuminate the other. One example already discussed was Wiser's and my study (1983) of the Florentine Academy's thermal concepts, especially heat and temperature, pursued in parallel with Smith's, Wiser's, and my study (C. Smith, Carey, & Wiser, 1985) of intuitive theories of matter, especially the concepts of weight and density. The Florentine Academy was peopled by Galileo's students, the most sophisticated scientists of the day. The members of the Academy were meta-conceptually aware and mathematically gifted experimenters and theory builders. Wiser and I wanted to know whether, in spite of the manifest differences between children and such adults, there are a set of questions that receive the same answers in cases of conceptual change involving both groups. How do successive conceptual systems differ from one another? What counts as evidence for conceptual change in each case? In what sense is CS2 descended from CS1? What, in representational detail, is an "undifferentiated concept." As sketched in chapter 10, we argued that the differentiation of heat from temperature in the history of science and the differentiation of weight from density in childhood provide parallel cases in which these questions receive comparable answers. The analysis of local incommensurability developed in this book is the fruit of cognitive-historical analysis.

Example of Cognitive-Historical Analysis: Darwin

A collaboration between psychologist Howard Gruber and historian Paul Barrett (Gruber & Barrett, 1974), in a case study of Darwin's notebooks, especially the Transmutation Notebooks, provides another example of cognitive historical analysis). Gruber and Barrett discovered that Darwin first formulated a theory of evolution (the Monad theory) that was incommensurable with natural selection. According to the Monad theory, a group of species related by a common ancestor is seen as analogous to an individual animal; the Monad originates (is born) and eventually dies. Environmental factors act directly on individuals to cause adaptation; extinction is explained by the natural end of a Monad life line. Within this framework, Darwin could (and did, for years) work on his description of the exquisite adaptation of species to local environmental variation. Notice that the Monad theory exemplifies the features of pre-Darwinian theories of evolution described by the biologist and historian of biology Ernst Mayr (1982). For example, the Modad theory held that adaptive processes operated vertically, from parent to child, ensuring that offspring would be better adapted to their environments than are their parents (Mayr, 1982; see Shtulman, 2006, for evidence that mastering the theory of natural selection requires conceptual change, and that students initially assimilate it to a system of concepts shared by pre-Darwinians, including the Monad theory).

In sum, Gruber and Barrett discovered that Darwin worked with a novel pre-Darwinian theory of evolution for many years. Darwin needed a theoretical framework within which to think about how well adapted animals are to their environments (the main phenomenon his empirical work explored), and it is no surprise that he began with the assumptions common to all biologists at the time who even entertained the possibility of evolution.

Gruber and Barrett also mined Darwin's notebooks to draw lessons about the dynamics of conceptual change. They emphasized that there is no one moment of conceptual change. Dramatically, Darwin had a page in the Transmutation Notebooks where he wrote "Three principles will account for all," and then articulated the three main premises of natural selection (heredity, variation, selection):

1. Grandchildren like grandfathers.
2. Tendency to small change, especially with physical change.
3. Great fertility in proportion to support of parents.

This page was embellished with exclamation points, stars, and other evidence of Darwin's great excitement (see Gruber & Barrett, 1974, p. 156). Darwin then apparently forgot about these principles, continuing to work and write in his notebooks from the vantage point of the Monad theory for two more years. Gruber and Barrett dryly comment that these facts undermine the view of conceptual change on which it occurs as a single gestalt shift.

Gruber and Barrett did not have the main goal of characterizing the process through which Darwin changed from the Monad theory to natural selection. They endorse what others have said, pointing to his analogy between natural selection and artificial selection and his analogy between Malthus's analysis of the implications of human population explosions and resulting competition for scant resources and the effects of competition for scant resources among members of animal species. Thus, even without thorough cognitive analysis, one sees that Darwin engaged analogical processes in constructing the theory of natural selection. It is likely that if one took the Monad theory as CS1 and carried out a rich historical cognitive analysis, one would discover other aspects of bootstrapping processes.

Example of Cognitive-Historical Analysis: Kepler

Another case study of conceptual change within an individual scientist stands out in its attempts to explicate the mechanism of change in terms of the tools of cognitive science. Dedre Gentner and her colleagues (Gentner, 2002; Gentner, Brem, Ferguson, Wolff, Markman, & Forbus, 1997) have characterized Kepler's CS1/CS2 shift, focusing on one part of the bootstrapping process—Kepler's use of analogy.

Kepler was the transitional figure in physics and astronomy between medieval times and Newton. The goal of the medieval Ptolemaic system was mathematical: to characterize the motion of the planets and stars so as to explain the observed night sky. As is well known, the Ptolemaic system was earth-centered, and the motions were conceived as perfect circles, with thousands of epicycles (smaller circular orbits embedded within larger circular orbits). This cumbersome system was indeed exquisitely accurate in predicting the observed motion of celestial bodies. In the Ptolemaic system, the ontology of the heavens was entirely distinct from that of our world— made of a fifth substance (quintessence), as opposed to the four worldly substances of earth, air, fire, and water. Planets and stars were thought to be eternal and unchanging, embedded in nested crystalline spheres, their motion explained by the rotation of the rigid spheres themselves. The motion of each sphere was caused by the motion of the nearest more outer sphere, with the ultimate cause of motion being that of the outmost sphere (the prime mover; explanation has to stop somewhere).

As Kepler began his work, three important developments had undermined Ptolemaic/medieval astronomy. First, improved instruments, including telescopes, had permitted the discovery of a supernova and a comet, both contradicting the doctrine of the fixed heavens. Second, the comet went through the locations of supposed crystalline spheres, undermining their existence. The abandonment of the doctrine of the crystalline spheres left the explanation of planetary motion open, and Kepler considered the Stoic doctrine that the planets had some internal source of motion, which he dubbed "anima motrix" (moving soul). Third, Copernicus had published his monumental work overturning a geocentric universe. In the Copernican system, the center of the earth's supposed circular orbit was taken to be the center of rotation of most (but not all) celestial bodies; the vast number of cycles and epicycles needed to describe the motion of the six known planets and the sun in the Ptolemaic system was reduced to 34.

Kepler is known for his three laws of planetary motion, including the discovery that the orbits of the planets are ellipses, with the sun as one focus. Kepler, like all other astronomers, was concerned with getting the mathematical description of planetary motion right, and working with the unparalleled observations of Tyco Brahe, his discovery of the elliptical orbit of Mars was his first major achievement. In his system, the 34 Copernican cycles and epicycles that sufficed to describe planetary motion was further reduced to six ellipses. How and why Kepler discovered his three laws of planetary motion is a fascinating story in the history of science, but it is not the focus of Gentner and her colleagues' work. They stress that Kepler's importance in the history of science goes way beyond his discovery of these three laws. Kepler predated Newton's integration of celestial phenomena with earth-based physics, and formulated a precursor to the Newtonian concept of gravity. It is this major conceptual change that Gentner seeks to understand.

As in all cases of conceptual change, one crucial ingredient is the setting of a new explanatory agenda. On a grand scale, Kepler did so by seeking a physical explanation for why the planets revolved around the sun. This explanatory goal evolved through his long career, and the answer he formulated required conceptual change. More locally, early in his work on the mathematics of the motion of the planets, Kepler noted that the speed of the planets was slower the farther they were from the sun. This generalization holds both between planets and within the orbit of each. Of any two planets, the one more distant from the sun moves slower around the sun. And within each planet's orbit, the speed of the planet is less the farther from the sun it is. These generalizations are the consequence of Kepler's Second Law: a line from the sun to a planet sweeps out a constant area in a given amount of time. In thinking about this, Kepler wondered whether each planet's anima motrix got weaker the farther from the sun it was. This was not a very satisfactory explanation, for in some ways it just restated the phenomenon and it was an unexplained fact—a coincidence. The only other idea he could come up with (a bold abductive leap) was that there was only one anima motrix, in the sun itself, and that the sun's anima motrix caused the motion of the planets. For this explanation to work, it must be that the causal effects of the sun's anima motrix became weaker as the distance from the sun got greater. The explanation was more satisfactory, although it violated the core of the concept of an anima motrix, which explains the motion of the entity itself and not other entities. To develop this explanation and transform the concept of anima motrix, Kepler drew on a central analogy that he worked with for the rest of his career. Gentner and her colleagues have provided an analysis of how the analogy worked and what role it played in Kepler's conceptual change.

Kepler analogized the anima motrix emitted by the sun to light emitted by the sun. Figure 11.1 is Kepler's diagram, emphasizing that (1) light is emitted by the sun, (2) light becomes less dense as the distance from the source (the sun), (3) light illuminates planets upon reaching them, and (4) the illumination is dimmer if the light is less concentrated. By analogy to light, the anima motrix was hypothesized to become less powerful as the distance from the sun increases, thus explaining why the motion of a planet is slower the farther it is from the sun. This analogy did considerable work for Kepler. Most important, it played a role in Kepler's major conceptual change: the transformation of the anima motrix (motive soul) to the vis motrix (motive force) or virtu motrix (motive power). In Kepler's later writings he used the latter terms, conceptualizing the cause of the motion of the planets to be a physical entity emitted by the sun, just like light. Gentner and her colleagues argue that the

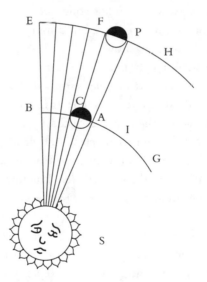

Figure 11.1. Kepler's diagram of the propagation of light from the sun, illuminating planets at different distances from the sun (redrawn from Gentner et al., 1997). Gentner, D., Brem, S., Ferguson, R. W., Wolff, P., Markman, A. B., & Forbus, K. D. (1997). Analogy and creativity in the works of Johannes Kepler. In T. B. Ward, S. M. Smith, & J. Vaid (Eds.), *Creative thought: An investigation of conceptual structures and processes* (pp. 403–459). Washington, DC: American Psychological Association. Adapted with permission.

depth of the analogy supports this conceptual change. That analogy supports a new ontology is a powerful point; virtu or vis motrix is a new kind of physical entity, a physical casual power that operates across space and influences the motion of the planets. As I said above, it is the precursor of the concept of gravity.

How did the analogy support this conceptual change? First, the analogy provided an existence proof that the effects of a central source could weaken with distance. Second, it provided a way of thinking about action at a distance. Kepler elaborated the analogy by pointing out that light is invisible as it passes through space, having a visible effect only upon reaching a surface to illuminate. So, by analogy, the causal power of the vis/virtus motrix could have no detectable effects as it moves through space—until, that is, it contacts a body that it causes to move. This aspect of the analogy was further elaborated by the observation that, although light travels instaneously through space, some of its effects (e.g., heating and fading the surfaces it contacts) take time because these effects require physical interactions with the bodies contacted. So too, the vis motrix travels instantaneously through space, but causing the motion of a body contacted involves an interaction with the body's matter, and thus unfolds over time. Third, light is conserved, merely becoming less dense with greater distance. Likewise, Kepler surmised, the vis motrix. Fourth, the analogy allowed Kepler to conclude that the vis motrix was not identical to light because light was blocked by intervening bodies (in eclipses), but motion was not so affected. And finally, the analogy provided a way of thinking about why the speed of a planet decreased linearly with distance from the sun, whereas brightness decreased by the square of the distance from a light source. Kepler's explanation was that it is a surface (two dimensions) that is illuminated by a source, but speed is in only one dimension. Thus, illumination decreases by the square of distance but speed decreases in proportion to distance.

I highly recommend the papers on Kepler's use of analogy by Gentner and her colleagues. They analyze the structure of the analogy between light and the vis motrix analogy's structure (e.g., what objects and relations are mapped on to each other across the source and target domains) and also provide an analysis of the role of this analogy, plus two others Kepler also drew on, in Kepler's conceptual change. As in all uses of analogies, Kepler highlighted the common structure between the source and target domains, and he used what Gentner calls "allignable differences" to illuminate the mechanisms involved (e.g., the 2-D/1-D difference, or the differential effects of eclipses on illumination and caused motion).

Compare Kepler's analogy with the analogy central to the bootstrapping account of the construction of the integers offered in chapter 8. Of course, we see all of the differences we might expect between a self-conscious, meta-conceptually aware, mathematically sophisticated genius and your average 3-year-old. Kepler was aware of analogizing, explicitly discussing the proper, productive use of analogies in theory building and explicitly distinguishing his analogies from the undisciplined and unsystematic analogies of contemporary alchemists. Nonetheless, as in other cases of comparing conceptual change in childhood with that of historical case studies, there are commonalities across the two. Kepler was engaged in Quinian bootstrapping, and his bootstrapping process exemplifies all of the key features of Quinian bootstrapping that I laid out in chapter 8. Kepler's initial abductive hypothesis—that something in the sun causes planets to move—was a placeholder structure. The resources of language allowed him to formulate that hypothesis, but the "something" was completely unspecified. Kepler rejected his first partial interpretation for this placeholder concept—*anima motrix*—in which the sun's anima motrix was hypothesized as capable of causing the motion of other bodies. This idea did violence to the concept of anima motrix, the hypothesized internal motive powers of the moving entities themselves. But at the beginning of the process of conceptual change, Kepler had nothing to replace the concept *anima motrix* with. Modeling processes—in this case especially, the analogy with light emitted by the sun and that "something"—filled in the placeholder. The analogy with light (and also magnetism) allowed Kepler to formulate a concept that was the direct precursor to Newton's concept of gravity—a physical force that determined the motion of the planets. These modeling activities drew upon concepts that were fairly well understood, and Kepler carried out considerable work on them in themselves. They were drawn from domains of phenomena that were initially totally distinct from the motion of planets —the domains of light propagation and of magnetic attraction. Kepler's modeling process combined the constraints from the phenomena being modeled (including his three laws of planetary motion) with the causal structure from his source analogy. The result was a new conceptual structure, with concepts interdefined in totally new ways, not expressible in the language of Ptolemaic/Aristotelian physics.

Nersessian's Cognitive-Historical Analysis: Example 3

Nersessian's goals for cognitive-historical analysis are much broader than accounting for conceptual novelty; she seeks to understand scientists' training practices, how scientists construct arguments and communicate, how they design and execute experiments (both real and thought), how they invent and use mathematical and other modeling tools, and how they invent scientific instruments. Here I am concerned with the lessons she draws from cognitive-historical analysis for understanding the mechanisms underlying conceptual change.

Nersessian originally formulated her cognitive-historical research program in a case study of Maxwell. I do not understand the physics or mathematics of this case well enough to give a feel for the conceptual change Maxwell achieved, but according to Nersessian (1992), the work of Faraday had already brought into question the Newtonian view that electricity and magnetism were separate phenomena. Maxwell accepted Faraday's conjecture that electricity and magnetism were aspects of the same phenomenon, and that electric and magnetic actions involve continuous transmission through space (Faraday) or the ether (Maxwell). Maxwell sought a mathematical treatment of these actions; and to achieve it, he had to invent a mathematics more powerful than the Newtonian calculus of differential equations (partial differential equations and the vector calculus). Maxwell had done work in the areas of fluids and electricity, where since it was too difficult to represent the underlying Newtonian forces in differential equations, scientists (including Maxwell himself) working in the field then called "continuum mechanics" had begun to invent the mathematics of partial differential equations.

Thus, Maxwell began with concepts of magnetic action and electrical action, and with Newtonian mathematics, and ended with concepts of electromagnetic fields with representations of forces that do not accord with Newton's three laws and a mathematics capable of expressing the concepts of quantum mechanics and relativity. I urge the mathematically sophisticated among you to read Nersessian's papers.

As in all cases of conceptual change, the incommensurability is local. Many of the concepts of CS2—electricity, magnetic attraction, charge, the speed of light, and so on—were known to Maxwell at the outset. What Maxwell did was to create a unified mathematical representation of the propagation of electric and magnetic forces with a time delay, and he calculated the velocity of the propagation. He discovered the mathematical form of the dependence of electric fields on magnetic ones (Maxwell's second equation), formulating the modern concept of electromagnetic field.

In this case study, Nersessian places analogical reasoning in a broader context of cognitive modeling activities. She notes the prevalence of analogies, visual representations, thought experiments, and limiting case analyses in Maxwell's work, and mentions also their prevalence in other episodes of conceptual change. She shows how all of these modeling activities are effective means of abstracting, examining, and revising the constraints on existing representational systems, in light of the constraints provided by a new target problem, and thus are effective means of generating a new conceptual structure.

Maxwell's work was initiated by a new explanatory agenda: to provide a mathematical account for electromagnetic phenomena discovered by Faraday. Any theory he constructed had to satisfy four constraints: (1) electric and magnetic actions are at right angles to each other, (2) the plane of polarized light is rotated by magnetic action, (3) there is a tension along the lines of magnetic and electric action (this was Faraday's speculation, and Maxwell accepted it), and (4) there is a lateral repulsion between lines of magnetic and electric action. Maxwell noted that there was a mechanical analogy consistent with these constraints: mechanical properties of fluid vortex media under stress. Maxwell was well versed in the new mathematical techniques relating to continuum phenomena, and his abductive leap was that these may be what are needed to model the phenomena Faraday discovered. Like Kepler's, Maxwell's use of analogy was self-conscious, deliberate, and central to his conceptual changes. He used what he called a "physical analogy": embodying the math in a physical form (e.g., specifying a fluid vortex, not just the equations). These physical analogies had a visual component or were often represented visually. In his words, these were easier to think with than were the formalisms.

By the end of this process, which extended over several years of solid work and involved three iterations of model building and the analogical mapping process, Maxwell had invented a mathematical representation more powerful and more general than Newton's. In Maxwell's final paper on the theory, he published the abstract schema that was the output of this process—the equations of electromagnetic theory. By the end of the process, he had created a schema that stood on its own as a basis for representing and explaining electromagnetic phenomena. But, as Nersessian points out, he would not have arrived at this point without the modeling processes he deployed. Maxwell's mathematical representation of a field, a non-Newtonian dynamical system, laid the groundwork for relativity theory and quantum mechanics. The bootstrapping process entailed changes in the representations of both the target and source domains.

Nersessian's account of how Maxwell used analogy draws on the cognitive literature on analogy, especially the slightly different analyses of Dedre Gentner and Keith Holyoak (see Gentner, Holyoak, Kokinov, 2001, for a recent review of cognitive science of analogy) Nersessian goes beyond the analyses in these papers, however, in addressing the use of analogy in conceptual change. As in all cases of conceptual change, at the outset of the process there was no source domain that had the full structure of electromagnetic theory or of the mathematics to represent it. The modeling processes Maxwell engaged in are central parts of Quinian bootstrapping. Nersessian shows how satisfying the constraints from both source and target domain served as an abstraction technique—the schema Maxwell ended with was the structure common to both domains that survived the iterations of mapping. She points out that other modeling processes, such as thought experimentation and carrying out limiting case analyses, are similarly abstraction and idealization devices. All of these techniques make use of the human capacity for simulation, engaging mental models in which some of the constraints are only implicitly or tacitly represented. Indeed, this is one of the sources of the usefulness of the visual dimension of the analogy that Maxwell used to represent the Newtonian forces in a fluid vortex. The visual representation was easier to use in thought than were the equations, and this is partly because constraints on computations over visual models are often merely tacit.

With these fruits of cognitive-historical analysis in hand, let us turn to the question of how children create a representation of number that transcends the positive integers, embracing rational number (NS2), and how they create a representation of matter in which weight and density are differentiated (PT2).

Bootstrapping a Representation of Rational Number and a Representation of Matter: A Paradox

An understanding of fractions, decimals, ratios, and proportionality is what divides scores on the SAT tests taken by college-bound seniors in high school above or below the median. That is, half of college-bound 17- to 18-year-olds have not fully consolidated NS2. Not surprisingly, then, figuring out curricular interventions that are effective in fostering the NS1/NS2 transition is one of the most heavily researched topics in math education. Educators working on this problem develop curricula that facilitate Quinian bootstrapping. A full characterization of the bootstrapping process involved is beyond the scope of this book, but I will say something about what is known and point you to some wonderful literature on the topic.

Not surprisingly, children do not initially understand the notational conventions that give symbols such as .5 or ½ their meaning. These notations thus serve the role of the explicitly represented placeholder symbols that are part of Quinian bootstrapping. Further, many authors have suggested that the process through which the new concept of rational number is created involves modeling numbers in terms of representations of physical quantity. Computations defined over representations of physical quantity include quantitative operations such as splitting, sharing, folding, comparing, and perceiving proportionality. These provide a qualitative appreciation of some aspects of the inferential role of rational numbers and ratios, and mapping physical quantity and these operations onto the placeholder symbols is part of the bootstrapping process. In this context, representations of physical quantities are the source domain, and mathematical representations are the target domain. The mathematics educators Joan Moss and Robbie Case, and also, independently, Jere Confrey, have implemented curricular interventions based on these ideas (Confrey, 1994; Moss & Case, 1999; see also Resnick & Singer, 1993).

As we will see below, bootstrapping curricula embodying the modeling techniques deployed by Maxwell have success in fostering the PT1/PT2 transition within a theory of matter. These curricula involve modeling weight in terms of number (NT2—number including rationals, infinitely dense) and density in terms of ratios. In this context, mathematical representations are the source domain and representations of physical quantity are the target domain. Hence, the paradox: mapping number to continuous quantities plays a role in coming to appreciate the NS2 concept of rational number, but at the outset of this process, children do not have a concept of continuous quantities. Mapping quantities like weight and volume to NS2's number plays a role in coming to appreciate the PT2 concepts of weight, volume, and density, but at the outset of this process, children do not have a concept of rational number. Although this seems paradoxical, this is how bootstrapping works. It is an iterative process, and often it involves co-construction of both source and target domains.

Constructing a Representation of Rational Number: NS2

Moss and Case's work can serve as an example of bootstrapping curricula developed to foster NS2. They argued that by the time children are 9 or 10 years of age, they have a global representation of proportions and a numerical structure that supports splitting and doubling. They further argued that coordinating these is part of the bootstrapping process that yields a representation of fractions and decimals. Their innovative 4th-grade curriculum begins with percents, as a way of numerically representing the qualitative notions of full, nearly full, half full, and nearly empty, as these apply to a beaker of water. Students are then led to coordinate intuitive understanding of halving physical quantities with learned numerical halving strategies. The curriculum subsequently moves to two-place decimal notation, and finally to fraction notation. Rigorous pretests and posttests have demonstrated that students using this curriculum outperform students using standard curricula.

The mapping between number and physical quantity is likely to be particularly important in children's coming to appreciate the existence of rational numbers and that they are repeatedly divisible. Although young children may deny that there is a number between 0 and 1, they can see that a line of unit length exists between the origin and the first unit on a number line. In Moss and Case's curriculum, measurement activities support the existence of quantities such as 1 ½ inches and ½ cup. Once children see how, through measurement, natural number maps onto quantities such as length or amount of matter, their representation of the physical quantity as repeatedly divisible could—if the mapping were maintained—support understanding number as repeatedly divisible.

Note that the learning process envisioned by such curricula is Quinian bootstrapping. Placeholder structures (mathematical notation) are initially uninterpreted. New expressive power derives from creating mappings between initially separate conceptual domains—in this case, representations of number and representations of continuous quantities. Initially, the computations defined over each of these separate domains are separate, and the curriculum supports mapping these to one another (e.g., halving, finding averages). In addition, each initial representational system makes explicit and salient different aspects of the resulting structure. When the final structure is built, the child has transformed his representations of the initial domains as well as created something new that is qualitatively different from either (see chapters 9 and 10 for defenses of the claims that each of these NS1–NS2 and PT1–PT2 transitions involve qualitative changes).

Remember the paradox. These bootstrapping processes presuppose that young children conceptualize some physical quantities as repeatedly divisible, so that their representations of physical quantity can serve as a base domain for modeling rational number. As we saw in chapter 10, children do not initially consider matter continuous in this sense, nor do they initially conceive of weight or different aspects of spatial extent (e.g., length, area, or volume) as continuous magnitudes. Studies that have examined children's reasoning about the infinite divisibility of material objects, the amount of space they occupy, and their weight show that young elementary- school age students can at best imagine only a limited number of divisions before the matter disappears and the amount of weight or occupied space goes to zero. Based on these findings as well as many other findings concerning children's concepts of weight, density, and material kind, chapter 10 argued that coming to conceptualize matter, weight, and volume as continuous physical quantities involves conceptual change, the construction of PT2.

In spite of this conundrum, I endorse Moss and Case's insights into how one might use representations of physical quantity as a source domain in bootstrapping a representation of rational number. As mentioned above, this is how analogy works when part of the bootstrapping processes that support conceptual change in mathematics and science. As has long been known, advances in mathematics and in physical theory proceed hand in hand—as witnessed by Newton's theory building in physics and his developmental of the calculus needed to represent his theory or by Maxwell's development of both electromagnetic field theory and the mathematics needed to represent it (partial differential equations).

Evidence for the Interdependence of PT2 and NS2

The studies described in chapter 9 of children's representations of rational number also included the tasks that diagnosed children's concepts of matter, weight, and space that were described in chapter 10. In a result of theoretical and practical importance, students' patterns of judgments on the tasks that diagnose a representation of number as infinitely divisible, and those that diagnose a representation of matter as infinitely divisible, are found to be strongly related. All (100%) students who showed the Never Get to Zero pattern described in chapter 9, judging that numbers could be divided ad infinitum, also judged that matter would continue to exist and take up space with repeated divisions. Similarly, 64% of the children who demonstrated that they understood the continuity of matter on this task also demonstrated that they understood that number is infinitely divisible. Indeed, some students who had infinitely divisible number and matter patterns explicitly justified their number answers by analogy to the matter questions (which had come earlier in the interview). For example:

- "Same as Styrofoam, could keep going forever" (S45, Grade 6)
- "There's an endless amount of numbers between 1 and zero; like Styrofoam, there's always something there" (S46, Grade 6)
- "It goes back to the matter thing. You could divide a molecule and keep dividing . . . an infinite number" (S47, Grade 6)

As can be seen by the above percentages, student judgment of the infinite divisibility of matter and the space it occupies *reliably preceded* their judgment of the infinite divisibility of number, as would be expected if mapping number to continuous quantity is an important part of constructing a representation of rational number. Roughly one-fourth of the children judged matter itself as infinitely divisible, concluding that it would always occupy some space, but judged number not to be infinitely divisible, whereas the reverse pattern never occurred. Thus, the intuition that an understanding of the continuity of physical quantity could possibly play an important role in the bootstrapping NS2 receives support.

Finally, these data reveal that, though student judgment of the infinite divisibility of matter itself and the space occupied by matter reliably precedes that of number, their judgment of the infinite divisibility of weight seems to occur at roughly the same time as that of number. Only 2% of students (1 of 50) understood the infinite divisibility of number and not that of weight, and only 4% (2 of 50) understood infinite divisibility of weight while having no insight about infinite divisibility of number (Get to Zero patterns). Further, those students with transitional patterns on number were in between in their understanding of weight: one half already understood the infinite divisibility of weight, while the other half did not. These results have implications for what could be a two-way process by which a conceptual change in one domain might reciprocally aid in the change in another, just as in Newton's or Maxwell's joint mathematical and physical conceptual changes.

The high level of coherence between children's thinking about the infinite divisibility of weight, on the one hand, and the infinite divisibility of number, on the other, is a form of mutual dependence that one would expect if change involves a conceptual bootstrapping process rather than simple knowledge accretion. At first glance, the mutual dependence may seem inflated by the fact that similar thought experiments probed children's concepts of number, matter, volume, and weight. While that is so, children's responses to the thought experiments predict other indications of their understanding of rational number (e.g., their abilities to order fractions or explain notation; see chapter 9) and other indications of their understanding of matter (e.g., their differentiation of weight from density, their sorting of entities as material versus nonmaterial, their appreciation that solid entities are material throughout, and their understanding of weight and volume measurement—see chapter 10). Thus, the thought experiments reflect conceptual changes in each case, and the two conceptual changes are indeed mutually supportive.

Bootstrapping Processes and Science Education

The fact that a sizable proportion of American adults have failed to construct either PT2 or NS2 is consistent with the claim that conceptual change is required in each case (evidence from difficulty of learning). But more to the present point, these facts reflect a major failure of math and science education in this country. These topics are repeatedly taught in the math and science curriculum (in the case of fractions and decimals, every year from grade 3 through high school).

Over the past 25 years, cognitive scientists and science educators have joined forces to document the failure of science and math education, to understand why, and to develop curricula that do better. Science and math education fail for many reasons, and some of them are of theoretical importance to the argument of this book. Science and math education require conceptual change. Very frequently, students bring a CS1 to the classroom that is incommensurable with the CS2 the teacher is presenting. For example, before encountering Newtonian mechanics in the classroom, adolescents have created an intuitive theory that shares much with the impetus theory of the Middle Ages; before encountering theories of thermal phenomena in the classroom, adolescents have created an intuitive theory that shares much with the Florentine Experimenters' source-recipient theory (see chapter 10); and before encountering Darwin's theory of natural selection in the classroom, adolescents have often constructed an intuitive theory of evolution that shares much with pre-Darwinian theories in which environmental factors cause adaptive changes within individual lineagesforces cause changes (e.g., for mechanics, Clement, 1982; McCloskey, 1983; Viennot, 1979; for thermal theories, Wiser, 1988; for evolution, Shtulman, 2006).

In each of these cases, qualitative problems have been devised that diagnose the student's initial theory. And what is universally found is that after one or two years of science instruction in high school, and even in college, many students' initial theories remain intact. These students have totally failed to assimilate CS2. How it is possible to pass (or even do well) in formal science courses without constructing the CS2 being taught is an interesting question, beyond the scope of this chapter. Basically, students memorize local factual information, equations, and problem-solving strategies without integrating these into coherent explanatory systems. When one sees science education as facing the problem of conceptual change, this finding is not entirely shocking (although the teachers shown these data from their own classrooms are invariably shocked). Science education is more likely to succeed if the curricula developers are aware of the systematic and deeply entrenched CS1s students bring to the classroom, and if the curricula are designed with what is known about the modeling and bootstrapping processes that underlie conceptual change in mind. The Moss and Case curriculum on fractions mentioned above is one example of the fruit of this work. Here, I describe the work of Carol Smith and her colleagues (Smith, 2007; Smith, Maclin, Grosslight, & Davis, 1997; Smith, Snir, & Grosslight, 1992; Snir, Smith, & Grosslight, 1993), exploring experimental curricula that support student construction of PT2.

The American public first faced the crisis in American science education in 1957, when the Soviet Union put a satellite, Sputnik, into orbit, when we Americans did not yet have the capability of doing so. The U. S./USSR space race was initiated in response to this blow to our intellectual and technological ego. Congress mandated huge spending on science education, and some of the finest scientists in the country turned their attention to the problem. One of the products of this effort was Integrated Physcial Science (IPS), a curriculum and textbook aimed at middle school/early high school students, that begins by teaching PT2. The first three sections of the IPS curriculum introduce measuring techniques for mass and volume, present these quantities as the fundamental properties of material entities, and characterize density as M/V and as a characteristic property that distinguishes material kinds. To ensure that these concepts are connected to the real world, students are engaged in hands-on activities, including inventing reliable measurement techniques and exploring phenomena that require PT2 to be properly represented and explained (e.g., exploring a variety of transformations such as thermal expansion, dissolving, and chemical reactions, to discover that mass is conserved even when volume is not, calculating the third variable of mass/density/volume when two are known). IPS is an elegant and well-thought-out curriculum that emphasizes formal definitions, precise measurement, and explicit quantitative calculations. However, this is not enough. When the qualitative tasks described in chapter 10 that diagnose children's concepts of weight, mass, volume, density, and matter are given as a pretest and posttest to these sections of IPS, one finds that the students who benefit from IPS are those who have already constructed PT2 before the beginning of the curriculum, at least on a qualitative level. Those in the grips of PT1 at the outset of the IPS curriculum hold PT1 at the end of it as well (Smith et al., 1997). Conceptual change is hard.

What went wrong? Two things. First, although the scientists and science educators who developed the elegant curricula in the wake of Sputnik understood the science deeply and recognized the importance of engaging students in hands-on activities, they did not explicitly grasp the problem of science education as one of conceptual change and therefore did not engage in the research of characterizing the CSIs their students brought to the classroom. In turn, they did not realize that, in addition to being provided formal definitions and paradigms of problem-solving activities involving these definitions, students need to engage in the modeling activities and bootstrapping processes required to create meaning for the terms in these formal definitions. I repeat myself: One cannot simply tell students "Matter is that which has mass and occupies space" and expect them to understand what is said. And without a continuous and extensive concept of weight, measurement procedures that presuppose that the weight of an entity is the sum of the weights of arbitrarily small constituents make little sense.

Curricula that draw on the modeling activities that have been discovered through cognitive-historical analysis are successful in inducing conceptual change. This is important for two reasons. First, in the present context, science education becomes a testing ground for theories of the bootstrapping processes and modeling activities that underlie conceptual change. Second, the research involved in creating and testing these innovative curricula points the way to effective means of fostering a scientifically literate public.

Bootstrapping Physical Theory 2 in a Classroom Context

We seek a characterization of the bootstrapping processes that underlie the transition from PT1 to PT2. A subset of the conceptual changes between these two theories include: (1) the extensive variable weight is differentiated from the intensive variable density, (2) weight comes to be represented as a necessary property of all material entities, (3) material entities are differentiated from nonmaterial physically real entities such as energy, heat, and light, (4) air is differentiated from the vacuum, and (5) solids, liquids, and gases are coalesced into the category of material entities. Although these changes are interrelated (necessarily so, since the concepts are interdefined), Smith and her colleagues have shown that one effective wedge into the process is working on developing an extensive concept of weight as a measure of amount of matter. Notice that this was also the intuition of the developers of IPS. But in Smith's hands, learning to measure weight (or mass) is seen as part of a series of conceptual changes resulting in the concept of weight as an extensive quantity. In contrast, the IPS developers assumed the extensive concept of weight and saw themselves as engaging children in understanding how scales measure weight in grams.

Smith deploys conceptual modeling processes. Here I draw on Smith's (2007) most recent study of the bootstrapping process. Learning to measure weight or volume requires creating a mapping between number (including fractions) and a physical magnitude that is not yet represented by the child. As in all episodes of conceptual change, a first step is the recognition of a new explanatory agenda. The explanatory goals of PT1 are to understand causal interactions among physical entities, and to distinguish physical entities from abstract and mental entities that do not causally interact with physical entities. The explanatory goals of all junior high school curricula on matter, in contrast, include distinguishing material from immaterial entities and constructing concepts of weight, mass and, volume as extensive properties of matter, differentiating these quantities from the intensive variable, density. Engaging students in the task of explaining the linear relation between weight and volume (given constant material), suggesting the possibility of different-size objects weighing the same (given contrasting material), explaining sinking and floating, explicitly distinguishing material from immaterial physically real entities, and so on motivates them in the curriculum. Of course, students with PT1 cannot consistently represent these phenomena, let alone explain them. Smith begins her curricular interventions with clinical interviews and written tests that diagnose students' physical theories, drawing on some of the qualitative measures described in chapter 10 (sorting entities into material and immaterial ones, the clay-ball task, weight and density ordering, the cutting Styrofoam task, measurement activities, drawing models of weight, density, and volume, and so on). In junior high school, many students have PT1, some are transitional, and a few have constructed a qualitative appreciation of PT2 even before instruction. These clinical interviews are very engaging to students, who recognize that there are inconsistencies among their concepts, and thus the pretest measures are a motivating factor in the curriculum.

The first part of the curriculum has five parts and extends over several weeks. First, students as a group sort entities into material and immaterial entities, arguing over unclear cases and attempting to formulate universal generalizations concerning necessary and sufficient conditions for being material. No consensus is reached. Second, as in IPS, techniques for the measurement of weight (or mass) and volume are introduced. One technique for measuring mass involves adding 1 gram weights to one side of a balance scale until the total weight is determined, and discovering some of the additive properties of weight and volume (e.g., the total weight of two objects is the sum of each of their weights, according to these measurement techniques). Comparable activities support measurement procedures and discoveries about the additive properties of volume. These activities also include deriving the mass and volume of small amounts of matter by division. Notice that these correspond to the central activity in the Moss and Case (1999) rational number curriculum. The children in Smith's studies are three to five years older than those in Moss and Case's, but not all have already created the relevant concepts of fractions. Thus, the bootstrapping is necessarily two-way.

These activities underlie the mapping of weight to number, beginning to draw out the extensive concept of weight from the undifferentiated weight/density concept of PT1. The curriculum then extends to cases where the derived measures exceed the limits of the measuring device (e.g., determining the approximate weight of a single lentil, given the weight of 50 lentils). These activities are supported by thought experiments. Children in the grips of PT1 maintain that a single lentil weighs nothing at all—0 grams—and they are challenged to explain how, then, 50 lentils can weigh something. This part of the curriculum culminates in a trip to a laboratory with an analytical balance, at which a fingerprint and a signature are weighed, further consolidating the differentiation of weight or mass from felt weight and providing a resolution of the lentil thought experiment in terms of the sensitivity of measurement devices. The final activities involve measuring the amount of space taken up by air in the lungs (lung capacity) and the weight of air in a balloon (comparing the weights of a full and empty balloon).

Posttests established that two-thirds of the students who go through this curriculum improve; all children who had begun to construct the relevant part of PT2 (weight conceptualized a continuous, extensive, property of all material entities) consolidated this theory, as did some who began firmly in PT1. Others who began with PT1 made progress, becoming transitional. Not all children progressed (one-third did not); conceptual change is hard. Smith showed that the prerequisites for progression were (1) some understanding of matter as continuous (though not necessarily as involves weight) and (2) some minimal understanding of number as infinitely divisible.

With these aspects of PT2 in hand, Smith and her colleagues have shown that an analogical mapping process structurally identical to that employed by Maxwell facilitates further conceptual change (e.g., Smith, Snir, & Grosslight, 1992; Smith & Unger, 1997). Smith and her colleagues employed visual analogies that embody the mathematics of intensive/extensive quantities as a source domain to facilitate middle-school children's differentiation of weight and density. The two extensive quantities in the source domain were number of dots and number of boxes, and the intensive quantity was density—number of dots per box. The curriculum includes meta-conceptual lessons about the nature of models and also lessons involving mapping dots per box models to extensive and intensive quantities already better understood (e.g., sweetness, where number of boxes represent volume of water, number of dots represent amount of sugar, and dots per box represents sweetness).

Remember the problem we are facing. In cases of conceptual change, at the beginning a person does not yet have the concepts in the target domain that will map onto the relevant concepts of the source domain. When children begin, they have an undifferentiated concept *weight/density*. If children have not yet differentiated weight from density (heavy from heavy kind of stuff), then how are they to map weight onto total number of dots and density of material onto number of dots per box? This is a deep problem and explains why the process takes so long— years when scientists are constructing mappings for the first time, and months in the science-education cases, where children are being guided by curricula designed by people who already understand the target theory and the mapping between it and the source domain.

Students are first introduced to the source domain—dots per box, number of boxes, number of dots. They see that they can predict the third variable from any two. For example, they can predict how many dots a figure will contain, given how many boxes and how many dots per box. They use the model to explain why there is a linear relation between number of boxes and number of dots, given a common density. After they have explored the source model, discussed the nature of models and modeled sweetness, they explore several phenomena in the domain of matter. These might include the linear relation between weight and volume given a constant material, the fact that two objects that are the same size might weigh different amounts, and the phe-nomena of sinking and floating. They then begin to map the target domain of matter onto the source domain. They are guided to map weight (or mass) onto number of dots, volume onto number of boxes. This is where the first part of the curriculum, described above, is essential, for it provides some wedge into extensive concepts of weight and volume. The dots/box modeling activities reinforce and consolidate the relevant extensive concepts. Furthermore, density is visible in the model in the form of dots per box. What remains is for students to see that there is a physical magnitude that does explanatory work that corresponds to dots per box. They can use the mapping to explain why two objects that are the same size might weigh different amounts, why the relation between weight and volume is linear given a single density, what the relevant variables are to explain sinking and floating, and so on. These modeling activities support the differentiation of weight from density, with weight providing a measure of amount of matter and density being a characteristic property of material kinds.

There are three crucial ingredients to such curricula. First, the child must master phenomena in the target domain for which an explanation depends on the differentiated concepts. Remember, incommensurability is only local, so some of these phenomena are represented by the same concepts across PT1 and PT2 and some are not. Second, they must see the analogy between these phenomena and the corresponding phenomena in the source domain. Finally, the visual analogy provides an anchor for the distinct roles each differentiated concept plays in understanding these phenomena.

In these pages I cannot begin to do justice to Smith's subtle and important work. In some versions of the curriculum, the lessons end with a challenge that requires changing the models deployed so far: thermal expansion. Up to this point, density has been modeled as a constant and characteristic property of material kind. Upon being introduced to the phenomenon of thermal expansion, students are engaged with modifying the models (there are many different ways this could be done), and also engaged in further reflection on the process of creating models in the service of theory building. These activities then support the differentiation of weight from density and the mathematics of intensive and extensive physical quantities.

This process is not magic. Not all children going through this process succeed in making the mapping. The first part of the curriculum provides a beginning inkling of the extensive concept of weight as a measure of amount of matter, and if children map this onto the extensive concept of number of dots, they are already part way there in distinguishing it from density. They must then grasp that there is a distinct physical variable in the domain of matter that corresponds to the variable dots per box, and the curriculum provides activities that support this insight. Smith and her colleagues have demonstrated that this curriculum outperforms curricula that do not deploy conceptual modeling techniques (including IPS, in Smith et al., 1997) in facilitating the construction of PT2, providing evidence for the role of bootstrapping processes in conceptual change.

Other important work in science education similarly draws on and informs the lessons concerning theory change that have emerged from cognitive-historical analysis. For example, Marianne Wiser (1988; 1995; Wiser & Amin, 2002) developed visual models similar to those used by Smith—models that embody the mathematics of intensive/extensive quantities and engaged high school students in using them to model thermal phenomena. She showed that this curriculum is more effective than others that do not engage Quinian bootstrapping in facilitating the differentiation of heat from temperature. She also explored the relations between these qualitative models and more realistic molecular models, and showed that children maintain PT2 (in this case of thermal phenomena) six months after the end of the curriculum, but forget the models. They truly are bootstrapping devices.

Quinian bootstrapping is central to these curricula. Formula such as $D = M/V$ or $D = W/V$ are placeholder structures, as are verbal statements such as "This steel ball weighs the same as this larger aluminum one," or "All matter has mass." Until the child has distinguished weight (or mass) from density, and material entities from physically real ones, these statements and formula can be at best only partly interpreted in terms of concepts already represented. Cognitive modeling processes create meaning for these placeholder structure—students model physical phenomena, creating analogical mappings between mathematical representations (and visual models of those mathematical representations) and the physical world, and engage in thought experiments and limiting case analyses. The meanings are constructed from the relations among concepts directly represented in the placeholder structures and from the computational and referential roles of the representations deployed in the modeling activities.

One purpose of Smith's and Wiser's work in science education is to explore the role of Quinian bootstrapping in conceptual change. The curricula succeed for several reasons, in addition to the modeling activities embedded within them. Students are explicitly engaged in conceptual change. That is, there is a meta-conceptual component to these curricula. Students are encouraged to become aware of their initial theories, to create explicit models of them, and to discover that other students have different models of the same phenomena. Lessons are built that encourage students to reflect on the role of models in scientific understanding, and students collaborate on building better models. Creating scientific understanding is a social process, and is about understanding the world in terms of consistent models that express universal generalizations. Curricula that create classrooms that engage students in these goals succeed in inducing lasting conceptual change.

They are an existence proof that the failure of science education is not inevitable (see Donovan, Bransford, & Pellegrino, 2000, for an excellent overview of the lessons from the cognitive science of conceptual change for science education). More important to my present purpose, the success of curricula built around Quinian bootstrapping processes provides evidence for the role of these processes in conceptual change.

Conclusion

Those who believe that there are important discontuities in knowledge structures over the course of conceptual development must characterize them. In what ways are later conceptual systems discontinuous with their ancestors? Chapters 8 through 11 provided two different answers to this question: Sometimes conceptual development results in representational systems with greater expressive power than their antecedents, and sometimes successive conceptual systems are locally incommensurable. Chapter 11, like chapter 8, took on the challenge of accounting for developmental discontuities of each type. Quinian bootstrapping underlies all of the conceptual discontinuities discussed in chapters 8 through 11, both in the course of historical changes and in the course of science and math education.

12

Conclusion I: The Origins of Concepts

I end with two concluding chapters. The first (chapter 12) summarizes the main points from the preceding 11 chapters. This chapter, along with the introduction (chapter 1), provides an overview of the argument and a road map through it. The second concluding chapter (chapter 13) steps back and considers the implications of the picture of conceptual development offered in these pages for a theory of concepts. Chapter 13 introduces new material, placing work on the origin of concepts in the context of selected controversies from cognitive science and philosophy concerning the very nature of concepts.

The Story so Far

Human beings, and only human beings, create deep, explicit, conceptual understanding. No animal but us can ponder the causes and cures for pancreatic cancer or global warming. Providing an account of where the concepts that articulate human understanding come from—concepts such as *cause, cancer,* and *global*—poses a formidable challenge. I believe that cognitive science, the disciples of psychology, philosophy, linguistics, and computer science, can meet this challenge; and my goal has been to illustrate the progress that has been made, illuminating the developmental history of many specific concepts—*object, agent, cause, positive integer, fraction, matter, weight,* and *density* being the most fully considered.

A full account of the origin of human concepts must appeal to three different time scales and three different types of processes. Over millions of years, evolutionary processes create innate representational capacities. Over hundreds of years, learning processes in a cultural–historical context create new representational resources that, in turn, are expressed and maintained in language and in the cultural products they make possible. And then, over years, each child must transcend the innately given representational capacities by mastering the culturally constructed ones.

I have said nothing about the evolutionary processes that create innate representational capacities; rather, I have appealed to data from infants and nonhuman animals for evidence concerning what some of these innate capacities are. Also, I have said little about the cultural construction of concepts, alluding only to the nature of theory change in historical time and to some of the bootstrapping mechanisms involved. My focus has been the third time scale—individual ontogenesis.

To explain the origin of concepts over ontogenetic time, one must specify the initial state, describe the changes that occur in development, and characterize the learning mechanisms that underlie change. The latter task is especially pressing if these changes involve the construction of concepts previously unrepresented (and even unrepresentable). With respect to characterizing the initial state, I argued that the innate stock of primitives is not limited to sensory, perceptual, or sensori-motor primitives. Rather, innate primitives include the representations that articulate core cognition, as well as central systems of representation that include concepts such as *cause* and that support language learning. With respect to developmental change, I argued that conceptual development includes episodes of qualitative change, resulting in systems of representation that are more powerful than, and sometimes incommensurable with, those of core cognition. And with respect to the origin of new representational capacities, I sketched and provided evidence for Quinian bootstrapping processes.

Core Cognition

Historical empiricists, such as Locke and Hume, and historical rationalists, such as Descartes, would all find comfort in what 21st-century cognitive science has to tell us about concept acquisition. As the rationalists insisted, there are innate input analyzers that compute perceptual representations —veridical representations of the distal world. Contrary to empiricist theories, these input analyzers are devices that do not have to be constructed by learning processes that operate over sensory representations. The example I alluded to in chapter 2 was depth perception.

Still, as the empiricists believed, an informational semantics (see chapter 13) seems appropriate for both sensory and perceptual representations. The input analyzers that create representations of color, of depth, and so on evolved to work as they do, and evolution is a process that is responsive to veridicality. That is, we have evolution to thank for guaranteeing that our representations of depth have the content they do and can fulfill the computational role required of them. Also, as the empiricists believed, garden-variety learning processes create previously unrepresented concepts from this initial stock of representational resources. What the empiricists did not envision were learning processes that create new primitives. But that is a long story, the story of this book.

Explaining the human capacity for deep conceptual understanding begins with the observation that evolution provides conceptual primitives much richer than the empiricists thought. The first half of this book characterized core cognition, for core cognition comprises most of infants' first conceptual representations. The domains of core cognition that are well supported empirically are: (1) the world of middle-size, middle-distant objects, including their paths of motion, spatial relations, and physical interactions (including contact causality; chapters 2, 3, and 6); (2) the world of agents, including their goals, communicative interactions, attentional states, and causal potential (chapters 5 and 6); and (3) the world of numbers, including parallel individuation, analog magnitude representations of the approximate cardinal values of sets, and set-based quantification (chapters 4 and 7).

Representations in core cognition differ from perceptual representations in their abstractness and their conceptual content. Two logically independent and empirically distinct properties of core cognition representations lead me to attribute them conceptual content. First, they cannot be reduced to spatio-temporal or sensory vocabulary. One cannot capture concepts such as *goal*, *object*, *approximately 10,* or *cause* in terms of primitives such as locations, paths of motion, shapes, and colors. Second, they have a rich, central, conceptual role. In this latter respect, the distinction between the representations of core cognition and those of perception is only a matter of degree. The output of perceptual processes such as representations of distance, color, and shape are centrally accessible, represented in working-memory models, and support action such as reaching. To successfully reach for an object, one must represent where it is, and to anticipate how one should grasp it, one must represent its shape. By 7 months of age, infants' reaches are guided by such representations. Thus, perceptual representations have some central computational role to play in explaining infant behavior. The representations in core cognition are similarly centrally accessible, represented in working-memory models, and support action such as reaching—for example, infants make a working-memory model of the individual crackers in each of two buckets and guide their choice of which bucket to crawl to from quantitative computations over those models. However, chapters 3 through 6 documented the very much richer conceptual role for the outputs of core cognition input analyzers. Indeed, a variety of quantitative computations are defined over working-model representations of sets of objects—infants can sum continuous quantities or compare models on the basis of 1–1 correspondence, and slightly older infants categorically distinguish singletons from sets of multiple individuals. Infants represent objects relative to the goals of agents, and infants' representations of physical causality are constrained by their conceptualization of the participants in a given interaction (as agents capable of self-generated motion or as inert objects). Thus, the conceptual status of the output of a given core cognition system is confirmed by its conceptual interrelations with the output of other core cognition systems.

In all other respects, the representations in core cognition resemble perceptual representations. Like representations of depth, the representations of objects, agents, and number are the output of evolutionarily ancient, innate, modular input analyzers. Like the perceptual processes that compute depth, those that create representations of objects, agents, and number continue to function continuously throughout the life span. And like representations of depth, their format is most likely iconic.

It is an empirical claim that there are systems of representation with these properties. While I believe all of the core cognition systems I discussed in chapters 3 through 5 have all of them, I emphasized the evidence for different properties in each example, and the current state of evidence is stronger with respect to some of the properties than to others. Let's look at each distinctive property in turn.

Dedicated Input Analyzers

A dedicated input analyzer computes representations of one kind of entity in the world and only that kind. All perceptual input analyzers are dedicated in this sense: the mechanism that computes depth from stereopsis does not compute color, pitch, or number. Similarly, the mechanism that computes north from the night sky, guiding indigo buntings' celestial navigation, plays no role in representing anything else of importance to indigo bunting life. It is a strong empirical claim about systems of core cognition that the entities in their domains are supported by innate dedicated input analyzers. Here, I separate the question of whether there are dedicated domain-specific input analyzers from the question about innateness, leaving innateness to the next section.

The nature of the mechanisms that identify the entities in systems of core cognition is a topic of ongoing research, and I touched on this research in each case study. With respect to core object cognition, much more is known about the adult perceptual input analyzers than those for infants, for object perception has been a topic of study since the time of the Gestalt psychologists. Still, as reviewed in chapters 2 and 3, we know that for both infants and adults, spatio-temporal evidence is privileged. This is one of the signatures that identifies infant object representations with those of mid-level object-based attention and working memory in adults (supporting continuity; see below). The spatio-temporal information that yields representations of objects includes being bounded in 3-D space, and the cost of noncohesion in tracking and forming memory representations of entities both for infants and for adults when attentional load is high is another signature that identifies these two systems as one and the same. These results (reviewed in chapter 3) also provide evidence for the claim that the input mechanisms are dedicated; perceptually very similar displays (pile-shaped objects, crackers) engage tracking mechanisms if cohesive, and fail to do so (piles of blocks, piles of sand, broken crackers) if shown to have a history of noncohesion. The visual perceptual devices that analyze input for 3-D boundaries and for spatio-temporal continuity create representations of just one class of entities—objects—just as those visual perceptual devices that analyze the input to the two eyes for disparity create representations of just one property in the world—depth. The input analyzers are dedicated to forming object representations.

Chapter 4 discussed in some detail what is known about the input analyzers that are dedicated to taking attended sets of individuals as input and outputting analog magnitude representations of number. I contrasted two possible types of such input analyzers—serial, iterative ones like the accumulator model of Meck and Church (1983), and parallel ones like that of Dehaene and Changeux (1993) and that of Church and Broadbent (1990). Each of these classes of devices is dedicated to number representations. The evidence favored the parallel models, for neither infants nor adults take longer to form analog magnitude representations of large rather than small sets. Chapter 4 provided further evidence for this position, as analog magnitude representations are formed, both by adults and infants, under conditions in which the individuals cannot be separately attended or tracked. Besides illustrating the research program that seeks to characterize the nature of the input mechanisms that compute the symbols that articulate core cognition, this discussion illustrated the importance of doing so in the quest for explaining the origin of concepts. The parallel systems do not implement counting algorithms, and therefore evidence that they underlie analog magnitude number representations makes it all the more unlikely that these in turn underlie explicit verbal counting (see chapter 8).

Chapter 5 raised different problems concerning the input analyzers that create representations of agents, agents' attentional states, and agents' goals. Evidence was presented that suggested that infants use spatio-temporal descriptions of the motions and interactions among objects to do so, but that the static appearance of the entities in an event (e.g., presence of eyes and hands) also plays a role in creating representations of agency. Chapter 5 left open whether one of these sources of information is primary. For example, infants may initially identify agents through patterns of interaction, and they may then learn what these agents look like. Alternatively, the innate face detectors infants have may serve the purpose of identifying agents, allowing them then to learn how agents typically interact. A third possibility is, like mother recognition in chicks, agency detection is such an important problem for human infants that evolution built in two dedicated input analyzers to do the trick.

Thus, just as for perceptual representations (color, depth, shape), specialized input analyzers identify the entities in the world that are in each domain of core cognition. Characterizing the nature of these input analyzers is an important part of the program of characterizing core cognition.

Innateness

Representations are mental symbols—states of the nervous system that refer to entities in the world. Although it is possible that infants think about things in the world before they've had any experience with them, this is not required for the representations to be innate in the sense I mean it. "Innate" simply means unlearned—not the output of an associative process, a hypothesis-testing mechanism, or a bootstrapping process—that is, not the output of any process that treats information derived from the world as evidence. What I mean for a representation to be innate is for the input analyzers that identify the represented entities to be the product of evolution, not the product of learning, and for at least some of its computational role to also be the product of evolution.

For the most part, the evidence reviewed in these pages for core cognition did not derive from experiments with neonates. There is good evidence for object representations by 2 months of age, for representations of causality by 6 months of age, for core cognition of intentional agency by 5 months of age, and for set-based quantification by 15 months of age. But 2 or 5 or 6 or 15 months is a lot of time for learning. Why believe that the representations tapped in these experiments are the output of innate input analyzers, and why believe that the demonstrated inferential role that provides evidence for the content of the representations is unlearned? I discussed this question in each case study, appealing to four types of arguments.

First, success at some tasks can be good evidence for some target representational capacity, whereas failure is not necessarily good evidence that the target capacity is lacking. This is because some other representational capacity, independent of the target one, may be needed for the tasks and may not yet be available (not yet learned or not yet matured). This obvious point does not buy us much—one can always say that some unspecified performance limitation is masking some competence an infant has. This move is of absolutely no interest without a specific proposal for what that performance limitation would be and without evidence that it is indeed playing a role in the failure. I gave several worked-out examples of successful appeals to performance limitations masking putatively innate competences. For instance, remember the explanation for why it is not until 2 months of age that infants create representations of a complete rod partially hidden behind a barrier when they are shown the protruding ends undergoing common motion. Specifying a single individual from patterns of common motion of parts is supposed to be part of core cognition and thus innate, but there is evidence that neonates fail to represent such arrays in terms of a single rod (chapters 2 and 3). One possible explanation for this failure is that below 2 months of age, infants cannot notice the common motion across the barrier, so they lack the critical input to the computation. Three types of evidence suggested that this may be the correct account. If the barrier is made thinner, younger infants succeed. Also, at the critical age, studies of eye movements show that infants who actually look at both ends of the rod succeed, whereas those who look at only one end of the rod fail, having focused on its motion relative to one boundary of the barrier. Finally, neonates succeed if the input is stroboscopic, thus preventing the infant's attention from being drawn to the misleading juncture between one portion of the rod and one edge of the barrier. Thus, it is possible to bring evidence to bear on the general hypothesis that performance limitations sometimes mask putatively innate representational competences.

A second type of evidence that a given representational capacity may be innate in humans, in spite of not being observed until some months after birth, is data that show that it is manifest in neonates of other species. Examples offered were depth perception, which emerges without opportunities for learning in neonate goats and neonate rats, and object representations, which are observed in neonate chicks. This line of evidence is obviously indirect, providing only an existence proof that evolution can build input analyzers that create representations with the content in question.

A third type of evidence I offered for the innateness of the input analyzers and computational machinery that constitutes core cognition was also indirect: the simultaneous emergence of different aspects of a whole system. As soon as infants can be shown to form representations of complete objects, only parts of which had been visible behind barriers, they also can be shown to use evidence of spatio-temporal discontinuity to infer that two numerically distinct objects are involved in an event, and also to represent object motion as constrained by solidity (chapters 2 and 3). Similarly, different aspects of intentional attribution emerge together; representing an entity as capable of attention increases the likelihood of representing its action as goal-directed, and vice versa (chapter 5). And so, too, are causal representations integrated as soon as they are evident at all (chapter 6). This developmental pattern provides indirect evidence that the relevant representational systems might be innate. The argument is simple: if the generalizations that underlie infants' behavior are learned from statistical analyses of the input (represented in terms of spatio-temporal and perceptual primitives), it is a mystery why all of the interrelated constraints implicated in the core cognition proposals emerge at once. Infants have vastly different amounts of input relevant to statistical generalizations over perceptual primitives. Relative to the thousands of times they have seen objects disappear behind barriers, 2-month-old infants have probably never seen rods placed into cylinders, and rarely have they seen solid objects placed into containers. Yet the interpretation of both types of events in terms of the constraints on object motion that are part of core cognition emerge together, at 2 months of age. Statistical learning would be expected to be piecemeal, not integrated.

Finally, I appealed to learnability considerations in arguing that the representations in core cognition are the output of innate input analyzers. If the capacity to represent individuated objects, numbers, agents, and causality is learned, that is, built out of perceptual and spatio-temporal primitives, then there must be some learning mechanism capable of creating representations with conceptual content that transcend the perceptual vocabulary. In the second half of the book, I offered Quinian bootstrapping as a mechanism that could, in principle, do the trick, but this type of learning process requires explicit external symbols (words, mathematical symbols), and these are not available to young babies. Associative learning mechanisms could certainly underlie the learning of regularities in the input, such as: if a bounded stimulus disappeared through deletion of the forward boundary behind another bounded stimulus, there is a high probability that a bounded stimulus resembling the one that disappeared will appear by accretion of the rear boundary from the other side of the constantly visible bounded surface. But such generalizations would not be formulated in terms of the concept *object*.

There is no proposal I know for a learning mechanism available to nonlinguistic creatures that can create representations of objects, number, agency, or causality from perceptual primitives.

Long Evolutionary History

Some of the first work on analog magnitude representations of number was carried out on rats and pigeons, using operant conditioning methods. Until recently, the methods used to explore the mental representations of animals and those of human infants have been very different. One cannot keep a baby at 80% body weight, highly motivated to work for food. Nor, obviously, would one want to. One cannot and would not want to carry out experiments that require days or even months of training, and thousands of test trials. Obviously, the animal methods permit much more detailed examination of the stimulus parameters that are guiding responses. Nonetheless, these methods provide evidence for some of the same systems of representation as make up core cognition in infants (see chapter 4 for data in support of analog magnitude number representations from both traditional animal training methods and methods that diagnose spontaneous representations).

Research with babies relies on spontaneous representations, diagnosing what draws their attention and what representations guide their actions. As reviewed in chapters 2 through 7, the same methods we use with babies—simple habituation methods, violation-of-expectancy looking-time studies, simple choice studies—also yield reliable data with nonhuman primates. These methods confirm that nonhuman primates as diverse as cottontop tamarins and *Rhesus* macaques spontaneously represent their world in terms of some of the same core cognition systems as underlie human infants' representations of their world. With respect to analog magnitude number representations, cottontop tamarins become habituated to a series of sequences of a constant number of tones that vary in all other parameters (total length of sequence, density of tones, total sound energy, and so on) just as babies do, dishabituating when a new number of tones is played. As for babies, discriminability is a function of ratio, implicating analog magnitude representations of number (chapter 4). With respect to parallel individuation, object representations with the same signatures as those that articulate human mid-level object-based attention and working memory, including the limits on parallel indi-viduation, have been demonstrated in cottontop tamarins and *Rhesus*, using both violation-of-expectancy looking-time methods and the two-bucket set-choice method (chapter 4). These methods also provide evidence for nonnumerical set-based quantification in both *Rhesus* macaques and pre-verbal babies (specifically the singular/plural distinc-tion; see chapter 7).

The evolutionary history of agent representations is more contro-versial. Recent work indicates that nonhuman primates including chimpanzees and *Rhesus* macaques do represent agents in terms of goals, attentional states, and even informational states like ignorance (he doesn't know the grape is there; see chapter 5). There is some evidence that primate representations of mental states may be encapsulated in more specialized computational systems (e.g., in the service of competition for food or mates) than are the general-purpose human representations of agents. Many scientists are at work trying to understand the limits of nonhuman primates' representations of agents relative to those of human infants. Are humans the only primates that cooperate widely, and thus monitor whether they are sharing attention to some external state of affairs, and thus seek to communicate, as Tomasello (Tomasello et al., 2005) now holds? Are humans the only primates that teach, and thus the only ones whose infants learn by imitation of cued demonstrations, as and Csibra and Gergely (2006) suggest? Perhaps. Nonetheless, the capacity for understanding agents in terms of intentional states preceded human evolution by a very long time (see chapter 5).

Clearly, addressing the evolutionary history of systems of conceptual representations is a central part of understanding the origin of concepts. To the extent that systems of representation are shared with nonhuman primates, it is unlikely that they were culturally constructed by human beings, drawing on human-specific symbolic capacities.

Iconic Format

A full characterization of any mental representation must specify its format as well as its conceptual role. W hat are the mental symbols like? How are they instantiated in the brain? For most mental representations, we know little about representational format. Of the core cognition systems discussed in these pages, the question of format is clearest for number representations, so my discussion of format was concentrated there (chapter 4).

I intend the distinction between iconic and noniconic formats to be the same distinction that was at stake in the historical debates on the format of representation underlying mental imagery Whether there are "imagistic" mental representations was hotly debated in the 1970s and 1980s. See Block (1981) for an overview of the early debate; see Kosslyn, Thompson, & Galin (2006) and Pylyshyn (2002, 2003) for their latest salvos. I take this debate to be settled in favor of the existence of both iconic and noniconic mental symbols. Iconic representations are analog; roughly, the parts of the representation correspond to the parts of the entities represented. A picture of a tiger is an iconic representation; the word "tiger" is not. The head in the picture represents the head of the tiger; the tail in the picture represents the tail. The "t" in "tiger" does not represent any part of the tiger.

The very name "analog magnitude representation" stakes a claim for its format. Analog representations of number represent as would a number line—the representation of two (————) is a quantity that is smaller than and is contained in the representation for three (————). We do not know how these analog representations are actually instantiated in the brain—larger quantities could be represented by more neurons firing or by faster firing of a fixed population of neurons, for example. Many plausible models have been proposed (see chapter 4). However analog magnitude representations are instantiated in the brain, their psycho-physical signatures strongly suggest this type of representational scheme. If nonlinguistic number representations were noniconic, as "7" and "8" are, there is no reason that it would take longer to judge that 7 is less than 8 than to judge that 5 is less than 6. That discrimination satisfies Weber's law (is a function of the ratio of set sizes) suggests that number representations work like length discrimination, time discrimination, brightness discrimination, loudness discrimination, and so on. All proposals for how these continuous dimensions are represented also deploy analog magnitudes.

I have claimed that all of core cognition is likely to be represented in iconic format. Although I believe this to be so, I admit this is a speculation. Consider the working-memory models that constitute the parallel individuation system of object representations. The fact that these representations are subject to the set-size limit of parallel individuation implicates a representational schema in which each individual in the world is represented by a symbol in working memory. This fact does not constrain the format of these symbols. A working-memory model for two boxes of different front surface areas, for instance, could be consist of imagelike representations of the objects (□□), or they could be abstract symbols whose parts do not correspond to parts of the objects [object (square, 3 square inches), object (square, 2 square inches)]. These models must include some representation of size bound to each symbol for each object because the total volume or total surface area of the objects in a small set is computable from the working-memory representations of the sets. This fact was demonstrated in the habituation studies in which infants are sensitive to total surface area in a set and not to number of objects in the set, and also in the cracker-choice studies in which infants choose the bucket with most cracker stuff rather than the most crackers (chapter 4). To me, the most plausible model for how this is done implicates iconic representations of the objects, with size imagistically represented, as well as shape, color, and other perceptual properties bound to the symbols iconically. As I envision it, the computations that are defined over working-memory models of this form include summing the continuous variables encoded iconically. Of course, it is possible that infants directly form analog magnitude representations of the continuous variables, and directly add them, but this alternative makes a mystery of the set-size signature. If infants could do that for three objects, what would prevent them for doing it for four or five or six? At the very least, the results presented in chapter 4 constrain the order of computations. The iconic alternative laid out in chapter 4 explains the set-size signature, even when continuous variables are driving the response.

I have several other reasons for suspecting that the representations in core cognition are iconic. Iconic format is consistent with (through not required by) the ways in which the representations in core cognition are perception-like; the dedicated input analyzers all make use of perceptual/sensory data and the content of the symbols is close to those data, while nonetheless going beyond them. They thus could easily have iconic format, with conceptual role providing the conceptual content. Second, just as static images may be iconic or symbolic, so too may representations of whole events. Consider an event in which a ball is dropped onto the stage floor. This event could be represented in iconic format, like a movie unfolding through time, in which the parts of the movie correspond to the parts of the event. Or it could be represented by any one of many natural language sentences, "It was the floor the ball fell onto to." If infants represent events in iconic format, this could help make sense of the apparently retrospective nature of the representations that underlie many violation-of-expectancy looking-time experiments (chapters 2–6). If the baby creates a movielike representation of an event that has just unfolded, when an outcome is revealed, he can consult that iconic representation in working memory, noting whether the outcome is consistent with it. Finally, that core cognition may be represented in terms of iconic symbols, with some of its content captured in encapsulated computations defined over these symbols, may help to make sense of the extreme lags between understanding manifest in infant looking-time studies and that manifest only much later in tasks that require explicit representations (see chapters 3, 5, 8–11).

The guess that the format of all core cognition is iconic is just that—a guess—but the considerations just reviewed lead me to favor this hypothesis. Whether this guess is right or not is a very important open question.

Constant Through the Life Span

There are many constraints to satisfy in creating useful and reliable systems of representation. Finding reliable enough clues to the presence of some entity and building representational formats that support the types of computations needed are not easy problems to solve. The distinctive signatures of processing within each core cognition system reflect how natural selection satisfied these constraints and allows us to examine whether core cognition representations are computed throughout the life span. Perhaps it is not surprising that they are. One might think that any representations important enough that evolution created dedicated perceptual input devices to detect specific classes of entities in the world, and important enough that evolution built specialized inferential machinery for thinking about those entities, should be useful for adults as well as children. However, this first thought is not necessarily correct. Some innate representational systems serve only to get development off the ground.

The learning processes (remember there are two) that support chicks' recognizing their mothers, for example, operate only in the first days of life, and their neural substrate actually atrophies when their work is done.

Another reason to doubt that core cognition systems would operate throughout the lifetime is that some of the constraints built into them are not actually true; it is not true, for instance, that one material entity cannot pass through the space occupied by a solid object such as a table or a person. Once one has undergone the conceptual changes needed to represent objects in terms of the particulate theory of matter, in which there is space between atoms for subatomic particles to pass through, it would be at least possible that the core cognition system would be overridden. It is most definitely an empirical question whether core cognition is constant throughout the life span. The core systems discussed in chapters 3 through 7 are. Core cognition input analyzers are modular and informationally encapsulated, protected from explicitly held conceptual knowledge. We may know that it is a color change that is necessary and sufficient for the motion of a color disk in a computer world, but we still perceive only the causality specified by Michottian launching (chapter 6). Similarly, we may know that ducks don't turn into cars, but we will compute numerical identity in an apparent motion experiment to make two instances of duck/car motions rather than two longer duck/duck and car/car paths (chapters 2, 3, and 7).

The evidence for continuity in the core cognition systems described in this book consisted of finding the same signatures of processing in adulthood and childhood. For analog magnitude representations of number (see chapter 4), these common signatures include: (1) discrimination is subject to Weber's law across the life span (although sensitivity becomes greater with age); (2) the input analyzers that create analog magnitude representations of cardinal values of sets operate in parallel over the individuals in the set; (3) many different types of individuals (sounds, events, objects) can be enumerated; (4) representations can be created even when the individuals are not resolvable. For object representations and parallel individuation (see chapter 3, 4, and 6), these common signatures include: (1) working-memory models are subject to absolute set–size limits across the life span (three in infancy, three or four in adulthood); (2) the same spatio-temporal criteria are privileged over property and kind information in the computation of individuation and numerical identity; (3) the same spatio-temporal parameters specify contact causality; (4) and the same stimulus parameters specify continued existence behind barriers versus ceasing to exist. Continuity has been least studied in the case of agent representations, but in the few cases that have been studied, adults establish teleological representations from motion of geometric stimuli under the same conditions infants do. Also, adults attribute attentional states of faceless robots under the same conditions infants do, and fail to do so when infants fail to (chapter 5).

Continuity through the life span is an important property of core cognition, for several reasons. The science of the mind seeks to characterize cognitive architecture that carves the mind into meaningfully different subsystems differentiated in terms of theoretically significant properties. Continuity is one such property; most conceptual representations are not continuous throughout development. Also, the property of continuity is most likely related to several other distinctive properties of core cognition, especially those that derive from the ways in which the representation resemble perceptual representations (innate input analyzers, possible iconic format).

Domain-Specific Learning Mechanisms

All of the core cognition systems I described are learning mechanisms. Their primary function, I would guess, is to enable the infant to acquire useful information about his or her immediate environment. Where is that object, so I can reach for it? What is my mother intending to do? Which container has more cracker-stuff? It is often overlooked that acquiring such information requires learning, and therefore, core cognition systems are learning mechanisms. Furthermore, the systems that acquire such information are domain specific; the mechanisms that pick out small sets of middle-size, separately movable objects, and that represent their properties, including quantitative variables, their locations, and their causal interrelations, are different from those that create representations about the particular goals of particular agents. Thus, core knowledge systems are domain specific learning mechanisms.

This being said, the least-studied aspect of infant core cognition systems is how they themselves are enriched by learning. How do object, agent, number, and causality representations themselves change as the child acquires knowledge of entities of these types? Although core cognition systems operate continuously through the life span, like perceptual systems, they are certainly not static and unchanging. There has been no research into whether core cognition includes specialized within-module learning mechanisms aimed at creating the representations that will be recruited in the episodic learning discussed above, akin to the learning process through which the indigo bunting identifies north in the night sky.

Beyond Core Cognition: Other Sources of Innate Concepts

The representations in core cognition are input to central reasoning processes, and it is certainly possible that there are also innate nonmodular central processes that yield conceptual representations. Chapter 6 considered the possibility that there may be an innate central mechanism for forming causal representations. Michotte suggested that causal representations arise in core cognition, part of the domain of object representations. He posited innate input analyzers that output causal representations on the basis of strictly limited spatio-temporal parameters of interactions among physical objects. Chapter 6 rejected Michotte's proposal on the grounds that causal cognition integrates across different domains of core cognition (object representations and agent representations) from as early in development as we have evidence for causal representations at all.

Innate central causal representations could come in either of two quite different varieties. There may be innate central processes that compute causal relations from patterns of statistical dependence among events, with no constraints on the kinds of events. Or there may be specific aspects of causality that are part of distinct core cognition systems (e.g., Michottian contact causality within the domain of core object cognition and intentional causality within the domain of agent cognition), and these may be centrally integrated innately. No evidence I know of would allow us to decide between these two broad types of possibilities. Further, they are not mutually exclusive; both types of central integration of causal representations could be part of infants' innate endowment.

I discussed that the developmental origins of causal cognition brings home the point that there is no reason to believe that core cognition systems are the sole source of innate conceptual content. Rather, just the opposite. One of the main reasons to believe that core cognition representations are conceptual rather than perceptual is their rich conceptual role—that they enter into inferences, including causal inferences, that integrates them. A natural consequence of this rich inferential role is the possibility of innate central representations whose content goes beyond that embedded in the systems of core cognition themselves.

Beyond Core Cognition: Public Symbols

Other animals do not create external public representations of quantifiers, sortals, epistemic states, causality, and so on. Other animals may represent their world in terms of such concepts, but they do not communicate about such things. I assume that domain-specific learning mechanisms, together constituting a language acquisition device (LAD), make possible language acquisition, but I have made no effort to summarize the current state of the art in characterizing the LAD. Whatever its nature, the LAD is another way innate cognitive architecture goes beyond core cognition, for the symbols in language are not iconic.

Language acquisition and conceptual development are intimately related. The representations in core cognition support language learning. They provide some of the meanings that lexical items and morphological and syntactic contrasts express. Chapter 7 considered how prelinguistic set-based quantification supports the learning of natural language quantifiers, and prelinguistic representations of individuals support the learning of terms that express sortals. Because I seek here an account of the origin of concepts, I focused mainly on the effects of language learning on conceptual development. Language learning makes representations more salient or efficiently deployed (chapter 7; so-called weak effects of language on thought). Language also shapes thought in the strongest possible way—Quinian linguistic determinism (chapters 8–11). Language learning plays a role in creating new representational resources that include concepts previously unrepresentatable.

Chapter 7 reviewed two cases in which very early language learning affects nonlinguistic representations. First, learning, or even just hearing, labels for objects influences the establishing/deploying of sortal concepts. In her original studies on object individuation, Xu (Xu and Carey, 1996) found that most 10-month-old infants do not yet comprehend the labels for the objects she used in her studies, but those who did (based on parental report) succeed at individuating the objects on the basis of the kind distinction alone. Xu also found that labeling the objects as they are shown to the babies one at a time (whether familiar kinds with familiar labels or novel kinds with novel labels) leads 9-month-old infants to succeed at establishing representations of two objects in the events, whereas in the absence of contrastive labeling or when the appearance of objects is associated with other contrasting noises, they fail.

The second case concerned morphological development. Chapter 7 reviewed evidence that mastery of explicit linguistic singular/plural morphology plays a role in deploying this distinction in nonlinguistic representations of sets. In the studies on set-based quantification, Barner and his colleagues (2007) found that 22- to 24-month-old infants spontaneously deployed a singular-plural distinction in a nonlinguistic object search task only if they were already marking plurality linguistically.

Chapter 7 argued that these are both most likely weak effects of language learning on thought. In both cases there is good evidence that prelinguistic infants have the representational capacity in question and deploy it under different nonlinguistic conditions. There are several different (and not mutually exclusive) mechanisms that could mediate such weak effects. Take the singular/plural case for an example. Learning a label for a contrast could simply increase the salience of that contrast, making it more likely to be deployed in any given nonlinguistic context. Alternatively, syntactic bootstrapping could be at work. The linguistic contrast might have been learned in some context in which the relevant semantic contrast is automatically deployed (as when sets move together as united wholes), and then when the child hears a plural applied to a case where she would spontaneously deploy parallel individuation alone, the presence of the plural marking causes her to analyze the set as a plurality. Having done so, she is more likely to spontaneously do so again in the future, even in the absence of linguistic input. And finally, plural marking provides an explicit linguistic symbol that may occupy a single slot in working memory, thus making encoding more efficient. In all these ways, language learning may effect the representations activated and deployed in nonlinguistic situations, even if language learning played no critical role in the creation of a representational resource with more expressive power than any available before (see chapter 7).

Although I believe that the two cases discussed in chapter 7 reflect at most weak effects of language on thought, Quinian linguistic determinism also occurs, as documented in chapters 8 through 11. Furthermore, "weak" does not mean the same thing as "uninteresting" or "unimportant." Creating representations whose format is noniconic paves the way for integrating the concepts in core cognition with the rest of language, and is a necessary prerequisite for the bootstrapping mechanisms that underlie Quinian linguistic determinism.

Discontinuity—The Descriptive Problem

Discontinuity in conceptual development arises at two different levels of abstraction. Most generally, explicit intuitive theories differ qualitatively from, and are thus discontinuous with, systems of core cognition. Most human conceptual representations differ from those in core cognition with respect to all those properties that characterize core cognition. Consider the concepts *planet* or *germ*. These concepts are not the output of innate input analyzers, and so are neither innate nor causally connected to the entities they represent as are the concepts in core cognition. They are neither evolutionary ancient nor the output of domain-specific learning mechanisms. Unlike core cognition representations, their format is certainly not iconic, and they are not embedded in systems of representation that are constant over development. Explicit conceptual representations can be, and often are, overturned in the course of conceptual development.

Chapters 8 through 11 provided evidence for conceptual discontinuities at a more specific level—discontinuities within particular content domains. I documented discontinuities in mathematical development, where "discontinuity" meant "more expressive power." I also documented historical discontinuities within explicit scientific theories and within intuitive theories, where "discontinuity" meant "local incommensurability."

Specific discontinuities of both types (more expressive power, incommensurability) usually involve two successive late-developing conceptual systems. But transitions from core cognition to later developing conceptual representations also display both types of discontinuity. The learning mechanisms that underlie specific developmental discontinuities also explain the construction of explicit representational systems with none of the properties of core cognition.

Increasing Expressive Power—Integers and Rational Number

Establishing conceptual discontinuity requires characterizing two successive conceptual systems (conceptual system 1, or CS1, and conceptual system 2, or CS2) and specifying the qualitative differences between the two. One must provide evidence that each underlies thought at particular successive historical or ontogenetic moments. Discontinuities involve systems of concepts and inferences, and so evidence for discontinuity must include evidence of within-child consistency over a wide range of probes of the underlying representational capacity. Also, mastery of CS2 must be difficult, and there should be initial assimilation of input couched in the language of CS2 in terms of the concepts of CS1. Chapters 4, 7, 8, and 9 illustrate two different cases of developmental discontinuity in the course of mathematical development, the first resulting in the capacity to represent positive integers and the second in the capacity to represent fractions. I review each case in turn.

Core cognition contains three systems of representation with numerical content: parallel individuation of small sets of entities in working-memory models, analog magnitude representations of number, and set-based quantification. The experiments that uncover the existence and nature of these representations, as well as showing that they reveal distinct processing signatures and are elicited in different contexts, are reviewed in chapters 4 and 7. These are the CS1s. The CS2, the first explicit representational system that represents the positive integers, is the verbal numeral list embedded in a count routine. Deployed in accordance with what Gelman and Gallistel (1978) call the counting principles, the verbal numerals implement the successor function. For any numeral that represents cardinal value n, the next numeral in the list represents n + 1.

Chapter 8 argued that CS2 is qualitatively different from each of the CS1s because none of the CS1s has the capacity to represent the integers. Parallel individuation includes no summary symbols for quantity at all, and has an upper limit of three or four on the size of sets it represents. Set-based quantification includes summary symbols for quantity (plural markers, symbols that express concepts like *some* or *all*), and importantly contains a symbol with content that overlaps considerably with that of "one" (namely, the singular determiner), but the singular determiner is not embedded within a system of arithmetical computations. Also, set-based quantification in the service of natural language quantifiers has an upper limit on the specific cardinal values that are expressed (e.g., with dual and trial markers). Analog magnitude representations include summary symbols for quantity that are embedded within a system of arithmetical computations, but they represent only approximate cardinal values; there is no representation of exactly 1, and therefore no representation of +1. Analog magnitude representations cannot even resolve the distinction between 10 and 11 (or any two successive integers beyond its resolving capacity), and so cannot express the successor function. Thus, none of the CS1s can represent 8, or 10, or 342. This analysis makes precise the senses in which the verbal numeral list (CS2) is qualitatively different from those representations that precede it: it has a totally different format (verbal numerals embedded in a count routine) and more expressive power than any of the CS1s that are its developmental sources.

Consistent with the claim that CS2 is qualitatively different from each of these three CS1s, it is indeed difficult to learn. American middle-class children learn to recite the count list and to carry out the count routine in response to the probe "How many...?" shortly after their second birthday. They do not learn how counting represents number for another year and a half or two years. As required by the claim that input stated in the language of CS2 is assimilated to CS1, chapters 7 and 8 reviewed several lines of evidence that verbal numerals are initially interpreted as quantifiers. "Two" is often analyzed as a generalized plural marker, and numerals higher than those for which the child has assigned exact meanings are often used as if they meant some or plural as well.

Subset-knowers (those children who have assigned numerical meanings for just a subset of the numerals in their count list) differ qualitatively from CP-knowers (those children who understand the counting principles and thus use counting to represent the cardinal values of sets). Children can be placed into a knower level on the basis of Wynn's Give-a-Number task, and this placement predicts performance on a very wide variety of other tasks. CP-knowers, but not subset-knowers, count to produce a set when asked to give the experimenter a particular number of objects (e.g., "five"), know how to fix a set if they've miscounted, correctly repeat the last word of a count when probed again "How many . . . ?" (rather than recounting, or producing a numeral that was not the last word of the count), and so on (see chapter 8). These tasks make vastly different information-processing demands on the child, and so the within-child consistency suggests that CP-knowers command a representational resource the subset-knowers lack—namely, the verbal numeral representation of integers.

Within-child consistency is found even within knower levels: "one"-knowers according to Wynn's Give-a-Number task reveal cardinal knowledge of only the numeral "one" on many other tasks as well. For instance, when asked to estimate sets, they apply numerals larger than "one" at random to sets larger than one, and when asked which of two cards depicts n objects, for any two cards with sets larger than one, they answer at random. Similarly, "two"-knowers on Wynn's Give-a-Number task can estimate the number of objects in sets of one or two, but produce higher numerals at random for larger sets, and when asked which of two cards depicts n objects, answer nonrandomly only if one of the sets contains one or two objects. Analogous patterns are shown by "three"-knowers and by "four"-knowers. In sum, the construction of the numeral list representation is a paradigm example of developmental discontinuity. How CS2 transcends CS1 is precisely characterized: CS2 is difficult to learn, adult language expressing CS2 is assimilated to CS1, and children's performance on a wide variety of tasks consistently reflects either CS1 or CS2.

Chapter 9 presents another parade case of developmental discontinuity within mathematical representations. The CS1 in this case is the count list representation of the positive integers, enriched with the understanding that there is no highest number. Explicitly asked about the existence of a highest number, 5-year-olds say no, and they explain that for any candidate highest number, someone could always add one to it. Also around this age children begin passing Piaget's conservation-of-number tasks, showing that they have an explicit awareness that 1–1 correspondence and only 1–1 correspondence guarantees numerical equivalence. Children also build models of addition and subtraction based on the successor function and 1–1 correspondence, they conceptualize multiplication as repeated addition, and they begin to explicitly understand base 10 notation. By ages 6 through 8, children's arithmetical understanding is very rich and very firmly built on the concept of number as positive integer.

In CS2, *number* means any point on a number line that can be expressed x/y, where x and y are integers. In CS2, rather than it being the case that integers are the only numbers, there are an infinity of numbers between any two integers, or, indeed, between any two rational numbers. The question of the next number after n (where n might be an integer or not) no longer has an answer. Thus, CS2 has more expressive power than CS1 (there are all of these extra numbers), and numbers are related to each other differently in the two systems. The new relation in CS2 is division. Division cannot be represented in terms of the resources of CS1, which model only addition, subtraction and multiplication of integers. CS2's division cannot be represented as repeated subtraction of integers.

Thus, CS2 is qualitatively different from and has more expressive power than CS1. Furthermore, as required by this analysis, CS2 is indeed extremely difficult for children to learn. The teaching of rational number is the most studied topic in the literature on mathematics education, reflecting both its importance and its difficulty. One-half of college-bound high school students taking the SAT exams do not understand fractions and decimals. Furthermore, as reviewed in chapter 9, explicit instruction concerning rational number is initially assimilated to CS1, and children are consistent over a wide range of probes as to how they conceptualize number. Whether children can properly order fractions and decimals, how they justify their ordering, how they explain the role of each numeral in a fraction expressed "x/y", whether they agree there are numbers between 0 and 1, and whether they believe that repeated division by 2 will ever yield 0 are all interrelated. What the child does on one of these tasks predicts what he or she will do on all of the others. CS1 and CS2 are each coherent conceptual systems, qualitatively different from each other.

In these two developmental episodes, one way in which each CS2 is qualitatively different from the preceding CS1s is that the CS2s have vastly more expressive power than the CS1s. At the end of each episode, children have constructed a representational system that can express an infinity of concepts not expressible before (integers in one case, rational numbers in the other). Before the construction of the numeral list, children cannot think thoughts formulated in terms of the concepts 7, 12, 348, and so forth; before the construction of rational number, children cannot think thoughts formulated in terms of the concepts 7/8 or 15/16 or 1/20, and so on, ad infinitum.

Local Incommensurability

In all of the other cases of conceptual discontinuities considered in these pages, there is no clear sense that there is more expressive power in CS2 than in CS1. Rather, the two conceptual systems are qualitatively different because they are not mutually translatable, because they are locally incommensurable. One cannot express the beliefs that articulate CS2 in the concepts of CS1 and vice versa. That the concepts of CS2 cannot be expressed in terms of the conceptual vocabulary of CS1 is one reason CS2 is so difficult to learn. Chapter 10 discusses the comparable difficulty holders of CS2 have understanding CS1, in both historical and developmental cases of conceptual change.

Incommensurability arises when episodes of conceptual development have required conceptual change. Conceptual changes arise when there is what Kitcher (1978) calls "mismatch of referential potential." There are multiple methods of reference fixing and many types of sustaining mechanisms that connect entities in the world with symbols in the mind. In cases of conceptual change, these fractionate, leading to change, but overlap, in content. Conceptual changes are of several kinds, including differentiations such that the undifferentiated concept in CS1 plays no role in CS2, and is even incoherent from the point of view of CS2, coalescences in which ontologically distinct entities from the point of view of CS1 are subsumed under a single concept in CS2, and changes in conceptual type and in content-determining conceptual cores.

Chapter 9 suggested that not only does the system of number representations including the rationals have more expressive power than the numeral list representation of the integers, the two can also be seen as incommensurable. Some of the conceptual changes involve the concepts of number, subtraction, and division. In CS1, division is not differentiated from subtraction, and ½ is not a number. There is a change in the core of the concept of number, from integer to point on the infinitely dense number line. As acknowledged in chapter 9, this is not a canonical example of incommensurability because the concept integer continues to play a role in CS2, and rational numbers can, of course, be defined in terms of integers, although not without the concept of division, which is not available in CS1.

Conceptual change occurs when sets of concepts that are interdefined are acquired together, en suite, with new concepts not representable in CS1 emerging and with content determining interconnections that differ from those in CS1. Kuhn's (1962; 1982) canonical examples of incommensurable theories were the phlogiston and oxygen theories of combustion. In chapter 10, I offered the historical change from the source-recipient theory of thermal phenomena to caloric theory as another example, focusing on the differentiation of heat from temperature. My worked-out example of conceptual change in childhood involved the construction of an intuitive theory of matter, and to draw out the parallels with historical cases, I focused on the differentiation of weight from density.

Chapter 10 described many phenomena that suggest that children's concepts of the physical world may be incommensurable with ours: their confidence that a small piece of Styrofoam weighs 0 grams, nonconservation of the amount of matter and of weight, the claim that dreams are made of air, that shadows exist in the dark but we just can't see them. Huh? If children's concepts are incommensurable with the target concepts of science instruction, the latter should be very difficult to master, and indeed they are. This is one of the domains in which very well thought out curricula fail to induce conceptual change. A large proportion of high school students have failed to construct a physical theory in which material substances are distinguished from nonmaterial physical entities that interact causally with material ones (e.g., heat), and in which weight is an extensive quantity that provides a measure of the amount of matter, and in which weight is differentiated from density. In CS2, density is an intensive quantity that is a characteristic property of material kinds.

At the heart of establishing local incommensurability is characterizing two successive physical theories, providing evidence that each is a theory children actually hold, and, of course, displaying the incommensurability. Chapter 10 characterized an initial theory (CS1), in which an undifferentiated concept *weight/density* functions coherently. A translator's gloss was provided, sketching the central concept *degree of heaviness* akin to the Experimenters' *degree of heat*, which was analogously undifferentiated between the concepts *heat* and *temperature*. A sketch of CS1's concept of *physically real/substantial*—the concept closest to CS2's *material*—was also part of the translator's gloss. The CS1's undifferentiated concept *degree of heaviness*, or *weight/density*, cannot be expressed in terms of any conceptual system that differentiates the two concepts, *weight* and *density*. It is incoherent from the point of view of CS2. Evidence for an undifferentiated concept *weight/density* is that there are no contexts where the child relies exclusively on one rather than the other, and also that the concepts of CS1 lead children to contradictions they cannot resolve. Finally, there is striking within-child consistency across the many disparate tasks that diagnose CS1 and CS2. These tasks included sorting entities as matter vs. nonmatter; judging whether matter would cease to exist upon repeated division (continuity-of-matter tasks); continuity of weight and volume; conservations; modeling weight, density, and volume of a set of objects; ordering objects with respect to weight, density, and volume; and measuring weight, density, and volume. Consistent performance on this wide range of tasks provides evidence that children actually hold CS1, as characterized.

Pondering children's responses on these tasks is what allows the reader to come to represent CS1. Constructing a set of coherent concepts that yield the same judgments as those of children with CS1 is a bootstrapping process. Aided by the translator's gloss, the reader must create a conceptual system in which the concept *degree of heaviness*, undifferentiated between *weight* and *density* functions coherently.

The concepts within CS1, like those in CS2, are mutually constraining because they are interdefined. This explains the striking within-child consistency we observe. To establish that CS1 and CS2 are incommensurable, chapter 10 characterized ancestor concepts in CS1 that are undifferentiated with respect to those in CS2. These undifferentiated concepts are not represented at all in CS2, even as superordinate concepts, because they are incoherent in terms of the concepts in the latter theory. The most fully worked-out example was *weight/density*; another touched on was *air/nothing*. Chapter 10 also characterized ancestor concepts in CS1 that represent kinds as ontologically distinct which CS2 unites under a single concept. An example is CS2's *matter*, uniting what are vastly different kinds in CS1 (object, liquid, air, or gas). Ancestor concepts in CS1 also differ from their descendants in CS2 in type and features taken to be essential. The essential features of CS1's undifferentiated concept of matter/physically real are perceptual access and causal interaction with other external physical entities. The essential features of the CS2's concept of matter are weight and occupying space. An interconnected change occurs within the concept of degree of heaviness. In CS1, degree of heaviness is a property of some material/ physically real entities, such as a large piece of Styrofoam but not a small piece. In CS2, weight is taken to be an essential feature of all material entities, a property that provides an extensive measure of amount of matter. The local incommensurability between CS1 and CS2 derives from simultaneous adjusting these concepts to each other. Differentiations implicating incommensurability never occur independently of simultaneous coalescences, nor do they occur independently of changes of the causally deepest properties represented within each of a set of interrelated concepts.

This analysis of local incommensurability illustrates the fruits of what Nancy Nersessian (1992) calls "cognitive historical analysis," in which philosophers and historians of science join forces with cognitive scientists to understand knowledge acquisition in both the history of science and the individual. It also illustrates the fruits of the theory-theory of conceptual development. The same questions can be asked of episodes of knowledge acquisition in individual children and historical theory changes, in spite of the manifest differences between scientists and children, and sometimes these questions receive the same answers. I juxtaposed a case of incommensurability between historical theories (the Florentine Academician's source-recipient theory of thermal phenomena and the caloric theory in which heat and temperature have been differentiated) and a case of incommensurability of between intuitive theories (the 6-year-old's theory of the physical world and that of the adolescent's, in which a concept of matter that supports the differentiation of weight from density has been constructed) to illustrate several such questions that receive the same answer. These include: What is an "undifferentiated concept"? What counts as evidence for lack of differentiation, as opposed to other representational states of affairs that might yield undifferentiated language? What distinguishes episodes of conceptual development that involve conceptual change from episodes involving only belief revision and knowledge enrichment formulated over a constant set of concepts?

Quinian Bootstrapping

Ultimately, learning requires adjusting expectations, representations, and actions to data—whether the learning mechanism is associative, Bayesian, or deductive. Abstractly, all of these learning mechanisms are variants of hypothesis-testing algorithms. The representations most consistent with the available data are strengthened; those hypotheses are accepted. However, in cases of developmental discontinuity, the learner does not initially have the representational resources to state the hypotheses that will be tested, to represent the variables that could be associated or could be input to a Bayesian learning algorithm. We seek a learning process that can create new representational machinery, new concepts that articulate hypotheses previously unstatable. Quinian bootstrapping is one such process.

The capacity for explicit symbolization makes possible the creation of mental symbols that are not yet connected to anything in the world. In Quinian bootstrapping episodes, mental symbols are established that correspond to newly coined or newly learned explicit symbols. These are initially placeholders, getting whatever meaning they have from their interrelations with other explicit symbols. As is true of all word learning, newly learned symbols must necessarily be initially interpreted in terms of concepts already available. But at the onset of a bootstrapping episode, these interpretations are only partial—the child (or scientist) does not yet have the capacity to formulate the concepts the symbols will come to express.

The bootstrapping process involves modeling the phenomena in the domain, represented in terms of whatever concepts the child or scientist has available, in terms of the set of interrelated symbols in the placeholder structure. Both structures provide constraints, some only implicit and instantiated in the computations defined over the representations. These constraints are respected as much as possible in the course of the modeling activities, which include analogy construction and monitoring, limiting case analyses, thought experiments, and inductive inference.

I drew on bootstrapping processes to explain all the developmental discontinuities sketched above. In the case of the construction of the numeral list representation of the integers, the memorized count list is the placeholder structure. Its initial meaning is exhausted by the relation among the external symbols: they are stably ordered. "One, two, three, four, ..." initially has no more meaning for the child than "a, b, c, d, ..." To illustrate that it is not difficult to describe bootstrapping processes that might effect a given CS1/CS2 transition, chapter 8 sketched two different ones that could yield numeral list representation of the integers. The two differed in the initial partial meanings children assign for the placeholder symbols in the list. On both theoretical and empirical grounds, I argued against the proposal that analog magnitude representations provide the input to the process. Rather, the details of the subset-knower period suggest that the resources of parallel individuation, enriched by the machinery of set-based quantification, provide the partial meanings children assign to the placeholder structures that get the bootstrapping process off the ground. The meaning of the word "one" could be subserved by a mental model of a set of a single individual {i}, along with a procedure that determines that the word "one" can be applied to any set that can be put in 1–1 correspondence with this model. Similarly "two" is mapped onto a longterm memory model of a set of two individuals {j k}, along with a procedure that determines that the word "two" can be applied to any set that can be put in 1–1 correspondence with this model. And so on for "three" and "four." This proposal requires no mental machinery not shown to be in the repertoire of infants—parallel individuation, the capacity to compare models on the basis of 1–1 correspondence, and the set-based quantificational machinery that underlies the singular/plural distinction and makes possible the representation of dual and trial markers. The work of the subset-knower period of numeral learning, which extends in English-learners between ages 2.0 and 3.6 or so, is the creation of the long-term memory models and computations for applying them that constitute the meanings of the first numerals the child assigns numerical meaning to.

Once these meanings are in place, and the child has independently memorized the placeholder count list and the counting routine, the bootstrapping proceeds as follows: the child notices the identity between the singular, dual, trial, and quadral markers and the first four words in the count list. The critical analogy that provides the key to understanding how the count list represents number is between order on the list and order in a series of sets related by an additional individual. This analogy supports the induction that any two successive numerals will refer to sets such that the numeral further along in the list picks out a set that is one greater than that earlier in the list.

This proposal illustrates all of the components of bootstrapping processes: placeholder structures whose meaning is provided by relations among external, explicit symbols, partial interpretations in terms of available conceptual structures, modeling processes (in this case analogy), and an inductive leap. It also captures what is known about the subset-knower period, and the ways in which subset-knowers differ from those children who have worked out how counting represents number. The greater representational power of the numeral list than that of any of the systems of core cognition from which it is built derives from combining the representational resources from the capacity to represent serial order (which gives the child the placeholder structure), set-based quantification (which gives the child singular, dual, trial, and quadral markers), and the numerical content of parallel individuation (which is largely embodied in the computations carried out over sets represented in memory models with one symbol for each individual in the set). The child creates symbols that express information that previously existed only as constraints on computations. Numerical content does not come from nowhere, but the process does not consist of defining "seven" in terms of symbols available to infants.

Chapters 10 and 11 further illustrate the fruits of cognitive historical analysis, as philosophers and historians of science have joined forces with cognitive scientists to illuminate the cognitive processes involved in conceptual change. Lessons from the analysis of the bootstrapping processes used by Kepler, Darwin, and Maxwell inform the curricular interventions of math and science educators, and the success of these interventions in turn provides evidence for the proposed bootstrapping processes.

In all three of these historical cases, the bootstrapping process was initiated by the discovery of a new domain of phenomena that became the target of explanatory theorizing. The phenomena were initially represented in terms of the theories available at the outset of the process, often with concepts that were neutral between those theories and those that replaced them. Incommensurability is always local; much remains constant across episodes of conceptual change. For Kepler, the phenomena were the laws of planetary motion; he sought to understand why these take the form they do. For Darwin, the phenomena were the variability of closely related species and the exquisite adaptation to local environmental constraints. For Maxwell, the phenomena were the electromagnetic effects discovered by Faraday.

In all three of these cases, the scientists created an explanatory structure that was incommensurable with any available at the outset. In all three cases, the process of construction involved positing placeholder structures and modeling processes that aligned the placeholders with the new phenomena. In all three cases, this process took years. For Kepler, the hypothesis that the sun was somehow causing the motion of the planets was a placeholder until the analogies with light and magnetism allowed him to formulate the concept *vis motrix*. For Darwin, the source analogies were artificial selection and Mathus's analysis of the implications of a population explosion for the earth's capacity to sustain human beings. For Maxwell, a much more elaborate placeholder structure was given by the mathematics of Newtonian forces in a fluid medium. These placeholders were formulated in external symbols: natural language, mathematical language, and diagrams.

Of course, the source of these placeholder structures is importantly different in the cases of conceptual change in the history of science and in the developmental cases. The scientists posited them as tentative ideas worth exploring, whereas children acquire them from adults, in the context of language learning or science education. This difference is one reason meta-conceptually aware hypothesis formation and testing are likely to be important in historical cases of conceptual change. Still, many aspects of the bootstrapping process are the same whether the learner is a child or a sophisticated adult scientist. Both scientists and children draw on explicit symbolic representations to formulate placeholder structures and on modeling devices such as analogy, thought experiments, limiting case analyses, and inductive inference to infuse the placeholder structures with meaning.

In the course of creating the theory of electromagnetic fields, Maxwell invented the mathematics of quantum mechanics and relativity theory. This illustrates an aspect of bootstrapping often seen in the development of the physical sciences; mappings between mathematical structures and physical ones have repeatedly driven both mathematical development and theory change. Another salient example is Newton's advances in the formulation of calculus in the course of his work on physics. Chapter 11 describes a bootstrapping process in the course of math and science education in which mathematical development and physical development go hand in hand, paralleling the historical cases. Constructing mappings between mathematical representations and representations of the physical world is an essential part of the processes through which both representations of rational number and representations of the physical world in which weight is differentiated from density are constructed. As predicted by this analysis, chapter 11 documents that the two conceptual changes constrain each other. The child's progress in conceptualizing the physical world exquisitely predicts understanding of rational number and vice versa. Children whose concept of number is restricted to positive integers have not yet constructed a continuous theory of matter nor a concept of weight as an extensive variable, whereas children who understand that number is infinitely divisible have done both.

The best evidence concerning the bootstrapping processes actually involved in each of these conceptual changes derives from studies of the effectiveness of curricula built upon them compared with control curricula that are not. The classrooms are randomly assigned to the experimental curriculum and control curricula that cover the same topics. In these studies, pretests diagnose students' initial concepts using the same kinds of tasks that allow us to describe the conceptual change in the first place. Posttests then establish the conceptual progress made; the curricula explicitly implementing bootstrapping processes greatly outperform otherwise excellent curricula that do not.

Chapter 11 briefly described Moss and Case's (1999) approach to the construction of rational number. The mathematical notations—percentages, decimals, and fractions—are initially placeholders, and modeling continuous quantities and computations over continuous quantities in terms of them is what infuses them with meaning. Moss and Case reversed the usual sequence of presentation of mathematical notation. They began with percentages, then moved to decimals and finally to fractions. This order of presentation was chosen because by 4th-grade children have a firm understanding of the count list from 1 to 100 and can fluently divide by 2. That is, although they do not yet fully understand division, they certainly know that half of 100 is 50, and that 75 is half-way between 50 and 100, and so on. This allows an initial mapping between the physical and mathematical worlds Moss and Case could promote— between the fullness of a cup and percentages. In this way, 100% is completely full, 50% is one-half full, and so on. After exploring this mapping, children were challenged to come up with ways of expressing one-half a quarter-full, and also to extend the mapping to other con-tinuous dimensions such as length. In these contexts, children were introduced to decimal notations and explored translating between these and percentages, solving problems that involve mapping each to con-tinuous quantities. The modeling process, which involves multiple iterations of mappings between the newly constructed mathematical notations and the physical phenomena, makes explicit in a common representation what was only implicit in the computations defined over physical quantities. Before the bootstrapping episode, children can carry out computations such as splitting and folding in half over physical quantities, and the bootstrapping process creates mathematical repre-sentations of division, percentages, decimals, and fractions to express and vastly expand these computations.

Carol Smith (2007) and Marianne Wiser (Wiser & Amin, 2002) each characterized the bootstrapping processes underlying conceptual change in intuitive physical theories, and each tested their proposals in teaching interventions. Because of the interrelation between the mathematical development of representations of rational number and the conceptual changes described in chapter 10 that results in material becoming dif-ferentiated from physically real and weight from density, chapter 11 illustrated their proposals by describing Smith's teaching interventions aimed at fostering this very conceptual change. Although developed independently of Nersessian's analysis of Maxwell's construction of electromagnetic theory, Smith's curriculum draws on all of the same components of the bootstrapping process. First, she engages students in explaining new phenomena—ones that can be represented as empirical generalizations stated in terms of concepts they already represent, even if not coherently. These include the proportionality of weight to overall size, explaining how different-size entities can weigh the same, predicting which entities will float in which liquids, and sorting entities on the basis of whether they are material or immaterial, focusing particularly on the ontological status of gases. She then engages students in several cycles of analogical mappings between mathematical representations (the mathematics of extensive and intensive variables, ratios, and fractions) and the physical world. Like Moss and Case, she begins with those aspects of mathematics best understood (the additive and multiplicative structures underlying integer representations) and begins with modeling the extensive quantities of weight and volume. The curriculum soon moves to calculating the weight and volume of very small entities, using division. These activities are supported by thought experiments (which are themselves modeling devices) that challenge the students' initial concept of weight as degree of heaviness (felt weights undifferentiated from density), densitys undifferentiated from, leading them into a contradiction between their claim that a single grain of rice weighs 0 grams and the obvious fact that 50 grains of rice have a measurable weight. These activities, along with measuring the weight of a fingerprint and a signature with an analytical balance, support conceptualizing weight as an extensive variable that is a function of the amount of matter. Understanding the implications of the limits of the sensitivity of the measurement device helps support the extensive concept *weight*.

Just as Maxwell used visual models to represent Newtonian forces in a fluid medium because these were easier to think with, to complete the differentiation of weight from density Smith makes use of visual models that represent the mathematics of extensive and intensive quantities. Visual objects are created out of numbers of boxes of a constant size and numbers of dots distributed equally throughout the boxes. Numbers of dots and numbers of boxes are the extensive variables, numbers of dots per box are the intensive variable. Students first explore the properties of these visual models as objects in themselves, discovering that they can derive the value of any one of these variables knowing the values of the others, and exploring the mathematical expression of these relations: dots per box equals number of dots divided by number of boxes. Students are guided to use these visual objects as models of physical entities, with number of boxes representing volume and number of dots representing weight. Density (in the sense of weight/volume) is visually represented in this model as dots/box, and the models make clear how it is that two objects of the same size might weigh different amounts—because they are made of materials with different densities, why weight is proportional to volume given a single material, and so on. The models are also used to represent liquids, and students discover the relevant variables for predicting when one object will float in a given liquid and what proportion of the object will be submerged. This activity is particularly satisfying for students because, at the outset of the curriculum, with their undifferentiated weight/density concept, they cannot formulate a generalization about which things will sink and which will float. Density as a characteristic property of material kinds does explanatory work in modeling the phenomena the curriculum challenges the students with. Differentiating weight from density in the context of these modeling activities completes the construction of an extensive concept of weight begun in the first part of the curriculum.

Just as Maxwell's modeling activities supported both mathematical and theoretical developments, through these modeling processes students consolidate the mathematics of intensive and extensive variables. Just as Maxwell engaged in several repeated episodes of analogical mapping in the course of developing a physical theory of electromagnetic forces, so Smith engages children in repeated episodes of model building in the course of creating a physical theory in which weight and volume are each extensive variables that provide a measure of the amount of matter, each being potentially infinitely divisible, and in which density is an intensive variable differentiated from weight.

The formula $d = w/v$ (density equals weight divided by volume) is a placeholder structure at the beginning of the bootstrapping process. The child has no distinct concepts of weight and density to interpret the proposition. As in all cases of bootstrapping, the representation of placeholder structures makes use of the combinatorial properties of language. Density here is a straightforward complex concept, defined in terms of a relation between weight and volume (division), and the child (if division is understood) can understand this sentence as "Something equals something else divided by something else." "Weight" and "volume" may be partially interpreted in terms of concepts in CS1 that are ancestors to those in CS2, but the child does not know the word "density" and when it is learned in this context it is mapped onto the same ancestor concept as that for "weight," namely, CS1's *degree of heaviness*. The dots per box model is also a placeholder structure at the beginning of the bootstrapping process, a way of visualizing the relations between an intensive variable (dots per box) and two extensive variables related by division, and thus provides a model that allows the child to think with, just at Maxwell's models allowed him to think with the mathematics of Newtonian mechanics as he tried to model Faraday's phenomena. At the outset of the process the child has no distinct concepts of weight and density to map to number of dots and number of dots/box, respectively.

Although straightforward conceptual combination plays a role in these learning episodes (in the formulation of the placeholder structures), the heart of Quinian bootstrapping is the process of providing meaning for the placeholder structures. At the outset, both "heavy object" and "heavy substance" are interpreted in terms of the child's undifferentiated concept *degree of heaviness* (see chapter 10). It is in terms of the undifferentiated concept of degree of heaviness that the child represents the empirical generalizations that constitute the phenomena she is attempting to model. The placeholder structure introduces new mental symbols (weight and density). The modeling processes, the thought experiments, and the analogical mapping processes provide content for them. The modeling process, using multiple iterations of mappings between the mathematical structures and the physical phenomena, makes explicit in a common representation what was only implicit in one or the other representational systems being adjusted to each other during the mapping. In Smith's most successful version of this bootstrapping process, the students first map weight and volume to number, and then use the dots per box models to represent a variety of physical phenomena, formulating an explicit concept of density and thus completing the differentiation of weight from density.

That bootstrapping processes with the same structure play a role in conceptual change among both adult scientists and young children is another fruit of cognitive historical analysis. As I have mentioned many times—a point bearing further repetition—this does not belie important differences between adult scientists engaged with meta-conceptual awareness in explicit theory construction and young children. Without denying these differences, chapters 8 through 11 illustrate what the theory-theory of conceptual development buys us. By isolating questions that receive the same answers in each case, we can study conceptual discontinuities and the learning mechanisms that underlie them, bringing hard-won lessons from each literature to bear on the other.

Conclusions. The Theory-Theory of Conceptual Development

The term "theory-theory" has many uses in cognitive science: some cognitive scientists speak of a theory-theory of conceptual development (as opposed to modular or maturational theories), and some of a theory-theory of concepts (as opposed to prototype or exemplar or information semantics theories), and some of the theory-theory of mentalizing (as opposed to modular or simulation theories). These are independent uses, which are confusing given the common designation of "theory-theory." The work reviewed in this chapter bears on the theory-theory of conceptual development; I will touch on the theory-theory of concepts in chapter 13. As I hope is clear, I endorse the theory-theory of conceptual development, although I do not believe that core cognition is in its domain. I believe in the existence and importance of framework theories, as these provide explanatory fodder, constrain inductive learning, and otherwise structure thought. Therefore, accounting for their acquisition is a central goal of cognitive development. The theory-theory holds that intuitive framework theories are similar to meta-conceptually held scientific theories in many respects, including important aspects of the mechanisms through which they are constructed. Engaging in cognitive-historical analyses of theory change, juxtaposing analyses of theory change in both historical and ontogenetic contexts, constitutes one way of making the theory-theory of conceptual development bear fruit.

The theory-theory of conceptual development is not actually a theory; it is way too underspecified. One way to see what it comes to is to consider the alternatives. The theory-theory is often contrasted with modular views, or with maturational accounts of the mechanisms underlying conceptual development. I agree with this abstract characterization of the theory-theory, but note that endorsing it does not require denying modular views, nor denying that maturational processes also play a role in conceptual development. The systems of core cognition fall under the umbrella of modular views, and it would be foolhardy to deny that maturation of executive function, for example, plays an important role in conceptual development. These positions are not competitors for understanding conceptual development unless each is posited to be the sole source of our conceptual repertoire and or the sole process driving developmental change. Clearly, there are many types of conceptual representations and many processes that underlie conceptual development. The contrast between those that articulate systems of core cognition, on the one hand, and those articulating explicit mathematical knowledge and explicit intuitive theories, on the other, has been central to the picture of conceptual development developed in these pages. Only the latter are in the domain of the theory-theory of conceptual development.

The theory-theory and modular views of knowledge acquisition may become competitors in any given case. Are the 4-year-old's representations of want-belief psychological causation the output of a Quinian bootstrapping process, or are they continuous with a system of core cognition, as Leslie and Fodor (chapter 5)? These are competing positions. Engaging these issues in each case requires subtle empirical and theoretical work, but it is important to recognize that even if we converge on an answer in any given case, we are not licensed to conclude that all cases of conceptual development will receive that same answer. I believe that systems of core cognition, as characterized in chapters 3 through 5, exist, and intuitive theories undoubtedly do. We distort our picture of conceptual development by adopting a one-size-fits-all stance toward the nature of and acquisition of systems of mental representation.

But what positive theses does the theory-theory of conceptual development commit us to? Sometimes it is taken to mean that knowledge acquisition is an evidence-driven process. Of course, this claim is only as interesting as what we have to say about evidence-driven processes is interesting. In recent years this work has become very interesting, indeed. Bayes-net representations of causal structure, together with Bayesian and other models of causal learning, have greatly enriched the study of causal cognition. Given the centrality of causal representations to theories, this work certainly has a lot to say about theory acquisition. It already has had a lot to say about hypothesis testing, theory choice, and causal learning. Here, I have taken an alternative, complementary approach to the question of theory acquisition. I have sought to understand where the representations that articulate the hypothesis space come from.

The positive thesis I have defended in these pages is that distinguishing theory changes that involve conceptual change from those that do not is as central to understanding individual conceptual development as it is to understanding theory acquisition in historical time. Conceptual change constitutes a form of genuine developmental discontinuity and thus poses a very difficult explanatory challenge. My answer to this challenge has been to flesh out Quine's bootstrapping metaphors, showing how these play a role in the acquisition of both intuitive theories during childhood and explicit theories during the history of science. Even within the theory-theory of conceptual development, within our accounts of evidence-based rational learning processes, there is room for quite different types of learning mechanisms. Endorsing the theory-theory, and choosing to work within it, is a commitment that understanding these different types of learning mechanisms will allow us to learn what it is we want to know about conceptual development. In my case, what I want to know is: How does the human capacity arise to think thoughts formulated in terms of concepts like *gene* and *atom?* The theory-theory gives us one type of purchase on this question. So, too, does the theory of core cognition.

13

Conclusion II: Implications for a Theory of Concepts

The previous chapters have sketched a theory of the origin of concepts. Building a theory of concept acquisition and a theory of concepts that fits with it is a single project. In this concluding chapter I ask you to accept, for the moment, my account of concept acquisition and consider where it leads in terms of a theory of concepts.

Beginning Assumptions

Concepts are mental symbols, and so a theory of concepts is part of a representational theory of mind. At least in principle, the theory must fit into a picture of what makes mental symbols *represent*—that is, what connects mental representations to the entities they refer to. It must also fit into a picture of how concepts function in thought. Mental representations enter into a variety of computational processes. They play a role in the inferences we draw, the predictions we make, and the explanations we build, so a theory of them must fit into an account of how it is they function. Finally, because concepts are merely a subset of all mental representations, the analysis must fit into an account of how to distinguish conceptual representations from nonconceptual ones.

First, some terminology. "Reference" is a relation between a symbol (e.g., the word "dog" or the concept *dog*) and the entities it symbolizes (i.e., Rover, Lassie, and the like); the referents of a symbol are the entities in the world it represents. "Conceptual content" is a philosopher's term of art that I will not try to explain here. My only claim is that the content of a concept is what it contributes to the meaning of the thought in which it figures. For example, the concept *dog* contributes to the meaning of the thought *John owns a vicious dog*. As I use the term, "content" is roughly synonymous with "meaning." Of course, different theories of concepts give different answers to the question of what determines the content of a concept, what the relations are between content and reference, and how concepts are to be individuated—what determines whether two symbols express the same concept or different ones. To explore how the theory of concept acquisition offered in these pages bears on adjudicating among theories of concepts, we need a better picture of the players. Therefore, I begin by providing a map, in very broad strokes indeed, of the lay of the land.

To get my work off the ground, I assumed that two types of processes figure in a theory of all mental representations, including conceptual ones: (1) causal processes that mediate between entities in the world and mental representations, at least partially determining what mental symbols refer to; and (2) internal computational processes defined over mental representations that explain their role in thought. The latter constitute what is called "conceptual role" or "inferential role."

Some have argued that conceptual role has three parts to play in a full account of concepts: a part in determining reference, a part in determining conceptual content, and, as its primary function, a part in determining the concept's contribution to thought. So far, separating the work of conceptual role into these distinct functions has not mattered. Rather, I have appealed to conceptual role as part of my evidence of *which* concepts monkeys, infants, and young children have. For example, that infants and monkeys use analog magnitude representations to support addition and the calculation of ratios provides evidence that these are number representations (chapter 4). Or, for another example, the ways that infants take into account the causally relevant properties of the participants in events in their representation of these events provides evidence that they are making causal attributions (chapter 6). Using inferential role in this way is surely justified, given the work concepts do in the computational processes that are thought, no matter what work conceptual role does in concept individuation and content determination. But for present purposes, specifying how, if at all, conceptual role plays a part in content determination matters very much, for it separates many philosophical theories of concepts (e.g., Dretske, 1981; Fodor, 1998; Kripke, 1972/1980; Putnam; 1975) from most theories psychologists and linguists are drawn to (e.g., Smith & Medin, 1981; Murphy, 2002).

What Phenomena a Theory of Concepts Is Responsible for

Many apparent disagreements about the nature of concepts are really disagreements about the central phenomena that will constrain a theory of them. Whenever I teach a class on concepts, I begin by asking students to say what phenomena—what data—a theory of concepts must be responsible for. The psychology students usually come up with three types: (1) data concerning categorization behavior, including the well-attested effects of prototypicality on ease of categorization; (2) data concerning inferential role; and (3) data concerning concept acquisition. Sometimes they also mention the phenomenon of conceptual combination—if concepts are the units of thought, the elements of beliefs, then a theory of concepts must be able to account for the construction of beliefs from concepts and for the productivity of thought.

The philosophy students, like the psychologists, also are concerned with understanding how concepts serve the productivity of thought and the role that concepts play in inference. But what always strikes me from this exercise is that psychology students almost never mention the phenomena that philosophers often take as the central challenges to a theory of concepts: (1) accounting for reference; (2) distinguishing concepts of entities in the world from beliefs about those entities (sometimes called distinguishing concepts from conceptions [e.g., Rey, 1983]); and (3) accounting for epistemological warrant. What role does a theory of concepts play in understanding the justification of belief? Analyticity (truth by virtue of meaning) is central to the epistemological project. If there are thoughts that are true in virtue of the concepts that compose them, a theory of concepts should allow us to understand why.

The second of these concerns, distinguishing concepts from beliefs (or distinguishing concepts from conceptions), bears further comment. On some theories of conceptual content, such as holistic versions inferential role semantics, everything we believe about the entities in a concept's extension contributes to the meaning of that concept. These theories have undesirable consequences (to say the least; see Fodor & Lepore, 1992). To mention just one obvious one, consider the intuition that I can disagree with people whose knowledge of tigers is vastly different from mine, including my past selves. You and I might disagree on whether wild tigers are to be found in China, for example, or on whether there are white tigers. If I now say that some tigers are white, how can I be disagreeing with myself of 10 years ago, when I thought all tigers were orange with dark stripes (or with you, if you believe the same)? If you share the intuition that people can disagree, then it cannot be that all of our beliefs play an essential role in determining content; if they did, we'd be talking past each other, meaning different things by both "tiger" and "white," rather than disagreeing about a given proposition (namely, that I take "tigers are white" to be true whereas you take it to be false). The challenge for a theory of concepts, then, becomes determining what, if not one's beliefs about the entities in the extension of a concept, does determine the concept's content.

In chapters 8 to 11, I argued that conceptual change is a real (indeed, common) phenomenon, so I am committed to the possibility that you and I might have different concepts (of matter, of weight, of heat, of number...). Any developmental psychologist, anthropologist, or intellectual historian who seeks to understand the historical development of concepts faces two urgent problems of concept individuation. When I say that you and I have different concepts of weight, there must be some way of picking out mental representations with enough overlap that they both express some concept we would both agree are candidates for being the same concept. And then, we must say why, nonetheless, these representations express different concepts. For example, one concept is really *weight* and the other is an undifferentiated *weight/density* concept. That is, I accept the urgency of distinguishing conceptual change from belief revision. In some cases of knowledge acquisition we merely change our beliefs about the world; in others we change the concepts in terms of which those beliefs are composed. If the arguments in chapters 8 through 11 are correct, then our theory of concepts had better allow us to distinguish concepts from beliefs, and concepts from conceptions.

The first phenomenon on a psychologist's list—categorization behavior—often does not even make it onto a philosopher's list at all. Philosophers do not deny the interest of the scientific project of understanding what leads to categorization decisions. These decisions are likely to draw upon all of what one knows about the entities one is categorizing, one's conceptions of and beliefs about those entities, as well as the concepts themselves, plus quick and dirty recognition routines developed to exploit statistically diagnostic and readily available evidence; and it is a wonderful project to figure out how this works. But understanding categorization behavior is unlikely to give us much purchase on the rest of the work we'd like a theory of concepts to do for us.

The list of phenomena that includes both the philosophers' and the psychologists' desiderata seems a good place to start as we think about a theory of concepts; and, indeed, the first worked-out theory of concepts —that of the British empiricists—sought to account for the whole set. There is no way of saying at the outset of theory building which phenomena will turn out to be in the domain of a worked-out theory. One way of looking at the history of the field, both within psychology and within philosophy, is that the search for a single theory of concepts that handles all of these phenomena has been fruitless. Still, as we review some of the moves that have been made, we should keep firmly in mind which phenomena are motivating them and which phenomena have been abandoned, at least for the moment, as we try to provide an explanatory account of the nature of concepts and how they function in mental life.

The Empiricists' Theory

For good reasons, discussions of concepts often begin with the British empiricists' theory. The empiricists' theory was extremely influential, directly impacting later philosophical work (e.g., the logical positivists of the Vienna circle [e.g., Carnap, 1932/1980] and the reactions against them, [e.g., Quine, 1953/1980; Wittgenstein, 1953/1958; Putnam, 1962; Kripke, 1972/1980]), as well as directly impacting the first systematic psychological work on concepts (e.g.., Vygotsky, 1934/1962; Bruner, Goodnow, & Austin, 1956). Creating the first important worked-out theory of concepts, the empiricists attempted to account for the whole range of both the psychologists' and the philosophers' phenomena listed above. Important for my project, the empiricists took concept acquisition to be an important source of constraint in theorizing about the nature of human concepts.

The philosophers Steven Laurence and Eric Margolis (1999) provide an excellent and psychology-friendly exposition of the empiricist theory of concepts. In the psychological literature, the empiricist's theory is often called "the classical view" (e.g., Smith & Medin, 1981), although the aspect of the theory taken up by psychologists under this designation (the central role of definitions in the analysis of concepts) is only part of the empricists' views. My account captures what I understand to be the common ground among quite different theorists, and it also modernizes some of the discussion. For example, the empiricists knew no mechanisms of conceptual combination other than association; I assume the machinery of logic and syntax as underlying conceptual combination.

The empiricists divided concepts into primitive concepts and complex ones, and they took the primitive concepts to be primitive in three different respects: developmentally primitive (they are the output of innate input analyzers), definitionally primitive (all other concepts are defined in terms of them), and interpretationally primitive (they are intrinsically meaningful, and all understanding requires unpacking complex concepts into the primitives from which they are comprised). Notice, these senses of primitive are actually quite different. On some modern versions of the classical view, the primitives from which definitions are built are not plausibly innate (e.g., the chemist's *element, atom,* or *charge* might be primitives in modern chemistry, figuring in definitions of other terms, but they are unlikely to be the output of innate input analyzers). Similarly, concepts might be interpreted without decomposition into other concepts, even if they could be defined in terms of some primitive vocabulary. The empiricists' primitives were primitive in all three senses. According to the empiricists' theory, complex concepts have primitive concepts as their constituents. Necessary and sufficient conditions for falling under a complex concept are stated in terms of primitive ones. Concepts and conceptions were easily distinguished: the definition specifies the concept; all other knowledge and beliefs about the entities in a concept's extension constitute the conception of those entities. People can share concepts in the face of widely different conceptions of and beliefs about the entities the concepts represent.

It was important part of the empiricists' theory that they took the primitive concepts to be sensory. They assumed that sensory representations are the output of innate sense organs, and that sensation provides causal connections between entities in the world and our representations of them. For example, the physics of light and the way that vision works guarantees that the representation *round* applies to round things. Similarly, the chemistry of salt and the physics and neural structure of taste representations ensure that *salty taste* applies to substances with salt in them. Thus, the empiricists provided something a bit like an information semantics for primitive concepts. It was also important to their project that all complex concepts are *defined* from primitives. They could thus account for the acquisition of all concepts: any given concept is either primitive, and thus innate, or composed from primitives. That primitive concepts are putatively sensory, and that complex concepts are putatively composed from primitives, also provides an account for how complex concepts refer. Complex concepts are causally connected to the entities they refer to because the primitives from which they are composed are.

The empiricists' view of how reference works is straightforward. Concepts (mental representations) *determine* their extensions in the world. Primitives refer directly: the entities that fall under a primitive concept are those that cause it to be activated in specifiable ideal circumstances. The entities that fall under a complex concept are those that satisfy the definition. This view led to a natural model of the categorization process; to decide whether a given entity is, for example, a cup, simply check whether it satisfies the definition of a cup, the necessary and sufficient conditions for being a cup.

Especially as developed by the logical positivists, these ideas were put to work in epistemology—the problem of justifying that our beliefs are true. How can we *know* that electrons have negative charge, that Tyrannosaurus rex once walked the earth, or that the universe is expanding? The logical positivists expanded the representations that ground cognition from sense data to include directly measurable properties of the world. According to their view, some knowledge (contingent knowledge) is justified by the logic of statistical warrant. The rest is warranted from the nature of concepts themselves. If sense data and the outputs of measurement devices ground our knowledge, and all other concepts are defined in terms of them, then epistemological warrant owing to our conceptual apparatus (as opposed to our contingent knowledge) has two components: (1) sense data and measurements are causally connected to the world, and (2) much other knowledge is analytic—true by definition. We know that bachelors are unmarried because this is part of what the word "bachelor" means. That is, "bachelor" means *unmarried man*. We have stipulated that in our language and thus the knowledge that bachelors are unmarried is justified conceptually. Similarly, "mass" and "acceleration" are primitives (we can directly measure them). We know that force is proportional to mass because "f = ma" is true by definition—this is what we have stipulated that the word "force" means—that physical magnitude obtained by multiplying mass by acceleration. The logical positivists held that it is not a discovery that f = ma (we have no independent concept of force because it is not directly measurable). Only if force is a primitive or definable in terms of primitives other than mass and acceleration can the fact that it equals mass times acceleration be a belief that is formed by empirical discovery. Rather, the positivists held, we define it so, and then explore how the physics works out.

The empiricists' theory could accommodate all of the other phenomena on our list as well. The problem of disagreement is solved by definitional structure. Primitive concepts are shared because innate input analyzers are common to all human beings, and as long as the correct definition for any complex concept is known, complex concepts are shared across time and among people. The productivity of thought is explained in terms of the processes that build complex concepts from primitive ones, including syntactically complex ones such as "brown cow" or "graduate student in psychology." Each constituent in such a phrase is either primitive or defined in terms of primitives, and syntax provides rules for building the meaning of the phrase from the meaning of the constituents. For example "black cat" refers to the intersection of black entities and cats.

As I said, the empiricists' theory was grand in scope. It provided a unified theory of concepts that accounted for reference, conceptual productivity, epistemological warrant, the inferences concepts support, categorization, conceptual stability and the possibility of disagreement, and acquisition. Of course, cognitive science has abandoned the theory as hopeless, and for good reason. But as we contemplate what has led to the abandonment of this grand theory, looking at the alternatives that have been offered, we need to keep the phenomena the empiricists' theory was responsible for in mind. Different theoretical perspectives will generally have a different idea of exactly which are the important phenomena to explain, but these must be argued for, and not merely assumed, and a justification given for which phenomena have been abandoned as belonging in the domain of any given theory.

The Psychologists' Response

This book is in part a response to the empiricists' theory of concept acquisition. The empiricists, as well as later thinkers like Quine and Piaget, had a theory about the developmental primitives from which all concepts are built—that they are perceptual, sensory, or sensori-motor. Chapters 2 to 7 of this book offered evidence that these writers mischaracterized the stock of original representational primitives. And chapters 8 to 11 offered a decidedly non-empiricist theory of how new concepts are acquired: certainly that they are not always learned by constructing definitions in terms of the stock of developmental primitives.

Two important books, one by Edward Smith and Douglas Medin (1981), and, more recently, one by Gregory Murphy (2002), summarize the psychological response to the empiricists' theory (the classical view). For the most part, the literature synthesized in these reviews was not concerned with the empiricist theory of concept acquisition. Psychologists working within or writing against the classical view did not consider the question of what the developmental primitives are, and therefore never endorsed or criticized the idea that all concepts can be defined in terms of sensory primitives. Rather, they were concerned with the structural claims about mental representations: that complex concepts are defined in terms of definitional and interpretive primitives, whatever these may be.

Some of the first experiments that undermined the classical view concerned the existence of definitional primitives that were also interpretative primitives. This work addressed the claim that comprehension of words requires recovering the primitives out of which they are built. If this is so, then there should be a processing cost of lexical complexity— that is, complex concepts should take longer to process than concepts that express their definitional components. Two laboratories in the 1970s, Walter Kintsch's and Jerry Fodor's/Merrill Garrett's, sought such evidence and failed to find any. In all of these studies, the techniques were shown to be sensitive to other linguistic expressions of formally identical complexity differences, when these did not rest on putative definitions. For example, negatives marked on the surface ("unmarried" or "not married") increased processing time in an inference task, whereas these same negatives, when supposedly part of a definition, as in "bachelor," did not (Fodor, Fodor, & Garrett, 1975; Fodor, Garrett, Walker, & Parkes, 1980; Kintsch, 1974).

One response to these studies was that concepts may be definitionally complex and yet not be decomposed during comprehension. Primitives may be definitional primitives without being interpretational primitives. The content of a concept could conceivably be captured by its definition in terms of primitives, even if in language these definitions have been compiled into units that subserve comprehension without decomposition.

The major attack on the classical view, however, concerned its theory of categorization. Without doubt, since concepts became a topic of study in psychological theories in the 1950s (e.g., Bruner, Goodnow, & Austin, 1956), categorization behavior has been the central phenomenon psychologists have sought to explain. Psychological research has decisively confirmed Ludwig Wittgenstein's claims that family resemblance structure, rather than a definitional structure that provides necessary and sufficient conditions for category membership, underlies categorization judgments. The psychologist Eleanor Rosch (1973, 1978; Rosch & Mervis, 1975) discovered that categorization decisions concerning a wide variety of concepts, from putative primitives such as *red*, to animal concepts, vehicle concepts, tool concepts, furniture concepts, and so on, reveal a prototype structure. Subjects find it natural to judge whether German shepherds are better exemplars of the concept *dog* than are Pekinese, and the ratings of exemplar goodness predict many details of the data from experiments on categorization. Subjects are faster to judge good exemplars to be category members than they are poor exemplars, children learn to recognize good exemplars before they recognize poor exemplars, and so on. Furthermore, when asked to list properties of instances of a category such as dogs, the properties listed of prototypical dogs overlap most of those listed of all dogs, and the properties listed of atypical dogs overlap least. Artificial-category learning experiments show that people can learn categories characterized probabilistically in terms of a primitive base specified by the experimenter, and that categorization reflects the typicality structure so created. The existence of prototypicality structure and its importance in the process of categorization are absolutely beyond doubt.

These phenomena led psychologists to adopt a theory of what concepts are that fits the categorization behavior. In particular, they have denied that categorization is a process of checking whether some entity satisfies the necessary and sufficient conditions for category membership. Rather, it was suggested that categorization reflects the probabilistic structure of concepts. According to the first theories that were developed in response to the classical view, a category is mentally represented by a set of features that members typically have, and categorization is determined by whether a given entity shares enough of those features (Rosch, 1978; see Smith & Medin, 1981, for an overview). As Murphy (2002) reviews, much of the subsequent controversy in the field has concerned adjudicating between prototype theories, in which a single summary representation encodes the features that probabilistically determine categorization judgments, on the one hand; and exemplar theories, in which particular category members are represented in terms of their features, and candidate category members evaluated in terms of their similarity to stored exemplars, on the other. For present purposes, the differences between these two classes of models need not concern us.

There is no doubt that prototype/exemplar theories account for a great deal of data from categorization experiments, and thus provide insight into the process of categorization (see below for caveats). However, they are not intended to account for most of the phenomena the empiricist theory covered. As already mentioned, they do not really take on the problem of concept acquisition, as there is no account of the origin of the features interms of which the prototypes or exemplars are specified. The features that enter into prototype or exemplar representations in psychological experiments (e.g., has a beak, has wings, flies) are not plausibly developmental primitives. These theories also make a mystery of shared concepts, failing to address the problem of disagreement: my prototype of a dog (or the dog exemplars I represent) must be different from yours, yet we both have concepts of dogs. We can agree that there are many species of dogs and disagree about whether wolves are a kind of dog. Relatedly, these theories offer no machinery to distinguish conceptual change from belief revision. Basically, "knowledge about dogs" and "concept of dogs" are treated as one and the same thing.

Indeed, one friendly amendment to prototype and exemplar theories —what Murphy (2002) calls the "knowledge view" of categorization— holds that all of one's knowledge of entities, especially causal/explanatory knowledge, is deployed in categorization. Murphy endorses the knowledge view and I believe that he is right; we do have summary representations of categories of entities, we do represent specific exemplars, and categorization draws on these as well as anything else we know about the entities to be categorized. Categorization is a kind of confirmation, and as Quine argued, confirmation is a holistic process. But that's exactly what should make categorization *not* the central phenomenon in a theory of concepts. Concepts are the units of thought—the building blocks of knowledge. If we use everything we know about dogs in categorizing an entity as a dog or a nondog, and if we take a theory of categorization *to be* a theory of conceptual representations, we cannot isolate the contribution of our concept of dogs to our ability to think and learn about dogs. The knowledge view explicitly denies the distinction between concepts and conceptions. As the philosophers Jerry Fodor and Ernie LePore (1992) argue in their passionate discussion of holistic theories of concepts, being forced by our data and theoretical commitments to this position is a cause for despair, not one to celebrate. As will become clear, Murphy's knowledge view is closely aligned with the theory-theory of concepts, and I shall argue for its place in a theory of concepts, while not giving up on distinguishing concepts from conceptions, belief revision from conceptual change.

Notice that whether one takes any possible objection to a given theory of concepts seriously depends upon one's own theory of concepts. Many embrace a holistic view of concepts and accept that concepts will therefore never be fully shared. If one identifies conceptual content with the output of categorization behavior, then one *must* accept that concepts are not completely shared (because people certainly disagree in their categorization judgments). As I wander through this conceptual landscape I do not lay out the answers holders of each view might give to an objection I am voicing. Rather, my point is that it is important to recognize the compromises our theories force on us. One's favored theory often requires abandoning some phenomenon that there is good reason to believe should be in the domain of a theory of concepts.

Some early responses to the demonstrations of prototypicality structure attempted to salvage the classical view. Sharon Armstrong, Lila Gleitman, and Henry Gleitman (1983) showed that the data revealing prototypicality structure in category decisions do not transparently reflect the nature of the concepts into which entities are being categorized. Prototypicality phenomena are observed in categorization decisions about what entities fall under clearly definitional concepts, such as *odd number*. Participants in their studies agreed upon a typicality structure for odd numbers (7 is a better example of an odd number than is 1 or 9 or 319), and the typicality structure predicted speed and accuracy of categorization decisions. But almost nobody would seriously think that our concept *odd number* is anything other than *integer not divisible by 2*, unless he or she were committed to denying utterly the distinction between concepts and conceptions, between content determining and merely associated representations. Participants could offer this definition, and their categorization decisions in the end reflected it. One initial response to these data was to posit a two-part structure to concepts: a classical core that determines conceptual content, as on the empiricists' theory, and a peripheral fast-and-dirty recognition routine that reflects all of our knowledge about odd numbers, our conceptions of them as well as of even numbers, prime numbers, and so on. This response missed the mark; these data do not show that *all* concepts have a definitional structure. Rather, they drive home the point that that data from categorization experiments that reflect prototypicality are not a pipeline to the nature of concepts (see also Diesendruck & Gelman, 1999, for evidence that considered categorization decisions dissociate from prototypicality judgments).

Psychological Essentialism and the Theory-Theory of Concepts

Even more damaging to the classical view, and to the prototype/exemplar view of concepts as well, are the many studies that show that we humans make some categorization decisions—those involving natural kind concepts—against an assumption of essentialism; that is, we assume that what makes an entity a dog is that it has the essential features of a dog, even though we might not know what those features are! See Gelman

(2003) for an extended defense of psychological essentialism. If we don't know what those features are, then categorization decisions cannot be made by checking whether an entity has those features, either in considered categorization or in fast-and-dirty categorization. If unknown, they are not represented and therefore cannot provide any criterion for category membership—neither definitional as on the classical theory nor probabilistic as on the prototype/exemplar theory.

Frank Keil (1989) provided the first empirical evidence for psychological essentialism. Keil's data also bring home the point that categorization decisions do not merely involve comparing the features of an entity to the stored features of a prototype. Participants in Keil's studies were shown pictures such as those in Figure 13.1a and asked what they depicted. Not astonishingly, they answered, "a raccoon." Keil then described a transformation of that animal involving plastic surgery and fur dyeing, implantation of a sac of smelly stuff, and behavior modification, so that the resulting animal looked like that in Figure 13.1b. Not only did it look like a skunk, it had all of the known behavioral features of skunks. That is, it matched people's prototypes of skunks exactly. Yet adults (and children starting around age 7) claimed that the animal in Figure 13.1b is a raccoon.

What makes an animal a skunk or a raccoon are not the properties that one ordinarily relies upon in classification tasks, nor the properties that account for the prototypicality structure of animals in feature listing experiments, nor similarity to stored exemplars of skunks and raccoons, but, rather, something deeper, something essential, something inherited from a creature's parents. We need not know what this essential property

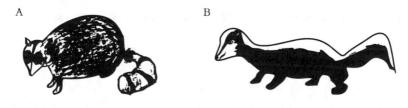

Raccon/Skunk

Figure 13.1. (From Keil, 1989). Keil, F. C. (1989). *Concepts, kinds, and cognitive development.* Cambridge, MA: MIT Press. Reprinted with permission.

is. (Something to do with DNA is our current best guess, but even biologists do not yet know exactly what it *is* about DNA that distinguishes skunks from raccoons.) Psychological essentialism reflects our assumptions about natural kinds, showing that we deploy our concepts of them in the absence of knowledge that would allow us to categorize entities under them. Notice that this characterization of psychological essentialism does not commit us to the claim that conceptual representations of kinds include placeholder symbols for the unknown essence (see Strevens, 2000). Rather, the claim is that our kind concepts are deployed against an assumption that what determines the entities of a given kind is a metaphysical question (something in the world, not in our minds), and that the current information we use to decide this matter is always up for revision.

The literature on psychological essentialism shows that natural kind concepts are deployed in a manner consistent with the following assumptions: (1) there are causally deep properties that explain a given entity's existence, kind, and superficial properties; (2) these causally deep properties are thus more important in interpreting what kind an entity falls under than superficial observable properties; and (3) this is so even if we do not know what those causally deep properties are. There are two crucial components of these assumptions that contradict the classical view. First, an entity's deepest properties, those that determine its kind, are not definitions. Rather than being stipulated by linguistic convention, they must be discovered. Second, our concepts are deployed against an assumption that our current beliefs about an entity's deepest properties, those that determine its kind, are revisable. They do not provide necessary and sufficient conditions for category membership. These representational assumptions are consistent with prototype/exemplar theories, but psychological essentialism also opposes those theories. Some of the tenets of psychological essentialism—such as the differential weighting of causally deep features in categorization decisions—can be seen as additions to prototype/exemplar views, friendly amendments as it were. But others, that there must be some mechanism of reference fixing that is independent of any of the known properties of the referents of the concept (unknown essential features), deeply undermine prototype/exemplar theories just as they undermine the classical view.

Psychological essentialism is closely aligned with Murphy's (2002) knowledge view of concepts, as well as with what some psychologists have called the "theory-theory" of concepts. Different theory-theorists mean rather different things by the term. I have been arguing for many years for one version of the theory-theory—namely, that many everyday concepts are terms in intuitive theories, and thus that whatever mechanism determines the content of the terms in scientific theories may also determine the content of these everyday concepts (e.g., Carey 1985b; 1991). Of course, this gets us nowhere toward an analysis of concepts without a specification of how the content of theoretical terms is determined. Others invoke the theory-theory to emphasize that the aspect of knowledge of entities that is particularly important in categorization decisions is causal and explanatory—just that type of knowledge embedded in intuitive theories.

One central tenet of the theory-theory is that conceptual role at least partly determines the content of concepts. Especially important is the role of each concept in the causal explanatory structure of the theory. Most psychologists (and philosophers criticizing the theory-theory) assume that the theory-theory is committed to the internal inferential role *completely* specifying content. I dub this the "internalist theory-theory," and, as I lay out below, I do not endorse it. Indeed, it is inconsistent with the evidence from the literature on psychological essentialism, which shows that people often deploy concepts assuming that they do not represent the features that determine which entities fall under them. But before sketching the particular version of the theory-theory I endorse, and showing how it is related to the theory of concept acquisition I have developed in these pages, I turn to the philosophical response to the empiricist theory, part of which was the historical source of the doctrine of psychological essentialism, and hence the theory-theory.

The Philosophers' Response

Even sketching the philosophical response to the empiricists' view of concepts is vastly beyond the scope of this book. Every part of the view has come under philosophical attack. Here I concentrate on two threads of the criticisms: those with the greatest impact on the psychological literature on concepts, the Kripke/Putnam arguments that the processes through which reference is determined are not mental, and Fodor's

arguments for conceptual atomism and radical concept nativism. I conclude with Ned Block's vision of a dual factor theory of the determinants
of conceptual content.

Wide Content and Information Semantics

Kripke (1972/1980) and Putnam (1975) took reference to be the central
phenomenon that a theory of meaning must account for. What determines the entities in the world that a given term in language (or concept
expressed by that term) picks out? Their radical denial of the classical
view (and also prototype, exemplar, and internalist theory-theory views)
is summed up by the statement, "Meanings are not in the head." By this,
Putnam meant that whatever mental representations, considered as purely
internal, support our use of a term do not also determine its content.
Intensions construed as purely internal do not determine extensions, at
least not for proper names or for natural kind concepts like *dog* or *gold*
or *star*. Kripke and Putnam deny that what we know about the entities
picked out by a concept or term determines which entities those are,
so long as that knowledge is thought of purely internally. In what
follows, it's important to focus on two quite separate aspects of the
Kripke-Putnam argument. Most of what follows focuses on one strand
of the argument: the reasons philosophers find the dictum that meanings
are not in the head at least plausible. I also briefly discuss the other strand:
their positive proposal for how meanings are determined.

The philosophical thought that culminated in Kripke's and Putnam's
work began with arguments against the existence of analytic truths
involving names, natural kinds, and terms in theories. According to the
classical view, analytic truths are true in virtue of meaning and are also a
priori. That is, our knowledge of analytic truths is not empirical. For
example, it is analytically true that all bachelors are unmarried, because
the relation between being a bachelor and being unmarried is a matter of
linguistic convention, therefore immune to reconsideration on any
empirical grounds. Similarly, mathematical and scientific definitions, such
as that of kinetic energy for Newtonians ($e = 1/2 \ mv^2$) were held to be
linguistic conventions and thus a priori true. Mass and velocity are
primitive concepts, according to the logical positivists, as they are the
output of measurement devices. We stipulate kinetic energy to be 1/2

mv^2 and then proceed to study kinetic energy empirically. Quine (1953/1980) and Putnam (1962) countered that this generalization was *not* a matter of linguistic convention and only seemed a priori because of the central role its truth played in an entire conceptual system. It was not only *revisable*; since Einstein, it has been *revised*. Quine and Putnam concluded that there are no nontautological analytic truths involving theoretical terms of science.

Consider our concept *tiger*. There is no definition of the concept (in sensory vocabulary or in any vocabulary) that provides analytically necessary and sufficient conditions for being a tiger, so knowledge of a definition cannot determine the extension of *tiger*. Putnam argues that neither similarity to our prototype of tigers (or to stored representations of tiger exemplars), nor our knowledge of or theory of tigers determines what our concept *tiger* refers to. What then *does* determine the extension of the concept *tiger* and, derivatively, the reference of the word *tiger*? Kripke and Putnam provide a two-part answer. First, what makes something a tiger inheres in tigers themselves, not in our concepts of tigers. Second, causal connections between tigers and our representations of them are involved in the determination of reference of natural kind terms.

What makes an entity a tiger is a metaphysical question, not a psychological one. In this respect, the Putnam-Kripke analysis dovetails with psychological essentialism, and indeed, historically was one of its sources. The philosophical analysis justifies psychological essentialism: what makes a tiger a tiger is a fact about the world, not a fact about our beliefs, knowledge, or mental representations of tigers. It is not a matter for definitional stipulation, and this is one way the classical view went wrong.

Kripke's analysis of proper names such as "George Washington" gives a feeling for the arguments that reference is not determined by what we know about the entities picked out by our concepts. Consider how the classical or prototype theories would explain how the referent of "George Washington" is determined. In the classical view, the meaning would be a set of descriptors that provide necessary and sufficient conditions for being George Washington (*was a person, was male, was the first president of the United States, was the general at the head of the Revolutionary Army during the War of Independence, was married to a person named Martha, and so on*). The unique entity that satisfies these descriptions is George himself. In the prototype view, these descriptors would merely probabilistically determine the referent—the person who best satisfies most of these descriptors is George himself.

Kripke (1972/1980) appealed to straightforward and compelling intuitions in his rejection of these mechanisms for reference determination. He pointed out that many of the components of any true description of George Washington fail to be necessarily true of him; they do not determine reference in the sense that they do not provide necessary and sufficient conditions for being George Washington across possible worlds. George Washington, the same George we have in mind, could have died as a child. If he had died, he never would have become a general or president, would never have married, and so forth. Thus known descriptions of George Washington are not part of the *meaning* of the term "George Washington," if meanings are what determine reference. The fact that we can imagine that the very child who became president might have gone on to be a carpenter, or even might have died in infancy, shows this is the case. We are entertaining these counterfactuals as descriptors that could have been true of George himself, so something other than the descriptions we are negating must be allowing us to use the term to refer to him. Notice that Kripke is appealing to psychological data in his theorizing; our intuitions are data. These intuitions provide evidence concerning how the concepts underlying the meaning of proper names work, how their content is determined.

If descriptions associated with proper names do not determine reference, neither definitionally or probabilistically, what does? Kripke's answer has two parts: (1) a baptism that initially establishes the referential relation, and (2) a causal chain between that baptized person (or place or other bearer of a proper name) and a successful act of reference. That I can successfully refer to George Washington is ensured by the right kind of causal chain between George, the baby, his parents who named him, and the elementary school teachers or my parents, whoever introduced the term to me and who used it supported by a successful causal chain of the same sort. Thus, Kripke's causal theory of reference appeals to social and historical factors to determine the content of an individual's mental representations.

Kripke's theory of proper names is especially important here because of its extension to other terms. Putnam and Kripke argued that the causal theory of reference applies to natural kind terms, such as *gold, water, tiger, star,* and *electron*, as well as to proper names. This makes sense of the division of cognitive labor we observe in our use of natural kind terms— we can and do defer to experts in determining the referents for them. Just as for proper nouns, Putnam and Kripke argued that the knowledge we have about natural kinds (whether in the form of classical definitions, exemplars/prototypes, or theories) does not determine the referents of natural kind concepts (e.g., Putnam, 1975). No part of any description of a natural kind term is necessarily true of that kind by virtue of the meaning of the term denoting it. This includes even such putative analytic truths as "cats are animals" or "gold is a metal." Essences cannot be stipulated as a matter of linguistic convention, and the current knowledge we have about the referents of natural kind terms, whether represented in the form of prototypes, exemplars, or theories, is always subject to revision in the course of scientific progress.

Putnam's Twin Earth scenarios complete the argument for "wide content." Wide content is that aspect of meaning that is in part determined by factors outside of the head. Putnam asks us to imagine a world exactly like ours, with each of us duplicated by a twin who has had identical experiences to us as he or she grew up. Let the time be before the advent of modern chemistry, in either world. The twin has all of the same mental representations as his or her earth version does, at least understood purely internally—the symbols in the twins' languages are the same and the twins have the same prototypes, theories, and exemplars represented. The only difference is that the stuff in the oceans and rivers that comes down from the sky, and that we call water on earth, is a totally different chemical compound (H_2O vs. XYZ) from the compound that plays the same role on Twin Earth. The internal processes underlying categorization would be the same for me and my twin, yet my "water" does not refer to the same stuff as does his or her "water," and indeed, if I traveled to Twin Earth and radioed home, "Lots of water here," the linguistic intuition of many (but not all) commentators dictates that I'd be saying something false. These intuitions complement those Kripke elicited in his proper name discussions in showing that the referents of a term or a mental representation are determined partly by the world itself and partly by the causal connections between the entities in the world and the speaker or thinker.

Psychologists might reasonably wonder why their theorizing should be constrained by impossible science fiction scenarios. (The one just mentioned is impossible, but others with the same sort of import are possible but not actual.) The intuitions these scenarios elicit are themselves data, much in the same way grammaticality judgments or moral intuitions are. They lay bare how our concepts work. More convincingly to psychologists, the data in support of psychological essentialism also point to the same conclusion. We can use a term to refer without knowledge that would allow us to represent (as part of a prototype, definition, or theory) the essential features that make it the case that the entities it refers to are in its extension. If that is so, something else besides our knowledge of those entities must determine reference; something determines reference that is not part of a definition, prototype, *or* theory we represent. Kripke's causal theory of reference sketches one way that wide content may be determined, but any theory on which reference is determined by some mechanism through which entities in the world are causally connected to our mental representations is a theory of wide content. Kripke's theory dictates that the causal history of a term is important to reference determination, but there is also a nonhistorical version called "informational semantics" that emphasizes causal covariation rather than causal history (Dretske, 1981; Fodor, 1998).

Putnam and Kripke took reference as the rock-bottom phenomenon that a theory of concepts must account for. Accordingly, the theory is silent concerning most of the phenomena of interest to psychologists. Inference, categorization decisions, conceptual combination, and language production and comprehension—conceived of as behaviors to be explained in terms of computational processes—simply do not fall under the theory, for these must be explained by what's inside the head. Psychologists' responses have been that, if this is so, they are not particularly interested in wide content. Psychologists are concerned with the format and computational role of mental representations, and if these do not determine the referents of concepts, so be it. Fine, but we psychologists must recognize that we are ignoring a central desideratum for a theory of concepts: what determines their extensions. Surely an adequate theory must get this problem right because, if our concepts of real entities (in contradistinction to fictional ones) are not appropriately connected to the world, they would not support learning about it. Unless we accept radical fictionalism about theoretical terms, we must agree that our physics and chemistry yield knowledge of gold and electrons, and that must be because the concepts we deploy refer to these entities. Furthermore, the data on psychological essentialism supports the Kripke-Putnam intuitions. We *do* deploy concepts in the absence of knowledge that would allow us to categorize entities under them, partly drawing on a division of cognitive labor, deferring to experts, and we do take our representations to be revisable. That is, we do not deploy our concepts as if our conceptions of and beliefs about the entities that fall under them determine reference, even probabilistically.

Theories of acquisition and theories of concepts are mutually constraining. The Kripke theory about how concepts are acquired is not intended as a psychologically adequate theory of the origin of concepts. According to the theory, what fixes the referent is what initially allows the language community user to glom onto the entities in the extension of a concept—a supposed baptism. This clearly applies only to external symbols, terms in language, and most transparently to proper nouns. What determines reference for any subsequent use of the concept is a causal chain between the baptism and the symbol in question. If one accepts the Kripke causal theory of reference, a theory of acquisition will be a theory of how a person's concepts come to have the right causal connections to the world. The theory is not remotely worked out enough to support such an account.

In my view, we must accept the arguments for wide content. As I have said, the evidence for psychological essentialism points to the same conclusion. However, in addition to accounting for the referential relations between symbols and their extensions, our theory of concepts should account for at least some of the other phenomena on our wish list for a theory of concepts, which leads me to endorse a dual-factor theory of conceptual content. But before turning to dual-factor theory, I discuss another version of a theory of conceptual content that puts reference as the core of content determination: Fodor's theory of concept atomism.

Concept Atomism

The philosopher Jerry Fodor (1998) favors information semantics over Kripke's causal history theory of reference. According to information semantics, content depends on idealized causal covariation. Fodor believes that what determines the content of a given mental representation, at least a primitive one, is a causal connection between the entities it refers to and the symbol itself, a connection that guarantees that the symbol ideally covaries with the entities in its extension. Fodor's view of wide content differs from Kripke's in that he emphasizes the role of processes inside the head as sustaining the causal relations. Fodor assumes that factors inside the head, such as perceptual mechanisms and inferential relations among symbols, will have an important part to play in the mechanisms that mediate the causal links that ensure that symbols covary appropriately with their referents. The literature on information semantics sometimes adopts the term "sustaining mechanism" to refer to the grab bag of processes that connect symbols to their referents. Historical and social factors, of the sort envisioned by Kripke, may be part of the sustaining mechanisms for the symbols of language and the concepts they express. Conceptual role may be also be part of the sustaining mechanisms that connect symbols to the world. Conceptual role simply isn't content determining in the traditional way this is understood, for reasons of psychological essentialism and the fact that no part of what we represent about the entities in the extension of a given concept is immune from revision.

Importantly, Fodor offers no theory of the sustaining mechanisms. He calls the sustaining mechanisms themselves "mere engineering," and assumes that an account of them will be very messy, indeed. Unlike Putnam and Kripke, whose arguments for wide content were the focus of their work, Fodor is concerned with the implications of accepting the arguments for wide content for a psychological theory of concepts. He argues that the considerations reviewed above that militate against the classical view of concepts (both the psychologists' responses and the philosophers' responses) show that a vast number of concepts are "atoms"—that is, they are without internal structure. Atoms are primitive in all of the empiricists' senses of the term. Primitive concepts, by definition, have no representational structure. They are the ultimate building blocks of beliefs, the atoms from which propositions are built. What makes conceptual atomism a radical theory is Fodor's claim that almost all concepts of the grain of single lexical items (including *electron, cancer, break, carburetor*) are primitive. They are *definitional* primitives (not constructed from other concepts, even probabilistically or in terms of their place in a theory). They are *developmental* primitives (innate). And they are *interpretational* primitives (not decomposed into other concepts in thought or in language production and comprehension). This is indeed a radical denial of the classical view of concepts, and also of all of the theories psychologists have offered in response to the classical view.

By now the arguments that concepts of this grain are definitionally primitive should be totally familiar. They are the well-rehearsed arguments that there are no definitions of most lexical concepts and that there need be no represented necessary and sufficient conditions, no prototypes, no theories, no knowledge, that determine whether an entity is an electron, a dog, or an exemplar of killing.

Fodor's picture of interpretational primitiveness is simple. Concepts are partly individuated by the symbols themselves. Suppose *couch* and *sofa* are synonyms, causally connected to the very same entities in the world. Nonetheless, they are distinct concepts because they are represented by distinct symbols. This, by the way, is how Fodor solves a critical problem for information semantics. Information semantics would seem to require that the content of *phlogiston* and *troll* be identical, since these two concepts have the same extensions (namely, none). But concepts are individuated, in Fodor's view, by the symbols themselves: *phlogiston* and *troll* are distinct concepts because they are represented by distinct symbols in the mind. It is these atomic symbols that enter into the inferential and compositional processes that constitute thought; they need not be (nor can they be) decomposed further.

Fodor accepts the empiricist distinction between primitive and complex concepts. Indeed, in addition to reference, Fodor takes compositionality as the central desideratum for a theory of concepts. Concepts are the unit of thought, and thought is productive. Complex concepts do have internal structure; the concept *purple cow* has each of the concepts *purple* and *cow* as components. According to Fodor, complex concepts are typically expressed with phrases in natural language. Here's a Fodorian example of compositionality: our lexical concepts allow us to think about all the grandmothers under age 40 who live in Boston, whose granddaughters are married to dentists. Composed concepts are complex (as in the classical view) and a theory of concepts absolutely must mesh with an explanation of the capacity for conceptual composition. Fodor argues that a virtue of the classical view is that it can handle composition, and that it is a problem for prototype theory, exemplar theory, and internalist theory-theory that they cannot.

Fodor assumes that for prototype theory or internalist theory-theory to explain compositionality, we must be able to derive the prototype or place in a theory of the complex concept from the prototypes or place in a theory of the constituents. Patently, we cannot do that. Many complex concepts do not even have prototypes or places in theories. We do not categorize the entities that fall under many complex concepts by matching current exemplars with stored representations of exemplars of those entities (for we often have no stored representations of exemplars). An example is *not a tiger*. Others have prototypes or exemplars or places in intuitive theories, but users of the concepts need not represent them. An example of this is *Paul Auster novel* (for those of us who have read none). Laurence and Margolis (1999) call this the "missing prototype" problem. Other complex concepts have prototypes and represented exemplars, but we cannot predict those exemplars or prototypes from our representations of the exemplars/prototypes/places in theories of their constituents. Examples are *pet fish, wooden spoon*. Similarly, our biological theory of tigers does not contribute to the prototype or exemplars we represent of "toy tiger" or "statue of a tiger." As Fodor says, prototypes/exemplars/theories don't usually compose, if by that one means that one can derive the prototype/exemplar/place in theory of the composite from those of the constituents (but see Smith, Osherson, Rips, & Kean, 1988, for progress in showing how one might do so, at least in some limited circumstances).

So how does Fodor's atomic version of information theory handle composition? Fodor does not try to derive the causal connections between complex concepts and their extensions from the causal connections between the primitives and their extensions plus laws of composition. Since we have no idea what kinds of causal connections ensure that symbols appropriately covary with the entities to which they refer (no theory of the sustaining mechanisms), we could not possibly provide such an account. Rather, Fodor gives a very different account of how the content of a primitive concept is determined (information semantics) and how the content of a complex, composed concept is determined. He assumes the empiricists, along with the linguistics, are on the right track for complex concepts. For example, the rules of compositional semantics determine that the extension of "not a tiger" is the complement of the extension of "tiger," and information semantics determines the extension of "tiger."

As Laurence and Margolis (1999) point out, this same move should be open to prototype/exemplar/theory theorists. However the content of lexical concepts is determined, we can appeal to the rules of compositional semantics to account for the content of phrasal ones. Because Fodor is not interested in mere engineering, he doesn't show us how the sustaining mechanisms for complex concepts can be derived from the sustaining mechanisms of their constituents. He holds the prototype, exemplar, and theories to a higher standard in explaining compositionality than he holds his own theory. Explaining the productivity of thought is a difficult task for any theory of concepts, and it is likely that the branches of cognitive science that will provide the most insight into this problem are formal linguistics and logic. Atomic theories of concepts are no better off here than are those theories that posit internal conceptual structure to lexical concepts.

I have dwelt on Fodor's theory for several reasons. Fodor is one of the few philosophers who places his theorizing about concepts firmly in the context of cognitive science and the representational theory of mind. He shows us most clearly how difficult it will be to find a single theory that accounts for all of the phenomena on our list of desiderata. But most important for my present purposes, he puts accounting for concept acquisition at center stage. I now turn to the third sense in which Fodor believes atomic concepts to be primitive: they are developmental primitives.

In his debates with Piaget at the famous Royamount conference, Fodor (1980) advanced the argument mentioned in chapter 1 that learning processes cannot create representations with more expressive power than their input. This follows, he argued, from the premise that learning is a form of hypothesis testing and confirmation, as well as from the premise that to test a hypothesis one must already have the resources to state it. Therefore, one cannot *learn* a logic with more power than its input, and thus Piaget's stage theory cannot be a correct description of cognitive development. Although I agree with Fodor's conclusion that Piaget's characterization of the stages of cognitive development is wrong, Fodor's argument does not successfully establish that this is so. Chapters 8 to 11 took on Fodor's challenge to cognitive science, demonstrating that there are discontinuities in conceptual development and fleshing out the bootstrapping mechanisms that underlie the construction of representational resources more powerful than their input.

Important for us here is Fodor's related argument that all lexical concepts must be innate. Fodor's conceptual atomism, according to which lexical concepts are primitive, led him to the conclusion that all 500,000 lexical concepts in the *Oxford English Dictionary* (plus all the concepts that all uncoined words express) are innate! Fodor painted himself into this corner, thus:

1. All learning mechanisms reduce to hypothesis formation and testing.
2. Hypotheses that play a role in learning new concepts must be formulated in terms of available concepts, using the machinery of compositional semantics.
3. Primitive concepts are not formulatable (definitionally or probabilistically) in terms of other concepts.
4. Therefore, primitive concepts cannot be learned, and thus must be innate.
5. Lexical concepts are primitive.
6. Therefore, lexical concepts must be innate.

Fodor argued that if we accept that lexical concepts are primitives (i.e., atoms, not composed out of other concepts), then we are forced to the conclusion that they are innate. Thus, Fodor's atomistic theory stands or falls with his nativist theory of concept acquisition.

Just as psychologists have not been much interested in wide content, neither have many concerned themselves with Fodor's argument that all lexical concepts must be innate. Since the conclusion of the argument is ridiculous, there must be something wrong with it. I agree that the conclusion is ridiculous, but I also agree with Laurence and Margolis (2002) that it is a serious challenge to cognitive science and, like other philosophical puzzles, such as Goodman's riddle about induction, it is important to see where the argument goes wrong.

Many cognitive scientists accept the argument that conceptual primitives must be innate (e.g., Jackendoff, 1989; Pinker, 1994), and they respond to Fodor's paradox by denying that lexicalized concepts are primitive (i.e., by denying premise 5). Others, including myself, have argued that the concept *primitive* must be differentiated (Carey, 1982). Definitional   or   interpretational   primitives   are   not   necessarily developmental primitives. My answer to Fodor's argument for radical concept nativism is the same as my answer to his more general argument against developmental discontinuities. Quinian bootstrapping mechanisms underlie the *learning* of new primitives, and this learning does not consist of constructing them from antecedently available concepts (they are definitional/computational primitives, after all) *using the machinery of compositional semantics alone*. Thus, I deny premises 1 and 2 of Fodor's argument.

The rest of this chapter develops my response to Fodor's paradox in the context of laying out the version of the theory-theory of concepts that I am led to by considering the problem of conceptual development. It is a two-factor theory, accepting the Kripke-Putnam arguments for wide content and the evidence for psychological essentialism, but asserting that aspects of the conceptual role must be seen as content determining as well. Many philosophers have advocated two-factor theories; here, I draw especially upon the work of Ned Block (1986, 1987).

The Dual-Factor Theory of Concepts

Information semantics, with its focus on wide content, is silent on most of the phenomena that psychologists look to a theory of concepts to explain. We must look inside the head to account for the productivity of thought, for how concepts can fit together to form thoughts, for the role of concepts in language comprehension and production, for the processes through which categorization is accomplished, and for at least part of the story about concept formation and acquisition. Many philosophers accept that at least some of the items on the psychologists' list of phenomena a theory of concepts should account for *are* in its domain, and whatever machinery accounts for the use of concepts will be an aspect of the determination of their contents. In response, they proposed a *dual-factor* theory of content determination.

Dual-factor theories posit two aspects of concept determination (or alternatively, two aspects of the determination of the meaning of terms), wide and narrow. Wide factors underlie the differences in concepts between me and my twin on Twin Earth—my concept *water* picks out H_2O and my twin's picks out XYZ. Narrow factors underlie those aspects of concepts that my twin and I share—every aspect of meaning that is determined by what's inside our heads. Of course, Putnam would not deny that I and my twin share mental representations with identical format and internal conceptual role; he depends upon this, after all, as he develops his science fiction scenario to argue that these internal factors don't suffice to individuate concepts. Putnam would also allow that mental representations do all the work psychologists want of them, *except* the epistemological and semantic work. At issue, then, between Putnam-Kripke and dual-factor theorists is whether on the one hand internal conceptual role is genuinely semantic, part of what determine the meanings of our terms, including mental symbols, or whether, on the other hand, internal conceptual role is merely part of the nuts and bolts of how concepts refer, as Jerry Fodor claims. Dual-factor theorists take the first of these paths, and so must spell out in what ways mental representations play a role in determining what a given mental symbol means.

I approach dual-factor theory in two steps. First, I summarize several considerations that favor the conclusion that inferential role plays a role in determination of the content of concepts. Second, I turn to the question of how we might separate the aspects of conceptual role that are content determining from those that have other parts to play in our theory of the mind.

Thinking about the content of at least one class of concepts provides an existence proof for narrow content. Conceptual role is the sole source of meaning for logical connectives—words like "if", "or" and "not." The meanings of logic connectives are exhausted by their role in conceptual combination. There are no entities in the world that cause "or" to be tokened. The concept *or* gets its meaning from its relations to other connectives ("and," "not") and the computations that allow one to derive the truth conditions from a complex proposition (*P or Q*) from the truth values of the constituent propositions *(P, Q)*. However the relevant theories of narrow content work out in the case of logical connectives, they might be drawn upon in theories of narrow content for terms with wide content for which information semantics applies—for concepts that would thus fall under dual-factor theory. Of course, we still need positive arguments for dual-factor theory in the case of concepts with wide content.

At issue in dual-factor theory is how the conceptual or inferential role of concepts figures in determining the meaning of those that are causally connected to entities in the world. One way inferential relations with other symbols plays a role in determining the content of a given mental symbol is by being part of sustaining mechanisms that causally connect entities in the world to it. As mentioned above, Fodor does not deny that the inferential role plays a part in sustaining mechanisms; rather, he insists that the information that is part of this is "mere engineering" and is not content determining. Following Putnam-Kripke, he argues that there is no information about the entities that falls under a concept that is analytically true of them, no prototype or theory that are part of what individuates a given concept. Dual-factor theorists need to counter with convincing arguments that some aspects of the inferential role that sustain the connections between entities in the world and mental representations are not *mere engineering*.

The philosopher Ned Block (1986, 1987) provides strong reasons for believing that internal conceptual role determines some part of true content. Block emphasizes the phenomena information semantics cannot account for—the productivity of thought, meaning-dependent inference, explaining incommensurability, and explaining the different between different terms which have the same reference—arguing that these phenomena are in the domain of a theory of concepts, and thus the aspects of conceptual role that account for them *are* genuinely content determining. In addition, he argues that even the information semanticists' sacred phenomenon—reference—cannot be accounted for without appealing to conceptual role. Take natural kind concepts like *tiger* or *gold*, for example. Block argues that although no particular component of the actual sustaining mechanisms that connects tigers to our concept *tiger* or gold to our concept *gold* may be constituitive of these concepts, conceptual role still determines the nature of these sustaining mechanisms. It does so by determining that psychological essentialism is true of our natural kind concepts. It is due to our mind, to our psychology, that natural kind terms pick out entities in the world that share hidden essences that we may never discover. Psychological essentialism is just that—*psychological*. It enables us to have concepts of entities whose nature may be hidden from us. As Block puts it, conceptual role determines the type of function between entities in the world and our types of representations of them, even if a variety of sustaining mechanisms can do the trick.

The force of Block's argument becomes clear when we consider a solution to Fodor's radical nativism paradox that was offered, independently, by the psychologist John Macnamara (1986) and by the philosophers Steven Laurence and Eric Margolis (2002). Taking on the difficult case of natural kind concepts, both groups pointed out that sustaining mechanisms can themselves be learned, although Macnamara did not use this terminology. Macnamara suggested that the mental symbol that represent tigers is *same natural kind as* [image/prototype/theory of tiger]. You can read the brackets as indicating demonstrative reference to an image or prototype or theory. The image/prototype/theory of a tiger can be learned by standard prototype extraction or theory learning procedures, and the resulting representational structure then subserves categorization and inference, as in standard prototype/exemplar/theory-theory analyses of concepts. This representation does not fall prey to the Putnam-Kripke objections to these theories because being tagged as a natural kind concept ensures concept holders do not take the stereotype/exemplars/theories they currently represent to *determine* the content of the concept; as they deploy the concept, they are committed to these being revisable. Thus, Macnamara presupposed psychological essentialism, although his work predated the research that falls under that description. The argumentative force of Macnamara's proposal is that we take a role slot we have for natural kind concepts and plug in a representation of an exemplar of a newly encountered natural kind, and what we get is a new concept. The exemplar-representation, or prototype abstracted from several exemplars, or representation of the kind constrained by its role in an intuitive theory, is thus part of the sustaining mechanism presupposed by information semantics. It helps ensure that our symbol *tiger* refers to tigers and not lions.

This proposal denies premises 1 and 2 of Fodor's argument for radical concept nativism. Although standard learning mechanisms that are varieties of hypothesis-testing processes underlie formation of the image/prototype/theory of tiger, and forming these does make use of standard processes for concatenating over antecedently available representations, this process does not exhaust learning the concept. The force of the role slot, *same natural kind as*, is that none of the features of tigers that constitute the representation of the prototype/exemplar/theory is nonrevisable. The force of this role slot is that these features do not *determine* category membership, even probabilistically.

Making essentially the very same proposal, Laurence and Margolis (2002) independently suggested that standard theories of prototype/ examplar/theory learning can be brought to bear on learning a "kind syndrome" that is then part of the sustaining mechanism that connects entities in the world, tigers, with the mental symbol *tiger*. Kind syndromes are those aspects of our mental representations of tigers that help us use our concept *tiger* to refer to tigers. These will be idiosyncratic from person to person and are learned through garden-variety learning processes, involving hypothesis testing over antecedently available concepts. This isn't to say that understanding these processes is easy, or that we have a complete theory (see Murphy, 2002), but this is the bread-and-butter work on the psychology of concepts. As in Macnamara's account, it is because the kind syndrome is deployed in the context of a commitment to psychological essentialism that these representations succeed in picking out natural kinds. The concept user is not committed to a kind syndrome's being nonrevisable. Quite the contrary; the concept user takes the concept to refer to entities whose existence, properties, and nature are determined by hidden causal processes—its essence—and is always open to revising the kind syndrome. That is, we have conceptual role machinery that treats words as placeholder kind terms; a conceptual role is generated by plugging a new term into that role and coordinating it with of members of the kind that have been ostensively defined by others in the language community. This is not a definition of the sort that the classical view envisioned, and creating such a representation is not exhausted by the hypothesis-testing processes that establish a representation of the exemplars. Rather, the mechanism of concept acquisition Laurence and Margolis envisioned, like that proposed by Macnamara, is a matter of using the term "tiger" as a placeholder which is linked to two things: an abstract role for natural kinds and then to an exemplar or prototype, the result being a new role. That process violates Fodor's premises 1 and 2.

Margolis and Laurence claim that their solution to Fodor's paradox is framed within Fodor's own theory of concepts, and that concepts can be learned because sustaining mechanisms can be learned. But, in fact, their solution is *not* framed within information semantics alone. Rather, it falls under dual-factor theory. Yes, some sustaining mechanisms—those involving the conceptual role—can be learned; but according to Fodor, these are not content determining, and Margolis and Laurence agree. That's why they put their solution in the context of the learner's commitment to psychological essentialism. But it is part of the *conceptual role* of the concept *tiger* that it falls under psychological essentialism. Not all concepts do, and that *tiger* does is necessary for the kind syndrome to properly sustain it. This is what Block means by the conceptual role determining the nature of the function between the entity in the world and the mental symbol.

Block offers an additional, closely related solution to Fodor's radical concept nativism paradox. He also denies that learning a concept involves stating it in terms of already understood concepts. As mentioned in chapter 11, Block gave the example of how a student learns the concepts *mass, force, energy, momentum,* and *acceleration.* He points out that one learns relations among these terms themselves, such as "Force equals mass times acceleration," without being able to define *force, mass,* or *acceleration* in terms of concepts that the learner already possesses. Block is appealing to Quinian bootstrapping here; the sentences and equations that express the relations among the concepts themselves are initially placeholder structures. The difference between this proposal and that described above is that it does not depend on an already established abstract conceptual role, *natural kind*.

The Quinian bootstrapping mechanisms discussed in chapters 8 to 11 put meat on the bones of Block's proposal. In those chapters I discussed how the placeholder symbols are generated and also the modeling activities through which these placeholders become meaningful. The bootstrapping proposal has two crucial parts. First, the creation of the placeholders is sometimes part of the process through which mental symbols themselves come into being. Before learning physics, there are no symbols in the mind that express the concept *mass* or the concept *acceleration*. This aspect of bootstrapping concerns the coining of new atomic primitives. As described in chapters 8 and 11, there are two processes through which these placeholder structures are created. When the bootstrapping is in the service of an individual's mastery of an already constructed theory, as when a physics students masters Newtonian mechanics, or a child masters the numeral list representation of the positive integers, then the placeholder structure is constructed through the combinatorial mechanisms of formal symbol systems but it is learned from others through ordinary processes of language acquisition. One can use the sentence "Force equals mass times acceleration" with a meaning exhausted by knowing what *equals* and *times* mean, plus understanding that the syntax of this sentence in English means that the variables are related, $F = MA$. In cases of the original, historical episodes of conceptual change, such as those achieved by Maxwell and Kepler (chapter 11), placeholder creation also draws upon the combinatorial mechanisms of formal symbol systems, but it is created as part of a tentative abductive leap and then explored through extensive modeling activities. In either case, at least some of the meanings in a pure placeholder structure are exhausted by relations among the symbols within it. These meanings are given by conceptual role. Next, modeling processes create new, richer, meanings for these symbols, and these modeling processes also crucially recruit conceptual role (see chapters 8 through 11).

Finally, I dwell on one last argument that the inferential role has an important part to play in determining conceptual content. Chapters 8 through 11 argued that accounting for the origin of concepts requires distinguishing conceptual change from belief revision that does not involve conceptual change. The reason that this distinction is crucial to the project of understanding the origin of concepts is that, in cases of conceptual change, new primitives are created, whereas belief revision always involves testing hypothesis that are stated in terms of already available concepts. Kitcher (1978) placed his analysis of incommensurability in the context of a theory of wide content. As he pointed out, there are multiple sustaining mechanisms, some involving conceptual role and some involving social practices. At any given time, the community assumes that all of these methods of reference determination connect a given symbol with the same class of referents. In cases of conceptual change, it transpires that some pick out different entities from others, and some, like the methods that identified phlogiston in the world, pick out nothing at all.

The analysis of conceptual change offered in chapters 8 though 11 is broader than that offered by Kitcher, for it assumes a dual-factor theory of content determination. Being a dual-factor theory, which allows for wide content, it can accept Kitcher's analysis as being part of the story. But an analysis of conceptual change in terms of certain types of differentiations, coalescences, and changes in conceptual types and cores concerns internal conceptual structure rather than wide content alone. To reiterate a point made above, consider again the concepts that articulate the successive physical theories described in chapter 10. Children with the first theory have not differentiated *weight* from *density,* and so have no mental symbol causally connected with weight. In the second theory, *weight* and *density* are interdefined and crucially depend on concepts of matter and material kind. That weight is an extensive variable, determined by amount of matter, is not merely the second theory's *conception* of weight. Without extensive concepts of matter and amount of stuff, the thinker can have no symbol causally connected to weight at all.

Of course, not everybody accepts that one must distinguish conceptual change from belief revision. To those who do not, I can only point to the analyses in chapters 8 through 11 and reiterate that doing so makes sense of those episodes of conceptual development that are so very difficult for people to achieve. The theory of the origins of concepts articulated in this book commits us to a dual-factor theory of concepts, and to the degree that that theory is supported by evidence and by engendering a fruitful research program, the dual-factor theory gains support.

Finally, the dual-factor theory I presuppose here allows for cases of conceptual change that a theory of meaning exhausted by wide content alone would not. If all content is wide content, and content is therefore determined by the extension of a concept, then so long as the extension of a symbol remains the same over historical or ontogenetic change, its meaning is the same. If Aristotle's Greek term that we translate as "water" referred to water, then its wide content is the same as modern chemistry's concept *water.* If meaning in exhausted by wide content, it is irrelevant to the meaning of the term *water* that today's concept is embedded in a chemistry articulated in terms of an ontology of atoms, molecules, and subatomic particles, and Aristotle's in terms of an ontology in which water was one of the four terrestrial basic elements (along with earth, air, and fire). These would merely be different beliefs about water.

From a dual-factor theory point of view, there is nothing inherently problematic with the possibility of conceptual change in these cases. Although many, if not most, examples of conceptual change involve changes both in wide and in narrow content, there could be changes within those aspects of conceptual role that determine narrow content alone. As I will argue below, the aspects of conceptual role that determine conceptual content include those conceptual roles that bring new primitives into existence. So changes in conceptual roles of existing concepts that relate them to new primitives are candidates for changes in narrow content. Aristotle's physical theory is incommensurable with the physics and chemistry of the 19th century or later, and that is mostly seen in the emergence of new primitives, such as *element, atom, electron,* and *matter.* The Aristotelian term we translate with *element* clearly expresses a concept different from Mendeleev's *element,* and the latter cannot be expressed in terms of concepts available to Aristotle. This analysis allows us to see a sense in which Aristotle's *water* shares wide content with modern chemistry's *water,* but differs in narrow content.

To summarize, dual-factor theory holds that both internal conceptual role and causal connections between entities in the world and mental symbols (both social/historical causal connections and physical causal connections involving perceptual mechanisms and inferential processes) play roles in determining content. Unlike the purely internalist psychological accounts of concepts, dual-factor theory denies that conceptual roles, whether specified in terms of definitions, exemplars, or theories, are *sufficient* to determine content. And it offers three different solutions to Fodor's concept nativism paradox. First, as Block argued, some aspects of conceptual role determine the nature of the mapping between entities in the world and symbols in the mind. Different types of symbols (e.g., symbols for natural kinds vs. symbols for logical connectives determine different types of mappings. Second, as Macnamara and as Laurence and Margolis argued, and as Fodor would agree, the causal processes that make information semantics work, the sustaining mechanisms, include conceptual role. These conceptual roles can be learned, and involve standard associative, prototype abstraction, and hypothesis formation and testing mechanisms. Third, concept learning mechanisms include Quinian bootstrapping processes, and these do not involve concatenation over a previously available set of concepts. In Quinian bootstrapping, conceptual role is necessary to content determination, because the content of some of the terms in the placeholders is exhausted by their conceptual role, and because the modeling processes that fill in the placeholders are constraint satisfying processes and the relevant constraints are part of conceptual role.

To conclude my highly selective review of the classical view of concepts and some psychologists' and philosophers' response to it, it is not going to be easy to come up with a theory that accounts for all of the phenomena on the empiricists' list, and it will not look like the empiricists' theory—the classical view. It will have a place for wide content and it will have a place for narrow content. At present, we do not have worked-out theories of either. We do not have a theory of the causal connections between entities in the world and mental symbols (Fodor's "mere engineering"), but there are good reasons to believe that both Kripke's historical and social factors and causal factors that operate within the body will be players. We also do not have a theory for which aspects of conceptual role are content determining.

This last point is important. Without being able to say *what* aspects of conceptual role determine narrow content and which merely reflect beliefs formulated over the concepts, one does not have a theory of the narrow content part of a dual-factor theory. My goal has been to show, in broad strokes, how understanding the origin of concepts motivates the dual-factor theory of concepts. I hereby acknowledge that I have no worked-out account of which aspects of the conceptual role are content determining, which are part of sustaining mechanisms, and which are merely part of the web of beliefs we hold about the entities in the world our concepts pick out. That a dual-factor theory of the sort I envision can be worked out is an article of faith, but no more so than any other broad view of concepts, including the Putnam-Kripke causal theory and the information semantics theory of wide content or purely internal, descriptivist views of the sorts psychologists favor. In the next sections, I offer some suggestions about how the dual-factor theory might be developed, first for the representations within core cognition, then for explicit mathematical representations, and finally for explicit repre-sentations within intuitive theories.

A Theory of the Symbols in Core Cognition

What theories of concepts apply to the symbols of core cognition? What determines their content (internal and external) and their role in infants' thought? It is in pondering these questions that the importance of the similarity between systems of core cognition and perceptual systems comes to the fore. The psychological theories of concepts (prototype/exemplar/knowledge/internalist theory-theory views) do not apply to perceptual representations. Consider depth representations. Depth representations are simply the output of perceptual analyzers. There is no prototype or exemplar of any given distance that plays a role in creating a representation of it. Nor is there any theory that is part of everyone's psychology in which distance is a theoretical term, although representations of distance clearly play a computational role in representations of size and shape and in navigation, reaching, and other activities. Similarly, prototypes, exemplars, and theories play no role in creating representations of objects. Infants can form representations of radically unfamiliar objects as subject to the constraints on object motion, just as they do for familiar toys and bottles. This does not mean that there are no represented exemplars of objects—of course, there are. But the processes of creating object files rely on spatio-temporal information that has no access to these exemplar representations. Similarly, analog magnitude representations of the approximate cardinal values of sets are imply the output of an innate input analyzer; this process does not involve prototype abstraction or representations of particular exemplars.

The story for agents is more complex. Presumably for infants as well as adults, humans are prototypical agents. Furthermore, as detailed in chapter 5, there is an innate representation of what human faces look like —an innate face schema—that clearly plays a role in recognizing faces as such, learning to identity one's mother's face, identifying eyes and the focus of gaze, and supporting facial imitation. We might think of this as an innate prototype, but this prototype does not provide the content for the concept. Rather, we might think of the innate face schema as part of the innate input analysis mechanism that allows the infant to identify agents in the world—part of the sustaining mechanism that connects agents to infants representations of them. Furthermore, the second input analysis mechanism—agency from action (see chapter 5)—makes use of no prototype. The representations in core cognition, like perceptual representations, are the output of dedicated input analyzers.

Dual-factor theory applies straightforwardly to the symbols of core cognition, just as it does to perceptual representations. Wide content has pride of place, and information semantics (rather than the social/historical theory of reference) is the relevant theoretical framework for thinking about wide content of core cognition's representational systems. The symbols in core cognition are not public, so they are not in the domain of the Kripke-Putnam social historical theory of wide content. Evolutionarily adapted perceptual analyzers ensure that the symbols of core cognition are causally connected to the entities in the world they represent. Computational role certainly is part of the sustaining mechanisms that connect entities in the world to the symbols of core cognition; the input analyzers themselves are computational devices. Nonetheless, the symbols of core cognition have narrow content as well as wide content. The core cognition concept *object* has the content it does partly because of within-module constraints on the models of events involving objects (e.g., the solidity constraint) but also perhaps because of innate or learned constraints on the representations that are the output of the core cognition modules (e.g., contact causality). For example, objects are categorized into those capable of self-generated motion and those that are not, and this categorization guides further inference (see chapter 5). Once infants have learned that unsupported objects fall, evidence that an entity does not fall when it is apparently suspended in mid-air is taken either to mean that it is not an independent object (i.e., it is part of an object it is adjacent to) or that it is capable of self-generated motion. Thus, post-module conceptual role is important to individuating objects and in placing them into their basic ontological kinds.

The question arises: which aspects of conceptual role are content determining, which part of sustaining mechanisms, and which merely part of the web of knowledge infants have about the entities in the domains of core cognition? On my account, the content determining computational role is that which is innately specified and never over-turned. This aspect of conceptual role is part of the sustaining mechanisms embodied in the input analyzers that underlie the causal connections between the symbols of core cognition and the real world entities in its domain. This aspect of conceptual role also guides domain-constituitive inferences. For object representations, this would include representations of spatio-temporal continuity, the solidity constraint, boundedness, and contact causality. For agent representations, this would include concepts of goals, perceptual and representational states, referential intent, and dispositional causal agency. For number representations, this would include the computations that support comparison and numerical computations like addition and multiplication. Notice that the Quine-Putnam arguments against narrow content that derive from the observation that no aspect of conceptual role is nonrevisable and thus no aspect of conceptual role can determine meaning, do not apply, as a matter of empirical fact, to the representations of core cognition. These are never revised. They may be overturned in our explicit theories of the world, but they continue throughout life to determine the content of the representations within core cognition.

In sum, we see that we have at least a sketch of the nature of the representations within core cognition, a sketch that includes both narrow and wide content and that satisfies all of our pre-theoretic desiderata for a theory of concepts. Representations of objects, agents, goals, approximate cardinal values of sets, and so forth, have the content they do because evolutionarily adapted perceptual analyzers and inferential devices ensure that they are causally connected to the entities in the world they represent. That these representations are, as a matter of empirical fact, never overturned makes the dual-factor theory of them play out differently from that for natural kind terms and explicit mathematical symbols. The representations of core cognition, when expressed in language, determine sufficiently shared content that people can disagree about the entities represented. The inferences core cognition supports are explained by innate computational structure, as well as learned generalizations stated over its symbols. Core cognition is productive. Some inferences supported by core cognition are instantiated within module, in the form of constraints on the processes that build iconic models of the world—for example, the solidity constraint. But the outputs of the core cognition modules are central and integrated. For example, infants represent agents as having objects as the goals of their reaches, and as interacting causally with each other and with objects. Core cognition may include processes that build complex iconic models, rather than language-like propositions, but it is nonetheless genuinely productive.

I turn now to how dual-factor theory might be fleshed out in the case of explicit conceptual representations.

A Theory of the Content of Explicit Symbols

Most concepts are *not* connected to the entities they represent by evolutionarily adapted input analyzers and innately specified sustaining mechanisms. Most concepts do not participate in innate domain-constituting inferences. Furthermore, as Quine and Putnam taught us, internal inferential relations among explicit symbols for natural kinds, at least, are always in principle revisable, and this applies even to those that begin life mapped to representations in core cognition. Modern physics allows us to see that objects like tables are not solid, and that other material entities can pass through the space occupied by tables. Although the *object* representations of core cognition continue to articulate our representations of the physical world throughout our lives, we can create explicit representations of objects that are incommensurable with core cognition (see chapter 10). How, then, do the explicit concepts in intuitive and formal theories get their meaning? What is the right semantics for public symbols that do not express developmental primitives and that are not definable in terms of developmental primitives? What determines the content of concepts such as *seven*, *a half*, and *matter*?

Mathematical Symbols

Space and expertise preclude a discussion of what gives mathematical symbols their meanings. Questions about the meanings of mathematical symbols are intertwined with questions about the ontology of mathematical entities. In some views, mathematics is entirely a formal enterprise, in the sense that mathematical symbols refer to nothing external to mathematical systems themselves. If we accept this view, then the meanings of the concepts that articulate the formalisms are exhausted by conceptual role

I doubt that anybody would oppose the claim that inferential role plays an important part in providing mathematical symbols with their meaning. After all, even Fodor agrees that the concepts in logic (*if, and, no, or*) get their meaning through their inferential role. Logical representations and mathematical ones are closely interrelated. The obvious question that arises in the case of mathematical concepts is whether *information semantics* could play any role in content determination. Perhaps dual-factor theory does not apply to them. Perhaps they have no wide content. Mathematical concepts represent abstract entities; how can there be causal connections between abstract entities and the concepts that represent them? Considering how mathematical concepts are acquired (concepts of fractions and integers being the cases considered in earlier chapters) shows us how dual-factor theory works out in this case. We see why we need inferential role semantics to characterize the content of mathematical symbols, and also we find a place for wide content.

Seven is a single lexical item. Clearly *seven* is definable in terms of other concepts (*1, number, add,* the concepts that articulate Peano's axioms), and thus it stands as an immediate counterexample to the claim that we can never provide a definition that supplies necessary and sufficient conditions for falling under a concept of the grain of a single lexical item. But that we can provide a definition does not mean that the definition we offer is stated in terms of developmental primitives, or that learning the concept was a process of testing hypotheses formulated in terms of those primitives. That all integers can be defined in terms of *0, 1,* and the successor function may be irrelevant to the processes that give meaning to symbols for integers. Surely children and non-mathematicians do not possess any explicit encoding of Peano's axioms. Furthermore, the primitives in Peano's axioms are not developmental primitives: there are no symbols in core cognition with the content *1* or *0* or *add* (although this content is embodied in the computations defined over parallel individuation and analog magnitude representations together).

Peano's axioms cannot be totally irrelevant to the meanings of symbols for integers. Even if the axioms are not explicitly represented, any representations of integers must be consistent with them. For example, Gelman and Gallistel's (1978) counting principles ensure that numerals satisfy Peano's axioms and thus represent integers. Bootstrapping the counting principles in turn ensures that *seven* has the content *one more than six, which is one more than five, which is one more than four,* and so on, even though this content is not explicitly stated as such over mental symbols. Inferential role (in this case in the form of the counting principles) gives verbal numerals their meaning, and that inferential role is learned via a bootstrapping process.

Inferential role plays three important parts in the acquisition of concepts for integers. First, it is central to the creation of the placeholder symbols. One step in the bootstrapping process involves learning the numeral list itself. Before this, the child has no atomic symbol (lexical or internal) that expresses any integer. At the beginning of this process the only content of these verbal numerals is provided by their place in a strictly ordered list. Second, inferential role provides the numerical meaning for "one," "two," and "three" in the subset-knower stage (in the form of long-term memory models of sets of 1, 2, and 3 objects and computations that compare these via 1–1 correspondence with working-memory models). These inferential roles are what allow the numerical meaning of the counting routine to be learned. Third, the numerical content of *seven* for cardinal-principle knowers (those children who have induced how counting represents number) is provided by its part in the count routine. Thus, inferential role is absolutely central to what makes the 4-year-old's "seven" represent the concept 7.

The place of inferential role in initially providing meaning for symbols for rational numbers (2/3, .5) parallels that for verbal numerals in every respect. Any rational number can certainly be defined in terms of other concepts; any rational number is one integer divided by another. But these primitives are not available at the outset of the bootstrapping episode; the child does not have the mathematical concept *divide*. As for integer representations, inferential role has three parts to play in the construction of symbols for rational number. The proposition that 2/3 is 2 divided by 3 is a placeholder structure. It tells the child that *divide* expresses some operation of one integer on another, and this is all it tells the child because the relevant concept *divide* must still be acquired. Second, inferential role provides the content for integer concepts available to the child at the outset of the bootstrapping process, as shown above. Inferential role also provides content for the precursors of the concept *divide*: splitting, finding midpoints, and sharing are all computations carried out over quantities (including integers, to a very limited extent). Finally, the numeral content of fractions at the end of the bootstrapping process is, appropriately, that each is one integer divided by another. This may be explicitly represented, or may remain implicit in the computations carried out over number representations after this episode of bootstrapping is complete.

Thus, the account of how concepts for integers and for rational numbers are acquired that was offered in chapters 8 and 11 confirms the importance of conceptual role to initially providing meaning for these symbols. But what of wide content? Collections of physical individuals exist, and the cardinal values that constitute the numerosities of those collections are among their real properties. Of course, physical collections and their cardinal values do not exhaust the mathematical concepts *set* and *integer*, but mathematical development never overturns the fact that the cardinal value of my set of hands is 2.

If we grant that collections of physical individuals are one instantiation of sets, and cardinal values of collections are one instantiation of integers, then the child's initial representations with numerical content are causally connected to the world through the innate input analyzers of the systems of core cognition. Three systems of core cognition (parallel individuation, analog magnitude number, and set-based quantification) have input analyzers that create represents of sets of individuals and support numerical computations over these representations. These numerical representations, for which information semantics definitely applies, get mathematical cognition off the ground. Thus, dual-factor theory applies to the representations that articulate numerical cognition. Conceptual role definitely plays a large part in determining the content of numerical symbols, but information semantics also has its place. Pairs of things are causally-informationally connected to our various concepts of pairs.

What I have just argued is that an appreciation of how Quinian bootstrapping works allows us to see how new primitive symbols are coined in the first place and how conceptual role provides meaning to those symbols. In addition, an appreciation of these processes allows us to address the question of what *aspect* of conceptual role determines the narrow content of symbols for integers and fractions. Distinguishing conceptions from beliefs, in this case, poses different problems from those in the case of concepts embedded within intuitive theories, for the inferences within mathematics are mostly deductive. Why do we think the information contained in Peano's axioms is constituitive of the concept *natural number*, whereas the fact that the squares of odd numbers are odd is not? Perhaps it does not much matter how we answer this question, because of the deductive relations between the properties of natural numbers. But one natural way to answer it is to suggest that the conceptual role we take to determine the narrow content of any symbol for an integer (e.g., *two* or *seven*) is the *minimum* needed to capture the work integers do in mathematics. Of course, there are different axiomatizations of natural number, with different primitives and thus different proposals about the minimum.

The question for psychologists is which, if any, of these anxiomatizations captures how the symbols people use get their meaning. In psychological work we seek to characterize the format, conceptual role, and extensions of the actual symbols people have (e.g., *seven, one-half*). The first representations with the content *natural number* are the count list, deployed in accord with Gelman and Gallistel's counting principles. That these capture the successor function is what ensures that they represent natural number. But surely we do not think that the content of *seven* for an adult or a professional mathematician is provided by the counting principles? No, but we can propose that it is constrained by them as follows: the part of the inferential role of *seven* that provides the narrow content of this symbol, even for adults, is that which ensures that their conceptual role is consistent with the counting principles.

Thus, we have at least a sketch of a dual-factor theory of the content of explicit mathematical symbols—one that satisfies all of the desiderata on our wish list for a theory of concepts. We can account for their acquisition (chapters 8 and 11), their role in inference and productive thought (through a characterization of their format and the computations defined over them), and their stability. (So long as we can characterize both wide and narrow content of mathematical symbols, then people share mathematical concepts so long as they have representations that satisfy that characterization.)

Natural Kind Concepts

The challenge for a theory of the semantics of explicit mathematical symbols is seeing a place for wide content. In contrast, the challenge for a theory of the semantics of natural kind concepts is seeing any place for narrow content. After all, externalist theories of wide content were developed in the arena of natural kind concepts, and these are the concepts to which psychological essentialism applies. The Kripke-Putnam arguments alluded to above, along with the evidence for psychological essentialism, convince me that wide content is important in our analysis of natural kind concepts. In laying out the arguments for dual-factor theory, I sketched the general arguments for narrow content as well as wide content, even for natural kind terms.

Some phenomena in the domain of theory of concepts necessarily depend on conceptual role (inference, conceptual combination, and others). In addition, conceptual role has a crucial part to play even in explaining how symbols refer. The sustaining mechanisms that mediate between entities in the world and mental symbols involve conceptual role, and conceptual role determines the nature of this function. In the case of natural kind terms, it is our mind that determines that the concept falls under the assumptions of psychological essentialism. Finally, the need to distinguish conceptual change from belief revision, and the characterization of Quinian bootstrapping as one of the mechanisms that underlies conceptual change, requires, and thus supports, a dual-factor theory of concepts.

In cases of Quinian bootstrapping of natural kind concepts, we see that conceptual role plays an essential part in concept acquisition, *beyond* being part of the kind syndromes that partially connect symbols in the head to kinds in the world. Seeing how this is so provides a wedge into the problem of characterizing what aspects of conceptual role determine narrow content. In bootstrapping episodes, inferential role enters the process of content determination in many different ways. Just as in the case of mathematical symbols, placeholder structures are the source of new symbols, and therefore are necessary for concept individuation. The content of placeholder structures is exhausted by conceptual role. That placeholder structures are the source of new symbols is seen from all of the conceptual changes documented in chapters 8 through 11. Before the child learns the words "weight" and "density," and placeholder relations such as "density equals weight divided by volume" and "weight provides a better measure of amount of matter than does volume," the child has no mental symbols that refer to these properties of physical entities. Before Kepler coined the term "vis motrix" as a placeholder for the force that is given off by the sun and causes the planets' motion, nobody had any concept that was even remotely connected to the concept *gravity*.

But, you might reply, isn't this true of all word learning? People encounter new words every day (hundreds of them, when they are young), and a new word may always be an invitation to form a concept. True enough, but it is an empirical question whether when children encounter a new term they already have a concept the term will express. In cases of fast mapping, where new words are mastered with virtually 1-trial learning, the learner often has already formed the concept: "I wonder what the animals that is the same natural kind as that [where "that" refers to an individual for which a kind syndrome has already been established] is called"—this is merely learning a label. Alternatively, the learner already has all the conceptual apparatus in place to connect the newly learned symbol with a newly represented kind upon first encountering a word applied to a member of a natural kind.

The cases of concept acquisition discussed in chapters 8 through 11 are most definitely *not* cases of fast mapping. The child has the symbol "two" as part of a count routine and as a quantifier with a meaning related to "some" or "plural" for six to nine months before assigning a cardinal meaning to it. Similarly "a half" and "heavy" are in the child's lexicon for years before they come to have the same meaning as do the adults' symbols with the same form. In cases like these, learning the placeholder structure provides symbols in natural language and also in the language of thought that did not exist before. And unlike learning a new term for a kind of animal or a kind of artifact, the only narrow content these newly coined symbols has is provided by inferential role (that is, determined by the relations to other symbols in the placeholder structure), plus whatever wide content is inherited from the social practices that play a role in the Putnam-Kripke causal theory of reference. These considerations lead to one broad answer concerning which aspects of conceptual role are content determining: those aspects that specify the meaning of the symbols in the placeholder structures that introduce them.

This proposal can't be quite right, because of the Putnam-Kripke-Quine arguments that all aspects of conceptual role for natural kind concepts are open to revision. These arguments apply to all conceptual roles, including those aspects of conceptual role that determine the content of the placeholder structures. I would amend the suggestion thus: in cases of conceptual change, there are clear ancestor/descendant relations among concepts. The aspects of conceptual role that are content determining are those that determine the content of the placeholder structures that introduce the concepts in the first place, plus those aspects of conceptual role that relate those concepts to new primitives that result from differentiations, coalescences, and changes in type and core that constitute the conceptual changes these concepts subsequently undergo.

This proposal avoids radical holism with respect to the aspect of conceptual role that is content determining by appealing to the conceptual roles through which new symbols are introduced into the language of thought and their subsequent developmental history, limiting the relevant conceptual role to relations to other concepts that indicate conceptual change. In the case of the thermal theories between Galileo and Black, the relevant suite of interrelated concepts are heat, cold, and temperature (chapter 10); in the case of conceptual change within the intuitive theory of matter that occurs in normal development between ages 6 and age 12, given the right input, the relevant suite of concepts includes weight, density, volume, mass, matter, liquid, solid, and gas (chapters 10 and 11).

This proposal is related to other natural proposals within the theory-theory of concepts for distinguishing those aspects of conceptual role that determine narrow content from those aspects that merely represent our beliefs about the entities the concepts refer to. Conceptual role is graded in centrality: some changes in conceptual relations would have great ramifications throughout the whole theory whereas others would not. The content determining aspects of conceptual role are the most central ones. In this version of distinguishing those aspects of conceptual role that determine narrow content from those that do not, the distinction is a matter of degree, allowing some degree of holism. The proposal is related to the previous one because the aspects of conceptual role that determine the meaning of the placeholder concepts are likely to be central in this sense, for the modeling processes that give meaning to these concepts are constrained to respect this structure as much as possible. Furthermore, those aspects of conceptual role that participate in conceptual changes are always central in this respect.

Another related proposal draws on the importance of causal structures in the theories in which natural kind concepts are embedded (Keil, 1989). Causal properties are ordered; some causally relevant features of entities derive from more fundamental ones. For example, we explain the capacity of some elements to chemically bind with oxygen by the structure of their electrons, rather than the reverse. The causally deepest features that articulate theories are among the most central ones in the sense of the previous proposal, and thus the two proposals would each suggest that the causally deepest features of the entities that fall under a natural kind concept are among those that determine narrow content. Indeed Ahn (e.g., Ahn & Kim; 2000; Ahn, Kim, Lassaline, & Dennis, 2000) provides evidence that participants are sensitive to causal status and weigh causally deeper features more than causally more peripheral ones in categorization judgments. The suggestion here is that this fact reflects something deep about concepts. Causally central features are part of what determines narrow content of natural kind concepts, as well as being an important part of what determines categorization decisions.

These related suggestions point to possible solutions to the problem of specifying what aspect of conceptual role may determine narrow content. The general arguments for the dual-factor theory of concepts, and the existence of narrow content, force us to accept that there must be *some* solution to this problem, but that solution is not likely to be simple or clean. Just as myriad factors enter into the processes that determine wide content (Fodor's "mere engineering"), so too myriad factors will probably conspire to separate those aspects of conceptual role that are content determining from those that are not. Furthermore, it is likely to be a graded rather than dichotomous distinction, in which case we will have to live with some degree of holism. However, considerations of how the content of the placeholder structures that introduce new primitives into the repertoire is determined (entirely by conceptual role), as well as a focus on just those episodes of conceptual restructuring that introduce new primitives and lead to new conceptual roles involving the ancestor symbols, their descendents, and these new primitives, allow us to identify an aspect of conceptual role that certainly is important in determining narrow content and may be all we need to do the trick of distinguish content determining conceptual role from mere belief.

The Theory-Theory of Concepts

The theory-theory of conceptual development was discussed in chapter 12. Intuitive theories of the physical, biological, social, and mental worlds are important conceptual structures, for they reflect our ontological commitments and contain representations of causal mechanisms, thereby constraining causal learning and inductive inference. Therefore, accounting for the acquisition of these framework theories is an important project in the discipline of cognitive development. However, my focus here is on a different version of the theory-theory: the theory-theory of concepts.

The two theory-theories are independent because it may be true that the key to understanding human knowledge acquisition is understanding the process of theory development, whereas it may *not* be true that theory-relative conceptual role plays a part in determining conceptual content. Those who endorse a single-factor theory of content determination (wide content alone), such as Putnam and Kripke and Fodor, would probably be happy to endorse the importance of explicit and intuitive theories to mental life, and thus the importance of these structures in the study of cognitive development, while at the same time denying the theory-theory of concepts.

As just discussed, my analysis of the origin of concepts commits me to a version of the theory-theory of concepts. A consideration of concept origins also provides some hints about how to distinguish the content determining aspects of conceptual role from mere beliefs the entities in the extensions of natural kind concepts. The two-factor theory of concepts I advocate here does not fall prey to the problems with purely internalist versions of the theory-theory, because there are two types of processes that determine conceptual content. The content of concepts is not entirely determined by their internal conceptual role; both wide and narrow content surely exist. With respect to inferential role, though, my version of the theory-theory contrasts with the classical view, with prototype/exemplar theories, and with entirely holistic pictures such as Murphy's knowledge theory.

Conclusions: The Origins of Concepts

For the most part, cognitive psychologists concerned with human concepts have abandoned the goal of accounting for their origins, for they ignore the question of developmental primitives. Developmental psychologists charting the conceptual repertoire of human infants, and comparative psychologists charting the conceptual repertoire of nonhuman animals, provide notable exceptions to this generalization, for they seek to characterize the representational resources that get human cognition off the ground, in both ontogenetic and evolutionary contexts. Chapters 2 through 7 synthesized what we have learned about the ontogenetic primitives from which our conceptual system is built. They are much richer and more abstract than empiricist theorizing would allow; we do not build all knowledge from perceptual or sensori-motor representations. However, core cognition is perception-like in many ways, and the representations within core cognition are therefore different in crucial respects from the later-developing explicit concepts that articulate human thought.

In addition to providing an abstract characterization of core cognition, these early chapters consisted of case studies of particular concepts: *object, agent, number,* and *cause.* Characterizing the conceptual repertoire of infants is difficult work, requiring convergent evidence from many methods. It also requires studying parallel suites of representations in order to ascertain which representations constrain other ones. Quite obviously, such work is absolutely necessary if we are to understand the origin of concepts. Only by charactering infants' quantificational representations can we ask whether integer representations transcend them. Only by characterizing infants' concepts of agents can we know whether infants represent others' epistemic states. Only by characterizing infants' representations do we know what work a theory of concept acquisition must accomplish.

A second project central to understanding where the human capacity to think thoughts formulated over concepts, such as *cancer, gold,* and *infinity,* is characterizing whether there are discontinuities in the course of conceptual development, and if so, what kinds there are. The second half of the book provided evidence for conceptual discontinuities at two different levels of abstraction. Abstractly, explicit concepts differ, qualitatively, from those in core cognition. More concretely, within a given domain of knowledge, conceptual development often results in representations with more expressive power, or representations incommensurable with, those that were their input. Chapters 8 through 11 documented discontinuities in conceptual development and characterized one learning process involved in each of these case studies—Quinian bootstrapping. The arguments in these chapters are central to understanding the origin of concepts, for Quinian bootstrapping is a mechanism through which new conceptual primitives are introduced into thought.

Just as for core cognition, the argument was illustrated through specific cases studies of conceptual development. Within intuitive mathematics, the worked examples were the origin of concepts of natural number and of rational number (chapters 4, 7, 8, 9, and 11). Within scientific theory development the most fully worked-out example was the description of the incommensurability between the thermal concepts of Galileo and his students (who invented the thermometer but failed to acquire the concept *temperature*) and Black (who distinguished *heat* from *temperature* and formulated the concepts of the caloric theory). Bootstrapping processes were illustrated in discussions of Kepler and Maxwell (chapters 10 and 11). With intuitive theory change, the fully discussed example involved conceptual changes in children's understanding of the material world, which involve differentiating the concept *matter* from the concept *physically real entity* and differentiating *weight* from *density*. In this case study I illustrated how data are brought to bear on characterizing the conceptual discontinuities and also how data are brought to bear in evaluating proposals for the Quinian bootstrapping process that underlies the change (chapters 10 and 11).

The human conceptual repertoire is a unique phenomenon on this earth, posing a formidable challenge to the disciplines of cognitive science: how are we to account for the human capacity for conceptual representations? I have sketched a response to this challenge, illustrating it through many case studies that show the interdependence of the projects of accounting for the origin of concepts and understanding what concepts are.

References

Adams, F., & Aizawa, K. (1994). Fodorian semantics. In S. Stich & T. A. Warfield (Eds.), *Mental Representation: A Reader* (pp. 223–242). Oxford, UK: Blackwell.

Aguiar, A., & Baillargeon, R. (1999). 2.5-month-old infants' reasoning about when objects should and should not be occluded. *Cognitive Psychology, 39*(2), 116–157.

Aguiar, A., & Baillargeon, R. (2002). Development in young infants' reasoning about occluded objects. *Cognitive Psychology, 45*(2), 267–336.

Ahn, W., & Kim, N. S. (2000). The role of causal features in categorization: An overview. In D. L. Medin (Ed.), *Psychology of Learning and Motivation, 40* (pp. 23–65). New York: Academic Press.

Ahn, W., Kim, N. S., Lassaline, M. E., & Dennis, M. J. (2000). Causal status as a determinant of feature centrality. *Cognitive Psychology, 41*, 1–55.

Alvarez, G. A., & Franconeri, S. L. (2007). How many objects can you track? Evidence for a resource-limited tracking mechanism. *Journal of Vision, 7*(13), 1–10.

Alvarez, G. A., & Franconeri, S. L. (2008). The allocation of visual short-term memory capacity: Evidence for a flexible storage mechanism. Manuscript submitted for publication.

Amso, D., Davidson, M. C., & Johnson, S. P. (2005). Selection and inhibition in infancy: Evidence from the spatial negative priming paradigm. *Cognition, 95*, B27–B36.

Antell, S., & Keating, D. P. (1983). Perception of numerical invariance in neonates. *Child Development, 54*, 695–701.

Armstrong, S., Gleitman, L. R., and Gleitman, H. (1983). What some concepts might not be. *Cognition, 13*, 263–208.

Aslin, R. N., & Johnson, S. P. (1996). Perceptions of object unity in young infants: The rules of motion, depth and orientation. *Cognitive Development, 11*(2), 161–180.

Au, T. K. (1994) Developing an intuitive understanding of substance kinds. *Cognitive Psychology, 27*, 71–111.

Au, T. K, Sidle, A. L., & Rollins, K. B. (1993). Developing an intuitive understanding of conservation and contamination: Invisible particles as a plausible mechanism. *Developmental Psychology, 29*, 286–299.

Baillargeon, R. (1986). Representing the existence and the location of hidden objects: Object permanence in 6- and 8-month-old infants. *Cognition, 23*, 21–41.

Baillargeon, R. (1987). Object permanence in 3.5- and 4.5-month-old infants. *Developmental Psychology, 23*, 655–664.

Baillargeon, R. (1993). The object concept revisited: New directions in the investigation of infants' physical knowledge. In C. E. Granud (Ed.), *Visual perception and cognition in infancy* (pp. 265–315). Hillsdale, NJ: Erlbaum.

Baillargeon, R. (1995). A model of physical reasoning in infancy. In C. Rovee-Collier & L. Lipsitt (Eds.), *Advances in Infancy Research* (pp. 305–371). Norwood, NJ: Ablex.

Baillargeon, R. (1998). Infants' understanding of the physical world. In M. Sabourin, F. Craik, & M. Robert (Eds.), *Advances in psychological science, Vol. 2: Biological and cognitive aspects* (pp. 503–529). Hove, England: Psychology Press/Erlbaum (UK) Taylor & Francis.

Baillargeon, R. (2001). Infants' physical knowledge: Of acquired expectations and core principles. In E. Dupoux (Ed.), *Language, brain, and cognitive development: Essays in honor of Jacques Mehler* (pp. 341–361). Cambridge, MA: MIT Press.

Baillargeon, R., & Hanko-Summers, S. (1990). Is the top adequately supported by the bottom object? Young infants' understanding of support relations. *Cognitive Development, 5*, 29–53.

Baillargeon, R., Needham, A., & DeVos, J. (1992). The development of young infants' intuitions about support. *Early Development & Parenting, 1*(2), 69–78.

Baillargeon, R., Spelke, E. S., & Wasserman, S. (1985). Object permanence in 5-month-old infants. *Cognition, 20*, 191–208.

Balaban, M. T., & Waxman, S. R. (1997). Do words facilitate object categorization in 9-month-old infants? *Journal of Experimental Child Psychology, 64*, 3–26.

Baldwin, D. A. (1991). Infant contribution to the achievement of joint reference. *Child Development, 62*, 129–154.

Baldwin, D. A., & Moses, L. J. (1994). Early understanding of referential intent and attentional focus: Evidence from language and emotion. In C. Lewis & P. Mitchell (Eds.), *Origins of an understanding of mind* (pp. 133–156). Hillsdale, NJ: Erlbaum.

Ball, W. A. (1973). The perception of causality in the infant. Paper presented at meeting of the Society for Research in Child Development. March 29 - April 1, Philadelphia, PA.

Barner, D., Thalwitz, D., Wood, J. N., & Carey, S. (2007). Children's ability to distinguish "one" from "more than one" and the acquisition of singular-plural morpho-syntax. *Developmental Science, 10*(3), 365–373.

Barner, D., Wood, J. N., Hauser, M., & Carey, S. (in press). Evidence for a non-linguistic distinction between singular and plural sets in rhesus monkeys. *Cognition*.

Baron, A., Barth, H. C., & Carey, S. (2005). *Children's pre-arithmetic representations of multiplication and division*. Paper presented at the 4th Biennial Meeting of the Cognitive Development Society, San Diego, CA.

Baron-Cohen, S. (1995). *Mindblindness.* Cambridge, MA: MIT Press.

Baroody, A. J. (1992). The development of preschoolers' counting skills and principles. In J. Bideaud, C. Meljac, & J.-P. Fischer (Eds.), *Pathways to number: Children's developing numerical abilities* (pp. 99–126). Hillsdale, NJ: Erlbaum.

Barth, H. C., Kanwisher, N., & Spelke, E. (2003). The construction of large number representation in adults. *Cognition, 86,* 201–221.

Barth, H. C., La Mont, K., Lipton, J., Dehaene, S., Kanwisher, N., & Spelke, E. S. (2006).Non-symbolic arithmetic in adults and young children. *Cognition, 98*(3), 199–222.

Bartsch, K., & Wellman, H. M. (1995). *Children talk about the mind.* Oxford, UK: Oxford University Press.

Bayley, N. (1969). *Bayley scales of infant development.* New York: The Psychological Corporation.

Behr, M. J., Wachsmuth, I., Post, T. R., & Lesh, R. (1984). Order and equivalence of rational number: A clinical teaching experiment. *Journal for Research in Mathematics Education, 15*(5), 323–341.

Berkeley, G. (1732/1919). *A new theory of vision and other select philosophical writings.* New York: Dutton.

Bernstein, M. H., & Sigman, M. D. (1986). Continuity in mental development from infancy. *Child Development, 57,* 251—274.

Berthier, N. E., DeBlois, S., Poirier, C. R., Novak, M. A., & Clifton, R. K. (2000). Where's the ball? Two- and three-year-olds reason about unseen events. *Developmental Psychology, 36*(3), 394–401.

Bijeljac-Babic, R., Bertoncini, J., & Mehler, J. (1991). How do four-day-old infants categorize multisyllabic utterances? *Developmental Psychology, 29,* 711–721.

Block, N. J. (1981). *Imagery.* Cambridge, MA: MIT Press/Bradford Books.

Block, N. J. (1986). Advertisement for a semantics for psychology. In P. A. French (Ed.), *Midwest studies in philosophy* (pp. 615–678). Minneapolis: University of Minnesota.

Block, N. J. (1987). Functional role and truth conditions. *Proceedings of the Aristotelian Society, 61,* 157–181.

Bloom, P., & Wynn, K. (1997). Linguistic cues in the acquisition of number words. *Journal of Child Language, 24*(3), 511–533.

Bogartz, R. S., Shinsky, J. L., & Speaker, C. J. (1997). Interpreting infant looking: The event set by event set design. *Developmental Psychology, 33,* 408–422.

Bonatti, L., Frot, E., Zangl, R., & Mehler, J. (2002). The human first hypothesis: Identification of conspecifics and individuation of objects in the young infant. *Cognitive Psychology, 44*(4), 388–426.

Booth, A. E., & Waxman, S. R. (2003). Mapping words to the world in infancy: Infants' expectations for count nouns and adjectives. *Journal of Cognition and Development, 4,* 357–381.

Boroditsky, L. (2001). Does language shape thought? Mandarin and English speakers' conceptions of time. *Cognitive Psychology, 43*(1), 1–22.

Boroditsky, L., Schmidt, L. A., & Phillipps, W. (2003). Sex, syntax, and semantics. In D. Gentner & S. Goldin-Meadow (Eds.), *Language in mind: Advances in the study of language and thought* (pp. 61–178). Cambridge, MA: MIT Press.

Bowerman, M. (1974). Learning the structure of causative verbs: A study in the relationship of cognitive, semantic, and syntactic development. *Papers and Reports on Child Language Development, 8.* Palo Alto, CA: Department of Linguistics, Stanford University, pp. 142–178.

Bowerman, M., & Choi, S. (2003). Space under construction: Language-specific spatial categorization in first language acquisition. In D. Gentner & S. Goldin-Meadow (Eds.), *Language in mind: Advances in the study of language and thought* (pp. 387–427). Cambridge, MA: MIT Press.

Bowerman, M., & Levinson, S. (2001). *Language acquisition and conceptual development.* Cambridge, UK: Cambridge University Press.

Boysen, S. T., & Bernston, G. G. (1989). Numerical competence in a chimpanzee. *Journal of Comparative Psychology,* 103, 23–31.

Braine, M. D. S. (1963). The ontogeny of English phrase structure: The first phase. *Language,* 1, 1–13.

Brannon, E. M. (2002). The development of ordinal numerical knowledge in infancy. *Cognition,* 83, 223–240.

Brannon, E. M., Abbott, S., & Lutz, D. J. (2004). Number bias for the discrimination of large visual sets in infancy. *Cognition,* 93, B59–B68.

Brannon, E. M., & Terrace, H. S. (1998). Ordering of the numerosities 1 to 9 by monkeys. *Science,* 282, 746–749.

Briars, D., & Siegler, R. (1984). A featural analysis of preschoolers' counting knowledge. *Developmental Psychology,* 20(4), 607–618.

Brooks, R., & Meltzoff, A. M. (2005). The development of gaze following and its relations to language. *Developmental Science,* 8, 535—543.

Brown, R. (1973). *A first language: The early stages.* Cambridge, MA: Harvard University Press.

Bruner, J., Goodnow, J., & Austin, G. (1956). *A study of thinking.* New Brunswick, NJ: Transaction.

Burge, T. (1979). Individualism and the mental. In French, P. A, Uehling, T. E., and Wettstein, H. K. (Eds.), *Midwest studies in philosophy IV* (pp. 73–121). Minneapolis: University of Minnesota Press.

Butler, S. C., Berthier, N. E., & Clifton, R. K. (2002) Two-year-olds' search strategies and visual tracking in a hidden displacement task. *Developmental Psychology,* 38, 581–590.

Butterworth, B. (1999). *What counts: How every brain is hardwired for math.* New York: Free Press.

Campbell, R., Heywood, C., Cowey, A., Regard, M., & Landis, T. (1990). Sensitivity to eye gaze in prosapagnosic patients and monkeys with superior temporal sulcus ablation. *Neuropsychologia,* 28, 1123–1142.

Campos, J. J., & Stenberg, C. R. (1981). Perception, appraisal and emotions: The onset of social referencing. In M. E. Lamb & L. R. Sherrod (Eds.), *Infant social cognition: Empirical and theoretical considerations* (pp. 273–314). Hillsdale, NJ: Erlbaum.

Cantlon, J., & Brannon, E. M. (2006). Shared system for ordering small and large numbers in monkeys and humans. *Psychological Science*, 17(5), 401–406.

Carey, S. (1972). *Are children little scientists with false theories of the world?* Unpublished Ph.D. dissertation, Harvard University.

Carey, S. (1982). Semantic development, state of the art. In L. Gleitman & E. Wanner (Eds.), *Language acquisition, state of the art* (pp. 347–389). Cambridge, UK: Cambridge University Press.

Carey, S. (1985a). *Conceptual change in childhood.* Cambridge, MA: MIT Press.

Carey, S. (1985b). Are children fundamentally different thinkers and learners from adults? In S. F. Chipman, J. W. Segal, & R. Glaser (Eds.), *Thinking and learning skills* (Vol. 2). Hillsdale, NJ: Erlbaum. Reprinted by Open University Press, Open University Readings in Cognitive Development.

Carey, S. (1991). Knowledge acquisition or conceptual change? In S. Carey & R. Gelman (Eds.), *The epigenesis of mind: Essays on biology and cognition* (pp.133–169). Hillsdale, NJ: Erlbaum.

Carey, S. (1999). Sources of conceptual change. In E. K. Scholnick, K. Nelson, S. A. Gelman, & P. Miller (eds.), *Conceptual development: Piaget's legacy* (pp. 293–326). Hillsdale, NJ: Erlbaum.

Carey, S., Evans, R., Honda, M., Unger, C., & Jay, E. (1989). An experiment is when you try and see if it works: Middle school conception of science. *International Journal of Science Education, 11,* 514–529.

Carey, S., & Smith, C. (1993). On understanding the nature of scientific knowledge. *Educational Psychologist, 28,* 235–251.

Carey, S., & Spelke, E. (1994) Domain-specific knowledge and conceptual change. In L. Hirshfeld and S. Gelman (Eds.), *Mapping the mind: Domain specificity in cognition and culture* (pp. 169–200). New York: Cambridge University Press.

Carey, S., & Spelke, E. (1996). Science and core knowledge. *Journal of Philosophy of Science, 63,* 515–533.

Carey, S., & Xu, F. (2001). Beyond object-files and object tracking: Infant representations of objects. *Cognition, 80,* 179–213.

Carlson, S. M., Moses, L. J., & Hix, H. R. (1998). The role of inhibitory processes in young children's difficulties with deception and false belief. *Child Development,* 69, 672–691.

Carnap, R. (1932/1980). The elimination of metaphysics through logical analysis of language. In A. Ayer (Ed.), *Logical positivism* (pp. 60–81). New York: Free Press.

Carpenter, M., Nagell, K., & Tomasello, M. (1998). Social cognition, joint attention, and communicative competence from 9 to 15 months of age. *Monographs of the Society for Research in Child Development, 63* (4, serial no. 255).

Carpenter, T. P., Corbitt, M., K., Kepner, H. J., & Lindquist, M. M. (1981). Decimals: Results and implications from the second NAEP mathematics assessment. *Arithmetic Teacher,* 28(8), 34–37.

Case, R. (1991). Neo-Piagetian theories of child development. In R. J. Sternberg & C. A. Berg (Eds.), *Intellectual development* (pp. 161–197). New York: Cambridge University Press.

Cheng, P. W., & Novick, L. R. (1990). A probabilistic contrast model of causal induction. *Journal of Personality and Social Psychology,* 58, 545–567.

Cheries, E. W., Feigenson, L., Scholl, B. J., & Carey, S. (2005). Cues to object persistence in infancy: Tracking objects through occlusion and implosion. Paper presented at the Vision Sciences Society, Sarasota, FL.

Cheries, E. W., Feigenson, L., Scholl, B. J., & Carey, S. (2008). Cues to object persistence in infancy: Tracking objects through occlusion vs. implosion. Manuscript submitted for publication.

Cheries, E. W., Mitroff, S. R., Wynn, K., & Scholl, B. J. (in press). Cohesion as a principle of object persistence in infancy. *Developmental Science.*

Chiang, W.-C., & Wynn, K. (2000). Infants' representation and tracking of multiple objects. *Cognition,* 77, 169–195.

Chierchia, G. (1998). Plurality of mass nouns and the notion of "semantic parameter." In S. Rothstein (Ed.), *Events and grammar* (pp. 53–103). Dordrecht, The Netherlands: Kluwer Academic Publishers.

Chomsky, N. (1965). *Aspects of the theory of syntax.* Cambridge, MA: MIT Press.

Church, R. M., & Broadbent, H. A. (1990). Alternative representations of time, number, and rate. *Cognition,* 37, 55–81.

Church, R. M., & Meck, W. H. (1984). The numerical attribute of stimuli. In H. L. Roitblatt, T. G. Bever, & H. S. Terrace (Eds.), *Animal cognition* (pp. 445–464). Hillsdale, NJ: Erlbaum.

Clark, E. V., & Nikitina, T. V. (in press). One vs. more than one: Antecedents to plural marking in early language acquisition. *Linguistics.*

Clearfield, M. W., & Mix, K. S. (1999). Number versus contour length in infants' discrimination of small visual sets. *Psychological Science,* 10, 408–411.

Clearfield, M. W., & Mix, K. S. (2001). Amount versus number: Infants' use of area and contour length to discriminate small sets. *Journal of Cognition and Development,* 2(3), 243–260.

Clement, J. (1982). Students' preconceptions in elementary mechanics. *American Journal of Physics,* 50, 66–71.

Clements, W.A., & Perner, J. (1994) Implicit understanding of belief. *Cognitive Development,* 9, 377–395.

Cohen, L. B., Amsel, G., Redford, M. A., & Casasola, M. (1998). The development of infant causal perception. In A. Slater (Ed.), *Perceptual developent: Visual, auditory, and speech perception in infancy* (pp. 167–209). East Sussex, UK: Psychology Press.

Cohen, L. B., & Chaput, H. H. (2002). Connectionist models of infant perceptual and cognitive development. *Developmental Science, 5*, 173–175.

Condry, K., Smith, W. C., & Spelke, E. S. (2001). Development of perceptual organization. In F. Lacerda, C. von Hofsten, & M. Heimann (Eds.), *Emerging cognitive abilities in early infancy* (pp. 1–28). Hillsdale, NJ: Erlbaum.

Condry, K., & Spelke, E. S. (2008). The development of language and abstract concepts: The case of natural number. *Journal of Experimental Psychology:General,* 137(1), 22–38.

Condry, K., Spelke, E., & Xu, F. (2000). *From the infant's number concepts to the child's number words.* Paper presented at the XIIth Biennal International Conference on Infant Studies, Brighton, UK.

Confrey, J. (1994) Splitting, similarity and rate of change: A new approach to multiplication and exponential functions. In G. Hared & J. Confrey (Eds), *The development of multiplicative reasoning in the learning of mathematics* (pp. 291–330). Albany: SUNY Press.

Corbett, G. G. (2000). *Number.* New York: Cambridge University Press.

Cordes, S., Gelman, R., & Gallistel, C. R. (2001). Variability signatures distinguish verbal from nonverbal counting for both large and small numbers. *Psychological Bulletin and Review, 8*, 698–707.

Csibra, G., Biro, S., Koos, O., & Gergely, G. (2003). One-year-old infants use teleological representations of actions productively. *Cognitive Science, 27*(1), 111–133.

Csibra, G., Gergely, G., Koos, O., & Brockbank, M. (1999). Goal attribution without agency cues: The perception of "pure reason" in infancy. *Cognition, 72*, 237–267.

Dehaene, S. (1997). *The number sense.* New York: Oxford University Press.

Dehaene, S. (2001). Précis of "The Number Sense." *Mind and Language, 16*, 16–36.

Dehaene, S., & Changeux, J.-P. (1993). Development of elementary numerical abilities: A neuronal model. *Journal of Cognitive Neuroscience, 5*, 390–407.

Deloache, J. S., Pierroutsakos, S. L., Uttal, D. H., Rosengren, K. S., & Gottlieb, A. (1998). Grasping the nature of pictures. *Psychological Science, 9*(3), 205–210.

Descartes, R. (1637/1971). The dioptrics. In E. Anscombe & P. T. Geach (Eds.), *Philosophical Writings: Descartes* (pp. 239–256). Indianapolis, IN: Bobbs-Merrill.

de Villiers, J. G. (2005). Can language acquisition give children a point of view? In J. W. Astington and J. A. Baird (Eds), *Why language matters for theory of mind.* Oxford, UK: Oxford University Press.

DeVries, R. (1986). Children's conceptions of shadow phenomena. *Genetic, Social, and General Psychology Monographs,* 112(4), 479–530.

Dewar, K., & Xu, F. (2007). Do 9-month-olds expect distinct words to refer to kinds? *Developmental Psychology, 43*, 1227–1238.

Diamond, A. (1991). Neuropsychological insights into the meaning of object concept development. In S. Carey & R. Gelman (Eds.), *The epigenesis of mind: Essays on biology and cognition.* (pp. 67–110). Hillsdale, NJ: Erlbaum.

Diamond, A., & Goldman-Rakic, P. S. (1989). Comparison of human infants and infant rhesus monkeys on Piaget's AB task: Evidence for dependence on dorsolateral prefrontal cortex. *Experimental Brain Research, 74,* 24–40.

Dickinson, A., & Shanks, D. (1995). Instrumental action and causal representation. In D. Sperber, D. Premack, & A. Premack (Eds.), *Causal cognition: A multidiscpilinary debate* (pp. 5–25). Oxford, UK: Clarendon Press.

Diesendruck, G., & Gelman, S. A. (1999). Domain differences in absolute judgments of category membership: Evidence for an essentialist account of categorization. *Psychonomic Bulletin and Review, 6,* 338–346.

Donovan, M. S., Bransford, J. D., & Pellegrino, J. W. (2000). *How people learn: Brain, mind, experience & school: Expanded edition.* Washington, DC: National Academy Press.

Dretske, F. (1981). *Knowledge and the flow of information.* Cambridge, MA: MIT Press.

Elman, J. L., Bates, E. A., Johnson, M. H., Karmiloff-Smith, A., Parisi, D., Plunkett, K. (1996), *Rethinking innateness: A connectionist perspective on development.* Cambridge, MA: MIT Press.

Emlen, S. (1975). The stellar orientation system of a migratory bird. *Scientific American, 233:* 102–111.

Estes, D., Wellman, H. M., & Woolley, J. D. (1989). Children's understanding of mental phenomena. *Advances in Child Development and Behavior, 22,* 41–87.

Everett, D. L. (2005). Cultural constraints on grammar and cognition in Pirahã: Another look at the design features of human language. *Current Anthropology, 46(4),* 621–646.

Fagan, J. F., & McGrath, S. K. (1981). Infant recognition memory and later intelligence. *Intelligence, 5,* 121—130.

Feigenson, L. (2005). A double-dissociation in infants' representation of object arrays. *Cognition, 95,* B37–B48.

Feigenson, L., & Carey, S. (2003). Tracking individuals via object files: evidence from infants' manual search. *Developmental Science, 6(5),* 568–584.

Feigenson, L., & Carey, S. (2005). On the limits of infants' quantification of small object arrays. *Cognition, 97(3),* 295–313.

Feigenson, L., Carey, S., & Hauser, M. D. (2002). The representations underlying infants' choice of more: Object files versus analog magnitudes. *Psychological Science, 13,* 150–156.

Feigenson, L., Carey, S., & Spelke, E. (2002). Infants' discrimination of number vs. continuous extent. *Cognitive Psychology, 44,* 33–66.

Feigenson, L., & Halberda, J. (2004). Infants chunk object arrays into sets of individuals. *Cognition, 91,* 173–190.

Feyerabend, P. (1962). Explanation, reduction, empiricism. In H. Feigl & G. Maxwell (Eds.), *Scientific explanation, space, and time* (pp. 28–97). Minneapolis: University of Minnesota Press.

Flavell, J. H. (1963). *The developmental psychology of Jean Piaget.* Princeton, NJ: Van Nostrand.

Flavell, J. H., Everett, B., Croft, K. & Flavell, E. (1981). Young children's knowledge about visual perception: Further evidence for the Level 1-Level 2 distinction. *Developmental Psychology, 17,* 99–103.

Flavell, J. H., Green, F., & Flavell, E. (1986). Development of knowledge about the appearance-reality distinction. *Monographs of the Society for Research in Child Development, 51.*

Flombaum, J. I., Junge, J., & Hauser, M. D. (2005). Rhesus monkeys (*Macaca mulatta*) spontaneously compute large number addition operations. *Cognition,* 97(3), 315–325.

Flombaum, J. I., & Santos, L. R. (2005). Rhesus monkeys attribute perceptions to others. *Current Biology,* 15, 447–452.

Fodor, J. A. (1975). *The language of thought.* Cambridge, MA: Harvard University Press.

Fodor, J. A. (1980). On the impossibility of acquiring " more powerful" structures: Fixation of belief and concept acquisition. In M. Piatelli-Palmerini (Ed.), *Language and learning.* (pp. 142–162). Cambridge, MA: Harvard University Press.

Fodor, J. A. (1983). *The modularity of mind.* Cambridge, MA: MIT Press.

Fodor, J. A. (1990). Information and representation. In P. I. Hanson (Ed.). *Information, language, and cognition* (pp. 175–190). Vancouver: University of British Columbia Press.

Fodor, J. A. (1998). *Concepts: Where cognitive science went wrong.* New York: Oxford University Press.

Fodor, J. A., Garrett, M. F., Walker, E. C., & Parkes, C. H. (1980). Against definitions. *Cognition,* 8(3), 263–267.

Fodor, J. A., & Lepore, E. (1992). *Holism: A shopper's guide.* Cambridge, MA: Basil Blackwell.

Fodor, J. D., Fodor, J. A., & Garrett, M. F. (1975). The psychological unreality of semantic representations. *Linguitic Inquiry,* 6, 515–532.

Frank, M. C., Everett, D. L., Fedorenko, E., & Gibson, E. (in press). Number as a cognitive technology: Evidence from Piraha language and cognition. *Cognition.*

Frye, D., Zelazo, P. D., & Palfai, T. (1995). Theory of mind and rule-based reasoning. *Cognitive Development,* 10, 483–527.

Fuson, K. C. (1988). *Children's counting and concepts of number.* New York: Springer-Verlag.

Gallistel, C. R. (1990). *The organization of learning.* Cambridge, MA: MIT Press.

Gallistel, C. R. (2000). The replacement of general-purpose learning models with adaptively specialized learning modules. In M. S. Gazzaniga (Ed.), *The cognitive neurosciences, 2nd ed.* (pp. 1179–1191). Cambridge, MA: MIT Press.

Gallistel, C. R., Brown, A., Carey, S., Gelman, R., & Keil, F. C. (1991). Lessons from animal learning for the study of cognitive development. In S. Carey & R. Gelman (Eds.), *The epigenesis of mind: Essays in biology and cognition* (pp. 3–39). Hillsdale, NJ: Erlbaum.

Gallistel, C. R., & Gelman, R. (1992). Preverbal and verbal counting and computation. *Cognition, 44,* 43–74.

Gallistel, C. R., & Gelman, R. (2000). Non-verbal numerical cognition: from reals to integers. *Trends in Cognitive Sciences,* 4, 59–65.

Garnham, W. A., & Ruffman, T. (2001) Doesn't see, doesn't know: is anticipatory looking really related to understanding of belief? *Developmental Science,* 4, 94–100.

Gelman, R. (1990). First principles organize attention to and learning about relevant data: number and the animate-inanimate distinction as examples. *Cognitive Science,* 14, 79–106.

Gelman, R. (1991). Epigenetic foundations of knowledge structures: initial and transcendent cognitions. In S. Carey & R. Gelman (Eds.), *Epigenesis of mind: Essays on biology and cognition* (pp. 293–322). Hillsdale, NJ: Erlbaum.

Gelman, R. (1993). A rational-constructivist account of early learning about numbers and objects. In M. D.L. (Ed.), *The psychology of learning and motivation* (Vol. 30, pp. 61–96). San Diego: Academic Press.

Gelman, R., & Baillargeon, R. (1983). A review of some Piagetian concepts. In J. H. Flavell & E. M. Markman (Eds.), *Cognitive development: Handbook of child development.* (Vol. 3, pp. 167–230). New York: Wiley.

Gelman, R., Durgin, F., & Kaufman, L. (1995). Distinguishing between animates and inanimates: Not by motion alone. In D. Sperber, D. Premack, et al (Eds.), *Causal cognition: A multidisciplinary debate* (pp. 150–184). New York: Claredon Press.

Gelman, R., & Gallistel, C. R. (1978). *The child's understanding of number.* Cambridge, MA: Harvard University Press.

Gelman, R., & Lucariello, J. (2002). Learning in cognitive development In H. Pashler & C. R. Gallistel (Eds.), *Stevens' handbook of experimental psychology,* 3rd ed. (Vol.3, pp. 395–443). New York: Wiley.

Gelman, R., & Meck, E. (1983). Preschoolers' counting: Principles before skill. *Cognition,* 13(3), 343–359.

Gelman, S. A. (2003). *The essential child: Origins of essentialism in everyday thought.* New York: Oxford University Press.

Gelman, S. A., & Markman, E. M. (1987). Young children's inductions from natural kinds: The role of categories and appearances. *Child Development,* 58(6), 1532–1541.

Gentner, D. (2002) Analogy in scientific discovery: The case of Jonannes Kepler. In L. Magnani & N. J. Nersessian (Eds.), *Model-based reasoning: Science, technology, values* (pp.21–39). New York: Kluwer Academic/Plenum.

Gentner, D., Brem, S., Ferguson, R. W., Wolff, P., Markman, A. B., & Forbus, K. D. (1997). Analogy and creativity in the works of Johannes Kepler. In T. B. Ward, S. M. Smith, & J. Vaid (Eds.), *Creative thought: An investigation of conceptual structures and processes* (pp. 403–459). Washington, DC: American Psychological Association.

Gentner, D., & Goldin-Meadow, S. (2003). *Language in mind: Advances in the study of language and thought.* Cambridge, MA: MIT Press.

Gergely, G., Bekkering, H., & Kiraly, I. (2002). Rational imitation in preverbal infants. *Nature, 415,* 755.

Gergely, G., & Csibra, G. (2006). Sylvia's recipe: Human culture, imitation, and pedagogy. In S. C. Levinson & N. J. Enfield (Eds.), *Roots of human sociality: Culture, cognition, and human interaction* (pp. 229–255). Oxford, UK: Berg Publishers Ltd.

Gergely, G., Nadasdy, Z., Csibra, G., & Biro, S. (1995). Taking the intentional stance at 12 months of age. *Cognition, 56,* 165–193.

Giaquinto, M. (2007). *Visual thinking in mathematics: An epistemological study.* Oxford, UK: Oxford University Press.

Gibson, E. J., & Walk, R. D. (1960). The "visual cliff". *Scientific American, 202,* 64–71.

Gleitman, L. R., Cassidy, K., Nappa, R., Papafragou, A., & Trueswell, J. C. (2005). Hard words. *Language Learning and Development, 1*(1), 23–64.

Godfrey-Smith, P. (1989). Misinformation. *Canadian Journal of Philosophy, 19,* 533–550.

Gopnik, A., & Astington, J. W. (1988). Children's understanding of representational change and its relation to the understanding of false belief and the appearance-reality distinction. *Child Development, 59,* 26–37.

Gopnik, A., Glymour, C., Sobel, D. M., Schulz L. E., Kushnir, T., & Danks, D. (2004). A theory of causal learning in children: Causal maps and Bayes nets. *Psychological Review, 111*(1): 3–32.

Gopnik, A., & Meltzoff, A. (1997). *Words, thoughts, and theories.* Cambridge, MA: MIT Press.

Gordon, P. (2004). Numerical cognition without words: Evidence from Amazonia. *Science, 306*(5695), 496–499.

Grimshaw, J. (1987). The components of learnablity theory. In J. L. Garfield (Ed.), *Modularity in knowledge representation and natural-language understanding.* (pp. 207–220). Cambridge, MA: MIT Press.

Gruber, H. E., & Barrett, P. H. (1974). *Darwin on man: A psychological study of scientific creativity.* New York: Dutton.

Haith, M. M. (1998). Who put the cog in infant cognition: Is rich interpretation too costly? *Infant Behavior and Development, 21,* 167–179.

Haith, M. M., & Benson, J. B. (1998). Infant cognition. In W. Damon (Ed.), *Handbook of child psychology: Cognition, perception, and language* (Vol. 2, pp, 199–254). Hoboken, NJ: Wiley.

Halberda, J., Sires, S. F., & Feigenson, L. (2006). Multiple spatially overlapped sets can be enumerated in parallel. *Psychological Science, 17*(7), 572–576.

Hamlin, J., Wynn, K., & Bloom, P. (in press). Social evaluation by preverbal infants. *Nature.*

Hanson, N. R. (1965). *Patterns of discovery.* Cambridge, UK: Cambridge University Press.

Hare, B., Call, J., Agnetta, B., & Tomasello, M. (2000). Chimpanzees know what conspecifics do and do not see. *Animal Behaviour, 59*, 771–786.

Hartnett, P., & Gelman, R. (1998). Early understandings of numbers: Paths or barriers to the construction of new understandings? *Learning and Instruction, 8*(4), 341–374.

Hartshorn, K., & Rovee-Collier, C. (1997). Infant learning and long-term memory at 6 months: A confirming analysis. *Developmental Psychobiology, 30*, 71–85.

Hauser, M. D., & Carey, S. (1998). Building a cognitive creature from a set of primitives: Evolutionary and developmental insights. In D. Cummins & C. Allen (Eds.), *The evolution of mind.* (pp. 51–106). Oxford, UK: Oxford University Press.

Hauser, M. D., & Carey, S. (2003). Spontaneous representations of small numbers of objects by rhesus macaques: Examinations of content and format. *Cognitive Psychology, 47*(4), 367–401.

Hauser, M. D., Carey, S., & Hauser, L. B. (2000). Spontaneous number representation in semi-free-ranging rhesus monkeys. *Proceedings of the Royal Society, London, 267*, 829–833.

Hauser, M. D., Chomsky, N., & Fitch, W. T. (2002). The faculty of language: What is it, who has it, and how did it evolve? *Science, 298*, 1554–1555.

Hauser, M. D., MacNeilage, P., & Ware, M. (1996). Numerical representations in primates. *Proceedings of the National Academy of Sciences, 93*, 1514–1517.

Heider, F., & Simmel, M. (1944). An experimental study of apparent behavior. *American Journal of Psychology, 57*, 243–259.

Held, R., Birch, E. E., & Gwiazda, J. (1980). Stereoacuity of human infants. *Proceedings of the National Academy of Science, 77*, 2272–2274.

Hespos, S., & Baillargeon, R. (2001). Reasoning about containment events in very young infants. *Cognition, 78*, 207–245.

Hiebert, J., & Wearne, D. (1986). Procedures over concepts: The acquisition of decimal number knowledge. In J. Hiebert (Ed.), *Conceptual and procedural knowledge: The case of mathematics* (pp. 197–223). Hillsdale, NJ: Erlbaum.

Hood, B., Carey, S., & Prasada, S. (2000). Predicting the outcomes of physical events: Two-year-olds fail to reveal knowledge of solidity and support. *Child Development, 71*(6), 1540–1554.

Hood, B., Willen, J. D., & Driver, J. (1998). Adults' eyes trigger shifts of visual attention in human infants. *Psychological Science, 9*(2), 131–134.

Hood, L. H. (1977). *A longitudinal study of the development of the expression of causal relations in complex sentences.* PhD dissertation, Columbia University.

Hood, L. H., Bloom, L., and Brainerd, C. J. (1979) What, when and how about why: A longitudinal study of early expressions of causality. *Monographs of the Society for Research in Child Development, 44*, 1–47.

Huntley-Fenner, G. (2001). Children's understandning of number is similar to adults' and rats': Numerical estimation by 5–7-year olds. *Cognition, 78*(3), B27–B40.

Huntley-Fenner, G., Carey, S., & Solimando, A. (2002). Objects are individuals but stuff doesn't count: Perceived rigidity and cohesiveness influence infants' representations of small groups of discrete entities. *Cognition, 85*(3), 203–221.

Hurford, J. (1987). *Language and number: The emergence of a cognitive system.* Oxford, UK: Blackwell.

Imai, M., & Gentner, D. (1997). A cross-linguistic study of early word meaning: Universal ontology and linguistic influence. *Cognition, 62,* 169–200.

Intriligator, J., & Cavanagh, P. (2001). The spatial resolution of attention. *Cognitive Psychology, 43*(3), 171–216.

Izard, V., & Dehaene, S. (2008). Calibrating the mental number line. *Cognition. 106*(3), 1221–1247.

Jackendoff, R. (1989).What is a concept? That a person may grasp it? *Mind and Language, 4,* 68–102.

James, W. (1890/1981). *The principles of psychology.* Cambridge, MA: Harvard University Press.

Jammer, M. (1961). *Concepts of mass.* Cambridge, MA: Harvard University Press.

Johnson, M. H., Bolhuis, J. J., & Horn, G. (1985). Interaction between acquired preferences and developing predispositions during imprinting. *Animal Behaviour, 33,* 1000–1006.

Johnson, M. H., & Gilmore, R. O. (1998). Object-centered attention in 8-month-old infants. *Developmental Science, 1*(2), 221–225.

Johnson, M. H., & Morton, J. (1991). *Biology and cognitive development: The case of face recognition.* Cambridge, MA: Blackwell.

Johnson, S. C. (2003). Detecting agents. *Philosophical Transactions of the Royal Society of London, Series B, , 358,* 549–559.

Johnson, S. C., Booth, A., & O'Hearn, K. (2001). Inferring the goals of a nonhuman agent. *Cognitive Development, 16*(1), 637–656.

Johnson, S. C., Shimizu, Y. A., & Ok, S. (2007). Actors and actions: The role of agent behavior in infants' attributions of goals. *Cognitive Development, 22,* 549–559.

Johnson, S. C., Slaughter, V., & Carey, S. (1998). Whose gaze would infants follow? The elicitation of gaze following in 12-month-olds. *Developmental Science, 1,* 233–238.

Johnson, S. P., & Aslin, R. N. (1995). Perception of object unity in 2-month-old infants. *Developmental Psychology, 31*(5), 739–745.

Kahneman, D., Treisman, A., & Gibbs, B. (1992). The reviewing of object files: Object-specific integration of information. *Cognitive Psychology, 24,* 175–219.

Kail, R. (1986). Sources of age differences in speed of processing. *Child Development, 57,* 969–987.

Kalish, C. W., & Gelman, S. A. (1992) On wooden pillows. Young children's understanding of category implications. *Child Development, 63,* 1536–1557.

Kanizsa, G., & Vicario, G (1968). The perception of intentional reactions. In G. Kanizsa & G. Vicario (Eds.), *Experimental research on perception* (pp. 71–126). Trieste, Italy: University of Trieste.

Karmiloff-Smith, A. (1990). *Beyond modularity: A developmental perspective on cognitive science*. Cambridge, MA: MIT Press.

Karmiloff-Smith, A. (1998) Development itself is the key to understanding developmental disorders. *Trends in Cognitive Science, 2*, 389–398.

Keil, F. C. (1989). *Concepts, kinds, and cognitive development*. Cambridge, MA: MIT Press.

Kellman, P. J., & Arterberry, M. E. (2000). *The cradle of knowledge: Development of perception in infancy*. Cambridge, MA: MIT Press.

Kellman, P. J., & Spelke, E. S. (1983). Perception of partly occluded objects in infancy. *Cognitive Psychology, 15*(4), 483–524.

Kerslake, D. (1986). *Fractions: Children's strategies and errors. A report of the strategies and errors in the secondary mathematics project*. Windsor, England: NFER-Nelson.

Kintsch, W. (1974). *The representation of meaning in memory*. Hillsdale, NJ: Erlbaum.

Kitcher, P. (1978). Theories, theorists, and theoretical change. *Philosophical Review, 87*, 519–547.

Kitcher, P. (1988). The child as parent of the scientist. *Mind & Language, 3*, 217–228.

Klahr, D., & Wallace, J. G. (1976). *Cognitive development: An information-processing view*. Hillsdale, NJ: Erlbaum.

Koechlin, E., Dehaene, S., & Mehler, J. (1998). Numerical transformations in five-month-old human infants. *Journal of Mathematical Cognition, 3*, 89–104.

Kosslyn, S. M., Thompson, W. L., & Ganis, G. (2006). *The case for mental imagery*. Oxford, UK: Oxford University Press.

Kosugi, D., & Fujita, K. (2002). How do 8-month-old infants recognize causality in object motion and that in human action? *Japanese Psychological Research, 44*(2), 66–78.

Kosugi, D., Ishida, H., & Fujita, K. (2003). 10-month-old infants' inference of invisible agent: Distinction in causality between object motion and human action. *Japanese Psychological Research, 45*(1), 15–24.

Kotovsky, L., & Baillargeon, R. (2000). Reasoning about collisions involving inert objects in 7.5-month-old infants. *Science, 3*(3), 344–359.

Kouider, S., Halberda, J., Wood, J. N., & Carey, S. (2006). The acquisition of English number marking: The singular-plural distinction. *Language Learning and Development, 2*(1), 1–25.

Kripke, S. (1972/1980). *Naming and necessity*. Cambridge, MA: Harvard University Press.

Kuhlmeier, V., Wynn, K., & Bloom, P. (2008). Attribution of dispositional states by 9-month-olds: The role of faces. Manuscript submitted for publication.

Kuhlmeier, V., Wynn, K., & Bloom, P. (2003). Attribution of dispositional states by 12-month-old infants. *Psychological Science, 14*, 402–408.

Kuhn, D., Amsel, E., O'Loughlin, M., Schauble, L., Leadbeater, B., & Yotive, W. (1988). *The development of scientific thinking skills*. San Diego: Academic Press.

Kuhn, T. (1962). *The structure of scientific revolutions*. Chicago: University of Chicago Press.

Kuhn, T. (1977). *The essential tension: Selected studies in scientific tradition and change.* Chicago: University of Chicago Press.

Kuhn, T. (1982). Commensurability, comparibility, communicability. In *Proceedings of the biennial meeting of the Philosohpy of Science Association, Vol. 2: Symposia and invited papers* (pp. 669–688). East Lansing, MI: University of Chicago Press.

Laurence, S., & Margolis, E. (1999). Concepts and cognitive science. In E. Margolis & S. Laurence (Eds.), *Concepts: Core readings* (pp. 3–82). Cambridge, MA: MIT Press.

Laurence, S., & Margolis, E. (2002). Radical concept nativism. *Cognition, 86,* 25–55.

LeCorre, M., Brannon, E. M., Van de Walle, G. A., & Carey, S. (2006). Re-visiting the competence/performance debate in the acquisition of the counting principles. *Cognitive Psychology, 52*(2), 130–169.

LeCorre, M., & Carey, S. (2007). One, two, three, four, nothing more: How numerals are mapped onto core knowledge of number in the acquisition of the counting principles. *Cognition, 105,* 395–438.

Leslie, A. M. (1982). The perception of causality in infants. *Perception, 11,* 173–186.

Leslie, A. M. (1984). Infant perception of a manual pick-up event. *British Journal of Developmental Psychology, 2,* 19–32.

Leslie, A.M. (1994). ToMM, ToBy, and Agency: Core architecture and domain specificity. In L. Hirschfeld and S. Gelman (Eds.), *Mapping the mind: Domain specificity in cognition and culture* (pp. 119–148). Cambridge, UK: Cambridge University Press.

Leslie, A. M., German, T. P., & Polizzi, P. (2005) Belief-desire reasoning as a process of selection. *Cognitive Psychology, 50,* 45–85.

Leslie, A. M., & Keeble, S. (1987). Do six-month old infants perceive causality? *Cognition, 25,* 265–288.

Leslie, A. M., Xu, F., Tremoulet, P. D., & Scholl, B. J. (1998). Indexing and the object concept: Developing "what" and "where" systems. *Trends in Cognitive Science, 2,* 10–18.

Levinson, S. (1997). From outer to inner space: Linguistic categories and non-linguistic thinking. In J. Nuyts & E. Perderson (Eds.), *Language and conceptualization.* (pp. 13–45). New York: Cambridge University Press.

Li, P., Dunham, Y., & Carey, S. (2008). Of substance: The nature of language effects on construal. *Cognitive Psychology.* Manuscript submitted for publication.

Li, P., Le Corre, M., Shui, R., Jia, G., & Carey, S. (2008). *Effects of plural syntax on number word learning: A cross-linguistic study.* Manuscript submitted for publication.

Li, P., Ogura, T., & Barner, D., Yang, S., & Carey, S. (in press). Does the conceptual distinction between singular and plural depend on language? *Development psychology.*

Link, G. (1987). Generalized quantifiers and plurals. In P. Gaerdenfors (Ed.), *Generalized quantifiers* (pp. 151–180). Dordrecht, The Netherlands: Reidel.

Lipton, J. S., & Spelke, E. S. (2003). Origins of number sense: Large number discrimination in human infants. *Psychological Science, 15*(5), 396–401.

Lipton, J. S., & Spelke, E. (2004). Discrimination of large and small numerosities by human infants. *Infancy,* 5(3), 271–290.

Lipton, J. S., & Spelke, E. (2005). Preschool children's mapping of number words to nonsymbolic numerosities. *Child Development,* 76(5), 978–988.

Locke, John (1690/1975) *An essay concerning human understanding.* Oxford, UK: Oxford University Press.

Lorenz, K. (1937). The companion in the bird's world. *Auk,* 54, 245–273.

Luo, Y., & Baillargeon, R. (2005). Can a self-propelled box have a goal? Psychological reasoning in 5-month-old infants? *Psychological Science,* 16, 601–608.

Luo, Y., Kaufman, L., & Baillargeon, R. (2008). Young infants' reasoning about physical events involving self- and nonself-propelled objects. Manuscript submitted for publication.

Luo, Y., & Baillargeon, R. (2007). Do 12.5-month-olds consider what objects others can see when interpreting ehir actions? *Cognition,* 105, 489–512.

Luo, Y. & Johnson, S. C. (in press). Recognizing the role of perception in action at 6 months. *Developmental Science.*

Macnamara, J. (1982). *Names for things.* Cambridge, MA: MIT Press.

Macnamara, J. (1986). *Border dispute: The place of logic in psychology.* Cambridge, MA: MIT Press.

MacWhinney, B. (2000). *The CHILDES project: Tools for analyzing talk,* 3rd ed. Mahwah, NJ: Erlbaum.

Mandler, J. (1992). How to build a baby: II. Conceptual primitives. *Psychological Review,* 99, 587–604.

Mandler, J. (2004). *The foundations of mind: The origins of the conceptual system.* New York: Oxford University Press.

Mandler, J., & McDonough, L. (1993). Concept formation in infancy. *Cognitive Development,* 8(3), 291–318.

Mandler, J., & McDonough, L. (1996). Drinking and driving don't mix: Inductive generalization in infancy. *Cognition,* 59(3), 307–335.

Mandler, J., & McDonough, L. (1998). Studies in inductive inference in infancy. *Cognitive Psychology,* 37, 60–96.

Marcus, G. (2001). *The algebraic mind.* Cambridge, MA: MIT Press.

Mareschal, D., Plunkett, K., & Harris, P. (1999). A computational and neuropsychological account of object-oriented behaviours in infancy. *Developmental Science,* 2(3), 306–317.

Margolis, E., & Laurence, S. (Eds.). (1999). *Concepts: Core readings.* Cambridge, MA: MIT Press.

Markman, E. M. (1989). *Categorization and naming in children: Problems of induction.* Cambridge, MA: MIT Press.

Markman, E. M. (1990). Constraints children place on word meanings. *Cognitive Science,* 14, 57–77.

Mash, C., Novak, E., Berthier, N., & Keen, R. (2006) What do two-year-olds understand about hidden-object events? *Developmental Psychology,* 42, 263–271.

Matsuzawa, T. (1985). Use of numbers by a chimpanzee. *Nature, 315,* 57–59.

Mayr, E. (1982). *The growth of biological thought: Diversity, evolution, and inheritance.* Cambridge, MA: Harvard University Press.

McCloskey, M. (1983). Intuitive physics. *Scientific American, 248*(4), 122–130.

McCloskey, M., Caramazza, A., & Green, B. (1980). Curvilinear motion in the absence of external forces: Naive beliefs about the motion of objects. *Science, 210* (4474), 1139–1141.

McCrink, K., & Wynn, K. (2004a). Large-number addition and subtraction by 9-month old infants. *Psychological Science, 15*(11), 776–781.

McCrink, K., & Wynn, K. (2004b). Ratio abstraction by 6-month-old infants. Paper presented at the International Conference on Infant Studies, Chicago.

McDonough, L., & Mandler, J. (1998). Inductive generalization in 9- and 11-month-olds. *Developmental Science, 1*(2), 227–232.

McKie, D., & Heatcote, N. H. V. (1935). *The discovery of specific and latent heat.* London: Edward Arnold.

Meck, W. H., & Church, R. M. (1983). A mode control model of counting and timing processes. *Journal of Experimental Psychology: Animal Behavior Processes, 9,* 320–334.

Medin, D. L., & Ortony, A. (1989). Psychological essentialism. In S. Vosniadou (Ed.), *Similarity and analogical reasoning* (pp. 179–195). New York: Cambridge University Press.

Meltzoff, A. N. (1988). Infant imitation after a 1-week delay: Long-term memory for novel acts and multiple stimuli. *Developmental Psychology, 24*(4), 470–476.

Meltzoff, A. N. (1995). Understanding the intentions of others: Re-enactment of intended acts by 18-month-old children. *Developmental Psychology, 31*(5), 838–850.

Meltzoff, A. N., & Borton, R. W. (1979). Intermodal matching by human neonates. *Nature, 282,* 403–404.

Meltzoff, A. N., & Moore, M. K. (1977). Imitation of facial and manual gestures by human neonates. *Science, 198,* 75–78.

Meltzoff, A. N., & Moore, M. K. (1983). Newborn infants imitate adult facial gestures. *Child Development, 54,* 702–709.

Meltzoff, A. N., & Moore, M. K. (1994). Imitation, memory, and the representation of persons. *Infant Behavior and Development, 17,* 83–100.

Meltzoff, A. N., & Moore, M. K. (1999). Resolving the debate about early imitation. In A. Slater & D. Muir (Eds.), *The Blackwell reader in developmental psychology* (pp. 151–155). Malden, MA: Blackwell.

Mervis, C., & Johnson, K. E. (1991). Acquisition of the plural morpheme: A case study. *Developmental Psychology, 27*(2), 222–235.

Michotte (1946/1963). *La perception de la causalite.* Louvain: Institute Superior de Philosophie, 1956, English translation of updated version by T. Miles & G. Miles, *The perception of causality.* New York: Basic Books.

Miller, K. F., Kelly, M., & Zhou, X. (2005). Learning mathematics in China and the United States: Cross-cultural insights into the nature and course of preschool mathematical development. In J. I. D. Campbell (Ed.), *Handbook of mathematical cognition* (pp. 163–178). New York: Psychology Press.

Minstrell, J. (1982). Explaining the "at rest" condition of an object. *The Physics Teacher, 20*(1), 10–14.

Mithen, S. (1996). *The prehistory of the mind: A search for the origins of art, religion, and science.* New York: Thames and Hudson.

Mix, K. S., Huttenlocher, J., & Levine, S. C. (1996). Do preschool children recognize auditory-visual numerical correspondences? *Child Development, 67*(4), 1592–1608.

Mix, K. S., Huttenlocher, J., & Levine, S. C. (2002). *Quantitative development in infancy and early childhood.* London: Oxford University Press.

Morton, J., Johnson, M. H., & Maurer, D. (1990). On the reasons for newborns' responses to faces. *Infant Behavior & Development, 13*, 99–103.

Moss, J., & Case, R. (1999). Developing children's understanding of rational numbers: a new model and an experimental curriculum. *Journal for Research in Mathematics Education, 30*, 122–147.

Movellan, J. R., & Watson, J. S. (2002). The development of gaze following as a Bayesiansystems identification problem. *UCSD Machine Perception Laboratory Technical Reports* 2002.01.

Moyer, R. S., & Landauer, T. K. (1967). Time required for judgements of numerical inequality. *Nature, 215*, 1519–1520.

Muentener, P., & Carey, S. (2008). Beyond Michotte: Infants' causal representations of state change events. Manuscript submitted for publication.

Munakata, Y., McClelland, J. L., Johnson, M. H., & Siegler, R. S. (1997). Rethinking infant knowledge: toward an adaptive process account of successes and failures in object permanence tasks. *Psychological Review, 104*, 686–713.

Murphy, G. (2002). *The big book of concepts.* Cambridge, MA: MIT Press.

Myowa-Yamakoshi, M., Tomonaga, M., Tanaka, M., & Matsuzawa, T. (2004). Imitation in neonatal chimpanzees (*Pan troglodytes*). *Developmental Science, 7*(4), 437–442.

Nakayama, K., He, Z. J., & Shimojo, S. (1995). Visual surface representation: A critical link between lower-level and higher-level vision. In S. M. Kosslyn & D. Osherson (Eds.), *Visual cognition: An invitation to cognitive science.* (Vol. 2, pp. 1–70). Cambridge, MA: MIT Press.

Needham, A., & Baillargeon, R. (1993). Intuitions about support in 4.5-month-old infants. *Cognition, 47*(2), 121–148.

Needham, A., & Baillargeon, R. (1998). Object segregation in 8-month-old infants. *Cognition, 62*, 121–149.

Needham, A., & Baillargeon, R. (2000). Infants' use of featural and experiential information in segregating and individuating objects: A reply to Xu, Carey and Welch. *Cognition, 74*, 255–284.

Nersessian, N. (1992). How do scientists think? Capturing the dynamics of conceptual change in science. In R. Giere (Ed.), *Cognitive models of science* (pp. 3–44). Minneapolis: University of Minnesota Press.

Nesher, P., & Peled, I. (1986). Shift in reasoning. *Educational Studies in Mathematics, 17, 67–79.*

Oakes, L., & Cohen, L. (1990). Infant perception of a causal event. *Cognitive Development, 5,* 193–207.

O'Neill, D., & Gopnik, A. (1991). Young children's ability to identify the sources of their beliefs. *Developmental Psychology, 27,* 390–399.

Onishi, K. H., & Baillargeon, R. (2005). Do 15-month-old infants understand false beliefs? *Science, 308*(5719), 255–258.

Pauen, S., & Trauble, B. (2008). How 7-month-olds interpret ambiguous motion events: Category-specific reasoning in infancy. Manuscript under review.

Pearl, J. (2000). *Causality, models,* reasoning, and inference. Cambridge, UK: Cambridge University Press.

Pepperberg, I. M. (1987). Evidence for conceptual quantitative abilities in the African parrot: Labeling of cardinal sets. *Ethology, 75,* 37–61.

Perner, J. (1991). *Understanding the representational mind.* Cambridge, MA: MIT Press.

Perrett, D., Harries, M., Mistlin, A., Hietanen, J., Benson, P., Bevan, R., Thomas, S., Oram, M., Ortega, J., & Brierley, K. (1990). Social signals analyzed at the single cell level: Someone is looking at me, something touched me, something moved! *International Journal of Comparative Psychology, 4,* 25–55.

Perrett, D., Smith, P., Potter, D., Mistlin, A., Head, A., Milner, A., & Jeeves, M. (1985) Visual cells in the temporal cortex sensitive to face view and gaze direction. *Proceedings of the Royal Society of London B, 223,* 293–317.

Peterson, M. A. (1994). Object recognition processes can and do operate before figure-ground organization. *Current Directions in Psychological Science, 3,* 105–111.

Phillips, A. T., Wellman, H. M., & Spelke, E. S. (2002). Infants' ability to connect gaze and emotinal expression to intentional action. *Cognition, 85*(1), 53–78.

Piaget, J. (1952). *The child's conception of number.* London: Routledge & Kegan Paul.

Piaget, J. (1954). *The construction of reality in the child.* New York: Basic Books.

Piaget, J. (1960). *The child's conception of the world.* Totowa, NJ: Littlefield.

Piaget, J. (1980). Language within cognition: Schemes of action and language learning. In M. Piatelli-Palmerini (Ed.), *Language and learning.* (pp. 163–183). Cambridge, MA: Harvard University Press.

Piaget, J., & Inhelder, B. (1974). *The child's construction of quantities: Conservation and atomism.* London: Routledge & Kegan Paul.

Piatelli-Palmarini, M. (1980). *Language learning: The debate between Jean Piaget and Noam Chomsky.* Cambridge, MA: Harvard University Press.

Pica, P., Lemer, C., & Izard, V. (2004). Exact and approximate arithmetic in an Amazonian indigene group. *Science, 306*(5695), 499–503.

Pinker, S. (1984). *Language Learnability and Language development.* Cambridge, MA: Harvard University Press.

Pinker, S. (1989). *Learnability and cognition: The acquisition of argument structure*. Cambridge, MA: MIT Press.

Pinker, S. (1994). *The language instinct*. New York: William Morrow.

Platt, J. R., & Johnson, D. M. (1971). Localization of position within a homogeneous behavior chain: Effects of error contingencies. *Learning and Motivation, 2*, 386–414.

Povinelli, D. J. (2000). *Folk physics for apes*. New York: Oxford University Press.

Povinelli, D. J., & Eddy, T. J. (1996). What young chimpanzees know about seeing. *Monographs of the Society for Research in Child Development, 247*.

Prasada, S., Ferenz, K., & Haskell, T. (2002). Conceiving of entities as objects and stuff. *Cognition, 83*, 141–165.

Preissler, M. A., & Carey, S. (2004). Do pictures and words function as symbols for 18- and 24-month-old children? *Journal of Cognition and Development, 5*(2), 185–212.

Putnam, H. (1962). The analytic and the synthetic. In H. Feigl & G. Maxwell (Eds.) *Minnesota Studies in the Philosophy of Science* (Vol. 3, pp. 350–397). Minneapolis: University of Minnesota Press.

Putnam, H. (1975). The meaning of meaning. In K. Gunderson (Ed.), *Language, mind, and knowledge* pp. 131–193). Minneapolis: University of Minnesota Press.

Pylyshyn, Z. W. (2001). Visual indexes, preconceptual objects, and situated vision. *Cognition, 80*(1–2), 127–158.

Pylyshyn, Z. (2002). Mental imagery: In search of a theory. *The Behavioral and Brain Sciences, 25*, 157–182.

Pylyshyn, Z. (2003). Return of the mental image: Are there pictures in the brain? *Trends in Cognitive Sciences, 7*, 113–118.

Pylyshyn, Z. W., & Storm, R. W. (1998). Tracking multiple independent targets: Evidence for a parallel tracking mechanism. *Spatial Vision, 3*, 179–197.

Quine, W. V. O. (1953/1980). Two dogmas of empiricism. In *From a logical point of view: Nine logico-philosophical essays* (pp. 20–46). Cambridge, MA: Harvard University Press.

Quine, W. V. O. (1960). *Word and object*. Cambridge, MA: MIT Press.

Quine, W. V. O. (1969). *Ontological relativity and other essays*. New York: Columbia University Press.

Quine, W. V. O. (1974). *Roots of reference*. New York: Columbia University Press.

Quine, W. V. O. (1977) Natural kinds. In S. P. Schwartz (Ed.), *Naming, necessity and natural kinds* (pp 89–108). Ithaca, NY: Cornell University Press.

Rakison, D. H., & Poulin-Dubois, D. (2001). Developmental origin of the animate-inanimate distinction. *Psychological Bulletin, 127*(2), 209–228.

Ravid, D., & Hayek, L. (2003). Learning about different ways of expressing number in the development of Palestinian Arabic. *First Language, 23*(1), 41–63.

Regolin, L., & Vallortigara, G. (1995). Perception of partially occluded objects by newborn chicks. *Perception & Psychophysics, 57*(7), 971–976.

Resnick, L., & Singer, J. (1993) Protoquantitative origins of ratio reasoning. In T. Carpenter, E. Fennema, & T. Romberg (Eds.), *Rational numbers: An integration of research* (pp. 107–130). Hillsdale, NJ: Erlbaum.

Rey, G. (1983). Concepts and stereotypes. *Cognition,* 15, 237–262.

Richardson, D. C., & Kirkham, N. (2004). Multi-modal events and moving locations: Eye movements of adults and 6-month-olds reveal dynamic spatial indexing. *Journal of Experimental Psychology: General,* 133(1), 46–62.

Rittle-Jonhson, B., Siegler, R., & Alibali, M. W. (2001). Developing conceptual understanding and procedural skill in mathematics: An iterative process. *Journal of Educational Psychology,* 93, 346–362.

Rochat, P., Morgan, R., & Carpenter, M. (1997). Young infants' sensitivity to movement information specifying social causality. *Cognitive Development,* 12(4), 441–465.

Rochat, P., Striano, T., & Morgan, R. (2004). Who is doing what to whom? Young infants' developing sense of social causality in animated displays. *Perception,* 33(3), 355–369.

Rosch, E. (1973). On the internal structure of perceptual and semantic categories. In T. Moore (Ed.), *Cognitive development and the acquisition of language* (pp. 111–144). New York: Academic Press.

Rosch, E. (1978). Principles of categorization. In E. Rosch, & B. Lloyd (Eds), *Cognition and categorization* (pp. 27–48). Hillsdale, NJ: Erlbaum.

Rosch, E., and Mervis, C. (1975). Family resemblances: Studies in the internal structure of categories. *Cognitive Psychology,* 7, 573–605.

Rose, S. A., Feldman, J. F., & Jankowski, J. J. (2001). Visual short-term memory in the first year of life: Capacity and recency effects. *Developmental Psychology,* 37(4), 539–549.

Ross-Sheehy, S., Oakes, L., & Luck, S. J. (2003). The development of visual short-term memory capacity in infants. *Child Development,* 74(6), 1807–1822.

Rovee, C. K., & Rovee, D. T. (1969) Conjugate reinforcement in infant exploratory behavior. *Journal of Experimental Child Psychology,* 8, 33–39.

Santos, L. R., Flombaum, J. I., & Phillips, W. (2007) The evolution of human mindreading: How non-human primates can inform social cognitive neuroscience. In S. Platek, J. P. Keenan, & T. K. Shackelford (Eds.), *Evolutionary cognitive neuroscience* (pp. 433–456). Cambridge, MA: MIT Press.

Santos, L. R., & Hauser, M. D. (1999). How monkeys see the eyes: Cotton-top tamarins' reaction to changes in visual attention and action. *Animal Cognition,* 2, 131–139.

Sarnecka, B. W., & Gelman, S. A. (2004). Six does not just mean a lot: Preschoolers see number words as specific. *Cognition,* 92, 329–352.

Sarnecka, B. W., Kamenskaya, V. G., Ogura, T., Yamana, Y., & Yudovina, J. B. (2007). From grammatical number to exact numbers: Early meanings of "one," "two," and "three," in English, Russian, and Japanese. *Cognitive Psychology,* 55(2), 136–168.

Saxe, R., Tenenbaum, J., and Carey, S. (2005). Secret agents: 10 and 12-month-olds infer an unseen cause of the motion of an inanimate object. *Psychological Science,* 16(12), 995–1001.

Saxe, R., Tzelnic, T., & Carey, S. (2007). Knowing who-dunnit: Infants identify the causal agent in an unseen causal interaction. *Developmental Psychology,* 43(1), 149–158.

Schaeffer, B., Eggleston, J. H., & Scott, J. L. (1974). Number development in young children. *Cognitive Psychology,* 6(3), 357–379.

Schlessinger, I. (1982). Steps to language: Toward a theory of language acquisition. New York: Erlbaum.

Schlottmann, A., Allen, D., Linderoth, C., & Hesketh, S. (2002). Perceptual causality in children. *Child Development,* 73, 1656–1677.

Schlottmann, A. & Shanks, D. (1992). Evidence for a distance between judged and perceived causality. *Quarterly Journal of Experimental Psychology,* 44A, 321–342.

Schlottmann, A., & Surian, L. (1999). Do 9-month-old infants perceive causation-at-a-distance? *Perception,* 28(9), 1105–1113.

Schnoor, B. C., & Newman, R. S. (2001, April). Infants' developing comprehension of plurals. Paper presented at the Society for Research in Child Development, Minneapolis, MN.

Scholl, B. J. (2001). Objects and attention: The state of the art. *Cognition,* 80, 1–46.

Scholl, B. J. (Ed.). (2002). *Objects and attention.* Cambridge, MA: MIT Press.

Scholl, B. J., & Leslie, A. M. (1999). Explaining the infant's object concept: Beyond the perception/cognition dichotomy. In E. Lepore & Z. Pylyshyn (Eds.), *What is cognitive science?* (pp. 26–73). Oxford, UK: Blackwell.

Scholl, B. J., & Pylyshyn, Z. W. (1999). Tracking multiple items through occlusion: clues to visual objecthood. *Cognitive Psychology,* 38, 259–290.

Scholl, B. J., Pylyshyn, Z. W., & Franconeri, S. (1999). When are spatiotemporal and featural properties encoded as a result of attentional allocation? *Investigative Ophtalmology and Visual Science,* 40(4), S797.

Sharon, T., & Wynn, K. (1998). Individuation of actions from continuous motions. *Psychological Science,* 9(5), 357–362.

Shimizu, Y. A., & Johnson, S. C. (2004). Infants' attrbution of a goal to a morphologically unfamiliar agent. *Developmental Science,* 7, 425–430.

Shtulman, A. (2006). Qualitative differences between naive and scientific theories of evolution. *Cognitive Psychology,* 52(2), 170–194.

Shutts, K., Keen, R., & Spelke, E. (2006) Object boundaries influence toddlers' performance in a search task. *Developmental Science,* 9, 97–107.

Siegler, R. S. (1991). In young children's counting, procedures precede principles. *Educational Psychology Review,* 3, 127–135.

Simon, T. J. (1997). Reconceptualizing the origins of number knowledge: A "non-numerical" account. *Cognitive Development,* 12, 349–372.

Simon, T., Hespos, S., & Rochat, P. (1995). Do infants understand simple arithmetic? A replication of Wynn (1992). *Cognitive Development,* 10, 253–269.

Slater, A., Mattock, A., & Brown, A. (1990). Size constancy at birth: Newborn infants' responses to retinal and real size. *Journal of Experimental Child Psychology*, 49(2), 314–322.

Slater, A., Morison, V., Somers, M., Mattock, A., & Brown, E. (1990). Newborn and older infants' perception of partly occluded objects. *Infant Behavior & Development*, 13(1), 33–49.

Sloman, S. (2005). *Causal models: How people think about the world and its alternatives*. New York: Oxford University Press.

Smith, C. L. (2007) Bootstrapping processes in the development of students' commonsense matter theories: Using analogical mappings, thought experiments, and learning to measure to promote conceptual restructuring. *Cognition and Instruction*, 25(4), 337–398.

Smith, C. L., Carey, S., & Wiser, M. (1985). On differentiation: A case study of the development of the concepts of size, weight, and density. *Cognition*, 21(3), 177–237.

Smith, C. L., Maclin, D., Grosslight, L. and Davis, H. (1997) Teaching for understanding: A comparison of two approaches to teaching students about matter and density. *Cognition and Instruction*, 15(3), 317–393.

Smith, C. L., Snir, J., & Grosslight, L. (1992) Using conceptual models to facilitate conceptual change: The case of weight/density differentiation. *Cognition and Instruction*, 9(3), 221–283.

Smith, C. L., Solomon, G., & Carey, S. (2005). Never getting to zero: Elementary school students' understanding of the infinite divisibility of number and matter. *Cognitive Psychology*, 51, 101–140.

Smith, C. L., & Unger, C. (1997) What's in dots-per-box? Conceptual bootstrapping with stripped down visual analogs. *Journal of the Learning Sciences*, 6(2), 143–181.

Smith, E., & Medin, D. (1981). *Categories and concepts*. Cambridge, MA: MIT Press.

Smith, E., Osherson, D., Rips, L., and Keane, M. (1988). Combining prototypes: A selective modification model. *Cognitive Science*, 12, 485–527.

Smith, L. B., Thelen, E., Titzer, R., & McLin, D. (1999). Knowing in the context of acting: the task dynamics of the A-not-B error. *Psychological Review*, 106, 235–260.

Snir, J., Smith, C. L., & Grosslight, L. (1993). Conceptually enhanced simulations: A computer tool for science teaching. *Journal of Science Education and Technology*, 2(2), 373–388.

Soja, N., Carey, S., & Spelke, E. (1991). Ontological categories guide young children's inductions of word meaning: object terms and substance terms. *Cognition*, 38, 179–211.

Sommerville, J. A., Woodward, A. L., & Needham, A. (2005). Action experience alters 3-month old infants' perception of others' actions. *Cognition*, 96(1), B1–B11.

Song, H., & Baillargeon, R. (2007). Can 9.5-month-olds attribute to an agent a disposition to perform an action on objects? *Acta Psychologica*, 124, 79–105.

Spelke, E. S. (1988). The origins of physical knowledge. In L. Weiskrantz (Ed.), *Thought without language*. Oxford, UK: Oxford University Press.

Spelke, E. S. (1998). Nativism, empiricism, and the origins of knowledge. *Infant Behavior & Development, 21*(2), 181–200.

Spelke, E. (2000). Core knowledge. *American Psychologist, 55*, 1233–1243.

Spelke, E. S. (2003). What makes us smart? Core knowledge and natural language. In D. Gentner & S. Goldin-Meadow (Eds.), *Language in mind: Advances in the study of language and thought* (pp. 277–311). Cambridge, MA: MIT Press.

Spelke, E. S., Breilinger, K., Macomber, J., & Jacobsen, K. (1992). Origins of knowledge. *Psychological Review, 99*, 605–632.

Spelke, E. S., Kestenbaum, R., & Simons, D. J. (1995). Spatiotemporal continuity, smoothness of motion and object identity in infancy. *British Journal of Developmental Psychology, 13*(2), 113–142.

Spelke, E. S., & Newport, E. L. (1998). Nativism, empiricism, and the development of knowledge. In R. M. Lerner (Ed.), *Handbook of child psychology, Vol. 1: Theoretical models of human development* (pp. 275–340). New York: Wiley.

Spelke, E. S., Phillips, A., & Woodward, A. L. (1995). Infants' knowledge of object motion and human action. In D. Sperber, D. Premack, & A. Premack (Eds.), *Causal cognition: A multidiscpilinary debate* (op, 44–78). Oxford, UK: Clarendon Press.

Spirtes, P., Glymour, C. & Scheines, R. (2000). *Causation, prediction and search (Springer Lecture Notes in Statistics)*. Cambridge, MA: MIT Press.

Starkey, P., & Cooper, R. (1980). Perception of numbers by human infants. *Science, 210*, 1033–1035.

Strauss, M. S., & Curtis, L. E. (1981). Infant perception of numerosity. *Child Development, 52*, 1146–1152.

Strevens, M. (2000). The essentialist aspect of naïve theories. *Cognition, 74*(2), 149–175.

Surian, L., Caldi, S., & Piredda, E. (2004). Agents' motion and the development of object individuation. Poster presented at the 9th biennial meeting of the International Conference on Infant Studies, Chicago, IL.

Surian, L., Caldi, S., & Sperber, D. (2007). Attribution of beliefs by 13-month-old infants. *Psychological Science, 18*(7), 580–586.

Swartz, K. B., Chen, S., & Terrace, H. (1991). Serial learning by rhesus monkeys: Acquisition and retention of multiple four-item lists. *Journal of Experimental Psychology: Animal Behavior Processes, 17*(4), 396–410.

Temple, E., & Posner, M. I. (1998). Brain mechanisms of quantity are similar in 5-year-olds and adults. *Proceedings of the National Academy of Sciences, 95*, 7836–7841.

Tenenbaum, J. B., & Griffiths, T. L. (2001). Generalization, similarity, and Bayesian inference. *Behavioral & Brain Sciences, 24*(4), 629–640.

Terrace, H. S., Son, L. K., & Brannon, E. M. (2003). Serial expertise of rhesus macaques. *Psychological Science, 14*(1), 66–73.

Thelen, E., Schoner, G., Scheier, C., and Smith, L.B. (2001). The dynamics of embodiment: A field theory of infant preservative reaching. *Behavioral and Brain Sciences*, 24, 1–86.

Tomasello, M., & Call, J. (1997). *Primate cognition*. Oxford, UK: Oxford University Press.

Tomasello, M., & Call, J. (2006). Do chimpanzees know what others see – or only what they are looking at? In S. Huley & M. Hudds (Eds.), *Rational animals?* (pp. 371–384). Oxford, UK: Oxford University Press.

Tomasello, M., Carpenter, M., Call, J., Behne, T., & Moll, H. (2005). Understanding and sharing intentions: The origins of cultural cognition. *Behavioral & Brain Sciences*, 28(5), 675–735.

Toulmin, S., & Goodfield, J. (1962). *The architecture of matter*. London: Hutchison.

Tremoulet, P., Leslie, A. M., & Hall, G. (2000). Infant attention to the shape and color of objects: Individuation and identification. *Cognitive Development*, 15, 499–522.

Uller, C., Carey, S., Huntley-Fenner, G., & Klatt, L. (1999). What representations might underlie infant numerical knowledge. *Cognitive Development*, 14, 1–36.

Uller, C., Hauser, M., & Carey, S. (2001). Spontaneous representation of number in cotton-top tamarins (*Saguinus oedipus*). *Journal of Comparative Psychology*, 115(3), 248–257.

Valenza, F., Gava, L., Leo, I., & Simion, F. (2004). *Perception of object unity at birth: The role of motion*. Paper presented at the Perception and Cognitive Processes Symposium, Trieste, Italy.

Van de Walle, G. A. (1999). Conceptual categorization in infancy: Membership in color vs. kind categories. Poster presented at the 63rd biennial meeting of the Society for Research in Child Development, Albuquerque, NM.

Van de Walle, G. A. (2008). *Perceptual contributions to category formation*. Manuscript submitted for publication.

Van de Walle, G. A., Carey, S., & Prevor, M. (2000). Bases for object individuation in infancy: evidence from manual search. *Journal of Cognition and Development*, 1, 249–280.

Van de Walle, G. A., & Hoerger, M. (1996). Perceptual foundations of categorization in infancy. Poster presented at the 10th biennial meeting of the International Conference on Infant Studies, Providence, RI.

Verguts, T., & Fias, W. (2004). Representation of number in animals and humans: A neural model. *Journal of Cognitive Neuroscience*, 16(9), 1493–1504.

Viennot, L. (1979). Spontaneous reasoning in elementary dynamics. *European Journal of Science Education*, 1, 205–221.

Vogel, E. K., Woodman, G. F., & Luck, S. J. (2001). Storage of features, conjunctions, and objects in visual working memory. *Journal of Experimental Psychology: Human Perception and Performance*, 27(1), 92–114.

Vosniadou, S., & Brewer, W. (1992). Mental models of the Earth: A study of conceptual change in childood. *Cognitive Psychology*, 24(4), 535–585.

Vygotsky, L. (1934/1962). *Thought and language*. Cambridge, MA: MIT Press.

Wagner, L., & Carey, S. (2003). Individuation of objects and events: A developmental study. *Cognition, 90*(2), 163–191.

Wagner, L., & Carey, S. (2005). 12-month-old infants represent probable endings of motion events. *Infancy, 7*(1), 73–83.

Waxman, S. R. (1999). Specifying the scope of 13-month-olds' expectations for novel words. *Cognition, 70*, B35–B50.

Waxman, S. R., & Booth, A. E. (2001). Seeing pink elephants: Fourteen-month-olds' interpretations of novel nouns and adjectives. *Cognitive Psychology, 43*(3), 217–242.

Waxman, S. R., & Booth, A. E. (2003). Mapping words to world in infancy: Infants' expectations for count nouns and adjectives. *Journal of Cognition and Development, 4*(3), 357–381.

Waxman, S. R., & Markow, D. B. (1995). Words as invitations to form categories: Evidence from 12- to 13-month-old infants. *Cognitive Psychology, 29*(3), 257–302.

Wellman, H. M., Cross, D., & Watson, J. (2001). Meta-analysis for theory-of-mind development: The truth about false belief. *Child Development, 72*(3), 655–684.

Wellman, H. M., & Gelman, S. (1992) Cognitive Development: Foundational theories of core domains. *Annual Review of Psychology, 43*, 337–375.

Wellman, H. M., Phillips, A. T., Dunphy-Lelii, S, & LaLonde, N. (2004). Infant social attention predicts preschool social cognition. *Developmental Science, 7*, 283–288.

Wellman, H. M., Lopez-Duran, S., LaBounty, J., & Hamilton, B. (in press). Infant attention of intentional action predicts preschool theory of mind. *Developmental Psychology*.

Wexler, K., & Culicover, P. W. (1983). *Formal principles of language acquisition*. Cambridge, MA: MIT Press.

Weyl, H. (1949). *Philosophy of mathematics and natural science*. Princeton, NJ: Princeton University Press.

Whalen, J., Gallistel, C. R., & Gelman, R. (1999). Nonverbal counting in humans: the psychophysics of number representation. *Psychological Science, 10*, 130–137.

Wilcox, T., & Baillargeon, R. (1998). Object individuation in infancy: The use of featural information in reasoning about occlusion events. *Cognitive Psychology, 37*, 97–155.

Wimmer, H., & Perner, J. (1983). Beliefs about beliefs: Representation and constraining function of wrong beliefs in young children's understanding of deception. *Cognition, 13*, 103–128.

Wiser, M. (1988). The differentiation of heat and temperature: History of science and novice-expert shift. In S. Strauss (Ed.), *Ontogeny, phylogeny, and historical development* (pp. 28–48). Norwood, NJ: Ablex Publishing Company.

Wiser, M (1995). Use of history of science to understand and remedy students' misconceptions about heat and temperature. In D. N. Perkins, J. L. Schwartz,

M. M. West, & M. S. Stone (Eds.), *Software goes to school: Teaching for understanding with new technologies* (pp. 23–38). New York: Oxford University Press.

Wiser, M., & Amin, T. (2002). Microworld-based interactions for conceptual change in science. In M. Limon & L. Mason (Eds.), *Reconsidering conceptual change. Issues in theory and practice* (pp. 357–388). Dordrecht/London: Kluwer Academic Publishers.

Wiser, M., & Carey, S. (1983). When heat and temperature were one. In D. Genter and A. Stevens (Eds.), *Mental models* (pp. 267–297). Hillsdale, NJ: Erlbaum.

Wittgenstein, L. (1953/1958). *Philosophical investigations.* New York: Macmillan.

Wood, J. N., Kouider, S., & Carey, S. (in press). The developmental origins of the singular-plural distinction. *Developmental Psychology.*

Wood, J. N., & Spelke, E. (2005a). Infants' enumeration of actions: Numerical discrimination and its signature limits. *Developmental Science,* 8(2), 173–181.

Wood, J. N., & Spelke, E. (2005b). Chronometric studies of numerical cognition in five-month-old infants. *Cognition,* 97(1), 23–39.

Woodward, A. L. (1998). Infants selectively encode the goal object of an actor's reach. *Cognition,* 69(1), 1–34.

Woodward, J. (2003). *Making things happen.* New York: Oxford University Press.

Wynn, K. (1990). Children's understanding of counting. *Cognition,* 36, 155–193.

Wynn, K. (1992a). Children's acquisition of the number words and the counting system. *Cognitive Psychology,* 24, 220–251.

Wynn, K. (1992b). Addition and subtraction by human infants. *Nature,* 358, 749–750.

Wynn, K. (1996). Infants' individuation and enumeration of actions. *Psychological Science,* 7, 164–169.

Wynn, K. (1998). Psychological foundations of number: numerical competence in human infants. *Trends in Cognitive Sciences,* 2, 296–303.

Wynn, K., Bloom, P., & Chiang, W. C. (2002). Enumeration of collective entities by 5-month-old infants. *Cognition,* 83(3), B55–B62.

Xu, F. (1999). Object individuation and object identity in infancy: The role of spatiotemporal information, object property information, and language. *Acta Psychologica. Special issue: Visual object perception.,* 102(2–3), 113–136.

Xu, F. (2002). The role of language in acquiring object kind concepts in infancy. *Cognition,* 85(3), 223–250.

Xu, F. (2003). Numerosity discrimination in infants: evidence for two systems of representations. *Cognition,* 89(1), B15–B25.

Xu, F. (2005). Categories, kinds and object individuation in infancy. In L. Gershkoff-Stowe and D. Rakison (Eds.), *Building object categories in developmental time* (pp. 63–89). Papers from the 32nd Carnegie Symposium on Cognition. Hillsdale, NJ: Erlbaum.

Xu, F., & Baker, A. (2005) Object individuation in 10-month-old infants using a simplified manual search method. *Journal of Cognition and Development,* 6, 307–323.

Xu, F., & Carey, S. (1996). Infants' metaphysics: the case of numerical identity. *Cognitive Psychology, 30*, 111–153.

Xu, F., & Carey, S. (2000). The emergence of kind concepts: A rejoinder to Needham and Baillargeon. *Cognition, 74*, 285–301.

Xu, F., Carey, S., & Quint, N. (2004). The emergence of kind-based object individuation in infancy. *Cognitive Psychology, 49*(2), 155–190.

Xu, F., Carey, S., & Welch, J. (1999). Infants' ability to use object kind information for object individuation. *Cognition, 70*, 137–166.

Xu, F., Cote, M., & Baker, A. (2005). Labeling guides object individuation in 12-month-old infants. *Psychological Science, 16*(5), 372–377.

Xu, F., & Spelke, E. S. (2000). Large number discrimination in 6-month old infants. *Cognition, 74*, B1–B11.

Xu, F., Spelke, E., & Goddard, S. (2005). Number sense in human infants. *Developmental Science, 8*(1), 88–101.

Zorzi, M., & Butterworth, B. (1997). On the representation of number concepts. In M. Shafto & P. Langley (Eds.), *Proceedings of the Nineteenth Annual Conference of the Cognitive Science Society* (p. 1098). Mahwah, NJ: Erlbaum.

Author Index

Subject Index